W9-CAE-106

Chris Argyris
Dr. Argyris has focused much of his attention on the topic of organizational development. He has made many key contributions to this important area. (Please refer to Chapter 16.)

Suzanne C. Kobasa
Dr. Kobasa's insightful research on stress (especially those factors that permit some persons to resist its negative impact) has received growing attention from organizational researchers in recent years. (Please refer to Chapter 9.)

Herbert A. Simon
A former Nobel prize winner, Dr. Simon is best known for his research on the nature of decision making. His distinction between programmed and nonprogrammed decisions, and his administrative model of decision making, have received widespread attention. (Please refer to Chapter 11.)

A SMALL SAMPLE OF MAJOR CONTRIBUTORS TO THE FIELD OF ORGANIZATIONAL BEHAVIOR

Shown here and on the inside back cover are a few of the many important contributors to O.B. We regret that space limitations and technical problems (e.g., the unavailability of suitable photos) make it impossible to include many other colleagues whose work is highly regarded, and who have also helped shape the development and current scope of our field.

William S. Ouchi
In his famous "Theory Z," Dr. Ouchi has called attention to a number of key differences between many American companies and their Japanese counterparts—differences that help explain the great success of the Japanese in competing for world markets. (Please refer to Chapter 15.)

Paul R. Lawrence
Dr. Lawrence's classic research on the impact of organizational structure (especially environmental uncertainty) played a key role in the development of the modern contingency approach. (Please refer to Chapter 15.)

Behavior in Organizations

Behavior in Organizations:

Understanding and Managing
the Human Side of Work

Robert A. Baron

Purdue University

With the special assistance of
Jerald Greenberg—Ohio State University
Angelo S. DeNisi—University of South Carolina

Allyn and Bacon, Inc.   Boston   •   London   •   Sydney   •   Toronto

Front cover painting:
MONDRIAN, Piet.
Broadway Boogie Woogie. 1942–43
Oil on canvas, 50 x 50''.
Collection, The Museum of Modern Art, New York.

© The Museum of Modern Art, New York.

Series Editor: Bill Barke
Production Editor: Joanne Dauksewicz

Photo research by Christy Rosso, Hamilton, MA, and Laurel Anderson, Salem, MA.

Chapter Opening Photo Credits
1 © Fredrik D. Bodin/Stock, Boston
2 Christian Simonpietri/SYGMA
3 Anestis Diako poulos/Stock, Boston
4 Peter Menzel/Stock, Boston
5 Michael Grecco/Picture Group
6 David Powers/Stock, Boston
7 Owen Franken/Stock, Boston
8 Cheryl A. Traendly/Jeroboam, Inc.
9 © Camerique
10 Courtesy Houghton Mifflin Co. and Boston Red Sox
11 © Mike Valeri/Picture Group
12 © Kevin Twombly/Picture Group
13 Christian Simonpietri/SYGMA
14 © Abigail Heyman/Archive Pictures Inc.
15 © Ellis Herwig, LXXIX/Stock, Boston
16 Randy Taylor/SYGMA

Copyright © 1983 by Allyn and Bacon, Inc., 7 Wells Avenue, Newton, Massachusetts 02159. All rights reserved. No part of the material protected by this copyright notice may be reproduced or utilized in any form or by any means, electronic or mechanical, including photocopying, recording, or by any information storage and retrieval system, without written permission from the copyright owner.

Library of Congress of Cataloging in Publication Data
Baron, Robert A.
    Behavior in organizations.

    Includes bibliographical references and index.
    1. Organizational behavior. I. Greenberg, Jerald.
II. DeNisi, Angelo S. III. Title.
HD58.7.B37 1983   658.3   82-20590
ISBN 0-205-07851-6
ISBN (International) 0-205-07955-5

Printed in the United States of America.
10 9 8 7 6 5 4 3   87 86 85 84

To Sandra, the girl who hears bells (and has the good sense to listen!)
and Jessica, the little ray of sunshine who—now and again—brightens up my life

Brief Contents

Contents

Special Inserts

Case in Point

A Note from the Author

ON THE BENEFITS OF CONCRETE GOALS

Books, like people, should have clear-cut goals. If they do not, they stand a very good chance of losing their way—of wandering off in several contradictory directions at once. Before I began work on *Behavior in Organizations*, therefore, I thought long and hard about what kind of book it should be. Who was its intended audience? What materials should it contain? How should it differ from (and perhaps improve upon) existing texts in the area? These are just a small sample of the questions I considered. After giving these and other issues careful thought, I decided that I should work toward the attainment of four distinct goals. I will now comment briefly on each.

Goal 1: Broad and Up-to-Date Coverage. The first and perhaps most important goal I sought was that of preparing a text offering *broad* and *current* treatment of Organizational Behavior. In order to attain the first of these features, I developed a questionnaire concerning topics for possible inclusion in the text. This was sent to over 1,000 colleagues currently teaching the course, and more than 400 kindly responded. The suggestions and feedback they provided were invaluable to me in writing a text that reflects the breadth and diversity of modern O.B.

With respect to currency of content, I made every effort to include recent findings and theories, as well as more "classic" materials. In this regard, I might note that more than 150 of the 800 citations present in the text are from 1980, 1981, and 1982. Thus, the book is as up-to-date and indicative of recent trends as possible.

Goal 2: Inclusion of Recent Advances in Related Fields. O.B. has always been an integrative field—one that benefits greatly from findings and advances in related disciplines. Consistent with this basic fact, I have attempted to include information on recent advances in such fields as social psychology, sociology, and management theory. And here, I might add, I discovered a number of interesting topics that had not as yet been incorporated into existing O.B. texts. Among these were the nature of escalating (and entrapping) conflicts, important new findings on social perception and attribution, "social loafing" (the tendency to expend less effort when working as part of a group than when working alone), and group polarization effects in group decision making. These and many other topics are included in *Behavior in Organizations,* and I believe that they will be of interest to students and colleagues alike.

Goal 3: Comprehensibility and Appeal to Students.

If my fifteen years of university teaching have taught *me* anything, it is this: when undergraduate students find a text undecipherable or dull, they will not read it. And even if they do, the information it contains will soon vanish without a trace. With this lesson in mind, I have taken several concrete steps to enhance the interest-value and appeal of the text. Briefly, these are as follows:

(1) *Informal Writing Style.* The text is written in a fairly informal style—one in which I often address readers directly. I have found that many students react positively to this approach, and I have adopted it here for this reason.

(2) *Inclusion of Special Inserts.* I have included three distinct types of special inserts (boxes) in the text. All are designed to enhance student involvement, as well as to present important materials. The first of these is labeled *"From the Manager's Perspective"* and seeks to clarify the implications of findings and principles covered for actual management settings. The second is titled *"Focus on Behavior."* Boxes of this type describe recent research findings or current methodological issues and refinements. The third type of insert is labeled *"Case in Point"* and offers cases specially chosen or created to illustrate important points made in the text. Together, these three types of inserts should enhance student interest in and involvement with the text.

(3) *Illustrations.* Having interacted with hundreds of undergraduates in recent years, it is my impression that they are highly "visual" people, who both enjoy and profit from graphics. For this reason, the text contains a larger number (and a greater variety) of illustrations than is true in many other O.B. texts. These include *graphs* depicting research findings, *tables, word diagrams, photos,* and *cartoons.* All the graphs contain special labels designed to call attention to the major points being shown. Word diagrams illustrate important processes and theories and are simple and straightforward. (Like all graphs, they have been specially created for this text.) Finally, photos and cartoons have been carefully selected so that they relate very closely to text material and illustrate important, basic points.

(4) *In-Text Aids.* The text also includes a number of specific aids designed to enhance its usefulness to students. Each chapter is preceded by an *outline* of the major topics covered and begins with a short *vignette* designed to capture reader attention and to set the stage for the materials that follow. (These vignettes can also be viewed as brief cases.) Each chapter ends with a detailed *summary* and a *glossary* in which all key terms are defined in clear and simple language.

Goal 4: Provide Assistance for Colleagues Teaching the Course.

My own experience in teaching large undergraduate courses suggests just how time-consuming and challenging they can be. For this reason, I have attempted to provide as much assistance as possible to colleagues faced with the task of handling undergraduate O.B. Along these lines, the text is accompanied by two ancillary items (both handled primarily by Jerri Frantzve): a comprehensive Instructor's Manual, and a Case/Experiential Exercise Handbook.

The *Instructor's Manual* provides the standard array of multiple choice, short-answer, and essay questions. In addition, it contains a number of innovative features. These include: (a) information helpful in preparing lectures (topics and sources not covered in the text); (b) a listing of new references published in 1982; (c) lists of films and other audiovisual aids (as well as where to obtain them); and (d) transparency masters, which can be used in producing illustrations for presentation in class. Finally, several cases and exercises are also provided.

Behaving in Organizations: Tales from the Trenches.   This ancillary text contains a wide assortment of cases and experiential exercises and offers several innovative features. Perhaps the most important of these is the fact that all cases presented were submitted by individuals who are now working in organizations or who have worked in them in the past. Hence the subtitle of the book. Other major features include (a) special guidelines on how to use and learn from case material and (b) sources students can consult for additional information on each topic covered. In addition, a special "grid" illustrates how each case and exercise can be related to several different topic areas considered in the text.

A Concluding Comment—
And a Request for Help

These, then, are the major goals I sought in preparing this text. Looking back, I can honestly say that I have spared no effort in my attempts to achieve them. But given the imperfect nature of all human endeavors, I'm sure that there is still much room for improvement. With this thought in mind, I openly invite—and eagerly await—your feedback and suggestions. I have always found such input valuable in the past, and would greatly appreciate receiving it now as well. So, please don't hesitate: Send your comments whenever (and in whatever form) you wish. Rest assured, they will *not* be ignored.

Robert A. Baron
385 Peirce Hall
Purdue University
W. Lafayette, IN 47907

ACKNOWLEDGEMENTS: SOME WORDS OF
THANKS

Setting one's thoughts down on paper is a solitary task, best carried out in quiet isolation. In an important sense, though, this is just about the only aspect of preparing a text that *is* solitary. At every other step along the way, I have been assisted by many talented persons. Given the many forms such aid has taken, it is probably impossible for me to thank all of these individuals here: my memory is simply not that good! But I do wish to offer my gratitude to all the persons listed below, and to everyone else who worked with me on this difficult (but ultimately rewarding) project.

First and foremost, I wish to express my appreciation to my friends and colleagues Angelo DeNisi and Jerald Greenberg, who contributed several chapters to the text. In addition, they acted as expert consultants, calling my attention to topics that should be covered and references that should be included. Finally, they read and commented upon each chapter as it was completed. For all their aid and valuable suggestions—and also for their good fellowship!—I wish to thank them here.

Second, I would like to express my appreciation to the colleagues who read and commented upon various portions of the manuscript. The remarks and comments they offered were thoughtful and informative. In addition, they were generally kind and constructive; who could ask for more? So, my special thanks to the people listed below:

Ted Valvoda
Lakeland Community College, Ohio

Paul Preston
University of Texas, San Antonio

Steve Ross
Marquette University, Wisconsin

Irving Herman
California State University, Sacramento

Ralph Katerberg
University of Cincinnati

Jim McElroy
Iowa State, Ames

Jerri Frantzve
SUNY—Binghamton

Bob Andrews
Simon Fraser, British Columbia, Canada

T. W. Bonham
Virginia Polytechnic

Hal Angle
University of Minnesota, Minneapolis

Third, I would like to thank my friend Irving H. Feuerman. It was he who first put the idea for such a book into my head. And his continued encouragement in the months that followed helped me to convert this idea into an actual volume. For his sage advice and unflagging faith, I wish to thank him sincerely.

Fourth, it is a distinct pleasure to acknowledge the aid of several outstanding individuals affiliated with my publisher. In this respect, special thanks are due to: Joanne Dauksewicz, my diligent, cheerful, and enthusiastic production editor—working with her has been a joy, and I am truly grateful for all her help; Christy Rosso, who once again devised an outstanding cover; and Dorothy Thompson for yet another excellent internal design.

Fifth, my sincere thanks to Dan Ilgen and Howard Weiss. Both offered many helpful suggestions and were more than generous in sharing their knowledge, expertise—and even libraries!—with me. I am indeed fortunate in having such outstanding colleagues, and gratefully acknowledge their assistance here.

Finally, I wish to thank my good friend and editor Bill Barke (alias *The Lithuanian Kid*). It is accurate to say that we planned the book together, and that his interest in and commitment to the project from the word "go" were major factors in its development. As they might well put it in Vilnius: "Way to go, Billy!"

To all of the persons listed above and to many others as well, a warm and heartfelt THANK YOU!

Behavior in Organizations

1

The Field of
Organizational Behavior:
An Introduction

ORGANIZATIONAL BEHAVIOR: A WORKING DEFINITION

ORGANIZATIONAL BEHAVIOR: A CAPSULE MEMOIR

Classical Theory: Scientific Management and the Early Years   The Human Relations
Movement: Work Settings as Social Systems   Organizational Behavior in the 1980s: A
Modern Perspective

USING THIS BOOK: A DISPLACED (BUT NOT *MIS*PLACED) PREFACE

SPECIAL INSERT

FOCUS ON BEHAVIOR   Common Sense: An Unreliable Guide to Human Behavior

KEY CONCEPTS

Organizational Behavior (O.B.)   Human Relations Movement
Organization   Human Resources Model
Scientific Management   Contingency Approach

□ □ □

It's a Thursday afternoon, and you are at a staff meeting held to discuss development of a new product. It will require a major investment in terms of equipment and production facilities, so the conversation is quite intense. As usual, Frank Blake and Jane McAllister—two officers in the Product Development Division—are on opposite sides of the issue.

"I don't know," says Frank. "It's a big chunk of money. And market research on product acceptance is pretty sketchy."

"Oh come on, Frank," replies Jane, with an obvious note of irritation in her voice. "We'll never get anywhere if we simply stand pat. You have *to take a chance sometimes, you know."*

The discussion continues, with Frank urging caution and Jane plugging away for boldness. You've witnessed this same scene over and over again, to the point where you can now predict the exact lines Frank and Jane will utter. As you sit listening to their statements, you begin to ponder the basic difference between them. Why is Frank so conservative and cautious, while Jane is so bold and daring? What makes them see the world through such different eyes? You continue thinking about these questions as the meeting drags on, and on, and on. . . .

□ □ □

"Oh no," you think as you look up from your desk. "It's Ellen Marks. Here comes trouble." Unaware of your thoughts, Ellen greets you with a big smile. "Hello Bill," she says cheerfully. "How's my favorite engineer today?"

For a couple of minutes, you and Ellen exchange small talk and then, finally, she comes to the point. "Look, Bill, I need your help. We're way behind on that Latham project. How about letting Stan Reynolds, Gloria Ippolito, and Tim Vilnis join our group for a couple of weeks?"

You are shocked; what a request! "Oh no, Ellen," you reply. "I can't possibly spare them now. You know this is the peak of our busy season."

"Well," she says, "If you can't spare all three, how about Gloria for just a couple of days?"

You experience great relief. This is more like it. "O.K.," you mumble without much enthusiasm. "I guess we can spare her. But just for a couple of days."

At these words Ellen smiles, says "Thanks," and beats a hasty retreat. After she leaves, you sit quietly for a moment. Then all at once, it hits you: she's done it again! When will you ever learn? Ellen set you up beautifully with her "ask for a lot, settle for a little" tactic. Just how many ways of getting what she wants does she know? You certainly haven't seen the limit yet!

□ □ □

4

Today marks the end of your first month in a new job. Just six weeks ago you accepted a position with a large Japanese company—one that has recently opened offices in the U.S. It's now the end of the day, and as you ease your car onto the expressway and head for home, you find yourself thinking about your new position. In some ways, it has turned out just as you expected. Your salary is high, and the company's brand new headquarters are very pleasant. But looking back over your first month, you realize that there have been some real surprises, too. A major one occurred during your first staff meeting. Several issues were discussed and, at one point, you described a decision you had reached about handling a special problem. To your surprise, the meeting ground to a halt and everyone stared at you in disbelief. Finally, after an uncomfortable pause, the division manager set you straight: "Listen, Tom, we don't do things that way around here. We try to make our decisions collectively, not as individuals. First we give everyone a chance to offer their views. And then we go ahead only when we've reached a consensus. Try to remember that here at Matsuhito we're all one big happy family." You realize now that he wasn't kidding about the "family" stuff. In other companies where you've worked, there has been a clear distinction between your job and your personal life. That's definitely not *the case here. Since joining Matsuhito, you and your family have been involved in a tremendous amount of company-sponsored socializing. Indeed, it's now clear that the firm actively encourages close personal ties among its employees and their families—ties that extend far beyond the work setting. This is a new pattern for you, and will certainly require some adjustment. In short, you've discovered that working for a Japanese company really* is *different. But are you going to like it over the long haul? Can you adjust to these many differences? You are still pondering such questions as you turn into the driveway of your home. . . .*

Do you think that you might ever encounter situations like these in your own life? We believe that you may. In fact, we would be quite surprised if you did *not* meet them (or ones very much like them) over the course of your career in the world of business. But why, you may be wondering, have we chosen to begin with this series of anecdotes? The answer consists of two parts. First, all of these situations are concerned with human behavior in organizations. Thus, there is indeed a common thread binding them together. Second, all focus attention on a basic principle we wish to emphasize at the very beginning: *In order to be an effective member of an organization, or to be a successful manager in it, it is essential for you to know something about human behavior.* In short, you must have a basic grasp of why individuals behave, think, and feel as they do in organizational settings (something the character in Figure 1-1 clearly lacks). The reason for this requirement is simple, but perhaps a bit surprising: as a manager, you will probably spend more of your time interacting with other persons than in any other single activity. Studies to determine exactly how managers spend their days indicate that, in general, they invest 60%–80% of their time in talking and listening to others.[1] Activities such as answering mail, touring plants, or simply thinking and planning occupy much smaller segments of their time. Given this daily pattern, it is obvious that a basic knowledge of behavior can often come in very handy.

"Merry Christmas, folks. And I want to say I couldn't be president of this great company without the support of each and every one of you, or people very much like you."

FIGURE 1-1   Basic Understanding of Human Behavior: A Key Requirement for Successful Managers

The final remark by the character in this cartoon indicates that he has little understanding of human behavior. Do you think he is an effective manager? (Source: Drawing by Wm Hamilton; © 1980 The New Yorker Magazine, Inc.)

As you may already know, human behavior is the primary focus of the field of **organizational behavior** (or **O.B.** for short). Briefly, O.B. seeks to comprehend the nature of behavior in organizational settings, primarily with an eye toward enhancing its effectiveness and that of the organizations themselves. Given the great diversity and complexity of human activities, it is far from surprising that O.B. addresses a number of intriguing topics. Thus, included in a small sample of the questions it has examined in recent years are the following:[2]

- What kinds of persons make the best leaders? What kinds of leaders are most effective in various settings?
- Do merit and incentive pay plans actually improve worker performance?
- What are the effects of physical work settings (noise, heat, crowding) on productivity?
- Do groups actually make more balanced or conservative decisions than individuals?
- How can women and members of minority groups overcome the lingering impact of prejudice?
- Whatever happened to the work ethic? Does its decline help explain recent drops in productivity?
- Does decentralization of authority in an organization actually improve employee morale? Productivity?
- What are the major sources of stress in work settings? How can the negative impact of such factors be reduced?
- In evaluating others' performance, do we assign more weight to their effort or their ability?

In the chapters that follow, we will present much information about these and many other questions of equal importance. Before turning to such topics, however, we believe it is important to provide you with certain background information—information that will prove useful in the remainder of this book. Thus, we will use the rest of this initial chapter for completing several preliminary tasks.

First, we will offer a formal definition of the field of organizational behavior. Our purpose here is simple: to provide you with a firm grasp of just what O.B. is and what it seeks to accomplish. Second, we will present a brief overview of the history and development of O.B. And third, we will comment on the structure of this book and on several of its special features. Armed with this basic information, you will be well prepared for what follows: careful consideration of many fascinating aspects of human behavior in organizational settings.

ORGANIZATIONAL BEHAVIOR: A WORKING DEFINITION

Earlier, it was noted that the field of O.B. seeks to comprehend the nature of human behavior in organizational settings. Further, we called attention to the fact that it does so with a constant eye toward application. That is, it seeks such information partly as a means of enhancing the effectiveness of individual behavior in organizations and of organizations generally. Together, these statements might seem to form the central core of a good working definition of O.B. By themselves, however, they are not quite sufficient. To see why this is so, let us return to the three anecdotes at the start of this chapter.

In the first incident, one individual noticed (and pondered) the existence of large differences in personality or temperament between two of his coworkers. In the second, one employee of a large company used a novel technique for influencing the behavior of another—who quickly realized that he had been "had" once again. Finally, in the third, an individual reflected on the important differences between an organization he had recently joined and others he had known in the past.

Taken together, these three anecdotes call attention to the fact that complete understanding of human behavior in organizations must include information about *individuals, groups,* and *organizational structure/function.* Thus, mention of these factors should—and will be—included in our working definition of the field.

In addition, there is one other feature of modern O.B. that should be mentioned. This aspect relates to the following basic question: How, precisely, can systematic information about the individual, group, and structural factors mentioned above be obtained? One answer—and a tempting one at that—involves reliance on "common sense." Down through the centuries, novelists, philosophers, and many other persons have focused their attention on the nature of human behavior. Because many of these individuals were brilliant, their writings provide us with a rich legacy of informal observation about human relations. Unfortunately, though, the richness of this material is greatly offset by major shortcomings. In particular, careful analysis of this "wisdom of the ages" reveals that often it paints an inconsistent or even contradictory picture of behavior in organizations. For example, consider the statement "Leaders are born, not made." Directly opposed to this view is the suggestion that individuals "rise to the situation"—demonstrate important and unexpected leadership qualities when conditions are "right." Similarly, consider the statements "Birds of a feather flock together" and "Opposites attract." The first suggests that attraction and liking (important forces within organizations) stem from similarity. In contrast, the second indicates that such reactions derive from differences between persons. In short, "common sense" and the "wisdom of the ages" offer intriguing and sometimes revealing speculations about human behavior. But they are *not* wholly satisfactory guides to its full comprehension. (For a demonstration of this fact, please see the **"FOCUS"** box on p. 10.)

Given this fact, it seems preferable to seek valid information about behavior in organizations through other means. One alternative approach in this regard is suggested by psychology, sociology, and other behavioral sciences. These fields have long employed the methods of science in an attempt to obtain systematic knowledge of human behavior. As you probably already know, they have attained considerable progress in recent decades. Given this success, it seems only reasonable to suggest that similar methods might also prove useful in the study of organizational behavior. In fact, this has turned out to be the case. An empirical, science-based approach is now widely accepted in the field of O.B. Indeed, it is a central characteristic of O.B. as it exists in the 1980s.

Taking this fact and the other points noted above into account, we can now offer the following working definition of O.B.: *Organizational Behavior is the field that seeks to comprehend and predict human behavior in organizational settings through the scientific study of individual processes, group processes, and organizational structure and function.* (Please see Figure 1–2 for a summary of these suggestions.)

FIGURE 1–2   The Field of Organizational Behavior

As shown here, the field of organizational behavior seeks to comprehend and predict
human behavior in organizational settings through scientific study of individual
processes, group processes, and organizational structure and function.

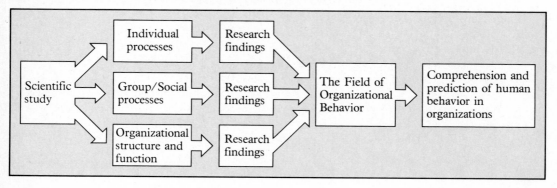

Our experience tells us that all too often, definitions are presented and then quickly forgotten. We hope, though, that you will take this one a bit more seriously. We have tried to adhere to it consistently in the remainder of this text. And in an important sense, it has helped determine just what materials are included. Thus, the definition is worth keeping firmly in mind as you move through the pages that follow.

A note on organizations.   In our comments so far, we have used the term "organization" repeatedly. Yet, we have not indicated just what we mean by this word. At this point, therefore, we will pause briefly to clarify matters. By the term **organization** we simply mean *any social structure consisting of two or more persons who are interdependent and who work together toward one or more common goals.* In simpler terms, organizations consist of persons who interact with one another (directly or indirectly), whose fates are somehow linked (i.e., what happens to one affects what happens to the other[s]), and who work together in an attempt to achieve some agreed-upon goals.

As you can readily see, this definition is quite broad in scope. Indeed, it suggests that a very wide range of social structures—everything from informal clubs or teams through giant corporations and huge government agencies—qualifies as organizations (see Figure 1–3). While this is certainly so, the field of O.B. generally focuses most of its attention on organizations in work-related environments. Thus, our interest, too, will be directed primarily to such organizations. But as

FIGURE 1-3   Organizations Take Many Different Forms

While both of these photos depict organizations, the field of O.B. focuses most of its attention on behavior occurring in ones such as that on the right—organizations in work-related environments. (Source: Photo (left) © Lionel Delevingne/Picture Group; photo (right) © Eli Heller/Picture Group.)

FOCUS ON BEHAVIOR

Common Sense: An Unreliable Guide to Human Behavior

Earlier, we noted that "common sense" and "the wisdom of the ages" often provide us with confusing and inconsistent suggestions about the nature of human behavior. Even worse, research findings suggest that in many cases, both are quite misleading: they point to false conclusions about behavior.

You can readily demonstrate this fact for yourself in the following manner. Simply ask several of your friends who have not taken a course in O.B. to answer the questions below. (It's also best to select friends who have not taken introductory psychology.) Because "common sense" suggests a ready answer to each, your friends will probably respond quickly and with considerable confidence. After they are done, compare their answers with the ones given below—answers based on the findings of actual research studies. In all likelihood, you will find that your friends have done quite poorly.

You may also want to take this quiz yourself before looking at the answers. If so, how did *you* do on it? (We are sure, by the way, that if you take it twice, right now and then again at the end of this course, you will do much better the second time around. In fact, after reading this text and attending lectures, you will probably score 100%.)

Instructions: Indicate whether you think each of the following statements is true or false by placing a *T* or *F* in the blank space next to each.

____ 1. If you pay someone for doing something they already enjoy, they will come to like this task even more.

____ 2. Women are more conforming and open to influence than men.

____ 3. Unpleasant environmental conditions (e.g., crowding, loud noise, high temperatures) produce immediate reductions in performance on many tasks.

____ 4. In bargaining with others, it is usually best to start with a moderate offer—one fairly close to the final agreement we desire.

____ 5. Directive, authoritative leaders are generally best in attaining high levels of productivity from their subordinates.

____ 6. In most cases, individuals act in ways that are consistent with their attitudes about various issues.

____ 7. Top executives are usually extremely competitive, hard-driving types.

____ 8. Most persons are much more concerned with the size of their own salary than with the salary of others.

____ 9. Direct, face-to-face communication usually enhances cooperation between individuals.

____ 10. Most persons prefer challenging jobs with a great deal of freedom and autonomy.

See page 23 for answers.   □

will soon become apparent, many of the principles and findings discussed apply to groups or organizations generally. This, we believe, is as it should be. In our view, human behavior in work-related organizations is continuous with human behavior in other kinds of organizations and in other types of settings. Further, we do not believe that it is possible to fully comprehend behavior in work-related organizations without understanding it in more general terms as well. Thus, while our attention in this text will certainly be work organization *focused,* it will by no means be work organization *bound.*

ORGANIZATIONAL BEHAVIOR:
A CAPSULE MEMOIR

Boats are launched amidst the shattering of champagne bottles. Tunnels, roads, and buildings are often dedicated in elaborate ribbon-cutting ceremonies. In contrast, new fields of study or new branches of science do not begin in such dramatic fashion. Rather, they often seem to take shape quietly, behind the scenes, and then to appear as fully "going concerns" without much fanfare or ritual. This is clearly the pattern shown by the field of organizational behavior. Even from the vantage point of the 1980s, it is difficult to select a particular date for its emergence as an independent discipline.

In an important sense, of course, O.B. is very, very old. Every civilization, from ancient times through the present, has shown interest in behavior within organizations. Indeed, a compelling case can be made for the view that the flowering and rapid growth of ancient cultures such as those in Egypt, Greece, and Rome stemmed, at least in part, from corresponding advances in the sophistication of organizations concerned with government and production.

Since there is little reason for embarking on a full-scale historical analysis, however, we will restrict our focus to a much shorter span of time. Briefly, we will search for the roots of modern O.B. within a period of about one hundred years—from the late nineteenth century through the present. Within this period, we will examine three major phases of development. First, we will focus on a relatively early approach, often known as *classical theory*. This period is exemplified by **scientific management,** which rose to prominence shortly after the turn of the current century. Second, we will consider the **human relations movement,** a profound shift of perspective within O.B. that occurred during the 1920s and 1930s. Finally, we will examine the modern approach—one characterized by the **human resources model** and a **contingency approach** to behavior in work settings.

Classical Theory: Scientific Management and the Early Years

Managers have always been concerned with improving the productivity of persons under their direction. Until quite recent times, however, attempts to accomplish this goal were far from systematic. Indeed, they generally depended on the intuition, experience, and common sense of individual managers rather than on any rigorous or scientific approach to the problem. In the closing decades of the nineteenth century, this picture began to change dramatically. At that time, a growing number of engineers realized that designing efficient machines was not, in itself, enough: attention had to also be directed to the persons who ran and used them. Efforts to take account of this new insight often led to time-and-motion studies—attempts to design each task of a job so that it could be performed in the most efficient manner possible. It was out of such work, of course, that the in-

FIGURE 1-4 Scientific Management: An Extreme That Never Was

One major goal of scientific management was that of designing jobs or tasks so that they could be performed as efficiently as possible. As shown in this scene from an early film, attempts along these lines by "efficiency experts" were often viewed with skepticism by the general public. (Source: Museum of Modern Art Film Stills Archive.)

famous "efficiency expert," a favorite villain of several early films, was born. (See Figure 1-4.)

This initial work on job design paved the way for the emergence of a major new approach known as **scientific management.** Although scientific management was supported and practiced by many individuals, its most forceful and influential proponent was Frederick W. Taylor. In a classic text entitled *The Principles of Scientific Management*, Taylor outlined the major features of his new approach.[3] Basically, it stressed two major themes.

First, he called for careful attention to *job design.* Many studies—including a large number performed by Taylor himself—suggested the need for planning work activities in a systematic manner. Only in this way, Taylor noted, could efficiency be maximized. Closely related to this principle were the suggestions that (1) employees be carefully selected and trained for their jobs, and (2) that tools and procedures be standardized in accordance with the results of careful studies. Both of these points make eminent good sense. After all, it is quite useless to devote detailed attention to the scientific design of jobs if they are then assigned at random to employees who may or may not be suited for their performance. And the efficiencies yielded by standardized tools and procedures are too obvious to require further comment.

Second, Taylor's approach focused on human motivation and on ways to maximize it in work settings. In this regard, he assumed that workers are primarily motivated by the desire for gain (i.e., money). Thus, he suggested that productivity could be increased by offering workers financial incentives for good performance. In addition, he called attention to the importance of providing each employee with a clear, assigned work quota. Taylor believed that when individuals possessed information about the specific amounts of work they were expected to accomplish each day, motivation would be enhanced. In short, he emphasized the benefits of clear-cut *goals*.

As noted recently by Locke, these themes in Taylor's approach to management—and several others as well—are readily visible in modern O.B.[4] Such techniques as careful design of jobs, standardized tools and procedures, and the scientific selection of personnel are all widely accepted today. And as we will see when we consider motivation in detail in Chapter 5, the importance of both individual incentives and clear-cut goals is widely recognized in modern management theory. Of course, all of these techniques and approaches are treated in a more sophisticated manner today than when Taylor first described them. But it is interesting to note that they have remained central to O.B. for several decades.

The methods outlined by Taylor and other supporters of scientific management were soon put to practice by industry. In many cases, results were gratifying. When jobs were designed to maximize efficiency and when attention was directed to maintaining high levels of motivation, productivity *did* often increase. Unfortunately, though, this was not always the case. Sometimes, the expected increments in efficiency failed to appear. In retrospect, the reason for this is clear: while the scientific management approach was certainly on the "right track" in several respects, it was also quite unsophisticated with respect to key aspects of human behavior. Thus, it overlooked important considerations such as the fact that human beings are motivated by many needs aside from that for financial gain (e.g., the need for security, need for social approval).

Given the undeveloped state of psychology and related fields at the turn of the century, scientific management certainly cannot be faulted for its somewhat simplistic view of human behavior. But its lack of sophistication in this respect did tend to limit its success in many settings. In any case, despite these problems, the scientific management approach represented an important step forward. By emphasizing the importance of the "human element" in the production equation, it focused attention on key factors that had previously been ignored. In this way, it prepared the ground for further advances toward a scientific field of organizational behavior.

The Human Relations Movement: Work Settings as Social Systems

As we have already noted, the scientific management movement did direct a degree of attention to the role of human behavior in work settings. Yet, it is obvious that it did not go far enough in this respect. If you have ever worked in an office, factory, or other organization, you are already aware of this fact. Job design and motivation are indeed important factors in such settings; but they are far from the entire picture. Performance is also strongly affected by many other conditions as well; and these include the nature of social relations among employees, their attitudes toward work, and so on. From the perspective of the 1980s, this fact is obvious and easy to grasp. Yet, in the early decades of the present century, it took some dramatic research findings to call it firmly to the attention of the practitioners of scientific management. The research that accomplished this important task—and so stimulated the development of the famous **human relations movement**—is known collectively as the *Hawthorne studies*. Because of the importance of this project in the history of O.B., we will now describe it briefly.

The Hawthorne studies: A brief description.   In the mid-1920s, a series of fairly typical scientific management studies were begun at the Hawthorne works of the Western Electric Company—a plant outside Chicago. The initial purpose of the research was straightforward: to determine the impact of level of illumination on worker productivity. Several female employees took part in the study. One group worked in a control room where the level of illumination was held constant; another group worked in a test room where brightness was varied in a systematic manner. Results were quite baffling: productivity increased in both the test and control rooms. Further, there seemed to be no orderly link between level of illumination and productivity. For example, worker output remained high in the test room even when illumination was reduced to that of moonlight—a level so dim that workers could barely see what they were doing!

Puzzled by these findings, officials of Western Electric called in a team of experts headed by Elton Mayo. These researchers set to work with considerable energy, and their findings proved to have a major impact upon management and the developing field of organizational behavior.[5] In an initial series of studies (the *Relay Room Experiments*), Mayo and his colleagues examined the impact of thirteen different factors on productivity. These included length of rest pauses, length of work day and work week, method of payment, place of work, and even provision of a free mid-morning lunch. Subjects were again female employees who worked in a special test room throughout the study. Once more, results were quite mysterious: productivity increased with almost every change of work conditions (see Figure 1-5). Indeed, even when subjects were returned to the initial, standard conditions that existed at the start of the research, productivity continued to rise. We should note that such findings were replicated several times, with different tasks, different groups of workers, and different settings. But what did these results mean? Why did productivity continue to rise in this totally unpredicted manner? These were among the many questions confronted by the team of researchers.

As if the findings we have just outlined were not puzzling enough, additional studies soon added to the confusion. For example, in one especially revealing investigation (the *Bank Wiring Room Study*), male members of an existing work group were carefully observed by members of the research team. No attempts were made to alter the conditions under which they labored, but employees were interviewed during non-work periods by another investigator. Here, results were quite distinct from those in the earlier studies. Productivity did *not* rise continuously. On the contrary, it soon became obvious that workers in this group were deliberately restricting their output. This was revealed both by observations of

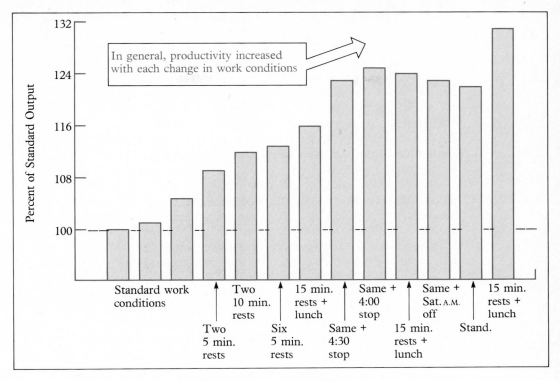

FIGURE 1-5   Results of One of the Famous Hawthorne Studies

As shown here, productivity among a group of female employees increased with each of a wide range of changes in work conditions. Indeed, it even rose when subjects were returned to initial, standard conditions. These and other findings of the Hawthorne studies pointed to the fact that on-the-job performance is strongly affected by a number of social factors. (Source: Based on data from Roethlisberger & Dickson, *Management and the Worker*. Cambridge, Mass.: Harvard University Press, 1939.)

their work behavior (e.g., all men stopped work well before quitting time) and by the interviews (almost all admitted that they could easily do more if they so desired). But why was this the case? Why did these findings differ so sharply from those obtained in the earlier studies? Fortunately, Mayo and his colleagues soon grasped the answer. On the basis of the findings we have already described, and those obtained in interviews with as many as 20,000 workers, they reached the following conclusion: *Work places are actually complex social settings.* Thus, in order to comprehend behavior in them, it is necessary to understand worker attitudes, social relationships, informal networks of communication, and a host of other variables.

Armed with this important insight, Mayo and his coworkers were soon able to interpret the seemingly contradictory findings obtained in their research. First, in terms of the initial Relay Room Experiments, it became clear that productivity rose continuously because subjects reacted favorably to the special attention they received and to the relatively free supervisory climate in the test room. In short, they knew they were being observed; and, because they experienced positive reactions to this attention, their motivation—and productivity—rose. In contrast, output was held low in the Bank Wiring Room Study because of other factors. The men in that investigation feared "working themselves out of a job," and raising the work standard (the amount to be completed each day) if their productivity was too high. In order to avoid such negative outcomes, they established informal but powerful rules governing conduct on the job—rules that operated to hold production down. Indeed, even sanctions against "rate busters" (men who worked too hard) were specified.

In short, Mayo and his colleagues concluded that social variables, such as group pressure to raise or lower production, relations between employees, and supervisory style, played a key role in generating the results of both sets of studies. In one case, these factors operated to enhance productivity; in the other, they acted to restrain it. However, in both instances, insight into on-the-job performance could be gained from attention to important aspects of human behavior.

Incidentally, we should note that effects such as those observed in the Relay Room studies—changes in subjects' behavior stemming mainly from their knowledge that they were participating in an experiment and were being observed—are quite common. Because their importance was first noted by Mayo and his associates, such changes are generally known as "the *Hawthorne effect*." And, unfortunately, they constitute just one of the many pitfalls researchers must avoid in their complex quest for knowledge about behavior in organizational settings (see Chapter 2).

The Hawthorne studies: Impact and interpretation.   At this point, we should note that the studies performed within the scope of the Hawthorne project were quite flawed by modern standards.[6] For example, essential control groups were often omitted, and no attempt was made to assure that subjects were representative of larger populations. (See Chapter 2 for further discussion of these points.) Despite these drawbacks, however, their impact was impressive. As we have already noted, the findings of these studies called attention to the fact that work settings are social situations. Further, they indicated that full understanding of behavior in organizational contexts requires attention to factors largely ignored by scientific management. As this basic principle gained recognition, a new perspective in management—the **human relations** approach—took form. This perspective devoted far more attention to human needs, motives, and relationships than had previously been the case. Indeed, it recognized that only through attention to such factors can organizational effectiveness and growth be encouraged. The human relations movement persisted for several decades, and it is influential in some quarters even today. Further, there can be little doubt that several of its basic ideas and concepts contributed heavily to the modern field of O.B. In this manner, the workers in that long-vanished plant outside Chicago have probably exerted a far more profound and lasting effect on modern organizations than they would ever have dreamed possible.

Organizational Behavior in the 1980s:
A Modern Perspective

It is often tempting to assume that the "modern approach" in any field of study is somehow radically different from what went before. In a sense, this is totally understandable. We all wish to feel that in contrast to those here before us, *we* are closer to the truth and more sophisticated both in our questions and in the answers we obtain. Certainly, O.B. is far from immune to such temptations. Indeed, like many other fields, it places great emphasis on what is "new" and "modern." But it would be a serious error for us to yield to such inducements. In a crucial sense, modern O.B. represents a logical and orderly extension of approaches and perspectives of the past. This is not to say that it is highly similar to these approaches—far from it. But as we hope to show, it is different in ways that reflect growth and refinement rather than radical change.

Basically, we feel that modern O.B. is characterized by four major features worthy of careful attention. First, it has adopted a somewhat more positive view of human beings in work settings than prevailed in the past. Second, by drawing on several related fields, it has attained a high degree of sophistication about human behavior—sophistication that often proves useful in practical respects. Third, and partly as a result of the sophistication to which we have just referred, it has adopted a *contingency approach* to behavior in organizations—an approach that begins with the assumption that there are no simple answers. And fourth, it is *integrative* in nature. That is, it seeks to comprehend behavior in organizations by combining information from several different levels of analysis (individuals, groups, and organizations). We will now consider each of these features.

Modern O.B. and the human resources model. Suppose that you approached a number of managers and asked them, individually, to describe their basic view of human nature. What kind of answers do you think you would receive? Unfortunately, even today, the replies would probably be somewhat negative in tone. For example, many of the persons questioned might suggest that human beings are basically lazy, and either unwilling or unable to accept much responsibility. Further, they might note that the role of the manager is mainly that of giving such persons direction—keeping them on the "straight and narrow," so to speak. This traditional view (often known as *Theory X*) has prevailed for centuries and is, we're afraid, still very much with us (see Figure 1-6).

A sharply contrasting view was offered more than twenty years ago by Douglas McGregor.[7] This perspective—known as the **human resources model** or simply *Theory Y*—rejects the assumption that human beings are innately lazy and irresponsible. Instead, it suggests that under appropriate conditions, they are just as capable of showing self-direction and responsibility as they are of "goofing off" and avoiding unpleasant duties. Thus, two key tasks for managers are (1) to determine what these favorable conditions are and (2) to assure that they exist. When appropriate circumstances prevail, it is reasoned, employees will demonstrate many desirable behaviors. And then, important but previously untapped human resources will be brought into play.

"Faster!"

FIGURE 1-6   Theory X Strikes Again!

As suggested by this cartoon, managers have often viewed employees as lazy creatures, who must be coerced into work or responsibility. (Source: Drawing by Whitney Darrow; © 1977 The New Yorker Magazine, Inc.)

Please note: Theory Y—which reflects a perspective adopted by many practitioners of modern O.B.—does *not* assume that human beings are always responsible or productive. Rather, it simply suggests that they react to the conditions around them. If these are favorable (e.g., they are treated with respect and consideration by management), they may respond by working hard, accepting responsibility, and demonstrating many other desirable actions. However, if these are negative (e.g., they are treated in a condescending or exploitive manner), they may show far less desirable patterns of behavior. In short, modern O.B. does not view the world of work through rose-colored glasses, and is not given to bursts of Pollyanna-like euphoria. However, it *does* assume that there are no intrinsic, built-in reasons why employees cannot be encouraged to show positive actions and to accept high levels of self-direction and responsibility. In this respect, at least, it is considerably more optimistic in its outlook than the traditional view represented by Theory X. (We will consider yet another approach, *Theory Z,* later in this book.)[8]

Modern O.B. and behavioral science.   A second major feature of modern O.B. is its vastly increased sophistication concerning human behavior. Since O.B. seeks to comprehend behavior in organizational settings, it is only reasonable that it should draw heavily on the findings and principles of fields such as psychology, sociology, and anthropology. In fact, in the 1980s, this is very much the case. Indeed, modern O.B. may be viewed as a major beneficiary of recent progress in these and other behavioral sciences.[9] From psychology, O.B. has acquired considerable knowledge of basic individual processes such as learning, perception, and motivation. And from social psychology and sociology it has gained much information on group processes such as leadership, cooperation, communication, and social influence. Such "importation" of knowledge from the behavioral sciences certainly went on in the past; this trend is far from new. But it is our impression that it has increased in recent years, and that O.B. has benefitted greatly from it. At this point, we should hasten to note that O.B. is not simply a "consumer" of information about human behavior. Many scientists with a background in O.B. have contributed greatly through their own research projects. But regardless of the source of such information, the major point is clear: in the 1980s, O.B. brings considerable sophistication about human behavior to bear upon its central concern: behavior in organizational settings.

Modern O.B. and the contingency approach: Realizing that there are, in fact, no simple answers. Partly as a result of the growing sophistication we have just described, and partly as a result of its own work and insights, modern O.B. has come to the following conclusion: where behavior in organizations is concerned, there are—alas!—no simple answers. The processes studied by O.B. are too complex and are affected by too many different factors to permit us this basic luxury. Thus, to mention just a few examples of this perspective (usually known as the **contingency approach**), there is no single "best" style of leadership, method of communication, approach to decision-making, or organizational structure.[10] Rather, the most successful style, approach, method, or structure varies from situation to situation, from one set of circumstances to another. A central assumption of the contingency approach, then, is that key processes in organizational behavior cannot be understood in isolation. Instead, they must be examined against a complex backdrop of many interacting factors.

Because of its awareness of such complexity, the answers offered by the contingency approach are often more complex and so less appealing than those offered by earlier and less sophisticated perspectives. But they offer one key advantage that cannot be overlooked: current evidence indicates that they are considerably closer to the truth. For this reason, the contingency approach is widely accepted in O.B. at the present time. And indeed, we will return to it—and its interesting findings—at several points in this book.

Modern O.B.: An integrative field. A final feature of modern O.B. to which we'd like to call your attention involves its essentially *integrative nature.* As we have already noted, O.B. draws upon the principles and findings of several related fields (e.g., psychology, sociology, organizational theory). But it does much more than just this: it also *integrates* this information (as well as findings from its own research) into a unified framework for comprehending behavior in organizational settings. In this respect, it may be viewed as unique. The fields closely related to O.B., and on which it often draws, tend to focus almost exclusively on a single level of analysis. Thus, psychology directs its attention primarily to processes involving *individuals.* Sociology and social psychology focus on *social interaction*

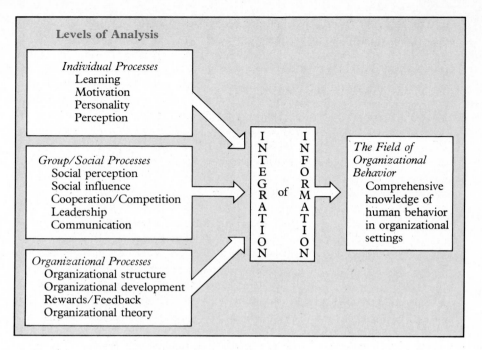

FIGURE 1-7   Modern O.B.: An Integrative Field

The field of O.B. combines information from three different levels of analysis (individuals, groups, organizations) into a unified view of human behavior in organizational settings.

and *group processes.* And organizational theory is primarily concerned with the structure and functioning of *organizations.*[11] To a large extent, each of these fields focuses on its chosen level of analysis, while largely ignoring, or at least deemphasizing, the others. This is *not* the case in O.B. In contrast, it actively seeks to integrate information from all three levels (see Figure 1-7). The result, we strongly believe, is a more complete, accurate, and comprehensive picture of human behavior in organizations than can be obtained by any other approach. In sum, we feel that the integrative nature of O.B. allows it to make a unique and important contribution—one whose value is increasingly recognized by business and by other fields of study.[12]

USING THIS BOOK: A DISPLACED (BUT NOT *MIS*PLACED) PREFACE

When was the last time you read the preface to one of your texts? If you are like most students, your answer is probably something like "Who remembers?" or even "Who cares?" Actually, this is unfortunate, for prefaces often *do* contain useful information—facts that can help you make more effective use of a particular volume. For this reason, we will now comment briefly on several features of this text.

First, we'd like to say a few words about its overall structure. We begin by considering some of the basic processes that underlie the behavior of individuals in organizations (e.g., learning, motivation, perception, attitudes, and stress). Next, we turn our attention to group or social processes affecting such behavior (e.g., communication, leadership, and decision making). And finally, we focus on the structure of organizations and on the techniques for enhancing their effectiveness. Thus, in general, we move from a focus on individuals to a focus on groups, and then to concern with organizations themselves.

Second, we wish to call your attention to several features of our text that are designed to make it easier and more convenient for you to use. Each chapter is preceded by an outline and a list of key concepts and terms. All chapters end with a summary of important points; and key terms (those listed earlier) are printed in **dark type like this** and are defined in a glossary following each chapter. We have also included a number of figures, charts, and graphs. All are designed to help you understand the concepts and findings presented, and all contain special labels that call attention to the major points being made. Third, we wish to note that we have made use of three distinct types of inserts, or "boxes," throughout the text. The first of these is labeled *From the Manager's Perspective*. Inserts of this type point out applications and implications of materials presented for actual management policy. The second type is called *Focus on Behavior* (see the one on p. 10). These boxes present descriptions of interesting lines of research or simple demonstrations you can perform yourself to gain first-hand experience with some of the facts and principles we cover. These demonstrations are all entirely safe and ethical, and we believe that you will find them interesting. The third type of insert is labeled *Case in Point*. These boxes describe actual (or in some instances, hypothetical) cases illustrating various aspects of organizational behavior. They are included to help emphasize important links between text materials and actual situations you may well encounter in the years ahead.

We hope that the features described above will help us to communicate a good deal of information about behavior in organizations in an interesting and useful way. Further, we hope that these features allow at least some of our own excitement with the field to come through in an undistorted manner. To the extent that we succeed in these tasks—and only to that extent—will we be satisfied that, as authors and teachers, we have done our part. The rest, of course, is up to you!

SUMMARY

The field of **organizational behavior** (O.B.) focuses upon human behavior in organizational settings. Specifically, it seeks to comprehend and predict behavior in organizations through the scientific study of individual processes, group processes, and organizational structure and function.

In a sense, the field of O.B. is very old; every civilization has shown interest in understanding behavior in organizations. However, it is only during the past hundred years that a systematic and science-oriented approach to this topic has emerged. *Scientific management*—one early predecessor of the modern field of O.B.—stressed the importance of designing jobs so that they could be performed as efficiently as possible. In contrast, the *human relations movement* emphasized the key role of social factors in work settings. This approach was stimulated, in part, by the famous Hawthorne studies of the late 1920s and early 1930s.

Modern O.B. is characterized by acceptance of a *human resources model*. This approach views human beings not as lazy creatures who must be coerced, but rather as individuals possessing important untapped resources. Within this perspective, the task of managers is seen as that of arranging conditions so that each person can perform to the fullest of his or her ability. Modern O.B. is also *science-oriented* in its approach and borrows much from related fields such as psychology and sociology. Finally, it is *integrative* in nature, seeking to combine information from several distinct levels of analysis (individuals, groups, organizations) into a comprehensive picture of behavior in organizational settings.

KEY TERMS

CONTINGENCY APPROACH   A perspective in modern O.B. that takes full account of the great complexity of behavior in organizational settings. Rather than searching for nonexistent "simple answers," the contingency approach seeks to understand the complex pattern of interacting factors that affect key aspects of organizational behavior.

HUMAN RELATIONS MOVEMENT   An approach to management and organizational behavior recognizing the importance of social factors in work settings.

HUMAN RESOURCES MODEL   An approach characteristic of modern O.B. In contrast to earlier views, the human resources model views human beings as capable of self-direction and as possessing important untapped resources.

ORGANIZATION   Any social structure consisting of two or more persons who are interdependent and who work together to attain one or more common goals.

ORGANIZATIONAL BEHAVIOR   The field that seeks to comprehend and predict human behavior in organizational settings through scientific study of individual processes, group processes, and organizational structure and function.

SCIENTIFIC MANAGEMENT   An early approach to management and organizational behavior that emphasized the importance of designing jobs and tasks so that they could be performed as efficiently as possible.

NOTES

1. Mintzberg, H. *The nature of managerial work.* New York: Harper & Row, 1973.
2. Staw, B.M., & Salancik, G.R. (Eds.) *New directions in organizational behavior.* Chicago: St. Clair Press, 1977.

3. Taylor, F.W. *The principles of scientific management.* New York: Harper & Brothers, 1911.

4. Locke, E.A. The ideas of Frederick W. Taylor: An evaluation. *Academy of Management Review,* 1982, *7,* 14–24.

5. Roethlisberger, F.J., & Dickson, W.J. *Management and the worker.* Cambridge, Mass.: Harvard University Press, 1939.

6. Franke, R., & Kaul, J. The Hawthorne experiments: First statistical interpretations. *American Sociological Review,* 1978, 623–643.

7. McGregor, D. *The human side of enterprise.* New York: McGraw-Hill, 1960.

8. Ouchi, W.G. *Theory Z: How American business can meet the Japanese challenge.* Reading, Mass.: Addison-Wesley, 1981.

9. Bonoma, T.V., & Zaltman, G. *Psychology for management.* Boston: Kent Publishing Co., 1981.

10. Schoonhoven, C.B. Problems with contingency theory: Testing assumptions hidden within the language of contingency "theory." *Administrative Science Quarterly,* 1981, *26,* 349–377.

11. Robey, D. *Designing organizations: A macro perspective.* Homewood, Ill.: Richard D. Irwin Co., 1982.

12. Stewart, R. A model for understanding managerial jobs and behavior. *Academy of Management Review,* 1982, *7,* 7–13.

Answers to Common Sense test (from the "FOCUS" box on p. 10)

1. F, 2. F, 3. F, 4. F, 5. F, 6. F, 7. F, 8. F, 9. F, 10. F

2

In Quest of Understanding:
Research Methods
in Organizational Behavior

KEY CONCEPTS

Experimentation   Demand Characteristics
Systematic Observation   Correlational Approach
Survey Method   Unobtrusive Measures
Case Method   Reliability
Independent Variable   Validity
Dependent Variable   Generalizability
Random Assignment

□ □ □

"Well, what are we going to do about Angel?" asks Terry, the manager of your department. "She's the kind of problem everyone likes, but we've got to do something about the situation—it's gone on too long already."

"I agree," says Irv, another member of your group. "She was hired as a technician, and she does a heck of a job at that. But she also writes those great programs. I'll bet she saved the company plenty with that last one. It really cut down on computer time. And the printout is much easier to read than the old format."

"It's a crazy situation, I'll admit," adds Larry. "Here we hire her to do one job, and she ends up doing that plus another. And in her spare time, no less. I think we've got to reward her in some way. Why don't we change her job description to include some program writing. Then we can give her a raise too."

"Sounds good to me," answers Terry. "If you all agree, I'll get on it right away."

At this point, Pam breaks in, although with obvious reluctance: "Gee, I don't know. That certainly sounds fair and all, but I'm wondering—if we change her job description so that she's supposed to write programs, won't that make it kind of like work? Right now she seems to enjoy playing around with the computer—it's a hobby. But if we make it part of her regular job, and give her a raise for doing it, maybe she won't enjoy it so much."

"Oh come on, Pam," answers Terry. "Everyone likes more money. I think the question is settled."

At this last remark, everyone laughs, and the informal meeting breaks up. But as you leave, you find yourself wondering whether this is really the best course to follow. Perhaps Pam is right. Giving Angel a raise is fair, but won't it change the way she feels about program writing? If only you knew for sure. . . .

Who is actually correct in this example—Terry and the others or Pam? Even more important, how can we ever find out? One approach to answering such questions is simple: we can proceed on the basis of common sense. That is, we can examine our own experience and informal knowledge for clues about human behavior. And then, we can apply such "knowledge" to the situation at hand. Unfortunately, as we noted in Chapter 1, this method often gets us into serious trouble. Common sense is quite unreliable as a guide to human behavior, and can lead us to many false conclusions (see Figure 2-1). This is the case in our example. A

FIGURE 2-1 Common Sense and Human Behavior: Trust It at Your Own Risk!

As suggested by this cartoon, common sense often leads us to false conclusions about other persons or their behavior. (Source: Reprinted by permission of the Tribune Company Syndicate, Inc.)

large body of research findings indicate that providing individuals with external rewards for performing activities they enjoy may sharply reduce their intrinsic interest in these activities.[1] Thus, it is quite possible that providing Angel with a raise for her program-writing may convert what is now an enjoyable hobby into a tedious chore—with all that this implies.

Given that common sense is unreliable in many situations, what alternative can we pursue? To repeat our comments in Chapter 1, we can adopt the methods of science and seek answers to our questions about human behavior through systematic research. In the present chapter, we will acquaint you with some of these techniques. That is, we will explain just how scientists wishing to uncover valid knowledge about behavior in organizations actually proceed. Our main purpose here is certainly *not* that of turning you into an expert in behavioral research. It takes several years to master such techniques.[2] But we do feel that a basic grasp of these methods will prove useful to you in the years ahead. In fact, we believe that such knowledge will help to make you a better manager in several respects. Our reasons for holding this view are summarized in the **"PERSPECTIVE"** box on pages 28–29. Please read it carefully before proceeding. We predict that when you do, your own ideas about the practical value of understanding research will change considerably.

In the discussion that follows, we will consider several different methods used by researchers to increase our knowledge of human behavior in organizational settings. These include **experimentation, systematic observation,** the **survey method,** and the **case method.**

THE EXPERIMENTAL METHOD: KNOWLEDGE THROUGH INTERVENTION

Because experimentation is generally viewed as one of the strongest weapons in the research "arsenal" of behavioral science, we will consider it first. Unfortunately, our past teaching experience suggests that many persons view this ap-

FROM THE MANAGER'S PERSPECTIVE

Understanding Research: Are There Any Practical Payoffs?

As we noted above, this chapter is designed to provide you with a basic grasp of some of the methods used to acquire knowledge about behavior in organizations. We plan to do our best to make the nature of these techniques clear and easy to grasp. But once you have read the chapter and acquired this information, what can you do with it? Will it prove useful to you in your career in business? In short, is there any reason why someone with your goals and plans should know about experimentation, systematic observation, and related issues? Our answer is an emphatic *"Yes!"* We firmly believe that there are important reasons for having a working knowledge of such techniques, even if you don't plan to use them yourself. Basically, these reasons fall under two major headings.

First, we feel that knowing something about such methods will make you a more effective evaluator (and user) of research findings. At many points in your life, you will read or hear statements about human behavior. Some of these will be based solely on "common sense" or informal observation. You already know how to interpret these—with a great degree of caution. Others, however, will be based on the results of research studies. For example, one day you may read an article in the newspaper noting that the findings of a recent medical study point to a link between coffee drinking and heart attacks: the more coffee people drink, the more likely they are to suffer cardiac arrest. Similarly, at a staff meeting you may hear that "studies suggest" that certain types of bonus pay systems are more effective in raising productivity than others. And often, you will encounter commercials claiming that "conclusive research evidence" indicates that the sponsor's product is best. How should you react to such statements? In our opinion, with a healthy degree of skepticism! Research, like all human endeavors, can vary greatly in qual-

proach as both mysterious and complex. Actually, though, this is far from the case. In its basic logic, the experimental method is surprisingly simple. To help you understand its use and value in the field of organizational behavior, we will first describe its basic nature. Then we will mention two conditions essential for its successful application. Finally, we will comment briefly on its use in two sharply different settings: the laboratory and the field.

Experimentation: Its Basic Nature

A researcher who decides to employ the experimental method in his or her work generally begins with a clear-cut goal: determine whether a given factor (variable) influences some specific form of behavior. In order to study this question, the researcher then follows two basic steps: (1) she varies the presence or strength of this factor in a systematic manner, and (2) she seeks to determine whether these variations have any impact upon the behavior under study. The essential idea behind these procedures is as follows: if the factor varied exerts such effects, individuals exposed to different levels or amounts of it should show different patterns

ity. Before accepting its conclusions, you should seek to learn something about the way in which it was conducted. And this, of course, is where a working knowledge of research methods will prove useful: it will help you to evaluate the basis for such statements and to decide whether they should be accepted or discounted. In short, a basic grasp of research methods will help you to separate valid findings and conclusions from ones that should be doubted, and this may often be of considerable practical value.

Second, having such knowledge at your disposal may well yield another payoff: it will make you a more sophisticated and versatile manager. Obviously, no one can be an expert in everything; indeed, attempts along these lines often backfire. But there *is* something to be said for having a basic idea of what people in other fields do and for being able to speak their language, at least to a degree. A basic knowledge of research methods may prove useful

to you in this respect. For example, in the years ahead, you may well find yourself having to interact with professionals in the field of human behavior (e.g., psychologists, sociologists). In particular, you may have to deal with these persons as expert consultants—people you have hired to help answer questions or solve various problems. In such cases, we believe, knowing something about research methods may prove helpful. At the very least, it will help you to communicate with these experts and to understand the basic strategies they are using in their attempts to solve the problems at hand.

In short, we believe that basic knowledge about research methods is far from an exercise in empty academics. On the contrary, we suggest that having such information will prove useful to you in several important respects. And while we believe that knowledge is a good thing, in and of itself, we also feel that knowledge that can be *used* is even better! □

---

of behavior. That is, exposure to a small amount of the factor should result in one level of behavior, exposure to a larger amount should result in another level, and so on.

Generally, the factor systematically varied by the experimenter is termed the **independent variable,** while the behavior studied is termed the **dependent variable.** In a typical experiment, then, subjects in several different groups (or conditions) are exposed to different levels of the independent variable (e.g., low, moderate, high). The behavior of these persons is then compared to determine whether it does in fact vary with different levels or amounts of the independent variable. If it does—and if two other conditions we shall mention shortly are met—it can be tentatively concluded that the independent variable does indeed affect the form of behavior being studied.

Since our discussion so far has been somewhat abstract, a concrete example may now prove useful. In this regard, let us consider an experiment designed to examine the *hypothesis* (an as yet untested suggestion) that interviewers' ratings of job applicants can be strongly affected by the personal characteristics of the applicants, quite apart from their experience, training, and other job-related qualifications. In particular, the researcher wishes to examine the prediction that applicants associated with a pleasant scent (i.e., those wearing cologne or perfume) will receive higher ratings than those not associated with such a scent. In order to investigate this possibility, researchers have subjects in the study play the role of a personnel manager and conduct a brief interview with another person, who plays the role of job applicant. Unknown to subjects, this individual is actually an accomplice of the researcher and appears for the interview in one of three states: (1) wearing no perfume or cologne, (2) wearing a mildly pleasant perfume or cologne, (3) wearing a very pleasant perfume or cologne. As you can see this constitutes manipulation of the independent variable. (Assume, by the way, that many perfumes and colognes have previously been rated by a large number of persons, and ones that induce the desired reactions have been selected for use in the study.)

After interviewing the applicant, subjects rate this person on a number of dimensions (e.g., suitability for the job, likelihood of success in this position, etc.). If the presence of a pleasant scent does in fact affect such ratings, we would expect them to vary across the three experimental conditions described earlier. Specifically, we would predict that ratings would be highest when the accomplice wears a very pleasant perfume or cologne, somewhat lower when this person wears a mildly pleasant scent, and lowest of all when the applicant wears no scent. If such results were actually obtained (see Figure 2-2), we could conclude, at least

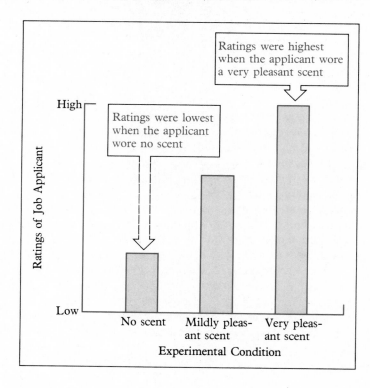

FIGURE 2-2   The Experimental Method: A Concrete Example

In the experiment represented here, subjects played the role of a personnel manager and interviewed job applicants who wore no scent, a mildly pleasant scent, or a very pleasant scent. Results indicated that ratings of the applicants were in fact affected by this independent variable.

tentatively, that pleasant scents do affect ratings of job applicants—a finding of considerable practical interest to interviewers and applicants alike. (Actually, several experiments have examined the impact of personal characteristics on the ratings received by job interviewees.[3] And one recent study has examined the impact of cologne and perfume on such ratings.[4] This research is discussed in Chapter 6.)

At this point we should note that the example just presented describes an extremely simple case—the simplest type of experiment one could conduct. In many instances, researchers seek to examine the impact of several independent variables at once. For example, in the research we have been describing, applicants' mode of dress and their sex might also be considered, along with the potential impact of pleasant scents. In any case, the most important point to bear in mind is this: regardless of the specific topic under investigation or the number of factors manipulated, the basic approach remains the same. One or more independent variables is systematically varied, and the effects of such variations upon behavior are examined.

Experimentation: Two Essential Conditions

Earlier (on p. 29), we noted that before we can conclude that an independent variable has affected some form of behavior, two important conditions must be met. Because a basic understanding of these is essential for evaluating the worth of any experiment, we will now describe them for you.

Random assignment of subjects to groups. The first condition involves what is generally termed **random assignment** of subjects to experimental groups. According to this principle, each person taking part in a study must have an equal chance of being exposed to each level of the independent variable. The reason for this rule is simple: if the subjects are *not* randomly assigned to each group, it may prove impossible to determine whether differences in their behavior stem from differences between subjects in the various groups—differences they brought with them to the study—or from the effects of the independent variable.

For example, returning to the study described above, consider what would happen if, for some reason, all the subjects assigned to the mildly pleasant and very pleasant scent conditions had terrible colds, while those in the no scent group did not. Here, results might well reveal no differences in the ratings given to the accomplice by subjects in these three conditions. If the researcher conducting the study were not aware of the fact that participants in the first two groups all had colds, she might conclude that perfume and cologne have no impact upon the outcome of job interviews. As you can readily see, though, this suggestion might well be false. After all, persons in the key experimental groups could probably not detect a pleasant scent even if they tried! In order to avoid such difficulties, it is crucial that subjects taking part in an experiment be randomly assigned to its various groups. (In the present case, of course, this would assure that about equal numbers of individuals in each group have colds.)

The absence of confounding variables.   The second condition to which we referred earlier may be stated as follows: all other factors that might also affect subjects' behavior aside from the independent variable must be held constant. To see why this is so, consider the following situation. In the study on the impact of pleasant scents described above, the researcher pays little attention to other variables. Thus, as bad luck would have it, the accomplices also vary their style of dress. Specifically, they dress very neatly and attractively when wearing either the mildly pleasant or very pleasant scent, but dress in a more casual manner when wearing no scent. (Assume that because of the lingering quality of the perfume and cologne used, it is necessary to conduct the no-scent, mildly pleasant scent, and very pleasant scent conditions on different days. Thus, the accomplices have an opportunity to vary their dress.) Results are as reported previously: subjects assign higher ratings to the job applicants (i.e., the accomplices) when they wear perfume or cologne than when they do not. What do these findings mean? Actually, we can't tell. There is no way of knowing whether these higher ratings stem from the presence of pleasant scents or from the accomplices' neater style of dress. In short, these two variables are *confounded*—the possible effects of each cannot be disentangled (see Figure 2-3).

In the case we have just described, such confounding between variables is easy to spot. In many instances, though, it can enter in more subtle and hidden ways.

FIGURE 2-3   Confounding of Variables: A Serious Pitfall for Unwary Experimenters

When factors other than the independent variable in an experiment are not held constant, it may be impossible to interpret the results. In the example shown here, the independent variable involved the presence or absence of pleasant scents (perfume or cologne). However, another factor—the applicant's style of dress—was also allowed to vary. As a result, it is impossible to tell why these persons received higher ratings in some cases than others.

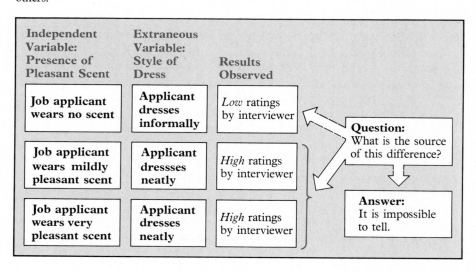

For this reason, researchers interested in human behavior in organizations must always be on guard to prevent its occurrence. The general rule they must follow is simply this: insofar as possible, all factors other than the one under study (i.e., the independent variable) should be held constant. Only when this is the case can the results of an experiment be interpreted with confidence.

Experimentation: Laboratory or Field?

Before concluding our discussion of experimentation, we wish to note that such research can be conducted in many different settings. Perhaps the most common location for experiments concerned with human behavior is the formal research laboratory. This was true in the study described above. Participants in that imaginary experiment reported to a laboratory, where they were exposed to the relevant independent variable (a pleasant or unpleasant scent) and worked on various tasks. The major advantage offered by this type of setting is obvious: when an experiment is conducted in a formal research laboratory, it is usually easier to avoid the type of confounding we mentioned above. That is, since the researcher has considerable influence over the conditions existing in his or her laboratory, factors other than the independent variable can be held constant or *controlled*.

While research laboratories offer this important advantage, however, they also suffer from certain drawbacks. For example, because they exist in special locations (often, on university campuses or in research institutes), they are physically removed from actual work settings. As a result, it is often difficult or impractical for employees to visit them in order to take part in an experiment. It is primarily for this reason that researchers often draw heavily upon groups of subjects who are close at hand, such as college students, or employees of their own organization. Needless to say, such persons may differ from the groups to which findings are to be generalized; and this can create important problems. (We will return to this crucial issue of *generalizability* on pp. 46–48.) In addition, because research laboratories are special and unfamiliar places, subjects may behave quite differently in them than they do in other, more natural settings. For example, they may often attempt to act in the way they think the researcher *wants* them to act. That is, they may try to guess the experimenter's hypothesis and then behave in ways that confirm such predictions. (Cues that reveal the hypothesis under study are known as **demand characteristics,** and they are often present in laboratory studies.) Needless to add, when subjects attempt to "help" a researcher in this manner, the findings of the project become invalid. After all, they now stem from the subjects' desire to confirm the major predictions—*not* from the impact of the independent variable.

While several methods for countering the impact of demand characteristics and other problems connected with laboratory research exist, many investigators in organizational behavior seek to lessen these difficulties by conducting their experiments in *field settings*. That is, they "set up shop" in natural locations where the subjects they wish to study normally spend part of their day. Factories, of-

FIGURE 2–4   Field Research: Studying Human Behavior in Natural Settings

In recent years, researchers have conducted field experiments on human behavior even in settings like this. (Source: Photo © Peggy McMahon/Picture Group.)

fices, and other work settings have frequently served as the site of such field experiments.[5] Adventurous researchers have also conducted investigations of human behavior in settings as varied as beaches, restaurants, subways, and even crowded bars (see Figure 2–4).[6]

The major advantages offered by field research are obvious. The participants in such experiments are clearly members of the groups whose behavior is of interest. Thus, the problem of generalizability is greatly reduced. Similarly, because the site of such research is both familiar and natural, subjects' behavior, too, may be quite close to what it usually is in these locations. Opposed to these benefits, however, is a major disadvantage: researchers working in field settings must often surrender some degree of control over extraneous factors—factors other than the independent variable that also may affect subjects' behavior. Because of this loss of experimental control, the findings of field research are sometimes more open to conflicting interpretations than those of laboratory studies.

We should also mention that field experiments often raise important *ethical issues*. Is it appropriate to expose subjects to independent variables without their prior consent? How can they be informed about the results of a study if they are

TABLE 2-1   Laboratory or Field? Often, the Choice Is Complex

Both field and laboratory research offer important advantages. Similarly, both suffer from certain disadvantages.

	ADVANTAGES	DISADVANTAGES
Laboratory Research	High degree of control over independent variables Impact of extraneous factors can be lessened or eliminated Rights and safety of subjects can be protected (informed consent and debriefing can be used)	Artificiality Potential impact of demand characteristics Generalizability of results may be problematic
Field Research	Realistic Participants are representative of the group being studied Potential impact of demand characteristics may be lessened	Lower degree of control over independent varibles More difficult to protect rights and safety of subjects (e.g., difficult to use informed consent and debriefing

no longer available when it is completed? These are complex questions with no simple answers. Yet, they must be taken into account when field research is planned.

As you can readily see, there is a definite trade-off involved in the choice between laboratory and field experimentation. Both offer advantages but both also suffer from specific problems (see Table 2-1). Fortunately, skilled researchers can usually maximize the benefits and minimize the costs associated with each. Thus, both techniques are useful to the field of organizational behavior and have added greatly to our knowledge of human behavior in work settings.[7]

THE CORRELATIONAL METHOD: KNOWLEDGE THROUGH SYSTEMATIC OBSERVATION

As we noted earlier, experimentation is generally viewed as one of the most powerful methods for conducting research on human behavior. Perhaps the major reason for this lies in its success in establishing cause-and-effect relationships. Briefly, if systematic variations in an independent variable produce systematic changes in some dependent variable, we can often conclude that a cause-and-effect bond exists between these factors. Changes in the independent variable are assumed to have *caused* changes in the dependent variable (i.e., in some form of behavior).

Often, though, practical or ethical constraints prevent the use of experimental methods. With respect to practical limitations, it is sometimes the case that systematic variation of the key independent factors is simply beyond an investigator's control. For example, consider a researcher who wishes to test the hypothesis that companies whose presidents possess certain personality traits will be more successful than companies whose presidents possess other traits. Obviously, there is no way in which he could replace the leaders of large organizations at will, in order to see how individuals with different patterns of traits affect the financial fortunes of these businesses.

Turning to ethical limitations, it is often the case that independent variables can, in principle, be varied; but doing so would raise serious ethical questions. For example, imagine a researcher who suspects that certain kinds of stress in work settings lead to heart attacks or other serious illness. Certainly, it would be unethical for him to expose employees to these conditions in order to determine if fatalities among them actually increase! Similarly, consider a researcher who suspects that certain types of inequity (unfairness) in pay lead to low morale and high turnover among employees. Could he ethically convince several companies to introduce such conditions in order to test this hypothesis? Again, our answer would be "no." In these and many other situations, then, use of the experimental method is not permissible.

Fortunately, when experimentation cannot be employed, it is not necessary for researchers to throw up their hands in despair. Instead, they can turn to an alternative method known as the **correlational approach.** We will now describe this basic method of research in organizational behavior and also call attention to its major liability—a degree of ambiguity with respect to the establishment of cause-and-effect relationships.

Correlational Research: A Brief Description

The correlational method, like experimentation, is quite straightforward in its essential logic. Briefly, it involves careful observation of two or more variables in order to determine if they are related in any manner. If changes in one are found to be consistently associated with changes in the other, evidence for a link between them is obtained. Please note that in contrast to experimentation, no attempt is made to vary one of the factors in order to observe its effects upon the other. Instead, naturally occurring variations in both are observed in order to learn whether they tend to occur together in some manner.

Perhaps at this point, a concrete illustration of the correlational method will be helpful. Let us return to our experiment on the impact of pleasant scents on the ratings of job applicants to see how the topic it considered might be studied by systematic observation.

Imagine that the researcher interested in this topic wants to work not with accomplices and subjects who know that they are participating in an experiment, but rather with real interviewers and real job applicants. Clearly, ethical considerations would prevent her from conducting an experiment. After all, she could not approach persons seeking a job and induce them to wear various scents (or no scent at all) simply to determine the impact of such actions on their chances of obtaining employment. But what could she do instead? An alternative method for conducting a useful study might involve the following procedures.

The researcher would enlist the cooperation of personnel managers or interviewers in a number of different companies. Through their good offices, she might arrange for job applicants to wait in a special room for a few moments prior to their interviews. This would provide her with an opportunity to rate the pleasantness of any cologne or perfume worn by these persons. (For example, the researcher might simply pass through this room in a casual manner, or be present in it when the applicants enter.) In addition, she would also obtain access to the employment ratings assigned to each person by the interviewers. (Needless to add, the anonymity of these individuals would be assured in some manner.) In a final step, the researcher would take these two sets of data (her ratings of the scents worn by applicants and the ratings they receive from the interviewers) and examine them carefully. Specifically, she would seek to determine whether they are related in any manner, probably through an appropriate form of statistical analysis. (She expects, of course, that the interviewers' ratings may become more favorable as the pleasantness of the scents worn by applicants rises.) Please note: she would *not* seek to vary either of these factors. Rather, she would simply gather systematic information on each and then determine whether changes in one are related in any manner to changes in the other.

As we hope this example suggests, the correlational method can be used to investigate a wide range of topics. Further, it offers several major advantages. First, it can readily be employed to study behavior in many practical settings. This is especially useful to O.B., which focuses its attention on behavior in a wide range of organizations. Second, it can be applied to topics and issues that, for ethical or practical reasons, cannot be studied by direct experimentation. Along with these "pluses," however, we must mention one major drawback. In contrast to experimentation, the findings yielded by the correlational approach are often somewhat uncertain with respect to cause-and-effect relationships. Since this is an important point, we will now expand upon it further.

Correlation and Causation: Why the First Doesn't Always Imply the Second

The major point we wish to make is this: If two variables are found to be related in a correlational study—even closely related—this tells us nothing about the existence of a direct causal link between them. The fact that changes in one variable are accompanied by changes in another does *not* necessarily imply that changes in the first *caused* changes in the second. (Please see Figure 2-5 for an amusing illustration of this point.) Perhaps the best way of clarifying this important fact is, again, through a specific example.

Assume that in a carefully conducted study, a researcher finds that there is a strong correlation between (1) hair length among male executives and (2) the sala-

GOOSEMYER   **by parker and wilder**

FIGURE 2-5   Why Correlation Does Not Necessarily Imply Causation

As shown in this cartoon, the fact that changes in one variable are accompanied by
changes in another does not necessarily imply that there is a causal link between them.
Despite Ms. Overberry's beliefs, it seems unlikely that changes in climate or volcanic
eruptions are caused by the election of Democrats! (Source: Goosemyer by Parker &
Wilder © 1981 Field Enterprises, Inc. Courtesy of Field Newspaper Syndicate.)

ries earned by these persons. The correlation is *inverse:* the longer the hair possessed by subjects in the study, the lower their salaries. What do these findings
mean? One possibility is that there is a direct causal link between the two factors:
shorter hair somehow causes a meteoric rise up the corporate ladder! Such a conclusion might make you wish to rush right out to the nearest barber shop, at least
if you are male. But as you can readily see, such an explanation seems unlikely.

A second possibility, and one that is far more reasonable, is as follows: both
hair length and salary are closely related to a third factor—age. That is, the older
individuals are, in general, the higher their salaries tend to be. (After all, they
have more experience and more time on the job.) And the older they are, the
shorter they tend to wear their hair. Thus, the correlation between hair length and
salary does *not* imply a direct link between these factors. Rather, this apparent
relationship actually stems from the influence of a third variable, to which both
hair length and salary are linked (see Figure 2–6).

In this example, the fact that a seemingly close relationship between two variables is actually produced by a third is fairly easy to spot. In other cases, though,
this task is far more difficult. Thus, the moral for researchers—and for consumers
of research findings as well—is clear: Always be on guard against interpreting
even a strong correlation between two variables as evidence of a direct causal link
between them. As we will have reason to note at several points in this text, jumping to such conclusions can be very misleading indeed! (For a discussion of a
technique often used in conjunction with correlational research, please see the
"FOCUS" box on pp. 40–41.)

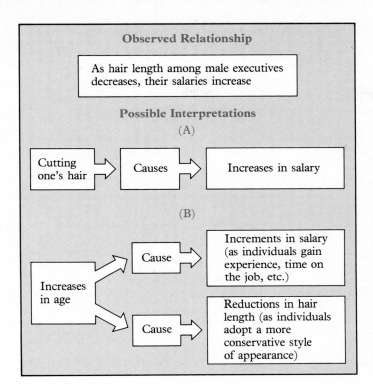

Observed Relationship

As hair length among male executives decreases, their salaries increase

Possible Interpretations

(A)

Cutting one's hair → Causes → Increases in salary

(B)

Increases in age → Cause → Increments in salary (as individuals gain experience, time on the job, etc.)

Increases in age → Cause → Reductions in hair length (as individuals adopt a more conservative style of appearance)

FIGURE 2-6   Correlation versus Causation

The fact that changes in one variable are accompanied by changes in another does not necessarily imply that they are causally linked. In the example presented above, salaries earned and hair length appear to be related: as hair length decreases among a group of male executives, their salaries tend to rise. As suggested in (A), this might indicate that cutting one's hair can yield a raise! A much more reasonable interpretation, however, is shown in (B). Here, it is obvious that both hair length and salaries are linked to a third factor—age— and to changes that occur as people grow older.

THE SURVEY METHOD: KNOWLEDGE THROUGH SELF-REPORT

A third major technique for conducting research in organizational behavior is one you will probably find familiar: the **survey method.** In this approach, individuals are asked to respond to a series of questions relating to some issue of current interest. Often, these are presented in a written survey or questionnaire. Alternatively, they can be posed during face-to-face interviews. In either case, the data collected involve subjects' responses to the questions: *self-reports* of their current views, feelings, attitudes, and so on.

Surveys can be used to study many important topics. For example, you are probably quite familiar with their use in political polling and in assessing public reaction to various government policies. Indeed, the results of such surveys appear almost nightly on the evening news (see Figure 2-8). In organizational behavior, surveys can be used to study many diverse issues. For example, they can question employees about their reactions to new incentive pay plans or their attitudes toward the institution of flex-time (flexible working hours). And they can even be used to measure the amount of stress individuals encounter on the job or their personal experience with prejudice and sexual harassment.

FOCUS ON BEHAVIOR
Unobtrusive Measures: Using the "Indirect Approach"
in Organizational Research

All scientists face a basic problem in conducting their research: often, their attempts to measure the phenomena they wish to study change or affect the phenomena in some manner. For example, light from a distant star may be distorted by the lens of a telescope. Similarly, chemical reactions can be changed by the containers in which they occur. Sad to relate, human behavior is no exception to this general rule. As we have already noted, subjects' behavior is often strongly affected by the knowledge that they are participating in an experiment and are being carefully observed. Similarly, when asked to complete a questionnaire, individuals often attempt to present themselves in a favorable light, or they give the answers they believe are most popular or appropriate. As you can readily see, effects of this type are important. Indeed, they can distort the findings of even carefully conducted research. But is there any way to avoid them? Fortunately, there is. When researchers are concerned about the potential impact of their measuring techniques on the data they collect, they can turn to the use of **unobtrusive measures.**[8,9]

Briefly, this term refers to measures of behavior that are collected in a relatively indirect manner, without disturbing or affecting subjects in any manner. A number of unobtrusive measures are based on the simple fact that human behavior often leaves traces—written records or effects on the physical environment. These can be studied at leisure, long after the persons who produced them have departed. And in many cases, they can be quite revealing.

A good example of the informal use of such measures is provided by an incident involving that master of observation, Sherlock Holmes. In one of his cases, the famous detective informs his client, a doctor, that he has a busier practice than his next-door neighbor, who is also a physician. When the good doctor expresses surprise at Holmes's knowledge of this fact, the detective quickly explains the

basis for his conclusion: the steps leading to the client's office are worn several inches lower than those leading to his neighbor's office. In short, Holmes employed the physical evidence left by thousands of former patients to estimate the volume of his client's practice.

In recent years, researchers have used similar techniques to uncover many intriguing facts about behavior in organizations. As an example of this work, let us consider the application of unobtrusive measures to the study of one interesting topic: the impact of *deadlines*. Informal observation suggests that deadlines exert a powerful effect upon human activity. Specifically, they seem to impose a kind of "rhythm" on the performance of various actions, assuring that these rise to a peak immediately before the deadline is reached. But is this actually the case? Or is it another instance in which "common sense" leads us astray?

The results of several studies employing unobtrusive measures are quite informative in this respect. For example, in one ingenious investigation, Grauer examined records of trading volume on the New York Stock Exchange.[10] Since the exchange closes at a specific hour, a clear deadline for trading exists. Thus, if deadlines do serve to "draw" behavior from the persons involved, it would be predicted that most trading would occur in the closing hours of the day. Further, it would also be expected that this effect would be more pronounced on Fridays, or before holidays, since the deadline would then have even more importance. As you can see from Figure 2–7, results offered strong support for these hypotheses. Trading did in fact rise to a peak during the final two hours of the day. And the slope of this rise was steeper on Fridays and on days preceding holidays than at other times.

Interestingly, such effects are not restricted to economic activities. They have also been observed with respect to the number of plays executed during professional football games.[11] Here, as most

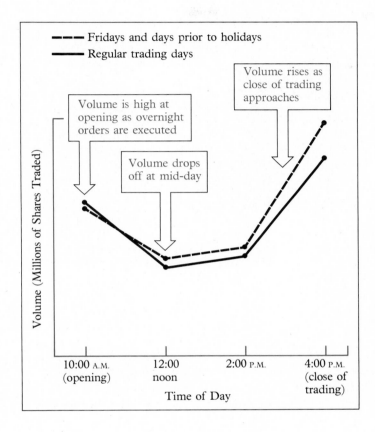

Fridays and days prior to holidays
Regular trading days

Volume rises as close of trading approaches

Volume is high at opening as overnight orders are executed

Volume drops off at mid-day

Volume (Millions of Shares Traded)

10:00 A.M. (opening)   12:00 noon   2:00 P.M.   4:00 P.M. (close of trading)

Time of Day

FIGURE 2-7   The Impact of a Deadline: One Unobtrusive Measure

As shown here, trading volume on the New York Stock Exchange seems to be affected by the presence of a deadline. On regular trading days, volume picks up sharply in the two hours prior to the closing bell. And this trend is even more pronounced on Fridays or days prior to holidays. (Source: Based on data from Grauer. In Webb, *Papers for the March 1973 Deadline Conference.* Unpublished manuscript.)

football fans would predict, the number of plays is highest during the second quarter—prior to the end of the half. And it is also higher during the final quarter than during the first or the third. (Since the team that is ahead often attempts to hold the ball during the closing minutes, though, there appear to be fewer plays during the final quarter than during the second quarter.)

We're sure that by now, you are convinced of the value of unobtrusive measures for organizational research. Often, they can be gathered with minimal effort—less than that required for the col-

lection of other types of data. And because they are not subject to the types of distortion that occur when subjects know that they are being studied or observed, such measures are often quite revealing. Of course, they are not applicable to every research setting or to every question about human behavior we wish to address. But given the obvious benefits they offer, it is far from surprising that during the past decade they have been applied to an ever-widening range of topics relating to organizational behavior.[12]

FIGURE 2-8   Political Polling:
An Example of the Survey Method

Political polling—one well-known
use of the survey method of
research—has become increasingly
popular in recent years. (Source:
Photo by Jerry W. Berndt/Stock,
Boston.)

The advantages offered by the survey method are impressive. First, surveys can be used to collect a large amount of information quickly and efficiently. Second, since surveys can often be constructed rapidly, they may be used to measure reactions to some event immediately after it has occurred. Third, because surveys can be specifically tailored to the populations for which they are designed and can focus directly on issues relevant to these persons, replies to them can often be quite revealing.

Opposed to these benefits, however, are several drawbacks. First and perhaps most important, surveys rely entirely on *self-reports*—subjects' answers to the questions posed. As you can probably guess, individuals may often change or alter their replies on a survey (or during an interview) in order to present themselves in a favorable light. Thus, results can sometimes be misleading for this reason. Second, surveys can only measure reactions to the specific questions posed. If some crucial aspect or dimension is omitted, information about it will not be obtained. Unfortunately, this is an all-too-common occurrence. Almost every researcher has had the experience of thinking of the truly key question for his or her survey *after* it has been completed by many subjects!

Despite these potential weaknesses, the survey method has proven quite useful in organizational research. Indeed, it is probably safe to state that, in the past, it was used with greater frequency than any other technique we have yet considered. This situation appears to have altered somewhat in recent years, as growing methodological sophistication has led many researchers to focus on alternative methods (experimentation, systematic observation). Even today, though, surveys continue to provide an important source of information about human behavior in organizational settings.

THE CASE METHOD: GENERALIZING FROM THE UNIQUE

A final technique for gaining knowledge about behavior in organizations is the **case method.** This approach is quite different in scope from the ones we have considered so far. In experimentation, systematic observation, and the survey method, data are collected from a large number of persons. Then, this information is used to reach general conclusions about some aspect of human behavior. In contrast, the case method focuses on one or, at most, a small number of persons. Further, it studies these persons in great depth and detail. The basic rationale behind this method is as follows: By carefully studying a few persons and their organization, we can uncover key factors affecting their behavior. And then, the impact of these factors on other persons in other work settings can also be examined. In short, the overall strategy is one of moving from conclusions about specific persons and organizations to conclusions about human behavior and organizations generally.

Often, the case method is chosen when a specific problem exists in an organization and no ready explanation or solution for it is apparent. In such instances, detailed study of the persons involved and the overall work setting may point to factors previously overlooked. For example, imagine that more than half of the young managers hired by a specific company resign within the first year. Pay is high, working conditions are excellent, and promotion possibilities abound. Why, then, are these talented people leaving in droves? The case method might help us to discover just what's going on. In particular, it might point to subtle factors, easily overlooked. (One possibility: all young managers receive the same raises and bonuses during their first year with the company. This leads many to conclude that there is no contingency between their performance and their outcomes. And since most persons prefer the presence of such links—see Chapter 4—they become dissatisfied and leave, despite the fact that in absolute terms, conditions are excellent.)

Successful use of the case method depends on several key factors. First, the investigator using it must adopt an open-minded, receptive approach. Only under these conditions will attention be drawn to new, previously overlooked factors. Second, the investigator must be skilled at integrating diverse information. The case method yields a wealth of detail, and it is up to the researcher to find the basic, underlying themes. Finally, the study must be thorough. If it is not, little in the way of new insights or information will be acquired.

If the case method is employed with skill, it can serve a unique function in the study of organizational behavior. Specifically, it can call attention to factors and relationships deserving of careful study, which have previously been ignored. And once such factors are identified, additional research employing experimentation, surveys, or systematic observation can be initiated. Thus, in an important sense, the case method often serves as the starting point, rather than as the conclusion, of research projects. In this respect, it can prove valuable indeed.

CHOOSING AMONG RESEARCH METHODS: DOES ONE HAVE AN EDGE?

In our discussion up to this point, we have examined a number of different techniques for conducting systematic research. When used with skill and care, all can yield valuable information (and important insights) about human behavior in organizational settings. Further, as we have tried to point out, all offer major advantages—and all suffer from certain drawbacks. How, then, can we choose among them? Does one method have a decided "edge" over the others? Basically, our answer is "no." While individual researchers differ greatly in their preference for one method or another, taken as a whole the field of O.B. is quite pragmatic on this issue. Indeed, it is our impression that most investigators in it seem to adopt the following perspective: in selecting a specific research method, let your questions—and the practical constraints involved in studying human behavior in work settings—be your guide. In short, select the approach that seems most appropriate for answering the basic questions under investigation. In some cases this will be experimentation; in others, systematic observation; and in still others, it may involve the use of surveys or even case analysis. Rather, flexibility should be the byword. In sum, when it comes to selecting a specific research method, O.B. is both eclectic and pragmatic. Given the crucial nature of the issues it seeks to study and its strong commitment to application and practical benefits, this approach seems fitting as well as effective.

EVALUATING THE FINDINGS OF RESEARCH: RELIABILITY, VALIDITY, AND GENERALIZABILITY

At the beginning of this chapter (in the *"Perspective"* box on pp. 28–29), we suggested that one of the major reasons for learning about basic methods of research is as follows: such information will help you to assess the value of research findings. We hope that by now, you realize that this is an important task. The volume of research in organizational behavior is increasing, and the chances are good that you will encounter it—or at least recommendations based upon it—in your own future work. But how, precisely, can you evaluate such information? How can you separate the wheat from the chaff, so to speak? Knowing something about the basic methods themselves certainly helps. Armed with this knowledge, you can determine whether a given study has used appropriate techniques and incorporated needed safeguards. But this knowledge, useful as it is, is not quite enough. You also need something more. In this final section, we will try to provide it. In particular, we will describe some general rules or criteria you can use for evaluating the worth of almost *any* piece of research (or research report) you encounter. These criteria involve **reliability, validity,** and **generalizability.**

Reliability: Consistency Counts

Suppose that at some unhappy time in the future, you are advised by your doctor to lose twenty pounds. To reach this goal, you go on a strict diet and also begin a painful program of jogging and exercise. After a month of hard work, you step onto your bathroom scale to see if you've made any progress. When you began, you weighed 175 pounds, so you're hoping your weight has dropped well below that level. When you look down, though, you receive a horrible shock: the needle actually points to 182! Dazed, you step off the scale. All your hard work seems to have been for nothing. But then, you have an idea. Quickly, you get back on the scale. This time, the needle reads 163. You'd like to believe this second number, but is it correct? To find out, you stand on the scale once more. This time, it reads 171. At this point, you give up in disgust. Obviously, your scale has outlived its usefulness. In order to keep track of the success (or failure) of your diet, you'll have to buy another.

This simple example—one you might well encounter yourself—helps to emphasize an important point. In order to be of any use, measuring devices must be *reliable.* That is, they must yield the same (or at least similar) results when they are applied to the same quantity. If they do not, the information they provide is unreliable and tells us very little. Clearly, the scale in our example performed very poorly in this respect. Each time it was used to weigh the same person, it yielded different results. Since the dieter's bulk could not change from one second to another, we must conclude that the scale was unreliable.

The same principle applies to any other type of measuring instrument or device—not just to ones designed to assess weight or other physical properties. For example, if several individuals complete a survey in the morning and then take it again that same afternoon, their scores should be quite similar on the two occasions. If they are not, we may begin to suspect that the survey is unreliable. (It may contain confusing questions, and so elicit sharply different answers each time it is taken.) Similarly, if several employees receive different scores on a laboratory test of job performance each time they take it, we can begin to question the reliability of *this* measuring instrument. Once again, we would expect these scores to be similar, if not identical, on each occasion.

By now, the moral for evaluating research findings should be clear: Always try to determine whether the surveys, tests, tasks or other measures used in a study are reliable. If they are, you can proceed to consider the other criteria we will outline. If they are not, stop right there—any findings reported are probably of little value.

Validity: Does Research Really Measure What It Claims to Measure?

Suppose that a researcher wishes to develop a technique for identifying persons who are "born leaders." After much trial and error, she devises a task that yields highly reliable results. Each time a given person takes it, he or she attains the same (or a highly similar) score. Moreover, different persons, who might well differ in leadership ability, do obtain contrasting results. The task is both simple and appealing; it involves playing a computer game similar to "Space Invaders." The researcher reasons that this may well be a useful measure of leadership ability. After all, don't leaders have to make quick decisions, behave aggressively, and defend their territory against would-be invaders? Thus, she assumes that scores on this test provide an accurate index of leadership skills.

Now, imagine that the researcher administers this task to two different groups of persons: a number of top executives, known for their great success as leaders, and a group of clerks, who have held the same job for more than five years. Results indicate no difference between the two groups on the task; both respond with equal skill. The researcher is crushed—and with good reason: her supposed measure of leadership ability is invalid. That is, it does not seem to measure what it is intended to measure. (For another example of a task or device that does not measure what it claims to measure, see Figure 2-9.)

This example brings us face to face with a second major criterion for assessing the value of research findings: *validity*. Only if we have grounds for assuming that the measures employed in a study really assess what they claim to assess do the findings have any value. That is, only if the measures are *valid* should we attach much weight to the reported findings. But what evidence should we seek in this quest for validity? Basically, two types are crucial. First, as suggested above, people known to differ with respect to the trait or behavior in question should attain different scores on the measure being used. If they do, evidence for validity is provided. If they do not, validity may be lacking. Second, different scores on the test or measure should predict different levels of the behavior in question. For example, people who score high on a measure of leadership ability should really turn out to be better leaders than those who score lower. Only when one or both of these types of evidence is available should you place much faith in the findings of a research study. And if they are lacking, please proceed with caution; the findings reported may have little if anything to do with the topic supposedly being studied.

Generalizability of Results

A final question you should always raise when seeking to evaluate the findings of any research project is this: Are the findings *generalizable?* That is, can they be generalized from the specific subjects who participated to a much larger group— for example, to all auto salespersons, junior executives, or production-line workers? If the answer is "no," the findings are obviously of limited value; they apply only to the subjects in the study itself. Thus, this is an important question. But how can we tell whether findings are generalizable? The answer involves the *representativeness* of the sample of subjects employed. Briefly, research findings can be generalized beyond the subjects who took part in a study only to the extent that these persons are representative of the larger group. That is, they must re-

FIGURE 2-9   An Example of Low Validity

Does this equipment really measure what it claims to measure? We doubt it. (Source: Photo © 1982 Larry Lawfer.)

semble such persons in many respects (e.g., age, education, years on the job, etc.). If they do not, generalization may be totally unwarranted. For example, suppose that a researcher conducts a study to determine the temperature level preferred by most office workers. Results indicate that this is surprisingly low—about 55°F. So far, these findings sound intriguing. Indeed, they seem to imply that businesses can save large amounts of money by lowering their thermostats, at least during the winter months. But now consider this fact: the study was conducted in Alaska, and most of the participants in it belong to a group of Eskimos famous for their love of cool temperatures. This added information places the findings in a very different light. Since the subjects in the study may well differ from other office workers in important ways, the findings cannot be generalized to this larger group. In fact, doing so may be quite misleading.

Obviously, this is an extreme example. In most cases, the subjects employed in studies you encounter will *not* differ from other employees to the degree noted here. But the basic principle remains very much the same: The results of a research project can be generalized to a larger group only to the extent that participants in it are representative of that group.

SUMMARY

In order to acquire systematic information about human behavior, researchers make use of several different methods. *Experimentation* involves procedures in which one or more factors (the independent variables) are systematically varied in order to determine if such changes exert any impact upon another factor (the dependent variable). Two essential conditions for successful experimentation are the random assignment of subjects to each experimental group, and the absence of confounding factors. *Systematic observation,* a second basic approach, involves careful observation of two or more variables in order to determine if naturally occurring changes in one are accompanied by changes in the other. Systematic observation is useful in many settings. However, it suffers from one major drawback: the findings it yields are somewhat ambiguous with respect to cause-and-effect relationships.

A third technique for obtaining information about behavior in organizations involves the use of *surveys* or *questionnaires*. These provide information about the attitudes, reactions, and feelings of large numbers of persons. A final approach sometimes used in organizational research is the *case method*. Here, detailed study is made of one or a few persons and the organization in which they work. This information is then used to identify key factors affecting behavior in that particular setting.

In evaluating the findings of any research project, attention should be directed to three major criteria: *reliability, validity,* and *generalizability*. Reliability refers to the extent to which measuring devices yield the same or equivalent results each time they are applied to the same quantity. If the measuring devices employed in a research project are not reliable, its findings are of no scientific value. Validity involves the question of whether a research project really measures or studies what it claims to measure or study. Finally, generalizability refers to the extent to which findings can be generalized from the specific sample of subjects who participate in a study to some larger group.

KEY TERMS

CASE METHOD A method of research in which one (or a few) individuals and the organization in which they work are studied in great detail. This detailed investigation may then suggest key factors affecting behavior that previously have been overlooked.

CORRELATIONAL APPROACH A basic method of research involving systematic observation. One or more variables are carefully studied in order to determine whether naturally occurring changes in one are accompanied by changes in the other(s).

DEMAND CHARACTERISTICS Any cues serving to communicate the hypothesis under study in an experiment to subjects. Demand characteristics, if uncontrolled, can render the findings of an experiment invalid.

DEPENDENT VARIABLE The variable in an experiment (usually some aspect of behavior) that is studied in order to determine whether it is affected in any manner by variations in the independent variable.

EXPERIMENTATION A basic method of research in which one or more factors (independent variables) are varied systematically to determine if such changes exert any impact upon one or more aspects of behavior (dependent variables).

GENERALIZABILITY Refers to the extent to which the findings of a research project can be generalized from the subjects who participated in it to some larger group.

INDEPENDENT VARIABLE The factor that is systematically varied in an experiment. (Usually, interest is focused on determining whether such changes affect some aspect of subjects' behavior—the dependent variable.)

RANDOM ASSIGNMENT TO GROUPS An essential condition for successful experimentation. This principle requires that all participants in the study have an equal chance of being assigned to each of the experimental conditions (groups).

RELIABILITY Refers to the extent to which measuring devices yield the same or equivalent results each time they are applied to the same quantity. Only if the measuring devices employed in a research project are reliable do its findings have any scientific value.

SURVEY METHOD A method of research in which large numbers of individuals respond to a series of questions relating to some issue of current interest.

SYSTEMATIC OBSERVATION (See Correlational Approach)

UNOBTRUSIVE MEASURES Indirect measures of behavior that can be obtained without disturbing or affecting research subjects in any manner. Often, unobtrusive measures involve the physical traces of past behavior or written records of human activities.

VALIDITY Refers to the question of whether a research project actually measures or studies what it claims to measure or study. Only if evidence for validity exists can the findings of a study be viewed as having scientific value.

NOTES

1. Fazio, R.H. On the self-perception explanation of the over-justification effect: The role of the salience of initial attitude. *Journal of Experimental Social Psychology,* 1981.

2. Sommer, R., & Sommer, B. *A practical guide to behavioral research.* New York: Oxford University Press, 1980.

3. Imada, A.S., & Hakel, M.D. Influence of nonverbal communication and rater proximity on impressions and decisions in simulated employment interviews. *Journal of Applied Psychology,* 1977, *62,* 295–300.

4. Baron, R.A. The impact of pleasant scents on ratings of job applicants in simulated employment interviews. Unpublished manuscript, Purdue University, 1982.

5. Luthans, F., Paul, R., & Baker, D. An experimental analysis of the impact of a contingent reinforcement intervention on salespersons' performance behavior. *Journal of Applied Psychology*, 1981, *66*, 314–323.

6. Pennebaker, J.W., Dyer, M.A., Caulkins, R.S., Litowitz, D.L., Ackerman, P.L., Anderson, D.B., & McGraw, K.M. Don't the girls get prettier at closing time: A country and western application to psychology. *Personality and Social Psychology Bulletin*, 1979, *51*, 122–125.

7. Weick, K.E. Laboratory experimentation with organizations: A reappraisal. *Academy of Management Review*, 1977, *2*, 123–127.

8. Webb, E., & Weick, K.R. Unobtrusive measures in organizational theory: A reminder. *Administrative Science Quarterly*, 1979, *24*, 650–659.

9. Webb, E.J., Campbel, D.T., Schwartz, R.D., Sechrest, L., & Grove, J.B. *Nonreactive measures in the social sciences* (2nd ed.). Boston: Houghton Mifflin, 1981.

10. Grauer, F.L. On deadline effects: Intraday trading volume on the New York Stock Exchange. In E.J. Webb (Ed.), *Papers for the March 1973 Deadline Conference*. Unpublished manuscript, Graduate School of Business, Stanford University.

11. Fischer, P.C. *A report on the influence of deadlines on the behavior of the professional football team.* Unpublished manuscript, Graduate School of Business, Stanford University.

12. Abrahams, N.M., Atwater, D.C., & Alf, E.F., Jr. Unobtrusive measurement of racial bias in job-placement decisions. *Journal of Applied Psychology*, 1977, *62*, 116–119.

3

Learning:
Adapting to—and Changing—
the World Around Us

KEY CONCEPTS

Learning

Classical Conditioning

Operant Conditioning

Modeling

Extinction

Positive Reinforcers

Negative Reinforcers

Punishment

Schedules of Reinforcement

Fixed-Interval Schedule

Variable-Interval Schedule

Fixed-Ratio Schedule

Variable-Ratio Schedule

Partial Reinforcement Effect

Learned Helplessness

Behavior Modification

O. B. Mod.

□ □ □

It's mid-morning, and you are hard at work. A large number of letters requiring your attention arrived in the first mail, and you are gradually working through the pile. But now, you are interrupted by an all-too-familiar voice: "Say Jean, I hate to bother you, but could you run through the procedures for an international purchase order one more time? I'm not sure whether to use the form 89-K or 106-M."

Looking up, you see that it is Charlie Hartmann. Charlie is one of those people who seem to be totally confused by regulations. As a result, he's been a perpetual thorn in your side—always asking for help and advice. Normally, you wouldn't mind. But Charlie asks the same things over and over again. Actually, you're a bit surprised to see him today, for you refused to let him interrupt you the last three times he's come by. In fact, yesterday you were quite gruff and let him know in very certain terms that you didn't like being bothered while deep in thought.

This time, though, you decide to give him the information he wants. So with a sigh, you run through the procedures in question for the tenth time. After Charlie leaves, you find that you are too stirred up to go right back to work. Instead, you walk over to the coffee pot and pour yourself a cup. "Why does he keep bothering me?" you wonder. "I thought I'd finally turn him off by refusing most of the time. Hope must really spring eternal, because he keeps coming back." Suddenly, a new thought occurs to you. Could you yourself be responsible for Charlie's actions? Perhaps by agreeing to help him only part of the time, you are actually encouraging him to pester you. After all, the way things stand, he never knows whether you'll say "yes" or "no." And this may make him feel it's always worth a try. Pondering the unsettling possibility that you have somehow taught Charlie to bother you, you return to your desk. . . .

Human beings (and all other organisms) possess the ability to profit from their experience. In a word, they can *learn.* Because of this capacity, they can usually acquire needed behaviors, information, and skills in a rapid and efficient manner. And as a result of such learning, they can function effectively in many complex environments—including those relating to the world of work. But what, precisely, is this process? What, in essence, *is* learning? Most experts on this subject define it in the following manner: ***Learning*** *is any relatively permanent change in behavior* *produced by experience.*[1] In short, it involves changes in the way we behave, think, or feel resulting from our contacts with the world around us. Note that learning should not be confused with temporary changes, such as those induced by drugs or illness, or with changes resulting from such factors as fatigue or physical growth. And also note that it is *not* synonymous with "improvements" in behavior. As the story on page 54 suggests, learning can often yield undesirable as well as desirable outcomes.

You are probably quite familiar with learning as a basic process; after all, each of us has faced the tasks of acquiring new skills and studying for exams. But there is a good chance that you do not as yet appreciate the breadth of its impact on human behavior or its key relevance to O.B. In a sense, the influence of learning cannot be overstated. It appears to play a role in everything we do—from reading these words to falling in love and from mastering the complexities of a new word processor through the formation of preferences and opinions (see Figure 3-1). In short, it is a central process in human behavior—perhaps *the* central process.

FIGURE 3-1   Learning: A Basic—and Central—Process in Human Behavior

Learning plays an important role in all of the activities shown here. (Source: Photo [top left] © Larry Lawfer; photo [top right] by Kirk Williamson; photo [bottom left] © 1981 Mike Blake.)

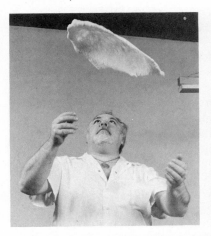

Given this general impact, we might well expect learning to play a major role in organizational behavior. And this is certainly the case. To mention just a few examples of its influence, learning is involved in all aspects of job training. Similarly, it is involved in what has been termed *socialization into an organization*— the process through which we gain knowledge of the unspoken rules governing behavior and interpersonal relations in work settings.[2] Learning also shapes our relationships with others and plays a key role in the development of our major motives and personal characteristics. Finally, we should note that techniques based on this central process can often be used to influence others' behavior— especially to direct it into desired patterns or ends. Taking all of these powerful effects into account, there can be little doubt that learning is an important process, fully worthy of our careful attention in this text.

As we have already noted, learning exerts varied and far-reaching effects on human behavior. Despite this great diversity, however, it appears to take only three major forms. These are known, respectively, as **classical** or **Pavlovian conditioning, operant** (or **instrumental**) **conditioning,** and **modeling** (or **observational learning**). We will now examine each, attempting, as we proceed, to underscore their implications for the field of organizational behavior.

CLASSICAL CONDITIONING: LEARNING THROUGH ASSOCIATION

Imagine the following situation. You've just joined the staff of Computech, a new firm with a bright future. As the newest employee in the office, you've been given the worst desk—one right next to a hall connecting with the loading and delivery area. It's winter, and each time someone enters from the delivery zone, a cold blast of air races down the hall and reaches your desk. When it hits you, you experience negative sensations and pull back in an automatic manner, just as you might withdraw from any other unpleasant stimulus (e.g., a hot object).

Now, consider these events. The door from the loading zone is an automatic one, and right before it opens, it emits a loud humming sound. (The motor that operates it is in need of servicing.) Would you react to this sound in any manner? In all probability, at first you'd show no reaction to it. Over a period of time, however, this situation might well change. Although the humming sound occurs *before* the cold air reaches your desk, you might soon come to respond to it quite strongly. Specifically, you might experience negative reactions and begin to flinch when you hear it. In short, you might gradually come to respond to the sound in much the same manner as you do the cold air itself. (Please see Figure 3-2 for a summary of these events.)

This simple situation provides a clear example of the process of *classical conditioning*. Briefly, it illustrates the manner in which a stimulus that is at first incapable of eliciting a given response may gradually acquire the ability to do so when it is repeatedly paired with another stimulus—one that *can* evoke this re-

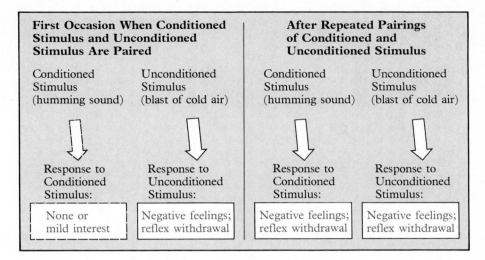

First Occasion When Conditioned Stimulus and Unconditioned Stimulus Are Paired		After Repeated Pairings of Conditioned and Unconditioned Stimulus	
Conditioned Stimulus (humming sound)	Unconditioned Stimulus (blast of cold air)	Conditioned Stimulus (humming sound)	Unconditioned Stimulus (blast of cold air)
Response to Conditioned Stimulus:	Response to Unconditioned Stimulus:	Response to Conditioned Stimulus:	Response to Unconditioned Stimulus:
None or mild interest	Negative feelings; reflex withdrawal	Negative feelings; reflex withdrawal	Negative feelings; reflex withdrawal

FIGURE 3-2   Development of a Conditioned Response

At first, the humming sound from an automatic door would have little effect upon an individual's behavior. After it had been paired with cold blasts of air on a number of occasions, however, it might evoke strong reactions from this person.

action. Thus, in our example, the humming sound gradually came to evoke reactions that were, at first, produced only by the blasts of cold air. Scientists who have studied this basic form of learning in detail generally refer to the stimulus that evokes reactions at first, in a seemingly automatic manner, as the *unconditioned stimulus (UCS)*. In contrast, they refer to the stimulus that acquires this ability gradually, through repeated pairings with the UCS, as the *conditioned stimulus (CS)*. In a similar manner, the response evoked by the UCS is described as the *unconditioned response (UCR)*, while that elicited by the CS is termed a *conditioned response (CR)*. (For another example of classical conditioning, see Figure 3-3.)

As you probably know, learning of this type was first studied in detail by Ivan Pavlov, a famed Nobel-prize-winning physiologist, at the turn of the twentieth century. His studies with ringing bells and salivating dogs are probably so familiar that they require no detailed description. Instead, we will focus on two other tasks we feel are more important. First, we will describe some of the basic principles of classical conditioning uncovered by Pavlov and many other researchers.[3] Second, we will attempt to indicate the relevance of this basic form of learning to human behavior in general and to organizational behavior in particular. As you will soon see, classical conditioning appears to play an important role in such diverse reactions as strong fears, several types of sexual hang-ups, and the formation of preferences and attitudes. Thus, it is far more general in its effects than you probably now imagine.

FIGURE 3-3   Classical Conditioning: An Unusual Example

While the events shown here are a bit far-fetched, they illustrate the basic nature of classical conditioning. Sgt. Snorkel's facial expression and posture probably could not elicit Beetle's collapse the first time he saw them. Through repeated pairing with the Sgt.'s punches, though, these stimuli have gradually acquired the capacity to elicit this response. (Source: © King Features Syndicate, Inc., 1979. World Rights Reserved.)

Classical Conditioning: Some Basic Principles

In the example presented earlier, we mentioned that a tendency to react to the humming sound of the door would be acquired in a gradual manner. In fact, this is actually the case. As the number of pairings between the hum and blasts of icy air increased, your tendency to react to this sound would also rise. At first, the strength of this tendency would increase fairly rapidly; but then, it would level off and rise more slowly. We should note that this pattern—rapid initial gains followed by slower or smaller ones—is characteristic of most forms of learning, not simply of classical conditioning. Thus, it can be observed in a wide range of situations (e.g., among employees learning how to use new equipment, among sales trainees learning how to deal with customers, etc.)

Now, imagine a change in the situation we have been considering. Because of many complaints, the hallway outside your office is protected from icy blasts in some manner (e.g., an outer door is installed). As a result, these unpleasant stimuli no longer reach your desk. However, the humming sound still occurs each time the automatic door opens. Would this shift produce any change in your behavior? Probably it would. Gradually, you would stop responding to the humming sound. You would stop experiencing negative reactions to it and would stop flinching whenever it occurred. This process is known as **extinction,** and it tends to occur whenever a CS is no longer followed in a regular manner by a UCS. (Interestingly, if the CS is presented again at a later time, after extinction has occurred, it often tends to elicit a CR once again—an effect known as *spontaneous recovery.*) The adaptive value of extinction should be obvious: it permits us to eliminate reactions to stimuli which no longer signal important events (i.e., presentation of a UCS). In short, it permits us to get rid of "excess behavioral baggage."

FIGURE 3-4 An Example of Stimulus Generalization

Do you experience positive reactions upon examining these stimuli? If so, this may be due to *stimulus generalization.* These objects are similar, in several respects, to others with which you are familiar and to which you have already acquired positive reactions. (Source: Photo © 1982 Larry Lawfer.)

Before proceeding, examine the photo in Figure 3-4. Did you experience a positive reaction to the stimuli shown? If so, you have just gained first-hand exposure to another basic feature of classical conditioning—*stimulus generalization.* This process refers to the fact that once we have acquired a conditioned response to a given stimulus, we often tend to respond in the same way to other, similar stimuli. The opposite of generalization is known as *discrimination.* It occurs when we gradually learn to respond to one stimulus, but not to other, similar ones. An example of discrimination can sometimes be observed in busy offices. Here, each person may react only to the ringing of his or her own phone; similar sounds evoke little or no reaction. Both generalization and discrimination are useful processes; and with a little effort, you can probably observe both in many situations in your everyday life.

Classical Conditioning: Its Relevance to Human Behavior

By now, you probably understand the basic nature of classical conditioning and some of the principles that influence its occurrence. But you may still be wondering about why we have chosen to discuss it here. In short, what is its relevance to human behavior generally and to organizational behavior in particular? Actually, we already hinted at the answer when we noted that classical conditioning plays a key role in several important forms of behavior. In fact, growing evidence suggests that this process strongly affects such diverse reactions as strong fears, certain types of sexual responses, and many attitudes and preferences.[4,5] Clearly, any process that causes such diverse effects is worthy of our attention. But how, precisely, can this seemingly simple process affect so many reactions? As a concrete illustration of such influence, we will examine the role of conditioning in the development of attitudes.

As we will note in Chapter 7, attitudes consist of clusters of reactions to the world around us—to people, events, objects, and issues. One key component of such clusters, however, is an evaluative dimension. Attitudes involve positive and negative feelings toward attitude objects, whatever they happen to be. And it is here that classical conditioning often plays a crucial role. In particular, such conditioning often serves as a basis for the acquisition of strong feelings or emotions. A dramatic illustration of its role in this process is provided by the formation of racial prejudice among children.

Initially, most youngsters have little or no emotional reaction to the members of racial groups disliked by their parents: the traits of these persons (e.g., skin color, hair texture) are fairly neutral to them. On numerous occasions, however, they observe their parents showing signs of anger or hatred when in the presence of these individuals. Such reactions induce strong, negative emotions among the children. Thus, as such incidents are repeated, classical conditioning takes place. Briefly, members of the disliked group acquire the capacity to evoke similar, negative emotions among the children largely because of their repeated association with such reactions on the part of the parents. The final result: youngsters show such reactions to a particular racial group even when their parents are absent (see Figure 3–5). An additional step in the process may then involve the

FIGURE 3–5   Classical Conditioning and the Development of a Racial Prejudice

At first (left panel) a child shows no strong reaction to members of a group disliked by his parents. However, he does react strongly to signs of fear or anger on the part of his mother and father. After repeated pairings between such reactions by his parents and members of the disliked group (right panel), the child reacts negatively to these persons themselves, even when his parents are not present.

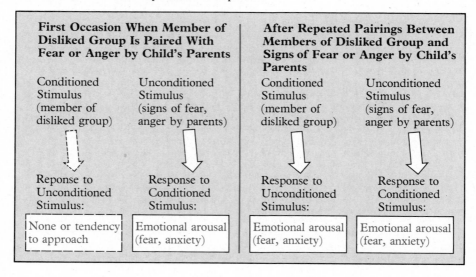

adoption of supporting beliefs that help the children "explain" their strong, negative feelings about the members of this group. If classical conditioning plays a role in the development of such attitudes—and there is considerable evidence that it does—there can be little doubt concerning its important impact on human behavior.[6] And in view of the role of racial, ethnic, and sexual prejudice in organizational settings, it is also apparent that this process has important implications for the field of O.B.

But given that classical conditioning exerts far-reaching effects on key aspects of human behavior, does knowledge of this process offer any concrete benefits for managers? We believe that it does. In many cases, persons unfamiliar with classical conditioning seem to assume that human beings have a great deal of control over their emotional and affective reactions. "If they want to," these persons reason, "people can readily overcome their silly fears and/or prejudices. All that's needed is clear thinking." As you can now see, this is not really the case. Reactions of this type often stem from associations acquired through classical conditioning—associations not easily or quickly altered. Comprehension of this basic fact can help managers avoid the trap of assuming that the workers in their charge can readily eliminate seemingly "irrational" attitudes or feelings simply on demand. Actually, more systematic steps, including the advice of experts in this area, may be needed. In short, we believe that a basic grasp of the nature of classical conditioning can help make managers more sophisticated about important aspects of human behavior. And as we noted at the start of this book, it is our conviction that this will make them more effective. (For an example of classical conditioning in an organizational setting, see the **"CASE IN POINT"** insert on p. 62.)

OPERANT CONDITIONING: LEARNING BASED ON CONSEQUENCES

A second major type of learning—perhaps the most important from the point of view of organizational behavior—is based upon a simple and obvious fact: the actions we perform often result in some consequence. For example, saying "I love you" to someone we admire will set one chain of events in motion. Saying "Beautiful day, isn't it?" may begin another (and far less interesting!) one. Similarly, writing a check when the balance in our account is zero will produce one effect; performing the same behavior when the balance is large will have other results. Because of the *contingency* that often exists between what we do and the outcomes we experience, we often learn to behave in certain ways.

First, we learn to engage in behaviors that produce positive outcomes or stimuli—ones we find pleasant. For example, we often acquire behaviors that permit us to obtain money, status, approval, and satisfaction of our physical needs. Such stimuli are termed **positive reinforcers** and their effect upon behavior is

CASE IN POINT   Guilt by Association

The rain is coming down in buckets, so you are grateful when your bus finally arrives. "Darn car," you think as you mount the steps and pay your fare. "It always acts up just when the weather's at its worst." Without further thought, you take the first empty seat you see and slide into it. You haven't even noticed the person sitting next to you, so you are surprised when he addresses you by name. "Hello Ms. Vacaro. How are you today?" Turning, you see that it's Larry Flambard, a young man who works at your company. "Oh nuts," you think, "why did I have to take this seat? I sure don't want to talk to *him*." But Larry is unaware of your negative feelings, and tries to engage you in conversation. Only gradually does he realize that you are not going to be friendly. Then, he turns away, and the minutes pass in cold, strained silence. Finally, after what seems like an eternity, Larry reaches his stop and hurries off with hardly a nod.

"Boy, am I glad he's gone," you muse. And then, it hits you: why *do* you have such a strong aversion to poor Larry? Actually, you hardly know him. At work, you only see him once or twice a week, and you've never exchanged more than a few words at one time. And really, he seems to be a fairly pleasant young fellow. So why do you dislike him? Gradually, the truth begins to dawn. Larry works in the Audit and Oversight Department, and he only visits your office (the Claims Department) when the people down there have found some special problem—some claim they view as questionable or poorly prepared. Each of these special cases requires a lot of work from the claims representative to whom it is assigned. So Larry's presence is really not something calculated to brighten anyone's day. In fact, each time he appears, he leaves behind a trail of angry and disgruntled people. "Ah ha!" you exclaim. "It's really not Larry himself. It's what he stands for—what his presence signals. Whenever I see him, it means extra work and bother. *That's* why I don't like him. It's just a case of 'guilt by association.'"

You are still thinking about this possibility when the bus arrives at your stop, and you exit into the cold, damp night.   □

Questions:

1. Through what basic process did Ms. Vacaro acquire her negative feelings about Larry?
2. What would happen if Larry brought something quite different to the Claims Department each week—for example, pay checks?
3. Is there anything Larry can do to change these negative reactions to him?
4. Can you think of a situation in your own life where you either grew to like or dislike another person as a result of conditions similar to the ones described in this case?

straightforward: generally, they strengthen responses that precede them or lead to their occurrence. The impact of positive reinforcement can be readily observed in organizational settings. For example, salespersons often work very hard to exceed their established quotas and so earn a bonus. Similarly, young executives may stay at their desks late into the night and even show up on weekends if they believe that this will enhance their image and assist them on their climb up the corporate ladder. Individuals at all levels engage in flattery, ingratiation, and even complex forms of organizational politics in order to advance their careers. In all of these cases, the basic principle remains the same: The persons in question will engage in whatever behaviors are necessary to attain (or at least move closer to) desired, positive outcomes.

Second, we learn to perform actions that permit us to avoid unpleasant outcomes or to escape from them once they occur. In this respect, we acquire responses that allow us to avoid unpleasant physical conditions (e.g., intense heat, uncomfortable cold), criticism from superiors, "loss of face" in front of others, reductions in earnings, and similar results. Outcomes of this type are termed **negative reinforcers** and, again, their impact upon behavior is clear: in general, they strengthen responses leading to their removal or termination. The impact of negative reinforcement, too, can be readily seen in most organizations. Thus, persons who hate to get up in the morning may learn complex techniques to help them accomplish this task—and so avoid the negative outcomes associated with being late. In a similar manner, individuals on a fixed expense account often learn many ways to avoid exceeding this limit, especially if doing so results in censure or worse (e.g., having to make up the difference out of their own pockets!). And most employees acquire behaviors that permit them to escape as quickly as possible from unpleasant outcomes such as undesired overtime or temper outbursts by their boss.

Finally, we also learn to avoid engaging in behaviors that lead to or produce negative outcomes. In short, we learn to refrain from performing actions that are punished. Please note that **punishment** is *not* identical to negative reinforcement. In the case of punishment, we learn to avoid negative outcomes by *withholding* behaviors we would like to perform (e.g., we don't punch our boss in the nose even when she criticizes us unfairly!). In the case of negative reinforcement, in contrast, we learn to *perform* responses that prevent or terminate the occurrence of unpleasant outcomes (e.g., we learn how to avoid getting into situations where we might wish to punch our boss in the nose). (Please see Figure 3-6 for a summary of the principles involved in positive reinforcement, negative reinforcement, and punishment.) We should also note that punishment, although it is often effective in getting individuals to refrain from certain behaviors, sometimes produces undesirable side effects. In particular, persons who receive it on a regular basis often become quite anxious and tense; and little wonder—they constantly face the strain of withholding behaviors they would prefer to perform. Second, they often show a pattern of inhibited activity. Thus, for example, a young editor who is constantly criticized by her boss for new ideas may soon learn to refrain from voicing them—with the result that many good thoughts never see the light of day.

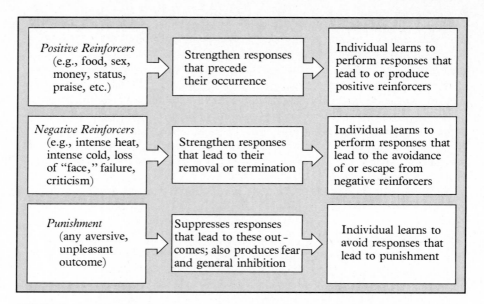

FIGURE 3-6   The Impact of Positive Reinforcers, Negative Reinforcers, and Punishment

As shown here, individuals learn to perform responses that lead to positive reinforcers, or that allow them to avoid or escape from negative reinforcers. In addition, they learn to refrain from responses that lead to punishment.

For these reasons, many practitioners in O.B. (including experts on operant conditioning) feel that punishment is a technique best avoided by managers in most situations.

   The type of learning we have been discussing so far is generally termed **operant conditioning.**[7] Because it exerts powerful effects upon a wide range of human behavior—including behavior in work settings—it has long been of interest to the field of O.B.[8,9] We will summarize several intriguing and practical applications of operant conditioning to organizational processes below. First, however, we will briefly outline some major features of this basic type of learning.

Operant Conditioning: Some Determining Factors

We should begin by noting that operant conditioning is affected by many of the same factors that affect classical conditioning. For example, as you might expect, the greater the number of occasions on which a given behavior is followed by reinforcement, the stronger our tendency to perform it. (In a sense, this corresponds to the number of CS-UCS pairings in classical conditioning.) Thus, the more often a manager praises a subordinate for some behavior (e.g., treating customers with courtesy), the stronger the tendency of this person to act in this manner. Similarly, the shorter the delay between performance of a given response and reinforcement, the stronger our tendency to engage in this activity. (In accordance with this basic principle, immediate praise for courtesy would be expected to produce stronger effects upon behavior than praise that is much delayed.) These and other similarities between operant and classical conditioning have led some experts to suggest that, despite their obvious differences, both forms of learning are closely related. Indeed, some believe that they may simply represent two aspects of the same basic process.

While the factors just mentioned exert strong effects upon operant conditioning, perhaps the one most deserving of our attention relates to the regularity and pattern with which positive or negative reinforcers are presented. This relationship is generally described as the **schedule of reinforcement.**

Schedules of reinforcement: The when and why of rewards.

As you know from your own experience, reinforcement does not always follow a particular response. For example, studying hard for exams sometimes yields high grades—and sometimes it does not. Similarly, taking a client out to dinner at an expensive restaurant and plying this person with excellent wine may help in closing an important deal, but not always. Also, keeping on top of your work and getting it done on time sometimes results in praise and recognition; at other times, though, it may be ignored. In many cases, the occurrence or absence of reinforcement following a given form of behavior seems to be quite random. In others, though, it is governed by definite rules. These rules are known as **schedules of reinforcement** and exert powerful effects upon behavior.

The influence of such schedules has been studied systematically for several decades by B.F. Skinner and his associates.[10,11] The key questions in such research have been these: How quickly and how often do subjects perform various responses under different schedules of reinforcement? Do such rates of responding vary from one schedule to another? In order to answer these questions, a large number of schedules have been examined. The simplest, of course, is one in which every response is followed by a reward—*continuous reinforcement.* Aside from this, however, the most basic schedules are ones in which the occurrence of reward is governed by a single rule. Four distinct schedules of reinforcement of this type exist.

In the first, the **fixed-interval schedule,** the occurrence of reinforcement depends largely on the passage of time. The first response emitted after a specific interval has passed yields reward. Schedules of this type generally produce a distinct pattern of behavior. Subjects show a very low rate of responding immediately after reward, but then gradually respond at a faster and faster rate as the time when reward can be obtained again approaches (see Figure 3-7). Apparently, this is because they learn that responses immediately after reinforcement do not bring further positive outcomes. Because most organizations pay their employees on a fixed-interval schedule (e.g., once a week or once a month), the pattern of behavior just described is quite common in work settings. For example, immedi-

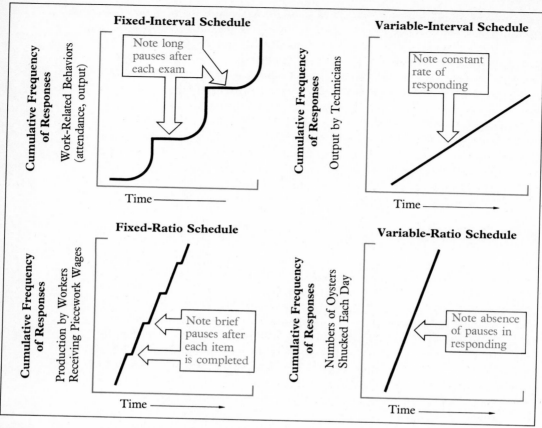

FIGURE 3-7   Four Simple Schedules of Reinforcement

Patterns of behavior (rates of responding) that might be observed under each of four simple schedules of reinforcement. Note that the steeper the lines, the higher the rate of responding by the persons involved.

ately after payday, attendance, effort, and output may all drop. Then, as the time for the next check draws near, such work-related behaviors may rise in frequency once again.

The availability of reinforcement is also controlled mainly by the passage of time in a **variable-interval schedule.** Here, though, the period that must elapse before responses will once again yield reinforcement varies around some average value. In some cases, reinforcement can be obtained after a short period has passed. In others, a much longer interval must elapse before it again becomes available. As a result of such uncertainty, variable-interval schedules of reinforcement generally yield moderate and steady rates of responding.

An example of behavior on this type of schedule might be provided by the actions of a group of technicians working for a large chemical company. Every so often—as his busy schedule permits—the head of the laboratory in which the technicians work personally examines the output and accuracy records of all employees. Then, he selects one for a special commendation and a substantial bonus: two weeks pay. Because the technicians never know when the head of the laboratory will have time to examine their records and make an award, they all work at a steady and fairly high rate. After all, as they've learned in the past, opportunity may knock at any time!

The occurrence of reinforcement is determined in a different manner in the **fixed-ratio schedule.** Here, it occurs only after a fixed number of responses have been performed. For example, it may be necessary for subjects to respond 20, 50, or even 500 times before obtaining each reward. Schedules of this type often yield a pattern of behavior in which subjects respond at a constant high rate, but pause briefly after each reinforcement (refer to Figure 3–7). Apparently, such pauses occur because the first few responses immediately after reinforcement are not associated with further reward. Fixed-ratio schedules are quite common in the world of business in the form of piecework systems of pay. Here, workers earn a fixed amount of money for completing a set number of items or operations. Because such schedules usually result in high rates of responding, this system is often quite attractive to management. It may be less popular with workers, though, especially when they feel that the ratio for various amounts of pay is set too high.

Reinforcement is also dependent upon the number of responses performed in **variable-ratio schedules.** Here, though, the number required varies around some average value. For example, reinforcement may be delivered after only 10 responses on one occasion, after 80 on the next, and after 150 on the next. On average, then, 80 separate responses must be performed before reinforcement occurs $(10 + 80 + 150 = 240) \div 3 = 80$. The actual number required varies greatly in each instance, however. As you might guess, variable-ratio schedules often yield very high and constant rates of responding (refer to Figure 3–7). Clear examples of variable-ratio schedules are Las Vegas or Atlantic City slot machines. These devices pay off after swallowing a variable number of coins. Since gamblers never know when they will be lucky, they often respond at a very high rate (see Figure 3–8). Another example of this type of schedule might be provided by the actions of workers in an oyster-processing plant. Every so often (no one can predict when), an oyster being opened is found to contain a pearl. Again, because the persons involved never know when fate will smile upon them in this manner, they work at a high rate, shucking as many oysters as they can each day.

As we have tried to suggest, these simple schedules of reinforcement actually operate in many real-life situations. Often, though, they are not present in "pure form." Instead, they are combined with each other, to produce more complex sets of contingencies. For example, consider the promotion policies in effect in many companies. Often, these involve both the completion of a number of responses (e.g., exceeding one's quota several times) *and* long-term service on the job. Only when both conditions have been met is promotion granted. In short, reinforcement (promotion) occurs only after the requirements of both a ratio and an interval schedule have been satisfied. As you can well imagine, simple schedules of

FIGURE 3-8   One Example of a Variable-Ratio Schedule of Reinforcement

Although they probably don't realize this is the case, individuals playing slot machines are operating under a variable-ratio schedule of reinforcement. The machines do finally pay off, but only after a variable number of plays. (Source: Photo courtesy of the Las Vegas News Bureau.)

reinforcement can be combined in many other ways as well—far too many for us to consider in detail here. However, this fact should in no way interfere with your firm grasp of two basic principles. First, in many real-life situations, reinforcement does not follow every appropriate response. Rather, it occurs only part of the time. Second, in such cases, the rules (schedules) determining its delivery exert profound effects upon behavior.

Patterns of reinforcement and extinction: The partial reinforcement effect. As we have just seen, schedules of reinforcement often exert a powerful effect upon ongoing behavior. They strongly influence the rate at which various responses are performed, as well as the overall pattern of such behavior. But what about extinction? Does prior exposure to various schedules of reinforcement also affect the persistence of behavior when reinforcement is no longer available? The answer is "yes," but with a surprising twist. Common sense might lead you to expect that if a form of behavior is always followed by reinforcement, it will be very resistant to extinction—more resistant than behaviors that are reinforced only part of the time. But beware: this is one of those cases we warned you about in Chapter 1. Actually, the pattern is precisely *opposite* to what common sense suggests; behaviors acquired under conditions of continuous reinforcement are often far easier to extinguish (eliminate) than ones acquired under partial reinforcement (e.g., one of the simple schedules of reinforcement described above). This surprising fact is often termed the **partial reinforcement effect,** and it can be observed in many situations.

For example, recall the story at the start of this chapter, in which a woman named Jean attempted to eliminate certain annoying behavior on the part of Charlie, one of her coworkers. For long periods of time, she refused his requests (i.e., withheld reinforcement). But then occasionally—just occasionally—she relented and gave in. The result, of course, was that extinction was prevented. Charlie was placed on a partial schedule of reinforcement, so he showed little tendency to stop pestering poor, long-suffering Jean.

One possible reason for the existence of the partial reinforcement effect is as follows. Conditions existing during extinction (the total absence of reinforcement) are more similar to those present under partial reinforcement than to those present under continuous reinforcement (when reinforcement is always available).[12] For this reason, behaviors acquired under partial reinforcement are more likely to persist during extinction than behaviors acquired under continuous reinforcement. Regardless of the precise basis for the partial reinforcement effect, though, it has intriguing implications for human behavior. Briefly, it helps explain why we often persist in performing actions that no longer work—no longer yield desired reinforcers. When it is realized that most of our behaviors are learned under conditions of partial reinforcement, such persistence loses much of its mystery. In short, what has often been described as human stubbornness may simply reflect the operation of a basic principle of operant conditioning. (Please see the **"FOCUS"** box on pp. 70–71 for a discussion of the unsettling effects that may occur when there is no contingency between individuals' behavior and their outcomes.)

OPERANT CONDITIONING AND ORGANIZATIONAL BEHAVIOR

Earlier, we noted that operant conditioning is based on a simple fact: behavior often produces consequences. The nature of these consequences, in turn, then determines whether specific actions are repeated or abandoned. Those yielding positive outcomes are strengthened; those followed by negative ones tend to be avoided. Implicit in these basic principles is an intriguing possibility. If the consequences yielded by behavior can be controlled in some manner, won't the behavior, too, be readily shaped or altered? The answer suggested by a large and growing body of research is "yes." When individuals are provided with positive reinforcers for engaging in some behavior, their tendency to perform this action increases. In contrast, when certain behaviors are followed by negative reinforcers, individuals soon learn to avoid their performance and adopt others in their place. Because procedures based on these principles seek to shape or mold human behavior, they have often been termed **behavior modification.** And they *do* work; that is, they are often highly effective in changing overt actions in many settings. For example, during the past two decades, techniques based on operant conditioning have been used to alter the bizarre actions of mentally disturbed persons and to help educate individuals who are severely retarded. Similarly, they have been employed to help children learn in school and to change the actions of youngsters who create disturbances in the classroom. Finally, they have been adapted to the task of helping individuals cope with many personal problems, such as excessive smoking, obesity, and shyness.[13]

The success of behavior modification in these and other fields led, quite naturally, to the suggestion that it might also be of use in organizational settings. One of the first individuals to call attention to this possibility was Walter Nord.[14] In an influential article, he noted that through the late 1960s, the field of organiza-

FOCUS ON BEHAVIOR

Learned Helplessness: When Contingency Fails

Throughout our discussion of operant conditioning, we have focused on situations in which there is a direct link between what an individual does and the outcomes he or she experiences. As we have seen, under such conditions, individuals can readily learn to perform responses that yield positive outcomes or allow them to avoid negative ones. But what about situations in which such contingencies are absent? In short, what happens when individuals are exposed to situations in which they cannot exert any control over their outcomes? This is an important question for the field of organizational behavior, for employees often perceive work settings in just this way. They believe that nothing they do really matters—they will be treated in much the same manner regardless of their effort or performance.

The impact of such situations has been the subject of a large amount of recent research.[15,16] Unfortunately, the findings of this work are far from comforting. It appears that, as a result of exposure to a lack of control, individuals often come to believe that their behavior and their outcomes are unrelated. If such beliefs were restricted to the situation in which they were acquired, this would not be too unsettling. But regrettably, they seem to generalize to other settings as well. Thus, after exposure to a lack of contingency in one situation, individuals often seem to give up and assume that they have no influence over their outcomes in other contexts—even ones in which such control *is* present.

Effects of this type have been demonstrated in many recent studies.[17] While the details of these experiments have varied greatly, most have used procedures of the following general type. First, two groups of subjects perform some task. For one group, outcomes are contingent on their behavior; there *is* a correct response, and subjects are rewarded when they perform it. For the second, such contingency is lacking; there is no correct response, and rewards are delivered in a random manner. (Usually, subjects in the second group receive the same number of rewards as those in the first. But of course, there is no link between their behavior and the delivery of such outcomes.) Following these procedures, both groups perform a second task—one in which behavior and outcomes are in fact related. As you might predict, individuals exposed to a lack of control on the first task usually do much worse on the second (see Figure 3–9). Several explanations for this finding have been suggested.[18] One that has gained wide acceptance is as follows. Exposure to the lack of contingency in the first part of the study leads subjects to conclude that they cannot influence their outcomes. This belief then generalizes to the second part; and by inducing passivity, reductions in self-esteem, and depression, it inhibits successful performance.[19,20]

As you can readily see, **learned helplessness** and the negative feelings that accompany it have important implications for managers. In particular, the findings we have just described suggest that exposing employees to situations in which they feel that they have no control over their outcomes can have important, negative effects. Such experiences may serve to reduce motivation, lower self-esteem, and induce depression, with the overall result that both morale and performance suffer. Unfortunately, conditions of this type are all too common in the world of work. Employees often believe that nothing they do really matters—they will receive

tional behavior had generally ignored operant conditioning and its potential applications to work settings. He then suggested that such techniques could actually be of substantial use in attaining many positive goals (e.g., more effective job design, improvements in organizational climate, better programs for employee com-

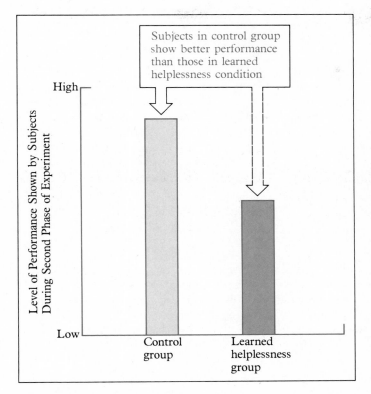

Subjects in control group show better performance than those in learned helplessness condition

High

Low

Level of Performance Shown by Subjects During Second Phase of Experiment

Control group

Learned helplessness group

FIGURE 3-9 Typical Results Obtained in Studies of Learned Helplessness

Many studies concerned with learned helplessness employ procedures consisting of two distinct parts. In the first, there is a link between performance and outcomes for one group (the *control* condition), but not for the other (the *learned helplessness* group). In the second part of the experiment, this type of contingency exists for both groups. Yet, because of their experience during the first phase, subjects in the helplessness group usually do more poorly than those in the control condition.

much the same rewards regardless of their actions. Similarly, they often perceive that merit pay, bonuses, promotions, and other rewards are not closely related to job performance. Given the negative effects that may stem from such feelings of helplessness and lack of control, it seems important for managers to devote careful attention to this issue. In particular, they should take every step possible to assure that contingencies *do* exist between employees' performance and the outcomes they receive and to assure that employees perceive their presence. Of course, union contracts, existing company practices, and other factors may often make it harder to attain this goal than to describe it. But given the benefits that may result when feelings of helplessness are avoided, we believe that steps in this direction will often be well worth the effort. □

pensation). According to Nord, one strategy for attaining these goals would involve the establishment, by managers, of appropriate *reinforcement contingencies*— that is, the establishment of conditions under which desired behaviors by employees would yield positive outcomes. In short, he recommended the use of operant conditioning as a technique for shaping effective behavior in persons in organizational settings.

This call for the direct application of operant conditioning to organizational behavior was soon criticized on several grounds. Some individuals felt that such conditioning ignored individuality, and treated all persons the same.[21] Others suggested that it restricted human freedom and allowed little room for personal choice.[22] We will return to such criticisms below. At the moment, we simply wish to note that despite its somewhat controversial nature, the operant conditioning approach has received growing attention and application in O.B.[23] But how, precisely, can such techniques be used? How can we apply principles of operant conditioning to behavior in work settings? One of the clearest answers has been provided by Fred Luthans and his colleagues.[24] These scientists have outlined a systematic approach to what they term **O.B. Mod.**—Organizational Behavior Modification. Further, they have put this approach to use and gathered considerable evidence for its value. In the discussion that follows, we will first summarize the major steps in O.B. Mod. as outlined by Luthans and then describe some recent evidence for its effectiveness. Finally, we will return to the controversy mentioned above and consider some of the ethical questions raised by O.B. Mod.

O.B. Mod.: Basic Steps

The first step in planning a successful program of O.B. Mod. involves identification of *critical behaviors,* ones that exert a strong effect upon key aspects of job performance. This can be accomplished in several different ways. For example, immediate supervisors can be asked to pinpoint those behaviors that are crucial for effective performance. Similarly, outside consultants can be hired to accomplish this task. Whatever method chosen, though, the result should be the same: a short list of behaviors that play a major role in job performance.

After critical behaviors have been identified, a second step, measurement of the rate at which these behaviors are occurring, is performed. Such measurement is crucial for without it, there can be no way to determine whether O.B. Mod. has actually been effective in changing job-related behaviors.

A third step—and a key one—involves what Luthans terms a *functional analysis* of the behavior. Basically, this analysis seeks to determine just what conditions lead to the occurrence of various actions being demonstrated by employees and what consequences follow from each. This knowledge is important, for O.B. Mod. derives largely from a basic principle of operant conditioning—that behavior is largely a function of the outcomes it produces.

The fourth step in O.B. Mod. focuses on development of a specific *intervention strategy*—specific steps for modifying the behaviors in question. In most cases, this involves determining what stimuli or events individuals find positively reinforcing and then arranging conditions so that attainment of such reinforcers is contingent on performance of the desired behaviors. As we have already seen, a very wide range of outcomes can serve as positive reinforcers—anything from money or improved work conditions, on the one hand, through social approval or increased status on the other. It is crucial, therefore, that effective reinforcers be selected for use in O.B. Mod. programs. After all, offering employees "rewards" they don't really desire is likely to have little impact on their job behavior. We should note that punishment can sometimes be combined with positive reinforcement to facilitate change. That is, conditions can be devised so that employees are rewarded with positive incentives for demonstrating desired behaviors, but punished with unpleasant outcomes (e.g., loss of pay, public criticism) for demonstrating undesirable ones. In many cases, though, punishment is best avoided. As we noted earlier, it often yields undesirable "side effects," such as a general inhibition of all behavior or resentment on the part of the persons who receive it. In any case, regardless of the specific techniques used, the major goal of an effective O.B. Mod. program is this: arranging the environment so that individuals are encouraged to engage in desired behaviors (those that contribute to productivity or morale) and discouraged from engaging in undesired ones.

A final step in O.B. Mod., one that places it on firm scientific footing, is that of systematic *evaluation* of the outcomes. Behavior prior to the start of the program is compared with that at its conclusion, in order to determine if the goals sought have actually been attained. A summary of the major steps in O.B. Mod. is presented in Table 3–1; please examine it carefully.

TABLE 3–1   O.B. Mod.: Some Crucial Steps

As shown here, effective use of O.B. Mod. involves careful attention to a number of different steps and procedures.

STEP	DESCRIPTION
Selection of Critical Behaviors	Selection of behaviors that play a key role in job performance. These can be suggested by immediate supervisors or identified by expert consultants.
Measurement of Base Rate	Determination of the rate at which critical behaviors are occurring. This information is necessary for evaluating the success of the O.B. Mod. program used.
Functional Analysis	Careful examination of current behaviors being shown by employees to determine what consequences each produce, what conditions lead to their occurrence, etc.
Design of Intervention Strategy	Development of specific steps for modifying the critical behaviors. This involves careful attention to identification of effective positive reinforcers and arranging conditions so that these are contingent upon performance of the desired behaviors.
Systematic Evaluation	Final behavior by employees is compared with that prior to the start of the project to assess changes produced by O.B. Mod. These should be in the directions desired.

O.B. Mod.: Some Supporting Evidence

In basic concept, O.B. Mod. is quite straightforward and easy to grasp. Further, it derives from basic and well-established principles of operant conditioning, as well as from a great deal of evidence concerning the application of such principles to the modification of human behavior. But does it actually work? Can it really produce beneficial effects in organizational settings? On the basis of evidence collected in recent years, our answer is, once again, "yes." Actually, a large number of studies have been conducted recently to assess the value of O.B. Mod. As an example of such work, we will consider an investigation by Luthans, Paul, and Baker.[25]

The goal of this project was that of improving the job performance of retail clerks working in a large department store. In accordance with the steps outlined on pages 72–73, critical behaviors first were identified. These included selling activities, stock work, idleness on the job (e.g., ignoring customers), and absenteeism. Next, the base rate at which each of these activities occurred was measured through careful observation. A functional analysis was then performed to determine just what behaviors should be reinforced during the O.B. Mod. program. This analysis suggested that it was crucial for salespersons to remain within about three feet of the merchandise on display, that they should greet customers within five seconds of their appearance, and that display shelves should be kept filled to at least 70% of capacity. An intervention program was then devised to encourage the clerks in an experimental group to act in these ways. In large measure, it consisted of offering them time off with pay and a chance to win a free vacation for attaining performance criteria related to the three behaviors outlined above. In contrast, clerks in a control group were never offered these incentives. The behavior of individuals in both groups was observed for 20 days while these incentives were available and during another 20 days after they were removed. As you can see from Figure 3–10, results were quite dramatic: on-the-job performance improved greatly and absenteeism dropped sharply in the experimental group. In contrast, however, similar changes were not observed for the control condition.

We should note that similar results have also been obtained in a number of other investigations, conducted in markedly different settings (e.g., a large hospital, an air freight company, several factories). Together, these findings suggest that principles based on operant conditioning can in fact be useful from the point of view of encouraging effective organizational behavior—especially when they are combined with other approaches emphasizing cognitive factors such as expectancies and goals.[26]

O.B. Mod.: A Continuing Controversy

Before concluding our discussion of the use of operant conditioning techniques in organizational settings, we should comment briefly on one remaining issue: are they really ethical? As we noted earlier, some critics have suggested that because O.B. Mod. and related procedures seek to "control" human behavior, they are

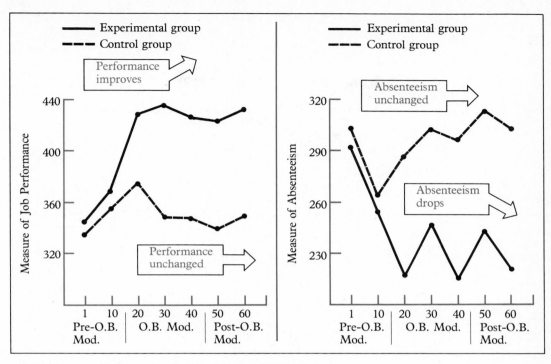

FIGURE 3–10   Evidence for the Effectiveness of O.B. Mod.

As shown here, O.B. Mod. can be quite effective. Subjects in the experimental group (those exposed to the new reinforcement contingencies) showed improved on-the-job performance and reduced absenteeism. In contrast, those in the control group failed to demonstrate similar changes. (Source: Based on data from Luthans, Paul, & Baker, *Journal of Applied Psychology*, 1981, *66*, 314–323.)

unethical and should be avoided.[27] Indeed, going further, some have noted that this approach represents a violation of basic human rights and freedoms. We view such arguments as largely spurious in nature. Briefly, it is our impression that they often stem from the erroneous view that O.B. Mod. and other operant techniques somehow *force* individuals to behave in certain ways. Actually, this is akin to arguing that the laws of physics force heavenly bodies to revolve around the sun. The principles of operant conditioning simply state basic facts about behavior. That is, they note that all organisms (including human beings) generally behave in ways that yield positive reinforcers, terminate negative reinforcers, or avoid punishment. The fact that such principles exist in no way implies coercion or force; rather, it simply describes reality. We should also note that attempts to influence human behavior have always existed and would doubtless continue without O.B. Mod. or operant conditioning. Thus, this and similar procedures simply represent an alternative approach to an age-old question: how can human beings be induced to behave in certain ways?

In our view, the key point concerning the ethical nature of O.B. Mod. and other operant procedures is actually this: what are the ultimate goals for which they are employed? If these involve exploitation of employees for the sole benefit of management or an organization, then serious questions can be raised about their use. If, instead, the goals sought are ones that benefit both groups (e.g., high productivity, improved morale, fairer distribution of rewards), then O.B. Mod. and similar approaches may well be acceptable. In sum, operant procedures, like any effective tool, are actually neutral in and of themselves. It is only the goals or ends for which they are employed that can be described as "good" or "evil." (For a discussion of the use of operant conditioning in organizational settings, see the **"PERSPECTIVE"** box on pp. 78–79.)

MODELING: LEARNING BY OBSERVATION

Suppose that at some time in the future, you are the manager of a small department in a moderate-sized company. A new employee has just joined your staff, and although he is well qualified in almost every respect, you discover that he is not familiar with the operation of the on-line computer terminal used in many tasks. What would you do to rectify this situation? One approach, of course, simply would be to hand him the manual that accompanies the terminal and instruct him to master the material in it. Another, probably more efficient, approach would be to have one of the members of your department who is already familiar with the equipment "teach him the ropes."

This latter strategy is based on a third major form of learning—one often known as **modeling** or **observational learning.** Briefly, it occurs when one individual acquires new forms of behavior (or the information necessary for such behavior) simply by observing the actions of others.[28] Of course, in the example just described, the person in question would also receive verbal instructions from his tutor. But the basic process would be one involving observation. In fact, if you listened in on the conversation between these two individuals, you might well hear the experienced person say to the beginner: "Now watch closely . . . "

Careful studies of observational (or *vicarious*) learning suggest that it involves four subprocesses. First, it is crucial that careful *attention* be directed to the model. Obviously, it is impossible to learn from others' behavior if we do not observe it. Thus, any characteristics of another person that attract our attention—high status, physical attractiveness, high expertise—will tend to facilitate modeling.[29] Second, *retention* of the model's behavior is crucial. Unless we can somehow retain an internal representation (a verbal description or visual image) of the model's actions, observational learning cannot occur. A third process involves our ability to reproduce the model's behavior. If we are unable to do so because of physical limitations or other factors, it may be difficult for vicarious learning to take place. Finally, *motivation* plays a key role. We must have some reason or encouragement for adopting the model's behavior. In the absence of such motivation, observational learning will probably not occur.

Additional research findings indicate that observational learning is actually a very common process. For example, children acquire much of their behavior and information through this process. They constantly observe their parents, teachers, and other children; and in this way, they learn a great many things. In most cases, the behaviors they acquire through modeling are useful and are approved by their parents. In other cases, though, they may acquire negative actions. In this regard, we are sure that you have read or heard about the controversy regarding *televised violence*. A large body of evidence suggests that, as a result of constant exposure to the mayhem occurring on T.V. screens each evening, children may acquire many new aggressive responses—and the willingness to put these into practice.[30] Clearly, this is one form of modeling that has important social consequences. Adults, too, often learn through observation. For example, to mention just one scintillating example (!), individuals who attend X-rated movies often report that, at least initially, they acquire new information about novel techniques of love-making in this fashion.

Observational learning is also quite common in work settings. First, as suggested by the example on page 76, it often plays a role in both formal and informal *job training*. New employees often seek to master their jobs by observing the actions of their more experienced co-workers. And more formal training programs often make use of systematic procedures in which inexperienced persons are paired with experienced ones, who then serve as models for these persons (see Figure 3–11). Research on the effectiveness of modeling as a training technique has yielded highly encouraging results. In general, it appears that programs in which employees (1) witness desired behavior, (2) have a chance to rehearse them, (3) are given positive feedback for performing such actions, and (4) are helped to apply them to their jobs can be quite successful. Indeed, they can help individuals master even difficult tasks in a rapid manner.[31,32]

Second, modeling often affects the setting of important, job-related goals. During the normal course of events, employees witness the performance of several other persons. On the basis of such information, they may then set goals for their own job performance. As we shall see in Chapter 5, such goals may then exert strong effects on actual performance and on satisfaction with it.

Direct evidence for such effects is provided by a recent investigation, carried out by Rakestraw and Weiss.[33] In this study, male college students first received instructions on how to perform a fairly complex card-sorting task. Half of the

FIGURE 3–11   Modeling: Often Useful in Business Settings

Modeling can often serve as a useful technique for on-the-job training. (Source: Photo © 1980 Richard Wood/The Picture Cube.)

FROM THE MANAGER'S PERSPECTIVE
Using Operant Conditioning: A Practical Guide

We trust that by now, you are convinced of the potential benefits of O.B. Mod. and related techniques. As we have tried to point out, such procedures—when used with skill and care—can yield dramatic results. Specifically, they can produce positive shifts in a very wide range of employee behavior. Unfortunately, though, systematic programs of this type usually require major investments of time and energy. For this reason, they are often easier to describe (or visualize) than to implement. This fact raises an important question: can practicing managers benefit from a working knowledge of operant conditioning, even in cases where full-scale programs of behavioral intervention are not practical? We think that they can. In fact, it is our firm belief that through attention to a small number of basic principles, managers can greatly enhance their effectiveness in guiding the actions of their subordinates into desired, beneficial patterns. Several of these principles, along with concrete suggestions for putting them to practical use, are listed below. Please consider them carefully, for together they may save you much unnecessary trouble in the years ahead.

1. *Clarify the contingencies.* One common "gripe" in many organizations is as follows: no one knows just what behaviors will yield important, valued rewards. In short, employees are uncertain as to just what they must do to gain raises, promotions, and other positive outcomes. Faced with such ambiguity, many become discouraged and conclude that they will never unravel the seemingly obscure "magic formula" for success within their company. The message for managers in such situations is obvious: if you want to be effective in guiding your subordinates' behavior, clarify such

contingencies for them. In other words, make sure that they know just what actions will—and will not—yield desired positive outcomes.

2. *Be sure to reward—not punish—desired behavior.* In many organizations, it is considered downright dangerous to have a totally clear desk. The reason for this is simple: being too much "on top" of one's work may actually yield negative results (see Figure 3-12). These can take the form of extra work, increased responsibilities, or negative reactions from one's peers. And all too often, such "punishments" are literally heaped upon the shoulders of the most energetic and conscientious members of work teams—those actually most deserving of reward. Needless to add, this pattern is counterproductive and should be avoided. As a manager, you should take active steps to assure that positive, desired behaviors by the persons working under your direction are rewarded rather than punished. If you don't, you may well encourage a high rate of turnover among your best subordinates.[34]

3. *Choose appropriate reinforcers.* Earlier, we noted that different persons seek different rewards. Some focus mainly on financial benefits, others crave praise and recognition, and still others place great value on interesting and varied work. As a manager, you should always try to take full account of these individual preferences. To the extent that you do, your efforts to shape the behavior of your subordinates through the delivery of positive reinforcement may be considerably enhanced.

4. *Punishment: handle with care!* Although it can often be effective in suppressing undesirable behavior, punishment frequently yields unwanted side effects. (For example, it may inhibit behavior generally and leave a lingering resentment in employees who receive it.) For this reason, you should

---

participants then practiced the task, while half did not. Next, all subjects watched a training film, ostensibly designed to help them master the task. In this film a male model performed the card-sorting task and achieved either a high level of performance or a relatively low level of performance. Following exposure to the

"By God, I'm so pleased with the way you handled that lousy, thankless job I gave you, Frawley, that I'm going to give you another one."

FIGURE 3-12   How *Not* to Use Operant Conditioning to Enhance Desired Organizational Behavior

In seeking to modify human behavior through operant conditioning, it is crucial to establish appropriate contingencies. That is, individuals must be rewarded—not punished— for engaging in desired behaviors. The manager shown in this cartoon is unaware of this fact. As a result, he will probably discourage just those actions he wishes to enhance. (Source: Drawing by Stan Hunt; © 1980 The New Yorker Magazine, Inc.)

avoid the use of this procedure if at all possible. And when you do find it necessary to employ punishment, be sure to administer it privately. The "loss of face" that can result from public criticism or censure is definitely something to be avoided.

5. *Avoid feelings of helplessness among employees.* When individuals conclude that there is no connection between their behavior and their outcomes, they may experience strong feelings of helplessness. These feelings, in turn, can lead to reduced motivation, lowered self-esteem, and even strong depression. Given the negative impact of such reactions on both performance and morale, managers should do everything in their power to avoid such situations. They should try to assure that clear connections between performance and reinforcement exist and that the persons working under their direction perceive them. To the extent such conditions prevail, employees will tend to view their fate as being largely in their own hands. And then, motivation, job performance, and satisfaction may all be strongly enhanced.   □

film, all individuals performed the card-sorting task themselves. In addition, they indicated their personal goals with respect to this task and their level of satisfaction with their own performance on it. Results indicated that exposure to the model (shown in the training film) exerted strong effects on all three variables.

As expected, subjects set higher goals for their own performance when they had witnessed a high level of performance by the model than when they had seen a lower level of performance. Similarly, the smaller the discrepancy between their own level of task performance and that shown by the model, the greater their reported satisfaction. Finally, among subjects who had *not* first practiced the task, those who watched the high-performing model achieved better performance than those who observed the low-performing model. This latter finding suggests that exposure to the performance of others may have stronger effects on inexperienced employees performing unfamiliar tasks than on experienced employees performing familiar and well-practiced tasks. In any case, taken as a whole, the findings reported by Rakestraw and Weiss and those obtained in other studies suggest that exposure to the behavior of others can often exert powerful effects upon the performance, goals, and satisfaction of employees.[35]

Finally, observational learning also exerts more subtle—but perhaps even more general—effects upon behavior in work settings. Because they possess high status, expertise, and competence, managers often serve as models for the persons working under their direction.[36] Thus, subordinates frequently emulate the job-related behaviors of their bosses. But such influence does not stop there. Often, they also adopt supervisors' actions which are not directly linked to work. These include mannerisms, style of dress, and even specific attitudes. In such instances, observational learning shades over into *conformity* and *social influence*—topics we will consider in Chapter 13. In any case, the key message for managers is this: whether they realize it or not, they often have a unique opportunity for shaping the behavior of their subordinates. How they use this opportunity, of course, can have a major impact upon the climate and effectiveness of their organizations.

SUMMARY

Human beings possess the capacity to profit from their experience through **learning.** This key process involves relatively permanent changes in behavior.

One basic form of learning is **classical conditioning.** It occurs in situations where one stimulus, not initially capable of evoking some response, is paired repeatedly with another stimulus that *can* evoke such reactions. As a result of such pairing, the first stimulus, too, acquires the capacity to evoke these responses. Classical conditioning appears to play a crucial role in the development of emotional reactions, such as strong fears or attitudes.

A second major form of learning, *instrumental* or **operant conditioning,** is based on the fact that behavior often yields consequences. As a result of this contingency, individuals learn to perform responses that yield desirable outcomes or that help them to escape or avoid undesirable ones. *Schedules of reinforcement*—rules determining the timing and frequency of reinforcement—exert powerful effects upon operant conditioning. Techniques based on this form of learning have been successfully employed in attempts to help human beings overcome many behavioral problems (e.g., excessive smoking, obesity). Recent studies indicate that they also prove useful in organizational settings.

A third major form of learning, *modeling* or *observational learning,* occurs in situations where individuals acquire new behaviors simply by observing the actions of others. Modeling plays an important role in the behavior of both children and adults. It often finds application in organizational settings as a technique for the training of new employees.

KEY TERMS

BEHAVIOR MODIFICATION   The use of conditioning principles and procedures to shape or mold human behavior.

CLASSICAL CONDITIONING   A basic form of learning in which one stimulus, not initially capable of evoking a specific response, is repeatedly paired with another that *can* evoke this reaction. As a result of such pairing, the first stimulus gradually acquires the capacity to evoke reactions similar to those elicited by the second stimulus.

EXTINCTION   The process through which conditioned responses are weakened and eventually eliminated.

FIXED-INTERVAL SCHEDULE   A schedule in which the first response following a set period of time yields reinforcement.

FIXED-RATIO SCHEDULE   A schedule in which reinforcement is delivered each time a set number of responses have been performed.

LEARNED HELPLESSNESS   Refers to situations in which individuals perceive that there is no contingency between their behavior and their outcomes. The feelings of helplessness so produced generalize to other situations (even ones in which such contingencies exist), and interfere with performance.

LEARNING   The process through which relatively permanent changes in behavior are induced through experience.

MODELING   A basic form of learning in which individuals acquire new responses simply by observing the actions and outcomes of others.

NEGATIVE REINFORCER   Any stimulus organisms find unpleasant. Negative reinforcers serve to strengthen responses leading to their removal or termination.

O.B. MOD.   Techniques for modifying organizational behavior derived from basic principles of operant conditioning. Recent evidence suggests that O.B. Mod. can be helpful in attaining many beneficial goals (e.g., increased productivity, improved morale).

OPERANT CONDITIONING   A basic form of learning (sometimes termed *instrumental conditioning*) in which responses that yield positive outcomes or eliminate negative ones are acquired and strengthened.

PARTIAL REINFORCEMENT EFFECT   Refers to the somewhat surprising fact that responses acquired under partial reinforcement are often more resistant to extinction than responses acquired under continuous reinforcement.

POSITIVE REINFORCER   Any stimulus organisms find pleasant. Positive reinforcers strengthen responses leading to their presentation.

PUNISHMENT   Refers to conditions in which the delivery of an unpleasant stimulus is contingent upon performance of a specific response. By refraining from this response, organisms can avoid the aversive stimulus.

SCHEDULES OF REINFORCEMENT   Rules governing the timing and frequency of reinforcement.

VARIABLE-INTERVAL SCHEDULE   A schedule in which the first response after the passage of a variable interval of time yields reinforcement.

VARIABLE-RATIO SCHEDULE   A schedule in which reinforcement is delivered only after the performance of a variable number of responses.

NOTES

1. Hulse, S.H., Deese, J., & Egeth, H. *The psychology of learning* (5th ed.). New York: McGraw-Hill, 1980.

2. Maanen, J.V., & Schein, E.G. Toward a theory of organizational socialization. In B.M. Staw (Ed.), *Research in organizational behavior.* Greenwich, Conn.: JAI Press, 1979.

3. King, D.L. *Conditioning: An image approach.* New York: Gardner Press, 1982.

4. Hygge, S., & Ohman, A. Modeling processes in the acquisition of fears: Vicarious electrodermal conditioning to fear-relevant stimuli. *Journal of Personality and Social Psychology,* 1978, *36,* 271–279.

5. Ohman, A., Fredrickson, M., Hugdahl, K., & Rimmo, P.A. The premise of equipotentiality in human classical conditioning: Conditioned electrodermal responses to potentially phobic stimuli. *Journal of Experimental Psychology: General,* 1976, *105,* 313–337.

6. Baron, R.A., & Byrne, D. *Exploring social psychology* (2nd ed.). Boston: Allyn and Bacon, 1982.

7. Bower, G.H., & Hilgard, E.R. *Theories of learning* (5th ed.). Englewood Cliffs, N.J.: Prentice-Hall, 1981.

8. Hamner, W.C., & Hamner, E.P. Behavior modification on the bottom line. *Organizational Dynamics,* 1976, *4,* 8–21.

9. Hamner, W.C. Reinforcement theory and contingency management in organizational settings. In H.L. Tosi, Jr. & W.C. Hamner (Eds.), *OB and management.* Chicago: St. Clair, 1974.

10. Ferster, C.B., & Skinner, B.F. *Schedules of reinforcement.* New York: Appleton, 1957.

11. Honig, W.K., & Staddon, J.E.R. (Eds.). *Handbook of operant behavior.* Englewood Cliffs, N.J.: Prentice-Hall, 1977.

12. Capaldi, E.J. Reinforcement level: An expectancy-associative approach to relative reinforcement and nonreinforcement effects. In J.E. Baerwaldt & G. McCain (Eds.), *The Arlington symposium on learning.* Stamford, Conn.: Greylock, 1980.

13. Grasha, A.F. *Practical applications of psychology.* Cambridge, Mass.: Winthrop, 1978.

14. Nord, W.R. Beyond the teaching machine: The neglected area of operant conditioning in the theory and practice of management. *Organizational Behavior and Human Performance,* 1969, *4,* 375–401.

15. Abramson, L.Y., Seligman, M.E.P., & Teasdale, J. Learned helplessness in humans: Critique and reformulation. *Journal of Abnormal Psychology,* 1978, *87,* 49–74.

16. Seligman, M.E.P. *Helplessness: On depression, development, and death.* San Francisco: Freeman, 1975.

17. Garber, J., & Seligman, M.E.P. (Eds.). *Human helplessness: Theory and application.* New York: Academic Press, 1980.

18. Black, A.H. Comments on "Learned helplessness: Theory and evidence" by Maier and Seligman. *Journal of Experimental Psychology: General,* 1977, *196,* 41–43.

19. Abramson, L.Y., & Alloy, L.B. Judgment of contingency: Errors and their implications. In A. Baum & J. Singer (Eds.), *Advances in environmental psychology* (Vol. 2). Hillsdale, N.J.: Erlbaum, 1980.

20. Klein, D.C., Fencil-Morse, E., & Seligman, M.E.P. Learned helplessness, depression, and the attribution of failure. *Journal of Personality and Social Psychology,* 1976, *33,* 508–516.

21. Locke, E.A. The myths of behavior mod. in organizations. *Academy of Management Review,* 1977, *2,* 543–553.

22. Hamner, W.C., & Hamner, E.P. Behavior modification on the bottom line. *Organizational Dynamics,* 1976, *4,* 8–21.

23. Adam, E.E., Jr. An analysis of changes in performance quality with operant conditioning procedures. *Journal of Applied Psychology,* 1972, *56,* 480–486.

24. Luthans, F., & Kreitner, R. *Organizational behavior modification.* Glenview, Ill.: Scott, Foresman & Co., 1975.

25. Luthans, F., Paul, R., & Baker, D. An experimental analysis of the impact of a contingent reinforcement intervention on salespersons' performance behaviors. *Journal of Applied Psychology,* 1981, *66,* 314–323.

26. Fedor, D.B., & Ferris, G.R. Integrating OB Mod with cognitive approaches to motivation. *Academy of Management Review,* 1981, *6,* 115–125.

27. Ashby, E. Can education be machine made? *New Scientist,* February 2, 1967.

28. Bandura, A. *Social learning theory.* Englewood Cliffs, N.J.: Prentice-Hall, 1977.

29. Weiss, H.M. Subordinate imitation of supervisory behavior: The role of modeling in organizational socialization. *Organizational Behavior and Human Performance,* 1977, *19,* 89–105.

30. Withey, S.B., & Abeles, R.P. (Eds.). *Television and social behavior: Beyond violence and children.* Hillsdale, N.J.: Erlbaum, 1980.

31. Latham, G.P., & Saari, L.M. Applications of social-learning theory to training supervisors through behavioral modeling. *Journal of Applied Psychology,* 1979, *64,* 239–246.

32. Manz, C.C., & Sims, H.P., Jr. Vicarious learning: The influence of modeling on organizational behavior. *Academy of Management Review,* 1981, *6,* 105–113.

33. Rakestraw, T.L., Jr. & Weiss, H.M. The interaction of social influences and task experience on goals, performance, and performance satisfaction. *Organizational Behavior and Human Performance,* 1981, *27,* 326–344.

34. Dreher, G.F. The role of performance in the turnover process. *Academy of Management Journal,* 1982, *25,* 137–147.

35. White, S.E., & Mitchell, T.R. Job enrichment versus social cues: A comparison and competitive test. *Journal of Applied Psychology,* 1979, *64,* 1–9.

36. Price, K.H., & Garland, H. Compliance with a leader's suggestions as a function of perceived leader/member competence and potential reciprocity. *Journal of Applied Psychology,* 1981, *66,* 329–336.

4

Personality:

The Uniqueness (and Consistency)

of Individuals

THEORIES OF PERSONALITY: CONTRASTING VIEWS OF INDIVIDUAL BEHAVIOR

Freud's Psychoanalytic Theory of Personality: Journey into the Unconscious   Learning-Oriented Theories of Personality: Experience as a Basis for Uniqueness   Humanistic Theories: Emphasis on Growth   Trait Theories: Identifying the Key Dimensions of Human Personality

PERSONALITY AND ORGANIZATIONAL BEHAVIOR: SOME SPECIFIC, NOTEWORTHY LINKS

The Type-A/Type-B Dimension: Who Succeeds—and Who Survives?   Machiavellianism: Manipulation as a Way of Life   Locus of Control: Are You the Master of Your Fate?   Other Aspects of Personality Related to Organizational Behavior: The Need for Achievement and the Need for Power

THE MEASUREMENT OF PERSONALITY: APPROACHES AND METHODS

Observational Techniques   Projective Techniques   Personality Inventories and Questionnaires   Using Information about Personality: A Brief Word of Caution

SPECIAL INSERTS

FOCUS ON BEHAVIOR   Is Personality Really Stable?
FOCUS ON BEHAVIOR   Measuring Machiavellianism: The Mach Scale
CASE IN POINT   "Say, Who Hired Him in the First Place?"

KEY CONCEPTS

Type A Behavior Pattern

Type B Behavior Pattern

Machiavellianism

Locus of Control

Id

Ego

Superego

Learning-Oriented Theories
of Personality

Social Learning Theory

Humanistic Theories
of Personality

Internal Control

External Control

Need for Achievement

Need for Power

Projective Techniques

Inventories

□ □ □

It's lunchtime and you've just left the line in the company cafeteria. You look around and notice that there's a place at a table occupied by three of your friends— Joe Barnes, Jennifer Tarantino, and Tim McGuire. You join this congenial group, and begin the usual small talk. After a couple of minutes, Jennifer breaks in with a surprising statement: "Say, have you fellows heard about Herb Rostkanski? He keeled over with a heart attack last Tuesday."

"No kidding!" Tim responds. "Gee, that's too bad. He's such a nice fellow."

Everyone agrees and expresses regret over Herb's misfortune. In fact, you decide to chip in and send flowers to him at the hospital.

At this point, Joe makes a somewhat unsettling remark: "You know, in a way, it's not all that surprising. I mean, if I ever saw a candidate for a heart attack, it's Herb. Always in a hurry, always uptight. I never saw anyone work so hard or take his job so seriously."

"Yeah," Jennifer agrees, "He really did seem driven."

"I think he always wanted to come out on top, no matter what," you add. "He's sure one of the most competitive guys I've ever known. And just the opposite of his partner Ken. Why, that guy is so relaxed you wonder how he stays awake!"

At this last comment, everyone laughs. Then, the conversation turns to other topics.

Later, after lunch is over and you are back in your office, you find yourself thinking about poor Herb once again. Everyone, including you, seems to agree that he was headed for a heart attack for a long time and that, in a way, he actually brought it on himself. But can this really be true? Is there actually a link between personality and health? If so, you decide, there are a couple of other people you know who will bear close watching. . . .

As this incident suggests, individuals differ greatly. Moreover, they do so in seemingly countless ways. Some are ambitious while others are lazy; some are friendly while others are hostile; some are generous, others stingy; some forgiving, others vengeful—the list goes on, and on, and on! As you know from your own experience, the existence of such differences is something of a mixed blessing. On the one hand, they are often a source of confusion. The people around us act in ways we find surprising or puzzling, and they frequently seem to see the world through eyes totally different from our own. On the other hand, such differences are stimulating and intriguing—truly "the spice of life" in several respects. In any case, we become aware of their existence at an early age and soon accept them as a basic feature of human behavior.

Fortunately, while people differ in many important ways, they also seem to show a degree of consistency in this respect. That is, although they are unique, the *pattern* of their uniqueness shows stability over time. Thus, characteristics demonstrated by specific persons at one time are often apparent at other times as well. We hasten to note that such consistency is far from perfect. However, recent evidence does tend to confirm informal observation in suggesting that a degree of stability exists.[1] In short, where at least some aspects of personality are concerned, the general rule is "Here today, here tomorrow."

The two themes we have just mentioned—uniqueness and consistency—actually form the core of our working definition of personality. Briefly, we will define this term as referring to *the unique pattern of characteristics and behaviors that sets each individual apart from others, but that is somewhat stable over time.* We believe that knowing something about this combination of uniqueness and consistency can be extremely useful to you in your future career. First, in order to predict and understand the behavior of other persons, it is essential to recognize their unique characteristics. A working knowledge of personality can enhance your sophistication in this respect and so assist you in dealing with others. Second, and perhaps even more important, there are several personal traits that appear to be directly related to organizational behavior. Familiarity with these and with their effects may be quite helpful to you in many situations.

As we are sure you will agree, personality is an intriguing topic. Partly for this reason, it has been the subject of extensive study for centuries. In the present discussion, we will provide you with an overview of some of the key points and findings uncovered in this continuing work. First, we will describe several contrasting *theories of personality.* These views have added significantly to our understanding of human behavior and are well worthy of careful attention. Second, we will focus on personality traits or characteristics that seem directly related to important forms of organizational behavior. Included here will be discussions of the **Type A behavior pattern** (a cluster of traits linked to increased risk of heart disease), **Machiavellianism,** and **locus of control.** Finally, we will comment briefly on several techniques for measuring personality.

THEORIES OF PERSONALITY: CONTRASTING VIEWS OF INDIVIDUAL BEHAVIOR

Why do human beings behave as they do? What accounts for individuality and uniqueness? How does personality grow and develop over time? It is to answer questions such as these that theories of personality are constructed. During the past century, literally dozens of such theories have been developed. Describing these views as diverse in nature is truly an understatement, for they range from an emphasis on the impact of learning and experience through a focus on the role of powerful inborn urges. Regardless of their specific details, however, all share a common theme: they are designed to enhance our understanding of individual behavior. In the present discussion, we will summarize a small sample of these views—ones that have proven influential in shaping modern thought and modern research concerned with personality.

Freud's Psychoanalytic Theory of Personality: Journey into the Unconscious

Perhaps the most dramatic—and in many ways most unsettling—theory of personality is the *psychoanalytic view* proposed by Sigmund Freud. Summarizing Freud's proposals in a few pages is virtually impossible—his insights and explanations are complex and do not lend themselves to such treatment. Basically, though, he felt that full understanding of human behavior must involve attention to three related topics: *levels of consciousness, the major structures of personality,* and *psychosexual stages of development.*

Levels of consciousness. As the captain of the ill-fated *Titanic* discovered, most of an iceberg lies beneath the surface of the sea; only a small tip is readily visible. According to Freud, the human mind can be viewed in much the same light (see Figure 4-1). Above the surface, and readily available for our mental (rather than visual) inspection, is the *conscious*. This includes our current

FIGURE 4-1   Freud's View of the Human Mind: Three Levels of Consciousness in the "Mental Iceberg"

Freud believed that the human mind consists of three distinct regions or levels: the conscious, preconscious, and unconscious. Note that the contents of these regions differ sharply.

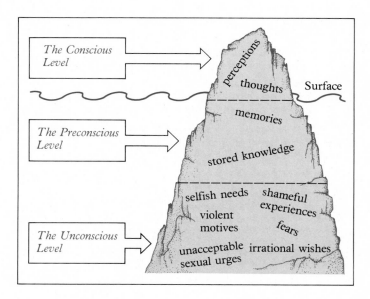

thoughts—whatever we are thinking about at a given moment. Beneath the conscious, and somewhat larger, is the *preconscious.* This portion of the mind includes memories that are not currently in our thoughts but that can be brought to mind if the need arises. Finally, beneath the preconscious, and forming the bulk of the human mind, is the *unconscious*—thoughts, desires, and urges of which we remain largely unaware. Some of this material was always unconscious. But Freud believed that much of it was *repressed,* thrust out of consciousness because it was too anxiety-provoking (e.g., unacceptable sexual desires, shameful experiences). From the point of view of this discussion of personality, the key point to remember about Freud's suggestions is this: because many thoughts, fears, and motives are unconscious, it is often difficult to identify the actual causes of an individual's behavior. In short, there is often much more to personality than at first meets the eye.

The structure of personality: Id, ego, and superego.

Have you ever seen a cartoon in which one of the characters is urged by his "good self" to take one course of action and by his "bad self" to take another? If so, you already have a rough idea of some of the major structures of personality described by Freud. Basically, he proposed that personality consists of three major parts—**id, ego,** and **superego.** (Freud could actually have labeled these structures *desire, reason,* and *conscience,* for they refer, in large measure, to these distinct aspects of human behavior.)

The id (desire) is the "motor" or energy source for human personality. It consists of our primitive, inborn urges for gratification of bodily needs. According to Freud, the id is totally unconscious and operates in accordance with the *pleasure principle,* the demand for immediate, total gratification. Unfortunately, the world offers few opportunities for unbridled pleasure. Indeed, frustration is a far more common experience than instant, total gratification.

It is out of this sad fact that the *ego* develops. Basically, the task of this structure is that of mediating between the desires of the id and the demands of reality. The ego operates in accordance with the *reality principle,* holding the impulses of the id in check until conditions are appropriate for their satisfaction. Only then is gratification permitted. As you might guess, the ego is partly conscious. But note that it is not entirely so. According to Freud, none of the structures of personality operate solely at the level of consciousness.

The final structure described by Freud is the *superego.* This structure, too, controls satisfaction of id impulses, permitting their gratification only under certain circumstances. In contrast to the ego, though, the superego is concerned with morality. That is, it can tell "right" from "wrong." Thus, the superego permits gratification of id impulses only when this is morally correct—not simply when it is safe and feasible, as required by the ego. The superego is acquired from our parents and represents our internalization of their moral teachings and the norms and customs of our society. Unfortunately, as you know, these moral teachings are often quite harsh and permit little room for gratification of our basic desires. Because of this fact, the ego faces another difficult task: it must mediate between the id and superego, striking a balance between our primitive urges and the moral constraints we have acquired. Freud felt that this constant struggle between our id and superego plays a key role in the development of personality—the topic to which we will turn next.

Psychosexual stages of development.   Now that we have outlined Freud's conception of the structure of personality, we can turn to a related topic: his ideas about psychosexual development. Briefly, he believed that between the time of birth and about age seven, all individuals pass through a series of distinct stages. These reflect the fact that as we grow, different parts of the body become the focus of the id's continual quest for pleasure. First, we seek pleasure primarily through our mouth—this is the *oral stage*. Next the id is focused upon the process of elimination, and we enter the *anal stage*. From about the age of three until about five, our genitals become the primary source of pleasure, and we are in the *phallic stage*. Then, from about age five or six until puberty, we enter the *latency period*—a seemingly quiet stage during which id impulses appear to be at a low ebb. Finally, with puberty, we enter the *genital phase*, during which pleasure is sought primarily through satisfactory heterosexual relationships.

At each of these stages, the struggle between the id and superego takes place. (For example, during the phallic stage, the child must contend with intense desires for sexual pleasure and prohibitions upon such activities derived from his or her parent's commands.) If the struggle is successfully mediated by the ego, healthy development proceeds. In some cases, though, this does not take place. An individual can become *fixated* at a given stage, unable to progress beyond the focus of pleasure it involves. When this occurs, the individual may be psychically scarred for life and never attain full maturity. For example, an individual who attains too much gratification during the oral stage may become overly dependent, conforming, and trusting. In contrast, a person who fails to attain sufficient gratification at this stage (because his superego is too strong), may become aggressive, suspicious, and assertive (see Figure 4-2). Similarly, a person who attains too much gratification during the anal stage may turn out to be chronically sloppy and disorganized; one who experiences too little gratification may become overly concerned with cleanliness and neatness.

Regardless of the specific outcome, the important general principle is this: Freud believed that many of the traits we show as adults can be traced to early struggles between our conscience and our primitive desires and to the precise way in which these struggles are resolved through mediation by our ego.

Psychoanalytic theory: Is it of practical use?   As you can readily see, Freud's theory of human personality is both absorbing and provocative. But does it have any bearing on practical matters? More specifically, does it tell us anything that we can use in our attempts to understand and deal with other persons? This is a difficult question, for Freud, it should be recalled, was a mental health practitioner primarily concerned with understanding the roots of neurosis and other personal problems. Thus, he was certainly *not* concerned with many of the prac-

FIGURE 4-2   Fixation at the Oral Stage: Two Contrasting Patterns

According to Freud, either too much or too little gratification at any given stage of development can lead to later personality problems. For example, too much gratification during the oral stage can result in an overly dependent, trusting personality (Lou Costello, left photo). Too little gratification at this time can result in a verbally aggressive personality (Don Rickles, right photo). (Source: Photo [left] from Culver Pictures, Inc.; photo [right] by Peter Borsari/Camera 5.)

tical issues you will soon face in organizational settings. Also, we must note that relatively little systematic research has been conducted to examine the accuracy of his views—a surprising state of affairs, given their widespread acceptance. Despite these facts, however, we believe that several of Freud's insights help increase our sophistication about human behavior and are well worth bearing in mind. The most important of these are as follows:

1. Many of the thoughts, motives, and memories that affect human behavior are unconscious. Thus, in many cases, individuals are not aware of the basis for their own actions or characteristics.
2. Important aspects of human personality may be formed quite early in life. Further, they may be difficult to change at later times. (Existing evidence is not entirely clear on this latter point, but some findings do point to this conclusion.)[2]
3. A healthy personality is characterized by balance; excesses in the direction of either too much gratification or too much control may be signs of existing or potential personal problems.

Other analytic theories.   Before concluding our discussion of Freud's work, we should note that his theory soon gave rise to a number of related views—many offered by Freud's former students who later broke with him and rejected part of his teachings. Space limitations make it unfeasible for us to describe all these other *analytic theories* in detail. However, in order to give you a general idea of their nature and focus, we have summarized several in Table 4-1. Please take a moment to examine this table, for some of these views are quite famous and we are sure that you will encounter them in one form or another in the years ahead.

TABLE 4-1   Other Analytic Theories: A Summary

As indicated by this table, analytic theories of personality vary greatly in their details and major concepts. However, in general, they perceive human beings as passing through various stages of development, each involving a different type of crisis or conflict.

AUTHOR OF THEORY	MAJOR POINTS/CONCEPTS
Carl Jung	Human beings possess a permanent store of memories passed on by their ancestors, the *collective unconscious.* This contains *archetypes,* symbols that appear over and over again in art, literature, mythology. (Superman, the Bad Witch from the Wizard of Oz, and Darth Vadar from *Star Wars* are examples.) Human beings are born as either *introverts,* who are primarily concerned with the self, or *extraverts,* who are more concerned with the outside world.
Erik Erikson	At each stage of development, there is a crisis or conflict. The way in which this is resolved determines the kind of person we become. For example, in the first stage (sensory stage), we learn feelings of trust or mistrust. If our mother is kind and dependable, we learn trust; if she is unkind and undependable, we learn mistrust.
Erich Fromm	Society is seen as an attempt on the part of people to resolve the basic contradiction of human nature: we are part of nature but also separate from it. In contrast to animals, we have needs aside from basic physiological drives. In particular, we have needs for relatedness, association with others, security, and a sense of identity. Five basic personality types exist: receptive type, exploitative type, hoarding type, marketing type, and productive type.
Harry Stack Sullivan	This theory stresses the importance of interpersonal relationships. Our interactions with others are a major determinant of our personality. We pass through a series of stages (infancy, childhood, juvenile, preadolescence, early adolescence, late adolescence, maturity). In each, we learn to play specific roles (e.g., bully, good boy/good girl, clown) and to interact with others. Our personal problems arise because other persons create them for us by what they do or fail to do.

Learning-Oriented Theories of Personality: Experience as a Basis for Uniqueness

In Chapter 3, we noted that learning plays a major role in human behavior. Indeed, as we hope you recall, we pointed out that this process affects everything from attitudes and anxieties, on the one hand, through work and love-making, on the other. Given this powerful and general impact, it seems reasonable to pose the following question: does learning also play a role in personality? Several different theorists believe that it does. Briefly, these experts suggest that personality, too, is shaped or molded by learning. Indeed, some have even gone so far as to suggest that personality consists primarily of patterns of learned behavior.[3] But how, you may be wondering, can learning account for the central aspects of personality described at the start of this chapter? Specifically, how can it account for the uniqueness of individuals and for the consistency they often demonstrate over time? Actually, the answers to both questions are quite straightforward.

With respect to uniqueness, learning theorists simply note that each individual is exposed to a unique set of experiences and environmental conditions throughout life. Since these experiences are unique, it is far from surprising that human beings, too, demonstrate large individual differences. Turning to consistency, recall that learning is defined as *relatively permanent* changes in behavior produced by experience. Given that these changes are permanent, it is only to be expected that patterns of behavior, once acquired, will tend to persist. This, in turn, accounts for the stability of personality. In short, learning theorists contend that human personality rests largely upon, and simply reflects, our unique learning experiences. Understand these experiences, they suggest, and the mystery of human personality, too, can be unraveled.

Although all learning-oriented theories agree on the general points mentioned above, they have tended to focus on contrasting aspects of personality. For example, some have stressed the influence of classical conditioning and have examined the role of this process in the development of conditioned fears. In contrast, others have stressed the impact of operant conditioning and have focused on the role of this basic form of learning in both adaptive and maladaptive patterns of behavior. Because it is closely related to important topics we will consider later, we will now describe a slightly different learning-oriented theory, the **social learning** approach proposed by Julian Rotter.[4]

Rotter's social learning theory: Expectancies and human behavior. Rotter contends that much of human behavior can be understood through careful attention to two basic factors: *expectancies* and *reinforcement value*. Expectancies refer to an individual's estimate of the probability that a given behavior will lead to a specific outcome in the present situation. Needless to say, they are based on past experiences in similar situations. (Incidentally, we will examine the role of expectancies in work motivation in Chapter 5.) Reinforcement value involves the subjective value an individual attaches to various reinforcements, assuming that these are equally likely to occur. For example, one person might prefer concrete

FIGURE 4-3   Rotter's Social
Learning Theory

According to this theory, the
probability that a behavior will
occur can be predicted from
information about two factors:
expectancy (the individual's
estimate of the probability the
behavior will lead to
reinforcement) and *reinforcement
value* (the subjective value he or
she attaches to this reinforcement).

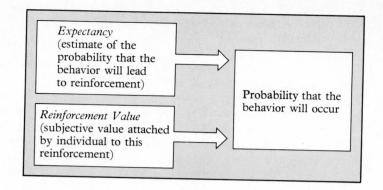

payoffs, such as a raise or bonus, to more subtle ones, such as increased status or
approval. Another might show the opposite pattern.

As you can readily see, both expectancies and reinforcement value will vary
from individual to individual, even in the same situation. Thus, Rotter's theory
has little difficulty in accounting for human uniqueness. And since expectancies
and reinforcement value tend to persist (once developed), it also accounts for consistency over time. In any case, according to Rotter's theory, the behavior of a
given person in a specific situation can be predicted with a high degree of accuracy, provided we know the behaviors available to this person, the reinforcements
that can be obtained in the situation, and this person's expectancies and reinforcement value (see Figure 4-3).

Before concluding our discussion of Rotter's theory, we should call your attention to one further point. In addition to specific expectancies regarding outcomes
in a given situation, individuals can also develop more generalized ones. Most importantly, they can come to believe, on the basis of a wide range of past experience, either that they can control their outcomes or that they are powerless in
this respect. As we will soon see, such generalized expectancies represent an important aspect of personality and have major implications for organizational behavior.

Humanistic Theories: Emphasis on Growth

At first glance, the analytic theories proposed by Freud and several of his followers probably strike you as being totally different from the learning-oriented theories we have just described. Actually, though, these seemingly opposite views
share a common theme. In each, behavior is seen as being *predictably determined*
by specific internal and external factors. In the case of analytic theories, these variables involve unconscious motives and a continuing struggle between the id, ego,
and superego. In learning theories, by contrast, the key factors are past experience
and basic processes such as classical and operant conditioning. Both approaches,

however, concur on the following point: once we obtain sufficient knowledge about the crucial factors, behavior can be accurately predicted. In short, both adopt what has often been termed a *mechanistic* view.

Humanistic theories of personality reject this basic assumption. In sharp contrast, they hold that, even if we attain complete knowledge of all the internal and external factors noted above, we will still be unable to predict or understand the behavior of other persons. This goal can only be attained, it is suggested, when we also comprehend how these persons perceive the world around them. In sum, we can fully understand other human beings only if we adopt their point of view or perspective.

Another key feature of humanistic theories is their emphasis on positive aspects of personality. Supporters of this approach object strongly to the fact that many other theories (especially analytic theories) focus on personal problems and mental illness. Humanistic theorists contend that in reality, human beings possess a strong tendency toward growth or *self-actualization,* toward improvement and health. Only when negative environmental conditions block this tendency do personal difficulties arise. Thus, a key task is that of assuring that conditions serving to promote self-actualization prevail. As an example of humanistic theories of personality we will now briefly summarize the *self-theory* proposed by Carl Rogers.[5]

One humanistic approach: Rogers's self-theory. According to Rogers, the key to understanding personality (and all human behavior) lies in the *self-concept,* all the attitudes and beliefs each person holds about himself or herself. Rogers suggests that when the self-concept is realistic (accurately reflects an individual's experience), good adjustment exists and the tendency toward self-actualization can proceed. However, when the self-concept is unrealistic (is inconsistent with some portion of experience), serious problems may develop. Unfortunately, it is relatively easy for such distortions in one's self-concept to develop. For example, imagine a scene in which parents instruct a child that "nice girls don't act that way or have such feelings." The child knows that she *does* have these feelings and *does* want to act in some manner. But now, she must deny their presence and distort her self-concept. The greater such inconsistency between an individual's self-concept and his or her experience, the greater the strains on personality (see Figure 4-4). But how can such problems be avoided? Rogers's answer is straightforward: by providing each individual with a healthy degree of love and respect— what he terms *positive regard.* Briefly, it is crucial to separate disapproval of specific feelings or behaviors on the part of others from disapproval or rejection of them as persons. The former is permissible; the latter can be extremely harmful. To the extent each person is assured that he or she is valued as an individual, distortions in the self-concept will be avoided. And then, the result will be continued growth toward health and self-actualization.

As you can readily see, there is an important message for managers in these suggestions. Rogers's theory implies that criticism should always be focused on unacceptable or inadequate performance—*never* on the employees involved. The

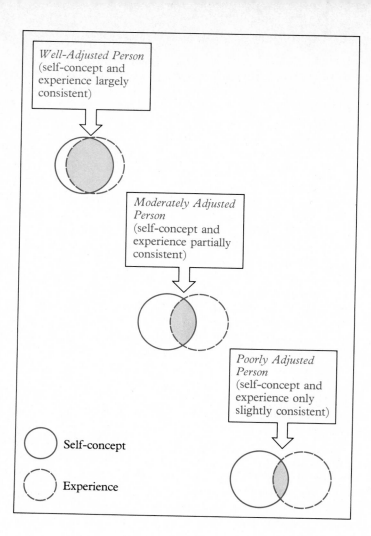

FIGURE 4-4   Rogers's Self Theory

According to Rogers's self theory, good adjustment occurs when an individual's experience is consistent with his or her self-concept. The greater the disparity between these two factors, the greater the strains on personality.

Well-Adjusted Person (self-concept and experience largely consistent)

Moderately Adjusted Person (self-concept and experience partially consistent)

Poorly Adjusted Person (self-concept and experience only slightly consistent)

Self-concept

Experience

former may serve as valuable feedback and can help individuals improve; the latter may threaten their self-esteem and produce many undesirable effects. In sum, Rogers, like other humanistic theorists, emphasizes the positive. Growth, health, and personal happiness can be readily attained; all that's needed, he suggests, is a reasonable amount of tender, loving acceptance.

Trait Theories: Identifying the Key Dimensions of Human Personality

Suppose that you were asked to prepare a written description of some person working under your direction for inclusion in his personnel file. How would you go about this important task? The chances are good that you would begin by coming up with a relatively short list of words, each describing what you perceived to be an important trait or characteristic of this person. For example, you might note that he is ambitious, assertive, considerate, well-organized, and out-spoken. And then, you would go on to expand upon each term, perhaps by citing an example of an incident relating to it.

Your strategy in this situation actually suggests the basic nature of a final group of personality theories we will consider—*trait theories.* Trait theories note that although human beings differ in a very large number of ways, some of these are probably more important than others. Thus, they seek to map personality by pinpointing the key dimensions along which individuals differ. But do such dimensions exist? Several trait theorists believe that they do.

For example, on the basis of extensive research, Raymond Cattell and his associates have concluded that there are only sixteen basic dimensions of personality (or *source traits,* as these are termed).[6] These include such familiar dimensions as dominance versus submissiveness, confidence versus timidity, conservatism versus radicalism, and composure versus tenseness. Cattell further suggests that these source traits interact with one another to yield an almost infinite number of distinct behaviors, which he terms *surface traits.* Thus, he contends that human behavior, varied as it is, actually derives from a relatively small number of basic characteristics.

Since the dimensions identified by Cattell have been verified in dozens of studies involving the participation of thousands of subjects, they do seem to represent important clues for understanding human personality. Further, research on a number of different traits (some suggested by Cattell and some by other investigators) indicates that differences along these dimensions can exert important effects upon behavior. We will examine several of these, and their impact on organizations, in the next section. Before turning to this task, however, we will comment briefly on a closely related issue: the joint role of traits and situations in shaping human behavior.

Traits or situations? Why both are important.   The main point we wish to make is this: while human beings do differ along many dimensions, and these differences often affect their behavior, situational factors, too, play a key role. Specifically, behavior is often shaped by conditions in the world around us as well as by our individual preferences and dispositions. Indeed, in many cases, these external factors and pressures overwhelm specific traits and dominate our actions. For example, consider what happens when the president of a large company visits a specific branch office: everyone smiles and greets him warmly—even persons known for their cold and hostile nature. Similarly, when the plant manager is on patrol, all employees perform at a high rate and keep their minds very much on their work—even those notorious for their lack of ambition and tendency to "goof off." In these and many other cases, situational factors constrain behavior and either mask or override even large differences in personality. Of course, in other cases, the opposite may be true: individuals possessing strong or central traits tend to behave in very much the same manner even across a wide range of situations. The important point to keep in mind, therefore, is this: in most cases, behavior is determined *both* by traits and by external, situational factors. Indeed, it is the complex interaction between these two groups of variables that makes human behavior so complex—and so intriguing. Please see the **"FOCUS"** box on pp. 100–101 for a discussion of an important—and basic—question: Is personality really stable?

PERSONALITY AND ORGANIZATIONAL BEHAVIOR: SOME SPECIFIC, NOTEWORTHY LINKS

Over the course of your career, you will encounter hundreds—perhaps thousands—of people. Almost certainly, these individuals will differ in a very large number of ways. Indeed, it is probably safe to assume that each will present you with a unique combination of behaviors and traits. Many of these differences will be interesting in themselves but will have little bearing on behavior in organizational settings. In contrast, others will be extremely important in this respect. Because we believe that it is useful for you to be aware of some of these key, O.B.-related traits, we will now examine several in some detail.

The Type A/Type B Dimension: Who Succeeds —and Who Survives?

Think back over your acquaintances. Can you recall a person who, like Herb in the story at the start of this chapter, always seems to work under great pressure, is hard-driving, competitive, and both impatient and aggressive? Now, in contrast, try to think of someone who shows the opposite pattern—an individual who is relaxed and easy-going, sociable, and not very competitive. The two persons you now have in mind represent contrasting patterns of behavior labeled, respectively, Type A and Type B. While these are clearly extremes on a continuous dimension, research findings suggest that most people actually seem to fall into one category or the other.[7] Specifically, about 40% of the general population is Type A and 60% Type B. For this reason, most persons have little difficulty in answering questions such as the ones in Table 4-2, items similar to ones on a test designed to classify adults as Type A or Type B.[8]

Clearly, the differences between Type A and Type B persons described above have important implications for organizational behavior. For example, we would expect hard-driving competitive individuals to behave very differently from relaxed, easy-going ones in many job-related activities. In addition to these obvious contrasts, though, Type A and Type B persons also differ in other key respects that are less apparent. The most important of these involve personal health, social relations, and performance on many tasks.

The Type A pattern and personal health.
Actually, initial interest in the Type A/Type B distinction was sparked by an unsettling finding: *persons showing*

TABLE 4-2   Identifying Type A and Type B Individuals

Answers to questions such as these (which are similar to items on the Jenkins Activity Survey) indicate whether an individual is best classified as Type A or Type B. As you can probably guess, Type A individuals generally choose a, a, and c in responding to questions 1, 2, and 3.

---

1. How rapidly do you usually eat?
   a. I am usually the first one finished.
   b. I eat a little faster than average.
   c. I eat about as quickly as other people.
   d. I eat more slowly than most other people.
2. How was your temper when you were younger?
   a. Fiery and hard to control.
   b. Strong, but still controllable.
   c. No problem.
   d. I rarely became angry.
3. How often do you bring work home from the office to complete at night?
   a. Rarely.
   b. Once a week or less.
   c. More often than once a week.

---

the Type A cluster of traits are more than twice as likely as those showing the Type B cluster to experience serious heart disease. Similarly, they are more likely to suffer another heart attack following one that is not fatal and to show more extensive hardening of the arteries leading to the heart.[9] In short, Type A individuals appear to pay a very high price for their hard-driving, high-pressure life-style!

Additional research findings help explain why Type A's are more likely to experience serious heart disease than Type B's. Briefly, it appears that Type A individuals have higher resting pulse rates than Type B's in a wide range of situations. Even worse, they seem to react to several types of stress (e.g., threat of failure) with larger increments in blood pressure than Type B's.[10] Given these factors, it is not at all surprising that Type A's are much more likely than Type B's to experience life-threatening breakdowns in their cardiovascular system.

The Type A pattern and interpersonal relations.   In addition to differences in personal health, Type A and Type B persons also demonstrate sharply contrasting patterns of social behavior. For example, Type A's tend to be more impatient with others and grow angry when these persons hold them back in any way. Similarly, Type A's generally report feeling less comfortable around other persons than Type B's. When given a choice, they often prefer to work alone rather than as part of a team. Perhaps most important, Type A individuals tend to be more irritable and aggressive than Type B's. For example, in one recent exper-

FOCUS ON BEHAVIOR

Is Personality Really Stable?

Typically, we assume that human behavior is stable. That is, we believe that other persons, and we ourselves, act in a fairly consistent manner across time. Needless to add, all of the theories of personality we have considered so far make a similar assumption; if they did not there would be little justification for their existence. But now for the crucial question we wish to pose: is this suggestion really as reasonable as it sounds? In a word, is human behavior actually consistent? You may be surprised to learn that this issue has recently been the subject of a considerable amount of controversy.

Actually, until a few years ago, the weight of existing evidence seemed to argue *against* the presence of much consistency. Scores on psychological tests designed to measure specific traits did not correlate closely with behaviors supposedly reflecting these traits. And behaviors in one situation did not even seem to correlate closely with related behaviors in other situations. Findings such as these led Walter Mischel, an expert on personality, to conclude that human behavior is far from consistent and that stable personality traits or dispositions do not exist.[11] Going further, he suggested that the reason we accept the presence of such consistency is that we are "set" to perceive it, even when it does not really exist. For example, he noted that once we form an overall impression of another person, we tend to cling to it tenaciously—even in the face of new, inconsistent information. Indeed, we often tend to distort or alter such information so that it appears to offer support for our initial views. Further, Mischel suggested that, once we perceive other persons as possessing certain traits, we may act toward them in specific ways—and so actually produce the consistency we anticipate! In sum, as recently as the mid-1970s, it appeared that behavior was much more strongly affected by specific situational factors than by enduring traits or characteristics.

As you can readily see, the implications of this conclusion for work on personality are chilling. After all, if people show little consistency in their behavior, there is not much point in trying to identify the key dimensions along which they differ, or measure these systematically. Rather, our attention should be focused primarily on the host of social and physical conditions that affect behavior, and cause it to change from one context to another.

Fortunately, though, this distressing conclusion has recently been reversed. Convincing evidence for the presence of a considerable amount of consistency both in behavior and in personality has begun to accumulate. The reason for this apparent reversal is actually quite simple. In earlier studies, very small samples of subjects' behavior were collected. For example, a single score on a personality test would be related to behavior in one artificial laboratory situation; or, behavior in one setting would be related to behavior in one other situation. Given these procedures, it is not at all surprising that little evidence for consistency was obtained. After all, there was ample room for random fluctuations to mask any underlying stability. More recent investigations, in contrast, have gathered much larger samples of behavior. And here, evidence for a healthy degree of consistency has emerged. For example, in one series of carefully conducted studies, Epstein obtained records of subjects' behavior over a period of several weeks.[12] A number of different variables were recorded, including participants' self-ratings of their positive and negative emotions, measures of their heart rate, and even the number of errors and erasures on their exam sheets. In each case, results were the same: the greater the length of the observation period, the greater the degree of stability apparent.

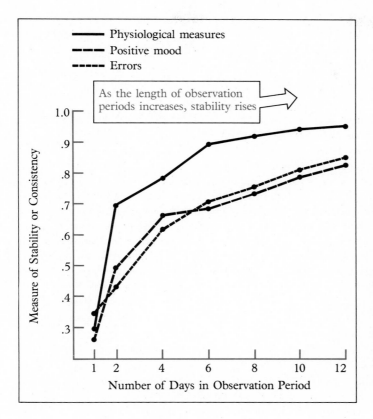

FIGURE 4-5 Human Behavior: Evidence for Its Stability over Time

The greater the length of the observation period, the greater the degree of stability shown in several aspects of behavior. This finding lends support to the view that human behavior is in fact influenced by enduring traits or characteristics. (Source: Based on data from Epstein *Journal of Personality and Social Psychology*, 1979, *37* 1097–1126.)

(See Figure 4-5 for a graphic representation of these results.)

At this point, we should hasten to note that these findings and those in other studies do not imply that situational factors are unimportant—far from it.[13] As we noted earlier, external conditions in the world around us often overwhelm even strong traits or dispositions. Thus, we *do* act differently in contrasting settings; and consistency in our behavior, while present, is far from perfect. But recent evidence suggests that human behavior is influenced by enduring traits, too. Thus, the high level of consistency or stability predicted by common sense is often present. In order to observe it in systematic research, however, we must give it a chance to emerge.   □

iment, individuals previously classified as Type A or Type B were provided with an opportunity to aggress against a stranger.[14] (They could deliver electric shocks of varying strength to this person each time he made an error on a simple learning task.) In one condition, subjects were provoked and frustrated by the stranger, while in another they were not. Results were quite clear: when provoked or frustrated, Type A individuals chose to direct much higher levels of aggression against the helpless victim than Type B's. (In contrast, such differences failed to emerge in the absence of provocation.) The moral in these findings is straightforward: If you annoy a Type A person, watch out. The reaction is likely to be a strong one.

The Type A pattern and performance. A third difference between Type A and Type B persons that is closely linked to organizational behavior involves their performance on many different tasks. As you might expect, Type A's and Type B's differ greatly in this respect. Surprisingly, though, the pattern of these differences is quite complex. On the one hand, Type A's appear to work faster on many tasks, even when no pressure or deadline is involved.[15] Similarly, they generally complain less about hard work and describe themselves as feeling less tired when done than Type B's.[16] Finally, they appear to be better able than Type B's to handle tasks involving multiple demands. This latter point is illustrated clearly in a recent experiment by Fazio and his colleagues.[17] In this study, Type A and Type B individuals worked on a proofreading task, requiring them to spot errors in a typed manuscript. Half of the subjects performed only this task; the remainder were also instructed to perform another task simultaneously. (They had to keep a running tally of the number of times the word "object" appeared.) As you can see from Figure 4-6, results pointed to an advantage for Type A's. That is, while Type B's showed a substantial drop in performance when asked to perform multiple tasks, Type A's were able to maintain or even actually to improve their accuracy. These and related findings suggest that Type A's may well have an advantage over Type B's in the performance of certain tasks.

On the other hand, however, additional findings suggest that Type A's may not always have the advantage. For example, they frequently do more poorly than Type B's on tasks requiring delayed responses. (They are simply too impatient to wait!)[18] More importantly, informal surveys reveal that most members of top management are Type B's, not Type A's.[19] Several factors may contribute to this finding. First, and most directly, it is possible that many Type A's simply don't last long enough to rise through the corporate ranks—they are eliminated from the race early on by the health risks noted above. Second, it is possible that the impatient, always-in-a-hurry style of Type A's is incompatible with the skills needed to function effectively at top management levels. As you know, such positions generally require considered judgment and the ability to weigh a large array of complex input carefully. Type A's do not appear to be well-suited to such tasks and may be absent from top-level jobs for this reason.

Taking all the available evidence into account, the following pattern seems to emerge. Type A's may well do better than Type B's on some tasks—especially

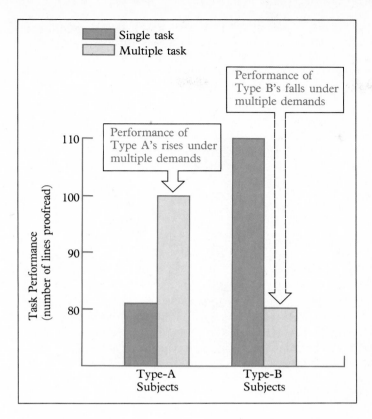

FIGURE 4-6   Dealing with Multiple Task Demands: When Type A's Have an Edge

When exposed to extra task demands, Type A individuals were able to maintain or even improve their level of performance. In contrast, exposure to extra demands reduced the performance of Type B persons. (Source: Based on data from Fazio et al., *Personality and Social Psychology Bulletin,* 1981, *1,* 97–102.)

ones involving time pressure, multiple demands, or solitary work. However, they may actually do *worse* than Type B's in tasks that involve complex judgment, accuracy rather than speed, and working as part of a team. In sum, neither pattern seems to have an overall edge. Rather, the nature of a task may be crucial in determining whether Type A's or Type B's will be a better bet.

Machiavellianism: Manipulation as a Way of Life

More than four hundred years ago, the Italian philosopher Niccolo Machiavelli wrote a book entitled *The Prince,* in which he outlined a general strategy for obtaining and holding power. The basic idea behind this approach was simplicity itself: other people can be readily and easily manipulated for our own ends. And, needless to add, Machiavelli went on to provide detailed suggestions on how best to accomplish this goal. For example, among the principles he recommended were the following: "A prudent ruler ought not to keep faith when by doing so it would be against his interests"; "Humility not only is of no service, but is actually harmful"; "It is better to be feared than loved." More generally, he urged those who desired power and influence over others to adopt a totally pragmatic, amoral approach. Let other people be swayed by loyalty, friendship, or morality, he suggested. The truly successful leader would be above such influences. He or she would simply do *whatever was required to attain his or her ends.*

Machiavelli and the princes he advised are, of course, long departed. But the basic ideas he proposed are still very much with us. Indeed, they are readily apparent in several books that have recently made their way onto the best-seller lists—volumes such as Korda's *Power: How to Use It* and Ringer's *Winning through Intimidation.* The existence of these and related books suggests that people are as fascinated by Machiavelli's approach today as they first were in the 1500s. Clearly, though, it is one thing to be intrigued by such tactics and quite another to put them to practical use. Are there actually individuals capable of living by the ruthless, self-centered creed outlined by Machiavelli and others? Unfortunately, a growing body of evidence suggests that there are.

Machiavellianism: Its measurement.   In order to study tendencies toward the adoption of an approach such as that outlined by Machiavelli, two psychologists, Richard Christie and Florence Geis, developed a brief questionnaire termed the *Mach Scale* (see the **"FOCUS"** box on pp. 106–107).[20] High scores on this scale are indicative of tendencies toward a ruthless, self-centered strategy in interpersonal relationships. For example, high scorers on the Mach Scale (labeled, appropriately, High Machs) report such beliefs as these: no one is to be completely trusted; it is perfectly acceptable to lie to others; the best way to handle other persons is to tell them what they want to hear. In contrast, low scorers (Low Machs) disagree with these views and report believing that most people are basically good, that actions should be taken only when they are morally correct, and that it is possible to get ahead by honest means. We would like to be able to report that most people score low on this scale—that they show little tendency toward a Machiavellian approach. Unfortunately, though, this is not the case. When the Mach Scale is administered to large groups of persons, researchers have little difficulty in identifying persons who would warm Machiavelli's cold heart. Indeed, High Machs appear to be present even among ten-year-olds![21] In short, Machiavellians are very much with us—so much so, that we confidently predict you will encounter many during your own career in business.

Machiavellianism: How it operates.   But given that High Machs exist, what is their modus operandi? In short, how do they succeed in manipulating others and using them for their own ends? Research findings point to several important factors. First, in contrast to most other persons, High Machs tend to show a pattern of cool detachment in their dealings with others. While the persons around them often give way to their emotions and let their hearts rule their heads, High Machs almost never behave in this fashion. Instead, they work cooly and pragmatically toward the goals they are seeking. Of course, they may often pretend to be experiencing strong emotions. But this is pure sham. All that truly concerns them is getting what they want. Second, High Machs appear to be both highly resistant to influence from others and skilled in exerting such influence themselves.

Thus, they are not easily swayed by their opponents. Rather, they usually succeed in influencing *them*. In this regard, we should note that recent findings point to the conclusion that High Machs are more effective liars than Low Machs; when persons in both categories tell a lie, High Machs are perceived as considerably more truthful than Low Machs.[22] Similarly, High Machs are more likely to use such tactics as *ingratiation* (i.e., false or exaggerated praise) than Low Machs.[23] Finally, as recommended by Machiavelli, High Machs do not allow themselves to be swayed by the kind of considerations that affect most persons—factors such as loyalty, friendship, past promises, and so on. While they often pay lip service to such factors, they readily ignore them if they get in the way of their progress. As you can see, this gives High Machs a tremendous edge over other persons who *do* often place these considerations above their own interests or gain.

Perhaps we should conclude with a brief description of one experiment illustrating the great success High Machs often attain in their dealings with others.[24] In this study, ten $1.00 bills were placed on a table in front of groups of three subjects. These persons were told that the money would belong to any two of them who agreed on how to divide it; the third individual would be totally "cut out." One of the three persons in each group was a high scorer on the Mach Scale, one a medium scorer, and one a low scorer. Who do you think did best? As you can see from Figure 4-7, the High Machs won hands down. Indeed, they obtained several times as much as the Low Mach players. We think there is an important moral for you in this and many related studies: Try to recognize High

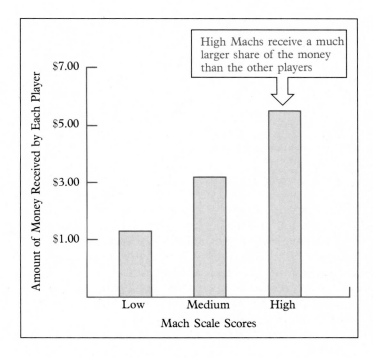

FIGURE 4-7 High Machs: Formidable Opponents

In an intriguing study, ten $1.00 bills were placed in front of groups of three persons (a High Mach, a Medium Mach, and a Low Mach). They were told that the money would belong to any two persons who could agree on how to divide it. As shown here, High Machs did much better in this situation than Medium or Low Machs: they walked off with a larger share of the money. (Source: Based on data from Christie & Geis, *Studies in Machiavellianism.* New York: Academic Press, 1970.)

FOCUS ON BEHAVIOR

Measuring Machiavellianism: The Mach Scale

Now that we have considered Machiavellianism and noted some of its consequences, you may find it interesting to find out just where *you* stand on this dimension. You can do this by responding to the statements in Table 4-3. Simply indicate how much you agree or disagree with each by circling one number.

To obtain your score, add the numbers you have circled for statements 1, 3, 4, 5, 9, and 10. For statements 2, 6, 7, and 8, reverse the scoring so that 5 becomes 1, 4 becomes 2, and so on. Then add the values for these two sets of statements together. An average score on this short form of the Mach Scale is 25, so if you scored well above this value, you are a High Mach. If you scored well below 25, you are a Low Mach. You may also find it interesting to

administer the test to some of your friends, preferably ones who haven't read this book and don't know anything about the Mach Scale or Machiavellianism.

One final word of caution: scores on the Mach Scale, like those on any other personality test, are far from perfect. They can vary greatly from one time to another and can be affected by many factors other than the personality trait being measured. Thus, please don't assume that a high score on this scale necessarily indicates a cold and ruthless approach to social relations or that a low score necessarily reflects rejection of such a strategy. Single scores on brief questionnaires like this one rarely provide the basis for reaching such firm conclusions. □

Mach persons when you meet them. And when you do, be prepared for the worst. If you are not careful, you may well end up as one of their many "victims." (To measure your own Machiavellianism, see the **"FOCUS"** box above.)

Locus of Control: Are You the Master of Your Fate?

Before proceeding, please examine the statements in Table 4-4. For each, decide whether you feel that choice (a) or choice (b) is closer to your own beliefs.

If you consistently chose (a), you are probably a person who believes that there is a direct link between your behavior and the outcomes you experience. In short, you have a generalized belief in **internal control.** In contrast, if you consistently chose (b), you probably believe that what happens to you is influenced by factors beyond your control, such as luck or fate. That is, you have a generalized belief in **external control.** You may recall that we discussed such generalized beliefs or expectancies briefly on pages 93–94, while examining Rotter's social learning theory. At that time, we noted that such expectancies have important implications for organizational behavior, and we will note some of these here.

The items in Table 4-4 are actually quite similar to ones on a personality test for measuring such expectancies, a test known as the *I-E Scale.* High scores on this scale suggest a belief in external control; low scores are indicative of a belief in internal control. When individuals complete the I-E Scale, large differences in

TABLE 4-3   A Short Form of the Mach Scale

Indicate your reactions to each of the statements shown above by circling one number for each. If you agree strongly with a given statement circle 5; if you agree, but to a lesser extent, circle 4, and so on.

	DISAGREE		NEUTRAL	AGREE	
	A LOT	A LITTLE	NEUTRAL	A LITTLE	A LOT
1. The best way to handle people is to tell them what they want to hear.	1	2	3	4	5
2. When you ask someone to do something for you, it is best to give the real reasons for wanting it rather than giving reasons which might carry more weight.	1	2	3	4	5
3. Anyone who completely trusts anyone else is asking for trouble.	1	2	3	4	5
4. It is hard to get ahead without cutting corners here and there.	1	2	3	4	5
5. It is safest to assume that all people have a vicious streak and it will come out when they are given a chance.	1	2	3	4	5
6. One should take action only when sure it is morally right.	1	2	3	4	5
7. Most people are basically good and kind.	1	2	3	4	5
8. There is no excuse for lying to someone else.	1	2	3	4	5
9. Most men forget more easily the death of their father than the loss of their property.	1	2	3	4	5
10. Generally speaking, men won't work hard unless they're forced to do so.	1	2	3	4	5

their scores are regularly noted. That is, people appear to range all the way from those who believe that they are fully in control of their own fate (Internals) to those who believe that there is virtually no link between their own actions and the outcomes they experience (Externals). But given that such differences exist, how do they arise? The answer seems to lie in past personal experience. Individuals who are exposed to a home environment in which effort and accomplishment are rewarded in a systematic manner tend to develop expectancies of internal control. In contrast, those raised in an environment where rewards seem to occur randomly, in an unpredictable way, tend to develop expectancies of external control.

TABLE 4–4   Items Similar to Those Used in Measuring One Important Aspect of
Personality

For each of the items shown below, indicate whether you feel that choice (a) or choice (b)
is closer to your own beliefs.

1. (a) I am the master of my fate.
   (b) A great deal of what happens to me is probably a matter of chance.

2. (a) Promotions are earned through hard work and persistence.
   (b) Making a lot of money is largely a matter of getting the right breaks.

3. (a) In my experience, I have noticed that there is usually a direct connection between
       how hard I study and the grades I get.
   (b) Many times the reactions of teachers seem haphazard to me.

4. (a) People like me can change the course of world affairs if we make ourselves heard.
   (b) It is only wishful thinking to believe that we can really influence what happens in
       society at large.

5. (a) Getting along with people is a skill that must be practiced.
   (b) It is almost impossible to figure out how to please some people.

Whatever their precise origins, once such expectancies develop, they exert important effects upon behavior. For example, Internals tend to engage in more attempts at self-improvement (such as physical fitness programs) than Externals.
Similarly, they are more likely to use seat belts and to care for their teeth and
other parts of their bodies.[25] More important from the point of view of organizational behavior, Internals show higher levels of motivation than Externals. Thus,
research findings suggest that they earn more money, hold higher-status jobs, and
advance in their careers more quickly than do Externals.[26] All this, of course, is
quite reasonable. If an individual believes that what he or she does makes a difference, then it makes good sense to try—to work hard and seek to succeed. On the
other hand, if an individual believes that what he or she does makes no difference,
then why bother? Thus, an individual's position along the Internal-External dimension can have important effects upon his or her performance in a wide range
of settings.

Sad to relate, growing evidence suggests that beliefs in internal control have
been on the wane in recent years. In fact, scores on the I-E Scale actually rose
from an average of about 8 in the early 1960s to an average of about 12 in the
mid-1970s.[27] (Remember: higher scores indicate greater belief in external control.) Fortunately, this trend seems to have leveled off in recent years. But it is interesting to speculate about two issues relating to this change. First, could this
drift toward belief in external control be related to factors such as the rising complexity of modern society, the Viet Nam war, and even the actions of OPEC? Second, could this shift be related in any manner to recent drops in productivity and
the decline of the work ethic in the U.S. and several other countries? (See Figure

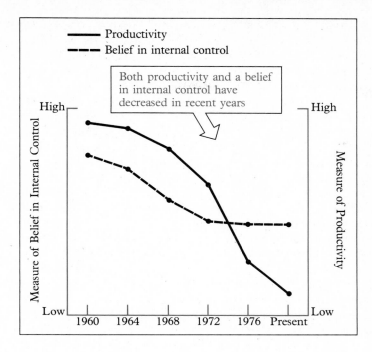

Productivity
Belief in internal control

Both productivity and a belief in internal control have decreased in recent years

High

Measure of Belief in Internal Control

Low

1960   1964   1968   1972   1976   Present

High

Measure of Productivity

Low

FIGURE 4–8   Productivity and Changes in Locus of Control: A Possible Link?

In recent years, both productivity and belief in internal control have fallen in the U.S. Is there a link between these two factors? No firm evidence on this issue exists, but the possibility is certainly intriguing food for thought. (Please note: the relationship suggested by this graph is only *correlational* in nature.)

4–8.) No firm evidence on these points yet exists, and we should emphasize that the relationships in question are only correlational in nature. Jumping to conclusions about causality is totally unwarranted. Yet, the possibility of such links remains and seems worthy of further study.

Since our discussion of locus of control so far has been a bit discouraging, we will close on a more positive note. Expectancies for internal or external control are *not* set in stone; they can be changed. Thus, effective managers can make a difference in this respect. If conditions in an organizational setting are such that excellence is both recognized and rewarded, even persons holding strong beliefs of external control can be led to change these expectancies. And to the extent such shifts occur, positive effects on performance, productivity, and morale may result. For this reason alone, careful attention to the I-E dimension may often be worthwhile.

Other Aspects of Personality Related to Organizational Behavior: The Need for Achievement and the Need for Power

The aspects of personality we have considered so far have all received a great deal of attention. Yet, they are by no means the only ones closely related to organizational behavior. Several others, too, are important in this respect. Space limitations prevent us from considering all of these in detail, but we can at least briefly mention two: the **need for achievement** and the **need for power.**

Need for achievement: Variations in the desire to excel. Individuals differ greatly in terms of their desire to excel—to do something better than others do it. In short, they differ greatly with respect to what has been termed the *need for achievement.*[28] Because this need or motive appears to be closely linked to a wide range of business or economic activities, it has long been of interest to the field of O.B. Research on achievement motivation has yielded many interesting findings. For example, as you might predict, persons highly motivated to achieve tend to be more successful in gaining promotions than those who aren't as motivated.[29] Similarly, high need achievers tend to achieve better grades in college and to choose higher status careers than low need achievers.[30]

Somewhat more surprising results have been obtained with respect to the impact of need for achievement on managerial success. Contrary to what common sense might suggest, persons high in this motive do *not* seem to make excellent managers; in fact, they are often poor ones.[31] The reason for this unexpected pattern is straightforward: persons high in need for achievement often show characteristics that interfere with managerial competence. For example, they usually want to do everything themselves—an approach that is inappropriate in large and complex organizations. Similarly, they usually desire concrete, short-term feedback on their performance. This is unavailable in many organizations, and its absence can exert adverse effects on the behavior of high need achievers. In short, it appears that persons high in the need for achievement may be better suited for the role of entrepreneur (e.g., starting their own business) than for that of manager. Apparently, they are too concerned with self-improvement and personal accomplishment to make good team players.

Need for power: The desire to influence others. A second key dimension of personality that is closely linked to organizational behavior is the *need for power.* This refers to the desire to influence or control others. Differences along this dimension are truly huge, with some people seeking power above all else and others seeking to avoid such influence, even when it is offered to them (see Figure 4-9). But what is the relationship between this characteristic and managerial effectiveness? Research points to some intriguing conclusions. Briefly, persons high in the need for power can be very effective managers, but only when three key conditions are met.[32] First, their need for power must be focused outward on the organization, not inward on self-aggrandizement. That is, they must desire to influence others for the good of their company, not their own benefit. Second, they must be relatively low in the need to be liked (at least, lower than they are in the need for power). And third, they must possess a considerable amount of self-control. When these conditions are met, persons high in need for power can be highly effective managers. However, when they are not, such persons can actually interfere with group productivity. For example, recent evidence suggests that they may suppress the flow of information—especially facts that contradict their preferred course of action—and so interfere with effective decisions.[33] Clearly, then, high need for power is a mixed blessing where leaders or managers are concerned.

"I have to take one three times a day to curb my insatiable appetite for power."

FIGURE 4-9 The Need for Power: Another Dimension along Which Human Beings Vary

As suggested by this cartoon, individuals differ greatly in their need for power over others. (Source: Drawing by Dana Fradon; © 1977 The New Yorker Magazine, Inc.)

A concluding note. In closing, we wish to add that need for achievement and need for power by no means exhaust the list—many other aspects of personality, too, are related to organizational behavior. (For example, growing evidence suggests that a cluster of traits involving high intelligence, the need to be perfect, competitiveness, and the desire to be in total control can lead individuals to rub fellow employees the wrong way. In short, these traits equip them with an *abrasive personality,* almost certain to damage their careers.)[34] Even without considering such traits, however, the main point we wish to make should be clear: many aspects of personality exert powerful effects on organizational behavior. Thus, attention to such factors can often prove helpful in gaining a fuller understanding of human behavior in work settings. (Please see the **"CASE IN POINT"** box on pp. 112–113 for an illustration of such effects.)

THE MEASUREMENT OF PERSONALITY: APPROACHES AND METHODS

Physical traits such as height and weight can be measured in a straightforward manner. But how can we assess various aspects of personality? How, for example, can we discover whether a given individual has an accurate self-concept, a weak superego, or a strong need for achievement? Obviously, rulers, scales, and similar measuring devices are of no use in this regard. Yet, if individual differences of the type we have discussed throughout this chapter exist, some means for measuring them must be obtained.

Fortunately, a number of potential solutions to this puzzling task have been devised. Many techniques for measuring personality now exist and can be put to practical use. In this final section, we will consider several of these, comment briefly on their relative merits, and insert a word of caution about their use in or-

"Say, Who Hired Him in the First Place?"

Hal Williams has had a meteoric rise to the top. In only five years he has moved from being a new and junior member of the firm just out of school to the point where he is now being considered for a Vice Presidency. Hal's rise is easy to understand. He is brilliant and creative. He gets the job done—generally with a flourish. He is always well-prepared, often to the point of being downright intimidating. And he is one of the most persuasive people you've ever met. There's only one problem in this rosy picture: just about everyone with whom he comes into contact grows to hate him!

The reason for this reaction is also clear. Hal uses people the way others use equipment or possessions. When he can benefit from a relationship, he enters into it eagerly, with assurances of loyalty and friendship. But as soon as he feels that it is no longer helping him toward his goals, he tosses these pledges out the window without a second thought. He has repeated this pattern over and over again. Yet somehow, each new victim falls for Hal's routine just like the ones before, assuming that it will be different for *him*. It never is. Hal extracts all the benefits and mileage he can from his new associate and then simply abandons this person. He is also the kind of individual who always seems to come out on top. No matter what the situation, Hal gets pretty much what he wants—often at the expense of others. Even worse, when things go well, he always manages to get the credit. When they go poorly, he assures that others take the blame. In sum, his brilliant rise has left a chain of angry, broken people in its wake. But what should the company do about him? This is the subject of the meeting now in progress.

"Well," says Jim Turley, president of the company, "What are we going to do about Hal? This is the moment of truth. If we promote him now, we're going to have him around for a long, long time. If we don't, he'll leave. I understand that he already has feelers from Comcon and Accuscan."

"He sure is a problem," agrees Fran Jenkins, vice-president for Marketing. "The guy is obviously talented—a real powerhouse. But wow, does he make waves! I can't figure out why he does these things to people. Like poor Beth

---

ganizational settings. Also, please note that each of these techniques is useful only to the extent that it is both *reliable* and *valid*. That is, each technique we discuss is useful in assessing personality only to the degree that it yields the same (or at least similar) measurements each time it is applied to a given person, and only to the extent that it actually measures what it purports to measure. (As you may recall, we discussed the concepts of reliability and validity in some detail in Chapter 2.)

Observational Techniques

One of the oldest techniques for assessing personality—but one that is still in widespread use—is based upon direct observations of an individual's behavior.

Klein. She really gave him her all and then, as soon as she made one mistake and the going got a little rough, he showed her the door. Maybe his problem is that he's basically insecure. I think that if he were really sure of himself deep down inside, he wouldn't have this urge to use people."

"I don't know that I agree," interrupts Don Lantanimo, production manager. "I think he's just too damn competitive. He can't stand to lose, so he does anything he can to come out on top—no matter what. What we have here is someone who's *too* aggressive for his own good or for the company's."

At this point, Bernie Halsey comments. "No, I don't go along with either of those ideas. I think Hal's problem is that he just has no conscience. Things that would bother other people don't seem to mean anything to him. Why, I don't think he even knows the meaning of the word guilt!"

"That's probably true," you agree. "But I really think his problem is simple: he's just a manipulator. He'll do *anything* to get what he wants. Sometimes he pretends to care about others, but I don't think he ever does. All he wants is to get from here to there. And if he has to step on a few people to do it, why that's O.K. with him. Yeah, he's just a classic manipulator. We'd better watch it or he'll sell us all the Brooklyn Bridge one of these days."

At this, everyone laughs. Then Jim says: "Well, whatever the reasons, we've got to make a decision. Do we promote him or let him go? God, what a dilemma. *Say, who hired him in the first place?*"   □

Questions:

1. On the basis of the information presented above, what do *you* think is Hal's basic problem? Is he too competitive? Is he an abrasive personality? Does he suffer from a missing superego (conscience)? Is he a High Mach?
2. Do you think there's any chance that Hal could change? If so, what might be done to make him more responsible in his dealings with others?
3. Would you vote to promote him? If so, why? If not, why?

The basic idea is that a person's major traits or characteristics will be revealed in his or her actions and that these can be assessed through careful observation.

Perhaps the most common application of this approach in business settings is the *employment interview.*[35] Here, applicants for a position are interviewed by a representative of the company who selects the one most suited for the job (see Figure 4–10). While such interviews can sometimes be of doubtful reliability and validity, their usefulness can be greatly enhanced by several steps.

First, each person should be rated on specific characteristics, in a specific way. Overall, global impressions are best avoided, for they may be based on different and noncomparable characteristics in the case of different individuals. Second, the observations themselves should be structured. For example, interviews should be

FIGURE 4-10 Employment Interviews: One Observational Technique for Assessing Personality

Interviews are one example of observational techniques for assessing personality. It is assumed that the answers and behavior of the interviewee will reveal much about his or her major traits. (Photo by Talbot Lovering, Allyn and Bacon Staff Photographer.)

planned so that the same (or at least similar) topics are covered and the same questions posed to each applicant. Finally, the setting or situation, too, should be standardized. Holding some interviews in an office, others in a restaurant, and still others at the beach (!) would introduce a great deal of confusion into the process and make interpretation of the results difficult. If the steps outlined here are followed carefully, interviews and other observational techniques can yield useful information on at least some aspects of personality.

Projective Techniques

A markedly different approach to the measurement of personality, **projective techniques,** is based on an intriguing assumption. If we present individuals with ambiguous stimuli and then ask them to tell us what they see, each person will "read" different meanings into these stimuli. And the pattern of their responses will tell us much about hidden aspects of their personalities.

One technique based on this assumption with which you are probably already familiar is the famous *Rorschach inkblot test.* The basic procedure here is simple: individuals are shown a series of inkblots and are asked to describe what they see. Presumably, their responses reveal much about their personalities.

A second projective technique used extensively is the *Thematic Apperception Test* (or *TAT*). This consists of a series of ambiguous drawings, and persons taking the test are asked to make up a story about each (see Figure 4-11). Presumably, their responses reveal much about their personalities and motives. The TAT is often used to assess two aspects of personality we have already considered: the need for achievement and the need for power.

Personality Inventories and Questionnaires

While observational techniques and projective tests are both in current use, many experts believe that the most reliable and valid means for assessing personality in-

FIGURE 4-11   The TAT: One Projective Technique for Measuring Personality

When individuals complete the TAT, they make up stories about ambiguous pictures such as this one. These stories are then scored for imagery relating to need for achievement, need for power, and other aspects of personality. What do *you* think is happening here? (Source: David C. McClelland et al., *A Brief Scoring Manual for Achievement, Affiliation, and Power Motivation.* Boston: McBer and Company, 1970.)

volves **inventories** or questionnaires. We have already described several of these in our discussion of O.B.-related traits. Basically, such inventories consist of a series of questions to which individuals respond. Their answers to the test are then scored, according to a predetermined key, to assess their relative standing on one or more characteristics. (That is, their answers reveal whether they are high, moderate, or low on the traits being measured.) Please refer to Tables 4–3 and 4–4 for examples of the kind of items often used on personality questionnaires or inventories.

Using Information about Personality:
A Brief Word of Caution

Personality is clearly a fascinating topic. We are all interested in other people, and insights into their uniqueness are certainly intriguing. Further, many personality traits appear to have important effects upon organizational behavior. In view of these facts, it is hardly surprising that managers (and others) have often sought to use such information in employee selection, employee placement, and even performance appraisal. While we fully understand the temptation to proceed in this fashion, there are several reasons for exercising a degree of caution in this regard, and we wish to call them to your attention.

First, many measures of personality are of doubtful reliability and validity. To the extent this is so, it is unwise to base important decisions about employees on them. Second, even when measures of personality are known to be reliable and valid, the relationship between the traits they assess and behavior in organizational settings is often complex. For example, common sense may suggest that some trait (e.g., assertiveness) is closely linked to an important aspect of organizational behavior (e.g., leadership ability). In reality, however, the relationship between them may be far more complex than assumed. Thus, caution is appropriate for this reason. Third, when using information about personality, it is all too easy to fall into the trap of viewing human beings as mere collections or clusters of traits. Certainly, enduring aspects of personality *do* affect behavior. But situational factors, too, are crucial. Placing too much emphasis on traits or needs may cause us to overlook the impact of such factors and to ignore the great capacity of individuals for flexibility and change.

For all these reasons, it is important to exercise caution in the use of information about employees' personality. Such information can be revealing and may be useful in many contexts. Before using it though, you should ask yourself three questions: (1) is the information itself to be trusted (i.e., is it reliable and valid)? (2) does it really have a direct bearing on performance or other aspects of organizational behavior? and (3) do I have sufficient knowledge and sophistication to interpret it adequately? If your answer to any of these is "no," or even "maybe," our recommendation is clear: proceed with care.

SUMMARY

Personality refers to the unique pattern of characteristics and behaviors that set each individual apart from others and that are stable over time. Many theories have been advanced to account for such individuality and to explain how personality develops. One of the most famous is Freud's *psychoanalytic theory*, which focuses on three major structures of personality: *id* (desire), *ego* (reason), and *superego* (conscience).

Freud believed that personality develops out of the continuing struggle between these structures. In contrast, *learning-oriented theories* of personality suggest that human individuality stems from the impact of past experience and basic processes of learning. *Humanistic theories* emphasize the view that human beings have strong tendencies toward health and growth. Only when these are blocked by a negative environment do personal problems arise. *Trait theories* seek to identify the key dimensions along which individuals differ and, in this way, to identify the basic traits of which personality is composed.

Several aspects of personality appear to be closely related to organizational behavior. The *Type A pattern of behavior,* characterized by an impatient, hard-driving, competitive life-style, is linked both to health and task performance. Type A's are more than twice as likely to suffer serious heart disease as their more relaxed counterparts (Type B's). Type A's outperform Type B's on tasks involving time pressure or multiple demands. However, they do more poorly than Type B's on tasks involving delayed responding or considered judgment.

Individuals who possess a highly manipulative orientation toward others are known as *Machiavellians.* Such persons show a pattern of cool detachment in their social relations, coupled with a high degree of persuasiveness. As a result of these characteristics, they get their own way in many situations.

Individuals differ greatly in their beliefs about their ability to influence their own outcomes. *Internals* believe that they can exert a great deal of control over their outcomes, while *Externals* believe that they cannot. As might be expected, Internals often attain higher levels of success in their careers than Externals.

Several methods for measuring personality exist. *Observational techniques* are based on careful study of actual behavior in specific situations (e.g., during interviews). They can be useful if certain safeguards are carefully followed. *Projective techniques* assume that in responding to ambiguous stimuli, individuals will reveal important aspects of their personalities. These have been useful in studying several topics (e.g., the need for achievement). Most researchers prefer *personality inventories* or *questionnaires* to other methods. This is the case because they appear to be higher in reliability and validity than other techniques for assessing personality.

KEY TERMS

EGO   The structure of personality that, according to Freud, represents reason. The ego is reality-oriented and holds impulses from the id in check until it is safe and appropriate to satisfy them.

EXTERNAL CONTROL   Refers to the belief that the outcomes we experience are not influenced (controlled) by our actions.

HUMANISTIC THEORIES   Theories of personality that emphasize the essential goodness of human beings and their basic tendency toward health.

ID   The structure of personality that, according to Freud, is the source of our primitive urges and motives.

INTERNAL CONTROL   Refers to the belief that the outcomes we experience are influenced (controlled) by our actions.

LEARNING-ORIENTED THEORIES   Theories of personality suggesting that human individuality and stability both stem from experience and basic processes of learning.

LOCUS OF CONTROL   Refers to beliefs held by an individual concerning his or her ability to control the outcomes he or she receives.

MACHIAVELLIANISM   A personality trait involving tendencies to manipulate or use others in order to reach one's goals.

NEED FOR ACHIEVEMENT   The need to excel—to do something better than others do it. Surprisingly, individuals who are very high in the need for achievement often do not make successful managers.

NEED FOR POWER   The need to exert influence over others or control their behavior. Individuals high in need for power can be excellent managers, but only if they also possess considerable self-control and have little need to be liked.

PERSONALITY INVENTORIES   Tests designed to measure specific aspects of personality. These consist of a number of questions and subjects' answers to these items supposedly reveal much about their personalities.

PROJECTIVE TECHNIQUES   Techniques for measuring personality based on ambiguous stimuli (e.g., inkblots). Because the stimuli themselves are ambiguous, subjects' interpretations of them are assumed to reveal much about their personalities.

SOCIAL LEARNING THEORY (ROTTER'S)   A theory suggesting that behavior in a given situation can be predicted from knowledge of an individual's expectancies that an action will result in reinforcement, and the subjective value he or she attaches to that reinforcement.

SUPEREGO The structure of personality that, according to Freud, corresponds to our conscience.

TYPE A BEHAVIOR PATTERN A pattern of behavior involving impatience or time-urgency, competitiveness, and a hard-driving life-style. Individuals showing this pattern are more than twice as likely as persons not showing it to develop serious heart disease.

TYPE B BEHAVIOR PATTERN A relatively relaxed, noncompetitive pattern of behavior involving the absence of characteristics shown by Type A individuals.

NOTES

1. Epstein, S. The stability of behavior: II. Implications for psychological research. *American Psychologist*, 1980, *35*, 790–806.

2. Byrne, D., & Kelley, K. *An introduction to personality* (3rd ed.). Englewood Cliffs, N.J.: Prentice-Hall, 1981.

3. Skinner, B.F. *Science and human behavior*. New York: Macmillan, 1953.

4. Rotter, J.B. Generalized expectancies for internal versus external control of reinforcement. *Psychological Monographs*, 1966, *80* (1, Whole No. 609).

5. Rogers, C.R. *Carl Rogers on personal power: Inner strength and its revolutionary impact*. New York: Delacorte, 1977.

6. Cattell, R.B., & Dreger, R.M. (Eds.). *Handbook of modern personality theory*. Washington, D.C.: Hemisphere, 1977.

7. Glass, D.C. *Behavior patterns, stress, and coronary disease*. Hillsdale, N.J.: Erlbaum, 1977.

8. Jenkins, C.D., Zyzanski, S.J., & Rosenman, R.H. Progress toward validation of a computer-scored test for the Type A coronary-prone behavior pattern. *Psychosomatic Medicine*, 1971, *33*, 193–202.

9. Jenkins, C.D. Recent evidence supporting psychologic and social risk factors for coronary disease. *New England Journal of Medicine*, 1976, *294*, 987–994; 1033–1038.

10. Pittner, M.S., & Houston, B.K. Response to stress, cognitive coping strategies, and the Type A behavior pattern. *Journal of Personality and Social Psychology*, 1980, *39*, 147–157.

11. Mischel, W. On the future of personality measurement. *American Psychologist*, 1977, *32*, 246–254.

12. Epstein, S. The stability of behavior: I. On predicting most of the people much of the time. *Journal of Personality and Social Psychology*, 1979, *37*, 1097–1126.

13. Costa, Paul T., Jr., McCrae, R.R., & Arenberg, D. Enduring dispositions in adult males. *Journal of Personality and Social Psychology*, 1980, *38*, 793–800.

14. Carver, C.S., & Glass, D.C. Coronary-prone behavior pattern and interpersonal aggression. *Journal of Personality and Social Psychology*, 1978, *36*, 361–366.

15. Burnam, M.A., Pennebaker, J.W., & Glass, D.C. Time consciousness, achievement-striving, and the Type A coronary-prone behavior pattern. *Journal of Abnormal Psychology*, 1975, *84*, 76–79.

16. Carver, C.S., Coleman, A.E., & Glass, D.C. The coronary-prone behavior pattern and the suppression of fatigue on a treadmill test. *Journal of Personality and Social Psychology*, 1976, *33*, 460–466.

17. Fazio, R.H., Cooper, M., Dayson, K., & Johnson, M. Control and the coronary-prone behavior pattern: Responses to multiple situational demands. *Personality and Social Psychology Bulletin*, 1981, *7*, 97–102.

18. Glass, D.C., Snyder, M.L., & Hollis, J. Time urgency and the Type A coronary-prone behavior pattern. *Journal of Applied Social Psychology*, 1974, *4*, 125–140.

19. Friedman, M., & Rosenman, R.H. *Type A behavior and your heart.* New York: Knopf, 1974.

20. Christie, R., and Geis, F.L. (Eds.). *Studies in Machiavellianism.* New York: Academic Press, 1970.

21. Kraut, R.E., & Paice, J.D. Machiavellianism in parents and their children. *Journal of Personality and Social Psychology*, 1976, *33*, 782–786.

22. Geis, F.L., & Moon, T.H. Machiavellianism and deception. *Journal of Personality and Social Psychology*, 1981, *41*, 766–775.

23. Pandey, J. Effects of Machiavellianism and degree of organizational formalization on ingratiation. *Psychologia—An International Journal of Psychology in the Orient*, 1981, *24*, 41–46.

24. Christie, R., & Geis, F.L. The ten dollar game. In R. Christie and F.L. Geis (Eds.), *Studies in Machiavellianism.* New York: Academic Press, 1970.

25. Strickland, B.R. Locus of control and health related behaviors. Paper presented at the XV Interamerican Congress of Psychology, Bogotá, Colombia, December, 1974.

26. Andrisani, P.J., & Nestel, C. Internal-external control as a contributor to and outcome of work experience. *Journal of Applied Psychology*, 1976, *61*, 156–165.

27. Rotter, J.B. Some problems and misconceptions related to the construct of internal versus external control of reinforcement. *Journal of Consulting and Clinical Psychology*, 1975, *43*, 56–67.

28. Atkinson, J.W. Motivation for achievement. In T. Blass (Ed.), *Personality variables in social behavior.* Hillsdale, N.J.: Erlbaum, 1977.

29. Andrews, J.D.W. The achievement motive and advancement in two types of organizations. *Journal of Personality and Social Psychology*, 1967, *6*, 163–168.

30. Raynor, J.O. Relationships between achievement-related motives, future orientation, and academic performance. *Journal of Personality and Social Psychology*, 1970, *15*, 28–33.

31. McClelland, D.C., & Burnham, D.H. Power is the great motivator. *Harvard Business Review*, March/April, 1976, 100–110.

32. Ibid.

33. Fodor, E.M., & Smith, T. The power motive as an influence on group decision making. *Journal of Personality and Social Psychology*, 1982, *42*, 178–185.

34. Levinson, H. The abrasive personality. *Harvard Business Review*, 1978, May-June, 86–94.

35. Jackson, D.N., Peacock, A.C., & Smith, J.P. Impressions of personality in the employment interview. *Journal of Personality and Social Psychology*, 1980, *39*, 296–307.

5

Motivation:
The Force Behind Behavior

KEY CONCEPTS

Motivation

Workaholic

Need Hierarchy Theory

ERG Theory

Equity Theory

Self-Actualization

Outcomes

Inputs

Inequity

Equity

Expectancy/Valence Theory

Expectancy

Valence

Intrinsic Motivation

Goal Setting

Job Enlargement

Job Enrichment

Job Characteristics Model

Motivating Potential Score (MPS)

□ □ □

It's a-quarter-to-five on a Friday afternoon. The Computech secretarial pool is ablaze with activity. Kathy Johnson is typing faster than ever. The bids on a new computer system have to be received before the weekend in order to be in the running for a new government contract. Mr. Stoker and Mr. Rafferty stayed up all through the night reworking their proposal to try to put together the most attractive bid. Now, it's all up to the secretarial pool to prepare and submit the final proposal on time. Kathy's eyes are burning and her fingers are aching as she wearily puts the finishing touches on that important proposal. For her, the whole day's been spent typing, proofreading, double-checking figures, and retyping.

The activity at the adjacent desk has been just as frenzied. Lucy Gato has been trying on new shades of eye shadow all afternoon. It hasn't been easy for her to decide just which shade would enhance that new look she's been trying to get for her date with Rick tonight. Her parading back and forth to the ladies room has transformed much of the office into a fashion show runway. Lucy's antics have attracted a good deal of attention among both her admiring and perspiring co-workers. While Kathy's eyes tire from overwork, Lucy's eyes burn from checking her image in the mirror and the hands of the time clock. Five o'clock is fast approaching. . . .

Does this scenario sound familiar to you? Perhaps you have had similar experiences with co-workers who have worked very hard or who hardly seemed interested in working at all. Although we have described rather extreme examples, they are not too far from reality. In fact, one O.B. expert has reported that, in most manufacturing jobs, the best workers produce about two to three times as much as the poorest workers and that even greater differences in magnitude can be found in other jobs.[1] This chapter is concerned with one of the major reasons why such great differences exist—**motivation.**

Why do you think Kathy and Lucy behave so differently? Is Kathy more motivated than Lucy? Are there different social pressures acting on them? Does the organization offer different rewards to each of them? These are all good possibilities. Indeed, the various theories that will be introduced in this chapter will look at motivation in these different ways.

Scientists studying organizational behavior are not merely content to develop theories of motivation; they also attempt to design and test ways of actually improving motivation in organizations. After discussing several major theories of motivation at work, we will discuss the various ways they can be applied. To balance the theoretical aspect of the chapter with a more practical side, several interesting and well-known techniques for enhancing motivation will be introduced.

Before we discuss the various theories and applications, however, we will begin by more formally introducing the concept of motivation. Specifically, we will begin by defining motivation and reviewing its importance in contemporary organizations.

HUMAN MOTIVATION: BACKGROUND

The concept of **motivation** has been central to organizational behavior and has been looked at in many different ways. For example, we have already described the idea of basic instinctual drives in Freud's psychoanalytic theory (Chapter 4), reinforcement theories of learning (Chapter 3), and McGregor's Theory X/ Theory Y (Chapter 1). All of these theories make important assumptions about what motivates people. However, rather than limit our conceptualization of motivation to any one theoretical perspective, we will offer a rather broad-based, general definition of motivation that will help us understand many different theories and applications.

What Is Motivation?

We define motivation as *a set of processes concerned with the force that energizes behavior and directs it toward attaining some goal.* In studying motivation we are interested both in what energizes behavior as well as what specific goal is sought. This process can be compared to the operation of an automobile; it is not only driven, but it is also steered in a certain direction. The hungry man, for example, will be motivated to eat (to reduce his drive), but may also choose between going to the refrigerator for an apple, preparing a sandwich, sending out for a pepperoni pizza, or going to *Chez Expensive* to enjoy a filet mignon.

Let's examine this process more closely as it is presented in Figure 5-1, which has been adapted from Dunnette and Kirchner.[2] The process begins with some need or expectation that a person has. The diagram shows a person who is lonely and is motivated to seek others' company. The drive to fulfill this need can be reduced in several possible ways. The person selects a possible behavior (e.g., visit Tom) and assesses whether or not it actually satisfies the need. Did visiting Tom make the person less lonely? If so, he or she won't be motivated to seek others. If not, the process will begin all over again.

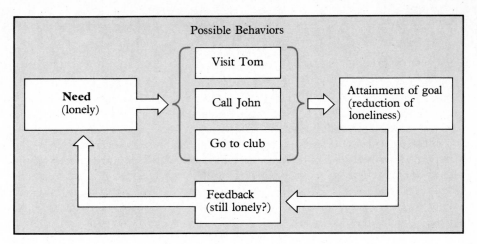

FIGURE 5-1   The Motivation Process: A General Framework

A person experiencing a need is motivated to reduce it and can usually do so in many possible ways. In this example, a lonely person can call or visit a friend or go to a club. This may reduce the need, and the person will no longer feel lonely. If not, the person will be motivated to engage in an alternative behavior. (Source: Based on data from Dunnette & Kirchner, *Psychology Applied to Industry.* New York: Appleton-Century-Crofts, 1965.)

This general way of looking at the process of motivation not only describes what motivation is but anticipates some of the more specific theories of motivation introduced in this chapter. Even though this framework is useful, there are some complexities that should be pointed out.[3] First, it is important to note that motives cannot be directly observed. Motives can only be inferred. An employee who works overtime may be doing it for the money, for the joy of work, for the social opportunities, or for many other reasons or combinations of reasons. Thus, while we may directly observe a person's behavior, we can only infer (or ask the person in question to infer) the underlying motives.

Second, there are usually many motives operating at once, making it difficult or impossible for all of them to be satisfied. Motives may even conflict (e.g., the motive to eat and the motive to get or stay thin), making it difficult to say exactly what a person may do. Accordingly, while motivation may be simply described as a general process, the actual study of motivation is far more complex. The research, theories, and applications that follow will certainly bear this out.

Motivation and the Changing Work Ethic

> This we commanded you, that if any would not work, neither should he eat. (2 Thessalonians 3:10)

Much has been written recently about the crisis of sagging productivity in American organizations.[4] Observers have attributed this problem to various causes, such as inflation, an unfair tax system, world market conditions, and the declining work ethic. Here we will focus on the last of these factors.

The polls clearly tell us that the meaning of work continues to change in American society. Late in 1971, the Secretary of Health, Education, and Welfare appointed a commission to study the role of work in American society. Some startling things were revealed in their report, *Work in America*.[5] A growing dissatisfaction with work, problems with alcoholism and drug abuse among workers, and a variety of other maladies were noted. A more recent survey by Yankelovich has shown that work values have continued to decline since the early 1970s.[6] He reports, for example, that from the early to the late 1970s, there has been a large decline in the number of people believing that hard work always pays off, or that work is at the center of their life. And disturbingly, this drop in the desire or motive to work has been matched by a parallel decrease in *managerial motivation* (the desire to become and act as a manager). Indeed, continuing, long-term studies suggest that such motivation dropped steadily among college students from the early 1960s through the mid-1970s. Fortunately, after that point, it appears to have either stabilized or even to have increased.[7,8] The presence of this fifteen-year-long downward trend, though, suggests that business may face a shortage of first-rate managerial talent for some time to come.

Returning to the topic of work motivation, we should note that the shifts mentioned above do not necessarily reflect a decline in commitment to the work ethic. Work may well be less important to individuals today than it was years ago because unemployment benefits and other forms of help for jobless workers ease the pressure to take any job just to survive. A recent *Los Angeles Times* poll reported that a vast majority of Americans were very satisfied with their jobs and felt they would continue to work even if they didn't have to.[9] Though today's workers are not less interested in working, they want more from their jobs than just a paycheck. Respondents rated having an "interesting job" as most important to them and rated money as their fourth priority. By contrast, a sample of blue-collar workers responding to a 1974 poll rated their pay as being most important and interesting work as fifth.[10] Thus, while today's workers appear to still have a strong work ethic, there has been a change in the values they attach to their jobs.

For the meaning of work to be changing is not a new phenomenon by any means; it has changed throughout the ages. For the ancient Greeks and Romans, work was associated with drudgery. To the Calvinists, work was an act of religious salvation—an ideology which formed the basis of the "Protestant work ethic" that motivated our colonial forefathers. It was the industrial revolution in the United States in the late 1800s that separated the religious values from the work values—a phenomenon that historians report worried many observers of the day as a threat to our moral character.[11] Just as the religious-based work values of the nineteenth century gave way to the industrial realities of the twentieth century, so too are today's work values shifting to accommodate new economic realities and changing social conditions. What we see happening in the work force today is no more than a continuing historical evolution of the values placed on work.

FOCUS ON BEHAVIOR

The Workaholic: Too Much Motivation?

As we have noted, many of today's workers do not seem interested in working very hard. Yet, there is a small segment of the population that loves to work, lives to work, and can't get enough of it—the **workaholics.** In her recent book, Marilyn Machlowitz identified the workaholic as "that blur of a person rushing by with the overflowing briefcase, dictating into a recorder, checking the time, and munching on a sandwich."[12]

You probably know, or have heard of, people who are at their desks hours before anyone else, who work through lunch, and who stay late every night—at least six nights a week. They are extremely well-organized, never take vacations, and, of course, never just sit around and do nothing. Naturally, you would think that workaholics would be sought after as prospective employees. Many managers seem to have bought the stereotype that workaholics may be somewhat sick but that they would make a valuable addition to their corporation. Consider the following poem:

Take My Word

by Richard Armour

A recent word is workaholic,
One caught by something diabolic.
But dangerous though it may be,
I'd like to have one work for me.[13]

Actually, despite their long hours of hard work, workaholics don't always make all that good a contribution to their organizations. A recent study of workaholics conducted at the University of California Medical School has shown that workaholics tend to work for work's sake and tend to be more addicted to the work itself than to achieving results. They are less likely to be successful corporate officers than persons who successfully integrate

---

The work values typical of employees in contemporary organizations can be characterized in several ways.[16]

Concern for "the good life."   To a large extent, the values of today's workers are changing because of the entry of the post-World-War-II "baby boom" into the work force. This generation, weaned on prosperity, is much more concerned with the enjoyment of work, leisure, and personal growth than the preceding generation, who was brought up during the depression. As a result, today's workers are used to having a comfortable life and are concerned about having an enjoyable work life. In fact, some 200 companies now have Quality of Work Life committees to help establish and maintain favorable working conditions in organizations (we will consider quality of work life in Chapter 16).

Adaptation to economic realities.   Today's workers are also concerned with earning money—although, as we said, this is not their primary concern. They want to earn enough to maintain their life-styles. Certain economic conditions such as inflation, declining economic opportunities, high interest rates, and recession make it difficult for workers to make as much financial progress as they may have once hoped. As a result, many of today's workers are not motivated to work very hard to become rich.

work with relaxation.[14] Moreover, they are poor at delegating authority and also create problems for their organizations by causing insecurities in their less ambitious co-workers.

Recent research also leads us to question the poem's suggestion that workaholism is "dangerous." Certainly, while there is evidence that working too hard may be a cause of heart disease, workaholics may not be working *too* hard, at least by their own standards.[15] For the workaholic, stress is caused by the pressures of their family and society to give up their work and to enrich their personal lives, *not* by the work itself.

Workaholics have little personal life, of course, since they have little time available for their families and few, if any, interests outside their work. But we don't mean to imply that workaholics are unhappy. On the contrary, Machlowitz found that the workaholics she interviewed were not frustra-ted, harried, unhappy persons. As a whole they were quite satisfied and content with their lives. They derive their life satisfaction from their jobs. When their jobs are going well, they are healthy and happy.

Should, or can, workaholics change their ways? Sometimes, of course, workaholism can cause or exaggerate problems. The hard-working executive can drive all the secretaries crazy, destroy his or her family life (e.g., answer the beeper while making love[!]), or ignore medical problems that require changing his or her pace of work. In these instances, workaholics need to change their ways. But can they? It is difficult for work addicts to change when they have to, but Machlowitz describes many success stories. The same kind of compulsive, driven characteristics that help many workaholics stop smoking and lose weight have often been channeled into making a better integrated person. □

Humanization of the work place. During the 1930s it was assumed that workers provided the labor and managers provided the "head work." Today, however, nonadversarial relations have developed between workers and managers, with workers providing considerable input into what goes on in organizations. More than ever, it has become fashionable for workers to exercise control over their jobs and to participate in the decisions involving them (see Chapter 12).

These aspects of today's work ethic are not important just because they chronicle changes in our social history. Even more crucial for the field of organizational behavior, they have key implications for the development of theories of motivation and the implementation of programs to enhance motivation in organizations. In Chapter 1 we described Taylor's "Scientific Management" philosophy—an approach to management that assumed that workers would be satisfied to earn as much as possible by working in the most efficient manner. However, given today's work ethic, scientific management would certainly be an inappropriate philosophy to use to motivate workers. As we will see in this chapter, contemporary theories of motivation and motivational programs are sensitive to the values today's workers place on work. (For a discussion of individuals who have their own, personal "work ethic"—and adhere to it with a vengeance!—see the **"FOCUS"** box above.)

MOTIVATION IN ORGANIZATIONS:
THEORIES AND RESEARCH

Our presentation of various theories of motivation in organizations will be centered around the scope of their analysis. We will begin by discussing *need theories* of motivation, which focus primarily on the individual. Next, we will introduce *equity theory*, which is concerned with comparisons between people—social processes. Finally, we will discuss the *expectancy/valence* theories of motivation. These are the most encompassing and take into account organizational-level processes.

As we will soon see, these theories are quite distinct and focus on different aspects of motivation in organizational settings. (Indeed, the lack of integration between them has sometimes been a source of criticism.[17]) Yet, all have been of major interest to researchers, who have sought to test and refine them. Further, these contrasting views of human motivation have also been of concern to organizational practitioners, who have sought to apply them to a key task: enhancing worker effort. Needless to add, we will take full account of both approaches in this discussion.

Need Theory: Motivating Individual Behavior

One of the most basic approaches to motivation assumes that persons are motivated to satisfy their needs. Probably the best known need theory of motivation is the one developed by the clinical psychologist Abraham Maslow.[18] Based on clinical work in the 1940s on the development of personality, Maslow's theory became popular among organizational theorists in the 1960s.

Description of the theory.   There are two basic premises of Maslow's **need hierarchy theory.** First, the theory assumes that people are motivated to satisfy several different needs. Second, the theory assumes that these various needs are arranged in a hierarchy such that people attempt to satisfy some needs before moving on to others.

There are five general types of needs in Maslow's system, and these are arranged into two categories (see Figure 5–2). The most basic category of needs are *deficiency needs,* which refer to needs that have to be satisfied in order for someone to be healthy and secure. The three types of deficiency needs are: physiological needs, the need for safety, and the need to belong. The most basic of these are *physiological needs,* such as the need for food and water. A second type of deficiency needs are *safety needs.* This refers to the need to be physically and psychologically safe from threats of injury. A third and final type of deficiency need is the *need to belong.* This refers to our need to be social, to have friendships, and to be loved and accepted by others. All of these are considered deficiency needs because if they are not met, the individual will fail to develop a healthy personality.

In contrast, Maslow's next two types of needs are called *growth needs.* These are needs to grow and develop to one's full potential. The two types of growth

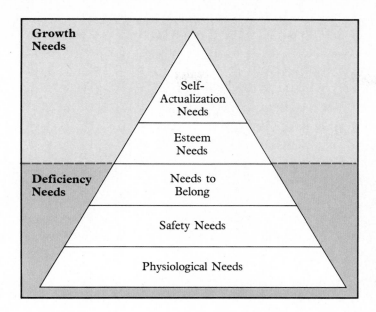

FIGURE 5-2   Maslow's Need Hierarchy

According to Maslow's need hierarchy theory, there are five basic needs arranged in a hierarchical order. The most basic needs (toward the base of the triangle) must first be satisfied before the higher needs (toward the apex of the triangle) are activated.

needs are: esteem needs and **self-actualization** needs. *Esteem needs* refer to an individual's tendency to try to maintain self-respect and to attain the respect and admiration of others. Finally, Maslow identifies the need for *self-actualization* which refers to the need to find out who we really are and to develop our potential to the fullest extent possible.

As we noted before, and as shown in Figure 5–2, these needs are arranged in a hierarchy. This means that only after the lowest-level needs (physiological needs) are met will individuals be motivated to fulfill the next-higher-level needs (safety needs). Maslow asserts that after a certain need is fulfilled, the next-higher-level need in the hierarchy will be activated. The desire to fulfill a particular need will arise only once all needs falling below it in the hierarchy have been satisfied. Thus, once all three of a person's deficiency needs are satisfied, he or she will become interested in satisfying the higher-order growth needs. Ultimately, a person strives to become self-actualized, the need at the top of the hierarchy.

Applying the theory.   Maslow's theory has been quite popular among some managers, probably because it is so simple and intuitively appealing.[19] It is easy to understand that a worker who cannot feed himself and have adequate housing will be less interested in achieving his potential than one who has these basic needs satisfied. The implication for managers appears clear: Create conditions in which employees' lower-order needs can be satisfied so that they will be motivated to reach their potential—to self-actualize. Indeed, we see this in many organizations, especially in the upper echelons of management, where a self-actualized manager would be one who would most benefit the organization with great creativity and productivity.

FIGURE 5-3   Satisfying Executives' Needs: One Route to Creativity?

Executives whose lower needs are met are free to self-actualize and to benefit their companies most. Accordingly, organizations often utilize ways of satisfying lower needs. Country club memberships help satisfy the need to belong. Awards banquets help satisfy self-esteem needs. (Source: Photo [left] from Polaroid Corp.; photo [right] by Terry McKoy/The Picture Cube.)

How do organizations do this? First, they pay their executives well enough to have all their physiological and safety needs fulfilled. Many companies even provide facilities for employees to exercise in—this takes care of both physiological needs and the need to belong. Sometimes top executives are even given country club memberships to ensure their belongingness needs. Awards banquets and various organizational honors are often bestowed upon employees to fulfill their self-esteem needs. According to Maslow's theory, these things should make it possible for workers to become self-actualized and to benefit their organizations as a result (see Figure 5-3).

Evidence—and an alternative.   Despite its intuitive appeal, the theory has received only the most general support. For example, Porter found that upper-level managers (who tend to have challenging, autonomous jobs) were more likely to have their growth needs satisfied than were lower-level managers (who had more routine jobs that made it difficult for growth needs to be satisfied).[20] However, a thorough review of research on Maslow's theory has shown that the theory actually receives little support in its present form.[21] There is little evidence to prove that there are five basic needs that are activated in the hierarchical manner suggested by Maslow.

As a result of the lack of support for Maslow's model, Clayton P. Alderfer has suggested a simpler reformulation.[22] Alderfer's **ERG theory** proposes that there are three basic needs: *existence* (physiological and safety needs), *relatedness* (need for meaningful social relations), and *growth* (need for developing one's potential). These are, of course, merely abstractions of Maslow's five categories. However, in addition to simplifying Maslow's model, Alderfer's model is less rigid in that it proposes that several needs may exist at one time. ERG theory recognizes that the basic needs may *not* be activated in any hierarchical order. Any one need may become activated regardless of whether or not the others are fulfilled. Thus, ERG theory represents a simplification of Maslow's need hierarchy theory, not only by reducing the number of need categories but by eliminating the restriction about the order in which they are activated.

Because studies have shown that there may be fewer than five different types of needs and that the activation of one need is not negatively correlated with the activation of other needs (as Maslow theorizes), Alderfer's simpler, less restrictive model better fits the results of research studies than Maslow's model.

Although need theorists are not in agreement about the exact number of needs that are important and what the exact interrelationships between them may be, they have had an important impact on the field of organizational behavior.

We have seen how certain theories explain motivation as a process of individual needs gratification. Now, let's take a look at other theories that take a broader perspective and recognize the importance of the social environment in which people work.

Equity Theory: Motivation through Social Comparison

One of the most popular theories of organizational motivation today is Adams's **equity theory.**[23] Basically, the theory asserts that people are motivated to maintain fair relationships with others and will attempt to rectify unfair relationships by making them fair.

Description of the theory.   According to the theory, one of the key elements in determining the fairness of one's relationships with another is *social comparison.*[24] For many years, psychologists have believed that one of the major ways by which people come to know about themselves is by comparing themselves to other people. Equity theory proposes that workers make comparisons between themselves and other workers with respect to what they get out of their jobs—referred to as **outcomes**—and what they contribute to their jobs—referred to as **inputs.** In work organizations, outcomes include such things as pay, fringe benefits, or the prestige one receives (see Figure 5-4). Inputs can include factors such as how long or how hard one has worked or any special features of a person's background or training.

The theory states that people compare their inputs and outcomes to those of others in the form of a ratio. That is, they compare the ratio of their own out-

"A raise is out of the question, Hicks, but I will move you up a notch in the pecking order."

FIGURE 5–4 Outcomes at Work: Varied in Nature

As the cartoon suggests, there are many different rewards one may receive in exchange for making contributions to an organization. (Source: Drawing by Stevenson, © 1976 The New Yorker Magazine, Inc.)

comes/inputs to the outcome/input ratios of other people. This comparison process can result in three different conditions:

1. If the person finds that his or her own ratio is greater than another's ratio, then he or she will experience **overpayment inequity.** In other words, the person gets more out of the job relative to what he or she puts in compared to another.
2. If the person's ratio is less than the other's ratio, then the person will experience **underpayment inequity.** In this case, the person gets less out of the job relative to what he or she puts in compared to another.
3. If the person's own ratio is equal to the other's ratio, the person will experience **equity.** This means that both persons get the same relative gain for their contributions.

Suppose, for example, that Sam and Joe are two equally well-trained inspectors who do the same work in two different divisions of a company. Suppose further that Sam is paid $300 each week, and Joe is paid only $250 a week. One day they meet and discover this discrepancy. How will they react? According to equity theory Sam will feel inequitably overpaid relative to Joe, and Joe will feel inequitably underpaid relative to Sam. Both Sam and Joe will feel upset by this inequity, but it will take different forms. Sam will feel *guilty* for being overpaid, and Joe will feel *angry* for being underpaid. Equity theory asserts that these are negative states which persons are motivated to escape.

How can Sam and Joe escape the inequity and bring about equity in their relationship? The theory mentions several ways of doing so, and these fall into two categories—behavioral and psychological. For example, Sam can actually do more or better work than Joe and Joe can do less or poorer work, since this would equalize their ratios. In this case, both workers have behaviorally adjusted their inputs. By raising his inputs Sam effectively lowers his ratio, making it closer to Joe's; and by lowering his inputs, Joe effectively raises his ratio, making it closer to Sam's. One way of lowering one's inputs in an organization is to be absent from work. Recent research has shown that the more workers believe they are unfairly underpaid, the more likely they are to lower their inputs by being absent from work.[25]

It is also possible for Sam and Joe to attempt to adjust their outcomes. Sam can fail to accept pay raises, and Joe can ask for a raise. Joe may even steal a few pencils or paper clips from the company in order to raise his outcomes. If Sam lowers his outcomes and Joe raises his, they equalize their ratios and help to establish an equitable relationship. One extreme way of redressing the inequity is by getting out of the relationship completely. If either Sam or Joe were to quit, that would end the inequity between them. Indeed, evidence exists that shows that inequitably paid workers are more prone to quit their jobs than equitably paid workers.[26]

These are all ways in which Sam and Joe can behaviorally alter their outcomes and inputs to establish equity. However, as we said, Sam and Joe can also establish equity psychologically. In other words, they can think about their own or the other's outcomes and inputs differently. For example, Sam and Joe can rationalize and convince themselves that Sam actually works harder than Joe. If this is believed to be true, then Sam's inputs are seen as greater, and equity is established. Underpaid workers often convince themselves that they really aren't working very hard, thereby establishing equity between themselves and higher-paid coworkers. These psychological inequity-resolution strategies help demonstrate the essentially perceptual nature of equity theory. What really matters is what is perceived. Inequity is only experienced based on how the persons themselves perceive their own and others' inputs and outcomes.

Equity theory research. Numerous experiments supporting equity theory have been conducted in organizational settings. One of the most interesting and ambitious of these was performed by Pritchard, Dunnette, and Jorgenson.[27] These experimenters created an environment simulating an actual small company in which male employees worked part-time on a clerical task over a two-week period. There were three different payment conditions. First, there was an *equity* condition in which workers were paid at the advertised hourly rate of $2.00. To create *underpayment,* the experimenters told the workers that they usually paid workers $2.50 an hour for working at these jobs but that they would only pay them $2.00 an hour because they responded to an advertisement announcing that as the rate of pay. Finally, some workers were led to believe that they were being *overpaid.* The experimenters accomplished this by telling subjects that workers usually get paid $1.65 an hour, but since they responded to an advertisement announcing a $2.00 an hour rate of pay, they would be paid the higher rate.

The partial results shown in Figure 5-5 clearly reveal support for the theory. Underpaid workers were less productive than equitably paid workers, and overpaid workers were more productive than equitably paid workers. As noted earlier, equity theory also says that inequity is a negative state. It should not be surprising, then, that the study also found inequitably paid workers to be less satisfied with their jobs than equitably paid workers. As shown in Figure 5-5, equitably paid workers were more satisfied with their jobs than either overpaid or underpaid workers.

More recent research has shown that workers can feel inequitably paid not only relative to others but relative to themselves at earlier points in time. This is clearly shown in a study of major-league baseball players by Lord and Hohen-

FIGURE 5-5   Inequity: Its Effects on Performance and Job Satisfaction

Hourly paid employees in a bogus company performed in accordance with equity theory. Relative to equitably paid workers, overpaid workers were more productive and underpaid workers were less productive. In addition, equitably paid workers were more satisfied with their jobs than inequitably paid workers, whether the inequitable payment was too high (overpayment) or too low (underpayment). (Source: Based on data from Pritchard, Dunnette, & Jorgenson, *Journal of Applied Psychology,* 1972, *56,* 75–94.)

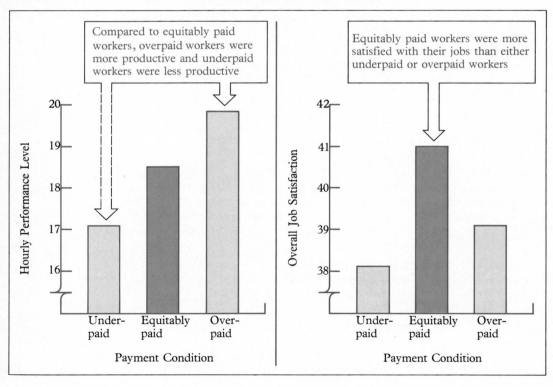

feld.[28] They examined the records of twenty-three players who, because they played out their options, were paid lower salaries in the 1976 season than they were in 1975. Equity theory would predict that these players would feel underpaid and perform at a lower level in the 1976 season. Indeed they did. The underpaid players had lower batting averages and hit fewer home runs and runs-batted-in in 1976 than they did in 1975. This interesting study shows us that people can judge the equity of their pay based on internal standards as well as external standards.

Before concluding our remarks on equity theory, we should note that the importance of equity in organizations has also been demonstrated in another way. The studies we've reviewed so far have shown that workers respond to inequities by behaving so as to restore inequity. However, another line of research has established that managers often strive to create equity in the first place by distributing pay (and other outcomes) in accordance with workers' inputs.[29] As we will see in Chapter 8, equity is a very important consideration in administering wage-incentive plans. Because equity is such an important concern both of workers and managers, it is not surprising to see such prevalent examples of concern for equity throughout organizations.

Expectancy/Valence Theory: Motivation through Beliefs about the Organization

As we stated earlier, **expectancy/valence theory** is the broadest in scope of the three different theories discussed in this chapter. Rather than focusing only on individual needs or social comparison, expectancy/valence theory attempts to explain motivation in terms of the overall environment in which people are working. Basically, the theory assumes that people are motivated to work when they have the **expectancy** that the work environment will provide them with the things they're looking for. There have been several different versions of expectancy/valence theory that have been popular in organizational behavior, including those of Vroom, and Porter and Lawler, just to name a few important pioneers of the theory.[30,31] However, rather than differentiate between the various versions of the theory, we will review it in its most general form.

One of the most important features of expectancy/valence theory is that it characterizes workers as being rational, thinking beings. Workers think about what they have to do to get rewarded and how much the reward means to them before they perform. Of course, the theory is much more specific. It says that performance results from several factors, one of which is motivation.

Description of the theory. Expectancy/valence theory defines motivation, or the force to perform, in a very specific way (see Figure 5–6). There are three determinants of motivation:

1. *The expectancy that effort will result in performance.* Sometimes workers believe that how hard they work will determine how productive they are, but

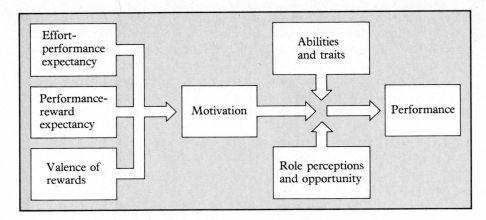

FIGURE 5–6   Expectancy/Valence Theory

According to expectancy/valence theory, motivation combines with other factors to determine performance. (Source: Adapted from a figure in Porter & Lawler, *Managerial Attitudes and Performance;* © 1968 by Richard D. Irwin, Inc. By permission.)

    this isn't always so. Thus, they will be motivated to work only to the extent that they expect high levels of effort to be reflected in high levels of performance.

2. *The expectancy that performance will result in reward.* Workers will be motivated by the belief that their performance will ultimately lead to pay-offs for them. Failure to believe that one's performance will be rewarded will inhibit motivation.

3. *The valence of rewards.* **Valence** refers to the personal value workers place on the rewards they believe they will receive for performing. Even if a worker believes his efforts will be rewarded, there will be little motivation to perform if these rewards hold little value for him. High valence of rewards is necessary for high motivation.

Most expectancy/valence theorists agree that these three determinants of motivation are combined *multiplicatively* to determine the overall level of motivation. The implication of this theoretical assumption is that all three factors must be high in order for a worker to be highly motivated. If any one determinant is zero, then there will be no motivation to perform. This makes intuitive sense since workers cannot be expected to work if their efforts fail to account for their performance, if their performance is not rewarded, or if the resulting rewards are not valued.

    The theory also states that motivation is just one of three determinants of performance. Ultimately, performance will also depend upon two other factors:

1. *Abilities and traits.* A worker's capacity to perform is partly determined by the various skills and characteristics that he or she possesses. Verbal skills

and intellectual capacity, for example, will surely help determine a manager's performance.

2. *Role perceptions and opportunity.* How well a worker performs is also determined by what the worker perceives to be his or her responsibilities, and by what opportunities exist to perform these responsibilities. For example, in order for a salesperson to perform well, she must recognize that her job is to sell and there must be a market to buy.

Thus, in conjunction with motivation, performance is determined by a worker's abilities and traits, as well as by role perceptions and opportunity.

In view of the many fascinating components of expectancy/valence theory, it is probably not too surprising that it has been the subject of a great many experimental tests.[32] Unfortunately, though, empirical support for the theory has been rather weak, and theorists have pointed to several problems with it.[33] Regardless, there seems to be a general acceptance that the theory will remain an important one in the field of organizational behavior because of the crucial implications it has for managerial practice. (For another, contrasting view of motivation in work settings, see the **"PERSPECTIVE"** box on pp. 138–139.)

Some practical implications.   Several useful messages are clearly suggested by expectancy/valence theory.[34] Specifically, the theory suggests that managers should do the following things:

1. *Determine what rewards each employee values.* What turns your workers on? Skillful managers find out what rewards are valued by their employees on an individual level since all rewards are not equally valued by all employees. Programs in which workers are free to select their own rewards, such as cafeteria-style pay plans, certainly help employees to work for rewards that are highly valuable to them (see Chapter 8).[35]

2. *Define desired performance.* It is important for workers to know exactly what is expected of them. How else will they know if they have done a good job?

3. *Make desired performance attainable.* What is expected of a worker must not only be known but must be seen as possible and reasonable. By specifying an expectancy that effort leads to performance, the theory suggests that workers have to feel that it is possible for them to perform adequately given some level of effort. Impossible performance expectations will, no doubt, lower motivation.

4. *Link valued rewards to performance.* Managers should let their subordinates know exactly what they will get for doing what they do. If it is clear to workers that they will be rewarded for performing at a certain level, then they should perform at the desired level. Only when the links between performance and reward are clear will workers be motivated to perform.

FROM THE MANAGER'S PERSPECTIVE

Intrinsic Motivation: When Does Pay Lower Motivation?

Pay has played a central role in the theories we have discussed in this chapter. It can help satisfy a person's lower-order needs. It is one of the major job outcomes workers compare to assess the equity of their pay. And it is one of the major sources of reward about which many expectancies are based. Indeed, pay is a major determinant of motivation in work organizations.

Yet, despite these facts, researchers have uncovered some surprising relationships between pay and work performance. These findings suggest that pay may sometimes *lower* a person's motivation to perform.[36] This was first demonstrated in a classic experiment by Edward L. Deci and has since been corroborated by others.[37,38] In Deci's study, college students worked on solving some interesting puzzles. After one work session, some of the subjects were paid for successfully solving the puzzles while others were not paid. However, subsequently none of the workers were paid for their work. Interestingly, those who were previously paid for their work performed much worse after the pay was taken away than those who were never paid at all.

Deci reasoned that this occurred because the pay caused the workers to alter their beliefs about *why* they were working. Those who worked for free could believe that they were intrinsically interested in solving the puzzles. Those who were paid for their labor probably came to believe that they were working for the money. Therefore, once the money was withdrawn, the level of work dropped. Deci's experiment suggests, then, that extrinsic rewards such as pay can lower performance by undermining workers' **intrinsic motivation.** On this basis, Deci has argued that organizations should be discouraged from using pay systems that make payment contingent upon performance.[39]

However, we must not apply Deci's findings to all types of organizations. Some important differences exist between the conditions created in Deci's study and those found in most work organizations. Deci's subjects were performing exceptionally interesting tasks, whereas many workers find their jobs far less appealing. Theorists have claimed that this may make a difference and that Deci's results probably wouldn't hold in situations in which workers performed uninteresting tasks.[40]

This has been shown in an important experiment by Calder and Staw.[41] Their subjects solved either interesting jigsaw puzzles (photos from *Life* and *Playboy* magazines) or uninteresting ones (blank photos) for which they were either paid or not paid. Afterwards, they were asked how much they enjoyed the task and how much future time they would be willing to volunteer to work on similar future tasks without pay. As shown in Figure 5-7, paid workers decreased their liking for and motivation to perform an already interesting task but increased their liking for and motivation to perform uninteresting tasks. Apparently, paying people to work only lowers motivation when the work is intrinsically interesting. When the work is uninteresting, however, pay actually enhances the motivation to perform.

Another difference between the conditions in Deci's study and those in most organizations is that it is normal for people to be paid for working but not for taking part in experiments. It is interesting to think that pay may be a motivator simply because it is expected in many organizations. But this isn't the case in voluntary organizations. Among voluntary workers we may find that payment for services reduces intrinsic interest in working.

For example, a political candidate who decides to pay his campaign workers in order to "motivate" them may find they will do very little campaigning once the budget runs out. In the words of one team of researchers, paying people to perform interesting, voluntary jobs can "turn play into work."[42] While the voluntary campaign workers may justify their efforts on the grounds that they are working for someone they believe in, the introduction of pay provides an additional justification to work—one that helps them revise their reasons for work-

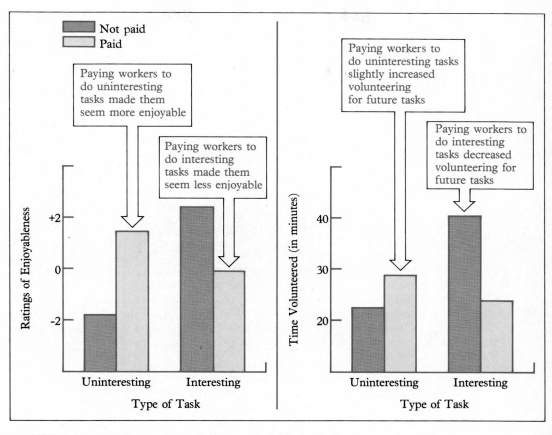

FIGURE 5-7 When Does Payment Lower Intrinsic Motivation?

Whether or not paying workers to perform lowers intrinsic motivation depends on how interesting the task is. Payment lowers motivation to perform interesting tasks but raises motivation to perform uninteresting tasks. (Source: Based on data from Calder & Staw, *Journal of Personality and Social Psychology,* 1975, *31,* 479–486.)

ing. Paying voluntary workers will cause them to feel that they are working for the pay instead of for the cause.

To summarize, paying people to work may lower performance by undermining intrinsic inter-est on the job. However, this only occurs in cases in which the task is so interesting that no additional justification to perform is needed and in which it is not usual to be paid for working. □

IMPROVING MOTIVATION IN ORGANIZATIONS: PRACTICAL APPLICATIONS

Now that we've examined several different theories of motivation, we will turn our attention to the practical problem of how to improve motivation. In drawing upon some of the theories and research, we will first focus our attention on ways in which managers can help improve motivation in their day-to-day encounters with workers. We will then focus on ways in which organizations can be designed to improve motivation.

What Managers Can Do: The Importance of Setting Goals

A program of research by Edwin A. Locke and his associates has shown that one of the most effective things a manager can do to motivate employees is to engage in **goal setting**.[43] Goal setting involves making it clear to workers exactly what goals they will be expected to achieve in performing their jobs. We will review some of this important work here by way of pointing out some practical suggestions for managers.

Assign specific performance goals.   Probably the best established finding from research on goal setting is that setting specific goals is a better way to motivate effective performance than setting general goals.[44] This was clearly shown in a study of teams of Oklahoma loggers by Latham and Baldes.[45] The loggers were responsible for cutting the trees, loading them onto trucks, and driving them to the mill. It was discovered, however, that the loggers were only loading the trucks with about 60% of their legal maximum weight before driving to the mill. During the period before goal setting began, the workers were simply told to try to do their best. Later, a specific goal was established for the loggers—to bring in 94% of the legal maximum weight. This specific goal was considered a difficult, but reasonable one. The workers were told that they wouldn't be given special rewards for meeting the goal, nor would they be punished for failing to meet the goal.

How did setting the goal affect task performance? As you can see from Figure 5-8, setting specific goals resulted in very large performance increases that remained stable for several months. Before the performance leveled off near the specified goal there was a dramatic improvement followed by a decline. Interviews with workers about this period of decline revealed that they were testing management to see if they would be true to their promise not to punish workers for lower performance. After the workers saw that this was the case, performance increased once again.

The effectiveness of this program saved the company over a quarter-of-a-million dollars in potential costs for new trucks, fuel, and new manpower expenses. Apparently, setting specific goals for workers can result in dramatic improvements in the motivation to perform.

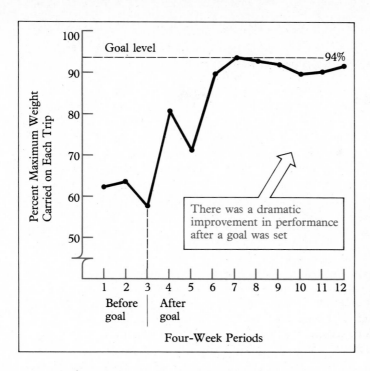

FIGURE 5-8   Goal Setting: Results at a Logging Camp

As shown here, the performance of loggers loading timber onto trucks markedly improved after a specific, difficult goal was set. The percentage of the maximum weight of timber loaded onto trucks rose from around 60% before any goal was set to close to 94%—the goal level—after the goal was set. (Source: Adapted from Latham & Baldes, *Journal of Applied Psychology*, 1975, *60*, 122–124.)

Assign difficult—but acceptable—performance goals.   The Latham and Baldes study just described showed that specific goals were better than general goals. But note that the goal set in their study was a difficult, though reasonable, one. The workers found it hard to achieve, but they accepted it as being possible. What would happen if the goals were too easy or too difficult? Several studies have shown that difficult goals lead to better performance than easy ones, as long as these goals are accepted.[46,47]

For example, in one recent study, subjects performed a clerical task while attempting to attain either an easy goal (to score higher than their previous *average* score) or a difficult goal (to score higher than their previous *best* score).[48] Participants were almost twice as productive when they had a difficult goal than when they had an easy one. Similarly, in another recent investigation, individuals showed higher performance on a creativity task when striving to attain hard or moderate goals than when attempting to reach easy ones.[49]

Other studies have qualified this idea by showing that setting goals that are too difficult to attain is not likely to result in improved performance. To study this process Zander and his associates compared communities that had met their previous goals in United Fund campaigns with those that had not.[50] They found that successful communities tended to set difficult, but reasonable, goals. Unsuccessful communities, however, set goals that were too difficult—ones that were generally not accepted and were therefore not attained. It is not surprising that campaign officials and community members were turned off to too difficult goals. One would have little reason to attempt to attain unreasonable, impossible goals.

The implication for enhancing on-the-job motivation is clear; Set difficult but acceptable goals. Consulting with employees about this would appear to be an excellent way of gaining their support.

Provide feedback on goal attainment. In addition to setting difficult but acceptable goals, recent research has shown that goal setting can be more effective when workers have clear feedback about the extent to which their goals have been obtained.[51] In one study, for example, Kim and Hamner examined the performance of telephone company service workers who worked under set goals without receiving any feedback on how close they came to meeting them. They compared these performances with those of workers whose goals were set and who received formal performance feedback.[52] Among other things, they found that the workers who received feedback performed their jobs more safely and at less cost to the company than those receiving no feedback.

Comparable results were also obtained by Nemeroff and Cosentino in a study comparing ways of training managers to handle performance appraisals of their subordinates.[53] The managers were trained in how to improve their interviewing skills and were either given specific goals to achieve, along with feedback about how successful they were in meeting the goals, or only feedback without any specific goals. There was also a control condition in which managers received neither specific goals nor feedback about their performance. The managers were judged in several ways, among them: (a) how successful their subordinates thought the interview was, (b) how motivated to improve the subordinates felt after the interview, and (c) the subordinates' rates of absenteeism following the interviews.

As you can see in Figure 5-9, the combination of specific goals and feedback brought about the greatest success. That is, the subordinates felt the interview was more successful, they felt more motivated to improve, they were more satisfied with the interview, and they were absent less frequently under this condition. Interviewers were less successful when they did not attempt to attain specific goals or when specific goals were not set and no feedback was provided.

Accordingly, we may recommend that feedback about goal attainment be incorporated into any successful program of goal setting. Although either feedback about performance or goal setting may be effective in improving performance, recent evidence suggests that combining goal setting with feedback brings about even better results.

What the Organization Can Do: Designing Jobs to Enhance Motivation

In addition to supervisors motivating workers by setting goals for their subordinates, it is also possible to motivate workers by designing jobs in certain ways. We may consider Taylor's philosophy of scientific management described in Chapter 1 as being an early approach to designing jobs to stimulate productivity. Taylor analyzed the minute motions of work to discover the most efficient ways

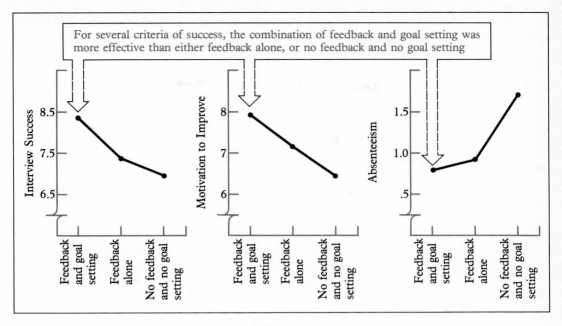

FIGURE 5-9   The Benefits of Combining Feedback and Goal Setting

Managers trained to give performance appraisal interviews were more successful when they received feedback and used goal setting than when either feedback alone was used or when no feedback and no goal setting were used. Under this condition the interviewers' subordinates believed the interview was most successful, they were most motivated to improve, and had the lowest rate of absenteeism. (Source: Based on data from Nemeroff & Cosentino, *Academy of Management Journal,* 1979, *22,* 566–576.)

of doing things and rewarded workers for behaving in a productive manner. The problem with such an approach, of course, is that it makes work highly routine and monotonous. Workers get bored, and this leads to high absenteeism and turnover.[54]

   In response to such problems, many organizations have designed jobs that motivate workers in more humane ways. Organizations today are more apt to motivate workers by involving them with their jobs. Several approaches have been employed, including the techniques of *job enlargement* and *job enrichment,* which were popular in the 1950s and 1960s, and the *job characteristics model* of the 1970s and 1980s.

Job enlargement.   One of the first modern ways of motivating behavior in organizations through job design was by way of **job enlargement.** Job enlargement may be defined as the expansion of the content of a job by increasing the number and variety of tasks performed.[55] In performing enlarged jobs, workers get to do a wider variety of tasks at the same level.

There have been several studies showing the positive effects of job enlargement in organizations. For example, Kilbridge compared the performance of workers assembling water pumps before and after their jobs were enlarged.[56] Prior to job enlargement each worker performed a single operation on an assembly line. The enlarged job required workers to perform all of the many tasks that were necessary to make and test an entire pump. As you can see in Figure 5-10, job enlargement was successful in reducing assembly time and production costs.

Job enrichment. An approach that expands upon job enlargement is **job enrichment,** a concept popular in the 1960s.[57] (Incidentally, we should note that one of the major determinants of interest in this topic was the theory of work motivation developed by Herzberg. However, since Herzberg's theory focuses heavily on the determinants of job satisfaction, we have reserved discussion of it until Chapter 7.) Job enrichment is like job enlargement, except that it not only gives workers more jobs to do, but gives them more complete control over the entire process, from planning and organizing through evaluating the final results.[58] Thus, enriched jobs enable workers to perform not only more varied tasks but tasks at a higher level—ones that give them greater responsibility over their work.

Consider, for example, the job enrichment program instituted in 1971 when General Foods opened a new pet food plant in Topeka, Kansas.[59] Work teams were set up in which all team members learned all the jobs to be done. Time

FIGURE 5-10   Job Enlargement: Some Concrete Benefits

After the jobs of water pump assemblers were enlarged, there was a reduction in the time it took to assemble each pump and in the annual costs of production. (Source: Based on data from Kilbridge, *The Journal of Business,* 1960, *33,* 357–362.)

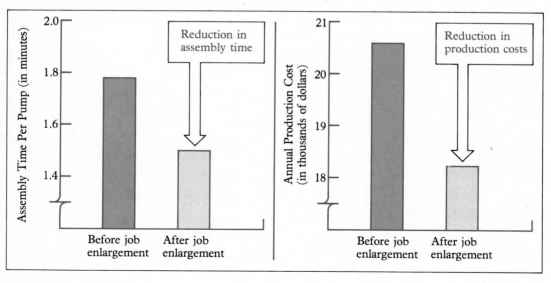

clocks and status symbols were eliminated. Teams did everything, from making decisions about setting appropriate levels of performance and determining pay rates for their teams to correcting customer complaints. The results of this program were quite successful. The vast majority of the employees felt that the quality of their life at work improved with job enrichment. Moreover, after a year and a half of job enrichment, overhead was reduced by 33%, absenteeism was below the industry norm, turnover was considerably below average, and productivity was 40% higher than in other General Foods plants.

However, despite these impressive figures, observers have noted that it has often been difficult to institute job enrichment plans in many organizations. For example, even General Foods was surprisingly slow to spread the impressive innovations of the Topeka plant to its other plants.[60] The Topeka plant was small, new, and not unionized. The cost of changing over large old plants could be very great. Moreover, acceptance by unions and management may be difficult to attain.[61] In general, the economic costs of such changeovers coupled with the problem of acceptance of the new system has resulted in a rather narrow application of job enrichment—at least in the United States.[62] (As explained in the **"CASE IN POINT"** box on page 146, the situation is not the same in Sweden.)

The job characteristics model. A recently developed approach to motivation at the organizational level has been Hackman and Oldham's **job characteristics model.**[63,64] Essentially, this model is an outgrowth of job enrichment. It specifies exactly how and why jobs should be enriched in order to yield the best results. The basic assumption of the model is that jobs can be redesigned, enriching them so as to "help individuals regain the chance to experience the kick that comes from doing a job well, and . . . once again *care* about their work and about developing the competence to do it even better."[65]

According to the model there are five core job dimensions, creating three critical psychological states, that, in turn, lead to several beneficial outcomes for the worker and the organization. The model is diagrammed in Figure 5-12 on page 149. As shown in that diagram, three job dimensions—skill variety, task identity, and task significance—contribute to a task's experienced meaningfulness. A task is considered meaningful if it is experienced as important, valuable, and worthwhile. The model specifies that this will be the case when jobs have a great deal of the following:

- *skill variety*—the extent to which a job requires the use of several different skills and talents,
- *task identity*—the extent to which a job requires completing a whole piece of work from beginning to end, and
- *task significance*—the degree of impact the job is believed to have on other people.

Another basic job dimension—autonomy—is said to contribute to experienced responsibility for the outcomes of the work performed. When a job is designed so that a worker feels autonomous (i.e., has a great deal of freedom and discretion to

CASE IN POINT

Job Enrichment at Volvo

In 1971 when Peter Gyllenhammar took over as Volvo's managing director, he inherited a 40% annual turnover rate and a 20%-25% rate of absenteeism.[66] Soon thereafter, Gyllenhammar developed a keen interest in job enrichment and instituted the program in an automobile factory in the southern Swedish town of Kalmar.

The plant is composed of many small workshops in a large star-shaped factory. Each point of the star houses a separate work group of about fifteen to twenty-five employees charged with working on a separate part of the car, such as the electrical system, the interior, the motor. Each group even had its own rest and meeting areas. Unlike assembly-line auto factories, the cars at this plant stand still as the people work on them. As a result, the workers can have social contact with each other. (See the photograph in Figure 5-11.) There are no inspectors; each team does its own quality control.[67]

The impact of job enrichment at Volvo's Kalmar plant appears to be generally positive, but not completely so. For example, absenteeism dropped from 40% to 25%, although economic factors may have accounted for this as much as the job enrichment program. There was also a significant drop in turnover, which is particularly important in Sweden because, unlike in the U.S., there is not a waiting pool of replacement workers.[68] At the same time, the Kalmar plant cost more to build than conventional plants and has higher operating costs. The output is much lower than that of conventional plants, although the quality is considerably higher. Nonetheless, Volvo's management appears quite enthusiastic about its job enrichment program and has successfully instituted it in its other plants.[69] Apparently, Volvo's job enrichment program is well-received by workers, who turn out high quality products (albeit at a high cost).

There is some evidence that the successfulness of Volvo's job enrichment program may not be completely generalizable to American workers or those in other countries. In the mid-1970s the Ford Foundation sponsored a project in which they flew six Detroit auto workers to Sweden for a month of work in an enriched Saab plant as engine assemblers. Afterwards, five of the six workers reported preferring the traditional assembly line. To quote one worker, "If I've got to bust my ass to be meaningful, forget it; I'd rather be monotonous."[70] Apparently, these individuals found that the demands of an enriched work environment (e.g. the need to schedule their own work, make many decisions ordinarily left to management) more than offset any positive feelings induced. Of course, it should be emphasized that only six individuals were involved, and it is not clear that they were fully representative of the millions of persons now at work on American assembly lines. However, these findings are still worth noting for they call our attention to the fact that what "works" in one culture or setting will not necessarily succeed in another.

FIGURE 5-11   Volvo's Work Team Alternative to the Assembly Line

Members of work teams at Volvo's Kalmar plant share the various tasks to be performed and have social contact with each other while working. (Source: Photo courtesy of Volvo of America.)

It should also be noted that Sweden's workers have exceptionally powerful unions that have been successful in influencing the government to pass legislation supportive of their continued interest in enriched jobs.[71] For example, the Democracy at Work Act was passed in 1977, which called for full consultation with employees regarding organizational decisions. Such laws certainly make Sweden a unique environment for the development and refinement of a wide range of job enrichment programs. But they also raise doubts about the extent to which the findings uncovered in such programs can be generalized to other countries. Every nation cannot, of course, be like Sweden—far from it. Yet *something* must clearly be done to arrest and reverse recent declines in productivity experienced by many companies in the U.S. and elsewhere. For this reason alone, careful evaluation of every potential lead seems necessary and justified.   □

carry out the job as desired), the job makes workers feel that they are personally responsible and accountable for the work they perform.

A final job characteristic—feedback—contributes to an individual's knowledge of results about the job performed. When a job is designed so that it provides workers with information about the effects of their work, they will be better able to develop an understanding of how effectively they have performed.

If jobs are designed so that they contain these core dimensions, the critical psychological states will come into being and various beneficial personal and work outcomes will result. For example, Hackman and Oldham state that workers will be highly motivated to work and will perform very well. They will also be highly satisfied with their jobs and will be unlikely to be absent from or resign from their jobs.

To summarize the various motivating characteristics of any job, Hackman and Oldham combine the various dimensions into a single index called the **motivating potential score (MPS).** Arithmetically, the MPS is defined as:

$$\text{Motivating Potential Score (MPS)} = \left[\frac{\text{Skill Variety} + \text{Task Identity} + \text{Task Significance}}{3} \right] \times \text{Autonomy} \times \text{Job Feedback}.$$

Through responses to questionnaire items, the various job dimensions are assessed, and then combined mathematically to form this index. The MPS reflects a job's potential to promote self-generated motivation among the workers. The higher the MPS of any given job, the greater will be the likelihood of experiencing the positive personal and work outcomes specified.

Because the model is new, it is now just beginning to be the subject of empirical research attention.[72] One recent study by Orpen shows some particularly promising support for the model.[73] In this experiment an attempt was made to redesign the jobs of clerical workers employed in a federal agency in South Africa. Their jobs were enriched with respect to each of the five core dimensions specified by Hackman and Oldham. For example, the employees were given the opportunity to choose what kind of tasks they wanted to perform (skill variety), they were able to perform the entire job (task identity), they were instructed as to how their job fit into the organization as a whole (task significance), they were free to set their own schedules and inspect their own work (autonomy), and they kept records of their daily productivity (feedback). In contrast, there was also an equivalent control group of workers whose jobs were not enriched along these lines.

After a six-month period, workers performing the newly designed jobs were compared to those performing the original jobs. Various questionnaire items were administered to measure job satisfaction and internal motivation. Objective measures were also taken of productivity, absenteeism, and turnover (resignations). As

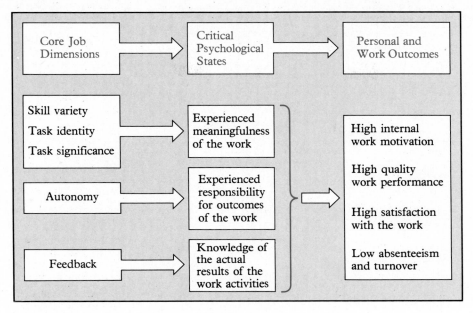

FIGURE 5-12   The Job Characteristics Model

Hackman and Oldham's job characteristics model stipulates that certain core job dimensions create certain critical psychological states, which lead to certain positive personal and organizational outcomes. (Source: Adapted from a figure in Hackman & Suttle [Eds.] *Improving Life at Work;* © 1976 by Goodyear. By permission of Scott, Foresman and Company.)

shown in Table 5-1 (page 150), the redesigned jobs generally brought improvements in the types of personal and work outcomes predicted by the job characteristics model. Specifically, workers on the redesigned jobs were more motivated and more satisfied, were absent less frequently, and were less likely to resign compared to workers on the traditional jobs. However, inconsistent with the model, workers performing the redesigned jobs did not perform any better than those performing the traditional jobs. Thus, although the model receives a great deal of support from this study, it is not completely confirmed. This partial support is, nonetheless, very impressive for such a new approach to motivation. Further research promises to continue to refine and extend this approach.[74]

In closing this section, we would like to point out some specific principles for redesigning jobs to enrich them.[75] These principles represent various things that can be done in organizations to enhance each of the core job dimensions (see summary in Table 5-2, page 150).

TABLE 5-1   The Job Characteristics Model: Results of an Experimental Test

An experiment comparing workers performing traditional jobs with those performing redesigned jobs generally supported the job characteristics model. Workers on redesigned jobs were more motivated to perform, more satisfied with their jobs, were absent less often, and were less likely to resign. However, performance levels were about equal on both traditional and redesigned jobs. (Source: Based on data from Orpen, 1979.)

PERSONAL OR WORK OUTCOME	TRADITIONAL JOB DATA	REDESIGNED JOB DATA	DESCRIPTION OF RESULTS
Internal Motivation	4.61	5.38	Workers were more motivated to perform the redesigned jobs
Work Satisfaction	8.60	12.10	Workers were more satisfied with the redesigned jobs
Absenteeism	3.94	2.56	Workers performing the redesigned jobs were absent less often
Turnover	3.75	2.01	Fewer workers resigned from the redesigned jobs
Productivity	5.86	6.02	Workers performed equally well on both jobs

TABLE 5-2   Principles for Redesigning Jobs

There are various principles for redesigning jobs that will help create the core job dimensions in the job characteristics model of work motivation. Note that some principles influence more than one job dimension. (Source: Based on information in Hackman and Suttle, 1976.)

CHANGE PRINCIPLES	CORE JOB DIMENSIONS
Combining Tasks	Skill Variety
	Task Identity
Forming Natural Work Units	Task Identity
	Task Significance
Establishing Client Relationships	Autonomy
	Feedback
Vertical Loading	Autonomy
Opening Feedback Channels	Feedback

Principle 1: Form natural work units. This principle requires that work should be distributed so that each person performing a task is identified with the job. So, for example, instead of having various members of a typing pool type different parts of one report, work can be distributed so that one typist types the whole report. As a result, the typist will better identify with the job and will understand its significance.

Principle 2: Combine tasks. Instead of having several workers each performing a separate part of a whole job, it would be better to have each worker perform the entire job. For example, Hackman describes how jobs were redesigned among workers assembling laboratory hot plates at the Corning Glass Works in Medford, Massachusetts.[76] Formerly, workers used to assemble part of the hot plate; but after the change, each worker assembled the whole unit. As a result, the newly designed jobs provided greater skill variety and task identity.

Principle 3: Establish client relationships. Usually, the performer of a service or the manufacturers of a product have little contact with the ultimate users. However if such contact were established, employees could benefit in several ways. First, they could receive important feedback about their work. Second, they could improve their interpersonal skills by having to deal with clients (skill variety). Finally, they would be given greater autonomy by being given the freedom to manage their own relationships with clients.

Principle 4: Load jobs vertically. Vertical loading means giving employees greater responsibility for their jobs. Workers usually perform a task while management controls it. However, vertically loading a job involves giving individuals some control over their own work, and it thereby increases a job's level of autonomy.

Principle 5: Open feedback channels. Every job has some way in which feedback can be provided to workers. In addition to receiving feedback from clients, jobs can be changed so that feedback is provided by the work itself. For example, workers operating computerized equipment (such as CRT terminals) can be given feedback about the number of errors they make by virtue of a few simple programming changes. On other jobs, records can be kept of daily performance, or supervisors can tell workers how they've performed on a regular basis. Workers have to know how they're doing in order to be motivated to do better.

SUMMARY

People in organizations are motivated by the desire to attain certain goals. Continuing changes in the work ethic suggest that workers in today's organizations are less motivated by an interest in attaining money than they are in having an interesting, meaningful job and pleasurable working conditions.

Various theories of organizational motivation have been proposed. Maslow's **need hierarchy theory** suggests that people strive to fulfill various personal needs on their jobs. A broader approach to motivation is taken by **equity theory.**

It asserts that workers are motivated to maintain fair relationships between themselves and others in the organization. The broadest approach to motivation is offered by **expectancy/valence theory,** which proposes that performance is motivated by a worker's beliefs about the extent to which an organization is likely to provide desired rewards.

A successful way for managers to motivate workers is to set goals. Research has shown that goals that are specific, difficult (but not impossible), and for which feedback is provided yield the greatest success in motivating workers. Motivation can also be enhanced at the organizational level through programs of *job enlargement* (giving workers more and varied tasks at the same level) and *job enrichment* (giving workers greater control over doing their jobs). The *job characteristics model* is a new and promising recent approach to redesigning jobs. It proposes that five core job dimensions lead to critical psychological states and that these, in turn, lead to positive results for the organization and its employees.

KEY TERMS

EQUITY   The state in which one worker's outcome/input ratio is approximately equal to that of another worker with whom this person compares himself or herself.

EQUITY THEORY   The theory that workers strive to maintain ratios of their outcomes (rewards) to their inputs (contributions) that equal the outcome/input ratios of workers with whom they compare themselves.

ERG THEORY   Alderfer's theory stating that there are three basic human needs: existence, relatedness, and growth.

EXPECTANCY   The beliefs that an individual holds about the likelihood of certain events occurring. A worker's expectancies that effort will affect his/her performance and that performance will lead to rewards are components of the expectancy/valence theory.

EXPECTANCY/VALENCE THEORY   The theory that a worker's motivation to perform is based on his or her beliefs about the probability that effort will lead to performance, multiplied by the probability that performance will lead to reward, multiplied by the valence (perceived value) of reward.

GOAL SETTING   The process of determining specific levels of performance for workers to attain.

INEQUITY   The undesirable condition in which a worker's outcome/input ratio is not equal to that of another who is used for comparison. If this inequality favors a person, the result is *overpayment inequity;* and this leads to guilt feelings. If it is to a person's disadvantage, the result is *underpayment inequity;* and this leads to feelings of anger.

INPUTS   A worker's contributions to his or her job (e.g., experience, hours worked, etc.).

INTRINSIC MOTIVATION   The desire to perform a task because of its own inherent interest, not because of the external rewards it may provide.

JOB CHARACTERISTICS MODEL   A framework proposed by Hackman and Oldham suggesting that five core job dimensions (skill variety, task identity, task significance, autonomy, and job feedback) produce critical states that then lead to positive results for the person (e.g., high job satisfaction) and the organization (e.g., high performance).

JOB ENLARGEMENT   The practice of expanding the content of a job so as to include more and varied tasks at the same level.

JOB ENRICHMENT   The practice of giving workers a high degree of control over their work, from planning and organization through evaluating the final results.

MOTIVATING POTENTIAL SCORE (MPS)   A mathematical index describing the degree to which a job is designed so as to motivate workers.

MOTIVATION   A set of processes concerned with the force that energizes behavior and directs it toward attaining some goal.

NEED HIERARCHY THEORY   Maslow's theory that there are five basic needs (physiological needs, safety needs, needs to belong, esteem needs, and self-actualization needs) and that these are arranged in such a way that lower, more basic needs have to be gratified before higher-level needs become activated.

OUTCOMES   The rewards a worker receives from his or her job (e.g., salary, recognition, etc.).

SELF–ACTUALIZATION   The need to find out who we really are and to develop to our fullest potential.

VALENCE   The value a person places on the rewards he or she expects to receive from the organization.

WORKAHOLIC   The person who works as if work were the most important thing in life.

NOTES

1. Lawler, E.E. *Motivation in work organizations.* Monterey, Calif.: Brooks/Cole, 1973.

2. Dunnette, M.D., & Kirchner, W.K. *Psychology applied to industry.* New York: Appleton-Century-Crofts, 1965.

3. Steers, R.M., & Porter, L.W. *Motivation and work behavior.* New York: McGraw-Hill, 1979.

4. Davis, K. Low productivity? Try improving the social environment. *Business Horizons,* June 1980, pp. 27–29.

5. *Work in America: A report of a Special Task Force to the Secretary of Health, Education, and Welfare.* Cambridge, Mass.: M.I.T. Press, 1973.

6. Yankelovich, D. New rules in American life: Searching for self-fulfillment in a world turned upside down. *Psychology Today,* April 1981, pp. 35–37; 39; 40; 43–44; 46–47; 50–52; 54–55; 58–60; 69; 72; 74; 76–78; 80; 82; 85–86; 89; 91.

7. Miner, J.B. & Smith, N.R. Decline and stabilization of managerial motivation over a 20-year period. *Journal of Applied Psychology,* 1982, *67*, 297–305.

8. Bartol, K., Anderson, C.R., & Schneier, C.E. Sex and ethnic effects on motivation to manage among college business students. *Journal of Applied Psychology,* 1981, *66*, 40–44.

9. The Los Angeles Times. Work still a labor of love. *The Columbus Dispatch,* April 20, 1981, p. 1.

10. Quinn, R.P., Staines, G.L., & McCullough, M.R. *Job satisfaction: Is there a trend?* Washington, D.C.: U.S. Department of Labor Manpower Research Monograph No. 30, 1974.

11. Rodgers, D.T. *The work ethic in industrial America: 1850–1920.* Chicago: University of Chicago Press, 1978.

12. Machlowitz, M. *Workaholics: Living with them, working with them.* Reading, Mass.: Addison-Wesley, 1980, p. 35.

13. Armour, R. Take my word. *The Wall Street Journal,* December 29, 1978. Reprinted by permission of the author.

14. Why Workaholics Work. *Newsweek,* April 27, 1981, p. 71.

15. Weiman, C.G. A study of occupational stressors and the incidence of disease/risk. *Journal of Occupational Medicine,* 1977, *19,* 119–122.

16. The new industrial relations. *Business Week,* May 11, 1981, pp. 84–87; 89–90; 92; 94; 96; 98.

17. Mitchell, T.R. Motivation: New directions for theory, research, and practice. *Academy of Management Review,* 1982, *7,* 80–88.

18. Maslow, A.H. *Toward a psychology of being* (2nd ed.). New York: Van Nostrand, 1968.

19. Tuzzolino, F., & Armandi, B.R. A need-hierarchy framework for assessing corporate social responsibility. *Academy of Management Review,* 1981, *6,* 21–28.

20. Porter, L.W. *Organizational patterns of managerial job attitudes.* New York: American Foundation for Management Research, 1964.

21. Wahba, M.A., & Birdwell, L.G. Maslow reconsidered: A review of research on the need hierarchy theory. *Organizational Behavior and Human Performance,* 1976, *15,* 212–240.

22. Alderfer, C.P. *Existence, relatedness, and growth.* New York: Free Press, 1972.

23. Adams, J.S. Inequity in social exchange. In L. Berkowitz (Ed.), *Advances in experimental social psychology* (Vol. 2). New York: Academic Press, 1965.

24. Goodman, P.S. An examination of referents used in the evaluation of pay. *Organizational Behavior and Human Performance,* 1974, *12,* 170–195.

25. Dittrich, J.E., & Carrell, M.R. Organizational equity perceptions, employee job satisfaction, and departmental absence and turnover rates. *Organizational Behavior and Human Performance,* 1979, *24,* 29–40.

26. Finn, R.H., & Lee, S.M. Salary equity: Its determination, analysis and correlates. *Journal of Applied Psychology,* 1972, *56,* 283–292.

27. Pritchard, R.D., Dunnette, M.D., & Jorgenson, D.O. Effects of perceptions of equity and inequity on worker performance and satisfaction. *Journal of Applied Psychology,* 1972, *56,* 75–94.

28. Lord, R.G., & Hohenfeld, J.A. Longitudinal field assessment of equity effects on the performance of major league baseball players. *Journal of Applied Psychology,* 1979, *64,* 19–26.

29. Freedman, S.M., & Montanari, J.R. An integrative model of managerial reward allocation. *Academy of Management Review,* 1980, *5,* 381–390.

30. Vroom, V.H. *Work and motivation.* New York: Wiley, 1964.

31. Porter, L.W., & Lawler, E.E. *Managerial attitudes and performance.* Homewood, Ill.: Irwin, 1968.

32. Mitchell, T.R. Expectancy models of job satisfaction, occupational preference and effort: A theoretical, methodological and empirical appraisal. *Psychological Bulletin*, 1974, *81*, 1096–1112.

33. Campbell, J.P., & Pritchard, R.D. Motivation theory in industrial and organizational psychology. In M.D. Dunnette (Ed.), *Handbook of industrial and organizational psychology*. Chicago: Rand McNally, 1976.

34. Nadler, D.A., & Lawler, E.E. Motivation: A diagnostic approach. In J.R. Hackman, E.E. Lawler, & L.W. Porter (Eds.), *Perspectives on behavior in organizations*. New York: McGraw-Hill, 1977.

35. Lawler, E.E. *Pay and organization development*. Reading, Mass.: Addison-Wesley, 1981.

36. Lepper, M.R., & Greene, D. *The hidden costs of reward*. Hillsdale, N.J.: Erlbaum, 1978.

37. Deci, E.L. The effects of externally mediated rewards on intrinsic motivation. *Journal of Personality and Social Psychology*, 1971, *18*, 105–115.

38. Pritchard, R.D., Campbell, K.M., & Campbell, D.J. Effects of extrinsic financial rewards on intrinsic motivation. *Journal of Applied Psychology*, 1977, *62*, 9–15.

39. Deci, E.L. The effects of contingent and noncontingent rewards and controls on intrinsic motivation. *Organizational Behavior and Human Performance*, 1972, *8*, 217–229.

40. Staw, B. *Intrinsic and extrinsic motivation*. Morristown, N.J.: General Learning Press, 1976.

41. Calder, B.J., & Staw, B.M. Self-perception of intrinsic and extrinsic motivation. *Journal of Personality and Social Psychology*, 1975, *31*, 599–605.

42. Lepper, M.R., & Greene, D. Turning play into work: Effects of adult surveillance and extrinsic rewards on children's intrinsic motivation. *Journal of Personality and Social Psychology*, 1975, *31*, 479–486.

43. Locke, E.A. Toward a theory of task motivation and incentives. *Organizational Behavior and Human Performance*, 1968, *3*, 157–189.

44. Latham, G.P., & Yukl, G. A review of research on the application of goal-setting in organizations. *Academy of Management Journal*, 1975, *18*, 824–845.

45. Latham, G.P., & Baldes, J.J. The practical significance of Locke's theory of goal setting. *Journal of Applied Psychology*, 1975, *60*, 122–124.

46. Mento, A.J., Cartledge, N.D., & Locke, E.A. Maryland vs. Michigan vs. Minnesota: Another look at the relationship of expectancy and goal difficulty to task performance. *Organizational Behavior and Human Performance*, 1980, *25*, 419–440.

47. Latham, G.P., & Yukl, G. A review of research on the application of goal-setting in organizations. *Academy of Management Journal*, 1975, *18*, 824–845.

48. Matsui, T., Okada, A., & Mizuguchi, R. Expectancy theory prediction of the goal theory postulate, "The harder the goals, the higher the performance." *Journal of Applied Psychology*, 1981, *66*, 54–58.

49. Garland, H. Goal levels and task performance: A compelling replication of some compelling results. *Journal of Applied Psychology*, 1982, *67*, 245–258.

50. Zander, A., & Newcomb, T.T., Jr. Group levels of aspiration in United Fund campaigns. *Journal of Personality and Social Psychology,* 1967, *6,* 157–162.

51. Erez, M. Feedback: A necessary condition for the goal setting-performance relationship. *Journal of Applied Psychology,* 1977, *62,* 624–627.

52. Kim, J.S., & Hamner, W.C. Effect of performance feedback and goal setting on productivity and satisfaction in an organizational setting. *Journal of Applied Psychology,* 1976, *61,* 48–57.

53. Nemeroff, W.F., & Cosentino, J. Utilizing feedback and goal setting to increase performance appraisal interviewer skills of managers. *Academy of Management Journal,* 1979, *22,* 566–576.

54. Hulin, C.L., & Blood, M.R. Job enlargement, individual differences, and worker responses. *Psychological Bulletin,* 1968, *69,* 41–55.

55. Aldag, R.J., & Brief, A.P. *Task design and employee motivation.* Glenview, Ill.: Scott, Foresman, 1979.

56. Kilbridge, M.D. Reduced costs through job enlargement: A case. *The Journal of Business,* 1960, *33,* 357–362.

57. Herzberg, F. *The managerial choice.* Homewood, Ill.: Dow Jones-Irwin, 1976.

58. Chung, K.H., & Ross, M.F. Differences in motivational properties between job enlargement and job enrichment. *Academy of Management Review,* 1977, *2,* 113–122.

59. Walton, R.E. How to counter alienation in the plant. *Harvard Business Review,* 1972, *50,* 70–81.

60. Walton, R.E. The diffusion of new work structures: Explaining why success didn't take. *Organizational Dynamics,* Winter 1975, *3,* 3–22.

61. Giles, W.F., & Holley, W.H., Jr. Job enrichment versus traditional issues at the bargaining table: What union members want. *Academy of Management Journal,* 1978, *21,* 725–730.

62. Fein, M. Job enrichment: A reevaluation. *Sloan Management Review,* Winter 1974, *16,* 69–88.

63. Hackman, J.R., & Oldham, G.R. Motivation through the design of work: Test of a theory. *Organizational Behavior and Human Performance,* 1976, *16,* 250–279.

64. Hackman, J.R., & Oldham, G.R. *Work redesign.* Reading, Mass.: Addison-Wesley, 1980.

65. Hackman, J.R. Work design. In J.R. Hackman & J.L. Suttle (Eds.), *Improving life at work.* Santa Monica, Calif.: Goodyear, 1976, p. 103.

66. Job design on the assembly line: Farewell to blue-collar blues? *Organizational Dynamics,* 1973, *2*(2), 51–67.

67. Gyllenhammar, P.G. *People at work.* Reading, Mass.: Addison-Wesley, 1977.

68. Gyllenhammar, P.G. How Volvo adapts work to people. *Harvard Business Review,* July-August 1977, 102–113.

69. Ibid.

70. Goldman, R.B. *A work experiment: Six Americans in a Swedish plant.* New York: The Ford Foundation, 1976.

71. Gyllenhammar, P.G. How Volvo adapts work to people. *Harvard Business Review,* July-August 1977, 102–113.

72. Roberts, K.H., & Glick, W. The job characteristics approach to task design: A critical review. *Journal of Applied Psychology,* 1981, *66,* 193–217.

73. Orpen, C. The effects of job enrichment on employee satisfaction, motivation, involvement, and performance: A field experiment. *Human Relations,* 1979, *32,* 189–217.

74. Champoux, J.E. A three sample test of some extensions to the job characteristics model of work motivation. *Academy of Management Journal,* 1980, *23,* 466–478.

75. Hackman, J.R. Work design. In J.R. Hackman & J.L. Suttle (Eds.), *Improving life at work.* Santa Monica, Calif.: Goodyear, 1976, p. 103.

76. Ibid.

6

Perception:
Knowing the World Around Us

KEY CONCEPTS

Perception

Social Perception

Figure-Ground

Constancies

Illusions

Nonverbal Communication

Attribution

Actor-Observer Effect

Self-Serving Bias

Halo Effect

☐ ☐ ☐

Geotherm Oil has recently undergone a major shift in top management. The President and several of his key people left suddenly to accept attractive offers from a new and much smaller company. After intense negotiations with several candidates, a new chief executive has been appointed. Today, you've seen and heard him for the first time at a briefing held especially for junior-level executives such as yourself. At this meeting, the new President, Elton McGregor, introduced himself and outlined his long-range plans for the growth of the company. His talk ended about an hour ago, and now you and several of your friends have adjourned to a nearby bar to compare notes. John Felton starts the ball rolling with an upbeat remark: "Well, I think McGregor is pretty impressive. I liked his style—cool and in command, but approachable. He's a pretty good speaker, too. And I like his plans for the future. Yeah, all in all, I think we could have done a heck of a lot worse."

At this mild statement, Terri Hastings pushes her chair back from the table, looks at John in utter disbelief, and replies: "Hey, come off it, John, you must be kidding. You actually liked him*? I thought he was terrible. I mean, what a bore! And those ideas of his. He sounded like a walking cliché. If he follows through on some of those plans, I think we've got big trouble."*

Hank Sandursky breaks in. "Hmmm . . . I think that you're both all wet. He's not so great, but he's not a total disaster either. Just your ordinary, typical, $250,000-a-year man." At this remark, everyone laughs. (As usual, Hank is playing the role of tension-reducer.)

"But really," Terri continues, "He doesn't even look *like a company President. Short, dumpy, and that tie—I mean, you'd think he'd have better taste than that."*

John answers: "Are you serious? I thought he made a darn good appearance. What do you want, a movie star?"

The conversation continues as happy hour melts into early evening. It's obvious that everyone in the group has formed a sharply different first impression of the new President. But which one is most accurate? you wonder. . . .

Each of us assumes that we possess a clear and accurate view of reality. We feel that the world "out there" is pretty much the way we perceive it. This belief is very strong—so strong that under most conditions we don't give it much thought. Incidents like the one described above, however, serve to remind us that it isn't necessarily correct. Even when exposed to the same situation or event, different persons often report sharply different reactions. In short, they really *do* seem to look out on the world through different eyes (see Figure 6-1).

"Here's to the truth as perceived by you."

FIGURE 6-1   Perception: Seeing the World through Different Eyes

As suggested by this cartoon, individuals perceive the world around them in very different terms. (Source: Drawing by Vietor; © 1980 The New Yorker Magazine, Inc.)

In one sense, such diversity is beneficial. Different perspectives are in fact useful in many situations. But such diversity is also somewhat disconcerting. After all, learning that our views of the world contrast sharply with those of other persons—even ones with whom we are on close or intimate terms—can be quite unsettling. Such differences point to an important fact, central to the present discussion: in reality, we *don't* know the world around us in a simple and direct manner. Rather, our "picture" of it is actively constructed from information provided by our senses.[1]

The process through which we accomplish this task—that is, interpret and organize our sensory input—is termed **perception;** and it is upon this topic that we will focus in the present chapter. As you can readily see, perception often exerts powerful effects upon behavior. Indeed, it is probably safe to state that often, the way individuals act is largely a function of how they perceive the world around them. For example, returning to the incident at the beginning of the chapter, it is clear that because of her reactions to the new President, Terri may seriously begin looking for another position. In contrast, John will probably be content to remain just where he is, at least for the present. Thus, understanding the perceptions of these persons provides a useful clue to comprehending and predicting their overt behavior.

In our discussion of perception, we will first focus on this process as it applies to the physical world—how it helps us to make sense out of the countless stimuli around us. Then, we will examine **social perception,** the process through which we seek to know and understand other persons. As will soon become apparent, several aspects of social perception play a key role in organizational behavior and are well worthy of our careful attention.

PERCEIVING THE PHYSICAL WORLD

At any given moment, we are literally bombarded by input from our senses. Our eyes respond to many different wavelengths of light, our ears react to sounds of different pitch, and so on. Yet, we do not perceive the world as a random collection of such sensations. Rather, we recognize identifiable objects and orderly patterns of events. The basic reason for this lies in the fact that perception is an active process—one that imposes order and meaning on the vast array of sensations we experience. Generally, this process is so automatic that we are not aware of its existence. But careful study reveals that it involves strong tendencies toward *selectivity, organization,* and *constancy.*

Attention: Selectivity in Perception

If you've ever attended a noisy party, you are already familiar with the fact that perception is selective in nature. At such gatherings, you can easily screen out all of the voices around you except that of the person with whom you are conversing. While the words of this individual stand out and make sense, those of all the others present blend into the background and become an undifferentiated buzz. But if for some reason you decide that you wish to listen to what someone else is saying, you can readily shift your attention to *this* person. Indeed, you can even do so while continuing to look the first person in the eye—thus leading him to believe that he is still the center of your interest! But how, precisely, do we accomplish these impressive feats? More generally, what factors lead us to perceive certain stimuli, while ignoring many others? Basically, these seem to fall into two distinct categories, which can be described as internal and external in nature.

Internal factors affecting attention: The role of motives and learning. As suggested by the preceding example, we can often choose to pay attention to specific stimuli. In such cases, perception is truly an overt, active process. In many instances, however, it is affected by internal factors less directly under our control. First, it is often affected by current *motives.* For example, if you are hungry, you will be much more likely to notice restaurants, golden arches, billboards showing pictures of foods, and similar stimuli than if you are not hungry. Similar effects exist for many other motives as well. Thus, perception is often shaped and directed by these factors.

Second, perception is strongly influenced by learning and past experience. In essence, what we notice in a given situation is often shaped by our past history as an individual. Perhaps one example with direct implications for organizational behavior will help to clarify this important point. Imagine that three persons, an architect, a lawyer, and a real estate agent, approach a large building that is currently for sale. What will they notice? In all probability, distinctly different things. The architect may focus on the materials of which the building is constructed and on its overall style. The lawyer may notice that several new additions place it in violation of the zoning laws in this area. And the real estate agent may focus on its general condition and other factors that can affect its market price. In short, each person pays careful attention to different aspects of the same stimulus because training and experience orients him or her in these directions.

As you can probably guess, similar differences in perspective are quite common in large organizations. For example, in examining a competitor's product, marketing people may tend to notice features likely to appeal to prospective customers. Engineers may focus upon technical refinements. And production experts may concentrate on the steps used in its actual manufacture. As you can readily see, such differences in perspective can often lead to a serious lack of communication between such persons. Effective managers, of course, will take steps to avoid such problems. (For an example of such differences in perception, please see the **"CASE IN POINT"** box on pp. 164–165.)

External factors affecting attention.   In addition to the internal factors mentioned above, attention is often affected by external factors—various aspects of the stimuli themselves. That is, certain features of stimuli determine whether they are more or less likely to be noticed and perceived. Among the most important of these are *intensity, size, contrast, motion, and novelty.* In general, the more intense and larger a stimulus is, the more it stands out from its background, the more motion it shows, and the more novel it is, the more it tends to capture our attention. Advertisers are well aware of these basic principles and make much use of them in planning roadside signs, ads for magazines, and television commercials. Some intriguing applications of these principles are shown in Figure 6-2. As you can readily see, ignoring these stimuli would generally be a difficult task!

FIGURE 6-2   The Use of Attention-Getting Techniques in Advertising

Our attention is often captured by stimuli showing such characteristics as large size, motion, and novelty. For this reason, these techniques are often used in advertising. (Source: Photo [left] courtesy of the American Cancer Society; photo [right] by The Picture Cube.)

The Eye of the Beholder

It's 3:00 P.M., and some of the management of Pella, Inc., is gathered in the boardroom. The company runs a chain of stores specializing in luxury consumer goods (e.g., silver, crystal) and has been in business only eight years. The group is small, because Pella itself is small—a closely owned firm that has experienced steady but not dramatic growth. Everyone present has just witnessed a demonstration of the latest in automated office equipment, put on by a representative of Officetronics. Now, Pella's management must decide whether to order this equipment—a major step for a small company like theirs. Paul Pella, the CEO, starts the ball rolling: "Well, people, now you've seen the best. What do you say? Should we go with this stuff or not?"

Elena Kuczenka, head of Finance, is the first to reply. "Gee, I don't know, Paul. A lot depends on how quickly we can depreciate it. The tax laws on that sort of thing have just changed, so I'll have to do some careful checking. But you know our cash-flow situation right now. I think we should proceed with caution."

Next to answer is Bill Farrell, head of Marketing. "Well, I can understand Elena's concerns, but I'm all for it. I think it will be a big plus for sales. I can see the pitch now: Order from Pella, where efficiency is our middle name. We can feature pictures of our order people using this equipment in all our stores. And just think how great it will look in the annual report. That's something big stockholders like me weigh heavily!" At this everyone laughs, for Bill owns only a token number of shares in Pella.

Then, Joe Cohen, director of Personnel, comments: "It sure looks like nice stuff. But how long will it take people to learn to use it? I've heard some real horror stories about fancy word processors and computer equipment sitting around for months while everyone tries to figure out how to use them. I'll bet some of the

Organization in Perception

As we have already noted, we are rarely aware of single, isolated sensations. Rather, we tend to organize the information brought to us by our senses into meaningful patterns. Such organization generally occurs in accordance with several basic principles.

Perceptual grouping. A considerable body of research suggests that we possess powerful, innate tendencies to organize stimuli in certain ways. Several of these tendencies are illustrated in Figure 6-3. As you can see, we tend to group isolated stimuli together on the basis of *proximity* (nearness), *similarity, closure,* and *continuity.* In other words, we tend to perceive separate stimuli as clustering

people in the showrooms and warehouse will have their problems. I think we should go slow too."

Ben Turrell, the office manager at company headquarters, uses Joe's remarks as a starting point: "I agree with Joe. We ought to look into the training aspect. And another thing—there won't be a processor for everyone, right? So who gets what? You can sure stir up a lot of trouble when some people in an office have fancy new equipment and others don't."

After hearing these comments, Paul Pella chuckles. Then he answers: "Predictable, totally predictable. Elena zeros in on the tax aspects. Bill sees it as a marketing ploy, and Joe and Ben are worried about their people, just like a couple of doting mothers. I guess we all see the world through different eyes, eh? Well, I'm in favor of ordering this equipment for two reasons. First, I think it will pay for itself in increased productivity. Second, I think it's just good for our image. After all, our competitors installed it last year. . . . "   □

Questions:

1. All the people listed above watched the same demonstration of precisely the same equipment. Why did they focus on different aspects of it and react in such contrasting ways?
2. Do you think the fact that all these people noticed different things is a "plus" or a "minus" for the decision-making process?
3. Was the CEO wise in asking all these individuals to attend the demonstration and give their reactions? Or should he have simply had a private demonstration and reached his own conclusions?

together when they are near one another, when they are similar in some manner, and when organizing them in this fashion allows us to complete some relatively simple pattern.

Please note that the principles we have been discussing do not apply solely to simple stimuli such as the ones shown in Figure 6-3. Actually, they appear to be quite general in nature. For example, if several persons work near each other in a factory, they may be perceived as a "unit" by their manager, even if there is no rational basis for making this assumption. And then, he or she may be tempted to treat them all in the same fashion, despite large differences in their productivity, absenteeism, diligence, and so on. Similarly, when various issues are discussed, there is often a strong tendency to perceive everyone involved as being either

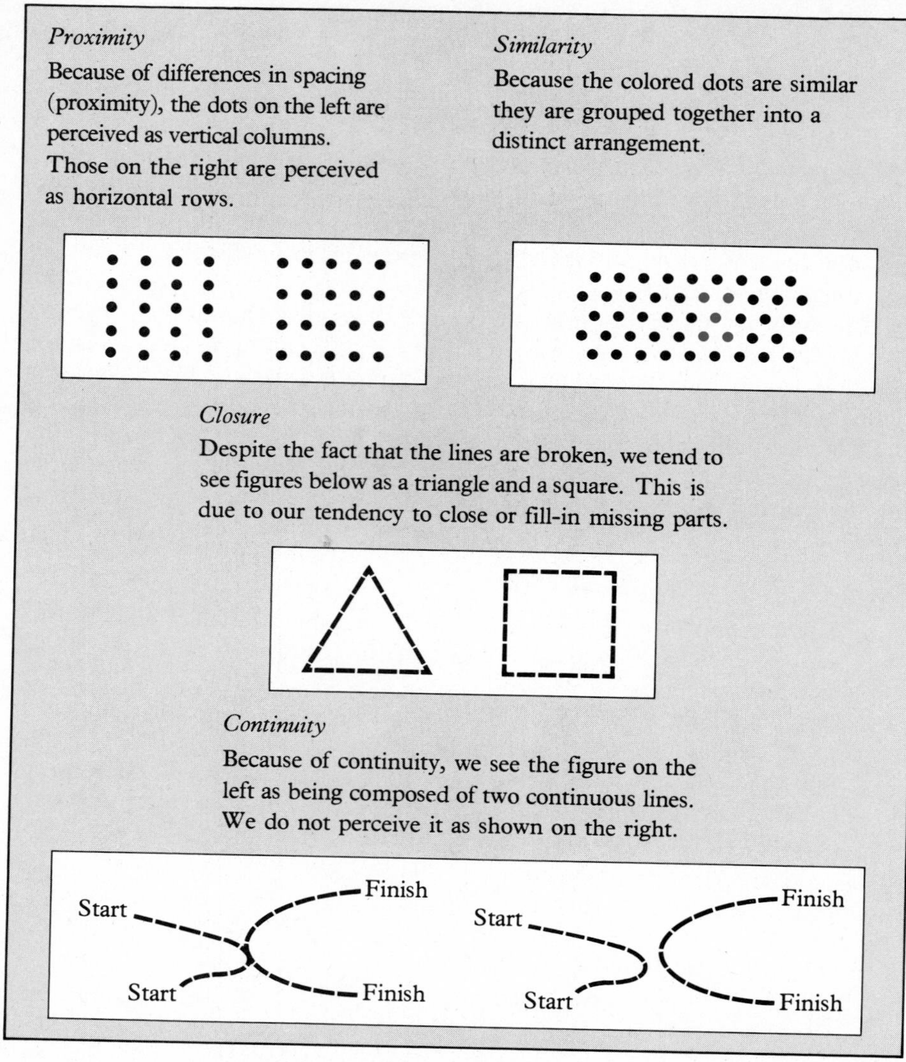
Proximity
Because of differences in spacing (proximity), the dots on the left are perceived as vertical columns. Those on the right are perceived as horizontal rows.
Similarity
Because the colored dots are similar they are grouped together into a distinct arrangement.
Closure
Despite the fact that the lines are broken, we tend to see figures below as a triangle and a square. This is due to our tendency to close or fill-in missing parts.
Continuity
Because of continuity, we see the figure on the left as being composed of two continuous lines. We do not perceive it as shown on the right.
Start
Finish
Start
Finish
Start
Finish
Start
Finish

FIGURE 6-3 Principles of Perceptual Grouping

We seem to possess built-in tendencies to group separate stimuli together on the basis of certain principles. Four of these are illustrated here.

"pro" or "anti," despite the fact that many different views or positions actually exist. (This is the familiar "you're either with us or against us" syndrome.) In these and many other cases, the general rule we seem to follow in forming perceptions of the world around us is this: Find—and use—the simplest pattern available.

Figure-ground. Another basic organizing principle in perception relates to our tendency to perceive any scene as consisting of objects (figure) and the space between them, or background (ground). For example, as you read this page, you do not perceive a random mixture of black marks and white space. Rather, you perceive letters or words standing out from a white background. The tendency to divide the world into figure and ground appears to be innate. When persons blind from birth recover their sight suddenly, through an operation or other form of medical treatment, they quickly show the **figure-ground** distinction.[2]

Intriguing illustrations of our tendency to divide the world into figure and ground are provided by reversible or *ambiguous figures,* visual patterns in which figure and ground can be readily interchanged. One of these is presented in Figure 6-4. When you first examine this drawing, you will probably see irregular colored shapes, separated by white spaces. But now, concentrate on the spaces themselves, and try to make *these* stand out as figures. When you do, you will soon form an entirely different perception. Actually, drawings such as this one serve to emphasize a basic point we have been attempting to make throughout this discussion. The physical world presents us with a complex array of stimuli and sensations. However, the patterns and organizations we perceive in these stimuli are largely of our own making.

Constancies: Invariance in a Changing World

In the case of both perceptual grouping and figure-ground relationships, we may be viewed as *adding* something to the information brought to us by our senses. That is, we impose our own internally generated order on sensations that do not intrinsically possess such organization. In contrast, another aspect of perception, known as **constancies,** may be viewed as involving a process in which we ignore or overlook certain aspects of our sensory experience. While this might at first appear to be wasteful or inefficient, it actually yields highly beneficial results. Briefly, it permits us to perceive various stimuli as constant and unchanging, even when the patterns of sensations they yield vary greatly. Several different perceptual constancies exist involving the *size, shape,* and *color* of physical objects.

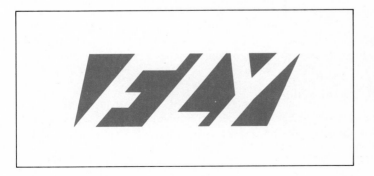

FIGURE 6-4 Figure-Ground: A Quick Demonstration

Concentrate on the colored shapes. Do they form any recognizable pattern? Now, try concentrating on the white spaces between the colored shapes. The sudden shift you probably experienced provides a good illustration of our tendency to organize the world into figure and ground.

Size constancy.   As you approach or move away from any object (e.g., a car, a tree, another person), the visual sensations it produces change. As you move toward it, the object casts a larger and larger image on your *retina* (the light-sensitive layer at the back of your eyes). As you withdraw, it casts an image of decreasing size. Yet, despite these changes, you do not perceive the object as varying in size. This is the phenomenon known as *size constancy.* One explanation for such constancy is that in estimating the size of any object we take both the extent of its visual image *and* its apparent distance into account. Thus, if two objects produce the same size image on your retina, the one that seems farther away will be perceived as larger. As with many aspects of perception, size constancy is largely automatic—it requires no active thought in most situations.

Shape constancy.   When you view various objects from different angles, they cast differently shaped images upon the retina. For example, a pen casts a round image when viewed from the top, but an elongated one when seen from the side. Despite these varying images, however, we do not perceive the objects themselves as changing in shape. Such *shape constancy* stems from the fact that, normally, experience makes us familiar with all the visual images a given object is likely to produce. Because of such familiarity, we then recognize each as relating to the same stable item. Only when we view an object from a new perspective do we show any confusion or doubt about what is being viewed.

Color constancy.   During the course of a single day, you may move back and forth between sunlight, fluorescent light, incandescent light, and perhaps (if you are lucky!) even candlelight. In each case, the rays of light reflected by your skin, hair, and clothing differ. Yet, in general, you do not perceive the color of these objects as changing. This phenomenon is known as *color constancy,* and, like both size and shape constancy, it is largely automatic in nature. That is, we seem to compensate for changes in illumination automatically when judging the color of various objects.

Together, the three types of perceptual constancy just described add a considerable degree of stability to our perceptions of the physical world. As you can probably see, such stability is quite useful to us. Without it, many forms of behavior, including jobs involving visual judgments or eye-hand coordination, would be very difficult. (For example, imagine the problems workers would face if they had to stop and identify their tools each time these were viewed from a different visual angle.) In the case of the perceptual constancies, then, our ability to overlook certain types of sensory information is actually quite adaptive.

Illusions: When Perception Fails

In our discussion of perception so far, we have emphasized the adaptive value of this basic process. In a sense, this is only reasonable. Generally, perception *is* adaptive: it helps us to interpret and make sense out of a complex and often confusing world. Before concluding, however, we should note that perception sometimes fails. That is, it leads us into errors concerning the world around us—errors that can have important consequences. We have already hinted at this fact in our discussion of perceptual selectivity. As you may recall, at that time we noted that perception can be strongly affected by our motives, expectancies, or experience. As a result, we may often perceive what we *want* to perceive or *expect* to perceive—not what actually exists. Perhaps the most dramatic illustrations of the fallibility of perception, however, are provided by **illusions.**

Illusions are simply perceptions not in accord with the true characteristics of an object or an event.[3] You are already familiar with several of these from your own experience. For example, have you ever noticed that the moon looks much larger when it is near the horizon than when it is overhead? Obviously, this must be an illusion; the moon does not change in size as it moves around the earth. Yet, even knowing this fact does not prevent the illusion from occurring. The moon *still* looks larger when on the horizon. Other illusions you have probably encountered are shown in Figure 6-5. If you pull out a ruler as you examine this figure, you'll soon find that sometimes you really *can't* trust your own eyes. In each case, your perceptions of the objects shown are quite inaccurate.

The basis for such illusions is quite straightforward. They arise when we apply rules that usually work—that usually yield accurate perceptions—in situations where this is not the case. For example, consider the moon illusion once again. Past experience has taught us that the horizon is quite far away. When the moon is near the horizon, it outlines and is clearly behind objects that are on the horizon (e.g., trees, buildings, etc.). Thus, there are strong perceptual cues suggesting that the moon must be very far away—further away than the horizon. For this reason, we perceive it as being large in size. When the moon is overhead, however, such cues are missing. The result: we perceive it as being somewhat smaller. Corresponding explanations exist for other visual illusions. In each case, they arise because we automatically follow rules of perceptual processing that usually work but that don't apply in the situation in question.

Illusions and other instances in which perception fails provide a powerful illustration of a major point we have made before, but which bears repeating. Despite our subjective feelings to the contrary, we do *not* know the world around us in a direct and simple manner. Rather, we actually construct an image or representation of it through an active perceptual process. This process, in turn, is strongly affected by our past experience, our motives, and our expectancies. Since these factors are unique for each person, the perceptual world we each construct is also, in some respects, unique. And therein lies a key message for managers and others who must deal with human beings on a regular basis. Since people really *do* perceive the world in distinct and different ways, it is crucial to take careful account of this fact. If you do not, you may run a very real risk of encountering misunderstandings, failures to communicate, confusion—or worse!

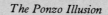

The Ponzo Illusion

Which of these three figures is largest?
If you measure them with a ruler, you will see that they are actually equal in size.

The Muller-Lyer Illusion

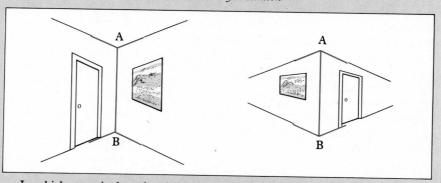

In which room is the colored line (A - B) longer?
If you measure both with a ruler, you will find that they are equal in length.

FIGURE 6-5   Illusions: Perception Gone Astray

Two well-known visual illusions. In both, our perceptions are not in accord with physical reality.

SOCIAL PERCEPTION: PERCEIVING—AND KNOWING—OTHER PERSONS

Accurate perceptions of the physical world are important. Indeed, without them we could not survive for very long. But important as such knowledge is, it is not, by itself, enough. In order to function effectively in a complex human society, we also need something else: accurate perceptions of the persons around us. Specifically, we require knowledge of their behavior, current moods, motives, and major traits. Information of this type is extremely useful and assists us in attaining predictable, orderly relations with others. Thus, we often expend considerable effort in our attempts to obtain it. The process through which we gather such knowledge is known as *social perception* and it often *does* yield accurate perceptions of other persons. As is the case with perception of the physical world, however, it is also subject to sources of error, bias, and distortion. In the present section, we will examine several aspects of social perception—aspects directly related to organizational behavior. Among these are **nonverbal communication** and **attribution.** (We will reserve discussion of another important topic, *stereotypes,* for Chapter 7.)

Nonverbal Communication: Perceiving the Temporary States of Others

One of the major tasks we face in our attempts to form accurate perceptions of the persons around us involves knowledge of their temporary states—their moods and emotions. Accurate information of this type can be very useful to us, for behavior is often strongly affected by such reactions. Individuals tend to behave very differently when they are in a good mood than when they are in a bad one. And their relations with us may vary greatly depending on whether they are experiencing anger, joy, sorrow, or some other emotion. Thus, knowing something about the current moods or feelings of others can often help us to interact with them in more desirable ways.

In many cases, we learn about the moods and emotions of other persons in a straightforward way: they simply tell us how they feel. In other instances, though, they do not provide such information—or they may seek to conceal their true reactions. Even then we can often learn much about them through careful observation of certain *nonverbal cues.* That is, we can still learn how they feel by studying their facial expressions, the position and movement of their bodies, and the pattern of their eye contact with us. But what, precisely, do such cues reveal? As we will now suggest, a great deal.

Facial expressions as guides to the emotional reactions of others. Perhaps the most obvious source of information about others' emotional states is their facial expression. It has long been assumed that emotions are mirrored on the face and can be "read" there with a high degree of accuracy. Recent research findings lend support to this view: most people do seem capable of identifying the emotional states of others—even total strangers—from their facial expressions.[4] In addition, such research has also revealed much more about the nature and role of this important nonverbal cue.

First, it appears that several facial expressions are universal in nature. That is, all over the world, people smile when they are happy and frown when they are sad, regardless of their specific culture.[5] Similarly, specific facial expressions are recognized as signs of the same underlying emotions everywhere. Taken together, these findings indicate that, in contrast to spoken language, the language of the face generally requires no interpreter.

Second, it has been found that distinct facial expressions relating to such emotions as happiness, sadness, surprise, fear, anger, and disgust arise very early in life. In fact, they are present by the time infants are only three or four months old.[6] The very early appearance of such expressions underscores their importance in human behavior.

Third, growing evidence indicates that human beings are often quite adept at distorting or changing their facial expressions in order to mislead others about their true emotional states. For example, individuals can often *falsify* their facial expressions—pretending to experience some feeling they don't have, showing no emotion when they are actually experiencing one, or substituting one reaction for another. Similarly, they can *modulate* their expressions so as to suggest that they are experiencing more or less of an emotion than is really the case.[7]

All of us seem to develop some degree of skill in these techniques. But as you can probably guess, certain groups of people become especially skilled in their use. For example, actors and confidence artists earn their living by accurately feigning (and concealing) various emotions. Similarly, diplomats, attorneys, politicians, physicians, and salespersons all find facial deceit helpful in their work. (See Figure 6-6 for an illustration of this fact.) And since practice does often make perfect, they frequently become quite expert in its use. Fortunately, addi-

FIGURE 6-6   Facial Deceit: A Useful Technique for Concealing Our Emotions

Because they often find it useful to disguise their true emotions, diplomats, attorneys, politicians, and salespersons often become highly skilled at facial deceit. (Source: UPI photo.)

TABLE 6-1   Detecting Facial Deceit

By paying careful attention to the cues described here, we can often recognize facial deceit on the part of others.

CUE	DESCRIPTION
Gaps in Total Pattern of Facial Reaction	One part of face suggests a given emotion, the other part does not. (Example: eyebrows are raised in surprise, but the mouth is not open as it usually is in genuine surprise.)
Timing of Facial Reaction	Genuine emotional reactions are mirrored on the face very quickly. If the interval between the emotion-provoking event and appearance of facial expression is too long, deceit should be suspected.
Microexpressions	Fleeting facial expressions (fraction of a second) that appear before deceit can be instituted. These may reveal true emotional reactions.

tional studies suggest that even the disguises of such persons can be penetrated if we pay careful attention to certain subtle cues. Some of these are summarized for you in Table 6-1. You may want to consider these carefully; after all, by keeping a careful watch for them, you can often avoid being "taken in" by others.

Gazes and stares.   Ancient poets frequently described the eyes as "windows to the soul." In an important sense, they were correct: we do seem to learn a great deal about others' internal states from the pattern of their eye contact with us. First, we use such cues as an index of other persons' overall emotional state. If they meet our gaze frequently and without hesitation, we often assume that they are experiencing positive emotions. If, instead, they try to avoid such eye contact, we usually conclude that they are experiencing some negative state, such as guilt or depression.[8]

Second, and perhaps of greater importance, we use the pattern of others' gazes as an indication of their feelings about us or other persons. In general, we interpret a high level of eye contact as a sign of friendliness and liking. A very low level of gazing, in contrast, is often interpreted as a sign of unfriendliness. Research findings confirm our beliefs in this regard: couples who report being in love spend more time gazing into each others' eyes than those who are only dating or who are strangers.[9] Thus, it does appear that eye contact is a useful guide to others' positive and negative feelings toward us.

At this point we should note that there is one important exception to the general rule that a high level of eye contact is suggestive of positive emotions or feelings. This exception is *staring.* As you probably know from your own experience, being stared at by others is unpleasant—something we prefer to avoid. The reason

for these negative reactions is clear: when another person gazes at us in a continuous manner and maintains such contact regardless of what we do, we interpret
this behavior as a sign of anger or hostility. And then, we generally react in one of
two ways: we accept this provocation or challenge and become angry ourselves, or
we seek to withdraw and avoid trouble.[10] Only if other factors place the stare in a
different context (e.g., as part of a plea for help) will we respond in other ways.[11]

In sum, others' eyes do often tell us much about their current mood, emotions,
or feelings. Little wonder, then, that we often pay close attention to this crucial
nonverbal cue.

Body language: Movements, gestures, and posture. Have you ever
shaken your fist at another person in anger or shifted your posture to sit very erect
when an important person entered the room? If so, you already know that individuals often reveal much about their current feelings through their bodies (see
Figure 6–7). Since slightly different information is provided by body movements,
gestures, and posture, we will mention all three.

Imagine that during an interview, the person being questioned moved about a
great deal. She fidgeted continuously, crossed and uncrossed her legs, clasped and
unclasped her hands, and so on. What would you conclude? Probably, you would
decide that she was quite nervous or ill at ease. This conclusion would probably
be correct, for one of the most important messages conveyed by body movements
involves overall arousal or tension. The higher the level of such movement shown
by another person, the more emotionally aroused or tense he or she generally is.
The moral in this finding is clear: When *you* are interviewed, try to avoid a high
level of body movement; if you engage in a great deal of such behavior, it may
well count against you.

While body movements reveal much about other persons' general level of
arousal or tension, more specific information on their emotional states is provided

FIGURE 6–7   Body Language: A Revealing Source of Nonverbal Cues

As suggested by this comic strip, individuals often reveal much about their current
emotional states through the movements and posture of their bodies. (Source: © 1980
King Features Syndicate, Inc. World Rights Reserved.)

by *gestures.* These are movements, often involving the hands or arms, that convey a specific meaning in a particular culture.[12] For example, in the United States, shaking one's finger at another person is usually a sign of irritation or annoyance; waving one's arm back and forth with the palm facing outward often means "Stop" or "No more"; and pointing one's thumb downward and moving the hand up and down indicates rejection or simply "No!" Gestures of this type exist in all societies; but, as you might expect, they vary greatly from one part of the world to another. This can create problems when diplomats or business people from various cultures meet. If they are not careful, they may well misinterpret one another's nonverbal cues.

Finally we should note that another person's overall posture—the position of his or her body—can often tell us much about emotional states. When others slump over, this can be a sign of depression or lack of interest or simply fatigue. And when they sit upright, attention and interest are suggested. Further, if two people seem to lean toward one another at a party or during a meeting, this is often an accurate sign of liking between them; the opposite reaction is suggestive of negative feelings.[13]

To conclude: body movements, gestures, and posture can tell us much about other persons. Often, they reveal others' emotions, communicate specific messages, and tell us how they feel about us. Given the usefulness of such information, it is clear that learning to "read" this unspoken language can be quite worthwhile. (For a clear illustration of the impact of nonverbal cues on important aspects of organizational behavior, see the **"FOCUS"** box on pp. 176–177.)

Communication through the use of physical space: Office design as a nonverbal cue. That human beings can communicate with others through facial expressions, gestures, eye contact, and body posture is hardly surprising. We have all had considerable experience with this nonverbal language and have learned (albeit to varying degrees) to both read and use it. But this is not the only technique available to us for communicating without words. Another, and perhaps more unexpected method involves the way we use physical space. Such communication is most readily apparent in organizations with respect to office layout or design. As you have probably observed, different persons arrange the furniture in their offices in contrasting ways. Do these differences tell us anything about them? Apparently, they do. The findings of a number of recent studies on this topic suggest that such differences can exert important effects upon the feelings of visitors and can also influence their perceptions of the office occupant. For example, it appears that visitors often feel more welcome and comfortable in offices where the desk is placed against the wall (an *open* arrangement) than in ones where it is placed between the occupant and visitors (a *closed* arrangement).[14,15] Similarly, visitors report perceiving office occupants as friendlier, more extroverted, and more interested in being of service in open offices than in closed ones (see Figure 6-9). Interestingly, neatness, too, seems to count. Thus, individuals feel more welcome in offices that are relatively neat than they do in ones that are either extremely neat or untidy. And they perceive persons with moderately neat

FOCUS ON BEHAVIOR

Nonverbal Communication and Organizational Behavior: Impact on Employment Interviews

Throughout our discussion of nonverbal communication, we have tried to call attention to the relevance of this subtle process for organizational behavior. In this regard, we noted that many persons practice facial deceit and provided you with some hints on how to penetrate such tactics. Similarly, we suggested that a high level of eye contact (except in the case of staring) can be used to communicate friendliness and positive feelings—messages you may find important in many situations. And we also noted that some forms of body language are best avoided, especially if you do not wish to appear nervous or ill at ease.

We believe that all of these applications to O.B. are important and may be quite useful to you in the years ahead. Before concluding our discussion of this intriguing topic, however, we wish to provide a more direct and specific illustration of the importance of nonverbal communication in organizational settings. In particular, we will now describe evidence suggesting that this aspect of social perception can play an extremely important role in employment interviews.

The impact of nonverbal communication on interviews has recently been studied in a systematic manner by Imada and Hakel.[16] These researchers asked subjects (undergraduate women) to conduct short employment interviews with a stranger. Actually, the person interviewed was an accomplice of the investigators, who had been trained to behave in one of two contrasting styles during the session. In one condition, she engaged in many nonverbal actions designed to induce positive reactions on the part of the interviewer. For example, she smiled at this person, sat upright, showed a high level of eye contact, and oriented her body directly toward the interviewer. In another condition, in contrast, she

engaged in nonverbal behaviors designed to induce less favorable reactions by the interviewer. Here, she did not smile, slouched in her chair, avoided eye contact, and oriented her body away from the interviewer.

After the session was over, the interviewer-subjects were asked to rate the accomplice on a number of job-related dimensions. These included the likelihood that she would be successful on the job, her competence, her level of motivation, her qualifications, and their overall recommendation about hiring her. It was predicted that subjects' reactions would be much more favorable when the accomplice engaged in positive nonverbal actions than when she engaged in negative ones. As you can see from Figure 6–8, results offered strong support for this prediction. On every dimension, the interviewee was rated more favorably when she performed positive nonverbal behaviors than when she performed negative ones. Indeed, this was even true with respect to ratings of her qualifications and motivation.

These findings have important implications for individuals seeking employment and for persons who conduct job-related interviews. With respect to interviewees, they suggest that efforts to present oneself in a positive nonverbal light may often reap handsome rewards. Indeed, success in this respect may often go a long way toward producing a favorable first impression. For interviewers, these results point to the need for caution: be on guard against placing too much emphasis on nonverbal cues. And certainly don't permit them to overwhelm other factors, such as an interviewee's qualifications or past experience. Regardless of whose perspective is considered, though, one fact is clear: nonverbal cues often exert a powerful effect upon this important form of organizational behavior.   □

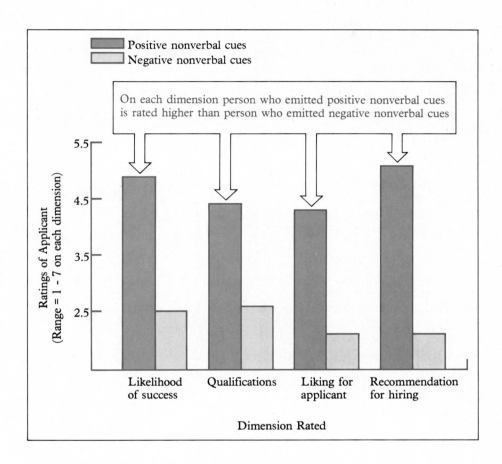

FIGURE 6-8   Nonverbal Cues and Employment Interviews

Interviewers responded much more favorably to an individual who emitted positive
nonverbal cues (e.g., a high degree of eye contact, alert posture) than to one who emitted
negative nonverbal cues (low eye contact, slouching posture). These findings suggest that
nonverbal cues may play a key role in many employment interviews. (Source: Based on
data from Imada & Hakel, *Journal of Applied Psychology,* 1977, *62,* 295–300.)

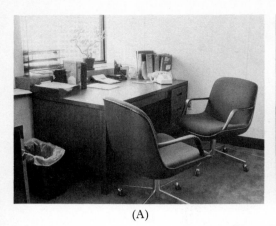 

(A)   (B)

FIGURE 6-9   Office Design: What Does It Reveal?

In which of these two offices, (A) or (B), do you think you would feel most welcome or comfortable? And which office do you think belongs to a person you would describe as being friendly and extroverted? Research findings suggest that you will probably answer (A) to both questions. (Source: Photos © Frank Siteman MCMLXXXII.)

offices as friendlier, higher in confidence, and more interested in helping than those with either very neat or untidy ones. On two other dimensions, though, having an extremely neat office may be a plus: persons with such offices are perceived as being busier and more organized than those with less neat ones.

Together, these findings suggest that the way in which you arrange your office, its neatness, and several other factors (e.g., the presence of status symbols, type of lighting) can communicate important messages about you to visitors. Further, there appear to be many trade-offs in this respect, so that no single arrangement is best. Rather, depending upon the type of information or "image" you wish to transmit, different approaches may be most useful. Unfortunately, we do not yet possess sufficient knowledge about the impact of office design to offer firm or general recommendations. One fact, though, is already clear: this subtle form of communication exists, and is probably well worth taking into account.

Attribution: Understanding the Causes of Others' Behavior

Accurate perception of others' emotions is often very useful. Yet, where social perception is concerned, it is only part of the total picture. Behavior is indeed often affected by current emotions or feelings. But it also stems from other, more lasting sources as well. For example, individuals often behave in certain ways not because they are experiencing a particular emotion, but because they possess certain traits or hold various motives and intentions. Information on such issues is essential if we are to understand other persons and predict their future actions.

But how do we go about acquiring such knowledge? In short, how do we form accurate perceptions of the causes behind others' behavior?

This complex process, generally known as *attribution,* has been a major topic of research in organizational behavior and related fields for several years. The volume of this work has been great—so great that we cannot possibly examine more than a small portion of it here.[17] In the discussion that follows, therefore, we will simply seek to acquaint you with aspects of attribution that seem directly relevant to organizational behavior. First, we will focus on *causal attribution,* a basic topic in attribution theory and research. The key question addressed here is as follows: how do we determine whether another's behavior stems mainly from internal causes (e.g., his or her traits and motives) or largely from external factors (e.g., situational conditions or luck). Second, we will examine several potential *sources of bias or error* in the attribution process. Unfortunately, these are quite common and can yield serious consequences in many settings. Finally, we will turn to specific findings concerning the role of attribution in organizational settings.

Causal attribution: How we answer the question "Why?"   Sometimes, individuals act the way they do because of *internal* causes. That is, their traits, abilities, motives, and similar factors lead them to behave in some manner. On other occasions, however, they act in specific ways mainly because of *external* causes. For example, situational constraints may make it impossible for them to behave in any other fashion. In our attempts to understand the persons around us, we are often concerned with this distinction. Two major reasons account for our interest in this regard. The first has to do with the informativeness of others' behavior. If they act as they do largely because of internal factors, then their actions tell us much about them as unique individuals; after all, this is the way they have *chosen* to behave. However, if they act as they do largely because of external factors, their behavior is far less informative. Under other circumstances, they might well behave very differently. The second reason for our interest in such causality involves the assignment of personal responsibility. If others act the way they do largely because of internal factors, we tend to hold them responsible for their behavior and for any outcomes it produces. If their actions stem mainly from external sources, in contrast, we are far less likely to assign such responsibility.

But given that we have important reasons for wondering about the causes of others' behavior, how do we go about attaining such knowledge? In short, how do we seek to determine whether others' actions stem mainly from internal or external causes? One widely accepted answer has been offered by Harold Kelley, a noted expert on attribution.[18]

According to Kelley, our attempts to answer the question "why" about other persons' behavior lead us to focus on three major factors. First, we consider *consensus,* the extent to which other individuals behave in a similar manner (in this situation) to the person in question. Second, we consider *consistency,* the extent to which this person behaves in the same manner on other occasions. And third, we consider *distinctiveness,* the extent to which this person acts in the same manner in other situations. Kelley further suggests that we are most likely to attribute another person's behavior to internal causes under conditions of low consensus, high consistency, and low distinctiveness. In contrast, we are most likely to attribute another's behavior to external causes under conditions of high consensus, high consistency, and high distinctiveness. (Please see Figure 6-10 for a summary of these suggestions.) Perhaps a concrete example will help us to illustrate the very reasonable nature of Kelley's theory.

Suppose that one day you attend the weekly staff meeting held by your department. During this meeting, one of your fellow employees continuously interrupts the proceedings. She asks one question after another, comments at length upon

FIGURE 6-10   Kelley's Theory of Causal Attribution

According to a theory proposed by Kelley, we take three different factors into account in deciding whether another person's behavior stems mainly from internal or external causes. These are *consensus, consistency,* and *distinctiveness.*

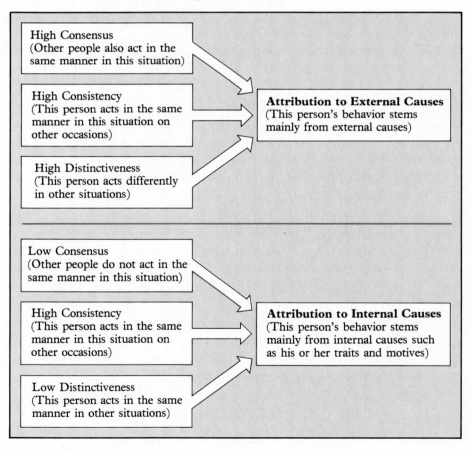

fairly trivial matters, and makes several silly jokes. Is her behavior due to internal or external causes? According to Kelley, your decision in this regard would depend upon the three factors mentioned earlier. Let us consider two contrasting patterns. First, assume that the following conditions prevail: (1) no one else acts in the same manner as this person (consensus is low), (2) you have seen her act in the same manner at other staff meetings (consistency is high), and (3) you have seen this person act in a similar manner at other types of meetings and in other situations (distinctiveness is low). Under these conditions, you would probably attribute her behavior to *internal* causes. For example, you might conclude that she likes to be the center of attention or simply enjoys long and tedious meetings.

Now, in contrast, assume that the following set of conditions exist: (1) several other members of your department act in the same manner during the meeting as this person (consensus is high), (2) you have seen her act in this manner at other staff meetings (consistency is high), and (3) you have seen this person act differently at other meetings and in other situations (distinctiveness is high). Here, Kelley predicts that you would attribute her behavior to *external* causes. That is, you might conclude that there is something about these staff meetings that induces such behavior among participants. (Perhaps they are so dull that the only hope is to stir things up a bit by asking questions and generating discussion.)

By now, the basic nature of Kelley's theory should be clear. In concluding our discussion of it, we wish to make two additional points. First, Kelley's suggestions have generally been confirmed in many different experiments.[19] Thus, his theory does offer a useful account of the manner in which we decide whether others' behavior stems mainly from internal or external factors. Second, it is important to note that our attributions in this regard have important implications for organizational behavior. For example, in evaluating a subordinate's performance, it is crucial to know whether it stems mainly from internal causes such as ability, or from external factors such as some aspect of the tasks being performed. We will soon return to this and to other applications of attribution theory to organizational behavior. For the moment, though, permit us to leave you with one final thought: the question of "why" is important for understanding the behavior of other persons in many different settings, and organizations are definitely no exception to this rule.

Causal attribution: Some potential sources of bias. So far, our discussion of causal attribution seems to suggest that it is a highly rational process. Presumably, we combine information about consensus, consistency, and distinctiveness in a totally logical manner and, on this basis, reach conclusions about the causes of others' behavior. Unfortunately, this is not actually the case. Causal attribution appears to be subject to important forms of bias—built-in tendencies that can distort the process and lead us into serious error. Two of these will now be considered.

The actor-observer difference. The first and perhaps most important source of bias we will consider can be readily illustrated. Imagine that, while going to work one day, you see another person rush toward an elevator, trip, and fall. How would you explain this behavior? While we can't say for sure, the chances are good that you would explain it in terms of this person's traits. You might conclude that he is careless or clumsy and often trips over his own feet when in a hurry. In short, you would attribute his actions mainly to internal causes. But now suppose that on another occasion the same thing happened to you. Would you explain your own mishap in the same manner? Probably you would not. Instead, you might assume that *you* tripped and fell because of external causes. For example, you might conclude that you stumbled because the floors in your building are waxed too often and are extremely slippery.

This tendency to attribute our own behavior to external or situational causes but that of others to internal causes—generally known as the *actor-observer difference* or **actor-observer effect**—has been noted in many different experiments.[20] For example, in one intriguing study on this issue, Nisbett and his colleagues asked male students to write brief paragraphs explaining why they liked their current girlfriends and why they had chosen their college major.[21] In addition, subjects were also asked to write similar paragraphs explaining why their best friend liked *his* girlfriend and had chosen *his* major. Both sets of paragraphs were then examined to determine how many situational or dispositional (internal) causes were mentioned. When this was done, large differences were noted between the paragraphs subjects wrote about themselves and the ones they wrote about their friends. In explaining their own choice of girlfriend or major, they tended to emphasize external factors (their girl's looks or behavior, the financial opportunities offered by the field they had chosen). In explaining their friend's choices, in contrast, they tended to emphasize internal causes (his need for a certain type of companion, personal traits that suited him for a specific field, etc.).

Similar effects have been obtained in many other studies. Thus, the actor-observer effect appears to be a real one. But why does it occur? One interesting explanation focuses on the fact that we usually possess different information about our own behavior and that of others.[22] We know that *we* have acted differently in other situations and realize that we would probably change our behavior under other circumstances. This knowledge of our own variability leads us to attribute our actions primarily to external causes. In contrast, unless we know someone else very well, we usually know little about their past behavior. Faced with this lack of information, we tend to assume that they have always acted very much as they do now. In short, we conclude that their behavior stems mainly from stable traits or other internal causes.

Regardless of the precise source of the actor-observer effect, it can lead us into serious attributional errors. On the one hand, it encourages us to overlook consistencies in our own actions—consistencies that might be quite revealing about our own personalities and abilities. On the other, it leads us to overestimate the stability of other persons' behavior. And this can set us up for some very unsettling surprises. We will comment further on the implications of these and related errors for organizational behavior in the **"PERSPECTIVE"** box on pages 186–187.

The self-serving bias: Taking credit for success, avoiding blame for failure.
While our tendency to perceive our own behavior as stemming mainly from situational factors seems to be quite general, it is sometimes overridden by a second
type of error in causal attribution, a form known as the **self-serving bias.** This
refers to our strong tendency to take credit for good or positive behaviors and
outcomes, while denying responsibility for bad or negative ones. In short, we tend
to attribute positive behaviors or results to internal causes—our own traits, effort,
or ability. But we attribute negative behaviors or outcomes to external causes—
other persons, the situation, bad luck, and so on. Both of these tendencies are easy
to spot. For example, imagine that you write a report for your boss, and she likes
it very much. How would you explain this outcome? Probably, you would assume
that it stemmed from such factors as your high level of intelligence, the hard work
you devoted to the report, and so on. But now, imagine that she rejects the report
as inadequate. How would you explain *this* result? The chances are good that you
would perceive it as stemming from external factors—her unreasonably high
standards, the extreme difficulty of the task, the lack of clear instructions about
what was needed, and similar causes. In short, we seem to be all too ready to take
full, internal credit for success but to deny personal responsibility for failure.

This self-serving or *hedonic* bias has been observed in a large number of experiments.[23] One of the most interesting of these, largely because it demonstrates the
operation of such bias in a real-life context, was conducted by Lau and Russell.[24]
These researchers examined newspaper articles dealing with major sports events
in order to locate statements by players and coaches about the causes of their
teams' wins or losses. Such statements were then coded as referring either to internal or external factors. Lau and Russell predicted that a self-serving bias would
be apparent in these remarks. That is, statements about wins would generally refer to internal causal factors (the players' skill, their high motivation); statements
about losses, however, would be more likely to mention external causes (actions
by the other team, poor condition of the playing field). As you can see from Figure 6-11, results offered support for these predictions. Players and coaches did
tend to explain wins largely in terms of internal factors, and they were more willing to refer to external ones in explaining losses. As you can probably guess, the
self-serving bias has important implications for organizational behavior. Please
refer to the **"PERSPECTIVE"** box on pages 186-187 for a discussion of some
of these.

Halo effects: Another source of bias in social perception. Before concluding our discussion of sources of bias in social perception, we will briefly mention one more: the **halo effect.** This term refers to the fact that once we form an
overall impression of another person, this global reaction may exert powerful effects upon our judgments of his or her specific traits. If you have ever heard the
phrase "Love is blind," you are already familiar with this phenomenon. The
meaning of this statement is clear: if we love another person, we are often totally
oblivious to all of his or her faults. Indeed, our powerful positive feelings about

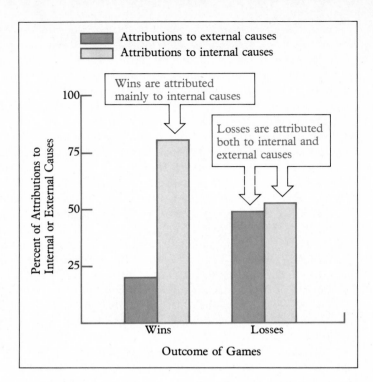

FIGURE 6-11   A Self-Serving Bias in the World of Sports

Players and coaches attributed successes (wins) largely to *internal* causes. In contrast, they were much more willing to attribute failures (losses) to *external* causes. (Source: Based on data from Lau & Russell, *Journal of Personality and Social Psychology,* 1980, *39,* 29–38.)

him or her may overwhelm our ability to notice, let alone evaluate, this person's specific traits.

Both informal evidence and experimental studies indicate that halo effects can be quite powerful. You have probably read or heard about mothers who cannot accept the reality that their children have committed horrible crimes. At best, they grudgingly admit that the crimes occurred but seek to explain them as stemming from external factors (e.g., the influence of a "bad crowd" on their beloved child). Similar, although less dramatic, effects have been noted in laboratory studies. For example, in one intriguing experiment, Nisbett and Wilson had subjects observe a videotape of a college instructor.[25] In one condition, he acted in a warm and friendly manner. In another, he behaved in an aloof and arrogant fashion. After watching one of these tapes, subjects rated the instructor's overall likability as well as several specific traits: his physical appearance, mannerisms, and accent. (He was Belgian.) As predicted, those who had seen the instructor behave in a warm and friendly manner reported liking him much more than those who had seen him act in a cold and arrogant fashion. Further, there was a large "spillover" from these global impressions to ratings of the instructor's specific traits. Subjects who had seen the "warm" instructor rated his appearance, mannerisms, and even his accent much more favorably than those who had viewed the "cold" instructor.

Unfortunately, halo effects are quite common. In fact, we are sure you have encountered them in one form or another in your own life. Even worse, they generally seem to go largely unnoticed. For example, in the study by Nisbett and Wilson, subjects were asked whether their overall impression of the instructor had affected their ratings of his traits. Disturbingly, an overwhelming majority denied that this was the case. Thus, they were totally unaware of the presence of a very pronounced halo effect. We will have more to say about such effects and their implications for organizations below. And we will return to them once again in Chapter 8, when we discuss *performance appraisal.*

Attribution and Organizational Behavior: Some Key Contributions

Attribution is clearly a key process in social perception; indeed, many experts would argue strongly that it is *the* process most deserving of our attention. Because of its obvious importance in understanding social perception and social behavior generally, it has been the subject of a great deal of study for more than two decades. As we have tried to note in the preceding pages, much information has been gained from this work. We now understand a great deal about attribution—how it operates, where it can go astray, and the major questions it addresses. Such information is interesting and valuable in its own right. But does it also have any direct bearing on organizational behavior? In short, can this large body of basic knowledge help us to understand important topics relating to organizations—topics we might otherwise find more puzzling? The answer, we believe, is definitely "yes." During the past few years, attribution theory has been applied to many key aspects of organizational behavior, often with impressive results. While a number of different topics have been examined in this manner, two seem most deserving of our attention at this point: the role of attribution in *evaluating performance* and the role of attribution in *behavior toward subordinates.*

Attribution and performance evaluation: It's not only how you perform that counts—"why" matters too.   Suppose that at some future time you are asked to evaluate the performance of two persons working under your supervision. Both are up for promotion, but only one can attain this goal, so your evaluations really count. When you examine the records of both persons, you find that they are about equal. But you also know that they have attained these results by very different routes. One is a highly talented individual who is coasting along, putting little effort into his work. The other is somewhat lower in ability, but has worked long and hard to attain good performance. Would your evaluations of these employees differ? In all likelihood, they would. There is a very good chance that you would give the "edge" to the hard worker of modest ability. The fact that you would illustrates a very important point: in evaluating others' performance, we do not consider only their actual behavior; the causes behind these outcomes matter too.

FROM THE MANAGER'S PERSPECTIVE

Bias in Social Perception: Implications for Organizational Behavior

As we have just seen, attribution—and social perception generally—are subject to several sources of bias. That is, they seem to be "slanted" in specific ways, so that we are more likely to reach some conclusions about other persons and their behavior than others. But given that such biases exist, do they have any implications for managers and for organizational behavior? We believe that they do.

First, consider the *actor-observer effect* mentioned earlier. As you may recall, this involves our strong tendency to perceive others' behavior as deriving mainly from internal causes, while we view our own as stemming primarily from external or situational factors. This erroneous "tilt" in our attributions can exert important effects upon our social relations and so upon effective organizational behavior. Our tendency to view others' behavior as stemming largely from internal factors may lead us to expect greater consistency in their actions than really exists. Thus, we may react with surprise—or even anger—when other persons do not show the high levels of stability we have come, quite erron-

eously, to expect. As you can readily see, this can be a major source of disruption within organizations.

Similarly, our tendency to view our own actions as stemming mainly from situational factors can have other important consequences. Because of this bias, we often tend to ignore consistencies in our own behavior and feelings. As a result, we fail to obtain a fuller understanding of these characteristics. For example, consider the case of a young woman who gets into repeated arguments with her supervisors and so loses one job after another. Because of the actor-observer effect, she may perceive the causes of these incidents as entirely external. That is, she blames bad luck or the inherent hostility of managers for her misfortunes. Actually, though, her run-ins with her bosses may stem from her own traits—stubbornness, unwillingness to compromise, or general abrasiveness.

Next, let us turn to the *self-serving bias*. This, too, can exert powerful effects upon behavior in organizational settings. Recall that it involves a tendency to attribute positive outcomes or behavior to

Actually, a large body of research findings indicates that when we attempt to evaluate others' performance, we pay close attention to four major factors: effort, ability, luck, and task difficulty.[27] As you can readily see, both effort and ability are internal causes, while luck and task difficulty are external factors. Further, while ability and task difficulty tend to be fairly stable over time, effort and luck are quite variable. But how do we combine information on these factors in evaluating others' performance? What rules do we follow in deciding when a given level of performance is deserving of praise and when it is deserving of criticism? Once again, research studies provide intriguing answers.

First, consider the internal cause-external cause dimension. Several investigations suggest that we take this carefully into account in judging overt performance.[28] Briefly, it appears that when others are successful in performing a given task, we evaluate their behavior more favorably if it stems from internal factors such as ability or effort than if it stems from external factors such as luck or an

internal causes (our own traits or effort) but failure and negative outcomes to external factors (bad luck, task difficulty, the actions of other persons). This tendency can often be the basis for interpersonal friction and conflict in organizational settings. In situations where two or more persons work together on a task, each will tend to perceive success as stemming largely from his or her contributions and perceive failure as deriving mainly from the shortcomings and flaws of their partners. Needless to say, such perceptions can have adverse effects on both morale and cooperation.

Finally, consider the *halo effect* described on pages 183–184. This powerful tendency in social perception has several implications for organizational behavior. First, it can lead to serious errors in the evaluation of performance and other job-related activities. Once an individual has acquired a "halo," it is as if he or she can do no wrong. Even mediocre performance by this person is rated favorably. And he or she often receives a larger share of available rewards than is strictly justified. While these errors are bad enough in themselves, their impact on other employees who are not fortunate enough to possess a halo, can be disastrous. Both their morale and performance may suffer. And in the end, an organization possessing too many halos may lose the services of talented and hard-working individuals who become discouraged and resign. Clearly, then, concrete steps to lessen the impact of such bias seem required.[26]

To conclude: several sources of bias in attribution and social perception appear to have major implications for organizations and organizational behavior. Because of these "slants" or tendencies, we often misunderstand other persons, reach false conclusions about their behavior, and hold them responsible for events they have not caused. Such errors, in turn, can exert adverse effects upon interpersonal relations in an organization and upon its morale and productivity. For these reasons, it seems important for managers to recognize these potential problems and to take active steps to combat them. The effort involved in this regard can be fairly high. But the benefits, we believe, can also be substantial.   □

easy task. In contrast, when others are relatively unsuccessful in performing a given task, we evaluate their work more favorably if it seems to stem from external factors (luck, a difficult task) than from internal ones (ability, effort). As you can see, this makes a great deal of intuitive sense. After all, it is reasonable to give others more credit for good performance when it stems from their ability or effort than when it is simply a matter of luck. Similarly, it makes more sense to overlook poor performance when it derives from bad luck or an extremely difficult task than if it stems from lack of effort or ability. Unfortunately, though, the situation is complicated by the existence of the actor-observer difference described earlier. Because of this form of bias, we tend to attribute others' behavior mainly to internal causes. And then, we often give them more credit for good performance—and more blame for poor performance—than they actually deserve. While such effects appear to be quite common, recent findings suggest that they can be readily overcome through a simple strategy: providing evaluators with direct experience in performing the tasks in question.[29] Apparently, such experience reminds evaluators of the importance of external, situational factors and so reduces the probability that they will fall prey to the actor-observer bias.

While this dimension of internal-external causes is important, however, it is by no means the entire story. As suggested by the example at the start of this discussion, we also pay close attention to the distinction between *ability* and *effort*. Specifically, we seem to assign more weight to effort than to ability in assessing performance in many situations. This fact is illustrated clearly by the results of an experiment conducted by Knowlton and Mitchell.[30] In this study, subjects were given the task of supervising three subordinates, all of whom were accomplices of the researchers. Two performed at an average level, while the third performed either well or poorly. Subjects were also provided with information suggesting that the "stand-out" person's performance stemmed mainly from ability or mainly from effort. After completing their role as supervisors, subjects were asked to evaluate the subordinate's performance along several different dimensions. It was predicted that when performance seemed to stem mainly from high or low effort, their ratings would be more extreme than when it seemed to stem primarily from high or low ability. As you can see in Figure 6–12, results offered support for this hypothesis. When the subordinate performed poorly, he received lower ratings when this seemed to stem from low effort than when it seemed to stem from low ability. And when he performed well, he received higher ratings when this success seemed to stem from high effort than when it seemed to derive from high ability. These findings and those of other experiments suggest that while we take both ability and effort into account in evaluating others' performance, we often attach greater weight to the latter. Needless to add, there is an important message for your own career in such results: if you want to attain high evaluations from your supervisors, be sure to keep your effort at visibly high levels. If you do not, even good performance may not yield favorable ratings. (Please note that we will devote full attention to the topic of *performance appraisal* in Chapter 8.)

Attribution and behavior toward subordinates.   Imagine that a person working under your direction makes a serious error. Several possible courses of action are open to you (e.g., you can criticize him, ignore the incident, and so on). Which should you select? The answer, of course, is: *it depends.* And what it depends upon, to a great extent, is your perception of the causes of this error. If these are largely internal (low effort, a lack of ability), you are likely to engage in actions designed to change the subordinate's behavior (criticism, training, feedback). If, instead, the factors responsible for the error appear to be largely external in nature (bad luck, an overwhelming burden of work), you will probably concentrate on changing the situation. In short, your behavior will be strongly determined by your attributions.

Direct evidence that attribution actually plays a key role in such cases is provided by the findings of several recent studies.[31] For example, in one ingenious experiment conducted by Mitchell and Wood, nursing supervisors read brief descriptions of hypothetical errors committed by hospital nurses.[32] Each incident

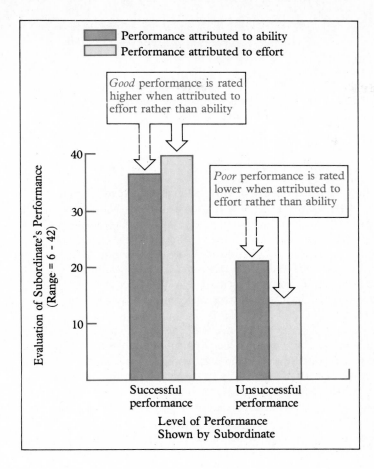

Performance attributed to ability
Performance attributed to effort

Good performance is rated higher when attributed to effort rather than ability

Poor performance is rated lower when attributed to effort rather than ability

Evaluation of Subordinate's Performance (Range = 6 - 42)

40
30
20
10

Successful performance   Unsuccessful performance

Level of Performance
Shown by Subordinate

FIGURE 6-12 Causal Attributions and Performance Evaluation

In evaluating others' performance, we take both effort and ability into account. However, as shown here, we often seem to give effort greater weight. Successful performance stemming mainly from high effort is rated more favorably than similar performance stemming mainly from high ability. Conversely, poor performance stemming mainly from low effort is rated more harshly than similar performance stemming mainly from low ability. (Source: Based on data from Knowlton & Mitchell, *Journal of Applied Psychology,* 1980, *65,* 459–466.)

was accompanied by information about each nurse's past work history, and this was varied so as to suggest either that the error stemmed from internal causes (lack of effort or ability) or external causes (a negative and demanding work environment). (We should note that the work history contained information on consensus, consistency, and distinctiveness—the three factors emphasized by Kelley.) After reading these materials, the supervisors were asked to indicate what kind of action they would take in the situation. Specifically, they were asked to indicate whether they would do something to change the nurse's behavior, or do something to improve the work situation. It was expected that when the error was attributed to internal causes, the supervisors would strongly endorse attempts to change the nurse's behavior. However, when it was attributed to external causes, they would recommend attempts to change the work setting. Results agreed with these predictions. Thus, causal attributions seemed quite important in determining how these actual supervisors would handle situations very much like the ones they faced in their daily work.

In sum, a growing and impressive body of evidence points to the conclusion that attribution plays a key role in several aspects of organizational behavior. It strongly affects evaluations of others' performance, determines the manner in which supervisors behave toward subordinates, and even appears to influence personal satisfaction with one's work.[33] For these and other reasons, it is a process that should be considered—and understood—by anyone concerned with the goals of enhancing organizational effectiveness and growth.

SUMMARY

In general, we believe that we know the world around us directly, through our senses. Actually, though, we construct a representation of it through the active process of **perception.** Perception is selective—we pay attention only to certain stimuli or events. In addition, it is organized—we impose order on the information brought to us by our senses. Our perceptions also show certain types of stability. Specifically, we perceive the shape, size, and color of various objects as constant even when sensory input about them varies. While perception is usually accurate, it sometimes fails. Dramatic illustrations of the fallibility of perception are provided by *illusions.*

While accurate perceptions of the physical world are important, it is also crucial that we acquire similar knowledge of the persons around us. One important aspect of such **social perception** involves our attempts to understand the moods and emotions of other persons. Often, we acquire such information from *nonverbal cues.* These include facial expressions, eye contact, and body positions and movements. Nonverbal cues play an important role in interviews and other aspects of organizational behavior.

Attribution is the process through which we attempt to understand the causes of others' behavior. One basic task in this regard is that of deciding whether other persons' actions stem mainly from internal or external causes. We accomplish this task by directing careful attention to the factors of consensus, consistency, and distinctiveness. While attribution often provides us with valuable information about the causes of others' behavior, it is subject to several types of bias. These include the *actor-observer effect,* the *self-serving bias,* and *halo effects.* In recent years, attribution theory and research have been applied to several key aspects of organizational behavior. Existing evidence suggests that attributions play a crucial role in performance evaluation and in guiding the behavior of supervisors toward their subordinates.

KEY TERMS

ACTOR-OBSERVER EFFECT Refers to the tendency to attribute our own actions to external or situational factors, but those of others to internal causes.

ATTRIBUTION The process through which we seek to determine the causes of others' behavior. Attribution is a central process in social perception.

CONSTANCIES (PERCEPTUAL)   Refers to the fact that we perceive the shape, size, and color of various objects as constant even when sensory information about them varies.

FIGURE-GROUND   Refers to our tendency to perceive any scene as consisting of objects standing out against a background.

HALO EFFECT   Refers to the fact that our overall impressions of others often influence our evaluations of their specific traits.

ILLUSIONS   Instances in which our perceptions are not in accord with the true characteristics of an object or event.

NONVERBAL COMMUNICATION   The process through which we infer the current emotional states or moods of other persons from cues involving their facial expressions, eye contact, and body positions or movements.

PERCEPTION   The active process through which we interpret and organize information provided by our senses. Through perception, we construct a representation of the world around us.

SELF-SERVING BIAS   Refers to our tendency to attribute positive outcomes or successes to internal causes (our own ability or effort), but negative outcomes or failures to external causes (bad luck, the actions of others).

SOCIAL PERCEPTION   The process through which we come to know and understand the persons around us.

NOTES

1. Levine, M.W., & Shefner, J.M. *Fundamentals of sensation and perception.* Reading, Mass.: Addison-Wesley, 1981.

2. von Senden, M. *Space and sight: The perception of space and shape in the congenitally blind before and after operation.* New York: Free Press, 1960.

3. Haber, R.N., & Hershenson, M. *The psychology of visual perception* (2nd ed.). New York: Holt, Rinehart, and Winston, 1980.

4. Buck, R. *Nonverbal behavior and the communication of affect.* New York: Guilford Press, 1983.

5. Ekman, P. Cross cultural studies of facial expression. In P. Ekman (Ed.), *Darwin and facial expression.* New York: Academic Press, 1973.

6. Izard, C.E., Huebner, R.R., Risser, D., McGinnes, G.C., & Dougherty, L.M. The young infant's ability to produce discrete emotion expressions. *Developmental Psychology,* 1980, *16,* 132–140.

7. Ekman, P., & Friesen, W.V. *Unmasking the face.* Englewood Cliffs, N.J.: Prentice-Hall, 1975.

8. Weitz, S. (Ed.). *Nonverbal communication: Readings with commentary* (2nd ed.). New York: Oxford University Press, 1979.

9. Rubin, Z. Measurement of romantic love. *Journal of Personality and Social Psychology,* 1970, *16,* 265–273.

10. Greenbaum, P., & Rosenfeld, H.W. Patterns of avoidance in response to interpersonal staring and proximity: Effects of bystanders on drivers at a traffic intersection. *Journal of Personality and Social Psychology,* 1978, *36,* 575–587.

11. Ellsworth, P.C., & Langer, E.J. Staring and approach: An interpretation of the start as a nonspecific activator. *Journal of Personality and Social Psychology*, 1976, *33*, 117–122.

12. Ekman, P. Biological and cultural contributions to body and facial movement. In J. Blacking (Ed.), *A.S. Monograph 15, The anthropology of the body*. London: Academic Press, 1977.

13. Clore, G.L., Wiggins, N.H., & Itkin, S. Judging attraction from nonverbal behavior: The gain phenomenon. *Journal of Consulting and Clinical Psychology*, 1975, *43*, 491–497.

14. Campbell, D.E. Interior office design and visitor response. *Journal of Applied Psychology*, 1979, *64,*, 648–653.

15. Morrow, P.C., & McElroy, J.C. Interior office design and visitor response: A constructive replication. *Journal of Applied Psychology*, 1981, *66*, 646–650.

16. Imada, A.S., & Hakel, M.D. Influence of nonverbal communication and rater proximity on impressions and decisions in simulated employment interviews. *Journal of Applied Psychology*, 1977, *62*, 295–300.

17. Harvey, J.H., & Weary, G. *Perspectives on attributional processes*. Dubuque, Iowa: Wm. C. Brown, 1981.

18. Kelley, H.H. The process of causal attribution. *American Psychologist*, 1973, *28*, 107–128.

19. Zuckerman, M. Actions and occurrences in Kelley's cube. *Journal of Personality and Social Psychology*, 1978, *36*, 647–656.

20. Goldberg, L.W. Differential attribution of trait-descriptive terms to oneself as compared to well-liked, neutral, and disliked others: A psychometric analysis. *Journal of Personality and Social Psychology*, 1978, *36*, 1012–1028.

21. Nisbett, R.E., Caputo, C., Legant, P., & Marecek, J. Behavior as seen by the actor and as seen by the observer. *Journal of Personality and Social Psychology*, 1973, *27*, 154–164.

22. Eisen, S.V. Actor-observer differences in information inferences and causal attribution. *Journal of Personality and Social Psychology*, 1979, *37*, 261–272.

23. Carver, C.S., DeGregorio, E., & Gillis, R. Ego-defensive bias in attribution among two categories of observers. *Personality and Social Psychology Bulletin*, 1980, *6* 44–50.

24. Lau, R.R., & Russell, D. Attributions in the sports pages. *Journal of Personality and Social Psychology*, 1980, *39*, 29–38.

25. Nisbett, R.E., & Wilson, T.D. The halo effect: Evidence for the unconscious alteration of judgments. *Journal of Personality and Social Psychology*, 1977, *35*, 450–456.

26. Landy, F.J., Vance, R.J., and Barnes-Farrell, J.L. Statistical control of halo: A response. *Journal of Applied Psychology*, 1982, *67*, 177–180. *Social Psychology*, 1977, *35*, 450–456.

27. Wong, P.T.P., & Weiner, B. When people ask "why" questions, and the heuristics of attributional search. *Journal of Personality and Social Psychology*, 1981, *40*, 650–663.

28. Hargrett, N.T. Potential behavioral consequences of attributions of locus of control. *Journal of Applied Psychology*, 1981, *66*, 63–68.

29. Mitchell, T.R., & Kalb, L.S. Effects of job experience on supervisor attributions for a subordinate's poor performance. *Journal of Applied Psychology,* 1982, *67,* 181–188.

30. Knowlton, W.A., Jr., & Mitchell, T.R. Effects of causal attributions on a supervisor's evaluation of subordinate performance. *Journal of Applied Psychology,* 1980, *65,* 459–466.

31. Mitchell, T.R., Green, S.G., & Wood, R.S. An attributional model of leadership and the poor performing subordinate: Development and validation. In B.M. Staw & L.L. Cummings (Eds.), *Research in organizational behavior* (Vol. 3). Greenwich, Conn.: JAI Press, in press.

32. Mitchell, T.R., & Wood, R.E. Supervisors' responses to subordinate poor performance: A test of an attributional model. *Organizational Behavior and Human Performance,* 1980, *25,* 123–138.

33. Porac, J.F., Nottenburg, G., & Eggert, J. On extending Weiner's attributional model to organizational contexts. *Journal of Applied Psychology,* 1981, *66,* 124–126.

7

Attitudes:
Reactions to People, Issues,
and Work

KEY CONCEPTS

Attitudes

Likert Scaling

Persuasive Messages

Credibility

Cognitive Dissonance

Frequency-of-Exposure Effects

Job Satisfaction

Critical Incident Procedure

Motivator-Hygiene Theory

Motivators

Hygienes

Stereotypes

Prejudice

Discrimination

□ □ □

It's hard to believe: can five years really have passed since graduation? The answer must be yes, for here you are attending your first college reunion. It's great to see old friends and discuss old times. All in all, you're having a truly enjoyable visit. Just now, you spot your old chum Dan across the room. After the repeated warm hand-shakes and mutual back-slapping are over, you settle down to business: filling each other in on the major events in your lives over the past few years. At one point, your conversation drifts onto the subject of jobs and careers. You are very enthusiastic, for you like your job very much and foresee a rosy future in the years ahead. Unfortunately, Dan has a different and sadder tale to tell.

"Gee, I wish I were as lucky as you," he laments. "My salary is OK and I work in a nice new building; but that's as far as it goes. Every day I do the same dull things over and over, until I can hardly stand it. Heck, sometimes I'm so bored I feel kind of numb. Things would be much better if I could get promoted, but the company's already loaded with middle-level managers, so there's almost no chance of that. Worst of all, my boss really doesn't seem to care about me at all. I guess we're just on different wavelengths or something." And then, lowering his voice and glancing around furtively, he adds: "And she's a woman, just a couple of years older than I am. What a bummer! I've thought of quitting a hundred times. As soon as something comes along, I'll leave."

You are about to offer a kind word of comfort when Howard and Chris, two other old friends, approach. Soon you are all talking about other things. But every time you glance over at Dan, you can't help feeling sorry for him. No wonder he looks so worn down. It's really tough when you hate your work . . . .

What were the two main characters in this incident doing? The simplest answer, of course, is that they were holding a conversation. But look a bit deeper. What was the conversation about? To a large extent, it centered around personal reactions. Both participants described their feelings and beliefs about a crucial aspect of their lives—their jobs. As you probably know from your own experience, this type of discussion is far from rare. People often communicate with one another about their personal feelings. And this, in turn, is far from surprising. As thinking, feeling persons, we experience reactions to virtually everybody, everything, and every idea or issue that we encounter during our daily lives. While these reactions vary greatly in scope, most fall within three major categories. First, they are *affective*, involving positive or negative feelings. Second, they are *cognitive*, involving beliefs about the objects or persons involved. And third, they are *behavioral*, centering around tendencies to act in certain ways. These three components were clearly present in Dan's comments. He reported disliking his job (being dissatisfied with it). Similarly, he noted his belief that he could not obtain rapid promotion in it. And he also stated his desire to leave it as soon as possible. When these three general types of reactions cluster about a single object and are relatively enduring in nature, they are often described as constituting an **attitude.** Thus, when we use this term in the present and later chapters, we will be referring simply to *relatively lasting clusters of feelings, beliefs, and behavior tendencies directed toward specific persons, groups, ideas, or objects.*[1]

The fact that public attitudes or opinions are mentioned almost daily in newspapers and on the evening news suggests that they play an important role in human behavior. And literally thousands of studies of attitudes and their impact indicate that this is in fact the case. Attitudes have been found to exert powerful effects upon everything from the outcome of political elections and the decisions of consumers in the marketplace through the child-rearing practices of parents.[2] In this regard, organizational behavior is definitely no exception to the rule. On the contrary, attitudes also exert a powerful impact upon several key aspects of behavior in organizational settings (see Figure 7–1). Because of this fact, we think it is important for you to know something about them. Thus, in the present chapter, we will survey current knowledge about several aspects of human attitudes. First, we will provide you with some background information about attitudes in general—how they are formed, how they are measured, and how they can be changed. Second, we will focus on a key type of work-related attitude—**job satisfaction.** Here, we will consider the factors producing satisfaction or dissatisfaction, the prevalence of such reactions among employees, and the impact of satisfaction and dissatisfaction upon important forms of organizational behavior.

FIGURE 7–1   Attitudes: A Key Factor in Organizational Behavior

While they are rarely as extreme as the ones expressed here, attitudes often play an important role in many aspects of organizational behavior. (Source: © King Features Syndicate, Inc., 1977. World Rights Reserved.)

Finally, we will examine an especially unsettling type of attitude—**prejudice.** Such negative reactions toward the members of specific groups (e.g., minorities, women, the aged) exert powerful effects upon both individuals and organizations and have tremendous social significance. For these reasons, they are fully deserving of our careful attention.

ATTITUDES: THEIR MEASUREMENT AND CHANGE

Because of their role in a very wide range of human activities, attitudes have been the subject of intensive study for several decades. In fact, it is probably safe to suggest that in some fields (e.g., social psychology), more studies have been concerned with attitudes than with any other single topic.[3] Many different questions have been examined. However, two that have received a great deal of attention are: How can attitudes best be *measured?* and How can they be *changed?*

Measuring Attitudes: Methods for Getting the "Inside" Story

When we meet other persons for the first time, some things about them are readily apparent. Their age, style of dress, and physical characteristics are all open to our immediate inspection. In contrast, their attitudes are not visible in the same direct manner. Usually, it is impossible to tell a conservative from a liberal or a satisfied employee from a dissatisfied one by means of a casual glance. Also, few persons go about announcing their views on important matters to every stranger; rather, most keep their attitudes to themselves and reveal them only to close friends or relatives. How, then, can we measure such reactions? In short, how can we make these internal clusters of feelings, beliefs, and behavior tendencies visible? Several different techniques for accomplishing these goals have been suggested. For example, some scientists have attempted to study attitudes through careful attention to subtle nonverbal cues.[4] As we noted in Chapter 6, such cues often reveal much about individuals' internal states. Thus, nonverbal cues can sometimes prove useful in the study of at least the affective (feeling) component of attitudes. However, the most common procedure for assessing attitudes involves the use of *attitude scales* or *questionnaires.*

Self-report measures of attitude: Ask—and sometimes—you shall know. The use of attitude scales or questionnaires is based on an eminently reasonable assertion: the best way to find out about others' attitudes is, quite simply, to ask them. Consistent with this view, attitude questionnaires contain numerous items that ask individuals to report on their feelings, beliefs, and behavior tendencies with respect to some topic (e.g., some issue, group, or object). It is assumed that the answers they provide will then reveal their attitudes about this topic. Under ideal conditions, this is indeed the case. If individuals complete the items on the scale honestly and accurately, their replies reveal much about their actual attitudes.

In other instances, though, sources of bias may exist. First, individuals completing the scale may wish to conceal their true reactions. (For example, they may wish to present themselves in a favorable light, and so may avoid expressing views that are currently out of favor.) To the extent this is so, their answers can be quite misleading. Second, it may not be possible for individuals to report accurately on their views even if they wish to do so. They may be uncertain as to what these really are; or the items on the scale may be phrased in such a way that none of the possible answers seem to apply.

Fortunately, a number of techniques for minimizing such problems exist. For example, subjects can be assured that their replies will be totally anonymous; scale items can be carefully refined so that they *do* allow subjects to report accurately on their views. Researchers in organizational behavior and related fields are very familiar with such precautions and generally employ them in their attitude surveys. Thus, you can be confident that the findings we report here were gathered in a manner that helps to assure their validity and accuracy.

Regardless of the topics on which they focus, attitude scales can be presented in many different formats. For example, the persons who complete them can be asked to indicate whether they feel that various statements about some issue are true or false. Alternatively, they can be asked simply to place a check mark along a line labeled at each end with contrasting phrases, in order to indicate their own position along this dimension. Perhaps the most common format, though, is one in which persons taking the scale indicate the extent to which they agree or disagree with various statements, or the extent to which they hold positive or negative views about the attitude object. This format is known as **Likert scaling,** and sample attitude items of this type are presented in Table 7–1. As you can see, these statements are designed to measure job satisfaction, and individuals respond to each by circling one number.

While the precise format of various attitude scales may vary, their overall goal remains the same: accurate and efficient measurement of respondents' attitudes toward some issue, object, person, or group. To the extent such scales are carefully constructed and cautiously administered, they can go a long way toward attaining this end.

Changing Attitudes: Persuasion, Dissonance, and Repetition

Once they are formed, attitudes tend to persist. Indeed, if left unchallenged, they may remain stable for many years. As you know from your own experience, though, this is rarely the case. Attempts to change our attitudes are extremely common. Almost every day we are exposed to advertisements urging us to buy various products or to vote for particular candidates. Similarly, we often receive direct pressure from co-workers, friends, and even loved ones, designed to alter

TABLE 7-1   One Type of Attitude Scale

In *Likert attitude scales*, individuals indicate the extent to which they agree or disagree with statements concerning some issue, person, or group. The items shown here are designed to assess *job satisfaction*—attitudes held by employees about their work. They are similar to the type of items included on one standard measure of such satisfaction (the Minnesota Satisfaction Questionnaire).

	NOT AT ALL SATISFIED	SLIGHTLY SATISFIED	SATISFIED	VERY SATISFIED	EXTREMELY SATISFIED
On my present job, this is how I feel about					
1. the variety of tasks I perform.	1	2	3	4	5
2. my responsibility for planning my work.	1	2	3	4	5
3. opportunities for advancement.	1	2	3	4	5
4. my rate of pay.	1	2	3	4	5

our views on many different topics. And we, in turn, do not sit idly by as the passive recipients of such attempts. On the contrary, we often try to affect the views of other persons. For example, at work we may seek to win support for our own plans or policies; in school, we may seek to convince our professors that we really *did* know the answers to certain exam questions; and at play, we may try to persuade attractive members of the opposite sex that we can provide just what they desire! In short, we both receive and initiate many attempts at attitude change on an almost daily basis.

But how, precisely, can attitudes be altered? What techniques are most successful in shifting the feelings, beliefs, and behavior tendencies of individuals? This is a practical question with important implications. As such, it has received a tremendous amount of attention from researchers in several different fields. The findings of their investigations suggest that many tactics can be successful in changing attitudes. However, two appear to be especially useful in this regard: **persuasive messages** and the induction of an uncomfortable cognitive state known as **dissonance**.

Persuasive messages: Hearing—sometimes—is believing. Perhaps the most common technique for inducing attitude change involves the use of *persuasive communications*. These consist of written, spoken, televised, or filmed messages that seek to alter attitudes through "logical" arguments and convincing "facts." As our quotation marks suggest, the arguments presented are often far from logical and the facts anything but accurate. In most cases, however, these flaws are concealed, and the messages presented maintain at least the appearance of reason and authority.

Many different factors influence the success of persuasive messages in altering attitudes—more than we could possibly mention here. The most important factors, though, involve certain characteristics of the *communicator* (who is doing the persuading?), the *communication* itself (what kind of information does it contain?), and the *recipients* (who are the persons who receive it?).

With respect to the communicator's characteristics, the dominant factor appears to be **credibility**—trustworthiness or believability. The higher a communicator is on this dimension, the more likely he or she is to succeed in inducing attitude change. Our impressions of a communicator's credibility, in turn, seem to depend largely on this person's apparent expertise and the motives that seem to lie behind his or her behavior (see Figure 7-2). Communicators who appear to be experts in the field they are talking about generally are perceived as being more credible, and so are more successful in changing attitudes than those who are perceived as being less expert. And communicators who seem to have little or nothing to gain from altering our views are often perceived as more credible than those who have much to gain from inducing such shifts.[5,6] For example, imagine that a sales representative with whom you are dealing on your job recommends that you purchase less costly equipment than you had planned, because it is actually more suitable to your company's needs. Under these conditions, you would probably be strongly influenced by her recommendation; after all, she has nothing to gain by making it, and may actually receive a smaller commission as a result. But now, in contrast, imagine that the same person tries to persuade you to order

FIGURE 7-2   Communicator Credibility and Persuasion

Communicators who are high in expertise and who have little to gain from changing their audience's attitudes are often perceived as high in credibility. As a result, they may be quite successful at persuasion. In contrast, communicators who are low in expertise and whose motives are questionable are perceived as low in credibility. Thus, they are usually far less effective in producing shifts in attitudes.

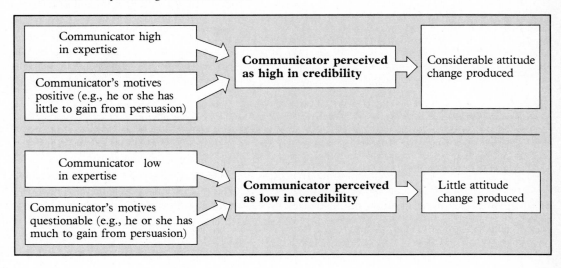

much more expensive equipment than you had planned. Here, you might well view her recommendations with skepticism and decide to stick to your original decision.

The *content* of a persuasive message is also important in determining its success in altering attitudes. Obviously, the more cogent and forceful the message, the more likely it is to induce attitude change. Further, some evidence suggests that messages that not only present one view but take pains to demolish opposing positions are often more effective in shifting attitudes than communications that present only one side of the issue. And a considerable body of research indicates that, when used with care, messages that attempt to induce fear or anxiety among recipients can be quite successful in changing attitudes.

It appears that such fear-inducing messages are most successful in altering attitudes when (1) they generate moderate levels of emotional arousal (if too weak, the messages have no impact; if too strong, they are often rejected); (2) the persons who receive them believe that the dangers cited are real; and (3) these persons also believe that the recommendations for avoiding these dangers will be effective.[7] A good example of the use of a fear appeal in an organizational setting might involve the following statement by a manager to employees: "If you people don't buckle down and work harder, this company is going to go broke and fold up. Then, you'll all be out of a job!"

Finally, the effectiveness of persuasive messages also depends upon the characteristics of the persons who receive them. As you might guess, highly intelligent persons are often less affected by such communications than those of lower intelligence. Similarly, persons high in self-esteem and confidence are less likely to change their attitudes in response to such messages than those lower in self-esteem or confidence.[8] We should also note that at one time in the past, it was believed that females were more readily swayed by persuasive communications than males. However, recent evidence indicates that this is definitely *not* the case.[9]

To conclude: spoken, written, and televised messages designed to alter attitudes can often succeed in this respect. Indeed, the existence of a giant and flourishing advertising industry and the increasing use of such appeals in political campaigns suggest that persuasive messages often do work. In order to be maximally successful, though, such appeals should be delivered by highly credible sources, should be as cogent and convincing as possible, and should be directed to appropriate audiences. When these and related factors are taken carefully into account, considerable attitude change can result.

When attitudes and behavior do not match: Dissonance as a basis for change.

Have you ever had the experience of saying something you didn't believe or of acting in a way contrary to your actual views? Probably you have. Often, factors such as family ties, good manners, or the desire to further our career leave us little choice in this respect. For example, imagine that your boss supports a specific policy—one with which you personally disagree. If he asks you to express your opinion about it at a staff meeting, in front of all other members of your department, what would you do? It's hard to predict with certainty, but the chances are good that you would avoid stating a position directly opposite to the one he supports; after all, it's important to be realistic!

But what happens in such situations? Are our attitudes affected in any manner? According to the theory of **cognitive dissonance,** they may be.[10] This theory argues that human beings dislike inconsistency. Specifically, it suggests that we dislike inconsistency in our attitudes or between our attitudes and our behavior. When such conditions arise, we experience an unpleasant cognitive state known as *dissonance*. And then, under certain circumstances, our attempts to reduce such feelings can result in considerable attitude change. To see why this is so, let us return to the example described above—the one in which your boss asks for your opinion at a meeting.

Imagine that in this incident, you do in fact "waffle." That is, when asked to express your opinion, you state that you are undecided or that you favor the boss's view—despite the fact that you are really dead set against it. What will be the result? According to dissonance theory, you will experience an uncomfortable state of dissonance. This will be the case because there is a large and noticeable gap between your true attitude and your behavior—what you really think and what you say during the meeting.

Will this dissonance then lead to shifts in your attitudes? The answer is: it depends. And what it depends upon, primarily, is the *magnitude* of the dissonance generated. If this is great, the pressure for attitude change will be intense. If it is small, this pressure will be much less. The magnitude of dissonance, in turn, depends primarily upon two factors. First, it is affected by the importance you attach to the cognitions in question. If you feel that the policy is unimportant, then dissonance will be low. If, in contrast, you feel it is important and has crucial consequences for the company and employees, dissonance may well be high. Second, it is affected by your reasons for engaging in attitude-discrepant behavior (for saying something you don't really believe). If you have many good reasons for endorsing your boss's position (e.g., the last person to contradict him was quickly fired!), then dissonance will be low. In contrast, if you have very few reasons for taking this stand (e.g., you know that your boss is fair-minded and encourages subordinates to speak their mind), dissonance will be high.

This last point, concerning the reasons behind attitude-discrepant behavior, leads to an intriguing prediction. If you wish to produce changes in others' attitudes by somehow getting them to voice support for views they don't hold, you should provide them with just barely enough inducement for doing so. If you offer more than this bare minimum, you will arm them with good reasons for having acted in this manner; thus, dissonance will be reduced. And if you offer them less, they may not engage in the attitude-discrepant behavior at all. In short, in some cases, "less" may lead to "more": smaller rewards or inducements for engaging in attitude-discrepant behavior may actually yield greater amounts of attitude change than larger ones (see Figure 7–3).

This somewhat surprising prediction has actually been confirmed in many studies. For example, in the first and most famous of these experiments, subjects were offered either a small reward ($1.00) or a large one ($20.00) for telling an-

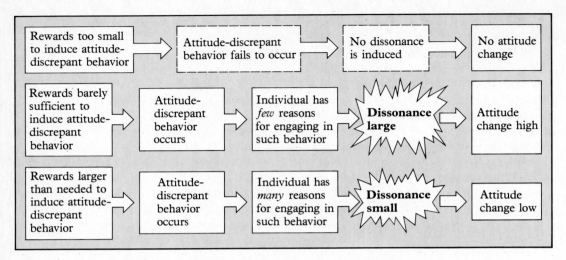

FIGURE 7–3   Why "Less" Sometimes Leads to "More" with Respect to Attitude
Change

When individuals are provided with rewards just barely sufficient to induce them to
engage in attitude-discrepant behavior, dissonance is maximized and considerable attitude
change may result (middle panel). When the rewards provided are either too small to
induce attitude-discrepant behavior (top panel) or are larger than needed to produce such
actions (bottom panel), dissonance and attitude change will both be lower.

other person that some dull tasks they had just performed were really very interesting.[11] (An example of these tasks: placing spools on a tray, dumping them out,
and repeating this process over and over again.) After engaging in this attitude-
discrepant behavior, subjects were asked to indicate their own liking for the tasks.
As predicted by the "less-leads-to-more" effect, they actually reported liking the
dull tasks *more* when they had received the small reward than when they had received the large one. Later research indicates that such effects tend to occur only
when individuals feel that they were free to choose whether to perform the attitude-discrepant behavior or not and when they feel responsible for any effects
produced by such actions.[12] Since these conditions often prevail, though, it appears that the "less-leads-to-more" effect may occur in many situations. In any
case, you should be aware of both dissonance and the effects of attitude-discrepant
behavior. In many cases, they can serve as the basis for important shifts in attitudes. For a discussion of another process that often exerts strong effects on attitudes, see the **"FOCUS"** box on pages 206–207.

JOB SATISFACTION: ATTITUDES TOWARD
WORK

Like it or not, work plays a dominant role in our lives. It occupies more of our
time than any other single activity. And for most of us, it is central to our self-

concept: we define ourselves, in part, by our careers or professions. Further, while fantasies of a life of total leisure are intriguing, few persons can really imagine a full and satisfying life that does not involve *some* productive work. It stands to reason that any activity of such central importance must evoke strong positive and negative reactions from us. And there is little doubt that this is the case. When asked, most persons can readily report feelings, beliefs, and behavior tendencies relating to their jobs. In short, they hold strong and well-established attitudes toward their work and specific aspects of it. Such attitudes are generally known as **job satisfaction,** and it is upon this important topic that we will now focus.

As you might readily guess, job satisfaction has been of major interest to the field of organizational behavior for many years. In fact, through the mid-1970s, more than 3,350 articles had been published on this topic—and the pace has certainly not slackened since then.[13] One major reason for this continuing interest in job satisfaction is obvious: positive and negative attitudes toward work may exert powerful effects upon many forms of organizational behavior. As we shall soon see, research findings indicate that this is definitely the case. But be prepared: there are some important surprises, too. While job satisfaction is closely related to some forms of work-related behavior, it does not seem to play a direct role in others. And it also seems to exert general and perhaps unexpected effects on behavior outside work settings.

In the remainder of this discussion, we will summarize existing knowledge concerning several key aspects of job satisfaction. First, we will indicate how such reactions are measured. Second, we will examine some of the major causes of job satisfaction. Third, we will consider its prevalence (the extent to which employees are generally satisfied or dissatisfied with their work). Finally, we will examine the consequences of job satisfaction—its impact upon a wide range of work-related behaviors.

Techniques for Measuring Job Satisfaction: Assessing Reactions to Work

As is true of other attitudes, job satisfaction can be measured by several different techniques. By far the most common approach, though, is one we have already described: rating scales on which individuals simply report their reactions to their jobs. A number of different scales of this type have been developed. Items similar to those used on one (the Minnesota Satisfaction Questionnaire) were presented in Table 7-1.[14] Another widely used scale is the *Job Descriptive Index.*[15] Individuals completing this scale are presented with lists of adjectives and asked to indicate whether each does or does not describe a particular aspect of their work. (They indicate their reactions by placing a *Y* for yes, *N* for no, or *?* for undecided next to each adjective.) One interesting feature of the JDI is that it assesses reactions to five distinct aspects of jobs: the work itself, pay, promotional opportunities, supervision, and people (co-workers). Items similar to those included on the JDI are shown in Table 7-2 (p. 208).

FOCUS ON BEHAVIOR

The Frequency-of-Exposure Effect: Does Sheer Repetition Count?

As we are sure you already know, advertisers place great faith in the view that repetition is an effective technique for changing attitudes. Indeed, they often repeat the same commercials over and over again, until most of us are literally "fed up" with seeing them. (How many times have you seen Ronald McDonald and his crew in recent weeks?)

But are such tactics really effective? Does repeated exposure really shift our attitudes toward various stimuli in a favorable direction? Growing evidence suggests that it does. Many studies—literally dozens—have reported that the more frequently a given stimulus is presented or viewed, the more it is liked or evaluated positively. Further, this effect—often known as the **frequency-of-exposure** phenomenon—appears to be quite general in scope. Thus, it occurs with stimuli as diverse in nature as art prints, simple drawings, music, and photos of faces.[16,17] As you might well guess, though, there do appear to be some limits to this relationship. Beyond some point, continued exposure may result in negative rather than increasingly positive reactions.

Clearly, the frequency-of-exposure effect has important implications for such fields as sales and advertising. But it also has more general implications—ones we find rather unsettling. Specifically, these relate to its potential impact upon the political process. If, as past research suggests, repeated exposure often leads to more favorable attitudes, it seems possible that political candidates, too, may be subject to such effects. And to the extent this is true, many elections may be won not by the most qualified or experienced individual but simply by the one who is most familiar to voters. That such effects actually take place is suggested by recent investigations conducted by Joseph Grush and his colleagues.[18,19]

In these studies, Grush and his associates examined the results of a large number of elections held in the United States (congressional and presidential primaries). They reasoned that if the frequency-of-exposure effect holds in politics as well as in other areas, two trends would be noted. First, in elections involving both famous and unknown candidates, the well-known individuals would frequently be victorious. Second, in elections involving only relatively unknown candidates, those who spent most on their campaigns—and so became most familiar to voters—would be favored to win. As you can see from Figure 7-4, results offered support for both suggestions. Incumbents and famous persons usually defeated their lesser-known rivals. And among relative unknowns, those with the greatest financial resources usually triumphed.

These findings have important implications. Briefly, they suggest that in politics, victory does not necessarily go to the best person for the job. Rather, as we have already noted, it may simply go to the most familiar.

In closing, we wish to add one thought. Although we do not currently know of any direct evidence on this issue, it seems possible that similar effects occur within organizations. That is, persons who are well-known and familiar to top decision-makers may often have a crucial "edge" in terms of promotions and other positive outcomes. Of course, many different factors play a role in such actions, and it seems likely that a number of these far outweigh the impact of mere familiarity. But it is also true that only persons who come readily to mind can be suggested and then considered for new positions or promotions when these opportunities arise. Thus, it is possible that being a "familiar face" to key people in an organization may be one more small plus aiding one's career.   □

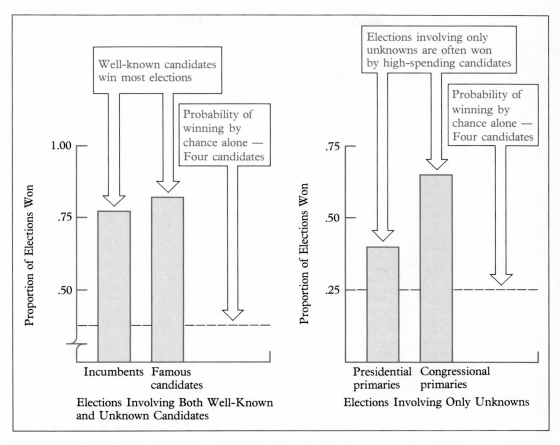

FIGURE 7-4   Frequency of Exposure and Politics

Elections involving both famous and unknown candidates are usually won by the well-known persons (left panel). Elections involving only relative unknowns are usually won by the candidate who spends most on his or her campaign (right panel). These findings suggest that the frequency-of-exposure effect exerts a powerful impact upon politics. (Source: Based on data from Grush, *Journal of Personality and Social Psychology*, 1980, *38*, 337–347 and Grush, McKeough, & Ahlering, *Journal of Personality and Social Psychology*, 1978, *36*, 257–270.)

TABLE 7-2   Items Similar to Those on the JDI

These items are similar to ones appearing on one standard measure of job satisfaction—the *Job Descriptive Index*. Individuals completing this measure indicate whether each of the adjectives shown does or does not describe some aspect of their work.

Place a *Y* (for yes), an *N* (for no), or a *?* (for undecided) next to each word to indicate whether it does or does not describe your job:

WORK	PAY
_____ Interesting	_____ Fair
_____ Unpleasant	_____ Appropriate for my level of skill
_____ Useful	_____ More than I deserve
_____ Simple	_____ Adequate for my current life-style
_____ Tiring	_____ Related to my performance

While self-report scales such as the JDI and MSQ are the most common technique for measuring job satisfaction, we should note that other approaches are also used for this purpose. One, known as *action tendency scales,* asks individuals how they feel like acting with respect to their job. Thus, employees may be asked to respond to such questions as: "Do you ever feel reluctant to go home from work at night because of the enjoyment you are getting from your job?" or "Do you ever feel like just walking out on this job for good?" One advantage of the action tendency approach is that it relies less on insight into one's own feelings than other types of attitude scales.

Another technique for assessing job satisfaction is the **critical incident procedure.** Here, individuals are asked to describe incidents relating to their work that they found particularly satisfying or dissatisfying. Their replies are then carefully analyzed to uncover underlying themes and reactions.[20] Finally, job satisfaction can also be assessed through interviews. Unfortunately, such procedures are often long and costly. Thus, they have not been used for this purpose very often. In closing, we should note that regardless of the specific approach adopted, the goal in assessing job satisfaction remains the same: uncovering the feelings, beliefs, and behavior tendencies of employees toward various aspects of their work.

Job Satisfaction: Some Major Causes

That job satisfaction varies greatly from employee to employee and from organization to organization is obvious. While some persons report overwhelmingly positive reactions to their work, others gripe continuously about real or imagined problems. Why, precisely, is this the case? What factors contribute to job satisfaction or dissatisfaction?

Attempts to answer these important questions have taken two basic forms. First, several investigators have sought to develop comprehensive theories of job satisfaction—theories that both identify the major determinants of such reactions and account for their impact on worker attitudes. Second, many researchers have adopted a more empirical approach, seeking simply to determine key factors affecting job satisfaction and dissatisfaction. Both strategies will now be considered.

Theories of job satisfaction: Maslow's need hierarchy and Herzberg's motivator-hygiene approach.   We have already described one theory relevant to job satisfaction—*Maslow's need hierarchy*—in Chapter 5.[21] As you may recall, this theory suggests that human beings have five basic categories of needs: physiological, safety, belongingness/love, esteem, and self-actualization. Further, it proposes that these are arranged in a hierarchy and that only when more basic needs are met do individuals seek to satisfy higher-level ones. When applied to job satisfaction, Maslow's theory suggests that workers will be most satisfied with their jobs when they permit them to satisfy the needs corresponding to their current position in the need hierarchy. For example, an individual seeking to satisfy physiological and safety needs would report satisfaction with his job to the extent that it helped him to meet these needs. In contrast, an individual whose basic needs had already been met might report satisfaction with his job only if it permits him to enhance his self-esteem or to achieve self-actualization.

While this view of human motivation in general and the source of job satisfaction in particular is intriguing, we must note that it has not been strongly supported by research findings.[22] Further, Maslow's theory appears to suffer from several logical flaws, including confusion between values and needs and a lack of clarity as to just what constitutes self-actualization. At present, therefore, its usefulness as a framework for understanding the basic causes of job satisfaction and dissatisfaction is open to question.

A second major theory, and one that has received considerably more attention, is the **motivator-hygiene approach** outlined by Herzberg.[23] This view developed out of a research project conducted with 200 engineers and accountants, employing the critical incident technique described earlier. Subjects were asked to describe times when they felt especially satisfied or dissatisfied with their jobs. Careful analysis of the incidents they reported then yielded an intriguing pattern of findings. Incidents involving the *work itself, achievement, promotion, recognition,* and *responsibility* were often mentioned as sources of satisfaction, but only rarely as sources of dissatisfaction. Herzberg termed such factors **motivators.** In contrast, incidents involving *interpersonal relations, working conditions, supervisors, salary,* and *company policies* were frequently mentioned as causes of job dissatisfaction, but only rarely as causes of satisfaction. Herzberg labeled this group of variables **hygienes.** Combining these results, he concluded that job satisfaction and dissatisfaction actually stemmed from different causes. Specifically, he argued that satisfaction derived mainly from motivators, or aspects of the work itself, while dissatisfaction stemmed primarily from hygienes, the context in which work is performed (see Figure 7–5).

These suggestions were soon investigated in a number of separate studies. Unfortunately, we must report that generally this work failed to offer strong support

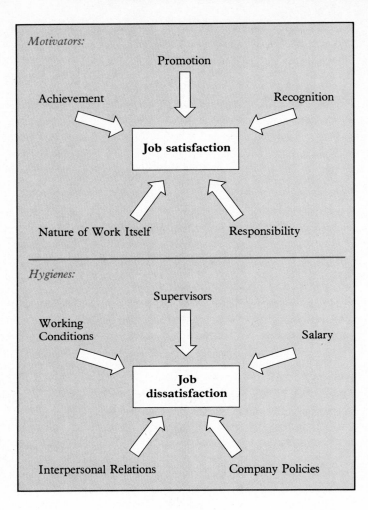

FIGURE 7–5   Herzberg's Motivator-Hygiene Theory

According to a theory proposed by Herzberg, job satisfaction stems largely from one set of factors (motivators), while job dissatisfaction stems from a different set of factors (hygienes). Research designed to test these proposals has yielded mixed results.

for the theory's accuracy. While some studies did yield findings similar to those reported by Herzberg, many others reported sharply contrasting results. Specifically, it was often found that hygienes and motivators exerted powerful effects upon *both* satisfaction and dissatisfaction.[24] Such findings, of course, are contrary to the theory's basic assertion that these positive and negative reactions stem from distinct and different clusters of variables. (We should note that several of these studies used methodology quite different from that employed by Herzberg. But even when similar methods were used, findings inconsistent with the theory were sometimes obtained.)

In view of this evidence, acceptance of Herzberg's theory as a fully adequate framework for comprehending job satisfaction does not seem justified. This is not to say, however, that it has been of little value. On the contrary, the theory has offered important contributions to the field of organizational behavior in other respects. Briefly, the hygiene-motivator theory served to call attention to the importance of psychological growth as a basic condition for lasting job satisfaction. And attention to this fact, in turn, led to much work concerned with the question of how jobs might be designed to foster such growth. Thus, in one sense, Herzberg's theory has served as the stimulus for valuable work on *job design* and *redesign,* as well as *job enrichment*—topics we covered in Chapter 5. For this reason alone, it is worth calling to your attention.

The causes of job satisfaction: Some consistent empirical findings. While neither of the theories we have just summarized seems to provide a thorough account of the causes of job satisfaction, much has been learned about this topic from empirical research. In particular, it is now clear that a large number of factors play a key role in enhancing (or preventing) job satisfaction. These variables are quite diverse in nature, but most seem to fall into two major categories: those relating to events and conditions in work settings and those pertaining more directly to the people in them.

With respect to events and conditions in work settings, job satisfaction is enhanced by work that is mentally challenging and interesting but not too tiring; company policies that permit individuals to reach important work goals; the presence of rewards for good performance (including raises and promotions); rewards that are fair and informative; and work conditions that are comfortable and that facilitate attainment of general work goals. (Interestingly, current evidence is mixed with respect to one recent innovation that might be expected to enhance job satisfaction—*flexitime.* While flexible working hours seem to enhance work group relations and reduce absenteeism, they do not appear to promote increased job satisfaction unless accompanied by other changes in management practices.)[25]

Turning to factors involving other persons, it has been found that job satisfaction is facilitated by supervisors, co-workers, and subordinates who share employees' major values; verbal recognition from superiors; supervisors who aid employees in attaining major work goals; good relations with co-workers; and participation in work-related decisions.

A summary of these and other factors is provided in Table 7–3 on page 214. As we have already noted, a large body of research findings points to their importance in determining employee satisfaction. Thus, to the extent that such factors are present, job satisfaction will probably be high. To the degree that they are absent, satisfaction will probably be low. Please see the **"CASE IN POINT"** box on pages 212–213 for discussion of still another factor that often exerts strong effects on job satisfaction.

The Prevalence of Job Satisfaction: Do People Generally Like Their Work?

Suppose that you approached a large sample of workers doing many different jobs in many different locations and asked them to rate their satisfaction with their work. What would you find? Would most report a reasonable degree of satisfaction, or would they deluge you with complaints and strong statements of dis-

Realistic Expectations . . . Or Shattered Dreams?

This is Georgina Carver's last day with General Industries, and right now, she is waiting for her exit interview with Mr. Bjornstadt, Director of Personnel Services. As she waits in his outer office, Georgina can't help remembering an earlier interview—one that took place just about a year ago. That meeting had been a very pleasant one and had led directly to her being offered, and accepting, a job at General. When she left the building on that spring day, her mind had been filled with visions of a challenging and rewarding career. Benefits, the type of work she would actually perform, the chance for advancement—all had seemed nearly perfect. For several days after the interview, she had sat by the phone, hoping it would ring. When it did and she learned that she actually had the job, she literally leapt into the air for joy.

And then came reality, with all its disappointments and disillusionment. Item: she had been promised a great deal of freedom and autonomy; none was forthcoming. Item: she had been offered rapid promotions and generous rewards; these too had failed to appear. Item: she had been promised work involving much contact with congenial colleagues; instead she found herself isolated from most social contact. And no one had bothered to tell her about the required overtime, the tedious travel, and the silly, time-consuming forms. Yes, she had been misled. And she was still angry about it. In fact, her anger was one of her major reasons for leaving.

Overall, conditions at General weren't all that bad, and the current job market was really tight. But she felt that she had been deceived, and this was a continuing source of irritation. If only they had told her the truth, she might be staying on.

---

satisfaction? Judging from depictions of the world of work in recent movies and magazine articles, you might predict the latter outcome. That is, you might expect to uncover huge pools of anger and discontent. After all, few characters in films are shown enjoying their work, and many articles in newspapers and periodicals focus on the boredom and despair experienced by industrial and even white-collar workers. Surprisingly, though, large-scale surveys of job satisfaction do not support this gloomy picture. On the contrary, most point to the conclusion that an overwhelming majority of persons are relatively satisfied with their jobs. For example, one survey that has continued for more than twenty years indicates that between 81% and 92% of employees are reasonably satisfied with their jobs (see Figure 7-6).[27] And other investigations stretching across even longer periods of time have obtained similar findings.[28] Thus, it appears that most workers are quite satisfied with their jobs.

The findings we have just described paint a comforting picture of conditions in the world of work. But how do they square with such facts as recent declines in

But they hadn't. The company obviously had a policy of misleading prospective employees, and *she* wasn't going to stand for it. Let them get someone else to play the sucker; she had had enough. . . .

At first glance, this situation may strike you as quite extreme. After all, why would any company choose to misrepresent basic working conditions so badly? Surely persons "in the know" would recognize the potential risks of such procedures and avoid them. Surprisingly, though, this is not the case. In their zeal to attract the best people, representatives of many large organizations tend to paint unrealistically rosy pictures of employment in them. And the result of such practices is much as you might expect: when new employees discover that they have been misled, they become angry, experience massive drops in job satisfaction, and often leave.

Such effects have been observed in several recent studies designed to compare the reactions of individuals given *realistic job expectations* and those given unrealistic or misleading ones.[26] In general, the results of such investigations indicate that persons provided with a realistic picture of their future jobs tend to show considerably higher satisfaction and morale than those offered an unduly positive picture of working conditions. These findings, and the general considerations mentioned above, point to the following general conclusion. In the long run, supplying prospective employees with realistic expectations about their new jobs may be a better policy than promising them far more than can actually be delivered. In a word, the costs of shattered dreams can be quite high where job satisfaction, morale, and employee turnover are concerned. □

---

productivity in many countries and high levels of absenteeism and turnover in many businesses? If workers are so satisfied with their jobs, why do such conditions exist—and persist? The answer, we believe, is this: the overall situation is far more complex than it seems.

First, while job satisfaction is generally high, these positive reactions are not uniform across all aspects of work and work settings. For example, satisfaction with pay is generally lower than satisfaction with quality of supervision or with having enough time, help, and equipment to get the job done properly. Thus, when we ask "how satisfied are workers generally," we may overlook important aspects of this issue.

Second, it seems that in some respects, at least, the high levels of satisfaction noted above may be more apparent than real. Briefly, they may stem as much from the way in which job satisfaction is measured as from high levels of positive reactions among employees. That this is in fact the case is suggested by the findings of recent studies in which employees were asked to indicate whether they

TABLE 7-3   Factors Affecting Job Satisfaction

All of the factors listed here have been found to exert important effects upon job satisfaction. Please note that this summary is far from exhaustive. Other factors, too, play a role.

FACTOR	COMMENT
Challenging Work	Work should be interesting, but not fatiguing
Rewards for Good Performance	Clear contingencies between performance and rewards are very desirable
Verbal Recognition	Most persons enjoy praise and positive feedback
Good Working Conditions	Physical working conditions should be comfortable and facilitate attainment of work goals
Concerned Supervision	Supervisors should demonstrate their concern with helping employees to attain important goals
Positive Interpersonal Relations	Satisfaction is strongly enhanced by friendly relations with co-workers and supervisors
Effective Company Policies	These should be designed to aid employees in attaining important work goals
Job Security	Employees should feel that if they perform adequately, their jobs are secure
Pay	Absolute level is important, but the belief that such benefits are fairly distributed may be even more crucial
Participation in Decision-Making	Employees generally feel that they know much about their jobs and should be consulted about them
Degree of Autonomy and Responsibility	The greater these are, the higher satisfaction tends to be
Role Ambiguity	Individuals wish to know just what is expected of them; ambiguity should be avoided

would choose the same work again if they could start all over. The results of such investigations have been considerably less encouraging than those we reported earlier. For example, only 41% of all white-collar workers surveyed reported that they would choose the same line of work again. And among blue-collar employees, the figure was only 24%.[29] In short, many persons seem to feel that they would be happier in some other type of work.

But if this is so, why do so many report that they are quite satisfied with their present jobs? Many factors probably play a role in producing this puzzling pattern (e.g., strong feelings about the necessity of holding a job, the desire to avoid looking like a constant complainer). In addition, it may also stem from the process of *cognitive dissonance*. Consider the following facts. Most persons realize that they will probably have to stay in the job they now hold or one quite similar to it—economic conditions usually do not permit the luxury of great mobility. Thus,

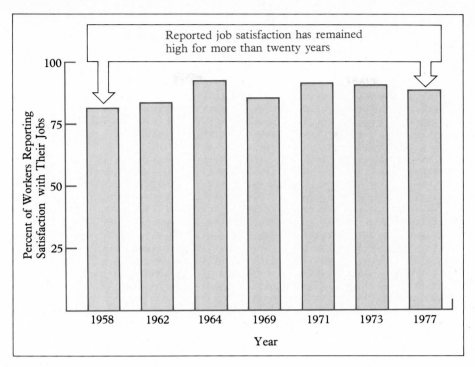

FIGURE 7-6   Reported Job Satisfaction: Consistently High

As shown here, most persons report being quite satisfied with their jobs. Further, such reported satisfaction has neither increased nor decreased greatly in recent decades. (Source: Based on data from Quinn & Staines, *The 1977 quality of employment survey.* Ann Arbor: Institute for Social Research, 1979.)

if they report being dissatisfied with their job, cognitive dissonance may result. After all, stating that one dislikes a job is inconsistent with the knowledge that holding it is a fairly permanent (and necessary) state of affairs. In order to avoid such inconsistency, therefore, many persons may choose to both describe and view their jobs in a relatively favorable light. In short, they may seek to avoid adding to their own discomfort by holding views that generate dissonance. We should hasten to add that direct evidence for these suggestions concerning the role of dissonance in reported job satisfaction is currently lacking. However, the large body of evidence pointing to the importance of dissonance in human attitudes suggests that its possible impact in this respect should not be overlooked.

A third important fact to bear in mind concerning the prevalence of job satisfaction is this: it varies greatly in different groups. As you might expect, managers, technical and professional workers, and the self-employed generally report higher satisfaction than blue-collar employees.[30] Similarly, older workers often report greater satisfaction with their jobs than younger ones (see Figure 7-7).[31] And members of minority groups indicate lower overall levels of satisfaction than

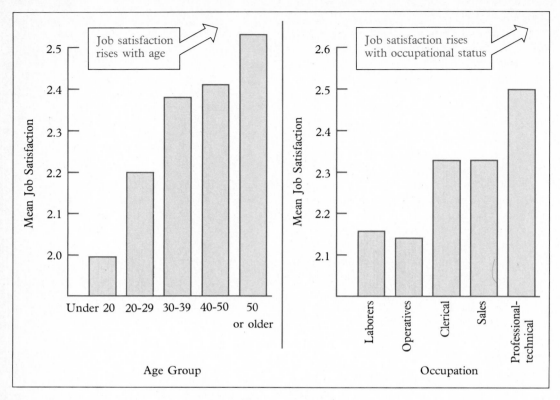

FIGURE 7-7   Job Satisfaction: Some Variations across Groups

As shown here, job satisfaction varies greatly among various groups of workers. For example, older persons report greater satisfaction than younger ones, and individuals in professional or technical jobs report higher satisfaction than laborers. (Source: Based on data from Weaver, *Journal of Applied Psychology*, 1980, *65*, 364–367.)

do others. We should also note that there appear to be some differences between males and females with respect to job satisfaction, although the pattern here seems to be in the process of change. In the past, it was often found that men reported considerably higher job satisfaction than women. However, recent investigations indicate that such differences may be declining, perhaps because of the removal of many barriers to female employment and advancement.[32] If this is indeed the case, then it seems reasonable to predict that such differences may totally vanish in the years ahead.

To conclude: workers in many different fields and locations report high overall satisfaction with their jobs. However, this finding should not be overinterpreted. While it may actually reflect positive reactions toward work on the part of many persons, it probably also stems from other factors too (e.g., strong feelings about the necessity of work, a desire to avoid dissonance). Further, it is important to note that job satisfaction varies considerably across different groups of employees. Thus, in answer to the question with which we began ("Do people generally like their work?"), we can reply: yes, they do—but there are many complications in the picture and these too should be considered.

Job Satisfaction and Dissatisfaction: What Are Their Effects?

Throughout this discussion of job satisfaction, and in our earlier treatment of attitudes generally, we made an important assumption: attitudes are related to overt behavior. We doubt that you find this suggestion surprising; but we must note that for many years, a heated debate raged in social psychology and other fields regarding the question of whether, and to what degree, it is true. Some studies seemed to suggest that the link between attitudes and behavior is weak, while others indicated that it is quite strong.[33,34] Fortunately, it appears that this issue has now been resolved. Growing evidence suggests that attitudes *do* in fact affect behavior; indeed, recent findings reveal that they are often the direct cause of a wide range of actions.[35] This is not to say that attitudes always translate into overt behavior in a direct or immediate manner—far from it. But there is now enough positive evidence to conclude that certain attitudes (especially ones that are specific in nature and were formed on the basis of direct contact with the attitude object) do affect relevant forms of behavior.

To the extent this is true, it is reasonable to expect job satisfaction to play a key role in several job-related activities. And in fact, this appears to be the case. We will now review some of these effects for you. But please be warned: as we have already stated, research on the behavioral effects of job satisfaction has provided some important surprises.

Job satisfaction, absence from work, and turnover. Imagine two employees, both of whom hate to get up in the morning and dislike fighting their way through the morning rush hour to work. One likes her job very much while the other dislikes it. Which is more likely to call in sick or miss work for other reasons? The answer is obvious: the one who dislikes her job is the better candidate. That job satisfaction does affect absence from work in this manner is suggested by the findings of many investigations. In general, these studies report a low to moderate *inverse* relationship between job satisfaction and absences. That is, the lower an individual's satisfaction with his or her job, the more likely is that person to be absent from work.[36]

Similar findings have been obtained with respect to employee turnover. Once more, the lower an individual's level of satisfaction with his or her job, the more likely this person is to resign and seek other opportunities. And again, the strength of this relationship is only low or moderate.[37] This raises an interesting question: why aren't the links between job satisfaction and both absenteeism and turnover even stronger? The answer is quite simple: these behaviors—as well as others pertaining to work—are affected by many different variables. Job satisfaction is only one of these. To mention just a few illustrations of this point, absence from work is probably affected by the distance employees live from their plant or office and by the severity of the climate in their area, as well as by job satisfaction. Similarly, turnover is probably affected by general economic conditions and the level of skills workers possess, as well as by their attitudes toward their jobs. Given the impact of these and many other factors, it is only to be expected that the relationship between job satisfaction and such behaviors would be moderate. Indeed, it would be far more surprising if this relationship were an overwhelming or all-powerful one.

Job satisfaction and productivity. It has often been assumed that happy workers are productive workers, and at first glance, this assertion makes good sense. After all, won't persons who are pleased with their jobs put out more effort than those who are unhappy and dissatisfied? Such arguments are persuasive, and even today most managers seem to accept them as valid. Actually, though, there is little support for their accuracy. Most studies designed to examine the possibility of a link between job satisfaction and productivity have yielded negative results. That is, contrary to what "common knowledge" suggests, productivity does not seem to rise with increased satisfaction or to fall with growing dissatisfaction.[38] Initially, this finding may strike you as quite puzzling, but there are several reasons for its existence. We will mention two of these here.

First, in many work settings, there is little room for large changes in performance or productivity. Jobs are structured so that the persons holding them must perform at a minimal level—if they do not, they cannot retain the position. But there is also little room for exceeding this standard. Even if a worker speeds up, the production line will continue to move at the same pace. And often, individuals are so dependent on others for part of their work materials that they cannot move ahead on specific jobs even if they wish to do so. Under these conditions, even extremely high levels of job satisfaction can do little to raise productivity; and the link between these variables is weakened.

Second, and even more important, it may actually be the case that job satisfaction and productivity are not directly linked. Rather, any apparent relationship between them may stem from the fact that both are related to a third factor—the receipt of various rewards. As outlined some years ago by Porter and Lawler, the situation may be as follows.[39] Past levels of performance lead to the receipt of both extrinsic rewards (e.g., pay, promotions) and intrinsic rewards (e.g., feelings of accomplishment). If these rewards are judged to be fair and equitable by employees, then they may come to perceive a contingency between performance and such outcomes. This, in turn, may result in relatively high levels of effort and performance. At the same time, the belief that rewards are provided in a fair manner and are contingent on one's actual performance may generate high levels of job satisfaction. In short, high productivity and high satisfaction may both stem from the conditions just outlined. The two factors themselves, however, are not directly linked. (Please see Figure 7–8 for a summary of these suggestions.)

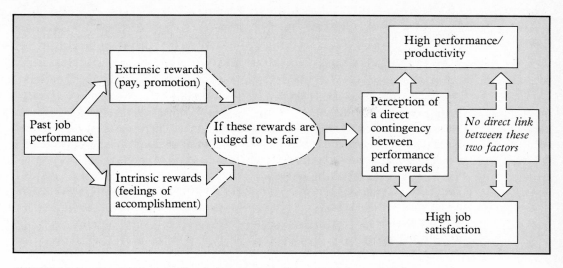

FIGURE 7–8   One Explanation for the Absence of a Direct Link between Job Satisfaction and Productivity

According to a theory outlined by Porter and Lawler, performance leads to both extrinsic and intrinsic rewards. If these are judged to be fair, employees may come to perceive a direct contingency between their performance and such rewards. This, in turn, can lead to both high performance/productivity and high job satisfaction. These latter two factors, though, are not directly linked. (Source: Based on suggestions by Porter & Lawler, *Managerial Attitudes and Performance.* Homewood, Ill.: Richard D. Irwin, 1968.)

For these and other reasons, job satisfaction may fail to exert direct effects upon productivity. As we have already noted, though, it does appear to influence both absenteeism and turnover. Further, it may also affect additional aspects of job performance, such as the rate at which new skills are mastered and the variability of both work output and work quality. In short, it is a factor well worthy of managers' careful attention.

Job satisfaction and early retirement.   In recent years, a number of organizations in both the private and public sector have adopted early retirement plans. Employees participating in such programs can retire before reaching age 65 if they have accrued a minimum number of years of service (usually 30) and have reached some minimum age (often 55). It seems reasonable to assume that attitudes toward or satisfaction with one's job might influence the decisions of such persons to either take advantage of this option or to continue working. And in fact, recent evidence gathered by Schmitt and McCune suggests that this is the case.[40] These investigators found that among a group of state civil servants, those who chose to retire early held less positive attitudes about their jobs than those who chose to continue working. For example, they viewed their jobs as less involving and challenging than nonretirees. Further, individuals in lower-level, less challenging positions were more likely to choose early retirement than those in higher-level, more challenging ones. Surprisingly, retirees and nonretirees did not differ in overall reported level of job satisfaction, as assessed by one standard measure of such reactions (the Minnesota Satisfaction Questionnaire). However, differences (although small) were in the expected direction. Taken as a whole, the findings reported by Schmitt and McCune suggest that individuals with negative attitudes toward or feelings about their jobs are more likely to choose early retirement than those with more positive ones—a finding with obvious practical implications for employers in both public and private sectors.

Job satisfaction and other aspects of behavior.   Before concluding this discussion, we should note that job satisfaction also exerts effects on behavior outside the work place. In particular, some research findings suggest it may be linked to both physical and mental health. With respect to physical well-being, it has been found that work satisfaction is linked to longevity: satisfied individuals tend to live longer than those who are dissatisfied with their work.[41] Clearly, this is an intriguing and potentially important relationship. Turning to mental health, other research indicates job satisfaction is related to several positive characteristics, such as low anxiety, high self-esteem, and good social adjustment.[42] Together, these findings suggest that the benefits conferred by job satisfaction may not be restricted to the purely economic "payoffs" of lower turnover and absenteeism. Rather, they indicate that being satisfied with one's work may exert more general beneficial effects. If managers needed one further inducement for paying close attention to the satisfaction of their employees (and themselves!), this should provide it. For some concrete suggestions concerning techniques for enhancing job satisfaction, see the **"PERSPECTIVE"** box on pages 222–223.

PREJUDICE: ATTITUDES THAT HARM

"Don't jump to conclusions" is a phrase we often hear and try to follow. Yet where other people are concerned, we somehow seem to forget all about its existence. In many cases, we *do* jump to conclusions about others. And often, these rest on the flimsiest foundation imaginable: their membership in some social group. That is, we reach conclusions about others' behavior or major traits simply on the basis of their ethnic, racial, religious, or sexual identity. This tendency to form judgments about others solely on the basis of their membership in various groups or categories lies at the heart of the topic we will now consider—*prejudice.*

Prejudice: Its Nature and Origins

In newscasts and magazine articles, the terms *prejudice* and *discrimination* are generally used as synonyms. But scientists who study these topics in a systematic manner usually distinguish between them. Briefly, they use the term *prejudice* to refer to negative attitudes of a special kind and the term *discrimination* to refer to the negative actions that often stem from such attitudes. We will adopt the same distinction here.

As we have just noted, prejudice can be viewed as a special type of attitude. Specifically, it is often defined in the following way: *Prejudice is an attitude* (usually negative) *toward the members of some specific group* (racial, ethnic, etc.) *that causes the person holding it to evaluate others solely on the basis of their membership in that group.* Thus, when we say that an individual is prejudiced against the members of some group, we mean that he or she tends to evaluate such persons in a negative manner simply because they belong to that group—*not* because of their individual characteristics or behavior.

As an attitude, prejudice possesses the cognitive, affective, and behavioral components we described earlier (see pp. 196–197). Because the first of these has received the greatest amount of attention in organizational behavior, however, we will focus exclusively on it at the present time.

The cognitive component of prejudice refers to beliefs and expectations held about the members of a particular group. Often, these beliefs form clusters of preconceived notions known as **stereotypes.** Stereotypes are of major importance, for once formed, they exert several powerful effects. First, they lead individuals to assume that all members of a given racial, ethnic, or other group possess similar traits or act in the same manner—assumptions that are often false. Second, they exert a powerful impact upon the processing of new social information. That is, they shape the interpretation of such information so that it is perceived as offering support for the stereotyped beliefs, even if this is not actually so.[43]

Unfortunately, stereotypes are both common and persistent. They exist with respect to racial groups, sex, occupational groups, age, and even physical beauty.[44,45] Further, considerable evidence indicates that they change very slowly, even over the course of several decades. That stereotypes often exert powerful effects upon important forms of organizational behavior is suggested by the findings of many recent studies. For example, consider the results of an intriguing investigation conducted by Rosen and Jerdee.[46] These researchers attempted to assess the impact of stereotyped beliefs about older workers upon several types of managerial decisions. In order to do so, they asked business school students to play the role of a Division Manager, and to make decisions/recommendations about six different incidents. (For example, one involved evaluating a candidate for promotion to a job requiring a high level of creativity. Another involved hiring someone for a job requiring the ability to make quick judgments under conditions of high risk.) In each incident, the key person involved was described as being either relatively young (in his 20s or 30s), or relatively old (in his 50s or 60s). Experience and qualifications were held constant in all cases. Rosen and Jerdee expected that stereotyped beliefs concerning older workers (e.g., that they are less creative and more cautious than younger persons) would exert strong effects upon subjects, decisions, and as you can see from Figure 7–10, this was definitely so. Thus, in the incident involving a job requiring creativity, 54% of the subjects recommended promotion of the younger candidate but only 25% recommended promotion of the older one. Similarly, in the incident involving hiring of

FROM THE MANAGER'S PERSPECTIVE

Job Satisfaction: Can It Be Enhanced?

By now, we're sure you are convinced of the value of inducing high levels of job satisfaction among employees. Such positive reactions on the part of workers can reduce turnover and absenteeism and so yield important economic benefits. Further, they can contribute to physical and mental well-being. And having happy and satisfied employees is certainly better for the image of one's company or organization than having dissatisfied and miserable ones (see Figure 7–9). But how, precisely, can job satisfaction be enhanced? Are there specific steps managers can take to encourage such feelings among their employees? Clearly, there is no magic formula for attaining this happy result. Many factors play a role in job satisfaction, and several of these are beyond the control of individual managers. (For example, there is no simple way of converting dull jobs into challenging ones.) Yet, we believe that managers are far from powerless in this regard. Through careful attention to several factors, they can substantially enhance job satisfaction. A number of specific steps that may prove useful in this regard are outlined below.

Assure clear contingencies between performance and rewards. In our experience, nothing reduces job satisfaction and morale as much as the feeling

"For God's sake, don't join this firm."

FIGURE 7–9   Job Dissatisfaction Strikes Again!

As suggested by this cartoon, dissatisfied employees can be a very bad advertisement for one's company or organization! (Source: Drawing by Stevenson; © 1976 The New Yorker Magazine, Inc.)

a person for a job requiring quick decisions, 25% recommended selection of the younger applicant and only 13% recommended choice of the older individual. In short, it appeared that beliefs about older workers did in fact strongly affect subjects' recommendations. To the extent such effects also occur in actual organizational settings (and there is every reason to believe that they do), they may often

that what one does on the job doesn't really count. After all, if there is no direct link between how one performs and the rewards one receives, there is little room for enthusiasm or related positive feelings. For this reason, managers wishing to encourage satisfaction among their employees should take great care to praise individuals for excellent work. And if this praise is public, all the better. Positive feedback of this type is usually appreciated and can do wonders for morale and satisfaction.

Demonstrate concern with workers' welfare. Employees do not expect their supervisors to be uniformly friendly or supportive, but they *do* expect them to care. Specifically, they expect their supervisors to be concerned with helping them to attain important work-related goals. Thus, managers interested in encouraging job satisfaction should take steps to convince their employees that they really *do* have their best interests at heart.

Provide opportunities for worker participation and input into decisions. Many employees feel—perhaps rightly so—that they know as much (or more) about their jobs as anyone else. Thus, they find it gratifying to be consulted by management about matters pertaining to their work. One effective means for raising job satisfaction, then, is encouraging worker participation in these respects. It seems possible that this factor plays an important role in the recent success of *Quality Circles*—small work groups charged with the task of improving the quality of company products. Because the members of such groups have full opportunity to advise management on work-related issues, their level of satisfaction may be high, with all the posi-

tive effects this often yields. In any case, managers concerned with raising job satisfaction should direct careful attention to worker participation and input.

Avoid task or role ambiguity. Human beings seem to dislike uncertainty almost as much as they dislike inconsistency. Thus, on the job, employees generally want to know just what is expected of them—what tasks they are expected to perform and what roles they are to play. Managers hoping to improve job satisfaction, therefore, should devote careful attention to avoiding ambiguity in these respects.

Encourage good interpersonal relations. One of the major sources of pleasure and satisfaction in employment settings is good relations with one's co-workers. For this reason, managers concerned with enhancing job satisfaction should take every possible step to assure the presence of such positive relations. This may mean transferring or even terminating workers who are a cause of interpersonal friction—steps no managers relish. But the benefits yielded may often make the anguish involved in such decisions worthwhile.

To conclude: we firmly believe that through these and related actions, managers can do much to enhance job satisfaction among their employees. We also realize, of course, that following these suggestions will often involve the expenditure of considerable effort. But given the many benefits derived from high levels of employee satisfaction, it is our view that this will usually be effort well spent. □

bias and distort managerial decisions. And the costs associated with such decisions are too obvious to require added comment.

The origins of prejudice: Some contrasting views.
Where does prejudice come from? Why do individuals so often hold strong negative attitudes toward

FIGURE 7–10 Evidence for the Impact of One Stereotype on Managerial Decisions

When asked to play the role of a division manager and make various decisions, business students were strongly influenced by stereotypes concerning the traits of older workers. As shown here, they were reluctant to promote an older person to a position requiring high creativity. And they were also less willing to hire an older than a younger worker for a job requiring quick decisions. In short, their stereotypes of older workers led them to strongly favor younger persons in several respects. (Source: Based on data from Rosen & Jerdee, *Journal of Applied Psychology,* 1976, *61,* 428–432.)

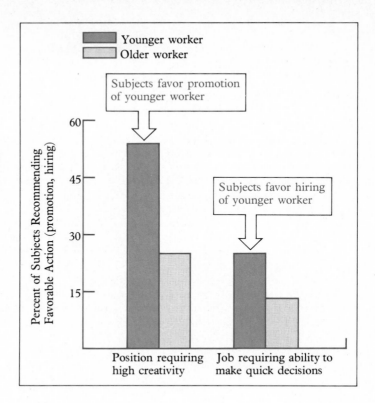

the members of groups other than their own? These are important questions, with many practical implications. Because prejudice is a complex process, several different answers have been offered. Among the ones receiving most attention have been the suggestions that prejudice stems mainly from (1) *intergroup contact,* (2) *the presence of certain personality traits,* or (3) *from learning experiences occurring early in life.*

With respect to intergroup conflict, it has been proposed that prejudice often arises when different groups strive for the same jobs, housing, and other resources. Since their contacts under these conditions are largely hostile and competitive, it is not surprising that these interactions give rise to strong, negative attitudes. Evidence for such effects has been obtained in a number of different studies. Briefly, these investigations suggest that when groups must compete, negative feelings akin to prejudice do often emerge.[47,48] And conversely, when contacts between various groups are largely friendly and cooperative in nature, such reactions are reduced.

Turning to personality as a basis for prejudice, it has been proposed that certain traits predispose individuals toward such attitudes. Perhaps the best known theory in this respect was offered several decades ago by Adorno and her colleagues.[49] These scientists suggested that prejudice is often related to—and stems from—a cluster of personality traits they termed the *authoritarian personality.* Briefly, authoritarian individuals are persons showing a pattern of submissive obedience to authority, punitive rejection of groups other than their own, and rigid, black-white thinking. Either you are a member of their own group and are for them or you are a member of some other, rejected group and must be against them. Unfortunately, authoritarian individuals are far from rare, and you will probably encounter many during your career. When you do, don't be too surprised if they express strong prejudice toward certain social groups. Considerable evidence indicates that their own personalities predispose them in this direction.

A final view as to the origins of prejudice rests upon the assumption that such reactions are learned. Basically, it suggests that children acquire negative attitudes toward various social groups either simply by observing such reactions on the part of their parents or through direct reward and training for expressing such views. While parents, teachers, and peers are probably most important in this respect, the mass media, too, may play a role. Until recently, members of racial and ethnic minorities appeared only rarely on T.V. and in movies. Further, when they did, they were often shown as holding low-status jobs, as living in slums, and as speaking with a heavy and incomprehensible accent (see Figure 7-11). Given repeated exposure to such materials, it is far from surprising that many children soon acquired negative attitudes toward such persons, even if they had never met any in real-life situations.

In sum, prejudice has been attributed to several different sources. Since evidence for the role of each exists, it is our view that all three probably contribute to such reactions. That is, prejudice probably stems from negative intergroup

FIGURE 7-11   The Mass Media: Past Contributors to Prejudice

In the past, members of minority groups were often portrayed in a negative or condescending manner by the mass media. (Source: Photo by Culver Pictures, Inc.)

contact, from specific personality traits or trends, and from early social learning experiences. Given the multiple origins of such negative reactions, it is little wonder that they are anything but rare.

Prejudice toward Females: A Special, Timely Case

Females constitute a clear majority of the world's population. Yet, despite this fact, they have been treated in much the same fashion as minority groups in most nations. They have been largely excluded from economic and political power. They have been the object of pronounced stereotyping. And they have often suffered from overt discrimination (e.g., females have often been barred from many jobs and social organizations). Fortunately, overt sexist practices such as these seem to be on the wane, at least in some places, and to some degree. Yet, there is little doubt that they continue to exist in many settings.[50] In the U.S. and other nations, recent government regulations (Equal Employment Opportunity rulings) now insist that females (and minorities) be given fully equal opportunities with respect to hiring, promotions, and other benefits. As a result, many businesses and organizations have found themselves grappling with these and other complex social problems. In order to acquaint you with some of the crucial aspects of these issues, we will now describe some of the factors that seem to work against female success and advancement in organizational settings. Then, we will turn to recent findings concerning the performance and behavior of women as managers.

Discrimination against females: Subtle but pervasive.   In the early 1980s women make up almost 50% of the total labor force in the U.S. This figure is even higher in other nations, and the trend toward growing female employment shows no sign of abating. As television, magazines, and movies suggest, women now find work in many fields once considered the sole domain of men. Yet, despite these gains, one crucial fact remains unaltered: women continue to be concentrated in relatively dull and dead-end jobs. At one time, this state of affairs stemmed primarily from overt discriminatory practices. Now, however, it seems to derive from other and more subtle factors. Among the most important of these are strong tendencies to devalue female achievement and certain internal barriers and conflicts faced by women as they mount the corporate ladder.

Devaluing female achievements: Does success stem from effort, ability, or luck?   When individuals perform some task, the success or failure they achieve can be attributed to several different causes. Specifically, a given level of performance can be attributed to internal factors, such as ability and effort, or to external factors, such as luck and task difficulty. As we noted in Chapter 6, most persons—including managers—feel that good performance stemming from ability or effort is more deserving of recognition than similar performance deriving from luck or an easy task. Thus, corporate rewards such as raises and promotions are frequently distributed to persons viewed as having succeeded because of high ability or outstanding effort; such "payoffs" are awarded far less often to persons perceived as having succeeded because of luck or because the job was easy. All this probably strikes you as being quite reasonable. But now, consider the following: several recent studies suggest that many persons tend to attribute successful performance by males and females to different factors. Successful performance by males is often attributed to their ability or effort. In contrast, successful performance by females is often attributed to luck or an easy task. (See Figure 7-12.)[51] Further, additional findings indicate that the more negative the attitudes held by individuals about women in management, the stronger these tendencies.[52,53] Needless to say, this form of bias in explanations for successful work operate against the advancement of women in organizational settings. Even when they achieve the same levels of success as their male counterparts, the outcome is not as favorable. After all, their success is seen as the result of having had an easy task or "lucky breaks." Clearly, an important task faced by many organizations in the years ahead is the elimination of this subtle—but powerful—type of bias.

   Internal barriers to advancement: Do women fear success?   Several years ago, Matina Horner conducted several intriguing and controversial studies.[54] In these investigations, she presented male and female subjects (college students) with the following brief statement, and asked them to write stories about it: "After first-term finals (Anne/John) finds (herself/himself) at the top of (her/his) medical class."
   For female subjects, the character was named Anne; for males, he was named John. Horner reported that many more women than men expressed ambivalence

FIGURE 7–12   Bias in Attribution: A Basis for Sexism

The results of several studies indicate that successful performance by females and males is often attributed to different causes. Specifically, good performance by males is attributed to ability or effort. Similar performance by females is often attributed to luck or an easy task.

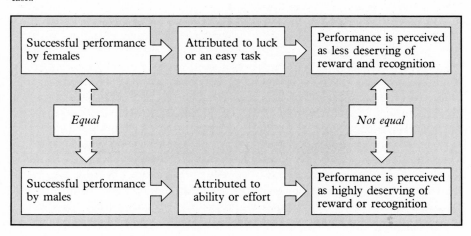

or conflict over success in this situation. Indeed, while fewer than 10% of the stories written by men contained any hint of such reactions, fully 65% of those written by females contained such themes. On the basis of these findings, she argued that because success and achievement conflict with certain aspects of traditional female sex roles, many women come to show fear of success. In short, they fear that if they are too successful or too competitive, they will sacrifice part of their own femininity.

While these are intriguing suggestions, we are happy to report that they have *not* been strongly supported by subsequent research. It now appears that fear of success—if it does in fact exist—is not as strong or common among women as Horner's findings indicate. And such reactions do not appear to be the sole property of females.[55] On the contrary, many males, too, seem to feel that far outpacing others may yield substantial personal costs as well as the obvious benefits. At present, then, it does not seem appropriate to conclude that fear of success is a major factor working against female advancement in organizational settings.

As noted by Terborg, however, other internal barriers to such success may exist.[56] For example, many women may view themselves—often incorrectly—as unsuited for managerial careers. It seems possible that recent shifts in traditional conceptions of masculinity and femininity, and in traditional sex roles, may do much to eliminate such barriers. But only time—and further careful research—will reveal whether this is indeed the case.

On the costs of being a "token."   The final barrier to female success and achievement we will consider is, perhaps, the most unsettling. This is the case because, surprisingly, it springs directly from attempts to *eliminate* discriminatory practices toward women. Permit us to explain. In recent years, many organizations have adopted *affirmative action programs.* That is, they have made special efforts to hire women (and members of various minority groups). On the surface, such programs seem quite beneficial. After all, they *do* lead to greater representation of women in jobs long dominated by males. But, it appears, these positive results may be gained only at some cost. The individuals hired through such programs may quickly come to conclude that their sex—not their job-related qualifications—are responsible for their employment. And this realization, in turn, may exert negative effects upon their morale, job satisfaction, and commitment. That such reactions actually occur is suggested by the results of a recent study conducted by Chacko.[57] In this investigation, young women holding managerial positions were asked to rate the importance of their sex, education, and experience in their hiring. In addition, they completed questionnaires designed to measure their organizational commitment and satisfaction with various aspects of their work. Results were quite clear: the greater the importance subjects assigned to their sex as a hiring factor, the lower their satisfaction and commitment. In short, to the extent they perceived that they were hired simply because they were female, both work satisfaction and organizational commitment suffered. These findings suggest that affirmative action programs, beneficial as they may be, can sometimes "backfire" in an alarming manner. While they may assist women in obtaining desirable jobs, they may also exert adverse effects upon their satisfaction with these positions and, perhaps, their actual performance in them. Needless to add, concrete steps must be taken to counter such effects if affirmative action programs are to accomplish their central goals.

Women as Managers: Some Revealing Recent Findings

Up to this point, the focus of our discussion has been on factors that operate against the advancement of females in organizational settings. In this final section, however, we will shift our attention to another issue—one, moreover, that will permit us to conclude on a much more positive note. The question we will address is this: once they have chosen management as a career, do women actually behave differently from men in this role? In short, do females manage differently from men? Stereotypes concerning masculine and feminine behavior would lead to the expectation that such differences exist.[58] Further, they would predict an advantage in favor of males. However, such predictions are *not* supported by the findings of a recent, large-scale study conducted by Donnell and Hall.[59]

These researchers conducted five separate but related investigations designed to uncover any differences in the behavior of male and female managers, should they exist. Almost 2,000 managers participated in the study, and in each case, comparisons between male and female managers were based on carefully matched samples—individuals who were similar in virtually all key respects except that of sex. Thus, subjects were matched in terms of age, rank within their organizations, the type of organization in which they worked, and so on.

Once matched samples were obtained, the behavior of male and female managers was compared along five key dimensions previously found by Donnell and Hall to be closely linked to managerial success. These included: (1) managerial philosophy—beliefs that shape an individual's approach to the management process; (2) motivational dynamics—the manager's own motives, and their effects upon his or her subordinates; (3) participative practices—the degree to which a manager is sensitive to the needs of subordinates; (4) interpersonal competence—the ability of a manager to deal effectively with others; and (5) managerial style—whether a manager is primarily concerned with people, with production, or both. The results of the project were clear and pointed to a firm conclusion: contrary to popular beliefs, women do *not* differ from men in terms of key aspects of their behavior as managers. Indeed, out of forty-three separate comparisons relating to the factors listed above, only two showed significant overall differences between males and females. And even here, one of the differences favored females (they were more achieving in their motivation profiles than males), while the other favored males (they were more open and candid with colleagues than females). In short, the findings of the study indicated that males and females behave in much the same fashion when serving as managers. Needless to add, this finding renders any vestiges of prejudice against women in the world of work even less defensible than would be the case if important differences did exist. After all, if male and female managers show virtually identical patterns of behavior, why should the question of gender enter into the picture at all? Our answer—and yours too, we trust—is simple: it shouldn't!

SUMMARY

Attitudes are relatively lasting clusters of feelings, beliefs, and behavior tendencies directed toward specific persons, groups, or objects. They are acquired through basic processes of learning and are often measured by means of self-report attitude scales or questionnaires. Attitudes can be changed through persuasive communications. In addition, they are often altered when individuals discover that their attitudes and their behavior are inconsistent, and so experience an unpleasant state known as *dissonance*. Repeated exposure to many different stimuli induces positive reactions to these stimuli. This phenomenon—known as the *frequency-of-exposure effect*—appears to play an important role even in the realm of politics.

Individuals usually hold strong and well-established attitudes toward their work. Such attitudes, known as **job satisfaction,** are often measured by means of self-report attitude scales. Job satisfaction is influenced by many different factors, including challenging, interesting work; the presence of rewards for good performance; recognition from superiors; and good relations with co-workers. Contrary to popular belief, most individuals report a high level of satisfaction with their jobs. However, some evidence suggests that such satisfaction may be more apparent than real. Job satisfaction is related to both employee turnover and absenteeism, but it does not seem to be directly linked to job performance. Several steps can be taken by managers to enhance satisfaction among their employees.

Prejudice is a negative attitude toward the members of some specific social group. Often, it results in negative behaviors toward the group. Such actions are known as *discrimination*. **Stereotypes,** the cognitive component of prejudice, appear to play an important role in many organizational decisions. Prejudice seems to stem from intergroup conflict, from specific personality traits, and from early learning experiences.

In recent years, overt discrimination against females has decreased. However, more subtle factors such as the tendency to attribute successful performance by females to luck remain and operate against the advancement of women within organizations. Recent findings indicate that women and men do not differ with respect to their behavior as managers.

KEY TERMS

ATTITUDES   Enduring clusters of feelings, beliefs, and behavior tendencies directed toward specific persons, groups, ideas, or objects.

COGNITIVE DISSONANCE   Refers to an unpleasant state produced when individuals notice that their attitudes or their attitudes and their behavior are somehow inconsistent.

CREDIBILITY   Refers to the perceived trustworthiness or believability of communicators. Credibility, in turn, is determined by a communicator's apparent expertise and motives.

CRITICAL INCIDENT PROCEDURE A method for measuring job satisfaction or dissatisfaction in which employees describe incidents relating to their work that they found especially satisfying or dissatisfying.

DISCRIMINATION The behavioral component of prejudice. Refers to negative actions taken by prejudiced individuals against the persons or groups they dislike.

FREQUENCY-OF-EXPOSURE EFFECT Refers to the fact that liking for many stimuli increases with their familiarity. This phenomenon appears to play an important role in politics.

HYGIENES In Herzberg's theory, factors that affect job dissatisfaction.

JOB SATISFACTION Attitudes held by employees about their work.

LIKERT SCALING A self-report technique for measuring attitudes in which individuals indicate the extent to which they agree or disagree with various attitude-relevant statements.

MOTIVATOR-HYGIENE THEORY A theory of job satisfaction proposed by Herzberg. According to this theory, different factors affect job satisfaction and dissatisfaction.

MOTIVATORS In Herzberg's theory, factors that affect job satisfaction. In general, these relate to aspects of the work itself.

PERSUASIVE MESSAGES Written, spoken, televised, or filmed messages designed to induce shifts in attitudes. Several factors relating to characteristics of the communicator, the communication itself, and the recipients appear to affect the success of such appeals.

PREJUDICE Refers to negative attitudes toward the members of some specific group that cause the person holding them to evaluate others negatively solely on the basis of their membership in that group.

STEREOTYPES Refers to the cognitive component of prejudice. Stereotypes lead the persons holding them to believe that all members of a given social group possess the same traits or show similar behaviors.

NOTES

1. Bem, D.J. *Attitudes, beliefs, and human affairs* (2nd ed.). Belmont, Calif.: Brooks-Cole, 1982.

2. Fazio, R.H., & Zanna, M.P. Direct experience and attitude-behavior consistency. In L. Berkowitz (Ed.), *Advances in experimental social psychology* (Vol. 14). New York: Academic Press, 1981.

3. Baron, R.A., & Byrne, D. *Exploring social psychology* (2nd ed.). Boston: Allyn and Bacon, Inc., 1982.

4. Knapp, M.L. *Nonverbal communication in human interaction* (2nd ed.). New York: Holt, Rinehart and Winston, 1978.

5. Maddux, J.E., & Rogers, R.W. Effects of source of expertness, physical attractiveness, and supporting arguments on persuasion: A case of brains over beauty. *Journal of Personality and Social Psychology*, 1980, *39*, 235–244.

6. Wood, W., & Eagly, A.H. Stages in the analysis of persuasive messages: The role of causal attributions and message comprehension. *Journal of Personality and Social Psychology*, 1981, *40*, 246–259.

7. Mewborn, C.R., & Rogers, R.W. Effects of threatening and reassuring components of fear appeals on physiological and verbal measures of emotion and attitudes. *Journal of Experimental Social Psychology,* 1979, *15,* 242–253.

8. Zellner, M. Self-esteem, reception, and influenceability. *Journal of Personality and Social Psychology,* 1970, *15,* 87–93.

9. Eagly, A.H., & Carli, L. Sex of researchers and sex-typed communications as determinants of sex differences in influenceability: A meta-analysis of social influence studies. *Psychological Bulletin,* 1981, *90,* 1–20.

10. Festinger, L. *A theory of cognitive dissonance.* Evanston, Ill.: Row, Peterson, 1957.

11. Festinger, L., & Carlsmith, L.M. Cognitive consequences of forced compliance. *Journal of Abnormal and Social Psychology,* 1959, *58,* 203–210.

12. Schlenker, B.R., Forsyth, D.R., Leary, M.R., & Miller, R.W. A self-presentational analysis of the effects of incentives and attitude change following counterattitudinal behavior. *Journal of Personality and Social Psychology,* 1980, *39,* 553–577.

13. Locke, E.A. The nature and causes of job satisfaction. In M. Dunnette (Ed.), *Handbook of industrial and organizational psychology.* Chicago: Rand McNally, 1976.

14. Lofquist, L., & Dawis, R.V. *Adjustment to work.* New York: Appleton-Century-Crofts, 1969.

15. Smith, P.C., Kendall, L.M., & Hulin, C.L. *The measurement of satisfaction in work and retirement.* Chicago: Rand McNally, 1969.

16. Zajonc, R.B. Attitudinal effects of mere exposure. *Journal of Personality and Social Psychology Monograph Supplement,* 1968, *9,* 1–27.

17. Mita, T.H., Dermer, M., & Knight, J. Reversed facial images and the mere-exposure hypothesis. *Journal of Personality and Social Psychology,* 1977, *35,* 597–601.

18. Grush, J.E. The impact of candidate expenditures, regionality, and prior outcomes on the 1976 Democratic presidential primaries. *Journal of Personality and Social Psychology,* 1980, *38,* 337–347.

19. Grush, J.E., McKeough, K.L., & Ahlering, R.F. Extrapolating laboratory exposure research to actual political elections. *Journal of Personality and Social Psychology,* 1978, *36,* 257–270.

20. Locke, E.A. The nature and causes of job satisfaction. In M. Dunnette (Ed.), *Handbook of industrial and organizational psychology.* Chicago: Rand McNally, 1976.

21. Maslow, A.H. *Motivation and personality* (2nd ed.). New York: Harper & Row, 1970.

22. Locke, E.A. The nature and causes of job satisfaction. In M. Dunnette (Ed.), *Handbook of industrial and organizational psychology.* Chicago: Rand McNally, 1976.

23. Herzberg, F., Mausner, B., & Snyderman, B. *The motivation to work.* New York: Wiley, 1959.

24. Schneider, J., and Locke, E.A. A critique of Herzberg's incident classification system and a suggested revision. *Organizational Behavior and Human Performance,* 1971, *6,* 441–457.

25. Narayanan, V.K., & Nath, R. A field test of some attitudinal and behavioral consequences of flexitime. *Journal of Applied Psychology,* 1982, *67,* 214–218.

26. Wanous, J.P. Tell it like it is at realistic job previews. *Personnel,* 1975, *52,* 50–60.

27. Quinn, R.P., & Staines, G.L. *The 1977 quality of employment survey.* Ann Arbor: Institute for Social Research, 1979.

28. Gallup, G.H. *The Gallup poll.* New York: Random House, 1972.

29. Kahn, R.L. The meaning of work: Interpretations and proposals for measurement. In A.A. Campbell & P.E. Converse (Eds.), *The human meaning of social change.* New York: Basic Books, 1972.

30. Weaver, C.N. Job satisfaction in the United States in the 1970s. *Journal of Applied Psychology,* 1980, *65,* 364-367.

31. Ibid.

32. Sauser, W.I., Jr., & York, C.M. Sex differences in job satisfaction: A re-examination. *Personnel Psychology,* 1978, *31,* 537-547.

33. Wicker, A.W. An examination of the "other variables" explanation of attitude-behavior inconsistency. *Journal of Personality and Social Psychology,* 1971, *19,* 18-30.

34. Kahle, L.R., & Berman, J.J. Attitudes cause behaviors: A cross-legged panel analysis. *Journal of Personality and Social Psychology,* 1979, *87,* 315-321.

35. Fazio, R.H., & Zanna, M.P. Direct experience and attitude-behavior consistency. In L. Berkowitz (Ed.), *Advances in experimental social psychology* (Vol. 14). New York: Academic Press, 1981.

36. Porter, L.W., & Steers, R.M. Organizational work, and personal factors in employee turnover and absenteeism. *Psychological Bulletin,* 1973, *80,* 151-176.

37. Michaels, C.E., & Spector, P.E. Causes of employee turnover: A test of the Mobley, Griffeth, Hand, and Meglino model. *Journal of Applied Psychology,* 1982, *67,* 53-59.

38. Locke, E.A. The nature and causes of job satisfaction. In M. Dunnette (Ed.), *Handbook of industrial and organizational psychology.* Chicago: Rand McNally, 1976.

39. Porter, L.W., & Lawler, E.E. *Managerial attitudes and performance.* Homewood, Ill.: Dorsey Press, 1968.

40. Schmitt, N., & McCune, J.T. The relationship between job attitudes and the decision to retire. *Academy of Management Journal,* 1981, *24,* 795-802.

41. Palmore, E. Predicting longevity: A follow-up controlling for age. *The Gerontologist,* 1969, *9,* 247-250.

42. Kornhauser, A.W. *Mental health of the industrial worker: A Detroit study.* New York: Wiley, 1965.

43. Hamilton, D.L., & Rose, T.L. Illusory correlation and the maintenance of stereotypic beliefs. *Journal of Personality and Social Psychology,* 1980, *39,* 832-845.

44. Sagar, H.A., & Schofield, J.W. Racial and behavioral cues in black and white children's perceptions of ambiguously aggressive acts. *Journal of Personality and Social Psychology,* 1980, *39,* 590-598.

45. Cash, T.F., Gillen, B., & Burns, D.S. Sexism and "beautyism" in personnel consultant decision making. *Journal of Applied Psychology,* 1977, *62,* 301-310.

46. Rosen, B., & Jerdee, T.H. The influence of age stereotypes on managerial decisions. *Journal of Applied Psychology,* 1976, *61,* 428-432.

47. Sherif, M., Harvey, O.J., White, B.J., Hood, W.R., & Sherif, C.W. *Intergroup conflict and cooperation: The Robbers' cave experiment.* Norman: University of Oklahoma Press, 1961.

48. Kerington, S.M. Intergroup relations and nursing. *European Journal of Social Psychology*, 1981, *11*, 43–59.

49. Adorno, T.W., Frenkel-Brunswik, E., Levinson, D.J., & Sanford, R.N. *The authoritarian personality*. New York: Harper, 1950.

50. Taylor, M.S., & Ilgen, D.R. Sex discrimination against women in initial placement decisions: A laboratory investigation. *Academy of Management Journal*, 1981, *24*, 859–865.

51. Heilman, M.E., & Guzzo, R.A. The perceived cause of work success as a mediator of sex discrimination in organizations. *Organizational Behavior and Human Performance*, 1978, *21*, 346–357.

52. Garland, H., & Price, K.H. Attitudes toward women in management and attributions for their success and failure in a managerial position. *Journal of Applied Psychology*, 1977, *62*, 29–33.

53. Stevens, G.E., & DeNisi, A.S. Women as managers: Attitudes and attributions for performance by men and women. *Academy of Management Journal*, 1980, *23*, 355–361.

54. Horner, M.S. Femininity and successful achievement: A basic inconsistency. In J.M. Bardwick et al. (Eds.), *Feminine personality and conflict*. Belmont, Calif.: Wadsworth, 1970.

55. Condry, J., & Dyer, S. Fear of success: Attribution of cause for the victim. In D.N. Ruble, I.H. Frieze, & J.E. Parsons (Eds.), Sex roles: Persistence and change. *Journal of Social Issues*, 1976, *32*, 63–83.

56. Terborg, J.R. Women in management: A research review. *Journal of Applied Psychology*, 1977, *62*, 647–664.

57. Chacko, T.I. Women and equal employment opportunity: Some unintended effects. *Journal of Applied Psychology*, 1982, *67*, 119–123.

58. Skrypnek, B.J. & Snyder, M. On the self-perpetuating nature of stereotypes about women and men. *Journal of Experimental Social Psychology*, 1982, *18*, 277–291.

59. Donnell, S.M., & Hall, J. Men and women as managers: A significant case of no significant difference. *Organizational Dynamics*, 1980, 60–77.

8

Performance in Organizations: Determinants, Appraisals, and Applications

KEY CONCEPTS

Performance Appraisal
Criterion Problem
Ultimate Criterion
Criterion Relevance
Criterion Deficiency
Criterion Contamination
Circadian Rhythm
Halo Error

Leniency Error
Central Tendency Error
Management by Objectives (MBO)
Merit-Pay Plans
Piece Rate
Commission
Scanlon Plan
Profit-Sharing

□ □ □

What a terrible day! You've just come out of the office of Mr. Barnett, your supervisor, where the two of you discussed your annual performance appraisal. The overall evaluation was a "good" one, but it was far from the "outstanding" evaluation you feel you deserved. Mr. Barnett tried to calm you down by pointing out this rating indicated he felt you were doing a better-than-average job, and that he wanted to give you some feedback so that you could do even better next time. But you weren't buying any of it. You realize that a "good" rating will get you only a cost-of-living salary increase with no merit raise, while an "outstanding" rating would have gotten you the raise you feel you deserve.

What really hurts is that you know Charlie Adams did get an "outstanding" rating, even though you know you're doing a better job than he is. The more you think about it, the more it hurts. What were those points that Mr. Barnett focused on? He talked about your lack of ingenuity and your weak leadership style. He couldn't even be specific. And, how would he know about those things anyway? The only specific incident he discussed was that order you were late in shipping last week. Of course, he forgot about that custom rush order at the beginning of the year that was so critical and that you got out ahead of schedule. Then you begin to wonder "Will I ever do the kind of job Mr. Barnett feels is 'outstanding'." You wonder if he personally dislikes you and so rates you lower than you deserve. Is it possible to ever overcome such a handicap? Well, that's for someone else to worry about. This is the final straw. Tomorrow you look for a new job.

Scenes like this happen every day. We are evaluated and we evaluate others on a regular basis. The waitress at lunch, the taxi driver, our friends, our family, and of course our subordinates are all under our scrutiny. Likewise, *we* are being observed by others, *our* performance is being duly noted, and we either reap the rewards or suffer the consequences of their reactions to our performance. Of course, as in the story above, we do not like being evaluated poorly. Even when such negative evaluations do not cost us money or other concrete benefits, we dislike being criticized. Further, we usually want to know *why* we received the precise rating we did. (It is interesting to note that most people also dislike *giving* criticism, so that this situation is really uncomfortable for everyone concerned.)

Performance appraisals are an integral part of life in a modern organization. We expect to be evaluated on a fairly regular basis, and we expect some re-

FIGURE 8-1   Performance Appraisal: A Key Process in Modern Organizations

Individuals working in modern organizations expect to have their performance evaluated. In contrast to the situation shown here, however, they also expect such appraisals to be fair—to be closely linked to their actual job performance. (Source: GOOSEMYER by Parker & Wilder © 1981 Field Enterprises, Inc. Courtesy of Field Newspaper Syndicate.)

wards to be tied to those evaluations. We also expect these appraisals to be linked to our performance, so that success and efficiency yield more favorable ratings than failure and inefficiency. In other words, we expect evaluations to be *fair*—to be based on job-related performance, *not* upon the way we look or upon a manager's selective memory (see Figure 8-1). Unfortunately, things are never as simple as we would prefer. There are actually many determinants of performance that can play a role in evaluations, aside from actual performance. As we shall also see, regardless of the type of rating scale used, most appraisals ultimately rely upon a fallible human judge. Thus, performance appraisals will never be perfect as long as raters can forget what they saw or make other types of errors.

In this chapter we shall discuss many of the problems associated with identifying, evaluating, and rating performance, as well as those associated with how performance evaluations are used in organizations. Specifically, we will first examine some *general issues* related to performance appraisal such as definitions of performance, the major determinants of performance in organizations, purposes for appraisals, dimensions for evaluations, and some common types of rating errors. Next, we will examine a number of *techniques* available for rating performance, as well as the issue of training raters in an attempt to reduce rating errors. Finally, we will discuss how performance information can be *used,* focusing especially on feedback interviews and procedures for tying performance to rewards.

GENERAL ISSUES RELATING TO PERFORMANCE IN ORGANIZATIONS

At first glance, performance appraisal may seem to be a trivial problem. If we want to evaluate a secretary's typing skills, we count the number of errors he makes in work he does for us; if we want to evaluate a store department manager's performance, we examine her sales figures for the last month. Unfortunately, few jobs lend themselves to such simple evaluations. For example, in the case of the secretary, since he performs many other duties besides typing (making airline reservations, scheduling appointments), evaluating his performance is not as simple as checking for typing errors. And in evaluating the store manager, we might also wish to consider employee turnover in her department and overall customer relations. The real issue, then, is deciding exactly what constitutes *good performance* on a particular job. Only after we've answered this question can we adequately evaluate performance. This is known as the **criterion problem** in performance evaluation, and we shall spend some time discussing the issues to keep in mind when attempting to deal with this problem.

Criterion-Related Issues: What to Measure When We Measure Performance

Let us begin by defining the **ultimate criterion**—that is, what we are ideally concerned with on the job. Psychologists have typically defined this as the sum total of a worker's contribution to an organization. Notice, we said this was an *ideal* since, obviously, we would have to wait until a person completed his or her time on the job before we could hope to measure *total* contribution. (Even then, there would be so many intangibles to consider we still would find the task extremely difficult.) While we are waiting, we need to rely on some alternative definition of performance that can be more easily measured and that we will call the *actual criterion*. This is not to say that any handy index of performance is necessarily a suitable criterion. In fact, let us suggest that any criterion should be:

1. reliable (that is, different people should be able to agree on the level of performance being exhibited by a worker);
2. realistic;
3. representative of the job as a whole;
4. acceptable to both workers and managers; and
5. measurable (that is, a number can be attached to a given level of performance).

Thus, criterion measures, such as words per minute typed, units produced by a factory worker, and dollar sales by a salesperson, are all acceptable for use in performance evaluation. In order to be able to distinguish between truly good and truly poor performers, however, our criterion measure needs to satisfy several other conditions as well.

Since we can never measure the ultimate criterion, and so have to settle for something less, we must always be concerned with the problem of **criterion relevance.** This is simply the degree to which the actual criterion overlaps with or corresponds to the ultimate criterion. Clearly, we wish to maximize criterion relevance, and we can do this by ensuring that the performance evaluation we use is related to the job the employee performs. On the other hand, our goal must also be to minimize two other factors: **criterion deficiency** and **criterion contamination.** Criterion deficiency is the extent to which our criterion measure lacks something that is a necessary part of the ultimate criterion. Thus, if we evaluated a waiter's performance only on the basis of the wine he recommended, we would be using a deficient criterion since his job involves so much more than that. Criterion contamination results when a part of the actual criterion is not also a part of the ultimate criterion. Using the example of the waiter again, he is not responsible for the way our food is cooked. If we include this as part of our evaluation of his performance (and this the size of the tip we left), we would be using a contaminated criterion. It does not require a great deal of imagination to come up with other sources of contamination such as the employee's age, race, and sex (all illegal as well as contaminating) or the way someone dresses or the books they read. For the time being, it would be safe to say that, generally speaking, criterion contamination is a more serious problem (both on the job and for society) than criterion deficiency. Figure 8–2 illustrates the relationship between criterion relevance, deficiency, and contamination. Please examine it carefully. (See the **"CASE IN POINT"** box on page 242 for a concrete example of the complexities involved in adequate performance appraisal.)

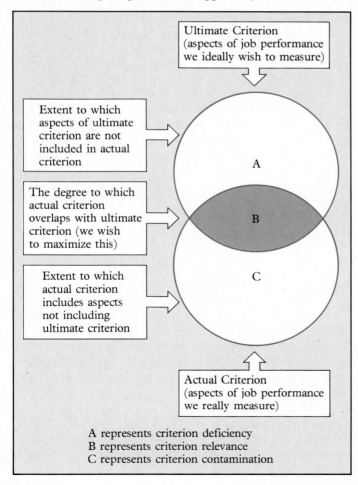

Ultimate Criterion (aspects of job performance we ideally wish to measure)

Extent to which aspects of ultimate criterion are not included in actual criterion

The degree to which actual criterion overlaps with ultimate criterion (we wish to maximize this)

Extent to which actual criterion includes aspects not including ultimate criterion

A

B

C

Actual Criterion (aspects of job performance we really measure)

A represents criterion deficiency
B represents criterion relevance
C represents criterion contamination

FIGURE 8-2   Ultimate versus Actual Criterion: The Ideal and the Real

One important goal in performance appraisal is that of maximizing *criterion relevance*—the extent to which actual measures of job performance overlap with or represent those aspects of performance with which we are concerned.

CASE IN
POINT

Hidden Assets . . . Or, The Many Faces of Good Performance

Phil Sakamura, Miriam Sedgewick, and Fred Storms are gathered in Phil's office, poring over the records of all managers at Robotronics below the rank of vice-president. It's their task to select individuals deserving of promotions, bonuses, or merit raises, and they take their job very seriously; after all, a lot is at stake. Right now, they're discussing Chuck Bolding, a Unit Manager in the Consumer Products Division.

"Well, Chuck's record looks about like it did last year," remarks Miriam. "He gets the job done, but he's not outstanding."

"Right," agrees Fred. "Production records for his unit are about average for the Division. And his quality rating and on-time index are both just a small shade above what's viewed as typical."

"Looks as though we can get through his folder pretty quickly," Miriam states. "I don't see much basis here for a major action one way or the other."

At this moment, Phil interrupts. "Hold on a second. I agree that the numbers aren't very exciting. But I have a hunch there's something else we should consider. The other day I had lunch with Harry Terner, from Research and Development. He mentioned that Chuck had sent them a good idea for a new valve they're designing. We got to talking about that kind of thing, and it turns out that Chuck actually does it on a pretty regular basis. About two or three times a year he comes up with an idea for an improvement in something we make or a new approach to producing it. And half the time, the guys in R&D find them useful. So, it looks as though he's been doing something that may not be in his job description, but that's pretty valuable to the company."

Major Determinants of Performance: What Causes Us to Perform the Way We Do

An issue that complicates the decision of what should be measured in performance evaluation is the fact that there are multiple determinants of any one person's performance on any one job. For example, some people's temperament is better suited for one type of job than another; some try harder; some get to work in more pleasant conditions; and some people are simply more capable than others. Although we can't always consider all of these factors when conducting an appraisal, it is important to understand the way different factors can help determine a worker's performance.

The physical environment.   One of the most important, yet overlooked determinants of job performance, is the physical environment in which the job exists. Although we often hear people discussing "working conditions," they are

For a few seconds Miriam and Fred look surprised. Then, Miriam responds: "Hmmm . . . you know, that makes a lot of sense. Unit Managers ought to be in a perfect position to provide that kind of input. I mean, if anyone knows the problems with our products, it's them. Maybe we've been missing something here."

"Yeah," adds Fred. "I think Miriam's right. Maybe this is the kind of thing we should expect from Unit Managers. And if Chuck's been doing it all along, we ought to recognize it. I'm for putting him up for a bonus."

I'll go along with that," says Phil. "And I'd go even further. Why don't we recommend adding this kind of information to the evaluation for Unit Managers? I think it ought to be considered along with the production numbers. Heck, it strikes me as a real important part of the job. . . . "   □

Questions:

1. Do you think it would make sense to add information of the kind described above to the evaluation of Unit Managers? If so, why?
2. What problems do you notice with respect to the evaluation criteria being used by Robotronics to appraise the performance of Unit Managers at present?
3. Would you go along with the recommendation to give Chuck Bolding a bonus? And if he receives one, how might other Unit Managers react, given that no one ever told them to offer suggestions to R&D?

usually not very precise in their use of the term. We would like to be quite precise and discuss four aspects of the physical environment that have been shown to affect job performance. These are (1) illumination, (2) temperature, (3) noise, and (4) work schedule. Although some may argue that work schedule is not, technically speaking, part of the "physical" environment, it is part of the work setting and it does affect performance.

Illumination is the first of these factors we wish to consider. As you may recall from Chapter 1, the original Hawthorne studies were designed, in part, to measure the effects of different levels of illumination on performance. Generally speaking, illumination levels for various tasks should be set such that both visual performance and comfort are assured. Of course, satisfying these two requirements involves different levels of illumination for different jobs, and we cannot go into the details of how those levels are determined. There are, however, several points about illumination worth noting.

First, it seems to be generally true that daylight provides the best illumination for work, although studies conducted with office workers indicate that the concern for daylight in offices has less to do with actual lighting conditions and more to do with the psychological desire for windows.[1] Other research further suggests that when artificial light is used, it should be as color-free as possible (although of the colored lights, yellow causes the least discomfort).[2] This research also points up the importance of glare for productivity. Glaring lights cannot only reduce productivity by increasing fatigue, they can also damage vision over time.

It is obvious that the level and quality of illumination is more important for some jobs than for others. Nonetheless, illumination represents one potentially important environmental determinant of performance.

Temperature is another environmental factor that has been found to influence performance. People are most comfortable when they are in a state of thermal equilibrium with their environment. Thus, when we are "hot," our bodies dissipate heat to the environment; and when we are "cold," they retain this heat. When we have to expend a lot of effort to maintain this equilibrium we might suspect that performance suffers, and that is in fact the case.

For example, the effects of heat on the performance of jobs involving strenuous physical activity is well known. A study conducted by Fine and Kobrick, however, demonstrated the effects of heat on the performance of *cognitive* tasks as well.[3] In this investigation, male soldiers (ages 18–25) performed several different tasks requiring thought and concentration (e.g., decoding messages, receiving and recording weather data). Subjects worked on these tasks under comfortable temperatures (70°F) and also under very hot conditions (95°F). As you can see from Figure 8–3, their performance deteriorated sharply in the presence of extreme heat, although there was actually a slight improvement in performance after workers became acclimated to the heat. Soon thereafter, however, performance decrements began and got progressively larger as the time of exposure to the heat increased.

Exposure to cold also has marked effects on performance, but there is little evidence to suggest that cold affects the performance of cognitive tasks. Manual tasks, however, do suffer as hand temperature drops in response to the cold. For example, Clark reported that manual performance begins to drop off when skin temperature drops below 55°F.[4]

Noise is generally considered to be a distractor and would therefore be expected to interfere with efficiency on the job. Contrary to popular belief, however, noise is not a major problem in most cases. Park and Payne suggest that a worker's *average* performance is not affected at all by the level of noise on most jobs; but the performance becomes more variable, and the worker is required to expend more effort to maintain the same level of performance.[5] Cohen further suggests that jobs requiring vigilance and concentration are much more susceptible to noise effects than are jobs involving simple, repetitive tasks.[6] Nonetheless, when noise levels get too high, not only does performance generally suffer, but employees run the risk of hearing loss and are more likely to miss work.[7] The effects of noise and similar factors will also be discussed as a source of stress in Chapter 9.

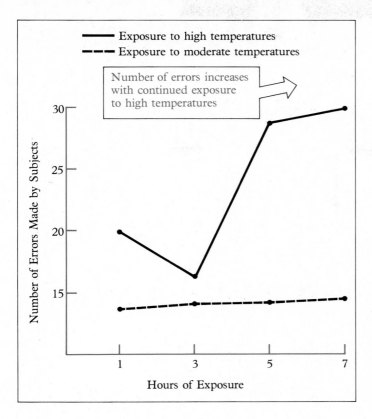

FIGURE 8-3   Heat: Its Negative Impact upon Task Performance

As shown here, performance of various cognitive tasks is impaired under high levels of heat. Further, these decrements in performance increase in size as duration of exposure to such conditions rises. (Source: Based on data from Fine & Kobrick, *Human Factors*, 1978, *20*, 115–122.)

    The final factor we want to consider here is *work schedule.* The major concern is the effect of shift work upon performance. Such a concern leads us to introduce the notion of the **circadian rhythm,** which is an internal "clock" that tells us when to eat, when to sleep, and when to get up. When this rhythm is disrupted, we tend to suffer sleep loss, lack of appetite, various digestive problems, and headaches that can lower our ability to concentrate on work.[8]

    The most serious problem relating to work schedules, though, is *rotating shifts.* Here, workers move back and forth between day and night shifts and their circadian rhythm never gets a chance to be established. Studies have found that workers on rotating shifts are eight times as likely to have ulcers as day-shift workers.[9] In a study done in Sweden, researchers reported that under a three-shift system, a very high number of errors occurred around 3:00 a.m. (the night shift ran from 10:00 p.m. to 6:00 a.m.).[10] Further, the number of errors did not seem to vary as a function of season or day of the week, and the number of errors was roughly the same on the first day of the shift as on the last day. Clearly, the weekly rotating shifts were not allowing workers enough time to adjust their rhythms and so there were problems.

    In conclusion, all of these environmental factors, as well as others we might suggest, can affect a worker's performance on the job. Should these factors be considered as part of the ultimate criterion and so play a role in performance evaluation? Probably so, for if they are not, it may be extremely difficult to compare the performance of workers on different jobs in the organization. In any event, these factors make the determination of a performance criterion much more complex.

Ability and motivation.   Imagine for a moment that you have recently begun taking guitar lessons, and you play for a friend. Your friend responds that you're not bad, but you're no George Benson. You might be annoyed by such a comment since, after all, you are not a professional musician. The point here is that we all differ in our *ability* to perform a given task. All other factors being equal, a person who has greater ability will outperform those with lesser ability. Perhaps, then, the major determinant of a worker's performance is his or her ability to perform the tasks required. Regardless of how hard you work or how long you practice, you will probably never be as good as George Benson—he is simply better able to play the guitar than most people. But is it fair to compare your playing with George's?

Perhaps we can better understand the problem by bringing in another factor—*motivation.* Theories of motivation were discussed in depth in Chapter 5; so for our present purposes, we will simply define motivation as the amount of effort a worker exerts on the job. One important issue, then, involves the interaction between ability and effort in determining job performance. If we are facing an impossible task—one for which we do not possess the necessary ability or skill—no level of effort can help: effort alone cannot produce success. In a similar fashion, if we possess a great deal of ability but put forth no effort at all, we are also unlikely to succeed. Here, though, there is hope: if we increase our effort, performance may well improve. In short, motivation is an important factor affecting performance only when an individual or worker possesses the required ability to begin with. In the total absence of ability to perform a given task, motivation has little if any effect.

But motivation does not simply determine level of performance; it also affects how performance is evaluated. Here, the key question is do we wish to reward workers (in the form of high evaluations and all that they imply) on the basis of mostly ability or mostly motivation? For example, suppose we are asked to evaluate two workers who are performing at about the same level. One is very capable, but is not really putting out maximum effort. The other is clearly less able, but *is* working as hard as he or she can. To whom do we assign higher ratings? As noted in Chapter 6, we might well be inclined to give the edge to effort. That is, assuming that actual performance is about equal (and at least adequate), we might assign higher ratings to the person whose success seems to stem mainly from effort than to the one whose success seems to derive mainly from ability. Of course, we should emphasize that this would be the case only if actual performance is equal, since we usually assign higher ratings to persons who show excellent performance than to those who show mediocre performance, regardless of the basis for such differences.[11]

Finally, we should also consider another aspect of the relationship between motivation and performance. Porter and Lawler have noted that if successful performance does in fact lead to organizational rewards, such performance can actually be a motivational factor for workers.[12] Under these conditions, they can see that their efforts *do* result in rewards. And as a result, they may become willing to exert higher levels of effort on the job. In sum, not only can motivation influence performance, performance (if followed by rewards) can influence motivation, too. In any case, the important point to consider is this: both effort and ability can play an important role in determining performance and in determining evaluations of it.

Personality. One determinant of performance we should briefly consider is the personality of the worker on the job. As discussed in Chapter 4, certain types of people are better suited for some jobs than for others. For example, we would not want to have someone susceptible to sensory overload and stress working as an air traffic controller. Conversely, there are many people who might find manufacturing jobs boring, and so would not perform as well as they should. Although this is basically a selection problem, there is an aspect that is particularly relevant for performance appraisal.

Leventhal and his associates have found that unexpected success tends to be over-evaluated.[13] If an individual does not seem to possess the characteristics needed for success but succeeds despite this fact, we tend to evaluate his or her work very favorably. After all, the person in question has done well despite an important handicap. An example of these effects is presented in Figure 8-4. As shown there, a shy, retiring person who succeeds as a salesperson may be evaluated more favorably than a bold, assertive one, for whom such success is expected.

FIGURE 8-4   Unexpected Success: Grounds for Positive Evaluations?

When individuals possess the traits or characteristics required for successful task performance, we expect them to succeed. Thus, when they do, we evaluate their performance in a moderately favorable manner (upper panel). When such persons do not possess the traits necessary for successful task performance, however, we evaluate good performance on their part more favorably. It is as if we award them "extra credit" for having succeeded in the face of adversity (lower panel).

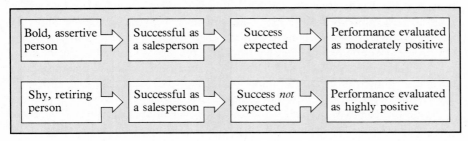

Each of these factors, then, plays a role in determining a worker's level of performance. A rater may or may not wish to consider all of them, but they are all factors nonetheless. We have discussed these determinants here primarily to call your attention to the fact that many different factors can and do influence performance. Unfortunately, these tend to complicate the evaluation process, and can lead to many types of inaccuracy. Another factor that has been found to be important in performance appraisal is the *purpose* for the appraisal. We will now turn our attention to that issue.

Purposes for Conducting Appraisals: Why We Evaluate Performance

At the outset of the chapter, we noted that people engage in some type of performance evaluation in many day-to-day settings. These evaluations may differ in one important aspect, however, which may be best illustrated through an example. When you are at a restaurant and you evaluate the performance of your waiter, you do so to help determine how large a tip you should leave. Thus, your evaluation has a very concrete outcome attached to it. Further, given societal norms, the waiter would probably have to make a major blunder (like spilling hot soup in your lap) before you would evaluate him so poorly that you would leave no tip. Now compare this situation with one in which a classmate asks you to read over the paper she wrote for her English class. She asks you to make comments and suggestions in the hope of improving her chances for a good grade. Now your evaluation has little in the way of concrete outcomes attached to it—a poor evaluation from you will cost your friend no money, nor will it cost her a poorer grade. Although she may be a bit upset if you had a lot of negative things to say about her paper, you still might look for all the weak points you could find—if she is aware of those points and corrects them, she will improve her chances of getting a good grade. Thus, in this case, assuming you handle the criticism well, a negative evaluation might really help her more than an unwarranted positive evaluation.

These examples parallel the two major purposes for conducting appraisals in organizations: *administrative decision making* and *feedback*. One of the more common reasons for conducting appraisals is to provide input for making decisions about salary increases, promotions, and other administrative actions. One special consideration for those using appraisals for administrative decision making is that the Equal Employment Opportunity Commission (EEOC) views appraisals in the same way as tests when an organization dispenses rewards and/or penalties on this basis. Thus, if the appraisals are found to have an adverse impact upon a "protected group" (a group specified in the Civil Rights Act), the organization may be liable in a legal action. There have, in fact, been cases where companies have been found guilty of discrimination because their performance evaluations were found to be biased (e.g., *Albermarle* vs. *Moody,* 1975).

The other common purpose for conducting evaluations is to provide workers with feedback concerning their performance and to point out areas where they

FIGURE 8-5   Feedback: A Key Facet of Performance Appraisal

We all like to know how we are doing. Thus, providing individuals with such feedback is one important reason for conducting performance appraisals. (Source: Drawing by W. Miller; © 1979 The New Yorker Magazine, Inc.)

might improve in the future. Since we all like to know how well we are doing, feedback is an important role for performance appraisals (see Figure 8-5). Additionally, several systems of management (e.g., Management by Objectives) employ feedback as an integral part of their approach.

Although these two reasons for conducting appraisals may seem distinct, a problem in many organizations is that, in practice, there is only one appraisal conducted to satisfy both objectives. Thus, it is often not possible to separate the two—a fact that researchers at General Electric found to cause problems.[14] Why problems? Let's go back to the two situations we described at the beginning of this section—evaluating the waiter and evaluating your friend's paper. In the first case, you might be likely to give the waiter the benefit of the doubt. In like fashion, when a worker's raise or promotion is on the line, a rater is likely to give that worker the benefit of the doubt and overlook some shortcomings. In the second case, you might go out of your way to point out problems in your friend's paper so that she could correct them and get an A in her course. A supervisor might likewise point out all of the areas in which a worker could improve so that he or she will eventually become an outstanding worker.

But what if the appraisal is being used for both purposes simultaneously? There seems to be a tendency to let the concern about costing an employee a raise or promotion override the concern for giving valuable feedback. As a result, the evaluation tends to overlook areas where there could be some improvement, thus reducing the utility of the feedback. How do we avoid this problem? The answer is deceptively simple: conduct two separate appraisals. One appraisal can be used for administrative decision making, and this should be made clear to everyone concerned. A second appraisal is then conducted simply to provide feedback to workers. The two appraisals should be kept distinct in time, and the results of one appraisal should not be allowed to influence the other. Although this may be difficult in practice (especially in terms of separating the two in the minds of raters and ratees), and would necessitate that two periods of time be set aside for evaluations, it does assure that both important functions of appraisals are well served.

Up to this point we have been discussing some general issues that deal with the underlying assumptions and context for performance appraisals. Before getting to the actual techniques available for conducting appraisals, however, there are two other general issues that must be discussed: *rating errors* and *dimensions for appraisals*. The first deals with problems that often occur with appraisals, while the second deals with the structure of those appraisals. Our concern with the first stems from a basic fact: even after we understand the determinants of performance and the purposes for appraisals, there are still many things that can—and often do—go wrong. Thus, we will now turn our attention to typical rating errors, such as the halo effect, leniency, and central tendency. Pinpointing these errors is easy, but finding out where they come from is, as we shall soon see, anything but simple.

Errors in Performance Appraisal: Why Evaluations Often Go Astray

As we noted in Chapter 6, **halo effects** involve the tendency to generalize from an overall impression of another person to his or her specific traits and behaviors. With respect to performance appraisal, then, halo errors generally center around the tendency to assume that individuals who do well (or poorly) on one job or aspect of a job will also do well (or poorly) on other jobs or aspects of a job as well. For example, consider the case of a young executive who closes a very important deal. On the basis of this success, he may acquire a positive "halo." And then, his supervisor may assume that he will do well on other tasks, too, even if she has no basis for making this assumption.

Advertisers often make use of halo effects to promote specific products. Thus, we are all familiar with ads in which an athlete recommends a specific brand of beer or other product. Is the athlete really an expert on the taste of beer? Does he even drink? We don't know, but the manufacturer hopes that we will make the "logical" connection between sports and beer or that our positive feelings about the athlete will spill over to the product he is promoting (see Figure 8–6). Either way, it would follow that we will buy the beer.

A great deal has been written about halo error and proposed methods for eliminating its effect. Unfortunately, as Cooper has recently pointed out, most of these methods have not been effective.[15] One of the nagging problems in the area has been the basis for the halo. Although our discussion thus far has been limited to halo as an error of judgment—as a cognitive error—there are other plausible explanations for halo error that have been proposed.[16] For one, if we observe someone working at different parts of a job and each time we do he or she is performing well, it would be reasonable for us to rate the person high on all aspects of the job. Is this an error? Perhaps. Perhaps we only watch this person at times when he or

FIGURE 8-6   Halo Effects: One Practical Use

Famous athletes and entertainers are often featured in ads for specific brands of beer and other products. Sponsors hope that positive feelings toward these persons will spill over onto their products, and so increase sales. (Source: Photo courtesy Miller Brewing Co.)

she is doing everything to impress us. The error, then, is in how we collect information, not in how we use it. (In this regard, recent findings suggest that the better or more accurate we are in observing others' behavior, the better or more accurate we are in evaluating their performance. Thus, accurate observation does seem to be a major foundation for useful evaluations.[17] There is yet another possible explanation for the halo—and this one is the most troublesome of all. What if, for example, good football players really *do* know more about beer or an outstanding professor really *is* good at everything. Then, a halo error would not be an error at all. Whatever the cause, though, the halo effect is usually seen as a source of inaccuracy in appraisals, and so we try to avoid it.

Closely related to this type of logical error is the problem that occurs when we rate someone's performance favorably because there is something about that person that seems "right" for the job or, at least, that is attractive to us. For example, we might rate individuals high because of the way they dress, the way they look, or the way they speak. Con artists capitalize on this variant of halo error. Further, studies have shown that workers tend to be evaluated more favorably when they are older,[18] when they agree with their supervisors on how the job should be done,[19] or when they are in some way supportive of their supervisors.

But what about variables such as race and sex? As noted in Chapter 7, some findings suggest that these factors affect ratings of performance in ways we might expect. That is, females often receive lower ratings than males, and blacks often receive lower ratings than whites (at least from white raters). But it is important to note that the evidence on such issues is far from consistent. In fact, there is some indication that under certain conditions, patterns opposite to those that might be predicted on the basis of "common sense" occur. For example, in one study reporting such results, Hamner and his colleagues asked college students to play the role of manager of a grocery store and to rate the performance of eight applicants for a job as stock worker.[20] The applicants performed either well or poorly, and were either black or white and male or female. Raters, too, varied in race and sex. As shown in Figure 8-7, the results were complex and contained several surprises. First, with respect to sex, female applicants actually received *more* favorable ratings than males. Further, this advantage was more pronounced

FIGURE 8-7   Sex and Race: Some Unexpected Effects on Performance Ratings

As shown here, female applicants for a job in a grocery store received higher ratings than male applicants—especially when their performance on a "work sample" test was high. In addition, black applicants received higher ratings than white applicants when their performance on the work sample was low. The reverse was true when performance on this screening test was high. (Source: Based on data from Hamner et al., *Journal of Applied Psychology,* 1974, *59,* 705–711.)

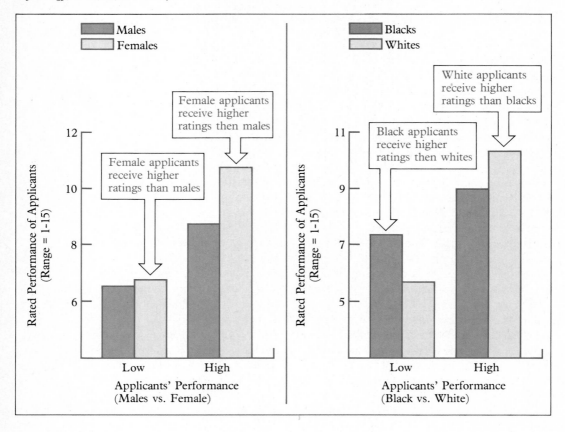

under conditions where applicants performed well than under conditions where they performed poorly. Second, as expected with respect to race, there was a tendency for raters to favor their own race: black raters assigned higher ratings to black applicants than to white ones, while this pattern was reversed for white raters. Another finding, however, was more surprising: under conditions of high performance, white applicants received higher ratings than black applicants. However, under conditions of low performance, black applicants were rated more favorably than white ones. (Recall our earlier discussion about unexpected performance, however, with regard to these results.) In sum, the findings of this study suggest that the race and sex of both raters and the persons they rate can affect performance appraisal. However, these effects seem to be much more complex than we might at first predict.

In addition to these variations of halo error, there are two other major types of errors raters often commit. **Leniency error** is simply the tendency to generally inflate ratings. We all know of instructors who give easy A's, just as waitresses learn who are the big tippers. (By the way, we can also mention *severity error,* which is literally the opposite of leniency.) Sometimes, in an effort to avoid making hard decisions we just give everyone a break. Of course, this has the effect of making high evaluations meaningless and essentially negates the entire appraisal process. Further, the existence of lenient and severe raters in the same organization produces a lot of resentment among workers being evaluated. Another way to avoid making tough decisions is simply not to make them. **Central tendency error** involves a rater's bias toward rating everyone "average." In this way, the rater completely avoids any real evaluation, and although no one receives outstanding evaluations, no one is rated poorly either.

Although these are not the only sources of rater inaccuracy, these errors are the ones most commonly associated with performance evaluations. Of course, to the extent that these problems play a major role in evaluations, neither the administrative nor feedback goals of evaluations will be served. Unfortunately, even the attempt to be a "nice guy" can result in legal problems for organizations (see the **"PERSPECTIVE"** box on pages 254–255). It is not surprising, therefore, that a great deal of effort has been aimed at reducing rating errors. We will now discuss the results of some of these efforts.

Dimensions for Appraisals: What We Rate Is Often as Important as How We Rate It

Since we cannot measure all aspects of performance and since we know that performance evaluations are often prone to a number of rating errors, can we help minimize these problems by focusing on certain dimensions of performance? The answer to this is not simple. Many of us intuitively feel that traits like creativity, loyalty, and perseverance should be rewarded. But focusing on performance "traits" such as these presents problems. What does creativity look like? Was Thomas Edison creative? How about the person who invents a utensil that slices

FROM THE MANAGER'S PERSPECTIVE

Inaccurate Ratings: Some Hidden, Unsettling Costs

Inaccuracy in performance ratings may seem to be solely the concern of employees being rated and researchers. But is inaccuracy important to managers/raters as well? The answer is a resounding yes. It may be difficult for a manager to motivate subordinates if his or her performance ratings are so inaccurate that poor performers are being rewarded (see Chapter 5 for a discussion of the theories that might explain this); but beyond that, inaccurate rating could lead to a law suit. How can this happen? Well, let's look at one possible case involving a middle-aged worker named Harry Benson. Perhaps this example will help illustrate why fair and accurate appraisals are important for a number of reasons.

Harry Benson has been on the job for 12 years. When he first came to work for your company, he was earmarked as someone with a lot of potential.

But, over the years, it became clear that Harry would never be your top man. In fact, for the last two years, his performance has really been quite poor. Everyone in the organization knows this; but Harry has been there a while, he has three children, and his wife has needed a series of operations recently. So, every year, you try to give Harry a reasonably good evaluation so that he will get the merit increase he needs so badly. You never give him the top rating in your department; he hasn't been promoted recently; and since everyone feels the same about old Harry, everything moves along smoothly—for a while.

One day, there is an announcement that the Board of Directors have called for a reduction in force. The president comes to see you; and, after some discussion, he suggests that you fire Harry. Although you argue for a while, you realize that the president is right: Harry is just not doing his

---

and chops your vegetables and sings you to sleep at night? Can we observe loyalty or perseverance? No; but the more serious question is *do we want to?* Although personality traits have typically been used as the dimensions of performance in appraisals, more recent thinking has been that performance appraisals should focus on job-related performance and *not* on the person doing the job.[21] Thus, when constructing a performance appraisal system, organizations should try to tie the appraisal back to the job. Although that may seem obvious, few organizations start building appraisals by first finding out what the worker is expected to do on the job.

Even at that, the dimensions used in a performance appraisal should be more than those indicated by a job analysis. Recall that earlier we said that criteria should be (among other things) *observable* and *measurable;* so should the things we want to consider in performance appraisals. By relying exclusively upon measurable, observable, job-related dimensions, then, we are more likely to be rating performance rather than personality, and we will evaluate performance in terms that workers can understand and agree upon. It makes feedback more meaningful, makes for more legally defensible appraisals, and helps to ensure that the worker who is the best performer receives the highest evaluation.

job well and the company can't afford to carry him any longer. So you fire Harry. It was unpleasant, especially considering that at 45, Harry might not find another job. But at least, you reason, it's over now.

You are wrong. In 1968, Congress passed the Age Discrimination in Employment Act. As later amended, it protects workers between 35 and 70 years old from any discrimination on the job. Harry sues you on the basis of this act. Of course, you are shocked. After all, everyone knew you were just carrying Harry for these past few years. Why would he sue? Could he win?

This little scenario describes an extreme case, but the problem is quite typical. The issue here is that Harry has been given good evaluations all this time and has received merit increases as well. When he was fired, it *appeared* to be unrelated to his performance on the job. The record, of course,

is in Harry's favor and so it will be difficult to defend this action. In fact, in this case, the organization will probably lose a costly suit.

What is the point of this example? Actually, there are two. First, it is important to give fair and accurate appraisals in order to promote good company morale. Second, it is crucial to keep complete and accurate records of an employee's poor performance; these can avoid costly litigation. Such information may come in very handy if legal action is taken by a disgruntled person over the outcomes of such performance. Since we never know how someone will react to being disciplined for poor performance, we should always be prepared to defend and document any action we take. In short, keeping careful records often pays off in the long run; being a "nice guy" can be quite costly!   □

TECHNIQUES FOR CONDUCTING PERFORMANCE APPRAISALS: MANY PATHS TO THE SAME GOAL

We have spent some time discussing the basics of performance evaluation, and especially trying to illustrate the types of issues that underlie all evaluations. Once we have come to grips with these issues, know why we are conducting an appraisal, and know what dimensions of performance we want to include, we then must select a technique for actually carrying out the appraisal. A great deal has been written about the techniques available, and most of this literature focuses upon the same problem: how can we conduct better evaluations of employees? In this section, then, we will address three issues. First, we will examine the various types of rating scales available. These include *graphic* and *forced-choice* scales, *behavioral checklists,* and *behaviorally anchored* rating scales. Second, we will consider techniques for improving ratings, such as *Management by Objectives.* Third, we will examine the issue of *rater training.* Together, this information should provide you with a good overview of the techniques available for appraising performance and of the steps that can be taken to enhance their effectiveness.

Types of Rating Scales: Rulers for Measuring Performance

Probably the most popular topic in the study of performance appraisals is the rating scale. A great deal of research has been devoted to developing better formats or approaches for such scales. Although we could devote much space to this topic alone, for our purposes we will simply describe a few of the more interesting types of scales and spend some time discussing how these are developed. Be advised, however, that in practice, each organization develops something that looks a little different and that can be called its own. Nonetheless, there are really only a handful of different types of scales that you need to know.

Graphic rating scales. This is the most commonly used type of rating scale and includes several statements about employee characteristics or behavior and a single statement about overall job performance. A continuous or discrete scale is then presented for each item, and the rater places a check, circles a number, or in some other way indicates the rating he or she feels is appropriate. Figure 8–8 illustrates three examples of graphic rating scales for a single overall performance item.

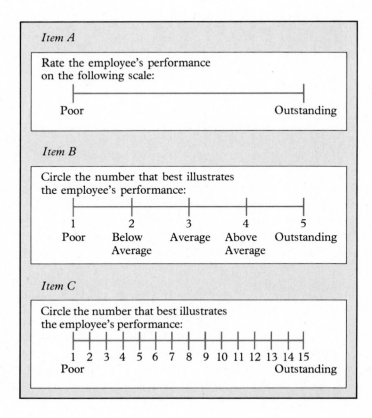

FIGURE 8-8 Graphic Rating Scales: Some Examples

In graphic rating scales, raters evaluate another person's performance by placing a check along a line or circling a number.

The first example employs a continuous scale, but this type is generally to be avoided since it is difficult for a rater to be very precise. The remaining examples employ discrete scales and deserve some further comment. Item B has five points and each is anchored with a descriptive adjective. Item C has 15 points with no anchors. Generally speaking, research on rating scales would favor item B on two counts. First, the use of descriptive anchors helps to ensure that different raters mean the same thing when they assign specific ratings. Second, most raters cannot adequately discriminate among the many different levels shown in item C. Thus, having so many points is more likely to result in confusion rather than in more precise ratings.[22]

Although graphic rating scales are the most commonly used type of scale, they are also prone to the rating errors discussed above. A variety of other approaches to rating scale development have therefore been proposed, mostly in an attempt to deal with some of these errors.

Forced-choice scales. An interesting approach, originally developed for personality testing, involves the use of forced-choice clusters.[23] Each cluster usually consists of two general statements about workers, and the rater is asked to choose the item that best describes the employees in question. The pairs of items are chosen to satisfy two conditions. The first has to do with an item's ability to differentiate between successful and unsuccessful performance on the job. This is determined by independent judges and is expressed as a *discrimination index*. The second has to do with an item's *desirability index* or the extent to which judges feel the statement is a favorable or unfavorable one to make about a worker.

Two examples of forced-choice pairs are presented in Figure 8–9. As can be seen, the point is to find a pair of items that are equally desirable or undesirable but in which only one item has a high discrimination index. The rater chooses one item in each pair (without the discrimination or desirability indexes included) and a rater's evaluation of a worker is calculated as the sum of the discrimination indexes for the items selected.

It should be noted that research on these scales reveals that raters dislike being kept in the dark about how their ratings will be used and so try to guess which item has a high discrimination index.[24] Eventually, they can determine which items get higher scores; thus, over time, this approach loses its usefulness.

Behavioral checklists. This approach to performance rating instruments represents a major departure from the others discussed in that here the rater only observes and records behavior; he or she is not required to judge that behavior.[25] Instead, a comprehensive list of behaviors encountered on the job is compiled, and a group of experts familiar with the job rate these according to how favorable or unfavorable each one is. The average favorableness rating for each item then serves as the scale value for the item, and a checklist similar to the one in Table 8–1 might be produced. (Items for which there is substantial disagreement should be dropped.)

FIGURE 8-9   Forced-Choice Scales: Some Examples

With *forced-choice* scales, raters are asked to choose the statement in each pair that best describes the employee being rated. Items in each pair are chosen to be equal in desirability, but different in how well they differentiate between good and poor performance. [Note: Both desirability and discrimination are rated on scales ranging from 0 (low) to 7 (high).]

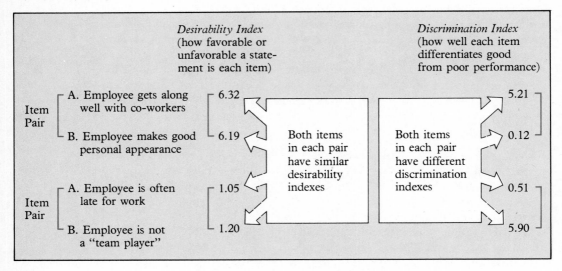

The behaviors (without the scale values) are then presented to the rater, whose only job is to record whether or not the worker engages in the behavior specified by each item. The overall evaluation is determined by summing the scores for each item checked. This approach, then, seeks to change the entire rating process, taking the rater out of the unpleasant role of being judge. In addition, the feedback function is facilitated, as the worker can see exactly what behaviors he or she did or did not engage in to obtain the rating received.

Behaviorally anchored rating scales.   Perhaps the most radical approach to rating scale development was proposed by Smith and Kendall in 1963.[26] Although a detailed explanation of this procedure is not appropriate for our present purposes, some discussion is worthwhile. The key requirement of this method is that the rater is fully involved in the development of the rating scale. Although there are variations on the basic procedures, a group of supervisors (or whoever else will eventually serve as raters) meet and generate a large list of concrete examples of effective and ineffective performance on the job. These are eventually collected in a smaller set of general categories and scaled. At each step in the process, any item for which general agreement cannot be reached is discarded. The resulting instrument consists of scales to rate performance in each area the raters agreed was important. The anchors on the scale (with appropriate scale val-

TABLE 8-1   Behavioral Checklist: An Example for an Administrative Assistant

A *behavioral checklist* is simply a list of behaviors one might observe on the job rated—in advance—by a group of experts. The rater is given the list without the scale values and checks those behaviors shown by the worker. (Note: Behaviors are rated for favorableness on a scale ranging from 0 to 7.)

ITEM	SCALE VALUE
Types letters making few mistakes	5.3
Socializes on the job	1.0
Does not guarantee hotel reservations	0.8
Determines air route with shortest layover	6.1
Composes polite responses to customer complaints	5.8
Loses patience over the phone	2.3
Uses easy-to-follow filing system	5.7
Office workers are often unhappy with policies	4.2

ues also agreed upon by the raters) are then actual behaviors rather than simply adjectives. The scales are usually worded in terms of behavioral expectations and are used as any other graphic rating scale. An example of such a scale developed for teacher evaluations (by students, incidentally) is provided in Figure 8–10.

These behaviorally anchored rating scales (sometimes referred to as Behavioral Expectation Scales) approach the whole problem of rater errors in a broader fashion than before. Basically, proponents of this approach maintain that by using only unambiguous performance dimensions and items and by getting the raters more fully involved in the entire rating process, rating errors will disappear. Unfortunately, this does not seem to be the case. Although the use of behaviorally anchored rating scales has been found to reduce some types of errors, there is some real question as to whether the benefits these scales offer are worth the time and expense needed to generate them.[27] While there is some residual feeling that the process of raters participating in scale development yields certain benefits, the evidence to date generally suggests that these and other innovative approaches to rating scale development (e.g., Behavioral Observation Scales,[28] and Mixed Standard Rating Scales[29]) offer little over prudently developed graphic scales. Thus, if we are to improve ratings, it would seem that we should focus on something other than developing new rating techniques. The remainder of this section considers some alternatives that have been proposed.

Management by Objectives: Progress as a Basis for Evaluation

Management by Objectives, or MBO for short, represents another general approach to performance appraisal that is more of a performance management sys-

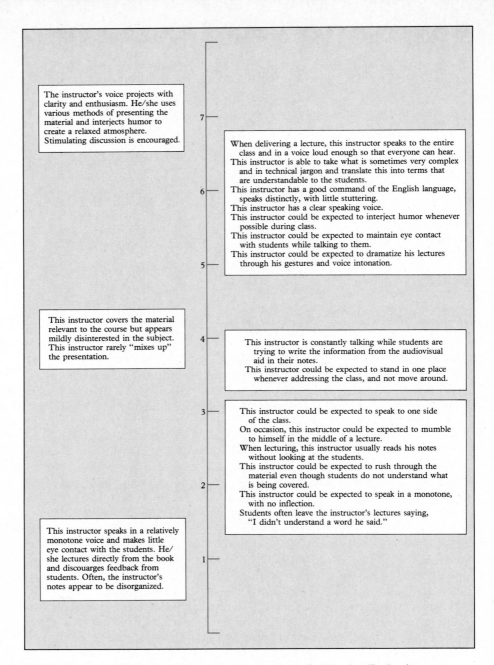

The instructor's voice projects with clarity and enthusiasm. He/she uses various methods of presenting the material and interjects humor to create a relaxed atmosphere. Stimulating discussion is encouraged.

When delivering a lecture, this instructor speaks to the entire class and in a voice loud enough so that everyone can hear.
This instructor is able to take what is sometimes very complex and in technical jargon and translate this into terms that are understandable to the students.
This instructor has a good command of the English language, speaks distinctly, with little stuttering.
This instructor has a clear speaking voice.
This instructor could be expected to interject humor whenever possible during class.
This instructor could be expected to maintain eye contact with students while talking to them.
This instructor could be expected to dramatize his lectures through his gestures and voice intonation.

This instructor covers the material relevant to the course but appears mildly disinterested in the subject. This instructor rarely "mixes up" the presentation.

This instructor is constantly talking while students are trying to write the information from the audiovisual aid in their notes.
This instructor could be expected to stand in one place whenever addressing the class, and not move around.

This instructor could be expected to speak to one side of the class.
On occasion, this instructor could be expected to mumble to himself in the middle of a lecture.
When lecturing, this instructor usually reads his notes without looking at the students.
This instructor could be expected to rush through the material even though students do not understand what is being covered.
This instructor could be expected to speak in a monotone, with no inflection.
Students often leave the instructor's lectures saying, "I didn't understand a word he said."

This instructor speaks in a relatively monotone voice and makes little eye contact with the students. He/she lectures directly from the book and discouarges feedback from students. Often, the instructor's notes appear to be disorganized.

FIGURE 8-10   A Behaviorally Anchored Rating Scale for Teacher Evaluations

Behaviorally anchored rating scales utilize pre-scaled behaviors as the anchors for evaluations. Since raters participate in the development and scaling of these anchors, rater acceptance and understanding of scales is maximized. The example illustrates such a scale to be used in teacher evaluation. (Source: Redrawn from a figure in Hom, DeNisi, Bannister, and Kinicki, *Effectiveness of Performance Feedback from Behaviorally Anchored Rating Scales.* Paper presented to the American Psychological Association, 1980.)

tem than simply another type of scale. Yet, it must be included in any discussion of appraisals. (We will return to MBO in the context of *organizational development* in Chapter 16.) This approach, originally offered by McGregor, is really based on the notions that (a) the clearer the idea a worker has of what he or she should accomplish, the greater the chances that it will be accomplished and (b) the only way to measure progress is in terms of the goal you are trying to reach.[30] With these two notions in mind, MBO programs usually begin with meetings between managers and subordinates to jointly determine the goals the subordinates should try to attain over some specified period of time. These goals must be realistic, and they also must be stated in terms that are as quantitative as possible. Thus, they probably wouldn't say that the goal is simply to improve productivity but rather that it is to reduce the number of rejects coming off the line by 20%. During this discussion, not only do the manager and subordinates develop mutually acceptable goals, but they also discuss procedures and methods for accomplishing those goals. Given this first step, performance appraisal becomes relatively simple. Employees are appraised relative to how much progress they have made in meeting their goals. The diagram in Figure 8-11 may help illustrate this process.

MBO programs have become extremely popular. And although MBO was originally proposed as a management tool, it obviously has much to offer as an evaluation technique. However, it's possible that the popularity of MBO programs has hurt as much as helped. Empirical research on the effectiveness of MBO has indicated a substantial number of failures, though these are usually due

FIGURE 8-11   The Management-by-Objectives Process

The MBO process begins with joint goal-setting between management and subordinate, as well as a discussion of procedures for accomplishing goals. At regular intervals, actual performance is compared to the goals set. If the goals are being met, new goals can be set and the process begins anew. If goals are not met, the parties jointly discuss what else needs to be done to accomplish the goals.

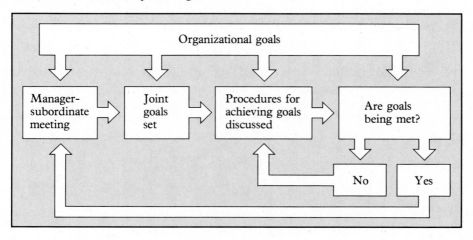

to misapplication.[31] MBO is probably not the answer for every organization and every job (and no one ever really suggested it was). But, as organizations try to get on the MBO bandwagon, they do not seriously attempt to determine if they are "right" for this approach. Clearly, there will be some types of jobs that defy setting goals in quantitative terms. Perhaps more seriously, however, MBO takes away some of management's prerogatives; it therefore requires a full commitment from top management on down, and the supervisors must not be afraid to work with subordinates.

These reservations aside, MBO appears to be an effective management tool and a potentially useful evaluation tool. There is a basic difference in the MBO evaluation philosophy, however, which must be recognized. Employees are evaluated on the basis of "bottom line" or what is actually accomplished. This is quite different from the other approaches we have discussed where the emphasis is on *how* the job is done, rather than what gets done. Some have argued that an exclusive focus on end product overlooks important information about employee future potential and that this focus, in the long run, may cause workers to go to any means to be sure the bottom line comes out right.

Rater Training Programs: Countering Inaccuracy

Regardless of the system used or the type of rating scale to be completed, it is the rater who is ultimately responsible for the quality of any rating. Therefore, it seems reasonable to attempt to train raters to do a better job of ratings. In fact, some fairly elaborate training programs have been developed and tested, and the results seem encouraging. For example, Latham, Wexley, and Pursell developed a program in which trainees (managers in a large corporation) viewed videotapes showing clear instances of several types of rating errors.[32] These included the *halo error* (a tendency to perceive all of an individual's traits in a favorable or unfavorable manner), the *similar-to-me effect* (a tendency by raters to assign more favorable ratings to persons similar to themselves), and the *contrast error* (a tendency to compare several applicants against each other, instead of with an established standard of performance). After viewing the tapes, these errors were discussed by subjects, and ways of reducing them were considered. In order to assess the success of these training procedures in countering such errors, subjects then rated several other persons (supposed applicants for a job) shown on a videotape. These tapes and accompanying information left considerable room for each of the errors noted above (e.g., background information on candidates capable of inducing a positive or negative halo effect was present). As you can see from Figure 8–12, however, the training program was highly effective in eliminating such errors. Subjects who had undergone this experience showed virtually no tendency to engage in halo, contrast, or similar-to-me errors. Those in a *control group* who had not undergone training, however, showed a considerable tendency to engage in such errors. These findings are encouraging, for they suggest that through appropriate training, raters can be taught to avoid common sources of bias in their assessments.

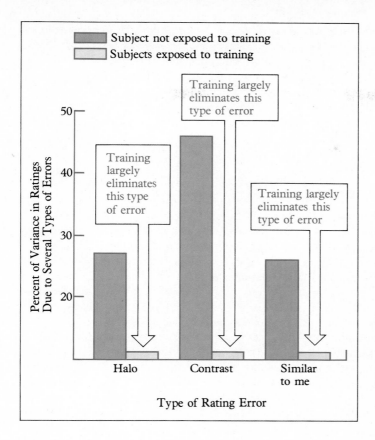

Subject not exposed to training
Subjects exposed to training

Training largely eliminates this type of error

Training largely eliminates this type of error

Training largely eliminates this type of error

Percent of Variance in Ratings Due to Several Types of Errors

50

40

30

20

Halo   Contrast   Similar to me

Type of Rating Error

FIGURE 8–12 Rater Training: Evidence for Its Effectiveness

When raters are shown clear examples of certain types of errors and then discuss the nature of these sources of bias, they may become much more adept at avoiding them. Indeed, the findings shown here indicate that several key forms of rater errors can be totally eliminated through such training. (Source: Based on data from Latham et al., *Journal of Applied Psychology*, 1975, *60*, 550–555.)

Although few persons would argue with the benefits of the type of rater train-ing we have just described, some have suggested that it may not go far enough. Specifically, Bernardin and Pence have argued that rater training must focus upon the entire rating process, not simply upon the examination of certain key types of errors.[33] This latter approach, they argue, could simply cause raters to lean over backwards and so err in the opposite direction. For example, they might fail to report high correlations among ratings on separate dimensions even when these exist, in an effort to avoid the halo effect.

In any event, simply getting raters to recognize rating errors is not the same as getting them to give accurate appraisals in practice. Rater motivation is an elusive construct that cannot be overlooked. Despite all the training and insight a rater may have, he or she may simply *choose* to give an inaccurate rating. For example, a rater may be perfectly aware of the inflated nature of a rating given to a friend but may do it anyway. Our earlier discussion touched upon the rater who felt sorry for the man with a family and so gave him unfairly favorable ratings. The appraisal process is complex; but if we want accurate ratings, we must be sure that raters are capable of evaluation, have insight into the rating process, understand the scales they are using, and want to give accurate ratings. Ultimately, we must consider the rater as a decision-maker and treat the problem as one in which a person needs to make a crucial decision with only limited information in the face of constraints and considerations that preclude collecting more information. From this perspective, it is not surprising that raters generally dislike giving ratings almost as much as employees dislike being rated. (See the **"FOCUS"** box on pages 266–267 for an intriguing view of the nature of the appraisal process.)

APPLICATIONS OF PERFORMANCE INFORMATION: USING THE OUTCOMES OF EVALUATIONS

We have now spent quite some time discussing performance appraisals, beginning with the determinants of performance and continuing through the problems of measurement and the different approaches to ratings. But what has all this gotten us? We hope, some insight into what is involved in the measurement and rating of performance, so that we have improved our chances of developing relatively fair and accurate evaluations. But now that we have come this far, we still need to discuss what to do with these ratings once they are obtained.

Earlier, we considered the major purposes for conducting appraisals: feedback and administrative decision making. In an important sense, these purposes dictate what is to be done with the ratings once collected. In the remainder of this chapter, we will focus on the *performance feedback process* and *tying rewards to performance*.

Feedback Interviews: Telling Others How Well They Have Done

If workers never receive feedback from their performance evaluations, they will not know where they stand, nor will they be able to do anything constructive to improve their performance. Clearly, then, performance feedback is critical. This feedback is usually given in an interview conducted once or twice a year; it not only gives the employee the opportunity to find out what his or her strengths and weaknesses are, but it also gives both manager and subordinate the opportunity to set goals for improving future performance. If handled well, the feedback interview is an ideal opportunity for employee development. If handled poorly, however, it can create a situation such as that described in the opening scenario, where defensiveness and resentment abound.

Since there has been a considerable amount of research on feedback interviews, it seems worthwhile to briefly discuss some points that have been made through research—ones that should be kept in mind when conducting these interviews.

The most comprehensive investigation of the feedback process was conducted in the mid-1960s at General Electric.[34] These studies revealed that the major problem in most feedback interviews was this: the manager spent too much time criticizing the subordinate and pointing out his or her shortcomings. Instead, the researchers suggest that the manager should be sure to emphasize positive points and praise accomplishments in addition to pinpointing problems. Furthermore, they suggest that the manager should draw the subordinate more fully into the discussion. Then, instead of the interview being a lecture by the manager about what is wrong, the interview could be a discussion focusing on what can be done to improve performance. Generally speaking, the researchers found that when the subordinate truly participated in the discussion and helped set future goals, there was a greater likelihood of lasting changes in behavior leading to improved performance.

An important point related to the quality of performance feedback is the *timing* of that feedback. As mentioned above, formal feedback interviews are usually held once or twice a year. The problem is that some managers give no feedback outside of these interviews. In some cases, this is why there is an emphasis on the negative aspects of performance; the manager has been saving his or her complaints for six months or a year, and here is the chance to get it all out. Feedback must be an ongoing process, as must appraisal. On a day-to-day basis managers observe good and poor performance, so they should occasionally communicate this to subordinates. Formal feedback may be infrequent, but informal feedback can be given on a regular basis.

Tying Rewards to Performance

The ultimate outcome of a performance evaluation, especially from the employee's point of view, is the reward associated with good performance. There are, of course, a number of non-financial rewards that an organization might dispense, but most of us tend to think of money first. Edward Lawler, an investigator well known for his efforts to clarify the relationship between pay and performance, has suggested that it is crucial for management to observe several basic rules when attempting to establish links between performance and pay.[35] Briefly, he contends that management must (1) create a belief among employees that good performance can lead to high pay, (2) reinforce the importance of pay, (3) minimize the negative consequences associated with good performance (such as being given additional work), and (4) create conditions such that rewards other than pay will also stem from good performance.

Of course, stating these principles is one thing; implementing them is quite another. And as Lawler himself notes, many complexities relating to their application exist. Yet, all are important and worthy of careful attention. From the organization's point of view, establishing a close link between performance and pay makes good sense. After all, it is only when such a link exists that pay can be used to motivate employee behavior. But the presence of such connections, in turn, has important implications for performance appraisal. Specifically, clear and direct bonds between pay and performance make it even *more* critical that such appraisals be fair and accurate and that they be perceived as such by all involved.

FOCUS ON BEHAVIOR

The Rater as Decision Maker

What *is* involved in the performance appraisal process for the raters? This question has been posed many times, and a number of researchers have offered answers. Recent papers by Meglino, Cafferty, DeNisi, and Youngblood,[36] Feldman,[37] and Cooper[38] propose models to answer this question that place almost all of the emphasis upon the rater. One model of this type is presented in Figure 8–13.

As can be seen, this model casts the rater as an active collector and processor of information in performance appraisal. If we begin with the worker performing some behavior, the process starts with the rater observing this behavior. The model further suggests that raters do not simply casually observe, but go out and seek information. Given a number of workers performing a number of different job duties, the rater must decide whom to observe and when.

What determines the choices made? Any number of things, really. For example, before ever actually seeing a person on the job, raters usually have some preconceived ideas about what kind of worker he or she is. Maybe the rater reviewed this employee's personnel file and saw previous evaluations. Perhaps someone told the rater something about the person. All this can influence the decision of whom to observe. So can the performance itself. Given a worker observed doing well and a worker observed doing poorly, whom do you choose to continue watching? It probably depends upon the purpose of the appraisal. For example, if you are trying to decide whom to promote, observing an incident of poor performance may be enough. Again, if you were somehow expecting good performance, poor performance might be perplexing and so you might want to look further.

In any event, this process of collecting information goes on until the time when evaluations are coming due. All along, bits and pieces of information are being stored away until they are needed. But information is not usually stored in memory without first being "tampered with" a bit. Quite often, what we store in memory is an impression rather than an act. That is why we often can recall not liking someone, although we cannot recall what the person did to provoke this reaction. Some things we see don't seem important at the time, and so we don't bother to take up precious "space" in memory with useless details.

Regardless of what gets into memory, it's clear that over the course of six months or a year, a lot of the information is forgotten or is so deep in our memory that we cannot recall it without a great deal of effort. Furthermore, there are things we want to forget and there are still other things that we don't remember correctly. That is, our memory can often play tricks on us, which is why the "old days" often seem to be so good.

All of this brings us to the rater about to make a decision. There are some things he or she didn't see, other things he or she never looked for, and still other things that he or she forgot or that were distorted over time. Armed with this scant ammunition, the rater now has to put it all together and make a decision. Of course, factors like personal feelings and biases can now come into play, as can any of the rating errors discussed earlier. Finally, a decision is made and then the rater must decide how to translate that decision into a specific rating.

When viewed in this way, the problem of inaccuracy in appraisals becomes complex indeed. It is not surprising that developing better rating scales doesn't help much, since the scale isn't a factor until the very end of the process. Similarly, training raters to avoid rating errors is only useful if the rater has already done a good job of collecting and remembering performance information. More adequate appraisals will only come when we help raters become better collectors of information, give them aids for more accurately remembering information, teach them how to combine information and avoid rating errors, and give them rating scales they can use.

Better performance appraisals are no simple matter, then; and organizations will have to commit much more time and effort to the appraisal process if they seriously expect to improve matters. □

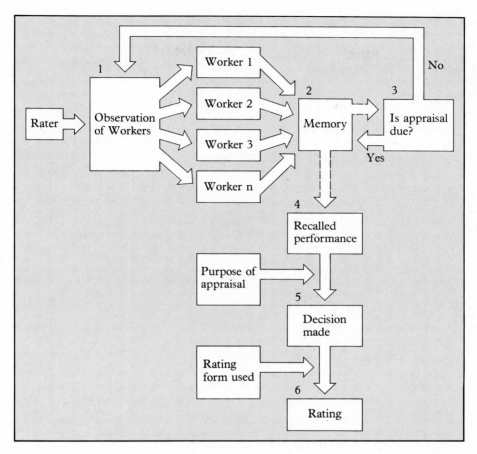

FIGURE 8-13   A Decision-Making Model of the Appraisal Process

In the model of performance appraisal shown here, the process begins with the rater observing some employee behavior (1). The evaluation of that behavior is then stored in memory (2) until needed. As the observation of behavior continues, the rater must ask if the appraisal is yet due (3). If not, the observation continues. When the appraisal is due, the rater recalls the evaluation information from memory (4) and reaches a decision about the worker's performance (5), after considering the purpose of the appraisal. This decision is then translated into a rating (6). (Source: Redrawn from a figure in Meglino, Cafferty, DeNisi, & Youngblood, "A Cognitive View of the Performance Appraisal Process." In *Cognitive Models in Industrial/Organizational Psychology.* Symposium presented at the APA Convention, 1981.)

Probably the most common type of plan that relates pay to performance is some form of **merit pay.** Under merit-pay plans each employee usually receives some base pay increase (often tied to the cost of living) and then is eligible for some additional increase based upon rated performance. For example, an organization might divide employees into four groups based upon their evaluations. The lowest two groups might receive only a cost-of-living increase (the lowest group might even be considered for termination); the next highest group might also receive a modest merit increase; and the highest group would also receive a fairly substantial merit increase. In this way, the basic survival needs of all employees are met and superior performance is rewarded. Unfortunately, budgetary constraints often dictate a small pot of money to be allocated for merit, and thus occasionally employees will not feel adequately rewarded for their performance.

Piece-rate plans are another procedure for tying rewards to performance, and, in fact, these plans establish the strongest relationships between pay and performance, since employees are paid only for units produced on a predetermined schedule. These plans are usually tempered by introducing some guaranteed hourly rate for a standard amount of production, with an accelerated rate paid for production over standard. Piece-rate plans are fairly popular on blue-collar jobs as they do clearly relate pay to performance. There is often a suspicion, however, that management would change the standard if too many workers exceeded it; so informal group norms keep performance below what it might otherwise be.

Somewhat related to a piece-rate system is the practice of paying salespeople on a **commission basis.** This simply involves paying people some predetermined percentage of the dollar-value of their sales. Although there are salespeople who are paid exclusively on a commission basis, it is not uncommon for organizations to guarantee some minimal hourly rate in addition to the commission.

These three plans have one important feature in common: the amount of the award an employee receives depends solely upon his or her performance. The advantage this offers is to make the performance-pay link as strong and as clear as possible. Unfortunately, these individual rewards have some disadvantages as well. Most importantly, these plans often foster competition among employees rather than cooperation.

Salespeople are especially well known for protecting "their" customers from others, and when situations require cooperation and teamwork, the organization suffers. Because of these problems, it has sometimes been suggested that rewards be tied to group or even organizational performance instead. In this way, employees will have an incentive to work together for the common good—so that they will all benefit. Unfortunately, by their nature, such plans weaken the link between an individual's effort and his or her reward. Productive workers might have to "carry" less productive workers, and peer pressure is the only weapon available to get people to work harder. Nonetheless, *group* and *organizational incentive plans* are quite popular, and several of these plans deserve discussion.

Scanlon plans, for example, are a fairly popular form of organizational incentive plan. Under such a program, employees are encouraged to submit suggestions for productivity and efficiency to a worker-management committee that then decides which plans to implement. The dollar value of improved efficiency (compared to a base period) is split between the organization and the workers and the workers' share is then put into a pot and divided (at given intervals) among all participants. It is interesting to note that these plans often have a contingency for dealing with a drop in efficiency (compared to some base period). In these cases, the workers' "account" is charged for the difference. These plans have often been effective, but usually only in smaller organizations with stable product lines. There are some reports of employee competition interfering with getting the job done, but there are also reports of janitors who earn $40,000 a year under these plans.

Profit-sharing plans involve paying the employees a certain percentage of each year's profits. The notion here is to demonstrate to workers that everyone benefits when the company is profitable. These plans result in the weakest perceived link between individual performance and pay, however, since profits are often subject to forces that are even beyond the organization's power to control.

A summary of the various plans we have discussed is presented in Table 8-2, along with the advantages and disadvantages each involves. As you can readily see, there are important trade-offs between individual and group or organizational

TABLE 8-2   Incentive Plans: An Overview

There are a variety of plans for tying rewards to performance. Several of these and their advantages and disadvantages are summarized here.

INCENTIVE PLAN	BASIS OF REWARD	ADVANTAGES	DISADVANTAGES
1. Merit Pay Plan	Individual performance	Strong link between individual performance and reward	Budgetary constraints often limit rewards Can lead to competition
2. Piece-Rate Plan	Individual performance	Strongest possible performance-to-reward link Easy to understand	Not applicable to all jobs Informal group norms often develop out of mistrust that standards will be changed Can lead to competition
3. Commission Plan	Individual performance	Strong link between individual performance and reward	Not applicable to all jobs Sales often due to external factors not under worker control Can lead to competition
4. Scanlon Plan	Savings due to improved efficiency	Emphasis on all workers pulling together to save money for the organization Large rewards possible	Weak performance-to-reward link Requires stable product lines Savings and money often interfere with job
5. Profit Sharing	Company profits	Ties individual's fate to organization's fate Large rewards possible	Weakest link between individual performance and reward

plans. In addition to the points made here, managerial styles, the precision with which individual performance can be measured, and external pressures (such as unions) are all factors to be considered when selecting the precise nature of the link between performance and pay.

SUMMARY

Measuring and rewarding effective performance is an important yet complex task facing all organizations. The first obstacle we face in this area is defining performance, and this is generally known as the **criterion problem.** Although we are interested in the *ultimate criterion,* which is the sum of a worker's contribution to an organization, we often settle for something less: the *actual criterion*—aspects of performance that can be readily measured. We try to maximize the *relevance* of this actual measure, but unfortunately some *criterion deficiency* and *criterion contamination* are unavoidable. One factor that complicates the criterion problem is that there are a variety of determinants of employee performance. Major among these are the *physical environment, ability,* and *motivation.* Since all have an impact on employee performance, pure measurement is impossible. And since not all are under the control of the worker, determining what constitutes effective performance is no simple matter.

Another factor complicating the appraisal process is the purpose for conducting a performance evaluation. There are two major purposes for appraisals: *administrative decision making* and *feedback.* The first involves making decisions concerning raises, promotions, and the like, while the second involves giving workers information about their strengths and weaknesses so they can eventually improve. Many organizations do not separate these two functions, with the result that employees fail to receive the feedback they need.

Unfortunately, performance ratings are also subject to a number of rating errors such as *halo error, leniency,* and *central tendency.* In attempting to reduce these errors, we should try to use only dimensions of performance that can be observed and measured, and we should use carefully constructed scales for rating performance. In fact, there have been many proposals for better rating scales, including *forced-choice scales, behavioral checklists,* and *behaviorally anchored rating scales.* However, these have not been found to offer much in the way of improvement—probably because the entire appraisal process is more complex than had been believed. In addition to proposals for new scales, *Management by Objectives* (MBO), which is really a system for performance management, and various types of *rater training* programs have also been proposed and have enjoyed some success.

After performance is evaluated, organizations still must apply the information in some way. Organizations need to use rating information as a source of worker feedback and as a guide for tying rewards to performance. This latter goal is often accomplished with an individual incentive plan such as a *merit-pay system, piece-rate,* or *commission plan,* or with a group or organizational incentive plan such as the *Scanlon plan* or a *profit-sharing plan*. Each has advantages and disadvantages, but all attempt to bring the results of appraisals back to the worker through rewards.

KEY TERMS

CENTRAL TENDENCY ERROR   The tendency to rate everyone as "average" and so, essentially, to avoid making decisions with respect to performance appraisals.

CIRCADIAN RHYTHM   An internal temporal program that "tells" us when to eat, sleep, etc. It takes time for the rhythm to become established, and this is one reason why individuals on rotating shifts often experience many difficulties.

COMMISSION   An individual incentive plan usually associated with salespeople in which employees are paid some predetermined percentage of the dollar value of the goods they sell.

CRITERION CONTAMINATION   Refers to the extent to which the actual criterion used to assess performance includes something that is not part of the ultimate criterion.

CRITERION DEFICIENCY   Refers to the extent to which the actual criterion used to assess performance does not include some portion of the ultimate criterion.

CRITERION PROBLEM   The general issue of what, precisely, to measure in performance appraisal.

CRITERION RELEVANCE   Refers to the amount of overlap between the actual criterion used to assess performance and the ultimate criterion.

HALO ERROR   A rating error that usually results from the tendency to assume that all aspects of performance are related. When this error operates, it is assumed that an individual who performs one part of a job well will perform other parts well too.

LENIENCY ERROR   The tendency to inflate ratings in performance appraisals. To the extent this error is present, all employees may receive favorable evaluations.

MANAGEMENT BY OBJECTIVES (MBO)   A management system in which managers and subordinates mutually agree upon goals for subordinates. These goals are stated in concrete, measurable terms, and methods for reaching them are also selected. Performance evaluation is then based upon the extent to which these goals are actually met.

MERIT-PAY PLANS   Individual incentive plans in which employees receive some fixed "cost-of-living" salary increase and then may receive an additional increment on the basis of excellent performance ratings.

PERFORMANCE APPRAISAL   Refers to the process by which job-related performance is assessed or evaluated. Performance appraisal is a key process in modern organizations.

PIECE RATE   An individual incentive plan in which workers are paid for each unit produced. Piece-rate plans usually include a provision for paying a fixed hourly rate for a standard amount of production and then paying at an accelerated rate for each unit over the standard.

PROFIT-SHARING   An organizational incentive plan in which all workers share profits with management.

SCANLON PLAN   An organizational incentive plan in which all workers share in cost savings produced by employee suggestions.

ULTIMATE CRITERION   The ideal criterion measure for assessing performance. This criterion considers the sum total of an employee's contribution to the organization over his or her entire working career. In practice, it is never possible to use the ultimate criterion. Thus, some imperfect actual criterion measure is substituted for it.

NOTES

1. Wells, B. W. Subjective responses to the lighting installation in a modern office building and their design implications. *Building Science,* 1965, *1,* 153–165.

2. Ferree, C. E., & Rand, G. Work and its illumination. *Personnel Journal,* 1940, *19,* 55–64.

3. Fine, B. J., & Kobrick, J. L. Effects of altitude and heat on complex cognitive tasks. *Human Factors,* 1978, *20,* 115–122.

4. Clark, R. E. *The limiting hand skin temperature for unaffected manual performance in the cold* (Tech. Rep. EP-147). Natick, Mass.: Quartermaster Research and Engineering Command, February 1961.

5. Park, J. F., & Payne, M. C. Effects of noise level and difficulty of task in performing division. *Journal of Applied Psychology,* 1963, *47,* 367–368.

6. Cohen, A. Noise effects on health, production, and well-being. *Transactions of the New York Academy of Sciences,* May 1968, *30,* 910–918.

7. Ibid.

8. Tufts College: Institute for Applied Experimental Psychology. *Handbook of human engineering data.* 1951.

9. Purach, A. Biological rhythm-effects of night work and shift changes on the health of workers. *Acta Medica Scandavia,* 152, suppl. 307, 1963.

10. Bjerner, B. Diurnal variation in mental performance. *British Journal of Industrial Medicine,* April 1955, 103–110.

11. DeNisi, A. S., & Stevens, G. E. Profiles of performance, performance evaluations and personnel decisions. *Academy of Management Journal,* 1981, *24.*

12. Porter, L. W., & Lawler, E. E., III. *Managerial attitudes and performance.* Homewood, Illinois: Irwin, 1968.

13. Leventhal, G. S. The distribution of rewards and resources in groups and organizations. In L. Berkowitz and E. Walster (Eds.), *Advances in experimental social psychology* (Vol. 9). New York: Academic Press, 1976.

14. Meyer, H. H., Kay, E., & French, J. R. P. Split roles in performance appraisal. *Harvard Business Review,* 1965, *43,* 123–129.

15. Cooper, W. H. Ubiquitous halo. *Psychological Bulletin,* 1981, *90,* 218–244.

16. Johnson, D. M., & Vidulick, R. N. Experimental manipulation of the halo effect. *Journal of Applied Psychology,* 1956, *40,* 130–134.

17. Murphy, K. R., Garcia, M., Kerkar, S., Martin, C., & Baizer, W. K. Relationship between observational accuracy and accuracy in evaluating performance. *Journal of Applied Psychology,* 1982, *67,* 320–325.

18. Svetlik, B., Prien, E., & Barrett, G. Relationships between job difficulty, employee's attitude toward the job, and supervisor ratings of employee effectiveness. *Journal of Applied Psychology,* 1964, *48,* 320–324.

19. Barrett, R. S. Influence of supervisor's requirements on ratings. *Personnel Psychology,* 1966, *19,* 375–388.

20. Hamner, W. C., Kim, J. S., Baird, L., & Bigoness, W. J. Race and sex as determinants of ratings of potential employees in a simulated work sampling task. *Journal of Applied Psychology,* 1974, *59,* 705–711.

21. Landy, F., & Farr, J. Performance ratings. *Psychological Bulletin,* 1980, *87,* 72–107.

22. Thorndike, R. L. (Ed.). *Educational measurement* (2nd ed.). Washington, D.C.: American Council on Education, 1971.

23. Sisson, E. D. Forced choice—The new Army rating. *Personnel Psychology,* 1948, *1,* 365–381.

24. Travers, R. M. A critical review of the validity and rationale of the forced-choice technique. *Psychological Bulletin,* 1951, *48,* 62–70.

25. Flanagan, J. C. The critical incident technique. *Psychological Bulletin,* 1954, *51,* 327–358.

26. Smith, P. C., & Kendall, L. M. Retranslation of expectations: An approach to the construction of unambiguous anchors for rating scales. *Journal of Applied Psychology,* 1963, *47,* 149–155.

27. Guilford, J. P. *Psychometric methods* (2nd ed.). New York: McGraw-Hill, 1954.

28. Latham, G. P., & Wexley, K. N. Behavioral observation scales for performance appraisal purposes. *Personnel Psychology,* 1977, *30,* 255–268.

29. Blanz, F., & Ghiselli, E. E. The mixed standard rating scale: A new rating system. *Personnel Psychology,* 1972, *25,* 185–199.

30. McGregor, D. *The human side of enterprises.* New York: McGraw-Hill, 1960.

31. Carroll, S. J., & Tosi, H. L. *Management by objectives: Applications and research.* New York: Macmillan, 1973.

32. Latham, G. P., Wexley, K. N., & Pursell, E. D. Training managers to minimize rating errors in the observation of rating. *Journal of Applied Psychology,* 1975, *60,* 550–555.

33. Bernardin, H. J., & Pence, E. G. The effects of rater training: Creating new response sets and decreasing accuracy. *Journal of Applied Psychology,* 1980, *65,* 60–66.

34. Kay, E., Meyer, H. H., & French, J. R. P. Effects of threat in a performance appraisal interview. *Journal of Applied Psychology,* 1965, *49,* 311–317.

35. Lawler, E. E., III. *Pay and organizational effectiveness.* New York: McGraw-Hill, 1971.

36. Meglino, B., Cafferty, T., DeNisi, A., & Youngblood, S. A cognitive view of the performance appraisal process. In *Cognitive Models in Industrial/Organizational Psychology.* Symposium presented at the American Psychological Association Convention, Los Angeles, 1981.

37. Feldman, J. M. Beyond attribution theory: Cognitive processes in performance appraisal. *Journal of Applied Psychology,* 1981, *66,* 127–148.

38. Cooper, W. H. Ubiquitous halo. *Psychological Bulletin,* 1981, *90,* 218–244.

9

Stress:
Its Nature, Causes,
and Control

STRESS: SOME MAJOR CAUSES

Organizational Causes of Stress   Personal Influences on Stress

STRESS: SOME IMPORTANT EFFECTS

The Physical Impact of Stress   The Psychological Impact of Stress   The Impact of Stress on Organizational Behavior

COPING WITH STRESS: SOME USEFUL TECHNIQUES

Personal Strategies for Coping with Stress   Organizational Strategies for Managing Stress

SPECIAL INSERTS

CASE IN POINT   Life in a Double-Boiler
FOCUS ON BEHAVIOR   Aftereffects: The Lingering (and Often Hidden) Costs of Stress
FROM THE MANAGER'S PERSPECTIVE   How Well Do You Cope? A Self-Assessment

KEY CONCEPTS

Stress
General Adaptation Syndrome
Role Conflict
Role Ambiguity
Overload
Underutilization

Cognitive Appraisal
Aftereffects
Social Support
Relaxation Training
Meditation

□ □ □

It's a delightful evening in June, and you are attending the annual barbecue held by the people on your block. Hamburgers, hot dogs, and chicken are sizzling invitingly on the grill, and dishes of homemade potato salad, baked beans, slaw, and other assorted goodies have been laid out on a long picnic table. "Ah, what a feast!" you think, rubbing your hands together in anticipation. Just then you are joined by two of your neighbors, Bill DeCecco and Ned Mueller. You've known both for years, but haven't seen much of either since last fall. Almost at once you are struck by the large difference in their appearance. Both men are the same age, and both face a lot of stress on their jobs (each holds a high-level position with a nearby company). Yet, Ned looks at least ten years older than Bill. Further, while Bill appears to be the very picture of good health, Ned seems to be in bad shape indeed. He seems run-down and looks nervous and tense. You've heard that he has been having problems with his digestion. And rumor has it that he's been drinking more than he should recently. Worst of all, the word is out that his work has begun to slip and that he may be in danger of losing his job. "What a shame," you think. "He's always been such a nice fellow." At this moment, someone rings the dinner gong, and you walk over to join your family. As you take your seat at the table, though, you can't help wondering about the difference between your two neighbors. Bill definitely seems to be handling the stress and strains of his job much better than Ned. But why is this the case? Can it be his physical exercise—jogging and tennis? And what about the serious personal blows Ned has suffered lately—the sudden loss of his brother in an accident and his temporary separation from his wife? Have these affected his ability to withstand the stress of his complex job? You continue to ponder such matters until they are driven from your mind by your first bite into a large, juicy hamburger.

Have you ever found yourself in a situation that seemed to be more than you could handle? If you have ever driven in frenzied commuter traffic, delivered a speech to a large, unfriendly audience, or searched frantically for your flight a few minutes before take-off in a bustling airport, your answer is certain to be yes. These and many other situations we all encounter on a regular basis share a common feature: they threaten to literally overwhelm our ability to handle or cope with them. When conditions of this type exist, we may be said to be experiencing

stress—an all too common aspect of life in the 1980s.[1] As one noted expert on stress, Joseph McGrath, has put it:[2]

> . . . there is a potential for stress when an environmental situation is perceived as presenting a demand which threatens to exceed the person's capabilities and resources for meeting it . . . (p. 1352)

While our reactions to stress vary greatly (everything from damp palms and shaking knees through intense feelings of despair), most fall under three major categories. First, we respond to stress *physiologically*. As noted by Hans Selye, a scientist who has studied stress for several decades, these reactions are ones designed to help us cope with threat or danger.[3,4] Thus, they include a rise in heart rate and blood pressure, increased respiration, and a diversion of blood to skeletal muscles—the ones used in "fight" or "flight" reactions. According to Selye, moreover, such reactions occur in three distinct phases which together constitute the **General Adaptation Syndrome**. Initially there is an *alarm reaction,* during which the body prepares itself for active coping. Next there is a *stage of resistance,* during which reserves are marshaled and coping occurs. Finally, if stress persists too long, we may enter a *stage of exhaustion,* in which our reserves have been drained. It is at this time that serious illness or damage often occurs.

While physiological reactions to stress are important, they are only part of the total picture. In addition, we react *psychologically.* We experience such feelings as fear, anxiety, and tension. And we actively seek to evaluate or *appraise* the stress-inducing situation, to determine just how dangerous it really is. Finally, we also respond to stress overtly, with a variety of *coping behaviors.* These range from attempts to gather more information about the stressful situation through direct steps to deal with it, and may also include *intrapsychic strategies*—ones designed simply to make us feel better (e.g., taking a drink; convincing ourselves that there really isn't much danger). A summary of our major reactions to stress is presented in Figure 9–1.

Because stress involves physiological responses, internal psychological states, and overt behavior, it has been studied by scientists in several different fields (e.g., biology, psychology, sociology). As we will soon see, this effort has been well spent, for growing evidence suggests that stress can affect our health, our relations with others, and our behavior in many different settings. (As you may recall, effects of all these types were mentioned in the story on p. 276.)

In the present chapter, we will focus most of our attention on the impact of stress upon behavior in organizational settings. But because stress is an important process with far-reaching effects, we will also seek to provide you with a broad introduction to current knowledge about it. First, we will describe some of the major *causes* of stress. These involve several aspects of organizations and also certain traits or characteristics possessed by individuals. Second, we will consider some of the major *effects* of stress, including its impact on health and work-related behaviors. Finally, we will examine techniques for *managing* stress—tactics for countering its negative impact on individuals and organizations.

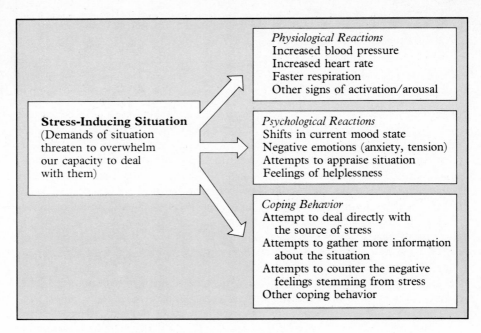

FIGURE 9-1   Reactions to Stress: An Overview

As shown here, we respond to stress on several different levels.

STRESS: SOME MAJOR CAUSES

When was the last time you experienced stress? In all probability, quite recently. As we have already noted, stress is a very common event. In fact, for most of us, hardly a week or even a day passes without some exposure to stress-inducing events. The reason for this high frequency of occurrence is obvious: stress stems from many different sources. Indeed, as suggested by Figure 9-2, it can involve virtually every aspect of our daily lives. In this discussion, though, we will focus primarily on two groups of factors that produce or influence stress: ones relating to aspects of organizations and ones involving the personal characteristics of individuals.

Organizational Causes of Stress

Stress is an unpleasant state and often exerts harmful effects on those who experience it. Despite this fact, however, job stress is exceedingly common in many organizations. Several factors that contribute to this unsettling state of affairs will now be considered.

Occupational demands: Some jobs are more stressful than others.   In the summer of 1981, more than twelve thousand U.S. air traffic controllers took a dramatic step—they went out on strike despite the fact that this action was viewed as illegal by both the federal government (their employer) and the general public (see Figure 9–3). One major reason behind this drastic decision was the controllers' concern with gaining better working conditions—ones that would help them cope with the tremendous pressures of their job. As evidence for the necessity of a shorter workweek and longer vacations, the striking controllers pointed to data indicating that few persons survive for ten or even five years in their job. And they also noted that those who do remain often pay a high price in terms of stress-related illnesses (e.g., high blood pressure, ulcers, skin disorders).[5] While some authorities have questioned the accuracy of these claims, it is clear that air controllers do face higher levels of stress than workers in many other fields, and their plight, in turn, calls our attention to a basic fact: some jobs are indeed much more stressful than others.

Systematic evidence on this issue is provided by a recent study of the level of stress in more than 130 occupations.[6] The results of this survey indicate that several occupations—e.g., physician, office manager, foreman, and waitress/waiter—are relatively high in stress. In contrast, other jobs, such as craft worker, maid, farm laborer, and (not surprisingly!) college professor, are much lower in this regard.

In addition to these differences in overall level of stress, it appears that jobs also differ in terms of the *pattern* of stressors they present. For example, evidence gathered by Parasuraman and Alutto suggests that high-level (managerial) jobs

FIGURE 9–2   Stress: A Basic Fact of Modern Life

Unfortunately, stress stems from many different sources. (Source: Drawing by Ed Fisher; © 1980 The New Yorker Magazine, Inc.)

FIGURE 9–3   One Response to Intense Stress

In 1981, U.S. air traffic controllers staged a controversial strike. According to the participants, one major reason behind their action was simple: they desperately needed relief from the intense stress associated with their jobs. (Source: UPI Photo.)

often involve stress from such sources as time pressure, too many meetings, or difficulties in attaining productivity standards.[7] In contrast, lower-level jobs more often involve stress deriving from technical problems (e.g., equipment breakdowns) or role frustration (e.g., low status, inadequate supervision). Similarly, holding job-level constant, equivalent positions in different departments or subsystems within a given company also expose their occupants to contrasting patterns of stress. Thus, the problems confronted by individuals in administration, production, sales, and supply tend to differ sharply.

In short, one major source of stress in work settings involves the nature and demands of various jobs. For this reason, persons considering a career in a specific field, or in a specific department within a company, would do well to take account of the level and pattern of stress it involves. Given the powerful, negative impact of stressors on physical and mental well-being, this is one case in which it may really pay to look before you leap.

Role conflict: Stress from conflicting—and often unreconcilable—demands.   When individuals occupy a given position within an organization, they are generally expected to behave in certain ways. For example, top executives are expected to be decisive and aggressive, while salespersons are expected to be friendly and cheerful, at least when dealing with potential customers. Together, such expectations constitute a *role*—a general set of guidelines indicating how persons holding certain positions should or ought to behave.[8] In many cases, the presence of such roles is beneficial: they save us the trouble of deciding what constitutes appropriate behavior in many situations. Often, though, roles can be the source of considerable discomfort and stress. This is especially likely in situations where different groups of people with whom an individual interacts hold contradictory expectations about how he or she should behave. Under these conditions, **role conflict** exists, and the person in question may find herself pulled in different and incompatible directions. For example, consider the case of a first-line manager. The employees working under her direction may perceive her job as that of helping them to reach their goals. Further, they may expect her to view them as friends and to "look out" for their interests at all times. In contrast, management may perceive her job as that of keeping employees "in line" and assuring that they follow company policy. As you can readily see, the person facing this situation probably cannot easily satisfy these contrasting expectations at the same time. The result: she may experience considerable stress stemming from role conflict.

Unfortunately, role conflict (in one form or another) appears to be quite common.[9] And growing evidence suggests that it is often quite stressful in nature. For example, in one ingenious study, French and Caplan monitored the heart rates of male employees while actually at work in their offices. (These data were gathered by means of miniature transmitters that did not interfere with regular work activities.) Results indicated that heart rate rose sharply at times during the day when role conflict occurred.[10] Additional findings suggest that role conflict is also linked to reduced job satisfaction and to reports of job-related tension.[11] Thus, it does appear to exert an important impact in job-related stress, and in this respect is worthy of careful attention.

Role ambiguity: Stress from uncertainty.   Even if an individual manages to avoid the strain associated with role conflict, he or she may still encounter an even more common source of on-the-job stress—**role ambiguity.** Briefly, role ambiguity occurs to the extent that individuals are uncertain about several matters pertaining to their jobs: the scope of their responsibilities, the limits of their authority and that of others, company rules, job security, and the methods used to evaluate their work.[12] As you can probably see, it is a fortunate employee indeed who possesses complete knowledge about all these issues. Thus, role ambiguity is quite common in organizational settings. In fact, it has been reported by thirty-five to sixty percent of the persons questioned about it in various studies.[13] Role ambiguity, like role conflict, produces several negative effects. To the extent it exists, job satisfaction is lowered, self-esteem may be reduced, and negative feelings of tension and futility may be generated. In short, such ambiguity can be a major source of job stress and should be avoided wherever and whenever possible.

Overload and underload: Doing too much, and doing too little.   When the phrase "job stress" is mentioned, many people envision a scene similar to the one shown in Figure 9–4. That is, they imagine a harried executive who is attempting to dictate a letter, talk on three phones, conduct an interview, and write a report—all at the same time! In short, they conjure up an image of someone

FIGURE 9-4   Overload: One Source of Job-Related Stress

Being asked to do too much on one's job—a condition known as *overload*—can
be an important source of stress. (Source: Photo by Susan Lapides.)

caught in the trap of trying to do too much in too little time. In this case, research
findings suggest that common sense is not too far off the mark. **Overload** is often
a major source of job-related stress. And while it rarely reaches the extremes just
described, more than half of all white-collar workers report experiencing it to
some degree in their jobs.[14] Further, persons who experience these conditions
show clear signs of stress: both their cholesterol and their heart rates are elevated,
relative to persons who do not encounter work overload. These and related findings seem to leave little room for doubt: being asked to do too much on one's job
is often a major source of stress.

We are fairly confident that you do not find the stress-inducing impact of overload very surprising. But now consider the following fact: being asked to do *too
little* in one's work can also be quite stressful. Such **underutilization,** as it is often termed, generally yields monotony and intense boredom, and these reactions,
in turn, can be quite stressful.[15] Many factors probably contribute to the link between underutilization and stress, but we will mention only two at this point.
First, most persons wish to feel useful and needed. Thus, when they discover that
they are doing very little and accomplishing next to nothing in their jobs, their
self-esteem may be threatened. And as we noted at the start of this chapter, threat
is a basic component of stress. Second, human beings appear to have a strong and
basic need for stimulation.[16] Their preferred state is definitely *not* that of staring
blankly into space. On the contrary, they prefer to interact with the world around
them. For this reason, a job that demands too little—and that provides too little in
the way of stimulation—can be unpleasant, boring, and stressful.

As you can now see, there are some good and basic reasons why under-utilization can serve as a source of considerable stress. It is little wonder, then, that persons who are "kicked upstairs" into secure but dull positions, and those who work on strictly routine and monotonous tasks, often show symptoms of stress quite similar to those who face opposite conditions.

Responsibility for others: Often, a heavy burden. In any organization there is a division of responsibility. Some persons deal primarily with financial matters (e.g., budgets, accounting); others handle the flow of supplies or the maintenance of equipment; and still others—supervisors and managers—deal primarily with people. Are there any differences in the level of stress associated with these contrasting types of responsibility? Research findings suggest that there are. In general, people responsible for other people—who must deal with them, motivate them, and make decisions about them—experience higher levels of stress than persons who handle other aspects of a business.[17] Such persons are more likely to report feelings of tension and anxiety. And they are also more likely to demonstrate "classic" symptoms of stress, such as ulcers and hypertension, than their counterparts in finance, supply, etc. The basis for this difference is easily discerned. Supervisors and managers must often deal with the human costs of their decisions. They must witness the anguish of persons who are fired or passed over for promotion. Similarly, they must witness the reactions of those given negative feedback on their work. As you can imagine, such experiences are often very stressful. As noted by the vice-president of one large company:

> Dollars, stockholders' dividends, market changes, all those are just numbers. They bother me, sure, but the decisions that eat away at me are the ones that involve people. If I have to lay off the father of a family . . . or call someone on the carpet, I'm a wreck for days.

In short, it appears that being responsible for other persons *is* often a heavy burden, one that exacts a major toll in terms of job-related stress.

Lack of participation: Stress from the absence of input. In our discussion of job satisfaction (see Chapter 7) we noted that most people feel they know quite a lot about their jobs and believe they should be consulted about decisions relating to them. When they are not, job satisfaction, and perhaps productivity too, can suffer. Here we simply wish to note that a lack of employee participation in such matters often has another negative effect as well—it can serve as an added source of tension and stress.[18] This seems to be true for two reasons. First, when they are not invited to take part in the decision process, many employees may feel "left out." This in itself is a negative experience. Second, because they have no opportunity to influence important events relating to their jobs, such persons may also experience feelings of helplessness or a loss of control. As we will soon note, such reactions often intensify the impact of stressful events. For these reasons it seems beneficial to permit as much employee participation in decisions as possible. After all, doing so may enhance job satisfaction, raise productivity, and eliminate at least one important potential source of stress.

Other organizational sources of stress: Evaluation, working conditions, and interpersonal relations.   The factors just described appear to be among the most important as sources of stress within organizations. However, several others also exist and should be at least briefly mentioned. First, there is the process of *performance appraisal* or evaluation described in Chapter 8. Being evaluated by others is often a stressful experience, especially when the results of such appraisal have important effects upon one's career. (We should also note that performing such evaluations can be quite unsettling.) Second, *working conditions* are sometimes an important source of stress. Extreme heat or cold, loud noise, crowding, and unpleasant smells can all act as physical stressors and exert powerful effects upon the persons exposed to them. Finally, stress can sometimes stem from *personal relationships* within an organization. When these are cordial and supportive, they can reduce or "buffer" the impact of various sources of stress and exert other beneficial effects.[19] When they are negative, however, they can elicit considerable amounts of stress. A summary of all the organizational sources of stress we have considered is provided by Figure 9–5. As this figure and our comments suggest, stress can stem from many different sources within an organization, and sev-

FIGURE 9-5   Organizational Sources of Stress: An Overview

Stress can stem from many different factors within an organization. Some of the more important ones are shown here.

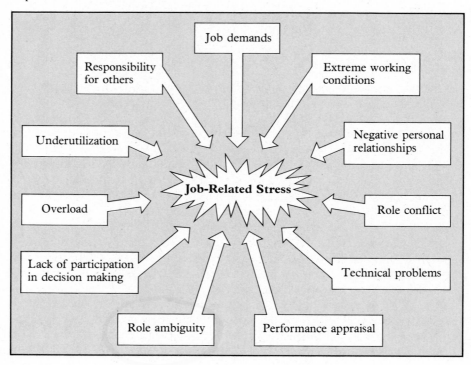

eral of these are difficult if not impossible to eliminate totally. Given these facts, it is far from surprising that stress is such a pervasive fact of life in the modern world of work.

Personal Influences on Stress

Organizations do not exist in a psychological or social vacuum; the behavior shown by individuals within them is often strongly affected by events occurring in other contexts. And as we noted in Chapter 4, it also reflects the traits and characteristics brought by individuals to the work setting. For these reasons, full comprehension of stress within organizations requires attention to individual and personal factors affecting this process. Several of these will now be examined.

The impact of life change.   Movies, novels, and plays often suggest that there is an important link between changes in one's life—especially traumatic ones—and later personal health. Specifically, they often portray individuals who have experienced stressful events (e.g., death of a loved one, divorce, loss of the family estate) as "pining away" until they become seriously ill and expire. Clearly, this suggestion of a link between stressful life events and health is intriguing. But does it have any basis in fact? The answer appears to be yes. Many investigations conducted during the past fifteen years suggest that this particular Hollywood or Broadway theme contains a substantial grain of truth. When individuals undergo extremely stressful changes in their lives, their personal health *does* often suffer.[20,21]

The initial work on this intriguing relationship was conducted during the 1960s by Holmes and Rahe.[22] These investigators asked a large group of subjects to rate numerous life events in terms of the amount of change they produced. On the basis of these data, they then prepared a *Schedule of Recent Life Events*, in which the amount of change associated with each entry is represented by a numerical value. (A later form of the schedule was titled the *Social Readjustment Rating Scale*.) As you can see from Table 9-1, the largest amount of change/stress is linked to the death of a spouse, followed by divorce and marital separation. In contrast, relatively low levels of change/stress are associated with vacations or minor violations of the law (e.g., a traffic ticket). In systematic research using this questionnaire, Holmes and Rahe then obtained evidence for a link between the occurrence of stressful life events and later illness. Thus, they noted that individuals reporting life changes totaling 150 points or less generally had good health during the following year. Those reporting changes totaling between 150 and 300 points had about a fifty-percent chance of developing a serious illness during this period. And among those scoring 300 points or more, the chances of a serious decline in health rose to fully seventy percent.

Subsequent research on the impact of stressful life events upon personal health has generally confirmed these initial findings.[23] However, we hasten to note that the strength of this relationship is far from overwhelming. In fact, correlations between magnitude of life change experienced and subsequent changes in health

TABLE 9–1   Various Life Events: How Stressful?

When individuals experience life changes such as those shown near the top of this list, they often experience considerable levels of stress. And this, in turn, can adversely affect their health. (Source: Adapted from the "Schedule of Recent Life Events," by Holmes and Rahe. *Journal of Psychosomatic Research,* 1967, *11,* 213–218.)

LIFE EVENTS	SCALE VALUE (RANGE = 1 − 100)
Death of a spouse	100
Divorce	73
Separation (Marital)	65
Death of close family member	63
Major personal injury or illness	53
Marriage	50
Fired from job	47
Retirement	45
Death of close friend	37
Foreclosure of mortgage or loan	30
Trouble with in-laws	29
Wife begins or stops work	26
Trouble with boss	23
Change in residence	20
Change in sleeping habits	15
Change in eating habits	15
Vacation	13
Christmas	12
Minor violations of the law	11

have generally been .30 or lower. One factor operating to hold this relationship to these modest levels is this: many persons exposed to highly stressful life changes do *not* become ill. That is, they seem impervious to the harmful effects often induced by such experiences. This fact raises an intriguing question: what is it about these individuals that permits them to cope so well? In short, what traits or characteristics help them to remain healthy in the face of extreme stress? A recent study conducted by Suzanne Kobasa has provided some intriguing answers to these questions.[24]

Kobasa reasoned that people who experience stressful life events without falling ill may differ, in terms of personality, from persons who *do* succumb to such stress. In particular, she reasoned that "stress-resistant" persons may possess three characteristics to a greater degree than those who are "stress-vulnerable." First, they may believe more strongly that they can exert *control* over the events they encounter. Second, they may be more deeply *committed* to the activities in their lives. And third, they may react more favorably to change, viewing it as an exciting *challenge* rather than as a source of threat. In order to examine these suggestions, Kobasa administered several questionnaires to all of the middle- and upper-level executives of a large public utility (some 837 men). One of the questionnaires was the Schedule of Recent Life Events developed by Holmes and Rahe, while another was designed to obtain information on any illnesses subjects had recently experienced. Additional questionnaires assessed the three personality factors previously listed—belief in personal control, commitment to one's activities, and reactions to change. On the basis of responses to all of these scales, Kobasa established two key groups of subjects: one consisting of persons who had experienced a great deal of stress but had not become ill, and another consisting of persons who had experienced a similar level of stress and *had* succumbed to serious illness. It was predicted that these two groups would differ sharply with respect to the three personality characteristics of control, commitment, and challenge. As you can see from Figure 9-6, this prediction was confirmed. Persons who remained healthy in the face of stressful life events did express a greater sense of control, greater commitment to life activities, and more positive feelings about change than those who became ill after such events. We should add that in another, related investigation, Kobasa and her colleagues have studied a large group of managers for several years.[25] The results of this long-term project can be readily summarized: the greater the degree to which the individuals involved possessed the traits described above (a cluster Kobasa terms *hardiness*), the smaller the negative impact of stressful life events upon their personal health. Together, these findings point to the conclusion that there *are* important individual differences in reaction to such events. While some persons are highly vulnerable to this form of stress, others are relatively resistant to it. And these differences, in turn, seem to reflect important underlying aspects of personality.

The Type A behavior pattern and reactions to stress.

In our earlier discussion of the Type A behavior pattern (see Chapter 4), we noted that Type A persons often pay a high price for their hard-driving, high-pressure life-style—they are more than twice as likely as Type B's to suffer from heart disease. Further, we also noted that this crucial difference in health may stem, at least in part, from underlying differences in the way in which Type A's and Type B's respond to stress. Briefly, A's seem to react more strongly to such conditions than B's. For example, when exposed to stress-inducing events, their heart rate and blood pressure increase to a greater degree than that of B's.[26]

At this point, we wish to expand upon our earlier comments by noting that A's and B's also differ in other aspects of their reactions to stress. In particular, recent evidence suggests that A's may be more likely to "give up" and feel helpless when confronted with certain types of stress than B's. And this, in turn, may lead them to demonstrate poorer and less adaptive behavior strategies than B's. Direct evidence for the presence of such differences has recently been reported by Brunson and Matthews.[27]

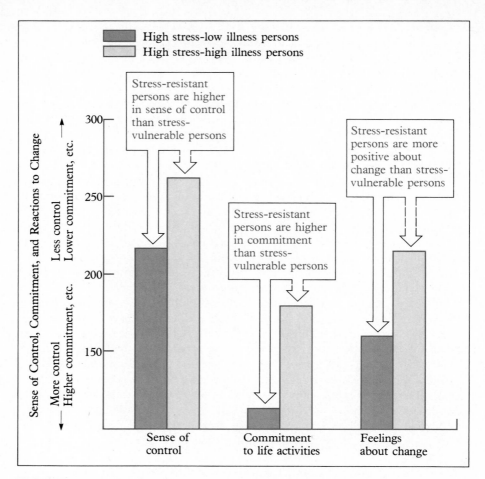

FIGURE 9-6   Personality: An Important Mediator of the Impact of Stressful Life Events

Individuals who experience a great deal of stress but do not become ill differ in several respects from individuals who experience similar levels of stress and do succumb to serious illness. Specifically, stress-resistant persons appear to be higher in the sense of control and commitment to their life activities and have more positive feelings about change in general. Note that higher numbers indicate *lower* control, commitment, and positive feelings about change. (Source: Based on data from Kobasa, *Journal of Personality and Social Psychology*, 1979, *37*, 1-11.)

These investigators conducted an ingenious study in which Type A and Type B persons (male students) were asked to work on several simple problems. (The problems involved determining which of several dimensions—size, shape, etc.— would permit subjects to choose the correct alternative in each of several pairs of drawings.) While working on the problems, subjects were asked to think out loud, to verbalize all of their thoughts and strategies. In this way, the researchers hoped to gather information on just how A's and B's handle stress.

The first four problems presented to subjects were readily solved, and at this time, no important differences in the behavior of Type A's and Type B's were noted. The final four problems, however, were insoluble. And here important and intriguing differences in the behavior of A's and B's emerged. When confronted with these problems, A's quickly began to adopt less effective problem-solving strategies. That is, they shifted from ones that could potentially yield a solution (assuming one existed), to strategies that could *never* yield a solution, even if the problem were actually solvable (see Figure 9–7). In contrast, Type B's showed less tendency to move in this inefficient direction. Further, the verbal comments made by Type A individuals suggested that they often blamed themselves for their failure on the insoluble problems. B's, in contrast, tended to blame the difficulty of the task or bad luck for their negative results.

In summary, existing evidence suggests that Type A persons react more strongly to stress than Type B's. As a result, they may often seriously damage

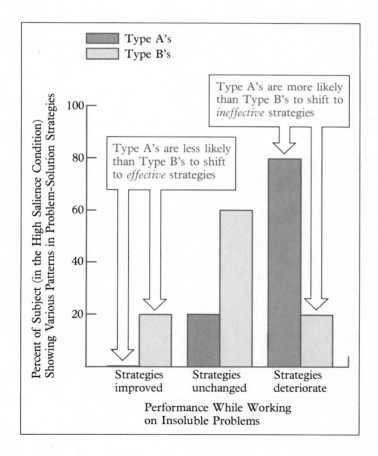

FIGURE 9-7 Type A Behavior Pattern and Reactions to Stress

When shifted to insoluble problems (a source of strong stress), Type A individuals were more likely than Type B individuals to adopt ineffective solution strategies. (Source: Based on data from Brunson & Matthews, *Journal of Personality and Social Psychology*, 1981, *40*, 906–918.)

their own health. Further, when they encounter stress, Type A's seem to respond less adaptively to it. And then, to make matters worse, they often blame themselves even for negative outcomes they have not produced. Type B's, in contrast, react with more effective behavior strategies and show less tendency to shoulder blame or responsibility that is not really theirs. Given these differences, it is little wonder that relatively few top-level managers are Type A's. On the one hand, they don't often survive long enough to rise to the highest ranks; on the other, if they do, they fail to handle as well as B's the stress so common at these heights. This is not to say that Type A's are always at a disadvantage. Competitiveness and achievement-striving *do* often yield positive results. But at the least, it appears that Type A persons should devote careful attention to techniques for coping with stress. If they do, the careers—and lives!—they save may well be their own.

Perceived control and reactions to stress. Imagine the following two sets of circumstances. In the first, you are scheduled, at unpredictable intervals, to present detailed reports on your work to a group of top executives in your company. Further, once the reports are scheduled, you have no choice but to give them; the dates cannot be moved. In the second situation, you must also deliver such reports. But here you are permitted to schedule them yourself and can change these appointments if you provide sufficient prior notice. Under which set of circumstances will you experience greater stress? Almost certainly, you would find the first far more disturbing. The reason for this is simple. While identical stress-inducing events occur in both, you have absolutely no control over their occurrence in the first case; in contrast, such control *is* present in the second.

That control over stressful events can often "cushion" our reactions to them is suggested by the findings of many recent experiments.[28] It has been repeatedly noted in such research that when individuals can control the onset or termination of a source of stress, they find exposure to it far less upsetting than when such control is lacking. Further, actual control does not appear to be crucial; merely *perceiving* that it exists may be sufficient. These findings, in turn, lead to another closely related point. As you may recall from our discussion in Chapter 4, individuals differ greatly in terms of their beliefs about their ability to control the world around them. Some (known as *Internals*) feel that they can readily affect such events and shape their own destinies; others (known as *Externals*) generally feel that their fates are determined by events and forces beyond their control. If feelings of control actually play a key part in determining reactions to stress, it seems reasonable to expect that Internals and Externals will differ greatly in this respect. And in fact, this seems to be true. For example, Internals generally describe their jobs as less stressful than Externals.[29] They also report lower levels of stress in many organizational settings than do Externals. In sum, a sense of personal control over stressful events can strongly affect reactions to such conditions. For this reason, individual differences along this dimension are worthy of careful attention.

Stress and cognitive appraisal: Stress—largely—is where we perceive it.
Before concluding, we should pause briefly to mention a final but important fact.
The amount of stress individuals experience in a given situation is *not* determined
solely by the objective conditions it involves. Rather, it is also strongly affected
by **cognitive appraisal** of these conditions.[30] In short, stress occurs only to the
degree that the persons involved in a situation perceive it to be harmful, threatening, or challenging. If, in contrast, they do not view the situation as possessing
these characteristics, stress will not occur—even if objective stress-inducing conditions actually exist. Perhaps the crucial role of such cognitive appraisals is most
readily visible in situations in which they are somehow "out of phase" with reality. For example, consider the events that occur in theaters, nightclubs, and similar settings when one or more persons suddenly—and falsely—perceive the presence of danger (e.g., fire). Here, panic may ensue, with the result that hundreds or
even thousands are injured, despite the total absence of any real threat (see Figure
9-8). Conversely, individuals can often suffer serious harm when they fail to recognize a real and imminent danger, and so take no steps to avoid it. These and related incidents serve to underscore the fact that our response to various stressors
is strongly shaped by our appraisal of their nature. And needless to add, the
process through which we appraise or evaluate potential sources of stress is affected by many variables, including our past experience with stressors, our attitudes about them, and several of our personal traits.

To conclude: stress, it seems, is largely where we perceive it. Thus, full comprehension of this important process cannot rest solely on knowledge of the exter-

FIGURE 9-8   Cognitive
Appraisal: A Key Process in
Reactions to Stress

When individuals falsely appraise
a situation as being dangerous or
threatening, tragic disasters such as
the one shown here can result.
(Source: UPI Photo.)

Life in a Double-Boiler

"Well," says Chris after hanging up the phone, "that was Joanne all right. She says she has another one of those terrible headaches and won't be in today. Gosh, that makes the third time in the past two weeks. And today is her meeting with old Merrill. He's not going to like this one bit."

"Yeah, it's a shame," answers Joe. "I don't know what's gotten into her lately. Hmmm . . . maybe it's the extra work load. She really has had it pretty rough since Hildy left. And she did pick up a lot of new responsibility after her promotion."

"That's right," Chris agrees. "And I don't think that working for 'Terrible Tom' helps. You know how he operates—he just goes ahead and makes decisions without talking them over with anyone. And then poor Joanne has to live with them. Even worse, she has to back them up with her staff even if she thinks they're rotten. Talk about being caught in the middle. . . . Whew!"

"And don't forget—she's also been having trouble with her husband. I think they're close to a split. And boy, would she ever be better off without him. What a drag. She deserves better."

"I'll say," replies Chris. Then, after a pause, she continues: "Gee, you know, taking everything into account, I can see why Joanne is having all those headaches. But I sure hope she pulls herself together. If she doesn't, it's really going to cost her."   □

Questions:

1. On the basis of the comments by Chris and Joe, can you identify potential organizational sources of stress Joanne currently faces?
2. Similarly, can you identify any personal sources of stress with which she must contend?
3. How would you recommend that Joanne deal with these sources of stress in her life? (You may wish to hold off on answering until you have read the section of this chapter dealing with the management of stress.)

---

nal factors that induce it. Rather, we must also know something about individuals and about the manner in which they perceive the world around them. (For a concrete illustration of the impact of stress in an organizational setting, please see the **CASE IN POINT** box above.)

STRESS: SOME IMPORTANT EFFECTS

We trust that our discussion so far has convinced you—if you needed any convincing—that stress is an extremely common aspect of life in organizations. At this point, therefore, we will shift our attention to another basic question: what are the specific effects resulting from exposure to stressful conditions? As we will soon see, stress actually exerts a powerful and far-reaching impact upon human beings. In fact, it is now known to influence our physical functioning, our psychological states, and several key forms of work-related behavior.

The Physical Impact of Stress

Stress, to paraphrase a poster popular in the 1970s, is definitely unhealthy for adults, children, and other living things. In fact, evidence gathered in recent years suggests that prolonged exposure to stressful conditions can produce serious disturbances in our basic bodily processes. We have already touched on evidence linking stress with heart disease. Here we will simply add that high levels of stress are also linked to the following negative effects: high blood pressure, high pulse rates, increased cholesterol levels, abnormalities in the electrical activity of the heart, peptic ulcers, and high levels of uric acid in the blood (a condition linked to gout and other ailments).[31] We should quickly note that at present it is not entirely clear that stress actually *causes* all these changes. The possibility exists that it merely accompanies them, and that both stress and these symptoms are produced by some other factor. Taking all available evidence into account, though, it seems reasonable to conclude that prolonged exposure to high levels of stress can result in physical changes that threaten our health and well-being.

The Psychological Impact of Stress

Most behavioral scientists now believe that mind and body are intimately linked. That is, events and conditions affecting one often affect the other as well. Given this basic view, it is not surprising to learn that as stress affects our basic bodily processes, it also influences our internal psychological states. A number of such effects have been uncovered in recent studies. First, as you might well expect, exposure to stress often induces negative changes in *mood* and *emotional state*. Persons experiencing it frequently report such feelings as anxiety, depression, fatigue, and irritation. Second, exposure to stress—especially stress relating to one's job—may result in *lowered self-esteem*.[32] Such effects may arise in the following manner. Individuals exposed to intense and prolonged job stress often feel that they cannot cope with the demands of their position. At the same time, these persons generally believe that such coping is essential. Indeed they may feel that the ability to handle one's job is closely linked to competence and self-worth. This gap between the way they feel things *should be* and current reality may then produce a downward shift in self-esteem.

Third, and perhaps most important, stress is often associated with reductions in *job satisfaction*.[33] Considering the negative and unpleasant nature of intense stress, such effects are far from unexpected. In any case, given the important links between job satisfaction and key forms of organizational behavior we described in

Chapter 7, it is clear that the impact of stress upon such feelings has important implications no manager should ignore.

The Impact of Stress on Organizational Behavior

Any factor that exerts powerful effects upon basic bodily processes and internal psychological states would normally also be expected to affect overt behavior. With respect to stress, this is definitely the case. A considerable body of research findings point to the conclusion that exposure to strong and continued stress exerts significant effects upon several types of organizational behavior.

First, and perhaps most important, stress affects the *performance* of many different tasks. It was once widely assumed that the relation between stress and job performance took the form of an inverted letter U or an inverted letter J. That is, at low levels of stress, performance actually improves (relative to no stress) because of the heightened arousal or activation generated. At higher levels of stress, however, negative effects (such as exhaustion or feelings of dissatisfaction) come into play, with the result that performance begins to decline. And at very high levels of stress such effects become dominant, and performance drops very sharply (see Figure 9-9).

Unfortunately, recent findings suggest that this description, appealing as it is, is probably not very accurate. In reality the relationship between stress and performance is considerably more complex. First, it is strongly affected by the level of difficulty of the task being performed.[34] And as noted recently by Beehr and Newman, its precise form probably varies with the specific stressor involved, the type of performance being measured, and several other personal and situational variables. In view of this more recent evidence, we cannot—alas!—provide a simple description of the overall relation between stress and task performance. Indeed, no single description of this relationship may be possible. We can, however, offer two general conclusions: (1) the performance of many tasks is in fact strongly affected by stress, and (2) such performance usually drops off sharply when stress rises to high levels.

In addition to task performance, stress also affects several other aspects of organizational behavior. For example, it is at least modestly related to absenteeism and turnover.[35,36] This is hardly surprising. After all, when individuals find a job highly stressful, they may well seek to avoid it, at least as much as possible. There is also some indication that high levels of job stress are linked to alcoholism and drug abuse on the one hand and to aggression and industrial sabotage on the other.[37] The fact that individuals sometimes attempt to cope with stress through the use of drugs accounts for the first of these findings. And the second is consistent with research suggesting that anger and aggression often follow exposure to certain stressors (e.g., intense heat, loud noise, crowding; see Chapter 13).

Before concluding, we should note that while most effects of stress upon organizational behavior are negative, there is one major exception to this general rule. The results of a recent study by Weiss, Ilgen, and Sharbaugh suggest that work-related stress (e.g., being transferred involuntarily, getting a new boss) can encourage individuals to engage in increased *information search* with respect to

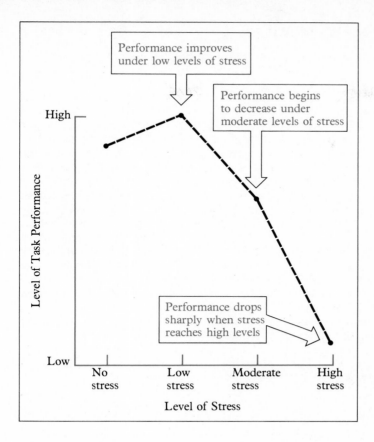

Performance improves
under low levels of stress

Performance begins
to decrease under
moderate levels of stress

High

Level of Task Performance

Performance drops
sharply when stress
reaches high levels

Low

| No | Low | Moderate | High |
| stress | stress | stress | stress |

Level of Stress

FIGURE 9-9 Stress and Task
Performance: An Earlier View

At one time, it was widely assumed
that the relationship between stress
and task performance is as shown
here. Recent findings, however,
suggest that the precise form of
this relationship probably varies
with task difficulty, the specific
forms of stress involved, and
several other factors.

their jobs.[38] That is, such conditions may encourage them to re-examine their
typical patterns of work behavior, to seek more input from co-workers, and so on.
Such actions, in turn, can yield many positive results. For example, they may assist individuals (and organizations) in altering outmoded patterns of behavior—a
key step in adapting to new environmental conditions. In such cases, the impact
of stress can be quite beneficial.

Aside from this exception, however, stress seems to exert largely negative effects upon organizational behavior. For this reason, it is often useful for managers
to devote careful attention to the task of reducing its presence both for themselves
and their employees. Please see the **"FOCUS"** box on page 296 for a description
of additional, unsettling effects stemming from stress.

COPING WITH STRESS: SOME USEFUL
TECHNIQUES

Because stress stems from many different sources, its complete elimination from
organizations seems unlikely. But even though it cannot be totally avoided, it *can*
be managed. That is, techniques for minimizing its adverse effects upon both in-

FOCUS ON BEHAVIOR

Aftereffects: The Lingering (and Often Hidden) Costs of Stress

During the course of each working day, most people are exposed to numerous forms of stress. Distracting and irritating noise is common in many work settings; temperatures often rise or fall to uncomfortable levels; and many of the other sources of stress we have considered may be present. Despite these conditions, however, individuals are generally able to perform their jobs in a fairly efficient manner. We have already noted the reason for this—stress does not seriously interfere with task performance until it reaches quite high levels. And in many cases, these are not present on a daily basis.

Unfortunately, though, this is not the only way in which stress can affect performance and other aspects of our behavior. Growing evidence points to the fact that, often, individuals can cope with stress while it is present—but only at a cost. When it ends, or when they leave its presence, they may often suffer from harmful **aftereffects.** In short, the impact of stress may well be moderated by intense effort when it first occurs, only to appear in full force at a later time.

Evidence for the existence of such effects has been gathered in many recent studies. For example, in an early and well-known series of experiments on this topic, Glass and Singer exposed one group of subjects to loud and irritating noise while they worked on simple tasks.[39] (The sounds were presented in a random manner, and could not be controlled by subjects.) In contrast, individuals in another condition (the control group) were not exposed to this noise. In a second phase of the investigation, subjects in both groups then worked on several additional tasks (e.g., proofreading; a task designed to measure tolerance for frustration, involving insoluble problems). The results obtained in five separate studies using this basic design were entirely consistent. In each case, subjects exposed

to the noise performed more poorly and showed lower tolerance for later frustration than those in the control group (see Figure 9–10).

Similar effects have also been observed following exposure to other forms of stress (e.g., crowding, high-demand tasks, frustrating experiences with a bureaucracy). And they seem to occur in natural as well as laboratory settings. For example, Cohen and his colleagues found evidence for negative aftereffects among children attending school in the flight paths of a busy airport.[40] Indeed, such effects did not entirely vanish even when the schools were later soundproofed. Finally, we should also note that aftereffects seem most likely to occur following exposure to stressors that are unpredictable or uncontrollable. When individuals possess real or even imagined control over the sources of stress, aftereffects may fail to occur.[41]

While aftereffects relating to task performance are certainly bad enough, we must also report that exposure to stressful conditions appears to leave other negative residues as well. First, individuals exposed to loud and irritating noise seem less willing to offer help to a stranger in need of their assistance than individuals not exposed to this form of stress.[42] Second, persons exposed to loud noise seem more willing to engage in dangerous acts of aggression than individuals not subjected to this unpleasant form of stress.[43] Together, these and related findings suggest that exposure to stressful circumstances may often reduce our later sensitivity to other persons—a social aftereffect with potentially serious consequences.

Taken as a whole, recent findings concerning the aftereffects of stress point to this unsettling conclusion: often, the immediate impact of such conditions may be only part of the total picture. Even when individuals manage to cope with strong and prolonged stress, they may pay a high price for

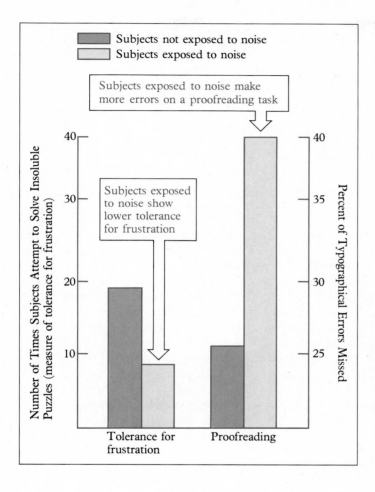

FIGURE 9-10 Stress and Negative Aftereffects

Individuals exposed to loud and unpredictable noise later showed poorer performance on several tasks than individuals not exposed to such noise. In short, exposure to this form of stress produced important negative *aftereffects*. (Source: Based on data from Glass & Singer, *Urban stress.* New York: Academic Press, 1972.)

their efforts. As suggested by Selye's General Adaptation Syndrome (discussed earlier in this chapter), the struggle to cope may leave them exhausted and less able to handle further sources of stress. In such cases, the aftereffects of stress, though less apparent than its immediate ones, may be no less costly. □

dividuals and organizations exist and can be put to practical use. Many different procedures for coping with stress have been developed. Most, though, fall into two major categories: *personal strategies,* approaches that can be applied by individuals to their own behavior, and *organizational strategies,* techniques organizations can follow to minimize stress among their employees. We will now consider several examples of each type.

Personal Strategies for Coping with Stress

Self-improvement and self-help have been popular themes during the past two decades. In fact, it is currently difficult to stroll down the aisles of any book store without encountering dozens of books focusing on these general goals. In this regard stress has certainly received its full share of attention. Many techniques for coping with its harmful impact have been proposed and strongly recommended. As we will now note, some of these focus on physical strategies for handling stress and others on psychological or behavioral approaches.

Physical strategies for coping with stress. As we have already seen, exposure to intense and prolonged stress can exert harmful effects on health and basic bodily processes. Given this fact, it seems reasonable to suggest that factors serving to enhance physical fitness might help individuals to withstand the adverse impact of stress. Consistent with this basic reasoning, it has often been suggested that *exercise* and *good diet,* two factors known to enhance physical fitness, may aid in coping with stress.[44] Indirect support for the accuracy of such proposals is provided by the fact that physically fit people are generally less likely to develop several types of illness (e.g., heart disease, stroke) than those who are less fit. Assuming that the level of stress encountered by both groups is approximately equal, these findings indicate that physical fitness may well be a buffer against the impact of stress. Unfortunately, no direct and systematic evidence on this possibility yet exists. Thus, at present this suggestion should be viewed as promising and reasonable, but still unverified.

Psychological strategies for coping with stress. While physical techniques for handling stress have received much attention in recent years, strategies based on psychological or behavioral factors have probably been even more in vogue. Among these the one that has probably received the greatest amount of firm support from careful research is the development of networks of **social support.** A number of studies suggest that persons who possess close, friendly ties with others in their organizations are often better able to cope with job-related stress when it occurs than individuals who lack such support.[45] Apparently this is so because persons possessing close ties with others are confident of receiving help in time of need. Consequently they tend to perceive many situations as less threatening than would otherwise be the case. And as we noted earlier, the level of stress experienced in any situation is strongly affected by such cognitive appraisals. Regardless of the specific mechanisms involved, however, it is clear that taking the trouble to develop close ties with one's fellow employees can often yield an important bonus—it may arm us with an effective weapon against the onslaught of job-related stress.

A second technique for coping with stress is both simple and effective—*plan ahead.* In many cases, it appears, individuals expose themselves to much unnecessary stress simply because they have not followed this basic rule. If, instead, they consider what events new situations are likely to involve and what future emergencies are likely to develop, they can prepare themselves for these contingencies. And since being able to predict the occurrence of stressors can sharply lessen their impact, being prepared in this manner can often render these events far less stressful when they actually occur.

A third strategy for dealing with stress is one you have probably heard recommended many times—take a vacation, adopt a hobby, or participate in other enjoyable activities. While such suggestions may strike you as a bit simplistic, growing evidence suggests that they are useful. The findings of several recent studies indicate that participation in enjoyable activities *can* enhance the ability to cope with even intense stress. Further, it appears that the persons most likely to benefit in this manner are those most in need of assistance—individuals who have recently experienced negative and upsetting life events.[46]

Two additional techniques for handling stress are closely related—**relaxation training** and **meditation.** Relaxation training involves an attempt to deal with stress through mastering techniques that induce deep muscle relaxation. Such relaxation seems to lower blood pressure, pulse, and other bodily functions. Thus, by employing this technique at times when they feel especially anxious or tense, individuals can help to minimize the impact of stress on their physical well-being.

Meditation is basically another technique for attaining similar goals. As you probably know, it received a great deal of popular attention during the 1970s, especially in a form known as *Transcendental Meditation.* Startling claims were made about the benefits of this technique, and it was soon adopted by hundreds of thousands of persons in the U.S., Canada, and elsewhere. In essence, the basic procedures of such meditation are fairly simple. After assuming a comfortable position, persons meditating close their eyes and attempt to clear all disturbing thoughts from their minds. Then they silently repeat a single syllable (or *mantra*) over and over again. As noted by Patricia Carrington, one expert on meditation, it is best to meditate in a quiet room, facing away from sources of light. And meditating in front of a plant or bouquet of flowers may be helpful.[47] In any case, silent chanting of a single syllable continues for twenty to thirty minutes.

Research designed to investigate the effects of such meditation has yielded interesting results. First, persons who engage in this practice often report such positive changes as increased feelings of well-being, higher reserves of energy, and greater clarity of thought.[48] Second, and even more dramatic, meditation appears to produce important changes in basic bodily functions. For example, in one study Wallace and Benson obtained careful records of the physiological reactions of thirty-six individuals before, during, and after meditation.[49] Results indicated

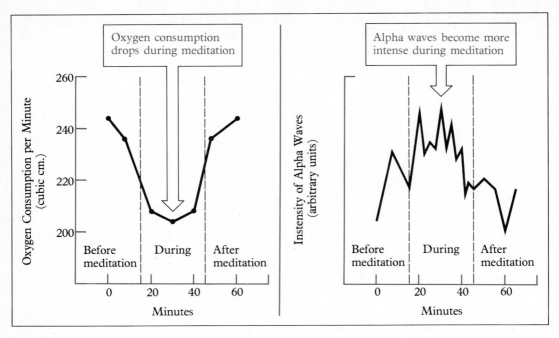

FIGURE 9–11   Some Physiological Effects of Meditation

During meditation individuals show reduced oxygen consumption (left panel) and an
increase in alpha waves (brain waves associated with a relaxed state; right panel). (Source:
Based on data from Wallace & Benson, *Scientific American,* 1972, *226,* 84–90.)

that thirty minutes of quiet meditation reduced subjects' oxygen consumption,
lowered their respiration, increased the electrical resistance of their skin (a change
linked to reduced emotional arousal), and shifted their brain waves toward a pattern reflecting calm relaxation (see Figure 9–11). In view of such findings, it
seems likely that meditation yields at least temporary benefits. However, the
question of whether these can be of practical use in dealing with job-related stress
is still to be investigated.

Organizational Strategies for Managing Stress

While personal strategies for coping with stress differ greatly, all center around a
common theme—arming individuals with techniques they can use for dealing with
stress when it occurs. In contrast, organizational strategies for managing stress
adopt a somewhat different approach. They seek to minimize such reactions by
removing factors that induce them from the work setting. Many of these techniques involve changes in the structure or function of organizations themselves,
while others focus primarily on changes in the nature of specific jobs.

Changes in organizational structure or function. As we pointed out earlier, a great deal of stress within organizations stems from certain aspects of their structure and function (e.g., the role ambiguity or conflict they induce; lack of participation in the decision-making process). Given this fact, it seems reasonable to suggest that the level of stress employees experience can often be reduced through judicious changes in these stress-inducing features. That this is actually the case is suggested by the findings of a relatively small but growing body of research.[50] Unfortunately, discussing all of the changes examined in this work would require more space than is available in this chapter. However, we can at least list several of the more important ones.

First, it has been found that job stress can often be reduced through *decentralization,* a dispersal of authority and responsibility throughout an organization. This process seems to alleviate feelings of helplessness and lack of control on the part of employees and so reduces overall stress. Second, job-related stress can be reduced through adjustments in the *reward systems* an organization uses. When performance appraisals are perceived as reasonable by employees, and when the distribution of rewards is seen as being fair, the stress stemming from concerns over such matters is minimized. Third, stress can be lowered by means of improved techniques for the *training* and *placement* of employees. More effective training helps individuals perform their jobs with a minimum of strain; and better placement minimizes the mismatch between persons and jobs that is so often a source of stress within organizations.[51] Fourth, stress can be reduced by arranging for employee *participation* in the decision-making process. And finally, it can also be minimized by improved lines of *communication.* To the extent these and related steps are implemented, the level of stress within an organization can be substantially reduced, with all the benefits in terms of performance, improved job satisfaction, and better personal health this can yield.

Changes in the nature of specific jobs. Additional organizational strategies for reducing stress center around adjustments in the scope and nature of specific jobs. For example, the stress often produced by performing boring and monotonous tasks can be lowered through *job enlargement,* broadening the scope of a given job to include more varied activities. Similarly, the stress stemming from feelings of helplessness and lack of control can be reduced by means of *job enrichment* procedures in which employees are afforded more autonomy and responsibility for planning and directing their own work. As you may recall, we examined these procedures in Chapter 5. Thus, for the present, we simply wish to note that job-related stress can often be minimized through careful attention to the general issue of effective and appropriate job design.

Techniques for coping with stress: A word of caution, and a word of optimism. As we have repeatedly noted, firm support for the effectiveness of many of the techniques we have described is currently lacking. That is, few rest upon the kind of firm, scientific evidence we prefer before reaching definite conclusions. Despite this fact, however, we are guardedly optimistic. Many of these

FROM THE MANAGER'S PERSPECTIVE

How Well Do You Cope? A Self-Assessment

Coping with stress is important. If we fail to handle it well, our personal health, psychological well-being, and ability to function effectively can all be affected. For these reasons, each of us should be concerned with the extent to which we are, or are not, coping with the sources of stress around us.

But how can we measure our success in this regard? One answer is provided by the *Coping Checklist,* a brief questionnaire developed by Albert McLean.[52] To gain some insight into just how well *you* are coping with common sources of stress, complete the questionnaire presented in Table 9–2. Simply indicate the extent to which each statement in it is true or not true about yourself. (You can also administer the Coping Checklist to people you know in order to learn how well *they* are coping with stress.)

Before providing you with instructions for scoring the Coping Checklist, we should say a few words about the characteristics it is designed to measure. According to McLean, persons who cope very effectively with stress show the following traits.

• First, they know themselves and accept their own strengths and weaknesses. In short, they possess a high degree of *self-knowledge.*
• Second, they have many interests outside the world of work. These include hobbies, sports, and a wide range of other leisure-time activities.
• Third, they are *flexible* and react to stressful circumstances differently at various times. In short, they are quite capable of adjusting their behavior so as to deal with a wide range of stress-inducing conditions.

• Fourth, they are aware that others have different values and accept this as a fact of life. Tolerance, it appears, is one of their major personal characteristics.
• Finally, they are active and productive at work without sacrificing similar activities at home or in the community. Such persons are not drained by their jobs; on the contrary, they seem to have adequate energy—and enthusiasm—left over for many other concerns.

You can obtain scores for yourself on each of these dimensions in the following manner:

• Self-Knowledge: Add items 4, 9, 13, 18
• Wide Interests: Add items 2, 5, 7, 16
• Flexibility: Add items 1, 11, 17, 19
• Acceptance of Others' Values: Add items 3, 8, 14, 20
• Active and productive: Add items 6, 10, 12, 15

On each of these dimensions, scores can range between 5 and 20. McLean notes that if you score higher than 12 on a given dimension, you may wish to direct special attention to that aspect of coping. Total scores can vary between 20 and 100.

If you score more than 60, you may be experiencing general difficulties in coping with stress. In that case you may wish to go back and select one of the personal strategies for managing stress described earlier in this chapter. Considerable effort may then be involved in adapting it to your own life, but remember—the person you help will be yourself!   ☐

TABLE 9-2   The Coping Checklist

Complete this short questionnaire to determine how well you are currently coping with common sources of stress. To what extent does each of the following fit as a description of you? (Circle one number in each line across.) (Source: McLean, *Work Stress.* Reading, Mass.: Addison-Wesley, 1980, pp. 126–127.)

	VERY TRUE	QUITE TRUE	SOME- WHAT TRUE	NOT VERY TRUE	NOT AT ALL TRUE
1. I "roll with the punches" when problems come up.	1	2	3	4	5
3. I spend almost all of my time thinking about my work.	5	4	3	2	1
3. I treat other people as individuals and care about their feelings and opinions.	1	2	3	4	5
4. I recognize and accept my own limitations and assets.	1	2	3	4	5
5. There are quite a few people I could describe as "good friends."	1	2	3	4	5
6. I enjoy using my skills and abilities both on and off the job.	1	2	3	4	5
7. I get bored easily.	5	4	3	2	1
8. I enjoy meeting and talking with people who have different ways of thinking about the world.	1	2	3	4	5
9. Often in my job I "bite off more than I can chew."	5	4	3	2	1
10. I'm usually very active on weekends with projects or recreation.	1	2	3	4	5
11. I prefer working with people who are very much like myself.	5	4	3	2	1
12. I work primarily because I have to survive, and not necessarily because I enjoy what I do.	5	4	3	2	1
13. I believe I have a realistic picture of my personal strengths and weaknesses.	1	2	3	4	5
14. Often I get into arguments with people who don't think my way.	5	4	3	2	1
15. Often I have trouble getting much done on my job.	5	4	3	2	1
16. I'm interested in a lot of different topics.	1	2	3	4	5
17. I get upset when things don't go my way.	5	4	3	2	1
18. Often I'm not sure how I stand on a controversial topic.	5	4	3	2	1
19. I'm usually able to find a way around anything which blocks me from an important goal.	1	2	3	4	5
20. I often disagree with my boss or others at work.	5	4	3	2	1

FIGURE 9-12   One Technique for Coping with Stress

As shown here, individuals often turn to alcohol and other drugs to cope with stress. (Source: © King Features Syndicate, 1974. World rights reserved.)

techniques *are* supported by well-developed theories and by sound logical arguments, and others receive at least indirect support from actual research findings. In view of these facts, we believe that as additional evidence accumulates, several will be found quite useful as strategies for minimizing the impact of stress. Until such evidence becomes available, of course, we must view them only as promising but as yet unverified procedures. Even under these conditions, though, it is our conviction that they are far preferable to other strategies commonly used by human beings to deal with stress, strategies such as the one shown in Figure 9-12. In this relative sense, at least, they possess current as well as potential value. (To see how well *you* cope with stress in your own life, see the **"PERSPECTIVE"** box on pages 302–303.)

SUMMARY

Stress occurs in situations in which we perceive that our ability to meet the demands they pose may be overwhelmed. Under such conditions we experience physiological arousal and psychological reactions such as tension and anxiety, and also engage in coping behaviors designed to deal with the stressful situation.

Stress stems from many different causes. Within organizations it may be produced by excessive job demands, role conflict, role ambiguity, and work overload or underload. It can also stem from responsibility for other persons, performance appraisal, and lack of participation in the decision-making process. Stress also derives from several *personal factors*. Major life changes can induce intense levels of stress. Type A persons seem more likely to experience stress than Type B's. And feelings of helplessness and lack of control may intensify reactions to stressful conditions.

Prolonged exposure to intense stress can exert harmful effects on health. With respect to psychological reactions, stress produces negative emotional states and may also lower self-esteem and job satisfaction. At one time it was assumed that the relationship between stress and task performance could be represented by an inverted letter J. However, more recent findings suggest that this relationship is quite complex and probably varies with the specific stressors involved, task difficulty, and several characteristics of individuals. While we can often cope with stress when it is present, we may experience serious *aftereffects* following its termination. These involve decrements in performance and lowered sensitivity to other persons.

Personal techniques for dealing with stress include exercise, developing networks of social support, planning ahead, and meditation. *Organizational strategies* for managing stress center around changes in organizational structure and function (e.g., decentralization, adjustments in reward systems) as well as changes in the nature of specific jobs (e.g., job enlargement and job enrichment).

KEY TERMS

AFTEREFFECTS   Refers to effects on behavior that persist after termination or removal of a stressor. Important aftereffects include reductions in performance and lowered sensitivity to other persons.

COGNITIVE APPRAISAL   The process through which individuals assess or evaluate potential sources of stress. Only to the degree that situations are perceived as dangerous or threatening will stress result.

GENERAL ADAPTATION SYNDROME   A model of physiological reactions to stress proposed by Hans Selye. According to this model, there is an initial alarm reaction, followed by a stage of resistance and then a stage of exhaustion.

MEDITATION   A personal technique for coping with stress in which individuals close their eyes and silently repeat a single word or syllable to themselves. Meditation appears to produce positive shifts in the sense of well-being and substantial reductions in physical arousal.

OVERLOAD   Refers to situations in which individuals are asked to do more work in a given period of time than they can perform. Exposure to overload can result in substantial amounts of stress.

RELAXATION TRAINING   Training in techniques for voluntarily relaxing major muscles of the body. Such relaxation reduces tension and physiological arousal and is one personal technique for coping with stress.

ROLE AMBIGUITY   The extent to which individuals are uncertain about several matters pertaining to their jobs, including the scope of their responsibilities, the limits of their authority, company rules, and job security. Role ambiguity is often a major source of job-related stress.

ROLE CONFLICT   The extent to which different groups of persons with whom an individual interacts hold conflicting expectations about his or her behavior. Role conflict is often a major source of job stress.

SOCIAL SUPPORT   Refers to the extent to which individuals form close, positive relationships with others within their organization. The existence of such relationships can help individuals cope with even intense stress.

STRESS   Physiological, psychological, and behavioral reactions experienced by individuals in situations where current demands threaten to overwhelm their ability to cope with these demands. Stress has important effects upon personal health, psychological states, and important forms of organizational behavior.

UNDERUTILIZATION Refers to situations in which the demands of an individual's job are insufficient to absorb his or her attention, energies, and abilities. Underutilization may result in intense boredom and thus can be quite stressful.

NOTES

1. Baum, A., Singer, J.E., & Baum, C.S. Stress and the environment. *Journal of Social Issues*, 1981, *37*, 4–35.

2. McGrath, J.E. Stress and behavior in organizations. In M.D. Dunnette (Ed.), *Handbook of industrial and organizational psychology*. Chicago: Rand McNally, 1976.

3. Selye, H. *The stress of life*. New York: McGraw-Hill, 1956.

4. Selye, H. *Stress in health and disease*. Boston: Butterworths, 1976.

5. Martindale, D. Sweaty palms in the control tower. *Psychology Today*, 1977, *10*, 71–73.

6. National Institute for Occupational Safety and Health, Department of Health, Education and Welfare, 1978.

7. Parasuraman, S., & Alutto, J.A. An examination of the organizational antecedents of stressors at work. *Academy of Management Journal*, 1981, *24*, 48–67.

8. Katz, D., & Kahn, R. *The social psychology of organizations* (2nd ed.). New York: John Wiley & Sons, 1978.

9. Beehr, T.A., & Newman, J.E. Job stress, employee health, and organizational effectiveness: A facet analysis, model, and literature review. *Personnel Psychology*, 1978, *31*, 665–699.

10. French, J.R.P., & Caplan, R.D. Psychosocial factors in coronary heart disease. *Industrial Medicine*, 1970, *39*, 383–397.

11. Miles, R.H., & Perreault, W.D. Organizational role conflict: Its antecedents and consequences. *Organizational Behavior and Human Performance*, 1976, *17*, 19–44.

12. McGrath, J.E. Stress and behavior in organizations. In M.D. Dunnette (Ed.), *Handbook of industrial and organizational psychology*. Chicago: Rand McNally, 1976.

13. Ibid.

14. French, J.R.P., & Caplan, R.D. Organizational stress and individual strain. In A.J. Morrow (Ed.), *The failure of success*. New York: Amacom, 1972.

15. Katz, D., & Kahn, R. *The social psychology of organizations* (2nd ed.). New York: John Wiley & Sons, 1978.

16. Weisler, A., & McCall, R.B. Exploration and play: Resumé and redirection. *American Psychologist*, 1976, *31*, 492–508.

17. McLean, A.A. *Work stress*. Reading, Mass.: Addison-Wesley, 1980.

18. Margolis, B.L., Krose, W.H., & Quinn, R.P. Job stress: An unlisted occupational hazard. *Journal of Occupational Medicine*, 1974, *16*, 654–661.

19. House, J.S., & Wells, J.A. Occupational stress, social support and health. In A. McLean (Ed.), *Reducing occupational stress*. Cincinnati: National Institute for Occupational Safety and Health, 1978.

20. McLean, A.A. *Work stress*. Reading, Mass.: Addison-Wesley, 1980.

21. Dohrenwend, B.S., & Dohrenwend, B.P. (Eds.). *Stressful life events: Their nature and effects.* New York: John Wiley & Sons, 1974.

22. Holmes, T.H., & Rahe, R.H. Social readjustment rating scale. *Journal of Psychosomatic Research,* 1967, *11,* 213-218.

23. Gunderson, E., & Rahe, R. (Eds.). *Life stress and illness.* Springfield, Ill.: Charles C. Thomas, 1974.

24. Kobasa, S.C. Stressful life events, personality, and health: An inquiry into hardiness. *Journal of Personality and Social Psychology,* 1979, *37,* 1-11.

25. Kobasa, S.C., Maddi, S.R., & Kahn, S. Hardiness and health: A prospective study. *Journal of Personality and Social Psychology,* 1982, *42,* 168-177.

26. Pittner, M.S., & Houston, B.K. Response to stress, cognitive coping strategies, and the Type A behavior pattern. *Journal of Personality and Social Psychology,* 1980, *39,* 147-157.

27. Brunson, B.I., & Matthews, K.A. The Type A coronary-prone behavior pattern and reactions to uncontrollable stress: An analysis of performance strategies, affect, and attributions during failure. *Journal of Personality and Social Psychology,* 1981, *40,* 906-918.

28. Cohen, S. The aftereffects of stress on human performance and social behavior: A review of research and theory. *Psychological Bulletin,* 1980, *88,* 82-108.

29. Gemmill, G.R., & Heisler, W.J. Fatalism as a factor in managerial job satisfaction, job strain, and mobility. *Personnel Psychology,* 1972, *25,* 241-250.

30. Lazarus, R.S., & Launier, R. Stress-related transactions between person and environment. In L.A. Pervin & M. Lewis (Eds.), *Perspectives in interactional psychology.* New York: Plenum, 1978.

31. Beehr, T.A., & Newman, J.E. Job stress, employee health, and organizational effectiveness: A facet analysis, model, and literature review. *Personnel Psychology,* 1978, *31,* 665-699.

32. McGrath, J.E. Stress and behavior in organizations. In M.D. Dunnette (Ed.), *Handbook of industrial and organizational psychology.* Chicago: Rand McNally, 1976.

33. McLean, A.A. *Work stress.* Reading, Mass.: Addison-Wesley, 1980.

34. Beehr, T.A., & Newman, J.E. Job stress, employee health, and organizational effectiveness: A facet analysis, model, and literature review. *Personnel Psychology,* 1978, *31,* 665-699.

35. Steers, R.M., & Rhodes, S.R. Major influences on employee attendance: A process model. *Journal of Applied Psychology,* 1978, *63,* 391-407.

36. Mobley, W.H., Griffeth, R.W., Hand, H.H., & Meglino, B.M. Review and conceptual analysis of the employee turnover process. *Psychological Bulletin,* 1979, *86,* 493-522.

37. Beehr, T.A., & Newman, J.E. Job stress, employee health, and organizational effectiveness: A facet analysis, model, and literature review. *Personnel Psychology,* 1978, *31,* 665-699.

38. Weiss, H.M., Ilgen, D.R., & Sharbaugh, M.E. Effects of life and job stress on information search behaviors of organizational members. *Journal of Applied Psychology,* 1982, *67,* 60-66.

39. Glass, D.C., & Singer, J.E. *Urban stress: Experiments on noise and social stressors.* New York: Academic Press, 1972.

40. Cohen, S., Evans, G.W., Krantz, D.S., Stokols, D., & Kelly, S. Aircraft noise and children: Longitudinal and cross-sectional evidence on adaptation to noise and the effectiveness of noise abatement. *Journal of Personality and Social Psychology,* 1981, *40,* 331–345.

41. Cohen, S. The aftereffects of stress on human performance and social behavior: A review of research and theory. *Psychological Bulletin,* 1980, *88,* 82–108.

42. Mathews, K.E., & Cannon, L.K. Environmental noise level as a determinant of helping behavior. *Journal of Personality and Social Psychology,* 1975, *32,* 571–577.

43. Donnerstein, E., & Wilson, D.W. The effects of noise and perceived control upon ongoing and subsequent aggressive behavior. *Journal of Personality and Social Psychology,* 1976, *34,* 774–781.

44. McLean, A.A. *Occupational stress.* Springfield, Ill.: Charles C. Thomas, 1974.

45. McLean, A.A. *Work stress.* Reading, Mass.: Addison-Wesley, 1980.

46. Reich, J.W., & Zautra, A. Life events and personal causation: Some relationships with satisfaction and distress. *Journal of Personality and Social Psychology,* 1981, *41,* 1002–1012.

47. Carrington, P. *Freedom in meditation.* Garden City, N.Y.: Anchor Press Doubleday, 1978.

48. Schultz, T. What science is discovering about the potential benefits of meditation. *Today's Health,* 1972, *50,* 34–37.

49. Wallace, R.K., & Benson, H. The physiology of meditation. *Scientific American,* 1972, *226,* 84–90.

50. Newman, J.E., & Beehr, T.A. Personal and organizational strategies for handling job stress: A review of research and opinion. *Personnel Psychology,* 1979, *32,* 1–43.

51. Caplan, R.D., Cobb, S., French, J.R.P., Jr., Harrison, R., & Pinneau, S.R. *Job demands and worker health: Main effects and occupational differences.* Washington, D.C.: U.S. Government Printing Office, 1975.

52. McLean, A.A. *Work stress.* Reading, Mass.: Addison-Wesley, 1980.

Part Three

Behavior in Organizations:

Group Processes

10

Communication in Organizations

WHAT IS COMMUNICATION?

The Process of Communication: A General Model

COMMUNICATION AND THE FORMAL STRUCTURE OF ORGANIZATIONS

Organizational Structure: The Framework for Communication   How Organizational Structure Influences Communication   How Communication Networks Influence Job Performance and Satisfaction

INFORMAL COMMUNICATION: HIDDEN PATHWAYS WITHIN ORGANIZATIONS

It's a Small World   Sociometry: Mapping Patterns of Informal Communication   Hearing It through the Grapevine

IMPROVING COMMUNICATION IN ORGANIZATIONS

Gauging the Flow of Information   Improving the Environment: Designing for Communication

SPECIAL INSERTS

CASE IN POINT   Giving the Pink Slip: A Case of the MUM Effect
FOCUS ON BEHAVIOR   Recipe for Controlling Rumors: Are There Really Worms in McDonald's Hamburgers?
FROM THE MANAGER'S PERSPECTIVE   Offices Without Walls

KEY CONCEPTS

Communication

Communication Networks

Encoding

Decoding

Organizational Structure

Organigram

Filtering Effect

MUM Effect

Discriminatory Buck Passing

Communication Network

Centralized Networks

Decentralized Networks

Saturation

Sociogram

Cliques

Isolates

Liaisons

Grapevine

Rumor

Overload

Gatekeeper

Filtering

Queuing

Distortion

Omission

Open Offices

□ □ □

"I can't believe our ratings have dropped so low!" exclaimed Wally Horton, producer of KRAF's "Afternoon Magazine" talk show. "We've got to get more interesting guests, or we'll never get any viewers." Horton's assistant producer, Len Cleaver, looked at the ratings book and nodded to his boss, "You're right, we need to book some sex researchers, an Elvis reincarnation, someone interesting, or we'll all be looking for new jobs!"

The door to the producer's office was open, and Patty Walker couldn't help but overhear Len saying something about "we'll all be looking for new jobs" as she entered the outer office to deliver the mail. "Could we be going out of business?" she said aloud as she closed the outer office door behind her. After thinking about it, it didn't seem too surprising at all, considering the way things seemed to be run at the station.

Catching her in thought in the hall, her friend Chuck Deaver asked what was going on. "Oh Chuck, I'm glad to see you," Patty said excitedly. "I think we're going out of business." "What? How'd you . . . " "It's true, I overheard Horton and Cleaver talking about it. They're looking for new jobs."

"Oh no!" said Chuck. "I'd better call my wife and tell her. We were gonna buy a new house; good thing you told me!" "I'll pass the word," said Patty, as Chuck ran to the phone.

What do you make of this incident of panic at KRAF? Maybe Patty overreacted. She really shouldn't have jumped to conclusions, especially such important ones, on the basis of such incomplete evidence. Of course, it's easy for us to condemn someone else in such a situation when *we* have all the facts.

Nevertheless, we all can probably think of times when we've been a party to an unsubstantiated rumor. Who hasn't listened to juicy tales around the water cooler and passed them on? Spreading information in this way is an important part of life in organizations, a fact that affects us all.

Our story points to several crucial aspects of information flow in organizations that interest us in this chapter on **communication.** It shows us how rapidly information can spread and how easily it can become distorted. The implications of these observations are fascinating. After all, the passage of information from one person to another is essential for an organization's well-being. Getting the right information to and from the correct others is necessary for an organization to function properly. Naturally, unfounded rumors and distorted messages that flow too rapidly, or accurate messages that are miscommunicated, can present serious problems for organizations.

Issues such as these will be examined in this chapter. Our presentation will begin by defining communication and describing the process by which it occurs. We will then focus on two different types of communication systems that operate in organizations—the *formal* system and the *informal* system. In studying formal communication, we will examine some of the organizational structures that affect the flow of communication. This will lead to a discussion of how various patterns, or **communication networks,** influence job performance and satisfaction. We will then contrast this with the informal ways organizations operate. In doing so, we will examine how *informal patterns of communication* develop and how the "grapevine" operates in organizations. Finally, we will close by exploring some common problems of organizational communication and by considering a few practical solutions to them.

WHAT IS COMMUNICATION?

It has often been said that speaking is not necessarily communicating. There is certainly much more involved in successfully communicating one's ideas than just speaking or writing. With this in mind, we may define communication as *the process by which one party (a sender) transmits information (a message) to another party (a receiver).* Communication occurs at many levels, as can be seen in Figure 10-1. It goes on within and between individuals, as well as within and between organizations.[1] Because this book focuses on individual behavior in organizations, we will deal primarily with interpersonal communication, although many of the basic processes we will present are relevant to other levels of analysis as well.

Now that we have a working definition of communication to guide us, let's take a closer look at the various steps in the communication process.

The Process of Communication: A General Model

As our definition suggests, communication is a process. Actually it is a continuing process, one that involves several steps that are repeated over and over again in cycles. We have summarized this process in diagram form in Figure 10-2.

This figure clearly reveals the steps that form the communication process.[2] The first element in the process is a source, or a *sender* of a message. This is the person who has the idea to be communicated. For the source to communicate his

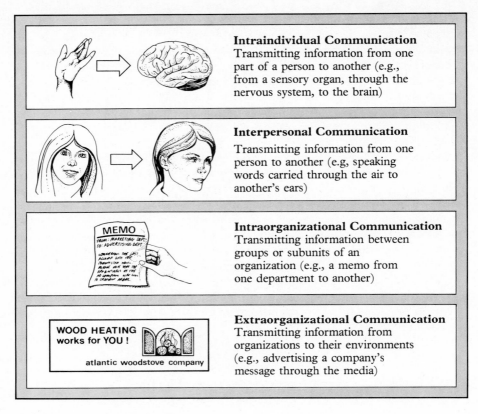

FIGURE 10-1   Levels of Communication
Communication occurs at many levels—within and between individuals, and within and between organizations.

or her idea, that information must first be translated into a recognizable form, such as spoken or written language. This is known as **encoding** information. Encoding is a very important process since an idea that is not adequately represented cannot accurately convey the sender's ideas. We've all encountered difficulties in encoding information at some times (see Figure 10-3). (Hopefully, we are not having this difficulty with you!)

After the message is encoded, the next step requires it to travel over channels to reach the intended receiver. *Channels of communication* may be telephone lines, mail routes, the air waves that carry the vibrations of your voice, or the light waves that enable us to see. They are simply the vehicles through which the encoded message travels to the receiver. We may send messages to other people, to organizations, to computers, or to any desired receiver.

Once the receiver gets the message, he or she begins **decoding**—that is, transforming it back into ideas. If the process worked accurately, these will be the same ideas the sender intended the recipient to receive. The decoding process can

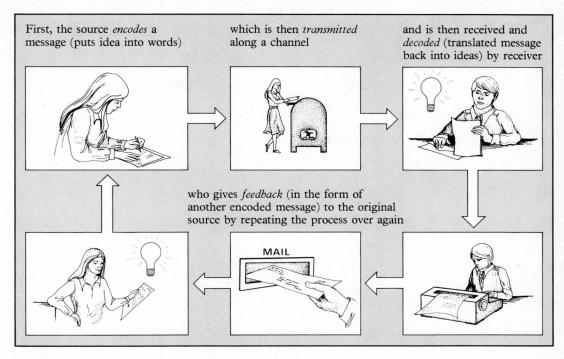

First, the source *encodes* a message (puts idea into words)

which is then *transmitted* along a channel

and is then received and *decoded* (translated message back into ideas) by receiver

who gives *feedback* (in the form of another encoded message) to the original source by repeating the process over again

MAIL

FIGURE 10-2   The Communication Process: A Summary

The process of communication is cyclical. A message is first sent from the sender in encoded form over channels to the receiver, who decodes the message and then provides feedback by starting the process over again.

involve many different subprocesses, such as reading words, understanding spoken language, interpreting facial expressions, and the like. All these processes work toward transforming the sender's message back into ideas the receiver can understand.

Once this has been accomplished, the *feedback* phase can begin. That is, the receiver can encode a new message and send it over channels to the original sender, who would then decode it. Of course, during the feedback phase, the former sender now becomes the new receiver, and the former receiver now becomes the new sender. The process then begins all over again until the cycle has been completed. For this reason we have characterized the process of communication as continuous.

An interesting aspect of the communication cycle in organizations is that it occurs on both a formal and an informal level. That is, organizations are designed in ways that require individuals in certain positions to communicate with each other. Also, as you probably know, people are not restricted by formal channels of communication and so develop informal patterns of communication as well. The next two sections will examine the communication process in its formal and informal contexts.

FIGURE 10-3   Encoding Messages: Often a Difficult Task

Writing is a common form of encoding messages in organizational communication. As the cartoon suggests, it doesn't always come easily for us. (Source: Reprinted by permission of United Feature Syndicate. Copyright © 1971.)

COMMUNICATION AND THE FORMAL STRUCTURE OF ORGANIZATIONS

Now that we have defined the concept of communication and have described the process by which it occurs, we are prepared to study how the communication process operates in organizations. Although the basic process of organizational communication is essentially similar to the communication process in other social contexts, there is a unique consideration in organizations that cannot be ignored—the structure of the organization itself. Organizations are designed in ways that often specify who may (and who may not) communicate with whom. The central question in this regard is this: How is the communication process helped or hindered by the structure of an organization?

Organizational Structure: The Framework for Communication

To begin addressing this question, we must first define what we mean by **organizational structure.** We use this term to refer to *the formally prescribed pattern of interrelationships existing between the various units of an organization.* Later in this book (Chapter 15) we will describe various models for designing organizations. Meanwhile, however, we will concentrate on the ways in which organizational structure influences communication.

An organization's structure is usually depicted in the form of an organizational chart, sometimes referred to as an **organigram.** Quite simply, an organigram is a graphic representation of an organization's structure. An example of an organigram is shown in Figure 10-4. We will use this diagram to make some important points about the structure of an organization and its implications for communication.

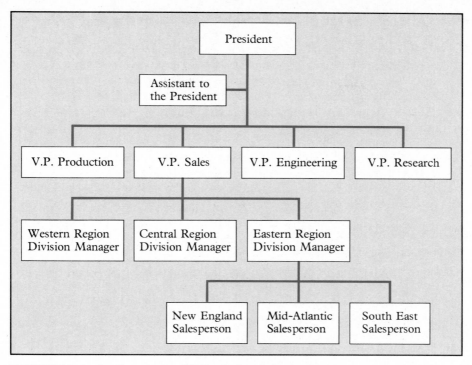

FIGURE 10-4   An Organigram: "X-Ray" of an Organization

An *organigram,* or organizational chart, of a hypothetical manufacturing company showing all levels of the hierarchy for one branch of a division.

You will immediately note the pattern of boxes and lines in the organigram. These tell a great deal about an organization's structure and have been likened to an X-ray of an organization.[3] The boxes in the organigram refer to various units within the organization—persons performing certain jobs. The lines connecting the boxes represent lines of authority; i.e., who answers to whom within the organization. Each person is *responsible to* (answers to) the persons at the next higher level to which he or she is connected, while simultaneously *responsible for* (gives orders to) the persons below.

Because the status and authority of persons in the organization differ, organigrams also show that the organization is a *hierarchy.* That is, all persons within the organization are *not* at the same level; some are higher up in terms of power, and others are lower down. A person's position in the organizational hierarchy may not always be obvious, but there are usually certain signs that immediately suggest a person's position. Military personnel, for example, wear stripes on their sleeves to display their position in the hierarchy. So, too, workers in private industry can be differentiated by their clothing. The expensive, well-tailored suit worn by the company president immediately sets him or her apart from the work shirt and overalls worn by workers on the loading dock.

We should make it clear that although it is composed of people, an organization's structure represents a pattern of formal responsibilities and job duties, and describes the roles people play in the organization, not the people themselves.[4] Although different persons may bring different characteristics and skills to their jobs, the structure of an organization does not change when employees leave their posts and are replaced by new ones. This keeps organizations stable and predictable. To function smoothly, each part of an organization must operate as required. An automobile's faulty transmission or a person's faulty heart needs repair or replacement to function properly. The same holds for organizations. The organigram is a blueprint of what job everybody has to perform so that the organization will operate properly.

How Organizational Structure Influences Communication

The link between organizational structure and communication is a very basic and important one. Simply put, an organization's structure dictates who can or must communicate with whom. An organization's lines of authority show the pathways through which messages have to flow within organizations.

Although the typical organigram doesn't show it, the lines connecting the subunits in an organization's structure operate as if they were two-headed arrows. That is, communication occurs up and down the organizational hierarchy.[5] However, as summarized in Figure 10–5, the same kinds of information do not flow in

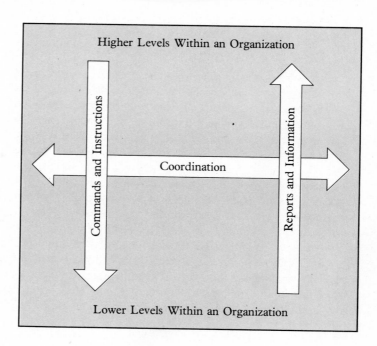

FIGURE 10–5 Types of Organizational Messages

Different types of messages are communicated in different directions in an organizational structure. Commands and instructions travel downward, reports and information travel upward, and coordination travels horizontally.

"Come in, Frank. I've been eager to communicate downward to you."

FIGURE 10-6 Downward Communication: A Frequent Event in Most Organizations

One of the easiest and most frequently occurring types of organizational communication is that from superiors to their subordinates. (Source: Drawing by Vietor; © 1975 The New Yorker Magazine, Inc.)

each direction. Instructions and commands flow *down* the hierarchy, while reports and information flow *upward*.[6] We can see this immediately if we think of an executive requesting sales figures from his or her secretary, who in turn passes them on to the executive. Each person's role in the hierarchy clearly defines his or her communicative duties in the organizational structure. Not only does one's position in the hierarchy dictate the others with whom communication is to occur, but also what *type* of communication is to occur.

We should also note another way in which the flow of information up and down the organizational chart is not equal. It has long been noted that communication occurs more frequently, and is easier, from superior to subordinate (down the hierarchy) than the other way around (see Figure 10-6).[7] One classic study, for example, found that the vast majority of assembly line workers initiated contact with their supervisors less than once a month, while their supervisors initiated contact with them very frequently.[8]

A common characteristic of upward communication is that it suffers from a **filtering effect.** That is, employees tend to withhold such potentially threatening or detrimental information as bad news, reports of mistakes, and unfavorable opinions. Because subordinates fear reprisals from their superiors, they tend to slant their upward communication in ways that place themselves in a favorable light. The result, of course, is that accurate reports of important negative information may fail to reach top management. (In this regard, please see the **"CASE IN POINT"** box on pages 320–321.) Research has shown that the tendency to distort upward communication is greater among persons who are more interested in achieving success. Moreover, distortion is less likely when employees feel their organizations allow them freedom over their work and are not ones in which there is little room for initiative and responsibility.[9]

CASE IN POINT

Giving the Pink Slip: A Case of the MUM Effect

We have noted that upward communication in organizations is frequently hindered by subordinates' reluctance to make themselves look bad by bringing negative information to their supervisors' attention. It should also be noted that supervisors are often reluctant to share bad news with their subordinates, as the following brief case history reveals.

"I'll have a double martini," Bill Martenson told the waiter at lunch. "Bill, since when do you drink?" queried Sam Thompson, a business associate and Bill's lunch partner. "I don't usually, but I've got to fire someone today, and I can use the courage." Through the rest of their meal Bill told Sam how he dreaded having to break the bad news to Mac Decker, a bright young manager who had only been with the company for three months. Bill received word from the corporate office that payroll had to be cut drastically and that newly hired personnel would have to be "given the pink slip." "It's not easy on me," Bill complained. "Decker's a good manager, and besides, I hate having to hurt the guy."

There was little Sam could say to make Bill feel any better. Sam was supportive, but still Bill agonized over the thought of having to fire Mac. Being a company vice-president sometimes conjured up in Bill's mind the image of being a tough, ruthless, efficient executive type, an image that Bill certainly didn't have of himself. Lunch was over, and the thought of having to fire Mac Decker consumed Bill the rest of the afternoon. He couldn't put it off any longer and stood up to summon Decker, but just then Decker walked in to see Bill on another matter.

"Mr. Martenson, you don't look so good," Mac observed. "What's wrong?" "I'm glad to see you," Bill replied. "Sit down, Mac, we have to talk. . . . "

This brief story may have left you feeling uneasy—not only for the person being fired, but for the person doing the firing. In fact, it is a well-established psychological phenomenon that people are reluctant to transmit bad news to those who are affected by it. This is known as the **MUM effect**.[11] We see a good example of the MUM effect in medical settings, in which very bad news all too frequently has to be communicated to patients and their relatives. Studies have

---

Horizontally across the organizational chart, persons at an equal level are friendly toward each other, and find it easier to talk to each other. Not surprisingly, they have more in common, understand each other better, and communicate in a manner that induces coordination (as opposed to the authoritative messages communicated downward). Yet, research has shown that horizontal communication tends to be discouraged in very large organizations with many levels of command.[10] In such organizations workers may feel that they are competing against each other for the rare opportunities to be heard at the upper ech-

shown that physicians prefer to avoid telling terminally ill patients that they are dying, even if they desire to know.[12]

The MUM effect has also been demonstrated in the context of communicating employment decisions. For example, in one study Rosen, Grandison, and Stewart had subjects play the role of personnel managers who were required to inform job applicants about whether or not they would be hired for a job.[13] Subjects had to pass on either good news (that the applicant got the job) or bad news (that the applicant didn't get the job). They could relate the news either directly by telling the applicants themselves, or by "passing the buck," delegating this job to their assistants. As you might expect, subjects tended to tell the applicants the good news themselves but had their assistant relate the bad news. This had been referred to as **discriminatory buck passing,** a variant of the MUM effect that appears to be quite widespread in organizations. Rather than not telling the bad news at all, certain persons in organizations may get others to do their dirty work for them.

While the existence of the MUM effect is intuitively obvious, there is no single obvious explanation for it. For example, it is possible that communicators are reluctant to transmit bad news because it makes *themselves* feel guilty or otherwise in a bad mood. It is also possible that the MUM effect results from the sender's fears about how the receiver may react. Bearers of bad news may not want the receiver to feel bad and may believe that this person would rather not hear the bad news.

Although scientists have yet to reach agreement as to exactly *why* the MUM effect occurs, it would seem worthwhile to note some of its implications for organizations. As we have already seen, feedback is crucial for the communication cycle to be complete. For persons in organizations to avoid giving negative feedback is to effectively avoid taking the first step toward solving problems. Negative information has to be transmitted, accepted, and acted upon for change to result. Hopefully, an understanding of the MUM effect will serve as the first step toward countering the negative impact—biasing and omission of information—that it might otherwise have on organizations.   □

elons of the organization. The result is that interest in coordination of effort with one's peers gives way to a competitive, antagonistic orientation.

How Communication Networks Influence Job Performance and Satisfaction

One of the most important and thoroughly researched topics in the field of communication involves the impact of patterns of contact between group members on their task performance. A great deal of research, beginning in the 1940s and continuing through today, has examined various fixed patterns of communication.[14,15] The name given to pre-established patterns dictating who can communicate to whom is a **communication network.** The central question confronting communication network researchers has been: Do certain communication networks provide more efficient ways of solving problems than others?

By seating experimental subjects in cubicles interconnected by slots in the walls, researchers have arranged conditions so that participants can communicate with each other only along rigidly defined patterns. Through these slots subjects pass written messages and information to each other in an attempt to solve a problem given to them by the experimenter. Many different configurations of networks have been studied using groups of different sizes. Some of the more commonly studied five-person networks are shown in Figure 10-7. Each circle represents one person in the network, and the lines connecting them represent two-way channels of communication between the persons.

There are some important differences between these various communication networks. You will note, for example, in the *Y,* the *wheel,* and the *chain* networks that messages have to flow through a pivotal person in the center of the network

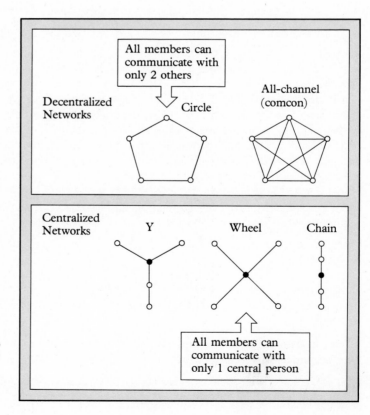

FIGURE 10-7   Communication Networks: A Few Basic Types

Some examples of five-person communication networks. Networks such as the circle and all-channel (comcon) allow all members equal opportunities to communicate with others and are known as *decentralized* networks. *Centalized* networks, such as the Y, wheel, and chain, contain members (marked by a filled-in circle) through whom messages must pass in order to reach others.

(marked by a filled-in circle in Figure 10-7). Because messages must flow to and from this central person, networks of this type are known as **centralized networks.** By contrast, in the *circle* and the *all-channel* (also known as the *comcon*), the members all have equal communication possibilities, and there is no central figure. Accordingly, these networks are referred to as **decentralized networks.**

Just how well centralized and decentralized networks perform depends on the difficulty of the tasks.[16] Different results have been obtained when groups perform simple tasks (e.g., identifying a symbol common to all the cards given to subjects) and complex tasks (e.g., solving arithmetic or word problems). In the typical communication network study, groups are given several problems to solve, one at a time, and the experimenter measures how long it takes the networks to solve them, how many errors are made, and how satisfied members are with the task.

Several conclusions have been reached on the basis of such studies (see summary in Table 10-1).[17] First, it is interesting that *centralized networks reach solutions faster and make fewer errors on simple problems, but decentralized networks reach solutions faster and make fewer errors on complex problems.* This can be explained in terms of **saturation.** The more information any one group member has to deal with at any one time, the more that person is said to be saturated. A person who is saturated is overloaded with information, and performance suffers. This is what appears to happen when a centralized network performs a complex task. The central person becomes so heavily saturated that the group is slowed down and many errors are made. On simple problems the central person automat-

TABLE 10-1   Different Communication Networks: Their Strengths and Weaknesses

As this table indicates, centralized and decentralized networks differ with respect to several important performance variables. On simple problems centralized networks work faster and more accurately, but on complex problems decentralized networks work faster and more accurately. Members of decentralized networks also show higher levels of job satisfaction.

PERFORMANCE VARIABLE	CENTRALIZED NETWORKS	DECENTRALIZED NETWORKS
Speed (number of problems solved)		
on *simple* problems	Faster ←———————	Slower
on *complex* problems	Slower ———————→	Faster
Accuracy (number of errors made)		
on *simple* problems	More accurate ←———————	Less accurate
on *complex* problems	Less accurate ———————→	More accurate
Job Satisfaction	Less satisfied ———————→	More satisfied

ically receives the information from all the other members of the network and can easily solve the problem alone. When the group members have several different options concerning where to send their messages (as in decentralized networks), it naturally takes longer for a solution to be reached.

A second conclusion from communication network research is that *members of decentralized networks are more satisfied with their work than members of centralized networks.* For example, members of circle networks tend to be the most satisfied, and members of the wheel are least satisfied. It appears that subjects enjoy having an equal say in the decisions made in the circle network and do not like having decisions made for them by the central person in the wheel. This explanation makes sense in view of a great amount of subsequent research showing that workers are most satisfied with their jobs when they have participated in making decisions about them (see also Chapter 11).[18]

One must be cautious about generalizing from these laboratory studies to "real world" communication networks. Of course, what an experimenter gains at the expense of realism in doing laboratory research is no more apparent in the case of communication network studies than in any other area of organizational behavior. However, there is one particularly important limitation of communication network research that should be noted. Namely, most studies on this topic examine performance over relatively brief periods of time—usually about an hour. This is in contrast to conditions in real organizations, where communication continues for months or even years. In this respect Burgess found, after several hundred tasks performed over a period of several hours, that the differences between centralized and decentralized networks disappeared.[19] It would appear that over time members of communication networks learned to overcome the limitations imposed on them by the restricted communication structure. They may have done this by learning to pass their information on to certain others who, in the past, have proven good at doing certain jobs.

This study suggests that our conclusions regarding the effects of communication networks must be limited to ones that exist for only brief periods of time. It also suggests that the effects of formal structure may be overcome by *informal* networks that grow and develop over time. In this regard, the character "Radar" O'Reilly on the T.V. show *M*A*S*H* comes vividly to mind. By unofficially trading supplies and equipment with other units, this resourceful corporal learned to operate informally within a large, formal military structure. We will now turn our attention to informal communication in organizations.

INFORMAL COMMUNICATION: HIDDEN PATHWAYS WITHIN ORGANIZATIONS

It is obvious that workers do not talk only to those to whom they are connected according to the organization chart. There are also more loosely structured informal interconnections between workers that can have profound effects on organizational functioning. Indeed, formal organizational structures only tell us part of the story of communication in organizations. They represent the way the organization is set up, but not how it actually operates. Our examination of this topic will focus on the patterns of informal communication that develop, and on the familiar "grapevine" that operates in organizations. Before getting to this, however, we thought it would be interesting to demonstrate just how prevalent informal patterns of communication can be.

It's a Small World

No doubt you've had an experience in which you met someone and found out that you have a third friend in common, maybe even someone who lives far away. "It's a small world," you said to yourself as you thought about this coincidence. Actually, this experience suggests a structure to the pattern of informal connections between people. You may not know that you know someone who knows someone who knows you, but the connection might be there nevertheless. This leads to an interesting question about informal patterns of communication. Suppose you choose a person who lives in one part of the country and another who lives in a different part of the country; through how many intermediary acquaintances would you have to go to connect the two persons? In other words, how many links are there in the social chain between them? This question was posed by psychologist Stanley Milgram and his associates, who conducted several studies to find out.[20]

We think you'll find it interesting to see how Milgram conducted this research. (As you are reading about it, think about the problem and try to predict the answer.) To begin, Milgram selected a volunteer starting person in Omaha, Nebraska, and a target person who lived in the Boston area. The starting person was sent the name of the target person and some information about him, and was asked to send a packet (provided by the experimenter) to the target person *if he was known personally*. If not, the starting person was instructed to mail the packet to someone known on a "first-name basis" who he thought was likely to know the target person. That person (i.e., the acquaintance) had to do the same thing until eventually the packet reached the target. To keep track of the packet at all times, subjects were asked to mail a postage-paid card provided in an envelope to the experimenter. This way, Milgram was able to determine how many links there were in the chain.

What do you think he found? The answer, summarized in Figure 10–8, may surprise you. Of the 42 chains completed, the median number of links to the target person was 5.5, probably much fewer than you would expect. As you can see from Figure 10–8, the shortest chain had only three links (there were several of these), while the longest had ten. Although this may seem surprisingly small, Milgram explains that this apparent closeness is actually very misleading. To be removed from another by five intermediaries is to be very psychologically distant from that person. Despite this, however, Milgram's study clearly demonstrates the very diverse informal social connections that exist between people.

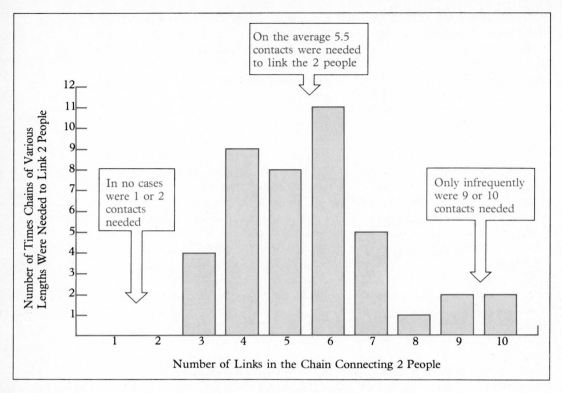

FIGURE 10-8   It's a Small World!: Some Experimental Evidence

In a study attempting to link a person in Omaha to another person in Boston, Milgram found that an average of 5.5 intermediary contacts were needed. (Source: Based on data from Milgram, *Psychology Today*, May 1967, 60–67.)

Sociometry: Mapping Patterns of Informal Communication

Not only is informal communication very far-reaching, as Milgram's work shows; it is also subject to analyses that often reveal established patterns. Messages do not flow randomly within organizations, nor do they necessarily follow only the pathways pre-established by the formal organizational chart. In all organizations people establish contacts with each other on an informal level. These relationships represent important pathways through which organizational messages are communicated. For this reason it is important to understand the patterns of informal communication that develop.

To study these informal pathways, social scientists have relied on a method known as *sociometry*.[21] In sociometry, members of a group or organization are questioned about the other members with whom they communicate. The diagram showing the resulting pattern of personal contacts is referred to as a **sociogram.** Just as an organigram shows the formal structure of an organization, a sociogram shows its informal structure. However, unlike organigrams, which are designed to control the pathways of communication, sociograms are developed after the fact to determine what pathways of communication have actually developed.

To help you understand and appreciate the nature of informal communication patterns in work groups and organizations, a sociogram of a hypothetical group is presented in Figure 10-9. Each numbered circle represents one person in the group; the lines connecting them are the pathways of communication. Some lines have arrowheads on one end (suggesting that one person passes information on to the other), while others have arrowheads at both ends (suggesting that giving and receiving information is reciprocal). By drawing sociograms for actual groups and organizations, social scientists have been able to recognize certain recurrent patterns of informal communication and special roles that are played in them.

We can note some of the regular patterns found in sociograms in Figure 10-9. For example, you may immediately see three clusters of individuals who all re-

FIGURE 10-9   A Sociogram

A diagram such as this, known as a *sociogram,* shows who actually communicates with whom. Each numbered circle represents a person. The lines show the paths of communication, with the arrows showing who receives the messages.

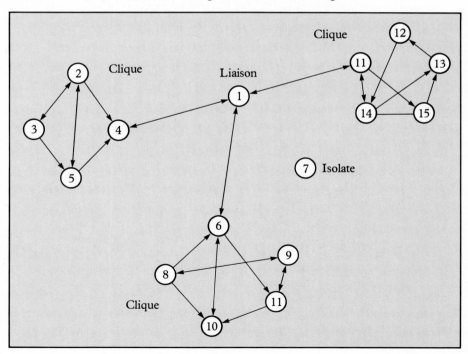

port frequently communicating with each other. Such groupings form what are known as **cliques.** Members of cliques tend to share information with each other and operate as a single unit. Sometimes cliques form because the individuals are forced to work together according to their job descriptions. However, it is also possible that social bonds, such as friendship, may determine the formation of cliques, and these may be unrelated to job duties.

By way of contrast, there are some persons who report having no contact with others; they neither give information to others nor receive it from them. Such individuals (e.g., person no. 7 in our sociogram) are known as **isolates.** Their lack of communication with others with whom they may be in potential contact functionally isolates them. Evidence suggests that being an isolate in a communication system may be a sign of disaffection. For example, in one study conducted in military organizations, it was found that isolates tended to be younger, lower ranking, and less educated than their cohorts.[22] They were also poorer performers, less committed to the military, and less satisfied. Apparently an association exists between being isolated from others in the organizational communication system and being negatively differentiated from them.

Some members of groups and organizations connect various cliques but are not themselves members of any clique. Such persons are known as **liaisons** (e.g., person no. 1 in our sociogram). Because liaisons are at the crossroads of the flow of information, they have been referred to as

> the "cement" that holds the structural "bricks" of an organization together; when the liaisons are removed, a system tends to fall apart into isolated cliques.[23]

Although the liaison may be considered a crucial role played in the *informal* communication networks of organizations, the function of connecting various parts of the organization is considered so strategic that the liaison role is sometimes *formally* built into the jobs of some personnel.[24] Indeed, some persons in most organizations, usually ranging from five to twenty percent, serve as liaisons between the various subunits or cliques. Organizations that have liaisons linking various departments tend to be more effective than those that do not.[25] While any person in an organization can potentially serve as a liaison, they are usually persons who have "been around" for a long time, and are usually administrators.[26] However, the industrial foreman also may be viewed as serving a liaison function.[27] By connecting the laborers with management, foremen are important organizational liaisons.

Hearing It through the Grapevine

The pathway of communication over which unofficial, informal information travels is often referred to as the **grapevine.** The use of the term grapevine is said to have originated during the U.S. Civil War, when telegraph lines strung loosely between trees resembled a grapevine. The resulting messages were often garbled and were said to have originated from the grapevine.[28] Today the grapevine is popularly believed to have a largely negative influence on organizations; some reportedly advocate its elimination.[29] However, according to Professor Keith Davis, an expert in organizational grapevines, they are a natural and inevitable part of organizational life. In fact, he says that it would be strange for employees *not* to take some part in exchanging informal information with their co-workers.[30]

Popular folk wisdom regarding the rapid speed with which messages travel over the grapevine is borne out by research. In one company studied by Davis, a plant supervisor's wife had a baby at 11:00 p.m. one night and by 2:00 p.m. the next day, only fifteen hours later, forty-six percent of the management had heard about it.[31] One reason for the rapid spread of grapevine information is that it is usually transmitted orally to several people. One person tells several others, who tell several others, and in short order many people have heard the message (see Figure 10–10). Written messages that travel from one person to another, and then another, would take some time to get around. Moreover the grapevine is not limited by the formal organizational structure. Anyone can pass the message on to anyone else in the organization.[32] Unlike official organizational business, it is not inappropriate for a mail deliverer to spread the word about an unofficial personal matter to a top executive.

It may be surprising to learn that most information communicated via the grapevine tends to be quite accurate. In one study, for example, it was found that

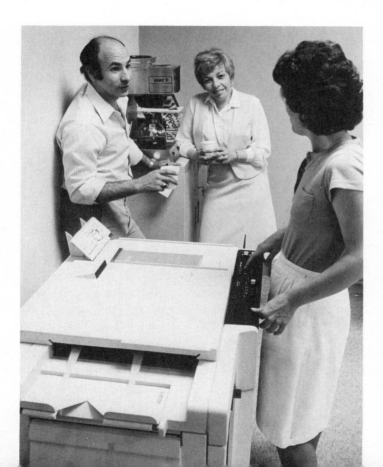

FIGURE 10–10 "I Heard It through the Grapevine"

Informal communication is a natural part of life in organizations. The pathways of informal communication are known as the *grapevine*. (Source: Photo © Frank Siteman MCMLXXXII.)

facts about the company communicated through the grapevine were eighty-two-percent accurate.[33] However, the problem with interpreting this figure is that the inaccurate or incomplete parts of the message are often very important and change the meaning of the rest of the message. For example, Davis found that in one plant grapevine he studied it was being communicated that a welder was marrying the general manager's daughter. The story was ninety-percent accurate in that the welder was getting married on the date and in the location specified by the grapevine. However, the one wrong detail was that though the bride-to-be had the same name as the general manager's daughter, she was actually someone else.[34] This one fact changed the meaning of the whole story. In fact, it is likely that this misunderstanding developed because it made the story so much more interesting. Indeed, Davis has speculated that highly personal or emotional information may be much less accurate than more mundane corporate information.

No doubt it is this undesirable feature that gives the grapevine such a bad reputation. The name commonly given to information transmitted over the grapevine for which there is very little secure evidence is **rumor.** A rumor is *not* the grapevine itself, as commonly thought; it is merely information transmitted over the grapevine that is not well substantiated. Rumors flourish when the information is both interesting and ambiguous.[35] If the message either is uninteresting or can be clearly disproven, it will not be subject to rumors. As we all know, rumors are changed and embellished as they pass from person to person. The result is often quite profound for both the person involved or the organization (see the **"FOCUS"** box on pages 332–333). Take, for example, the case of Mary Cunningham, a former administrative assistant at Bendix Corp., whose rumored romantic involvement with chairman William Agee during the fall of 1980 was claimed by some around the water cooler to be responsible for her rapid promotion to vice-president.[36] Unfortunately, such corporate gossip forced Ms. Cunningham to resign from Bendix, providing us with a good, if unsettling, example of the potential negative impact of a rumor in an organization.

IMPROVING COMMUNICATION IN ORGANIZATIONS

Thus far, our discussion of organizational communication has focused more on how the process works than on what difficulties may exist. Accordingly, to complete our presentation of this topic, we will now consider some communication problems that occur in organizations and some ways of solving them. We will avoid considering communication problems based at the individual level, such as problems of encoding information (using the right words) and decoding information (being a good listener). While these are vitally important skills, treating them adequately would require us to go quite far afield. Instead we will focus our attention on the other elements of the communication process—the information and the context in which it is transmitted. Specifically, we will focus on problems created by improper flow of information or by work environments that cause communication difficulties, and how both types of problems may be eliminated. This discussion will highlight the practical value of many of the concepts and research investigations we have already presented.

Gauging the Flow of Information

One of the most obvious communication problems of any organization concerns the flow of information—the amount of information with which any one person in the organization has to deal. Some executives, for example, are responsible for many workers and a considerable amount of money, and may be expected to have many people answering to them and many others to whom they must answer. There are two interrelated problems we can immediately identify. First, these employees may be overloaded and slow down the system. Second, they may tend to distort or omit important messages. Let's consider each of these problems and some possible solutions.

Overload: Too much, too quickly. The concept of **overload** describes a condition in which any unit in a communication system (e.g., a person, a committee, etc.) becomes bogged down with too much information. Just like a college student who has three final exams on the same day, persons in organizations may become overloaded by having to do too many things at once. Another example that immediately comes to mind is that of the tax accountant who gets busier and busier as the April 15 filing deadline comes along. Unfortunately, the structure of some organizations is such that some persons are required to be much busier than others. This is analogous to the person whose position in a centralized network may result in saturation. The result, as you might expect, is a sharp drop in efficiency. Not only are overloaded workers inefficient themselves; they can cause bottlenecks or a *restricted flow of communication* that makes the entire organization operate at a lowered level of efficiency.[37]

In recent years, top government officials have shown a great deal of interest in solving problems of restricted communication flow resulting from overload by reducing the usual level of routine paperwork and memos (see Figure 10–12). Just imagine the load at the top of a hierarchical structure if everyone below sends up just one unit of information, one memo! The load at the top would be—and usually is—tremendous. So what can be done?

Several solutions to overload have been proposed, and we will describe some of these here.[38] For the sake of convenience, we have summarized them in the top half of Table 10–2. One thing that is commonly done is to employ certain individuals to keep someone else from getting overloaded by controlling the flow of information. Such a person is known as a **gatekeeper.** The assistant to the president shown in our organigram (p. 317) serves as a gatekeeper, deciding who will see the president, when, and for how long. In a broader sense, television news directors and newspaper editors are also gatekeepers; they select the news to which the public will have access.[39] In both cases, the gatekeepers help the potential problem of overload by gauging the flow of information.

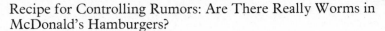

Recipe for Controlling Rumors: Are There Really Worms in McDonald's Hamburgers?

What's the best way to control a rumor? Refute it, right? Actually, a recent study by Tybout, Calder, and Sternthal has shown that refuting a rumor has almost no impact at all on people's beliefs about its truth.[40] Their investigation focused on a completely unfounded rumor circulated in the Chicago area in the late 1970s, stating that there were worms in McDonald's hamburgers. That's ridiculous, of course, but nonetheless sales in areas affected by the rumor dropped by as much as thirty percent. Naturally, McDonald's officials were alarmed and took immediate steps to counter the rumor. Letters from the Secretary of Agriculture were posted in stores assuring customers that the hamburger served was "wholesome, properly identified, and in compliance with standards prescribed by Food Safety and Quality Service regulations." Advertisements emphasizing that the hamburgers were "100% pure beef" were intensified. However, these tactics proved ineffective in combating the rumor, and sales continued to slump for a long time.

According to Tybout and her associates, the failure of McDonald's anti-rumor campaign is not surprising. They claim that the refutation served to remind people of the rumor, thereby strengthening it in their memories. Instead of refuting the rumor, they claim that it would have been more successful to encourage people to think about other, more positive aspects of McDonald's, or even to alter people's negative connotations about worms!

To test these ideas, subjects participated in a study alleged to investigate their reactions to television violence. They watched a one-hour episode of *Hawaii 5-0* interspersed with twelve commercials, including three for McDonald's. After the third McDonald's commercial, an accomplice posing as one of the four to six experimental subjects in each session casually remarked, "You know, these commercials remind me of that rumor about McDonald's—you know, that McDonald's uses worm meat in their hamburgers." There was also a control condition in which subjects were not reminded of the rumor.

The experimenter responded to the rumor in one of four different ways. In the *refutation* condi-

tion the experimenter said, "That's just not true! If nothing else, worms are too expensive—$8 a pound. Besides, the Food and Drug Administration did a study and found that McDonald's uses 100% pure beef." In the *retrieval cue* condition, the experimenter attempted to stimulate other thoughts, neutral or positive, that were unassociated with the worm rumor, and would therefore displace it from subjects' memories. To do this, the experimenter asked subjects a series of questions about McDonald's—the location of the restaurant they usually went to, how often they ate there, and whether or not it had indoor seating. There was also a *storage cue* condition in which the experimenters attempted to reduce the rumor's effect by creating a positive association with worms. Here, in response to the confederate's remark, the experimenter said, "That may sound funny to you, but last week my mother-in-law was in town, and we took her to Chez Paul (a posh Chicago restaurant) and had a really good sauce that was made out of worms." Finally, there was a *no response* condition in which the experimenter reminded the subjects to keep quiet but did not comment on the confederate's remark about the rumor.

To test the impact of the various responses to the rumors, subjects evaluated McDonald's by responding to questionnaire items assessing the quality of the food, the degree to which it fit their needs, and the certainty of their eating there. Subjects were also asked how likely the rumor was to be true.

The results, summarized in Figure 10-11, revealed a very clear and interesting pattern. As you might expect, subjects who heard the rumor evaluated McDonald's more negatively than those who heard no rumor at all, even though they said they didn't believe the rumor. Furthermore, the results showed that simply refuting the rumor caused no improvement in the way McDonald's was evaluated. However, both the retrieval and storage cues helped weaken the impact of the rumor, producing more positive evaluations. Subjects who answered the questions about their own experience at McDonald's, or who heard about the gourmet worm sauce, evaluated McDonald's more posi-

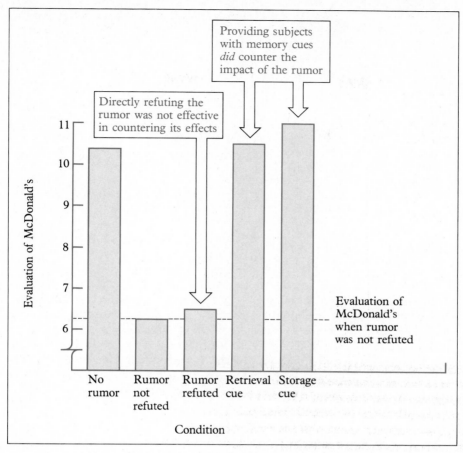

FIGURE 10-11   Countering a Rumor: Two Techniques That Work

How would you go about countering a rumor that there are worms in McDonald's hamburgers? A study showed that persons hearing the rumor evaluated McDonald's more positively if they were led to think other things about McDonald's, or if they were led to think of worms as gourmet food, than if the rumor was directly refuted. (Source: Based on data from Tybout, Calder, & Sternthal, *Journal of Marketing Research*, 1981, *18*, 73–79.)

tively than those who heard the rumor without any response to it by the experimenter, or those who heard a direct refutation of the rumor. In fact, subjects in the retrieval cue and storage cue conditions evaluated McDonald's as positively as those who heard no rumor at all.

In sum, the results of this study suggest that "protesting too much" may not be an effective way of countering a rumor. Refuting a rumor directly only serves to call attention to it. Getting people to think about other aspects of the subject of the rumor or changing their associations with the negative aspect of the rumor appear to be much more effective strategies.   □

FIGURE 10-12   The "Paper Explosion": One of the Major Causes of Overload

As this cartoon suggests, the seemingly endless flow of organizational paperwork can be a major contributor to the problem of overload. (Source: Reprinted by permission of the Tribune Company Syndicate, Inc.)

Using gatekeepers is not all that can be done, of course. Another solution to the potential problem of overload is **filtering.** Filtering simply refers to assigning some priorities to incoming information and deciding what will and will not be attended to. We have already mentioned in this chapter that subordinates tend to filter their upward communications so as to avoid making themselves look bad to their superiors. While such filtering may cause problems of distortion and omission of information (which we will consider next), it is usually necessary to do some filtering to avoid becoming overloaded. This is what we do when we are very busy and throw away "junk mail" without reading it. Dealing with too much incoming information has been described as a problem for many residents of very large cities who often have to filter out extraneous information (e.g., streets littered with garbage, panhandlers, and noise) in order to attend to what they're doing.[41]

TABLE 10-2   Communication Problems and Solutions: Gauging the Flow of Information

Overload, distortion, and omission, common problems in organizational communication, have to do with the flow of information. Some solutions to these problems are listed here.

Problem: Overload

Solutions: 1. Use *gatekeepers*—individuals responsible for controlling the flow of information
2. Make *filtering* decisions—decide what information will or will not be attended to
3. Use *queuing*—assigning priorities to incoming information

Problem: Distortion and Omission

Solutions: 1. Make messages *redundant*—transmit messages in another form, or over another channel
2. *Verify* messages—test their accuracy
3. *Bypass* intermediaries—send the message directly to the intended party

---

A final solution to the overload problem is **queuing.** A queue—a word more common in British English than American—is a line. When queuing is used to handle overload, the incoming information is lined up so it can be handled one piece at a time, in an orderly fashion. This occurs when we put off doing something at a particularly busy time and get to it when things are less hectic. Lining up incoming jets in a landing pattern approaching a busy airport, and taking a number for service at a busy shop are examples of handling potential overload by queuing. By putting communication inputs in a queue, we are lessening the chance that chaotic conditions will result from having to handle too much at any one time.

Distortion and omission.   A related set of problems resulting from the incoming flow of information are **distortion** and **omission.** Distortion refers to changing the content of a message. Omission refers to deleting all or part of a message. Remember Patty, KRAF's resident rumor starter in our opening story? She was responsible for distorting a message she heard. Anyone who has ever played the parlor game of "telephone" (in which one person whispers a message to another, who whispers it to another, and so on until it reaches the last person) has clearly experienced (or contributed to) the ways messages get distorted or omitted.

What is it about the structure of an organization that causes these problems? One obvious factor is that many organizations have a very *tall structure,* meaning that messages have to pass through many individuals up or down the hierarchy before reaching the intended recipient. With each successive pass, the chances become greater that a message will be distorted or ignored completely. A dramatic demonstration of this effect was reported in a study tracing the flow of information downward over five levels in one hundred organizations.[42] A significant loss of information occurred at each level. By the time the message reached the workers at the bottom of the hierarchy, approximately eighty percent of the information was lost!

Of course, if an organization has a *flat structure* (fewer levels of hierarchy), there would be less distortion and omission. Changing the otherwise efficient and well-established structure of an organization to avoid these problems would certainly be unwise, if not impossible. How then might organizations more directly attempt to avoid the problems of distortion and omission of communications? Some solutions suggested by Rogers and Agarwala-Rogers are summarized in the bottom half of Table 10–2.[43]

One suggestion involves increasing the *redundancy* of messages. Messages can be made more redundant by repeating them in a different form, or over different channels. For example, a message from a manager to his or her subordinates may be expected to receive greater attention if it is transmitted in a written memo and then followed up orally via remarks at a meeting. Distortion and omission can also be reduced through *verification* of messages. Messages received by astronauts, for example, are repeated to verify that they were accurately received. Another approach to reducing distortion and omission is *bypassing.* By eliminating intermediary parties in an organization, persons can direct their messages to the best possible receiver. Going right to the company president with an idea and by-passing the intermediary personnel is one thing workers might do to see that their ideas are neither misrepresented nor overlooked.

A problem with these solutions to the distortion and omission problem should be pointed out. Unfortunately, they contribute to the problem of overload.[44] Redundancy and verification are time consuming and may require additional paperwork. Bypassing others in an organization may create overload in the receiver, who normally has messages screened by the bypassed person. As a result, the solutions to the problems of distortion and omission may add to the problem of overload. The ultimate resolution to this dilemma is certainly not easy to see. While we do not intend to propose a way out, it seems an interesting problem to note because it underscores our point about the important role of structure in communication in organizations.

Improving the Environment: Designing for Communication

One important element in all organizational communication systems that is often overlooked is the physical environment in which communication occurs. Anyone who has ever had difficulty finding a suitable place at work for an important private conversation has directly experienced the impact of the work setting on communication. One aspect of organizations' physical environment that has been the subject of recent attention is the matter of the physical arrangement of individuals—how easily they can get to each other.

The importance of physical proximity in communication has long been recognized by social scientists due, in part, to the classic studies done by Festinger, Schacter, and Back at various housing developments after World War II.[45] Briefly described, these studies were designed, in part, to determine how the flow of communication was influenced by informal communication networks (friendship patterns), and the role of physical proximity in the formation of these networks. The study was conducted by interviewing the wives of the male students who lived in these housing units.

Not surprisingly, when asked whom they were most friendly with, the respondents usually identified someone with whom they frequently came into contact. These friendship patterns were found to serve as important lines of communication. To demonstrate this, the experimenters started two different rumors and told each to one member of two different friendship groups. Several days later, the residents were interviewed again to see how the rumors spread. As we would expect, the lines of friendship served as pipelines (what we earlier called the "grapevine") for the flow of information. Residents heard the rumor planted among their own friends, but not the other rumor started in another friendship group. This landmark study clearly demonstrates that physical closeness influenced the formation of friendships, which influenced the flow of information.

The same kind of thing happens in organizations as well. People become friends with those with whom they most often come into contact, and this largely

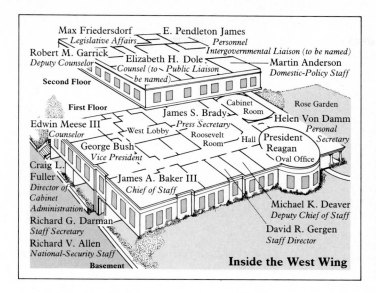

FIGURE 10-13   The Reagan White House: An Example of Designing for Communication

This floorplan of President Reagan's White House shows that the offices of the President's closest advisors and aides are located nearest to his own (e.g., Deaver, Gergen, Baker). Physical accessibility to others is an important facilitator of communication in organizations. (Source: Drawing by Ohlsson. Copyright 1981 by Newsweek, Inc. All rights reserved. Redrawn by permission.)

determines the flow of communication. In fact, in one study of a research and development firm, it was found that two employees who worked more than twenty-five feet apart on the same floor rarely had any significant communication.[46] The implications of this are quite profound if one considers that the effective flow of communication in organizations may require communicating with others who are physically distant.

To deal with this matter, organizations sometimes arrange employees in ways that match their position in the organizational structure. After all, if a worker has to answer to her supervisor and give orders to her subordinate, it would be useful to be located near both. A good example of this process is provided by the pattern of office assignments in President Reagan's White House (see Figure 10-13). (Please see the **"PERSPECTIVE"** box on pages 338–339 for a discussion of yet another technique for facilitating organizational communication.)

SUMMARY

The process of **communication** occurs when a sender of information encodes a message and transmits it over communication channels to a receiver, who decodes it, and then sends feedback. The structure of an organization helps determine who communicates to whom and what form that communication takes. Orders flow down the organizational hierarchy and information flows upward. However, that upward communication is often filtered so as to avoid transmitting negative information.

Formally imposed patterns of communication, called **communication networks,** influence job performance and satisfaction over brief periods of time. Some networks, known as *centralized networks,* have members through whom all

FROM THE MANAGER'S PERSPECTIVE

Offices Without Walls

One popular approach to alleviating problems caused by physical barriers to communication is represented by the **open office**.[47] The open office is literally an office without walls—a large room shared by many office workers. The idea of the open office, also known as a *landscaped office,* began in Germany and Sweden, and was introduced in the United States in the mid-sixties, although it is today still considered somewhat unconventional. Typically, open offices are large rooms with moveable desks and partitions that are arranged so that employees have easy access to each other (see photo in Figure 10–14).

The underlying philosophy of the open office is that workers will be able to arrange themselves close to others with whom they have to work, keeping only minimal physical barriers between them. Supervisors can have easy visual access to their subordinates. Anyone who has ever seen a newspaper room will recognize the open office design used there, one that has been popular for many years. The shared working space in the newspaper room may facilitate the high degree of coordination needed for working in such a setting.

Several large organizations have gone to the open office design, including some sections of the Ford Motor Company. According to one report, the reaction to the landscaped offices at Ford was quite positive.[48] The ability to have face-to-face contact with one's co-workers helped develop a sense of community among the workers. In the words of one Ford manager, the open office made it

> "easier to induce communication with people who would otherwise be reluctant to approach me. I did get to know many people better, and our rapport was unobstructed by artificial physical conditions."[49]

Similar positive reactions to open offices were noted in a survey of several hundred office workers in fifteen open offices in Switzerland.[50] Management in these companies reported an improvement in job-related communication. Moreover, sixty-three percent of the workers felt the landscaped offices helped them accomplish their work more easily and with greater efficiency.

Despite such evidence of success, we should note some drawbacks of open offices. Employees are usually forced to accept them. As a result, they tend to miss the privacy they once had.[51] In addition, open offices may appear messy and chaotic, and may be noisy.[52] These problems illustrate that open offices may not work for all organizations, and that they certainly are not a panacea for all communication problems in organizations. Despite these drawbacks, the open office nicely demonstrates the virtues of flexibility of working spaces in facilitating organizational communication.   □

---

messages have to travel. People in these networks perform better on simple problems. By contrast, in *decentralized networks* all members play an equal role in transmitting information. People in such networks perform better on complex tasks. Research has also shown that members of decentralized networks tend to be more satisfied than members of centralized networks.

Information also travels along informal pathways in organizations. Various patterns of *informal communication* flows can be depicted in the form of a sociogram. Through studying *sociograms,* one can note various individual communication roles, such as that of the liaison, who interconnects various cliques. Informal communication pathways are known as the *grapevine*. Information trav-

FIGURE 10-14   The "Open Office": Designing the Work Environment
to Facilitate Communication

An *open office*, such as this, is designed to separate work groups or individuals from each
other, while simultaneously allowing easy communication between them.
(Source: Photo © 1982 by Larry Lawfer.)

els very rapidly over the grapevine, although it is often incomplete or distorted in
important ways.

The problems of *information overload* and *distortion* and *omission* of information are serious and affect the flow of messages in organizations. Overload can be
relieved through using gatekeepers, by filtering, and by queuing incoming information. Distortion and omission can be reduced through making messages redundant, by verifying messages, and by bypassing intermediary parties. Communication can also be improved by designing work environments so as to allow
communicants easy access to each other. The open office design is one such
approach.

KEY TERMS

CENTRALIZED NETWORKS　　Communication networks that have some members through whom all information must pass to reach the other members (e.g., the "Y," the "wheel," and the "chain").

CLIQUE　　An informal aggregation of persons who frequently share information with each other more than with others.

COMMUNICATION　　The process by which one party (a sender) transmits information (a message) to another party (a receiver).

COMMUNICATION NETWORKS　　Pre-established patterns dictating who can communicate with whom (see *Centralized Networks* and *Decentralized Networks*).

DECENTRALIZED NETWORKS　　Communication networks in which all members play an equal role in the transmittal of information (e.g., the "circle" and the "all-channel").

DECODING　　The process of transforming messages back into ideas.

DISCRIMINATORY BUCK PASSING　　The practice of transmitting good news oneself, but using subordinates to transmit bad news.

DISTORTION　　The changing of the content of a message.

ENCODING　　The process of translating an idea into a recognizable form that can be transmitted to others.

FILTERING　　The assigning of priorities to incoming information in deciding what information will and will not be attended to.

FILTERING EFFECT　　The tendency for organizational members to distort upward communication by withholding negative information.

GATEKEEPER　　A person who controls the flow of information to others in an organization.

GRAPEVINE　　The pathways through which informal information travels. Messages transmitted through the grapevine are usually transmitted orally and may be exchanged between any persons, regardless of their position in the organizational structure.

ISOLATE　　A person who neither gives information to others nor receives information from others in a group or organization.

LANDSCAPED OFFICES　　See *Open Offices*.

LIAISONS　　Persons who connect various cliques, but who are not themselves members of any clique.

MUM EFFECT　　Refers to the reluctance to transmit bad news.

OMISSION　　The deletion of all or part of a message.

OPEN OFFICES　　Large office spaces shared by many workers, designed to promote accessibility to others and encourage communication, also known as landscaped offices.

ORGANIGRAM　　A diagram showing the formal structure of an organization.

ORGANIZATIONAL STRUCTURE　　The formally prescribed pattern of interrelationships between the various units of an organization.

OVERLOAD　　The condition in which any unit of an organization becomes bogged down with too much incoming information.

QUEUING The arranging of information one unit at a time so that it may be processed in an orderly fashion.

RUMORS Informally communicated information that is not well substantiated.

SATURATION The degree of information with which a member of a communication network must deal.

SOCIOGRAM A diagram showing the informal patterns of communication in an organization; who actually communicates to whom.

NOTES

1. Roberts, K. H., O'Reilly, C. A., Bretton, G., & Porter, L. Organizational theory and organizational communication: A communication failure? *Human Relations,* 1974, *27,* 501–524.

2. Shannon, C., & Weaver, W. *The mathematical theory of communication.* Urbana, Ill.: University of Illinois, 1949.

3. Argyris, C. *Behind the front page: Organizational self-renewal in a metropolitan newspaper.* San Francisco: Jossey-Bass, 1974.

4. Blau, P. M., & Meyer, M. W. *Bureaucracy in modern society.* New York: Random House, 1971.

5. Watson, K. M. An analysis of communication patterns: A method for discriminating leader and subordinate roles. *Academy of Management Journal,* 1982, *25,* 107–120.

6. Rogers, E. M., & Agarwala-Rogers, R. *Communication in organizations.* New York: Free Press, 1976.

7. Katz, D., & Kahn, R. L. *The social psychology of organizations* (2nd ed.). New York: Wiley, 1978.

8. Walker, C. T., & Guest, R. H. *The man on the assembly line.* Cambridge, Mass.: Harvard University, 1952.

9. Athanassiades, J. C. The distortion of upward communication in hierarchical organizations. *Academy of Management Journal,* 1973, *16,* 207–226.

10. Hage, J., & Aiken, M. *Social change in complex organizations.* New York: Random House, 1970.

11. Tesser, A., & Rosen, S. The reluctance to transmit bad news. In L. Berkowitz (Ed.), *Advances in experimental social psychology* (Vol. 8). New York: Academic Press, 1975.

12. Feifel, H. Death. In N. L. Farberow (Ed.), *Taboo topics.* New York: Atherton, 1963.

13. Rosen, S., Grandison, R. J., & Stewart, J. E., II. Discriminatory buckpassing: Delegating transmission of bad news. *Organizational Behavior and Human Performance,* 1974, *12,* 249–263.

14. Shaw, M. E. Communication networks. In L. Berkowitz (Ed.), *Advances in experimental social psychology* (Vol. 1). New York: Academic Press, 1964.

15. Shaw, M. E. Communication networks fourteen years later. In L. Berkowitz (Ed.), *Group processes.* New York: Academic Press, 1978.

16. Porter, L. W., & Roberts, K. H. Communication in organizations. In M. D. Dunnette (Ed.), *Handbook of industrial and organizational psychology.* Chicago: Rand McNally, 1976.

17. Shaw, M. E. Communication networks. In L. Berkowitz (Ed.), *Advances in experimental social psychology* (Vol. 1). New York: Academic Press, 1964.

18. Locke, E. A., & Schweiger, D. M. Participation in decision-making: One more look. In B. M. Staw (Ed.), *Research in organizational behavior* (Vol. 1). Greenwich, Conn.: JAI Press, 1979.

19. Burgess, R. L. Communication networks: An experimental reevaluation. *Journal of Experimental Social Psychology,* 1968, *4,* 324–337.

20. Milgram, S. The small world problem. *Psychology Today,* May 1967, pp. 60–67.

21. Moreno, J. L., & Jennings, H. H. *The sociometry reader.* New York: Free Press, 1960.

22. Roberts, K. H., & O'Reilly, C. A. Some correlates of communication roles in organizations. *Academy of Management Journal,* 1979, *22,* 42–57.

23. Rogers, E. M., & Agarwala-Rogers, R. *Communication in organizations.* New York: Free Press, 1976.

24. Likert, R. *The human organization.* New York: McGraw-Hill, 1977.

25. Lawrence, P. H., & Lorsch, J. W. *Organization and environment: Managing differentiation and integration.* Homewood, Ill.: Richard D. Irwin, 1969.

26. Schwartz, D., & Jacobson, E. Organizational communication network analysis: The liaison communication role. *Organizational Behavior and Human Performance,* 1977, *18,* 158–174.

27. Miller, D. C. Supervisors: Evolution of an organizational role. In R. Dubin, G. C. Homans, F. C. Mann, & D. C. Miller (Eds.), *Leadership and productivity.* San Francisco: Chandler, 1965.

28. Davis, K. *Human behavior at work* (5th ed.). New York: McGraw-Hill, 1977.

29. Baskin, O. W., & Aronoff, C. E. *Interpersonal communication in organizations.* Santa Monica, Calif.: Goodyear, 1980.

30. Davis, K. *Human behavior at work* (5th ed.). New York: McGraw-Hill, 1977.

31. Davis, K. E. Management communication and the grapevine. *Harvard Business Review,* 1953, *31,* 43–49.

32. Walton, E. How efficient is the grapevine? *Personnel,* 1961, *28,* 45–49.

33. Ibid.

34. Davis, K. *Human behavior at work* (5th ed.). New York: McGraw-Hill, 1977.

35. Allport, G. W., & Postman, L. *The psychology of rumor.* New York: Holt, Rinehart, & Winston, 1947.

36. "Bendix abuzz." *Time,* October 6, 1980, p. 83.

37. Lanzetta, J. T., & Roby, T. B. Group learning and communication as a function of task and structure demands. *Journal of Abnormal and Social Psychology,* 1957, *55,* 121–131.

38. Platt, J., & Miller, J. G. Handling information overload. *Ekistics,* 1969, *28,* 295–296.

39. Allen, T. J. The world, your company: A gate for information! Who guards the gate? *Innovation,* 1969, *3,* 33–39.

40. Tybout, A. M., Calder, B. J., & Sternthal, B. Using information processing theory to design marketing strategies. *Journal of Marketing Research,* 1981, *18,* 73–79.

41. Milgram, S. The experience of living in cities. *Science,* 1970, *167,* 1461–1468.

42. Nichols, R. G. Listening is good business. *Management of Personnel Quarterly,* Winter 1962, p. 4.

43. Rogers, E. M., & Agarwala-Rogers, R. *Communication in organizations.* New York: Free Press, 1976.

44. Ibid.

45. Festinger, L., Schacter, S., & Back, K. *Social pressures in informal groups.* Stanford, Calif.: Stanford University, 1950.

46. Allen, T. J. Performance information channels in the transfer of technology. *Industrial Management,* 1966, *8,* 87–98.

47. Brookes, M. H., & Kaplan, A. The office environment: Space planning and affective behavior. *Human Factors,* 1972, *14,* 373–391.

48. Zanardelli, H. A. Life in a landscape office. In N. Polites (Ed.), *Improving office environment.* Elmhurst, Ill.: Business Press, 1969.

49. Ibid., pp. 39–40.

50. Nemeck, J., & Grandjean, E. Results of an ergonomic investigation of large-space offices. *Human Factors,* 1973, *15,* 111–124.

51. Manning, P. (Ed.). *Office design: A study of environment.* Liverpool, England: University of Liverpool, The Pilkington Research Unit, 1965.

52. Brookes, M. H., & Kaplan, A. The office environment: Space planning and affective behavior. *Human Factors,* 1972, *14,* 373–391.

11

Decision Making in Organizations

KEY CONCEPTS

Decision Making
Programmed Decision
Non-programmed Decision
Rational-Economic Model
Rational Decisions
Bounded Rationality
Administrative Model
Satisficing Decision
Heuristics
Bounded Discretion
Implicit Favorite

Confirmation Candidate
Synergy Effect
Well-Structured Task
Poorly Structured Task
Brainstorming
Groupthink
Delphi Group Technique
Nominal Group Technique (NGT)
Risky Shift
Cautious Shift
Group Polarization

□ □ □

The caucus committee table was littered with crumpled papers and coffee cups, and the ash trays were filled with cigarette butts. The half-dozen or so party bigwigs who sat around the table had hours ago removed their jackets and loosened their ties. It was now nearly 1:00AM and no decision had been reached. Who was going to be their candidate for mayor? The deadline for filing their party's candidacy papers was 10:00AM, only nine hours away, yet they were no closer to making their final decision than they were several weeks ago.

Barry Archison looked okay on paper, but nobody seemed overly enthusiastic about him. The Bar Association's report showed him to be highly qualified, but some expressed uncertainty about his popularity with the voters. Others questioned his commitment to party ideals; he struck them as being a little too independent.

Who else was there? In some districts Sidney Yost was highly regarded. Although he was less experienced in government, he was considered a bright young attorney with a future ahead of him. He'd do a good job, to be sure, but would he be a vote-getter? If the opposition zeroed in on his lack of experience, it'd be an uphill fight for votes, and they couldn't risk that.

The pros and cons of each candidate were debated long into the night. Every time the caucus appeared certain to endorse one candidate, the pendulum would begin to swing the other way. No consensus was immediately forthcoming and a decision was crucial. By not filing any candidate's name on time, the party would not be represented in the election. So, failing to make any decision on time would effectively make the decision for them. Ten o'clock was fast approaching, and the caucus members were growing impatient with each other. Who would they decide upon? The decision wasn't easily made. . . .

Such dramas are played out every day in offices and boardrooms everywhere. People are always making decisions having profound implications for themselves and for their organizations. It can safely be said that decision making is one of the most important—if not *the* most important—of all managerial activities. We are hardly alone in making this observation. Herbert Simon, a scientist who won a

FIGURE 11-1   Decision Making: A Common Managerial Work Role

This manager's job requires him to make many decisions. Experts agree that decision making is one of the central aspects of managerial jobs. (Source: Photo © Robert V. Eckert, Jr./The Picture Cube.)

Nobel prize for his work on decision making, has described decision making as *synonymous* with managing.[1] Other management experts have agreed. Long ago, for example, Chester Barnard described decision making as one of the major functions of the executive.[2] Indeed this remains a commonly accepted axiom through the present day. Empirical studies have verified that decision making represents one of a manager's most common work roles (see Figure 11-1).[3]

This chapter will examine theories, research, and practical managerial techniques concerned with **decision making** in organizations. Specifically, we will explore the ways individuals make decisions, and then consider the decisions made by groups. We will compare individual and group decisions on a variety of different tasks. Before we get to this, however, we will begin by taking a look at the general process of decision making and the types of decisions made in organizations.

THE PROCESS AND SCOPE OF ORGANIZATIONAL DECISION MAKING

To understand decision making in organizations, we first have to understand the general steps decision makers go through in reaching decisions. Although we will see in the next section that experts disagree about what specifically goes on in decision making, there is agreement about the general nature of the process. After we take you through the general process of decision making, we will examine the variety of problems that confront managerial decision makers and give them an opportunity to practice their craft.

The Process of Decision Making: A General Model

Given the centrality of decision making in organizational life, it should not be too surprising that theorists have given a great deal of attention to attempting to understand the decision-making process. Indeed, many formulations have been proposed.[4] However, probably the most useful conceptualization for our purposes is Elbing's five-step model, which is summarized in Figure 11-2.[5]

The first step is *recognizing a problem.* By perceiving and observing the situation, individuals first become sensitive to potential problems. For example, by comparing what *is* to what *should be,* we become aware of an imbalance.[6] Once we recognize the problem, we may try to understand the cause of the problem, or *diagnose the problem.* As we noted in Chapter 6, perceiving the causes of behavior is an important and complicated process. Making judgments about the causes of problems is also very difficult, especially when the problems have no immediately obvious causes.[7] It is not surprising, therefore, that individuals often make premature judgments about the causes of problems and dwell on possible solutions, even before the cause is carefully considered.[8] Nevertheless, however unsound it

FIGURE 11-2   Decision Making: The Basic Steps

The decision-making process is concerned with identifying and solving problems, as well as the generation and selection of alternative solutions. (Source: From *Behavioral Decisions in Organizations,* Second Edition, by O. Alvar Elbing. Copyright © 1978 Scott, Foresman and Company. Reprinted by permission.)

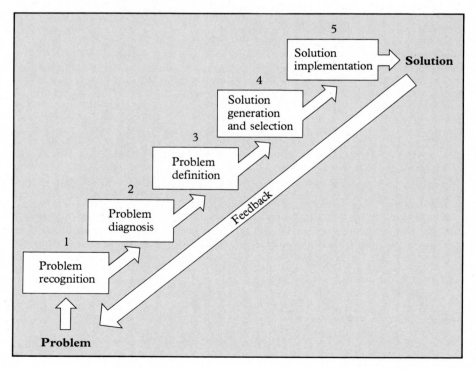

FIGURE 11-3   Selecting among Alternatives: Take Your Choice!

As this decision maker can probably attest, selecting from a vast array of alternatives is often the hardest part of decision making. (Source: Drawing by W. Miller; © 1976 The New Yorker Magazine, Inc.)

may be, some judgment about the cause of the problem leads to a *definition of the problem*. Such a statement of the issue is important, according to Elbing, because a problem is only a problem when it is recognized by someone. Therefore, he notes, "All problems are human problems."[9]

Now that a problem has been defined, the next step is the *generation and selection of solutions*. What alternative solutions are available for solving the problem? As the cartoon in Figure 11–3 illustrates, there is sometimes a bewildering array of choices to be made in making decisions. Research by Mintzberg and his associates has shown that people tend to seek out ready-made solutions to problems.[10] They tend to look for solutions that have been used in the past, either by looking through organizational records or by consulting outside sources (e.g., managerial consultants, government agencies) that might provide ready-made answers. When such alternatives prove unsuccessful, less familiar or novel solutions are generated. However, Mintzberg found that ready-made solutions to problems were only used about twenty percent of the time; eighty percent of the problems in the organizations he studied required unique, custom-made solutions. Not surprisingly, research has shown that newly generated solutions to problems tend to be better than ready-made ones that are applied automatically.[11]

Finally, after a possible solution is selected, the next step is *implementation of the solution*. That is, the solution is then put into action. Decision makers also have to monitor the effects of their acts to gauge their success. Did the decision work? Is it necessary to redefine the problem? In other words, the decision maker seeks *feedback* regarding the effectiveness of the implemented solutions.

This model makes it clear that decision making is more than just making choices (step 4); it is a broadly conceived process concerned with identifying and solving problems in organizations. Although some have conceived of decision making more narrowly, we, like others, prefer the broader approach outlined here.[12,13] We feel this model directs our attention to the context in which organizational decisions are made.

Varieties of Organizational Decisions

Managers—indeed just about all organizational personnel—have to make decisions, whether they are relatively simple and routine or extremely complex and monumental. (Please see the **"FOCUS"** box on pages 352–353 for a discussion of who, precisely, makes decisions in organizations.) It is helpful to our understanding of the decision-making process in organizations to look at the different types of decisions that are made. In doing this, we will be concerned with two major characteristics of all decisions—how structured or unstructured the situation is, and how certain the decision maker is about the outcomes of the decision.

Programmed versus non-programmed decisions. One very popular way to categorize organizational decisions is with respect to how routine or well-structured they are, as opposed to how novel or poorly structured they are. Some theorists conceptualize managerial decisions along a continuum ranging from those that are extremely well-structured to those that are extremely poorly structured, with partially structured decisions in between.[14] Herbert Simon initially conceived of the two end points—decisions he called **programmed** and **non-programmed,** analogous to what some have been calling, respectively, well-structured and poorly structured decisions.[15] A programmed decision is one that is made repeatedly, on a routine basis, according to a pre-established set of alternatives. An auto mechanic, for example, may immediately decide to perform a certain operation in response to a specified set of symptoms. Similarly, an order clerk may decide to request a certain amount of supplies as soon as the existing stock drops below a specified level. He makes a decision automatically on the basis of well-established information.

In contrast, a non-programmed decision is one that is new and unique for the decision maker, a decision made in a poorly structured situation—one in which there are no pre-existing, ready-made courses of action. For example, a biochemical researcher making a decision about the appropriate dosage of a radically new drug is making a non-programmed decision. His decision is not made automatically by recourse to pre-established alternatives.

Programmed and non-programmed decisions can be characterized in many ways (see Table 11–1). Most notably, the solutions to programmed decisions are designed and specified in advance by organizational guidelines—*policies* and *procedures.* If a certain problem arises, an employee need merely refer to the policy manual to carry out the most appropriate course of action; the decision was al-

TABLE 11-1   Characteristics of Programmed and Non-programmed Decisions: A Summary

Programmed and non-programmed decisions may be distinguished in terms of (1) the uniqueness of the problems, (2) the manner in which the solution is specified, (3) who make the decisions, and (4) the type of organization in which they are commonly made.

PROGRAMMED DECISIONS	NON-PROGRAMMED DECISIONS
Problems are routine and common	Problems are unique and novel
Solutions are specified in advance by organizational policies and procedures	Solutions are creatively determined after the problem is defined
Made by lower-level personnel	Made by higher-level personnel
Commonly made in organizations in which the market and technology are relatively stable, and many routine, highly structured problems must be solved	Commonly made in organizations in which situations are poorly structured, and the decisions made are non-routine and complex

ready made by the policy. The decision maker merely recognizes the problem and implements the predetermined solution. As a result, such decisions are highly routinized and are usually relegated to lower-level personnel.[16] Consequently, everyday problems can be handled efficiently and with a high degree of coordination and control. This safeguards against the possibility of someone making a very bad decision and ensures consistency of action across many decision makers in an organization. It should not be too surprising that programmed decisions are commonly made in organizations such as banks and insurance companies where the market and the technology are relatively stable and many routine, highly structured problems must be solved.[17]

Non-programmed decisions are unique and cannot be specified in advance. Because the situation confronting the decision maker is so novel, there are no pre-established policies or procedures to rely on. Instead, decision makers, usually senior level managers, have to rely on expert consultants and their own creativity in making non-programmed decisions. Not surprisingly, non-programmed decisions are more common than programmed decisions in such organizations as research and development firms, where situations are poorly structured and the decisions being made are non-routine and complex.[18]

No doubt, one of the determinants of making successful non-programmed decisions is the creativity of the decision maker. Interestingly, the organization can help breed an atmosphere conducive to creative decision making by encouraging the free expression of novel ideas. This is especially important in view of some evidence suggesting that individuals who are successful at solving novel problems are no more intelligent than those who are unsuccessful, but successful persons try harder—they attempt more solutions to the problem.[19] These are encouraging

FOCUS ON BEHAVIOR

Who Makes Decisions? Participation in Decision Making

Perhaps more than any other issue in the field of organizational behavior, the question of whether or not workers should be allowed a say in making managerial decisions is an ideological and moral one. People in most Western societies tend to think it is "right" and "good" to give workers a say in the decision-making process. Indeed, management systems that fail to stress participative decision making have been accused of being "dictatorial," "exploitative," and worse.[20] (Incidentally, the issue of how much leaders allow subordinates to participate in the decision-making process is so crucial that it forms the core of Vroom and Yetton's *normative theory* of leadership, one of the three modern views of leadership we will examine in Chapter 14.) The message is clear that participation in the decision-making process is often expected (by U.S. labor leaders), or demanded (by the striking Polish workers in 1981), or even legislated (in Sweden, where laws require workers to have a say in decision making). Despite the legal or moral implications of involving workers in managerial decisions, the question may be asked: What are the effects of participatory decision making on the decision makers and their organizations?

This simple question does not have such a simple answer. On the basis of a comprehensive investigation of the research in this area, Locke and Schweiger found that participatory decision making was associated with greater employee satisfaction, but with no greater productivity than in traditional organizations in which management makes decisions for the workers.[21] Apparently, workers enjoy being able to make decisions affecting them in the organization, but this does not always lead to improved performance. (As we already noted in Chapter 7, a happy worker is not necessarily a better worker.)

The results of one recent study suggest that participation in decision making may have some interesting effects on absenteeism from the job. Hammer, Landau, and Stern looked at the absenteeism rates of workers before and after they bought their small library-furniture-making company and gained a voice in the way it was run.[22] The investigators found no difference in the overall rate of absenteeism but found some very big differences when they compared *voluntary absences* (inexcused absences—absences for personal reasons) with *involuntary absences* (excused—absences such as sickness, jury duty, death in family, etc.). As you can see from Figure 11–4, voluntary absences dropped after ownership, but involuntary absences increased.

Why? The experimenters reasoned that the workers who now had a voice in decision making felt more responsible for the company and *legitimized* their absences by making them *appear* involuntary. So, for example, rather than just not showing up for work and going fishing, a worker would be prone to call in sick. Apparently, ownership in the company did little to reduce total absenteeism, but it had a great impact on the reasons given for absences.

In summary, having a say in the decision-making process doesn't tend to make workers any more productive or even to lower their rate of absenteeism. However, it does raise their satisfaction. Workers *want* to have a say in decision making, regardless of the results. Indeed, programs such as *flexitime* (an approach in which workers set their own working hours within certain limits) are becoming increasingly popular since they give employees a great deal of power to make decisions affecting them and the organization.[23] It should not be surprising that participatory decision-making practices are becoming increasingly widespread in the U.S. and England and are already quite prevalent in France, Israel, Sweden, and Yugoslavia.[24] □

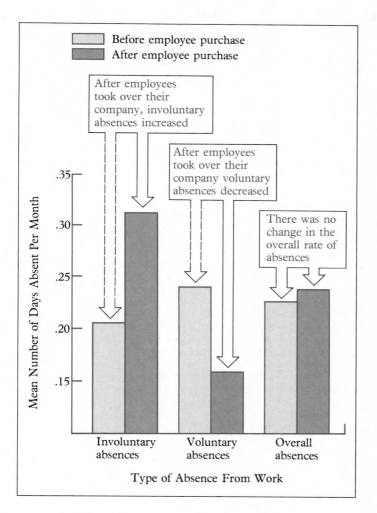

Before employee purchase
After employee purchase

After employees took over their company, involuntary absences increased

After employees took over their company voluntary absences decreased

There was no change in the overall rate of absences

Mean Number of Days Absent Per Month

.35

.30

.25

.20

.15

Involuntary absences   Voluntary absences   Overall absences

Type of Absence From Work

FIGURE 11–4 Employee Ownership: No Change in Absenteeism, but a Change in Excuses

A recent study compared the absenteeism rates of employees before and after they were given a voice in their company's decision-making policies by becoming owners of the company. While the average rate of absenteeism remained unchanged, the reasons given for the absenteeism changed drastically. There was a marked drop in voluntary (inexcused) absences. However, involuntary absences (such as illness or other good reasons) greatly increased. It appears that workers' obligations to the company's well-being led them to legitimize their absences by characterizing them as involuntary. (Source: Based on data from Hammer, Landau, & Stern, *Journal of Applied Psychology*, 1981, *66*, 561–573.)

findings since organizations can do little to improve the intelligence of their employees but may be able to create an atmosphere encouraging the expenditure of effort—get employees to try hard, even if they fail.

Decisions under certainty, uncertainty, and risk. Decisions can also be characterized with respect to the degree of certainty with which specific outcomes are likely to occur. An industrial foreman may know, for example, that only one machine in the plant operates fast enough to meet an impending production deadline. The decision to use that particular machine is made under conditions of certainty. The foreman knows its capabilities and can be certain about the outcome of the decision to put it into use.

By way of contrast, there is a high degree of uncertainty behind the U.S. government's decision to sell military weapons and equipment to certain foreign governments. Although we may hope for certain outcomes (and not others), we remain uncertain about exactly how and against whom the weapons will be used. The businessman who invests in a totally unknown company is making a decision under conditions of uncertainty. The outcomes of the decision are unknown in advance. Generally speaking, decision making under conditions of uncertainty is left to higher-level managers.[25] Moreover, such decisions are most likely to occur in organizations that have to change very frequently.[26] One thing is sure—decision making under uncertainty is very undesirable! Decision makers need information about the future to make high quality decisions. However, in many high technology organizations decision makers sometimes have to take a "stab in the dark" and make their choices under uncertainty.

Between the states of certainty and uncertainty lies the state of *risk*, the condition under which most organizational decisions occur. After all, decision makers are not likely to be completely certain about future conditions (although it's nice to imagine how rich we'd get from the stock market if we could be certain of future states). Nor are decision makers likely to make any decisions at all (if they don't have to) under *complete* uncertainty—even a "hunch" reduces our uncertainty.

Levels of risk are differentiated in terms of the probability of attaining certain outcomes. The probability of throwing a certain number in a dice game, for example, is known in advance to the gambler, who realizes how risky his or her bet is and can decide on the extent of the wager. These risks are based on *objective probabilities* of the likelihood of certain outcomes occurring. However, decision makers sometimes assign to certain outcomes *subjective probabilities*—personal beliefs or hunches about what will happen.[27] The T.V. weather forecaster who gives the probability for precipitation is reporting an objective probability of the occurrence of rain or snow based on objective statistics; when Uncle Otto says it is going to rain because he "feels it in his bones," he is offering a subjective probability. In either case these probabilities can help the decision maker decide whether or not to take an umbrella that day. (The riskiness of decisions made by individuals as compared to groups is an important topic that will be discussed later in this chapter.)

THE IMPERFECT ART (AND SCIENCE) OF INDIVIDUAL DECISION MAKING

How good are the decisions people make? Obviously the answer depends on how you judge the "best" possible decisions. In this section we will look at two different models of individual decision making. These approaches to decision making differ in their assumptions about how *rational* decision makers are. It is generally accepted that a rational decision is one that *maximizes the achievement of an individual's, group's, or organization's goals.*[28] As we will see, the two models presented here make quite different assumptions about the rationality of the individual decision maker.

The Rational-Economic Model: The "Ideal" Decision Maker

The model of the **rational-economic decision maker** is reminiscent of Adam Smith's eighteenth-century classical economic thought, assuming that decisions are perfect and completely **rational** in every way. The economically rational decision maker is assumed to make decisions that maximize his or her advantage (e.g., profits), and to do so by systematically searching and evaluating all possible alternatives.[29]

According to the rational-economic model, the process of decision making is assumed to follow these steps:

1. Symptoms of the problem are discovered.
2. The problem is identified and the goal to be reached is defined.
3. Criteria (objectives) are developed, against which possible solutions may be evaluated.
4. *All* possible courses of action are recognized.
5. The consequences of each course of action are considered.
6. Each course of action is then evaluated relative to the criteria.
7. Finally, the course of action that maximizes the criteria is selected and implemented.

This is certainly a rather idealistic, perhaps even naive, model of decision making. Indeed decision makers rarely, if ever, have access to perfect information. Knowing all possible alternatives and their consequences is not likely. Furthermore, being able to manipulate all this information mentally, as the model assumes, is also uncharacteristic of how people actually make decisions.

Thus, rather than saying that the rational-economic model is *descriptive* of how people actually behave, it is characterized by a *prescriptive,* or a *normative model,* describing how decision makers "ought to" behave. Generally, most economists claim that the main virtue of the rational-economic model is in predicting economic market conditions and prices rather than actual human behavior.[30] However, as recent experiences suggest, even economic forecasting may be considered highly imperfect.

The Administrative Model: The "Real" Decision Maker

On the basis of our discussion of the rational-economic model, it is probably no surprise that this view has not been widely accepted. One of its major critics has been Herbert Simon. Writing over a quarter of a century ago, Simon made the following observation (1957, p. 198):

> The capacity of the human mind for formulating and solving complex problems is very small compared with the size of the problems whose solution is required for objectively rational behavior in the real world—or even for a reasonable approximation to such objective rationality.[31]

More simply put, Simon's criticism is that human limitations make it impossible for people to make completely rational decisions, ones that optimize desired goals. Other decision scientists have also noted that practical limitations preclude completely rational, optimizing decisions in business organizations. For example, Anthony Downs has stated that human decision makers have a limited capability to process information, and they operate in organizational contexts that severely limit the time they can spend on making any one decision.[32]

As a result of such mental and organizational limitations, decision makers have to operate within conditions Simon has called **bounded rationality.** That is, decision makers are limited to settling for less than the ideal or optimal decision. Simon's **administrative model,** in contrast to the rational-economic model, assumes that decision makers are limited in the number of solutions they recognize, and that they are not perfectly aware of the consequences of each alternative solution they consider. (For a summary of differences between the two models, please see Figure 11–5.) The administrative model recognizes that people have only a limited, simplified view of the problems confronting them.

Because of these limitations, or bounds of rationality, decision makers strive to make decisions that are good enough rather than ideal. Such decisions are referred to as **satisficing decisions.** In making a satisficing decision, the decision maker examines each alternative as it becomes available and then selects the first one that satisfies all his or her requirements. Of course, it is much easier to *satisfice* than to *optimize.* As March and Simon have noted, rarely are decision makers concerned with making optimal decisions; satisficing is what generally occurs.[33] They note that *optimizing is like searching a haystack for the sharpest needle,* but *satisficing is like searching a haystack for a needle just sharp enough to sew with.* It should be clear from this analogy that it is often too inefficient or too costly to make optimal decisions in organizations. In selecting a new employee, for example, we might just hire the first applicant who meets all our minimal requirements since it would take a lot of valuable time to keep looking for the "ideal" employee.

In addition to making satisficing decisions, the administrative model also assumes that decision makers attempt to simplify the vast array of complex information confronting them by using simplifying decision rules called **heuristics.** A heuristic is a simple rule of thumb applied to making satisficing decisions. For example, the decision to punt on fourth down in football is a heuristic that helps the

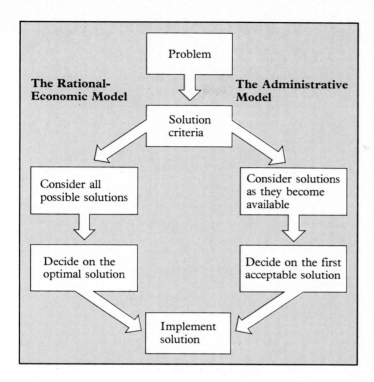

FIGURE 11-5 The Rational-Economic Model versus the Administrative Model: A Comparison

As the diagram shows, the rational-economic model requires the consideration of all possible solutions in order to decide on the optimal one, whereas the administrative model asserts that decision makers accept the first available alternative that meets their criteria.

team obtain victory because it helps bring about the desired outcome (moving the ball away from your goal so the other team cannot score as easily). It is simply a guideline to follow. Similar rules about when to "hit" in the game of blackjack, or when to buy and sell stock in the market, can also be considered heuristics. The administrative model assumes that decision makers use heuristics to reduce the complexity of large problems and thus make them more manageable.

Another limitation to making optimal decisions is imposed by moral and ethical restraints—what has been referred to as **bounded discretion.**[34] According to this idea, decision makers often limit their actions to those falling within the bounds of accepted moral and ethical standards. For example, some *possible* alternative solutions for a businessperson faced with bankruptcy include robbing a bank, borrowing from loan sharks, and defrauding the insurance company (see Figure 11-6). However, these possibilities may not generally be enacted or even considered by individuals operating within the bounds imposed by accepted societal standards. While this may be obvious, it suggests another limitation on the decisions that might actually be made.

Theorists agree that Simon's administrative model provides a useful approximation to how decision makers actually operate. Thus, in contrast to the rational-economic model, the administrative model can be called a descriptive model of

FIGURE 11–6   Bounded Discretion: Moral Limits to "Rational" Decisions

Why doesn't this woman steal the money in order to solve her personal financial problems? The concept of *bounded discretion* recognizes that decision makers often limit their consideration of alternatives to those falling within accepted moral and ethical standards. (Source: Photo © Margaret Thompson/The Picture Cube.)

decision making. (In many cases, individuals seem to adopt a general decision-making strategy somewhat different from both approaches described above. Please see the **"CASE IN POINT"** box on pages 360–361 for an example of this compromise strategy.)

GROUP VERSUS INDIVIDUAL DECISIONS: WHEN ARE TWO (OR MORE) HEADS BETTER THAN ONE?

If you are planning a career in management, you will doubtlessly spend thousands of hours in decision-making groups in the years ahead. Such groups, known by various names including *committees, study teams, task forces, review panels,* and others, are a well-established fact of organizational life.

As you might imagine, the vast scope and complexity of many organizational decisions require the use of decision-making groups whose members can offer varied perspectives on the problem at hand. One managerial observer has gone so far as to observe that "the multiple escalation of our potential through groups is the foundation of American industrial greatness."[36]

It is not too difficult to think of the possible advantages inherent in group decisions. Indeed, experts have identified several advantages decision-making groups are likely to have over individual decision makers.[37] One obvious advantage is that groups possess several individuals who may contribute many good ideas; that is, there may be a *pooling of resources*. Similarly, group members may stimulate and encourage each other through their mutual interaction, what is known as a **synergy effect.** It should also be apparent that group members may be able to divide the problem, leaving less work for any one person—"sharing the load," so to speak. They may also be able to capitalize on individual talents, allowing individuals to work on problems at which they are most adept—*specialization of labor*. (For a summary of these advantages, see Table 11–2.)

In contrast, it is also generally accepted that groups don't always make ideal decisions. This is suggested by the old aphorism, "a camel is a horse designed by a committee." The disadvantages of using decision-making groups are probably also familiar to you. One obvious disadvantage is that groups often waste more time than individuals. Groups may use a lot of time "clowning around" and getting organized. Similarly, they tend to invest a great deal of effort in what has been termed *the release of affect*—stating strongly held views and associated feelings. Recent evidence suggests that the energy spent on such activities is a drain on group resources, and can interfere with effective decisions.[38] Another potential problem with groups is that some members may be threatened or intimidated by others, and so be discouraged from freely expressing their ideas. And finally, a great amount of disagreement over reaching a decision can cause *conflict* and ill will between group members. These are just a few possible consequences of using groups to make decisions (refer to Table 11–2).

As the above observations suggest, advantages as well as disadvantages are associated with using groups to make decisions. These considerations make it difficult to offer any firm generalizations about whether "two heads are better than

TABLE 11–2   Group Decision Making: A Summary of Advantages and Disadvantages

Are "two heads better than one?" Or, do "too many cooks spoil the broth?" As this table summarizes, there are both advantages and disadvantages to group decision making.

ADVANTAGES OF GROUP DECISION MAKING	DISADVANTAGES OF GROUP DECISION MAKING
Possible pooling of resources	Likely to waste time and energy
Intellectual stimulation of one another—*synergy effect*	Presence of some group members may intimidate others
Specialization of labor	Disagreement may breed group conflict and ill will

Deciding on Implicit Favorites: Searching for a Confirmation Candidate

The administrative model of decision making faults the rational-economic model by noting that decision makers do not evaluate all possible alternatives, but stop the process after arriving at the first acceptable alternative. However, as the following case suggests, sometimes decision makers actually do something between these two extremes.

Gene was soon to graduate from State University with an M.B.A. in accounting. This was going to be his big chance to leave the boonies and head out to San Francisco, the city by the bay. Gene had always dreamed of living there and his first job, he hoped, was going to be his ticket.

It was only March, but the nearness of June graduation was heralded by the presence of the company recruiters who made their annual migration to campus in search of new talent. Gene eagerly filled out the recruitment application form, and with his excellent qualifications he hoped the job of his dreams would come his way. One of the first firms Gene signed up to see was Baxter, Marsh, and Hidalgo, a medium-size public accounting firm in San Francisco. The salary was right and the people seemed pleasant, a combination that excited Gene very much. Apparently the interest was mutual; soon Gene was offered a position.

Does the story end there? Not quite. It was only March and Gene felt he shouldn't jump at the first job that came along, even though he really wanted it. So, to do "the sensible thing," he signed up for more interviews. Shortly thereafter, Dixon, Timpkin, and Dinglethorpe, a local firm, made Gene an attractive offer. In fact, the salary was excellent, and there was every indication that the job promised a much brighter future than the one in San Francisco.

What would he do? Actually, for Gene there was not much of a dilemma. After thinking about it, he believed there was too much low-level work at Dixon, Timpkin, and Dinglethorpe, not enough exciting clients to challenge him. The starting salary wasn't really all *that* much better than Baxter, Marsh, and Hidalgo offered. And besides, he reasoned, who wants to live here in the middle of a corn-

---

one" or "too many cooks spoil the broth." Instead scientists have found it more instructive to ask: On what kinds of tasks will groups function more effectively than lone individuals as problem solvers or decision makers?

This question will guide our discussion in this section of the chapter. Earlier, in considering varieties of decisions, we distinguished between programmed and non-programmed decisions, and we will make a parallel distinction here. Specifically, we will compare group and individual decisions on both well-structured and poorly structured tasks—those in which programmed and non-programmed decisions are made, respectively. We will also identify tasks involving the taking of risks, and compare group and individual decisions on them.

field! The day after graduation Gene was on his way to his new office overlooking the Golden Gate bridge.

Think about Gene's decision-making behavior. Did he consider *all* alternatives—the rational-economic thing to do? Of course not; if he did, he'd still be interviewing! Did he succumb to bounded rationality and make a satisficing decision? Not really; he kept on looking after the first suitable alternative came along. Is Gene's behavior unusual? We think not. In fact, his case comes very close to describing the decision-making process of many people in similar situations.

This is evidenced by a study by Soelberg, who looked at the way students graduating with advanced degrees from M.I.T.'s Sloan School of Management went about making decisions about their first jobs.[35] Soelberg found that early in the recruiting process applicants identified the job they most wanted—their **implicit favorite.** However, like Gene, almost three-fourths of the applicants in the study kept looking for a job even after they had an offer from their implicit favorite. They were apparently searching for a **confirmation candidate,** a job they could compare to the one they really wanted in order to convince themselves that they made the right decision. They, too, psychologically distorted the information they had about the confirmation candidate, using it only to make unfavorable comparisons with the job they really wanted. Indeed usually only two factors, starting salary and job location, are used to develop implicit favorites; other information is largely ignored! Like Gene, eighty-seven percent of the M.I.T. students studied eventually selected their implicit favorites.

Apparently decision makers don't always stop considering additional alternatives after a satisficing alternative comes along, nor do they consider all possible alternatives. Instead, they sometimes keep searching for alternatives just long enough to convince themselves that whatever decision they implicitly favor is the right one! □

Well-Structured Tasks: When Groups Have the Advantage

Imagine a problem with several discrete steps and a solution that can be readily verified—e.g., an elementary arithmetic problem or an anagram puzzle. These would be considered well-structured tasks since certain steps are necessary to solve them; they are divisible into separate parts, and there is a definite right or wrong answer. Who would do better on such tasks—groups or individuals? One study conducted over fifty years ago found that groups were five to six times more likely to solve well-structured problems than were individuals.[39] Generally speaking, it has been established that *groups make better, more accurate decisions, but take more time in reaching them.*[40]

More recent research has confirmed this generalization. For example, in one study, Webber compared the performance of individuals and groups of five working on well-structured problems.[41] Specifically, he looked at the number of problems solved correctly and the length of time it took to solve them. As you can see from the results summarized in Figure 11-7, groups made more accurate decisions than individuals but were considerably slower in reaching these decisions.

Several important factors appear to account for these consistently observed findings.[42,43] Most obviously, groups have the advantage of being able to pool their resources and combine their knowledge. As a result they are likely to generate a wider variety of approaches to problems than any single individual, and can be expected to catch their own errors. It is this pooling of ideas that seems to provide the greatest advantage to groups over individuals in the performance of well-structured tasks.

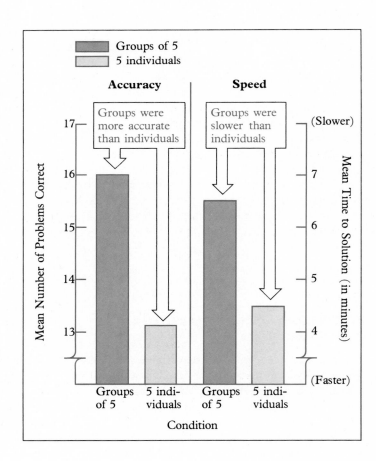

FIGURE 11-7   Group versus Individual Performance: An Experimental Comparison

Experimental evidence shows that groups are more accurate, but also slower than individuals when performing well-structured tasks. (Source: Based on data from Webber, *Academy of Management Journal*, 1974, *17*, 570–574.)

Group composition effects: Pooling resources or pooling ignorance?

If it is true that the *pooling of resources* gives groups an advantage over individuals, this should only happen when the group members have skills that they can contribute to the task. In short, for there to be a beneficial effect of pooling, there has to be something to pool. (In other words, two heads may be better than one, but only if there is something in one of those heads!)

This has been shown in a study by Laughlin and Johnson in which subjects performed a series of **well-structured** tasks, such as identifying synonyms and solving analogies.[44] About a week before subjects performed these tasks alone or in pairs, they were individually pretested and classified as low, moderate, or high with respect to their ability on these tasks. Then, subjects performed the tasks either alone or in pairs arranged in accordance with their ability level (i.e., in high-high, high-medium, high-low, medium-medium, medium-low, and low-low pairs).

The results for the most interesting conditions are summarized in Figure 11–8. As you can see, it was found that groups did better than individuals only when both individuals were able to contribute their skills to the task. Two highly able

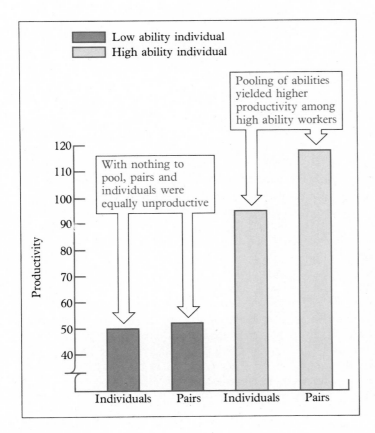

FIGURE 11–8 Pooling of Abilities: It Works Only When There Is Something to Pool

Pairs of individuals with low ability working together performed no better than a low ability individual working alone. However, pairs of high ability individuals working together performed better than a high ability individual working alone. (Source: Based on data from Laughlin & Johnson, *Journal of Experimental Social Psychology,* 1966, *2,* 407–414.)

individuals working together outperformed one individual of high ability, but pairs of low ability workers performed just as poorly as one individual with low ability. Apparently the "pooling of ignorance" will not facilitate group performance.

Although the skills the subjects contributed in this experiment were probably quite similar, the problems confronting employees of most organizations are usually highly complex and require diverse talents. Under these circumstances a group would appear to have an advantage if the skills pooled together are *complementary*. That is, groups of individuals each expert in a certain aspect of an organizational problem (e.g., taxes, labor relations, law, etc.) might benefit from pooling their diverse talents, offering many varied perspectives and areas of expertise, leading to a high-quality decision. For this reason, it is not surprising that researchers have found that groups composed of members with heterogeneous characteristics generally perform better than groups with more similar members.[45]

To summarize, in performing well-structured tasks, groups tend to perform better but more slowly than individuals. This appears to depend on the extent to which group members can contribute varied information or diverse perspectives on the task at hand.

Poorly Structured Tasks: The Advantage of Working Alone

In contrast to well-structured tasks that can be divided into several discrete parts and have a definite solution, other decision-making situations are more **poorly structured.** Any problem involving creative thinking provides a good example. Suppose an organization is faced with deciding what to do about the prospect of a declining market for its products in the coming years. There are many possible courses of action, and you would probably expect that a group would do a better job of handling such a problem than any one individual. However, this is generally *not* the case. Most of the research has shown that *on poorly structured, creative tasks, individuals show superior performance to groups.*[46] This generalization has particularly important—and potentially devastating—implications for organizations since some administrators spend as much as eighty percent of their time in committee meetings.[47]

A commonly employed approach to solving creative problems in organizations is **brainstorming.**[48] Brainstorming, a technique developed by an advertising agency executive, is designed to enhance creativity by encouraging the free discussion of ideas. Members of a brainstorming group are admonished against being critical and are encouraged to generate as many ideas as possible. (For a more complete listing of the basic rules of brainstorming, please see Table 11–3.)

As we have suggested, research has shown that group brainstorming is often ineffective. This is demonstrated quite dramatically in an important experiment conducted at the 3M Company by Dunnette, Campbell, and Jaastad.[49] The participants in the study were personnel from the research staff and the advertising

TABLE 11-3   The Four Essential Rules of Brainstorming

Brainstorming groups follow these rules to generate solutions to problems. (Source: Adapted from Osborn, *Applied Imagination*. New York: Scribner's, 1957.)

1. *No criticism!* Adverse judgments about your own or others' ideas are to be withheld.
2. *"Freewheeling" is invited.* No idea is too wild; the more far out the idea, the better.
3. *Quantity is desired.* Generate as many ideas as possible—one might just work!
4. *"Piggybacking" is encouraged.* Participants should build upon the ideas and suggestions of others and combine them with their own.

staff. They were required to generate solutions to two creative problems—how to encourage European tourism in the U.S., and how to ensure educational effectiveness in the face of a potential shortage of teachers. The workers generated solutions to both problems working either alone or in brainstorming groups. The number of solutions generated for the problems were counted, and the quality of these solutions were judged. The results are shown in Figure 11-9. As you can see, the groups averaged fewer solutions, and poorer ones as well!

It is interesting to consider the reasons why groups fare so poorly on creative tasks. The explanations all rest on the intriguing dynamics of group interaction. Various group processes seem to reduce the group's effectiveness. Let's now consider two of the major adverse influences.

The dominance of high-status group members.   The term *status* is used to describe the relative esteem given an individual on the basis of the position that person holds. It should come as no surprise that high-status persons in organizations, such as presidents, chief executive officers, and board chairpersons, are carefully listened to, and what they have to say is given high credence. As a result, high-status persons tend to dominate group situations, and their ideas are frequently accepted without question.[50] The result can easily be a group of "yes men/women" behind the single dominant force.

With an understanding of this phenomenon, former General Motors head Alfred P. Sloan, Jr. failed to attend the early phases of his groups' meetings.[51] He feared that his presence would discourage open and honest discussions of critical problems among other executives, who would instead try to please him. Sloan can be complimented on his insight into group dynamics. Indeed, there is every reason to believe that his high status would have had an undue impact on the group by inadvertently encouraging uniformity.[52]

Groupthink: Too much cohesiveness can be a dangerous thing.   Just as a group's esteem for a leader can lead its members to desire uniformity and a strong consensus behind that person, so too a group's own esteem for itself—its team spirit or *cohesiveness*—can create strong pressures toward uniformity within the group. The problem with this is that these desires toward oneness of spirit and

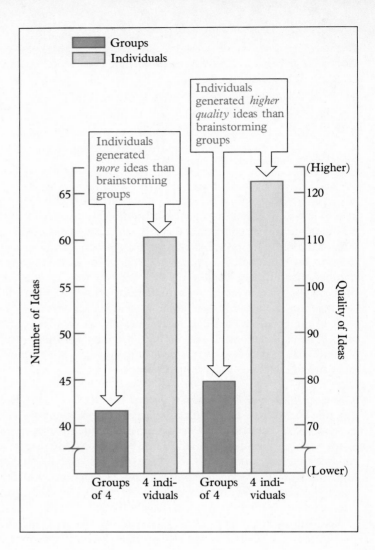

FIGURE 11-9 Brainstorming Groups: Not Always Effective

Research comparing individuals and brainstorming groups on creative problems revealed that individuals produced more ideas and better ideas than groups. (Source: Based on data from Dunnette, Campbell, & Jaastad, *Journal of Applied Psychology,* 1963, *47,* 30–37.)

action, like-mindedness, may well exceed members' concerns with making the best possible decision—a problem known as **groupthink.**[53] It is not that cohesive groups are bad, but that some groups may be so cohesive that they isolate themselves from outside correcting influences, and this can be detrimental.

More specifically, Janis defines groupthink as "a deterioration of mental efficiency, reality testing, and moral judgment that results from in-group pressures."[54] His observation was based on analyses of the ineffective decision-making processes involved in high-level U.S. government decisions that led to such fiascos as the Bay of Pigs invasion and the Japanese attack on Pearl Harbor.

In these cases and others, Janis believes that the President's advisors actually *prevented* the enactment of effective decisions. If a group is highly cohesive, its members usually have a great deal of faith in the group decisions, which they feel are superior to individual decisions. As a result, individuals tend to suspend their own critical thinking in favor of expressing ideas that conform to the group consensus. Members conform to the group out of the belief that it is invulnerable to bad decisions. Group members become so fiercely loyal to each other that they insulate themselves from qualified outsiders, thereby creating a strong sense of unanimity. The result is that the group's decisions may be entirely unrealistic, uninformed, irrational, or even immoral. President Nixon's advisors during the Watergate era provide a good example of this. As a practical guide to recognizing the warning signals of groupthink, we have summarized the symptoms in Table 11-4.

We wouldn't want to close this section on an entirely pessimistic note. Indeed there is hope for combating groupthink! Two successful techniques for avoiding groupthink are discussed in the **"PERSPECTIVE"** box on pages 368-369.

TABLE 11-4   The Eight Warning Signals of Groupthink

Groupthink is a phenomenon sometimes occurring in very highly cohesive groups in which group members are more concerned with maintaining group spirit than in making the most realistic decisions. The major symptoms of groupthink are listed and described here. (Source: Adapted from Janis, 1972.)

SYMPTOM	DESCRIPTION
1. Illusion of *invulnerability*	Ignoring obvious danger signals, being overly optimistic, and taking extreme risks
2. Collective *rationalization*	Discrediting or ignoring warnings that run contrary to group thinking
3. Unquestioned *morality*	Believing the group's position is ethical and moral while all others are inherently evil
4. Excessive negative *stereotyping*	Viewing the opposing side as too negative to warrant serious consideration
5. Strong conformity *pressure*	Discouraging the expression of dissenting opinions under the threat of expulsion for disloyalty
6. *Self-censorship* of dissenting ideas	Withholding dissenting ideas and counterarguments; keeping these to oneself
7. Illusion of *unanimity*	Sharing the false belief that everyone agrees with the group's judgments
8. Self-appointed *mindguards*	Protecting the group from the influx of adverse information that might threaten group complacency

FROM THE MANAGER'S PERSPECTIVE

Avoiding Groupthink with the Delphi and Nominal Group Techniques

In this chapter we have identified both advantages and disadvantages of group decisions. It would be ideal to combine the wide variety of ideas generated by groups with the speed and efficiency of individual decisions, while avoiding the problems of groupthink. Several techniques designed to bring about the "best of both worlds" have been widely employed in organizations and will be identified here.

One such approach, known as the **Delphi technique,** has been developed by the Rand Corporation.[55] This approach involves soliciting by mail the independent opinions of several experts on a problem, compiling these ideas and sharing them with other experts, and allowing the experts to comment on each other's ideas until a general consensus is reached. These steps are more specifically outlined in Figure 11–10.

The advantage of the Delphi technique is that it allows the organization to draw on the judgments of experts without the logistical difficulties of bringing them all together for a face-to-face meeting. However, as you might expect, the process may be *very* time consuming. It takes a long time for everyone to respond, for all the ideas to be transcribed and disseminated, and for a general consensus to be reached. Some experts have estimated that the *minimum* time it would take to use the Delphi technique is 44½ days.[56] One careful study found that the Delphi technique took five months to complete![57] Certainly this approach would not be appropriate for making decisions about an impending crisis. However, the Delphi technique has been successfully employed in a variety of situations, such as obtaining predictions of the impact of new land-use policies, technological forecasting, and identifying problems to be discussed at conferences.[58]

Another approach, known as the **nominal group technique (NGT),** is a cross between face-to-face brainstorming groups and the Delphi technique.[59] The NGT brings together small numbers of people (usually about seven to ten) who interact according to a controlled procedure. After a problem is identified, members write down their own ideas and individually present them to the group without any discussion. Each idea suggested is then listed on a flip chart and discussed, clarified, and evaluated. The participants then privately rank each of the ideas, and the idea with the highest ranking is taken as the group's decision. (See Figure 11–11 for a step-by-step presentation of the NGT procedure.) This approach is called the *nominal* group technique, because the individuals form a group *in name only* and are not allowed to interact directly with respect to each potential solution.

The NGT has several advantages and disadvantages.[60] On the practical side, an NGT session may take only two hours or so to complete. With respect to the process, the technique allows the evaluation of many ideas without pressures to conform to those of a high-status person. The major disadvantages are that using the technique requires the use of a trained group facilitator—a leader who runs the session—and that the technique allows for dealing with only one problem at a time.

The relative effectiveness of nominal groups and Delphi groups over conventional face-to-face interacting groups has been demonstrated in an important study by Van de Ven and Delbecq.[61] Twenty groups of seven members using the NGT were compared to an equal number of seven-member Delphi and interacting groups in their performance on a poorly structured problem—defining the job description of a university dormitory counselor. Nominal groups came out ahead with respect to the quality of ideas and perceived satisfaction. Specifically, nominal groups were slightly more productive than Delphi groups, but both were much more productive than interacting

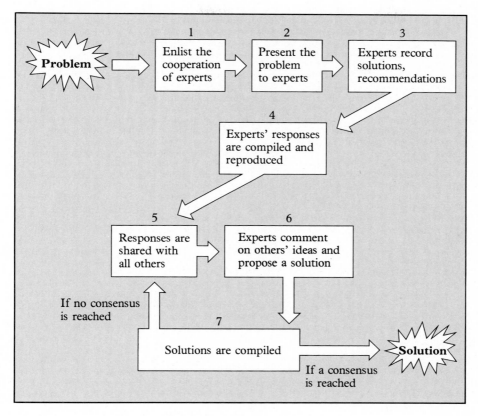

FIGURE 11-10   Steps of the Delphi Technique

The *Delphi technique,* outlined here, allows decisions to be made by several experts without the disadvantages of face-to-face discussion groups.

groups. Nominal groups were also more satisfied with their group than either Delphi or interacting groups. Consistent with this study, other investigations have also revealed the superiority of nominal groups with respect to decision quality.[62]

Thus, nominal groups and Delphi groups do indeed appear to offer techniques for gaining the advantages of groups while minimizing their disadvantages.   □

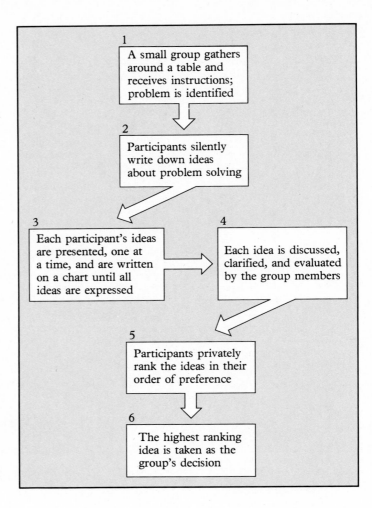

1
A small group gathers around a table and receives instructions; problem is identified

2
Participants silently write down ideas about problem solving

3
Each participant's ideas are presented, one at a time, and are written on a chart until all ideas are expressed

4
Each idea is discussed, clarified, and evaluated by the group members

5
Participants privately rank the ideas in their order of preference

6
The highest ranking idea is taken as the group's decision

FIGURE 11–11   Steps in the Nominal Group Technique

The nominal group technique allows for the exchange of ideas between individuals, while eliminating some of the problems inherent in face-to-face interacting groups.

Making Risky or Cautious Decisions: Groups Are More Extreme

Suppose a decision had to be made that involved a certain amount of risk. Say it concerned choosing between two investments, one that was unlikely to succeed but would pay off big if it did, and another that would be more of a sure thing but wouldn't yield as much profit. Suppose further that this decision was being made by a committee or by an individual acting alone. Who do you imagine would choose the riskier alternative, the group or the individual? Most people would probably say the individual, thinking that the group would have to make a more conservative, middle-of-the-road decision in order to accommodate the varied perspectives of the group members. However, this is generally *not* so! Systematic research over the last two decades actually suggests that *groups tend to make more extreme decisions than individuals.*[63]

This phenomenon was first noted in 1961 when James Stoner, a graduate student in management at M.I.T., reported such an effect in his Master's thesis.[64] Stoner composed a series of fictitious cases depicting a person faced with the dilemma of having to decide between a risky but attractive alternative, and a more conservative but less attractive one. In one of these, for example, subjects read of a character who was torn between accepting a higher-paying but less secure position with a new company and a lower-paying but more secure position with his present employer (see Table 11–5). The subjects' task was to imagine they were advising the decision maker and to report the *lowest* probability of success of the

TABLE 11–5   How Risky Are You? Decide for Yourself

On questionnaire items such as this, it has been found that groups tend to make riskier decisions than individuals, a phenomenon known as the *risky shift*. (Source: Adapted from Kogan & Wallach, *Risk Taking*. New York: Holt, Rinehart, & Winston, 1964.)

Mr. A, an electrical engineer, who is married and has one child, has been working for a large electronics corporation since graduating from college five years ago. He is assured of a lifetime job with a modest, though adequate, salary, and liberal pension benefits upon retirement. On the other hand, it is very unlikely that his salary will increase much before he retires. While attending a convention, Mr. A is offered a job with a small, newly founded company which has a highly uncertain future. The new job would pay more to start and would offer the possibility of a share in the ownership if the company survived the competition of the larger firms.

Imagine that you are advising Mr. A. Listed below are several probabilities or odds of the new company's proving financially sound.

Please check the lowest probability that you would consider acceptable to make it worthwhile for Mr. A to take the new job.

____ *The chances are 1 in 10 that the company will prove financially sound.*
____ *The chances are 3 in 10 that the company will prove financially sound.*
____ *The chances are 5 in 10 that the company will prove financially sound.*
____ *The chances are 7 in 10 that the company will prove financially sound.*
____ *The chances are 9 in 10 that the company will prove financially sound.*
____ *Place a check here if you think Mr. A should* not *take the new job no matter what the probabilities.*

riskier alternative (the new job) they would accept before advising the person to take that course of action. Someone advocating only a one-in-ten chance would be viewed as making a risky decision, while someone recommending a nine-in-ten chance of success would be making a rather cautious, or conservative choice.

Subjects first responded to a series of these questionnaire items alone; they were then formed into groups and asked to arrive at a unanimous decision. Repeatedly, it was found that groups recommended riskier decisions than individuals, a phenomenon that became known as the **risky shift.** That is, there was a shift toward riskiness among groups relative to the same decisions made alone by the individual group members.

We should note, however, that a shift toward riskiness has *not always* been observed. There appear to be some instances in which groups actually make more cautious, or conservative, decisions than individuals. For example, researchers found that groups made more cautious decisions than individuals in a case involving whether or not a couple contemplating marriage should go through with their plans despite some sharp disagreements they've been having.[65] Groups required a higher odds of success before recommending marriage than did individuals. Similarly, in another study, Stoner found that groups were more cautious than individuals in a decision involving protecting the endangered life of an expectant mother.[66] In both cases, groups made *more cautious* decisions than individuals (what may be called a **cautious shift**)—a finding that ostensibly contradicts the previously noted risky shift.

In attempting to reconcile these apparently inconsistent findings, scientists have come up with a very useful general explanation. Namely, when people interact with others in a group, they attempt to present themselves favorably by endorsing the *predominant cultural value.* That is, people want to appear certain to embrace the prevailing accepted standards in front of others. As a result, each individual is encouraged to present himself or herself to the group as endorsing the culturally accepted standard at least as much as the others in the group. Thus, group decisions tend to be more extreme in the direction of the prevailing social standard than are the decisions made by individuals.

Consider the case in which the man was deciding about the change of jobs (Table 11-5). It has long been accepted (and valued) in American society that to succeed in business, one has to take risks. Indeed, some of the greatest American industrial heroes, such as Ford, Carnegie, and Rockefeller, took risks and succeeded. Not surprisingly, when groups met to decide about the case in Table 11-5, each person in the group embraced this value by making a riskier decision. By contrast, in the previously mentioned cases of the uncertain marriage and saving the woman's life, the prevailing social standard was the exercise of caution instead of riskiness—playing it safe. Accordingly, group members attempted to appear at least as cautious as others, resulting in an extremely cautious group decision. In both cases, groups more strongly endorsed positions in the direction of prevailing societal standards.

In view of the tendency for both risky and cautious shifts to be observed in group decision making, scientists no longer believe that any specific bias toward risk or caution is inherent in group decisions. Instead, it is believed that these shifts are part of a more general phenomenon called **group polarization,** the tendency for group members to shift their views to ones that are more extreme, in the same direction, as the ones they originally favored.[67] Consider, for example, that panels of liberal judges tended to hand down over twice as many liberal decisions as individual liberal judges.[68] Similarly, in studies simulating the decision making of juries, individual jurors who originally believed a defendant was guilty or innocent before deliberating were found to hold even more extreme views in the same direction after the deliberations.[69]

We have already alluded to one major explanation of the group polarization effect—*social comparison.* Briefly, this explanation suggests that individuals shift to more extreme positions following group discussion because they wish to feel that they hold "better" views than other members—ones more closely aligned with accepted cultural values. But this is not the only way in which groups may induce shifts toward polarization among their members. Such effects can also arise from the *exchange of information* occurring during group discussion. Briefly, as these deliberations unfold, various members may be exposed to arguments they had not previously considered. And since most of these will favor the views initially held by a majority of the members, the end result may be a gradual shift toward extremity, as dissenters become convinced and join the "bandwagon."[70]

Regardless of the precise basis for group polarization effects, however, their existence has important implications for managers and organizations. The occurrence of such effects in many situations suggests that if decision-making groups are not careful, they may gradually drift into positions that are more and more extreme—and more and more dangerous. Clearly, this is a possibility that should not be overlooked. If it is, the results—for individuals and organizations alike—can be disastrous.

SUMMARY

Decision making is described as a multi-step process through which problems are recognized, diagnosed, and defined; solutions are generated and selected; and finally, these are implemented. There are several types of organizational decisions, including *programmed decisions,* those made in accordance with pre-existing guidelines, and *non-programmed decisions,* those requiring novel solutions. Other decisions can be characterized with respect to how certain the decision maker is about the outcomes of the decision. These can range from very *certain* to highly *uncertain,* with most decisions, those made under *risk,* in between.

Two major models of individual decision making have been identified. The **rational-economic model** characterizes decision makers as selecting the best alternative after systematically searching all alternatives. In contrast, the **administrative model** assumes that decision makers operate within a *bounded rationality* that limits their decisions to finding *satisficing* alternatives, ones that are just good enough rather than optimal. Decision makers are also limited by *bounded dis-*

cretion—restrictions imposed by ethical constraints—as well as by the tendency to use *heuristics,* simple decision rules that help provide easy answers to complex problems.

In comparing group and individual performance, it is known that groups perform better than individuals on well-structured tasks but are slower in reaching solutions. By contrast, on poorly structured tasks groups perform more poorly than individuals, partly because of **groupthink,** the tendency for groups to create strong pressures on their members to accept group solutions. In decisions involving risk, groups make more extreme decisions than individuals, whether such decisions are riskier or more cautious. This is known as the **group polarization** effect.

KEY TERMS

ADMINISTRATIVE MODEL   The model of decision making that recognizes that purely rational-economic decisions cannot be made. Instead, decision makers operate within a *bounded rationality.*

BOUNDED DISCRETION   Limitations imposed on decision makers arising from moral and ethical constraints.

BOUNDED RATIONALITY   The major assumption of the administrative model—that organizational and human limitations make it impossible for optimal decisions to be made. Instead of searching for optimal decisions, decision makers make *satisficing decisions.*

BRAINSTORMING   A technique designed to foster group creativity by encouraging interacting group members to express their ideas in a non-critical fashion.

CAUTIOUS SHIFT   The tendency for groups to make more cautious (or conservative) decisions than individuals.

CONFIRMATION CANDIDATE   An alternative to a problem that the decision maker considers in order to convince himself/herself that the *implicit favorite* is more desirable.

DECISION MAKING   The process through which problems are recognized, diagnosed, and defined; possible solutions are generated and selected; and then a course of action is implemented.

DELPHI GROUP TECHNIQUE   An approach to avoiding *groupthink* by soliciting the opinions of experts through the mail and then compiling their ideas to reach a solution.

GROUP POLARIZATION   The tendency for group members to shift to more extreme positions (in the direction they originally favored) following group interaction.

GROUPTHINK   The tendency for members of highly cohesive groups to succumb to group influences to the extent of isolating themselves from the potentially correcting influence of outsiders.

HEURISTICS   Simple decision rules ("rules of thumb") used to make quick decisions about complex problems.

IMPLICIT FAVORITE   A solution to a problem that the decision maker prefers, despite information suggesting the superiority of other alternatives.

NOMINAL GROUP TECHNIQUE (NGT)   An approach to avoiding *groupthink* by bringing together small groups of individuals who systematically present and discuss their ideas and then vote for their favorite. This is then taken as the group's decision.

NON-PROGRAMMED DECISION   A decision made about a highly novel problem for which there is no pre-specified course of action.

POORLY STRUCTURED TASK   A task requiring a creative solution, one that does not have a definitive solution.

PROGRAMMED DECISION   A highly routine decision made according to pre-established organizational policies and procedures.

RATIONAL DECISIONS   Decisions that maximize the achievement of an individual's, a group's, or an organization's goals.

RATIONAL-ECONOMIC MODEL   The model of decision making according to which decision makers consider all possible alternatives to problems before selecting the optimal outcome.

RISKY SHIFT   The tendency for groups to make riskier decisions than individuals.

SATISFICING DECISION   A decision made after selecting alternatives as they become available, and then selecting the first one that satisfies the decision maker's minimal requirements.

SYNERGY EFFECT   The intellectual stimulation of group members resulting from their interaction with one another.

WELL-STRUCTURED TASK   A task divisible into discrete steps having a readily verifiable solution.

NOTES

1. Simon, H. *The new science of management decisions* (2nd ed.). Englewood Cliffs, N.J.: Prentice-Hall, 1977.

2. Barnard, C.I. *The functions of the executive.* Cambridge, Mass.: Harvard University Press, 1938.

3. Mintzberg, J. *The nature of managerial work.* New York: Harper & Row, 1973.

4. Lang, J.R., Dittrich, J.E., & White, S.E. Managerial problem solving models: A review and a proposal. *Academy of Management Review,* 1978, *3,* 854–866.

5. Elbing, A. *Behavioral decisions in organizations* (2nd ed.). Glenview, Ill.: Scott, Foresman, 1978.

6. Reitman, W.R. Heuristic decision procedures, open constraints, and the structure of ill-defined problems. In M. Shelley & G. Bryan (Eds.), *Human judgments and optimality.* New York: Wiley, 1964.

7. Mintzberg, H., Raisinghani, R., & Theoret, A.D. The structure of unstructured decision processes. *Administrative Science Quarterly,* 1976, *21,* 246–275.

8. Kepner, C.H., & Tregoe, B.B. *The rational manager.* New York: McGraw-Hill, 1965.

9. Elbing, A. *Behavioral decisions in organizations* (2nd ed.). Glenview, Ill.: Scott, Foresman, 1978, p. 11.

10. Mintzberg, H., Raisinghani, R., & Theoret, A.D. The structure of unstructured decision processes. *Administrative Science Quarterly,* 1976, *21,* 246–275.

11. Maier, N.R.F. *Problem-solving discussions and conferences.* New York: McGraw-Hill, 1963.

12. Huber, G.P. *Managerial decision making.* Glenview, Ill.: Scott, Foresman, 1980.

13. MacCrimmon, K.R., & Taylor, R.N. Decision making and problem solving. In M.D. Dunnette (Ed.), *Handbook of industrial and organizational psychology.* Chicago: Rand McNally, 1976.

14. Radford, K.J. *Modern managerial decision making.* Reston, Va.: Reston Publishing, 1981.

15. Simon, H. *The new science of management decisions* (2nd ed.). Englewood Cliffs, N.J.: Prentice-Hall, 1977.

16. Radford, K.J. *Modern managerial decision making.* Reston, Va.: Reston Publishing, 1981.

17. Tosi, H.L., & Carroll, S.J. *Management* (2nd ed.). New York: Wiley, 1982.

18. Friedlander, F. The relationship of task and human conditions to effective organizational structure. In B.M. Bass, R. Cooper, & J.A. Haas (Eds.), *Managing for accomplishment.* Lexington, Mass.: D.C. Heath, 1970.

19. Raaheim, K., & Kaufmann, G. Level of activity and success in solving an unfamiliar task. *Psychological Reports,* 1972, *30,* 271–274.

20. Locke, E.A., & Schweiger, D.M. Participation in decision-making: One more look. In B.M. Staw (Ed.), *Research in organizational behavior* (Vol. 1). Greenwich, Conn.: JAI Press, 1979.

21. Ibid.

22. Hammer, T.H., Landau, J.L., & Stern, R.N. Absenteeism when workers have a voice: The case of employee ownership. *Journal of Applied Psychology,* 1981, *66,* 561–573.

23. Cohen, A.R., & Gadon, H. *Alternative work schedules: Integrating individual and organizational needs.* Reading, Mass.: Addison-Wesley, 1978.

24. Locke, E.A., & Schweiger, D.M. Participation in decision-making: One more look. In B.M. Staw (Ed.), *Research in organizational behavior* (Vol. 1). Greenwich, Conn.: JAI Press, 1979.

25. Mack, R.P. *Planning on uncertainty.* New York: Wiley Interscience, 1971.

26. Tosi, H.L., & Carroll, S.J. *Management* (2nd ed.). New York: Wiley, 1982.

27. Kassouf, S. *Normative decision-making.* Englewood Cliffs, N.J.: Prentice-Hall, 1970.

28. Einhorn, H.J., & Hogarth, R.M. Behavioral decision theory: Process of judgment and choice. In M.R. Rosenzweig & L.W. Porter (Eds.), *Annual Review of Psychology* (Vol. 32). Palo Alto, Calif.: Annual Reviews, 1981.

29. Simon, H.A. Rational decision making in organizations. *American Economic Review,* 1979, *69,* 493–513.

30. Machlup, F. Theories of the firm: Marginalist, behavioral, managerial. *American Economic Review,* 1957, *47,* 114–128.

31. Simon, H.A. *Models of man.* New York: Wiley, 1957.

32. Downs, A. *Inside bureaucracy.* Boston: Little, Brown, 1966.

33. March, J.G., & Simon, H.A. *Organizations.* New York: Wiley, 1958.

34. Shull, F.A., Delbecq, A.L., & Cummings, L.L. *Organizational decision making.* New York: McGraw-Hill, 1970.

35. Soelberg, P.O. Unprogrammed decision making. *Industrial Management Review,* 1967, *8,* 19–29.

36. Reeves, E.T. *The dynamics of group behavior.* New York: American Management Association, 1970, p. 334.

37. Kelley, H.H., & Thibaut, J.W. Group problem solving. In G. Lindzey & E. Aronson (Eds.), *Handbook of social psychology* (2nd ed., Vol. 4). Reading, Mass.: Addison-Wesley, 1969.

38. Guzzo, R.A., & Water, J.A. The expression of affect and the performance of decision-making groups. *Journal of Applied Psychology,* 1982, *67,* 67–74.

39. Shaw, M.E. A comparison of individual and small groups in the rational solutions of complex problems. *American Journal of Psychology,* 1932, *44,* 491–504.

40. Collins, B.E., & Guetzkow, H. *A social psychology of group processes for decision-making.* New York: Wiley, 1964.

41. Webber, R.A. The relationship of group performance to the age of members in homogeneous groups. *Academy of Management Journal,* 1974, *17,* 570–574.

42. Maier, N.R.F. Assets and liabilities in group problem solving: The need for an integrative function. *Psychological Review,* 1967, *74,* 239–248.

43. Plau, P., & Scott, W.E. *Formal organizations.* New York: Chandler, 1963.

44. Laughlin, P.R., & Johnson, H.H. Group and individual performance on a complementary task as a function of the initial ability level. *Journal of Experimental Social Psychology,* 1966, *2,* 407–414.

45. Hall, R. Interpersonal compatibility and work group performance. *Journal of Applied Behavioral Science,* 1975, *11,* 210–219.

46. Taylor, D.W., Berry, P.C., & Block, C.H. Does group participation when using brainstorming facilitate or inhibit creative thinking? *Administrative Science Quarterly,* 1958, *3,* 23–47.

47. Delbecq, A.L., Van de Ven, A.H., & Gustafson, D.H. *Group techniques for program planning.* Glenview, Ill.: Scott, Foresman, 1975.

48. Osborn, A.F. *Applied imagination.* New York: Scribner's, 1957.

49. Dunnette, M.D., Campbell, J.D., & Jaastad, K. The effect of group participation on brainstorming effectiveness for two industrial samples. *Journal of Applied Psychology,* 1963, *47,* 30–37.

50. Jewell, L.N., & Reitz, H.J. *Group effectiveness in organizations.* Glenview, Ill.: Scott, Foresman, 1981.

51. Sloan, A.P., Jr. *My years with General Motors.* New York: Doubleday, 1964.

52. Maier, N.R.F. Assets and liabilities in group problem solving: The need for an integrative function. *Psychological Review,* 1967, *74,* 239–248.

53. Janis, I.L. *Victims of groupthink.* Boston: Houghton Mifflin, 1972.

54. Ibid., p. 9.

55. Dalkey, N. *The Delphi method: An experimental study of group opinions.* Santa Monica, Calif.: The Rand Corp., 1969.

56. Delbecq, A.L., Van de Ven, A.H., & Gustafson, D.H. *Group techniques for program planning.* Glenview, Ill.: Scott, Foresman, 1975.

57. Van de Ven, A.H., & Delbecq, A.F. Nominal versus interacting group processes for committee decision-making effectiveness. *Academy of Management Journal,* 1971, *14,* 203–212.

58. Delbecq, A.L., Van de Ven, A.H., & Gustafson, D.H. *Group techniques for program planning.* Glenview, Ill.: Scott, Foresman, 1975.

59. Van de Ven, A.H., & Delbecq, A.F. Nominal versus interacting group processes for committee decision-making effectiveness. *Academy of Management Journal,* 1971, *14,* 203–212.

60. Ulschak, F.L., Nathanson, L., & Gillan, P.B. *Small group problem solving: An aid to organizational effectiveness.* Reading, Mass.: Addison-Wesley, 1981.

61. Van de Ven, A.H., & Delbecq, A.L. The effectiveness of nominal, Delphi, and interacting group decision making processes. *Academy of Management Journal,* 1974, *17,* 605–621.

62. Jewell, L.N., & Reitz, H.J. *Group effectiveness in organizations.* Glenview, Ill.: Scott, Foresman, 1981.

63. Lamm, H., & Myers, D.G. Group-induced polarization of attitudes and behavior. In L. Berkowitz (Ed.), *Advances in experimental social psychology* (Vol. 11). New York: Academic Press, 1978.

64. Stoner, J.A.F. *A comparison of individual and group decisions involving risk.* Unpublished master's thesis, M.I.T., Sloan School of Industrial Management, 1961.

65. Kogan, N., & Wallach, M.A. *Risk taking: A study in cognition and personality.* New York: Holt, Rinehart, & Winston, 1964.

66. Stoner, J.A. Risky and cautious shifts in group decisions: The influence of widely held beliefs. *Journal of Experimental Social Psychology,* 1968, *4,* 442–459.

67. Lamm, H., & Myers, D.G. Group-induced polarization of attitudes and behavior. In L. Berkowitz (Ed.), *Advances in experimental social psychology* (Vol. 11). New York: Academic Press, 1978.

68. Walker, T.G., & Main, E.C. Choice-shifts in political decision making: Federal judges and civil liberties cases. *Journal of Applied Social Psychology,* 1973, *2,* 39–48.

69. Kaplan, M.F. Judgements by juries. In M.F. Kaplan & S. Schwartz (Eds.), *Judgment and decision processes in applied settings.* New York: Academic Press, 1977.

70. Burnstein, E. Persuasion as argument processing. In M. Brandstatter, J.H. Davis, & G. Stocker-Kreschgauer (Eds.), *Group decision processes.* London: Academic Press, 1983.

12

Coordination and Incoordination in Groups: From Helping and Cooperation to Conflict and Aggression

KEY CONCEPTS

Helping (Prosocial Behavior)
Reciprocity
Social Responsibility
Diffusion of Responsibility
Fear of Social Blunders
Social Loafing
Cooperation
Competition
Conflict
Accommodation

Compromise
Collaboration
Avoidance
Bargaining
Superordinate Goals
Entrapping Conflicts
Aggression
Punishment
Catharis
Incompatible Response Strategy

□ □ □

It's late in the afternoon and you are going over some reports in your office when suddenly you hear the sound of someone clearing her throat. Looking up, you see that you have a visitor—Maureen O'Reilly. Her presence is a real surprise, for you are barely on speaking terms. The reason for this is simple: you and Maureen have always been head-on rivals. You both joined the company at about the same time, and ever since have been competing for the same raises, promotions, and other rewards. Because of this prolonged rivalry, you have avoided one another like the plague. Thus, you are amazed to see her standing in the doorway. But she doesn't give you much time to ponder the reasons for her presence. Smiling sweetly, she takes a seat and makes a surprising suggestion. "Listen, Bob" she says, "I've been thinking. We've been working against each other for more than two years now, and I don't see that it's gotten us much. What do you say to burying the hatchet? That big Houston deal is coming up next month, and I think you could be a lot of help to me in closing it. And I know that I could use my influence with Herb to help get you that extra staff position you've been wanting. How about it?" You are stunned. Maureen has been your chief rival for two years. Indeed, you can remember many occasions on which you were in direct conflict with her—times when you experienced an overwhelming urge to wring her long, slender neck! Now, suddenly, she's suggesting that you join forces. What should you do? "Gee, I don't know what to say," you stammer weakly. "I'll really have to think about that one. Why don't I sleep on it? Then we can talk it over at lunch tomorrow." "Good idea," Maureen answers. "Think about it tonight, and we'll talk more tomorrow. But think positive!" After she leaves, your thoughts are a blurred confusion. Maureen's offer is an enticing one. Together you really would make quite a team. But can you trust her? Is her offer real? Or is she simply setting you up for some kind of trap? "I'd better watch my step," you tell yourself. "This could be tricky. . . . "

Human behavior is tremendously diverse and varies along many different dimensions. As suggested by the preceding story, however, one of the most important of these involves a continuum stretching from positive actions and mutual coordination on one end, through negative actions and incoordination on the other. Lo-

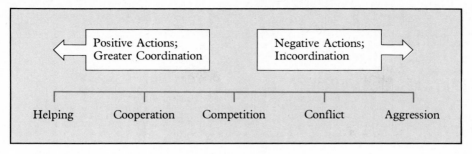

FIGURE 12-1   Positive and Negative Actions toward Others: A Basic Dimension of Human Behavior

Human behavior varies along a dimension ranging from positive actions and coordination (e.g., helping, cooperation) through negative actions and incoordination (conflict, aggression).

cated on the positive side are **helping** and **cooperation.** Further toward the middle (or perhaps beyond) is **competition.** And on the negative side of the dimension are **conflict** and **aggression** (see Figure 12-1). As you can readily see, all of these actions have major implications for organizations. Indeed, it is probably reasonable to assert that the degree of coordination or incoordination existing within a given organization usually exerts powerful effects upon its productivity, climate, and overall effectiveness. To see why this is so, consider the following imaginary companies. In one, mutual assistance between employees is common, cooperation is the general rule, and conflict is rare. In the other, mutual aid and helping are virtually unknown, extreme competition is the typical procedure, and conflict between individuals and departments is both frequent and bitter. In which organization would you prefer to work? And which do you think has a better chance of reaching its major goals? The answers are so obvious as to require no further comment. But perhaps the main point we wish to make *does* bear repeating: behaviors leading either to coordination or incoordination within organizations are important and worth taking into account. Indeed, as suggested by Figure 12-2, ignoring them can prove very costly! In the present chapter, therefore, we will provide you with some basic information on these forces. In particular, we will examine helping, cooperation, competition, and conflict, with special attention to the following issues: (1) What is the basic nature of each of these phenomena? (2) What factors encourage or discourage their occurrence? and (3) What is their potential impact on key aspects of organizational functioning?

HELPING: THE MOST DIRECT FORM OF COORDINATION IN GROUPS

Human beings frequently offer help to others. For example, the victims of accidents or natural disasters often receive aid from nearby communities; charities collect vast sums in contributions each year; and nations often provide military or

"I see by the current issue of 'Lab News,' Ridgeway, that you've been working for the last twenty years on the same problem I've been working on for the last twenty years."

FIGURE 12–2   Coordination: A Basic Requirement for Organizational Effectiveness

As shown here, a lack of coordination between individuals within the same organization can prove very costly. (Source: Drawing by Opie; © 1976 The New Yorker Magazine, Inc.)

economic aid to needy neighbors. Helping is also common within organizations. Thus, older and more experienced employees often take new ones under their wing and save them much time and effort by showing them "the ropes." Similarly when one member of a department or work group is ill or experiencing personal problems, his or her fellow workers may step in and shoulder more of the work until this person is able to function at peak efficiency once again. And of course, organizations themselves often engage in helping, especially in the form of contributions to charities or special foundations set up to assist the arts or sciences. In sum, there are many situations in which human beings seem willing to assist others, even in the absence of immediate or direct benefits for doing so.

Does this mean that we are basically altruistic creatures, overflowing with the "milk of human kindness"? Not necessarily. As you already know, when individuals help others, they often expect similar aid in return. That is, they count on later *reciprocity*. Thus, the workers mentioned above anticipate that the person they assist will help *them* if the need ever arises. And recent evidence indicates that organizations do not make contributions primarily out of philanthropic urges. Rather, they usually expect a hefty return in terms of free publicity or a boost to their public image.[1]

Even when reciprocity is not expected, persons who help others can obtain other, more subtle rewards for their seemingly "selfless" actions. For example, individuals who donate to charity may pat themselves vigorously on the back for having behaved in such a kind and responsible manner.[2] Similarly, those who give gifts or do favors for others may take vicarious pleasure in the recipients' positive reactions.[3] In short, while helping itself is quite common and easy to observe, establishing the motives for its occurrence is a more formidable task. Regardless of the ultimate motivation behind such behavior, though, helping clearly offers major benefits to organizations. Indeed, it seems reasonable to suggest that the greater the willingness of employees to assist one another, the more productive, pleasant, and efficient their organizations are likely to be. (Along these lines, William Ouchi has recently suggested that high levels of such coordination may play a major role in the phenomenal success of many Japanese companies.[4] See Chapter 15 for further discussion of this possibility.) But how, precisely, can helping be enhanced? What steps can managers take to increase such behavior among their employees? Research studies offer several intriguing answers. In considering this information, we will begin with factors that tend to facilitate helping, and then turn to ones that seem to inhibit such behavior.

Conditions That Enhance the Tendency to Help

We have already mentioned one major factor that enhances the occurrence of helping: strong expectations that such assistance will be returned. In fact, expectation of **reciprocity** may be the single most important condition predisposing human beings to offer aid to others. In view of this fact, managers wishing to encourage such behavior among their employees should take care to ensure that reciprocity actually exists. That is, they should assure that when employees "go out on a limb" or exert extra effort for them or for others, they can reasonably expect to be repaid. The reason for establishing the certainty of such reciprocity is simple: if employees doubt that favors or aid on their part will be returned, they may become far less willing to engage in such actions. After all, why should they do things for their manager, other workers, or the company if they will receive nothing in return? Thus, establishing firm expectations of on-the-job reciprocity is an important initial step toward greater organizational coordination. But reciprocity is far from the entire story. Several other factors, too, affect the frequency of helping in organizational contexts. Two of these are the presence of *helping models* and the *current mood* of potential helpers.

Models and helping: When kindness is contagious. Earlier (in Chapter 3) we noted that individuals are often strongly affected by exposure to the behavior of others. On the basis of such experience (often termed *exposure to social models*) they may acquire new behaviors, experience increases or decrements in motivation, and raise or lower their personal goals concerning performance on a given task.[5] Indeed, as we saw previously, exposure to aggressive models in the mass media can even enhance overt aggression among viewers. Given the breadth of such effects, it is not surprising that helping too can be influenced by this basic process. Specifically, it appears that exposure to *helping models*—other persons who act in a benevolent or helpful manner—can enhance similar behavior among the individuals who witness such actions. Effects of this type have actually been reported in many different studies conducted in a wide range of settings. For example, shoppers who witness a charitable model dropping coins into a Salvation Army kettle are more likely to make donations themselves than shoppers not exposed to such actions.[6] Similarly, persons who witness a theft in a store and then overhear another shopper state his intentions of reporting this crime are more likely to do so themselves than persons not exposed to such statements.[7] Such effects seem to stem mainly from the fact that when they are exposed to helping models, individuals are reminded of the norm of **social responsibility**—a general rule in most societies indicating that we should aid those in need of our assistance.[8] Such feelings of responsibility are quite general and exist in organizational settings as well as elsewhere. Thus, it is reasonable to expect that the type of modeling effects we have just described often occur within organizations. To the extent they do, a clear moral for managers is suggested. If you wish to encourage this type of positive behavior among your subordinates, be careful to demonstrate it in your own actions. If you do, you may discover that helping—like many other forms of social behavior—can be quite contagious.

The effects of mood: Positive feelings as a basis for helping.   Suppose that you want to obtain a favor from another person (e.g., your boss). When should you make your request: when she is in a good mood, or when she is in a bad mood? The answer seems obvious: try to catch her when she is in especially fine spirits. And by all means, avoid asking for your favor when she is feeling angry or irritable. These suggestions seem to make good sense and are consistent with our informal experience. But are they accurate? Research findings suggest that in general, they are. When individuals are in a good mood, they seem more likely to agree to do favors for others, to make donations to charity, or to yield to a salesperson's "pitch" than when they are in a bad mood.[9] Moreover, such effects seem to be fairly general, occurring in a wide range of contexts and situations. That they are also quite powerful is suggested by another finding: even seemingly trivial events capable of inducing only slight improvements in mood (e.g., finding a dime in a phone booth, receiving a free sample) seem to produce large increments in helping.[10] Thus, the link between mood and helping seems to be a strong one.

As you can readily see, this relationship has practical implications for organizational behavior. Briefly, it points to one additional reason for making work settings as pleasant as possible. When physical conditions are unpleasant (e.g., too warm, too cold, too noisy, crowded, dirty), unpleasant moods may be induced, with the result that helping and coordination are impaired (see Figure 12–3).[11] In contrast, when such conditions are pleasant, more positive feelings will occur, and helping may be enhanced. For similar reasons it is important for managers to set a positive emotional tone for their employees. If they are pleasant, friendly, and calm, managers may induce similar positive moods among these persons, and so increase their tendency to engage in beneficial, helping actions. In contrast, if they are irritable, tense, or abrasive, they may evoke similar negative feelings among their employees, and so reduce tendencies toward mutual helping. In sum, the powerful link between current mood and willingness to help others is one with practical implications for the field of organizational behavior. Moreover, given the relative ease with which such feelings can be altered, it is a relationship that

FIGURE 12-3   The Link between Mood and Helping: One More Reason for Making Work Environments as Pleasant as Possible

In which of these two offices do you think helping between employees might be more common? Research findings suggest that because it is a more pleasant environment in which to work, the office on the right might have an important advantage in this respect. (Source: Photo [left] by Mark Antman/The Image Works; photo [right] © Bohdan Hrynewych.)

thoughtful managers can often turn to their own, their company's, and their employees' ultimate advantage.

Conditions That Reduce the Tendency to Help

While some factors or conditions seem to enhance tendencies toward helping, others exert the opposite effect: they tend to reduce or inhibit our willingness to assist other persons. Again, several factors play a role in this regard. Among the most important, though, are **diffusion of responsibility** and the **fear of social blunders.**

Diffusion of responsibility: "Passing the buck" when others need our aid.   Imagine the following scene: you are working late one night. While walking through a section of the plant, you notice that Frank Peterson, a skilled lathe operator, is also working late in order to finish a special job. Just as you turn the corner and pass from sight, you hear Frank shout in pain and cry for help: he is being injured by one of his machines. What would you do? The answer is obvious: you would rush to his assistance at once. But now imagine the same scene with one major difference: it is the middle of the day, and when Frank cries out for help, there are more than two dozen other workers standing nearby. Would you be as likely to rush to his aid? The findings of a large number of experiments suggest that you would not. In fact, the results of these investigations indicate that the greater the number of other witnesses present on the scene, the slower or less likely you would be to aid the victim.[12] For example, in one such experiment Darley and Latané arranged for male subjects to overhear what seemed to be a dangerous epileptic seizure on the part of another person.[13] In one condition subjects believed that only they and the victim were present; thus, they were the only potential helper. In another, they believed that they, the victim, and one other person were present. Finally, in a third group subjects were led to believe that they, the victim, and four other persons were present. Results were clear: as the number of other potential helpers rose, subjects' tendencies to aid the apparent victim dropped sharply. Thus, eighty-five percent rushed to his aid when they believed that they were the only witness present, sixty-two percent did so when they believed that one other helper was available, and only thirty-one percent offered aid when they felt that four other persons were present. Similar results have been obtained in many other studies employing a wide range of "staged" accidents or emergencies (e.g., an apparent fire, an accident in which another person seems to experience a bad fall, or a dangerous electric shock from a high voltage line).[14] And such effects also seem to occur in non-emergency situations, too. For example, we are less likely to do a favor for another person (e.g., a fellow employee) when he can also ask several other persons for assistance than when we are the only one he can approach. Similarly, it is far easier to pass an individual collecting for charity without making a donation if we are part of a large crowd than if we are the only person on the street. Thus, this surprising inverse relationship between the number of persons present and helping seems to be a general one.

But why do such effects occur? Why are we less likely to help in the presence of others than when we are alone? The answer seems to involve a process known as diffusion of responsibility. Briefly, when other potential helpers are present, we seem to assume that one of them will do what's necessary, thus relieving us of all responsibility. In short, we seem all too willing to pass the buck to other persons, whether they agree to take it or not. Of course, in many situations, all potential helpers have much the same reaction—with the result that, ultimately, no one helps!

As you can readily see, such effects have important implications for organizations. For example, they may waste precious seconds during serious accidents or emergencies. And they may also tend to depress the overall willingness of employees to aid one another on the job. For these reasons, managers should attempt to minimize such influences whenever possible. Fortunately, one effective means for accomplishing this goal has been identified: obtaining a *prior commitment* to help from the persons involved.[15] When individuals commit themselves to helping before the need for such behavior arises, they seem less likely to "pass the buck." Thus, procedures in which employees practice giving aid in emergencies, fires, or other situations, and in which they explicitly agree (perhaps in group meetings) to assist one another on the job, can go a long way toward reducing the impact of such effects. In any case, since diffusion of responsibility seems to be a general tendency affecting productivity as well as helping (see the **"FOCUS"** box on pp. 390–391), it is worth considering in many situations.

Fear of social blunders: Helping and loss of face. A closely related factor that often serves to inhibit helping stems from the fact that many situations in which aid can potentially be given are somewhat ambiguous. Specifically, it is unclear whether, and to what degree, the persons involved really need aid. If they do, offering such help can result in positive outcomes for the helper. Such persons will receive approval from others and may even become heroic. But if need is absent or minimal, providing assistance can cause would-be helpers to look quite foolish. For example, consider the case of a worker who, hearing another employee cry out in what seems to be intense pain, rushes to his assistance—only to learn that this person has simply gotten a splinter. Similarly, consider the plight of a manager who, convinced by a tale of woe that would draw tears from a stone, agrees to reduce the workload on one employee—only to discover that this person is a perennial shirker, highly skilled at manipulating others. In such cases the persons offering aid may experience considerable loss of face: they have been made to appear silly or foolish in front of others. Because most individuals strongly wish to avoid such outcomes, they often hesitate before offering aid to others. After all, they want to be sure that such assistance is really needed and justified. For this reason, the fear of social blunders or *loss of face* is often another important factor that inhibits overt helping (see Figure 12-4).[16] Unfortunately, there is no simple

FIGURE 12-4 Diffusion of Responsibility and Fear of Social Blunders: Two Reasons Why Bystanders Often Fail to Help

Bystanders often fail to offer aid to the victims of accidents or other emergencies for two major reasons. First, they feel that others will take the responsibility for acting (*diffusion of responsibility*). Second, they fear that offering aid that is not really needed will cause them to appear foolish to others (*fear of social blunders*).

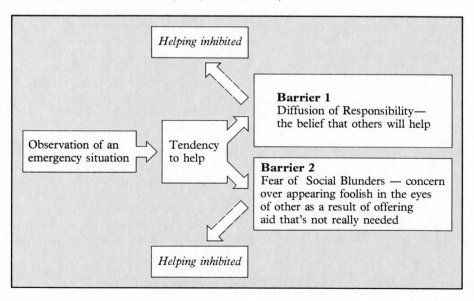

FOCUS ON BEHAVIOR

Diffusion of Responsibility and Group Productivity: Social Loafing

More than fifty years ago, a German scientist named Ringelmann performed an intriguing experiment. He asked workers to pull as hard as they could on a rope attached to a meter that measured the strength of their efforts. Subjects worked on this task alone, and in groups of two, three, and eight. Results were quite surprising. While the total amount of force on the rope increased as group size rose, the amount of effort by each person actually seemed to drop. Thus, while one person pulling alone exerted an average of 63 kg. of force, this dropped to about 53 kg. in groups of three and was further reduced to only about 31 kg. in groups of eight. In short, the greater the number of persons performing the task, the less effort each one expended.

At first glance this effect—often known as **social loafing**—is quite puzzling. Why should working on a task with several other persons reduce individual effort? Wouldn't the generation of "team spirit" be expected to yield the opposite result? One intriguing explanation for these puzzling findings has recently been provided by Latané and his colleagues in a theory of *social impact*.[17]

Briefly, this theory suggests that the impact or effect of any social force directed toward a group from an outside source (e.g., a manager) is divided among its members. Thus, the greater the number of persons in the group, the less the impact such force will have upon each. As you can readily see, this process is closely akin to *diffusion of responsibility,* which we discussed earlier. Because they are working along with several other persons, each group member feels that *they* will take up any slack resulting from reduced effort on their own part. And since all members tend to respond in this fashion, average output per person drops sharply.

Evidence for precisely this kind of effect has recently been reported by Latané, Williams, and Harkins in an integrated series of experiments.[18] For example, in the latest of these investigations, groups of male students were asked to shout as loudly as they could at certain times, supposedly as part of a study on the effects of sensory feedback upon sound in social groups.[19] They engaged in this unusual (but often enjoyable) activity either alone or in groups of two or six, and as you can see from Figure 12-5, social loafing definitely occurred: the amount of noise each person generated dropped as group size rose. In a second portion of the study—one designed to examine a potential means of eliminating social loafing—subjects were told that even when they worked in groups, their individual outputs could be identified. (It was explained that the system of microphones used in the experiment would allow the researchers to determine just how loudly each person shouted.) Here, as you might expect, social loafing all but disappeared: individuals working in groups performed nearly as well as those shouting alone. It appears then, that a key factor in social loafing actually *is* diffusion of responsibility. When such reactions are minimized (by making each member's output identifiable), the tendency to "take it easy" when working with others disappears.

Regardless of the precise mechanism underlying social loafing, though, its existence has important implications for organizational behavior. Specifically, it appears that when employees work together in groups or teams, individual levels of effort may drop. As you probably know, such team or group arrangements are extremely common in work settings, and their numbers seem to be rising as many companies seek ways of enhancing morale and productivity (see Chapter 5). Research on social loafing, then, suggests that such efforts may not yield uniformly positive results.

Of course, we should hasten to note that the boundaries of social loafing have not yet been established. For example, it is possible that such effects occur with respect to some types of tasks, but not with others. Similarly, some groups of employees may be far more susceptible to social loafing than others. Further research is clearly needed to

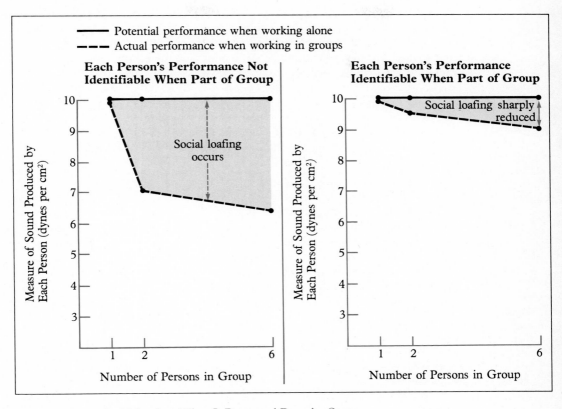

FIGURE 12-5   Social Loafing: When It Does—and Doesn't—Occur

When working on a task with one or five other persons, individuals exerted less effort than when they worked alone. Thus, *social loafing* occurred (left panel). However, when participants were told that individual performance could be identified, such effects disappeared (right panel). (Source: Based on data from Williams, Harkins, & Latané, *Journal of Personality and Social Psychology,* 1981, *40,* 303–311.)

examine these and related issues. Existing evidence, however, seems to point to the following conclusion: In some cases, at least, group effort or performance may represent a situation in which the whole is *less* than the sum of its parts. To the extent this is true, our tendency to take it easy when part of a task-performing group may have costly implications for productivity and efficiency.   □

or surefire means for eliminating the impact of this basic anxiety. But its impact can at least be reduced by tactics that minimize the ambiguity present in many helping situations. For example, very clear signals can be established for specific emergencies (bells, buzzers, specific words or phrases). Similarly, managers can do their best to assure that requests for help among their employees are legitimate, and to eliminate ones that involve attempts by one individual to take unfair advantage of one or more others. Through these and related steps, concern about loss of face through helping can be minimized, and the occurrence of this important form of organizational coordination increased.

COOPERATION AND COMPETITION: WORKING WITH—OR AGAINST—OTHERS

In our discussion of helping, we noted that individuals sometimes offer benefits to others without receiving anything obvious in return. They may well expect *some* benefit from their prosocial actions, but this is both subtle and delayed. While such one-way assistance does occur in many situations, it is probably less common than another type of behavior—one in which two or more persons work together to increase the outcomes received by each. Such mutual assistance is generally known as **cooperation** and represents a frequent and important form of social behavior. Within organizations it can be seen in a wide array of incidents, ranging from the efforts of several workers on the loading dock to move a heavy package, to the preparation of complex joint reports by two or more executives. In each case, the basic strategy is much the same: two or more persons seeking the same goal coordinate their actions and thereby perform better than they could by working alone. And once the goal is attained, it is shared among participants in some equitable (fair) manner.

Given the obvious benefits that result from cooperation, you might wonder why it sometimes fails to occur. Unfortunately the answer is obvious: often, the goals sought by two or more persons cannot be shared. Thus, pooling their resources or efforts makes little sense. For example, two employees seeking the same promotion cannot work together to attain it—the prize can go to only one. Similarly, sales representatives from different companies cannot join forces to close a major deal with a customer; only one of them can succeed. And in another but no less important sphere of life, two persons in love with the same individual usually cannot share the object of their desires (in most cultures, at least). In these and many other cases, cooperation is, literally, impossible, and an alternative form of behavior known as **competition** develops. Here, each person strives to maximize his or her own outcomes, often at the expense of others, and coordinated behavior is impossible. Because many attractive goals (status, promotions, love) are sought by more persons than can actually hope to attain them, competition too is a very common form of social behavior. Indeed, it is a basic fact of life in most modern organizations (see Figure 12-6).

FIGURE 12-6   Competition: A Basic Fact of Life in Modern Organizations

Because many goals cannot be shared, competition is an extremely common form of behavior in modern organizations. (Source: Photo by Sandra Johnson, Courtesy of Prime Computer, Inc. © 1981.)

In many situations the choice between cooperation and competition is an obvious one—indeed, there may really be no choice at all. But in others, the persons involved may find that they have some room for maneuver. That is, they can choose either to work *with* others or *against* them. (Recall the story at the start of this chapter.) This fact raises an intriguing question: What factors tip the balance one way or the other in such cases? That is, what conditions lead individuals to opt for cooperation and coordination or for competition and a "fight to the finish?" Much research has focused on this central question, and the answers it provides are both complex and revealing.

Group Cohesiveness: Liking as a Basis for Cooperation

People who work together do not necessarily like one another. Sometimes they do, sometimes they don't. And feelings in both directions can often be quite intense. Not surprisingly, the level of liking or disliking between group members—a factor often termed *group cohesiveness*—exerts powerful effects upon many aspects of work-related behavior. Among the most important of these is the level of intragroup cooperation. As you might expect, work groups in which members like one another, or feel attached to the group for other reasons, tend to show higher levels of cooperation than groups in which such positive feelings are absent or weaker. Such effects seem to be quite general, and have been observed among groups as diverse as carpenters and bricklayers, miners, factory workers, infantry squads, and air force maintenance crews.[20,21] In all these groups, the higher the level of cohesiveness present, the higher members' satisfaction and morale, the greater their acceptance of group goals, the better the communication between them, and the lower the hostility and tension. Thus, as a general rule, a high level of cohesiveness seems to facilitate cooperation and may yield important benefits in terms of group morale and productivity. We should note, however, that there seem to be definite limits to this relationship. If groups become *too* cohesive, coordination and productivity may actually begin to drop. The reason for this is simple: at very high levels of cohesiveness, group members may devote too much attention to socializing and not enough time to the work at hand. For this reason, moderate rather than extremely high levels of cohesiveness may often be best, at least from the perspective of maximum productivity.

Reacting to the Behavior of Others: Reciprocity and Cooperation

A second major factor that strongly affects the occurrence of cooperation in work groups and other contexts is one we have already discussed: *reciprocity*. Throughout our lives, we are often urged to "do unto others as we would have others do unto us." Despite such exhortations, though, we usually behave in another manner. Briefly, we treat *them* as they have treated *us* (see Figure 12–7). Thus, if others behave cooperatively, we tend to act cooperatively; if they choose to behave competitively, *we* do the same. This tendency to reciprocate cooperation or competition from others is quite strong. Indeed, many studies have found that individuals usually match very closely the level of cooperation they have received from others.[22] Only one major exception to this general rule seems to exist: If another person acts in a totally cooperative manner—chooses to cooperate with us no matter what we do—we may be strongly tempted to take advantage of this fact. And, unfortunately, such temptation seems hard to resist. Thus, in one intriguing study designed to investigate such effects, fully 129 out of 143 participants chose to exploit a stranger who behaved in a totally cooperative fashion.[23] The fact that cooperation is generally reciprocated, however, offers an important message for managers: often, such coordination is self-perpetuating. Once it has begun, it may

FIGURE 12-7   Reciprocity: A Major Factor in Cooperation

In deciding whether to cooperate with others, we often follow a general rule of *reciprocity*. That is, we behave toward them as they have already behaved toward us, or as we expect them to act in the future. Of course, as shown here, there is considerable room for error in such expectations! (Source: THE WIZARD OF ID by permission of Johnny Hart and Field Enterprises, Inc.)

tend to continue. The key task then is that of getting cooperation started. After this initial step, the stage may be set for continued coordination.

Reacting to the Motives and Intentions of Others: Attribution and Cooperation

At the beginning of this chapter, we described an incident in which a man faced a puzzling task: determining the true motives of a rival who suddenly—and unexpectedly—offered cooperation. Was she sincere? Could she be trusted? These are only two of the questions faced by the character in our story. While you may never confront a situation precisely like this one, there is little doubt that you will often have to grapple with questions such as these. The reason for this is simple. When we interact with others on the job and elsewhere, we are not simply concerned with their overt actions. In addition, we often pay careful attention to the motives and intentions behind these behaviors. Thus, in deciding whether to cooperate or compete in a given situation, we consider more than whether the others involved are currently cooperating or competing with us; we also try to determine *why* they are demonstrating these behaviors.[24] For example, if we decide that another person is cooperating out of a genuine desire to work together for mutual benefit, we may well reciprocate such behavior. In contrast, if we perceive that such cooperation stems from other motives (e.g., a desire to lull us into a false sense of security and exploit us), we may react quite differently.

Unfortunately, such judgments are often difficult to make. Other persons offering cooperation frequently seek to mislead us with respect to their true motives and intentions. For example, at a meeting or convention, a marketing manager from one company may offer to share vital information with his counterpart from a rival company, ostensibly so that both organizations (and both managers) can benefit. In fact, his ultimate goal may be that of acquiring more information than he transmits, in order to gain an important edge over the competition. Similarly, within a given organization, individuals maneuvering for power or influence may use offers of cooperation as a means of gaining support and strengthening their position. Once they have attained their goals, though, they may suddenly shift to a sharply different pattern. In these and many other situations, uncovering the true intentions of others—and the precise reasons why they offer cooperation or competition—is difficult. It *can* be accomplished, though, through careful attention to some of the factors we discussed in Chapter 6 (e.g., the degree of consensus, consistency, and distinctiveness shown by the persons in question). In any case, because of this complexity, you should probably never accept cooperation (or even competition) at face value. Rather, the best strategy is probably one of proceeding with caution and gathering all the information you can before making a definite commitment. Following such procedures may slow your decisions and might even conceivably lead you to miss out on a few opportunities for mutual coordination. But it may also save you from falling into traps leading to exploitation, and this may make it well worthwhile.

Communication: An Effective Technique for Enhancing Cooperation?

In a situation where cooperation could potentially develop but does not, the persons involved often blame its absence on a "failure to communicate." They suggest that if better or more direct communication were available, cooperation might well have occurred. This suggestion seems quite reasonable on the surface. Open communication between potential opponents may well convince them that cooperation is actually the best strategy. And communication *is* essential for the mutual coordination of behavior; indeed, in its absence, achieving such coordination may be impossible. In view of such considerations, most organizations establish special mechanisms for encouraging communication between their employees or departments (e.g., weekly staff meetings, newsletters). And for similar reasons, powerful nations have established direct "hot lines" between their capitals.

That some forms of communication do indeed enhance cooperation is obvious.[25] Yet it is equally clear that not all types produce such beneficial effects. In fact, the results of systematic research suggest that two types of contact between individuals—*threats* and *direct visual access*—can sometimes reduce rather than encourage cooperation.

Threats typically involve statements to the effect that if the recipient does not behave in some manner (or, alternatively, does not *refrain* from acting in some way), negative consequences will follow. As you probably know, comments of this type are far from rare in organizational settings. For example, managers frequently warn subordinates that unless their work improves, they will receive negative evaluations, smaller raises—or worse. Similarly, union officials frequently inform management that unless their demands are met, a costly strike will follow. Such tactics have mixed effects in the situations in which they are employed. Sometimes they succeed, and produce capitulation. In other cases they fail, and simply stiffen the resolve of the recipients to resist. In addition, growing evidence suggests that threats have important negative effects that may extend beyond the present situation. Specifically, it appears that they may sharply reduce the likelihood of cooperation at later times.[26] The reason for this is straightforward: most persons resent coercion. Thus, when subjected to threats, they become angry and hostile toward the persons who use this approach. Thus, even if they comply in the present context, they may nurse a lasting grudge and wait months or even years for a chance to repay the threatener in kind. Needless to add, as long as such feelings are present, cooperation will be difficult (if not impossible) to achieve. Indeed, once individuals (or groups) have been exposed to strong threats, the chances of establishing subsequent cooperation with them may almost vanish. The existence of such lasting effects has clear implications for managers and others who wish to enhance cooperation within organizations: try to avoid threats and similar tactics at all costs. While these procedures may work in the short run, they can leave lingering negative effects that discourage future coordination.

Turning to *direct visual contact* between individuals, we see that surprising results have been obtained. Contrary to what common sense might suggest, it appears that such contact between individuals sometimes results in *reduced* rather than enhanced cooperation. For example, in one careful study on this topic, pairs of male subjects played the roles of buyer and seller, and bargained over the price of several appliances.[27] In one condition, both persons could see each other during their discussions. In another, a barrier was present, and visual contact was blocked. Results indicated that cooperation was sharply *lower* when face-to-face contact was available. Thus, when participants could see one another, they engaged in more pressure tactics (threats, status slurs) and exchanged less information than when visual contact was prevented (see Figure 12–8). Further, their joint profit in the negotiations was lowered.

The mechanism underlying these results seems to be as follows. In situations where individuals can either cooperate or compete, they often use nonverbal cues as a means of dominating the exchange (see Chapter 6). For example, they may attempt to "stare down" the other person, to demonstrate firm resolve through their facial expressions, or to adopt a dominant body posture. Since both partici-

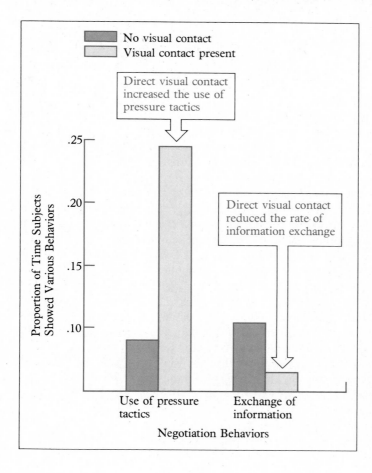

FIGURE 12–8 Face-to-Face Contact: Not Always Useful in Enhancing Cooperation

Surprisingly, face-to-face communication does not always facilitate cooperation. As shown here, when individuals playing the roles of buyer and seller in a bargaining situation could see each other, they actually showed less cooperation than when a barrier prevented such visual contact. (Source: Based on data from Carnevale, Pruitt, & Seilheimer, *Journal of Personality and Social Psychology*, 1981, *40*, 111–120.)

pants can employ these cues, and both can interpret them, the outcome is predictable: the situation quickly turns into a "macho" contest of wills, in which each side seeks to dominate the other. Of course, this pattern does *not* develop in every face-to-face interaction occurring in business settings—far from it. Yet, existing evidence suggests that it is frequent enough to warrant careful attention. In any case, the practical implications of research findings concerning the impact of such communication on cooperation are as follows. First, managers should try to be aware of the fact that subtle, nonverbal cues can often tip the balance toward competition instead of cooperation. Second, if coordination is of great importance, it may well be worth the effort to hold such cues to a minimum in your own behavior and to overlook them when they are emitted by others.

Individual Differences in the Tendency to Compete: Cooperators, Competitors, and Individualists

Think back over the many persons you have known in your life. Can you recall several who are highly competitive—persons who view every interaction as one in which they must "beat" their opponents? Similarly, can you recall some who are almost always cooperative—who refuse to compete under almost any circumstances? Probably you have no difficulty in remembering persons of both types. Our informal experience tells us that there are large individual differences in the tendencies to both cooperate and compete. And not surprisingly, the existence of such differences has been confirmed by systematic research. Basically, these studies suggest that most individuals fall into one of three major categories with respect to cooperation and competition tendencies.[28]

First, there are *competitors*—persons who seek to maximize their own gains relative to others. These individuals are primarily concerned with doing better than those around them, regardless of the payoffs at stake. Indeed, they are often more concerned with this goal than with obtaining positive outcomes. As a result, they will sometimes settle for negative results as long as these are better than those of other persons. Second, there are *cooperators*—individuals concerned with maximizing both their own gains *and* those of others. Such persons are interested in assuring that both they and their partners obtain positive results, and are most satisfied when all parties concerned obtain equal payoffs. Finally, there are *individualists*—persons primarily concerned with maximizing their own gains. Individualists have little concern for the outcomes of others, and could not care less whether these persons do better or worse than they. All they really care about is their own rewards, and they focus almost entirely on these. (Please see Figure 12-9 for a summary of the differences between individuals showing these three contrasting orientations.)

As you might well expect, cooperators, competitors, and individualists often behave in sharply different ways.[29] For example, competitors frequently try to exploit their opponents and will cooperate with them only on a temporary basis.

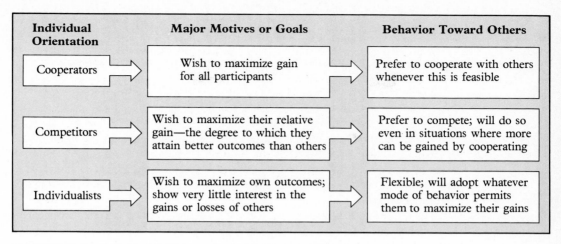

Individual Orientation	Major Motives or Goals	Behavior Toward Others
Cooperators	Wish to maximize gain for all participants	Prefer to cooperate with others whenever this is feasible
Competitors	Wish to maximize their relative gain—the degree to which they attain better outcomes than others	Prefer to compete; will do so even in situations where more can be gained by cooperating
Individualists	Wish to maximize own outcomes; show very little interest in the gains or losses of others	Flexible; will adopt whatever mode of behavior permits them to maximize their gains

FIGURE 12-9   Individual Differences in the Tendency to Cooperate or Compete

As shown here, some individuals prefer to compete, others prefer to cooperate, and still others will adopt whichever strategy permits them to maximize their own gains.

In contrast, cooperators prefer mutual coordination and adopt this pattern of behavior whenever it seems feasible. And individualists are quite flexible—they adopt whatever strategies serve to maximize their own outcomes. Another interesting difference between persons in these three categories concerns their perceptions of others. In general, competitors perceive everyone around them as highly competitive; indeed, they can hardly imagine that someone would prefer cooperation as a general mode of behavior! In contrast, cooperators seem more aware of the fact that individuals differ in this respect. That is, they realize that some persons are cooperative like themselves, while others prefer to compete.[30] We should add that these differences—where they exist—are only relative in nature. To a large degree, competitors, cooperators, and individualists all assume that most other persons behave much as they do—a basic assumption known as the *false consensus effect*.[31] But within the context of this general tendency, cooperators do seem more aware of individual differences than extreme competitors.

In sum, it appears that individual differences in the tendency to cooperate often play a key role in social relations. For this reason, it is important that you be aware of them in your dealings with fellow employees, bosses, customers, and friends. While "pure" cooperators, competitors, or individualists are rare, many persons do seem to possess *some* underlying preference for cooperation or competition. Thus, you should try to recognize these and take account of them when planning your own interpersonal strategies. And above all, always beware of persons who demonstrate what seem to be sudden shifts in their overall orientation; in most cases, the chances are quite good that these are not genuine. (For a concrete example of the type of effects that can stem from these contrasting orientations toward cooperation, please see the **"CASE IN POINT"** box on pp. 400–401.)

CASE IN
POINT

"With Winners Like These, Who Needs Losers?"

Al Jones, V.P. for sales, and Stu O'Shaugnessy, his top aide, are sitting in Al's office, discussing the monthly sales figures.

"Well," says Stu, "it looks like Jan's done it again. She's moved a bigger volume than the next three people combined. Why, she even got that giant Ampco order—the one that was really a long shot."

"Right," answers Al. "But a few more deals like that one and she'll put us out of business. Have you looked at the figures? I mean, on the terms she offered, we'll be delivering the units right at cost. And that agreement for spare parts, geez. . . . What comes over her in these situations? Does she lose touch with reality altogether?"

"I don't know. I think it's just that she's so darn competitive she can't bear to lose. When she's in there bidding against several other people, she forgets all about the bottom line. All she wants to do is win—beat the others at any cost."

"You're probably right. But doesn't she care about her own commissions? I mean, she knows darn well that if we don't make any money on a deal, she doesn't earn a nickel."

"No, I don't think that's too important to her. All that matters is winning. You know how she feels. If you say 'Hey Jan, take it easy. You don't have to win them all,' she comes back with 'Oh yes I do. And don't ask me to slow down. It's a dog-

---

Cooperation and Productivity: Is There a Link?

Throughout this discussion of cooperation, we have assumed that such coordination is good—that it is a desirable goal for organizations to seek. In one sense, this suggestion is almost a truism. When individuals work *with* rather than *against* one another, positive feelings often follow, and group cohesiveness can be enhanced. Thus, there is little doubt that cooperation yields positive effects in this regard. But what about productivity? Is cooperation superior to competition in this respect, too? This is a crucial question with important implications. Thus, you will not be surprised to learn that it has been investigated in great detail for several decades. The findings of such research have not been entirely consistent, but in general they point to the following conclusion: often, cooperation *does* have a major edge.

Support for this view is offered by the results of a detailed review conducted by Johnson and his colleagues.[32] These investigators examined the findings of more than 120 separate studies designed to compare productivity under three conditions: *cooperative, competitive,* and *individualistic* reward structures. (Cooperative reward structures involve conditions in which goal attainment by each group member facilitates goal attainment by the others. Competitive reward structures are ones in which goal attainment by each group member blocks such

eat-dog world, and my competitors will tear me to pieces if it looks like I'm slipping.' She really sees the world that way."

"Well, this has to stop. We can't afford it. Now you take a guy like Hank McKenzie. He wants to win, too. But he knows there are limits. And mainly, he wants to earn the biggest commissions possible. If that means dropping out of a particular deal, he's perfectly willing to do so. His motto seems to be 'Stay loose and shoot for the biggest gains.' He may close fewer orders than Jan, but in the long run he earns a heck of a lot more money for us."

"Probably so," answers Stu. And then, sighing, he adds: "You know, it's too bad people have to be so different in these ways. Jan's got a real talent—she can probably sell anything to almost anyone. If only we could make her see the big picture. . . . " □

Questions:

1. How would you describe Jan's orientation toward her job and toward her dealings with other people?
2. How does her orientation differ from Hank McKenzie's?
3. If you were Jan's supervisor, what steps would you take to change her behavior? Do you think they would have a reasonable chance of success?

attainment by the others. And individualistic reward structures involve conditions in which goal attainment by group members is unrelated.) The results of this careful review of existing evidence were quite revealing: in most cases, cooperation yielded higher group productivity than either competition or individualistic effort. (These latter two conditions did not differ from one another.) The superiority of cooperation over the other two reward structures was greater in small groups than in large ones, and was more pronounced when group members had to work interdependently rather than independently. However, this superiority appeared in studies that employed a wide range of tasks and many different groups of subjects, and that were performed in different settings (e.g., the laboratory, actual work environments).

Additional findings reported in recent experiments point to even stronger conclusions concerning the superiority of cooperation over competition in facilitating productivity. For example, in a series of studies focused on situations involving a mixture of cooperation and competition (conditions present in many work settings), Rosenbaum and his colleagues found that the addition of even a small element of competition to a cooperative situation can sharply lower productivity.[33] Indeed, these researchers noted that if eighty percent of the rewards available to a group for task performance are distributed cooperatively, but twenty percent are distributed competitively (assigned to the best-performing worker), productivity is significantly lower than if all rewards are distributed in a cooperative fashion. These findings suggest that the presence of even a small element of competition in a work setting can sharply disrupt coordination between group members.

As you can readily see, these findings concerning the impact of cooperation and competition on group productivity have important implications. Basically, they suggest that in many cases reward structures that emphasize interdependence between employees may be preferable to ones that pit them against one another, or that make their rewards totally independent. Of course, exceptions to this general rule probably exist. Some people—especially those in high-level jobs and those with professional training—may object to totally cooperative reward structures. And some tasks are probably best performed individually. Such exceptions aside, though, it appears that cooperation may often provide an important route to enhanced productivity. Thus, encouraging its occurrence through appropriate reward structures, and through the other techniques discussed in this section, may be well worth the effort.

CONFLICT: ITS NATURE, CAUSES, AND MANAGEMENT

Competition and conflict. Somehow, the words seem to go together. Yet at the same time, most of us have the impression that somehow they are different. In our opinion, this feeling is well-founded. While competition and conflict are closely linked and there are no fixed or definite boundaries between them, they do differ in important ways. First, they stem from somewhat different sources. Competition develops in situations in which two or more persons seek the same goal, and this goal cannot be shared. In contrast conflict usually develops in situations where one individual perceives that another has either frustrated or is about to frustrate some important concern he or she holds.[34] In short, competition involves the *potential* for thwarting major goals, while conflict often begins with such thwarting. Second, competition and conflict often arouse contrasting emotions. As you already know, competition can often be exhilarating and can evoke many positive feelings. Conflict, however, generally induces mainly negative emotions, such as anger or resentment. A third difference between these two processes centers around contrasting perceptions of one's opponent. In competition, the individuals involved often realize that their opponents have no choice but to compete with them. Thus, they do not hold them personally responsible for the events that follow. In conflict situations, however, markedly different perceptions may occur. Here, the persons involved often believe that it was not necessary for their opponents to thwart them; rather, they are seen as having acted out of malevolence or evil intent. For this reason, they (the opponents) are held personally responsible for the unpleasant situation.

In sum, competition and conflict are closely related processes, but they do differ in several respects. In general, we believe that these differences can be summarized as follows: conflict falls farther toward the negative end of our dimension of "positive actions—negative actions" toward others than competition. In this sense, it is potentially more dangerous and disruptive to organizations and groups. But please note: We are not suggesting that the effects of conflict are entirely negative. On the contrary, recent analyses of this process have called attention to the fact that it can often yield positive results.[35] For example, it can serve to arouse or activate individuals, and so enhance their performance on various tasks. Second, the confrontation of divergent views it involves can sometimes lead to the emergence of superior ideas or perspectives. And by calling attention to important problems within organizations, it can pave the way to their solution. In general, though, it seems reasonable to view conflict as a potentially dangerous process—one that often poses serious problems for organizations.

Conflict: Some Basic Causes

As we noted earlier, conflict generally develops in situations in which one or more persons perceive that one or more others either have frustrated their major concerns or are about to do so. Conflict itself, therefore, can be defined as the process which follows such thwarting, and involves specific perceptions, emotions, and behaviors on the part of the persons involved.[36] But what forms of frustration or thwarting serve to initiate conflict? Unfortunately, a great many. Individuals seek many different goals—everything from protection or enhancement of their self-esteem, through wealth, status, and power. Thus, many opportunities exist for one person or group to block the goal-attainment of other persons or groups. Indeed, the goals sought by human beings are so varied and complex, that it is all too easy for conflict to develop accidentally—in the absence of any conscious or overt desire by one individual to thwart the concerns of another. Some of the major sources of conflict within organizations are summarized in Table 12-1. We think it is worth becoming familiar with these for an important reason: once it begins, conflict is often exceedingly difficult to resolve. Thus, being able to recognize—and avoid—situations in which it is likely to occur may save you much unnecessary unpleasantness and trouble in the years ahead.

Conflict: Some Basic Patterns

Sad to relate, conflict is a basic fact of life in groups and organizations. As suggested by Table 12-1, there are simply too many opportunities for its occurrence for the situation to be otherwise. But given that conflict, in one form or another, is an inescapable aspect of group or social relations, how do individuals handle it? In short, what strategies or actions do they adopt once a conflict has begun? As you might guess, reactions to conflict vary greatly. Indeed, each person usually has his or her "pet" tactics for coping with such events. In reality, though, almost all of these turn out to be variations on five basic themes: **competition, accommodation, compromise, collaboration,** and **avoidance.**[37]

Competition, of course, refers to attempts to deal with conflict by overcoming one's opponent. Since we have already examined such behavior in detail, we will

TABLE 12-1   Conflict in Organizations: Some Major Causes

As suggested by this table, conflict within organizations can stem from many different sources.

GOAL SOUGHT	MODE OF THWARTING
Protection or enhancement of one's self-esteem	Slights to status; omission or removal of special "perks," derogation, criticism
Desire for personal autonomy	Ordering individual to behave in certain ways, restrictions on freedom, imposing needless regulations and rules
Economic benefits	Awarding smaller raise than person feels is deserved, blocking or delaying promotion
Compliance with certain norms (e.g., reciprocity, fair play)	Violation of these norms (e.g., breaking agreements, failing to reciprocate favors)
Enjoyable work	Assignment to dull, boring tasks
Self-actualization (personal growth)	Preventing such growth (e.g., retaining individual in dead-end job, blocking attempts at acquiring new job-related skills)
Free expression of personal values	Compelling individual to act in ways inconsistent with these beliefs
Good, friendly interpersonal relations	Transferring individual away from friends, interfering with informal social relations on the job

not comment further on it here. A sharply different response to conflict is *accommodation.* Individuals adopting this strategy simply surrender to their opponent, and let this person have his or her way. While accommodation might seem somewhat irrational, it often makes good sense. If it is clear to an individual that he or she can't win, the best approach may in fact be that of "cutting current losses" and surviving to fight another day. A third reaction to conflict is *compromise.* Here, each side attempts to satisfy some of its needs and goals, while permitting opponents to do the same. Because each gets at least part of what it desires, compromise is a very common strategy for handling conflict situations. *Collaboration,* a fourth general reaction to conflict, is far more elusive. Here, attempts are made to permit both sides to attain full satisfaction of their goals. Given the nature of life and the scarcity of many desired objectives, attempts to achieve this positive outcome are often doomed to failure. A final technique for handling conflict, one that seems relatively ineffective, is *avoidance.* When using this approach, individuals simply withdraw from the situation and attempt to take no part in the conflict. Needless to say, such evasion is not always possible, and even when it is, it may prove quite costly to those who adopt it.

In the past, these various reactions to conflict were often viewed as falling along a single dimension—one stretching from cooperative actions on the one hand to uncooperative behaviors on the other. More recently, though, it has been noted that a second dimension—one ranging from unassertive, passive behaviors at one extreme to assertive, active ones at the other—is also involved. Taking both into account, we can see that competition is uncooperative and assertive, accommodation is both cooperative and unassertive, and so on (see Figure 12-10). Kenneth Thomas, a researcher who has spent several years studying conflict, suggests that when both of these dimensions are considered, a more accurate and useful model for understanding such behavior is attained. That this is actually the case is suggested by the results of several recent studies. For example, in one, Ruble and Thomas presented stories describing a conflict situation to students.[38] The stories described a realistic situation in which two department managers had to divide available funds between their separate units. The specific strategies used by the characters for handling this conflict varied across different versions of the story, so that in one they used competition, in another compromise, and so on. After reading the stories, subjects rated the hypothetical persons in them on several different dimensions. Careful analysis of the results then revealed that the various strategies used by the characters were in fact perceived by subjects in the expected manner. That is, competition was seen as being both active and uncooperative, collaboration was perceived as being active and cooperative, and so on. The only major exception to this pattern was compromise: this strategy was seen as being even more cooperative than predicted (refer to Figure 12-10).

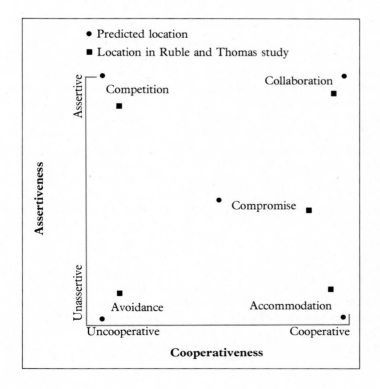

FIGURE 12-10 Five Basic Modes of Behavior in Conflict Situations

According to Thomas, individuals generally show five modes of behavior in conflict situations: *competition, accommodation, collaboration, compromise,* or *avoidance.* These can be viewed as varying along two dimensions: uncooperative-cooperative and unassertive-assertive. An experiment by Ruble and Thomas generally obtained results consistent with this model. Subjects reported viewing competition as uncooperative and assertive, collaboration as cooperative and assertive, and so on. However, they rated compromise as more cooperative than predicted. (Source: Based on data from Ruble & Tomas, *Organizational Behavior and Human Performance,* 1976, *16,* 143–155.)

These findings and those obtained in several other studies suggest that while conflict is a complex process involving many different factors, our reactions to it generally fall into a few discrete categories. And insight into these reactions, we believe, can often help us choose the best one for a given situation.

Conflict: Strategies for Its Resolution

As you already know, conflict can be costly. When it develops, individuals may be forced to spend much of their time dealing with their opponents. Further, they may be greatly upset and distracted by the strong emotions generated. Together these factors can result in substantial reductions in their performance of other vital tasks. Even worse, conflict—no matter what its outcome—often leaves a negative residue consisting of ill will, hostility, and the desire for revenge. These reactions can persist for long periods of time and disrupt important group or organizational functions. Given such costs, it seems important that conflicts be brought to a speedy and satisfactory conclusion. But what tactics can be used for this purpose? And which are most effective? Fortunately, research findings point to several strategies that may be useful in resolving interpersonal conflicts. Among the most important of these are **bargaining** and the induction of **superordinate goals.**

Bargaining: Compromise through discussion.   By far the most common tactic used for resolving interpersonal conflict is bargaining. Briefly, this process consists of a mutual trading of offers, counter-offers, and concessions between the parties involved or their representatives. If the process is successful, a solution acceptable to both sides is attained, and the conflict is brought to a close. The catch, of course, is that often the process is *not* successful. Negotiations frequently deadlock—with the result that conflict is intensified rather than reduced. A major question concerning bargaining, then, is this: What factors enhance or reduce its likelihood of success? Research findings indicate that a number of different variables play a role in this regard. With respect to the enhancement of agreement, it appears that intervention by a third party (a mediator or arbitrator) can be effective. And, comfortingly, the beneficial effects of this strategy seem to be greatest under just those conditions where it is needed most: when the conflict of interest between the individuals or groups involved is quite intense.[39] On the other side of the coin, unfortunately, several additional factors seem to reduce the success of bargaining. For example, if bargainers feel that they have an "out"—some other option aside from reaching an agreement with their opponent—they may refuse to grant concessions, and so block a solution.[40] Similarly, it appears that when negotiators represent others and are accountable to them for their actions during bargaining, they may adopt a "tougher" stance, and so render agreements more difficult to reach.[41] Perhaps the single most important determinant of the ultimate success of bargaining, though, involves negotiators' overall orientation toward the process.

In many cases, bargainers adopt a highly competitive approach to their negotiations. Each sees his or her task as that of "beating" the opponent—extracting a highly favorable agreement from this person. To the extent this orientation exists, solutions may be extremely difficult to achieve. Indeed, negotiators may become more interested in wringing concessions from their opponent than in maximizing their own potential gains. Luckily, though, this is not the only orientation toward bargaining that can exist. Another, and radically different perspective, views bargaining largely as a problem-solving task.[42] Within this approach, participants view their conflict as a solvable problem. Thus, they perceive their task simply as one of finding an agreement acceptable to both sides—one that affords positive outcomes to each. Adoption of such a problem-solving orientation, in turn, is accompanied by two major features. First, it encourages the *exchange of information* about values and priorities between participants. Such information is useful, for it aids bargainers in keeping both their own and their opponents' welfare in mind. Second, a problem-solving orientation enhances *heuristic trial and error*—a process in which both sides make an orderly series of proposals and counterproposals in a joint effort to find one acceptable to each. Such offers are accompanied by requests for information on the recipient's reactions, and by the granting of concessions on relatively low-priority issues in order to keep the process moving.

That the adoption of a problem-solving orientation toward bargaining may be helpful in reaching an agreement is supported by the findings of several studies.[43] In these investigations bargainers obtained better joint outcomes when they were encouraged to approach their discussions as centering around a solvable problem than when they were simply told to make as much individual profit as possible. Further, under the problem-solving orientation, bargainers showed more concern for each others' welfare, transmitted more accurate information to their opponents, and engaged in fewer pressure tactics designed to increase their own profit. Together, such findings suggest that inducing negotiators to adopt a problem-solving orientation toward their discussions can often be an effective strategy for resolving interpersonal conflict.

The induction of superordinate goals: Converting "them" into "us." A second general strategy for resolving conflicts stems from a basic aspect of social perception. Stated briefly, we seem to possess a strong tendency to divide the social world into two distinct categories: them and us. Persons falling into the former category are viewed as being different from ourselves, and usually evoke negative feelings and attitudes. In contrast, persons included in the latter category are seen as being similar to ourselves, and generally elicit positive reactions. In short, we divide the social world into "in-group members" and "out-group members," and demonstrate sharply different reactions to the individuals who fall into each of these two categories.[44]

This tendency, in turn, has important implications for many interpersonal conflicts. In such situations, each side tends to view its opponent as belonging to the out-group. As a result, they tend to hold negative attitudes toward these persons. A crucial step toward resolving many conflicts, then, involves eliminating these artificial barriers. But how can this be accomplished? Research findings point to the effectiveness of at least one basic strategy: arranging conditions so that the two sides must work together to attain some *superordinate goal.* That this strategy can often reduce conflict is readily apparent. For example, consider recent events in the U.S. automobile industry. Confronted with growing competition from foreign companies, labor and management have agreed to "bury the hatchet," at least temporarily, and work together to fend off this threat to their common livelihood. Thus, workers have agreed to reductions in pay and other benefits, and management has agreed to pass the savings so obtained onto consumers in the form of lower prices. More systematic evidence for the conflict-resolving properties of superordinate goals has been obtained in several research projects. For example, in a classic investigation of this topic, Sherif and his colleagues divided boys at a summer camp into two groups.[45] These groups were then pitted against each other in a series of competitive events until, as expected, they developed negative attitudes toward one another. In a final stage of the study, attempts were made to eliminate these feelings and to reduce intergroup conflict. The strategy that proved most effective in this respect was one based on superordinate goals. That is, when conditions were arranged so that the groups had to work together to achieve various shared goals or overcome common threats (e.g., they had to join forces to pull a disabled truck; they competed against a group of outsiders), conflict was greatly reduced. These and similar findings suggest that reminding the parties to a conflict of their shared goals—or actually establishing such objectives—can be highly effective in resolving their disagreements. Of course, this is not possible in all cases; sometimes true conflicts of interest make it impossible to establish shared goals. But it is our view that when conflict occurs within organizations, such superordinate goals usually do exist—the persons involved have merely lost sight of their presence. In such cases, taking steps to break down the artificial ingroup–out-group barriers mentioned above may go a long way toward re-establishing harmony and cooperation. (For further discussion of conflict, and some reasons why it is often so difficult to end, please see the **"FOCUS"** box on pp. 410–411.)

Beyond Conflict: A Note on Aggression

While conflict is disturbing and potentially harmful, there is another form of behavior lying even farther out along our dimension of "positive actions–negative actions" toward others: **aggression.** A detailed discussion of such behavior (which is generally defined as any action designed to harm a victim who is motivated to avoid this treatment) is beyond the scope of this chapter. But given its frequent occurrence in many settings (including organizations), we feel we should at least comment briefly on its nature and control.

Conflict versus aggression: Some basic distinctions. Earlier, we noted that competition shades imperceptibly into conflict. In a similar manner, conflict shades gradually into aggression. Thus, it is impossible to draw a hard-and-fast boundary between these two processes. Yet they do differ in several important respects. First, while conflict stems primarily from thwarting, aggression derives

TABLE 12-2 Aggression: Its Multiple Roots

Studies conducted during the past two decades suggest that aggression stems from a very wide range of factors and conditions. A number of these are summarized here.

FACTOR OR CONDITION	DESCRIPTION, KEY FINDINGS
Social Factors	
Direct Provocation	Physical provocation or verbal insult elicits aggression
Exposure to Social Models	Exposure to live or televised aggressive models enhances aggression
Presence of an Audience	Can either enhance or inhibit aggression, depending on nature of onlookers
Negative Attitudes	Negative attitudes (e.g., racial or ethnic prejudice) can facilitate aggression
Frustration	Thwarting goal-directed behavior can lead to aggression, especially if it is arbitrary or unexpected
Deindividuation	Being an anonymous member of a large group can often increase aggression
Situational and Environmental Factors	
Heightened Arousal	Can enhance aggression, especially if it is misinterpreted as anger; intense sexual arousal can exert similar effects, but mild sexual arousal may actually reduce aggression
Drugs	Alcohol can reduce inhibitions against aggression and increase sensitivity to provocation; marijuana seems to reduce aggression in some situations
Heat	Moderate warmth (e.g., temperatures in the mid-80s F can enhance aggression; higher levels of heat induce lethargy, and so tend to reduce overt aggression
Crowding	High levels of crowding can increase irritability, and so facilitate aggression
Noise	High levels of unpleasant noise can enhance aggression, especially in the presence of prior anger arousal
Personal Factors	
Personality Traits	Several personality traits (e.g., Type A behavior pattern) are associated with lower thresholds for anger and overt aggression
Abrasive Personality	Possession of a cluster of traits (e.g., the need to be in total control) increases the likelihood that such persons will become involved in aggressive exchanges with others
Sex	Females are less aggressive than males, but only in some situations; when aggression is approved or justified, such differences may disappear

FOCUS ON BEHAVIOR

Too Much Invested to Quit: Why Some Conflicts Are Entrapping

Many conflicts seem to demonstrate an unsettling tendency toward persistence. That is, once they begin, they tend to continue far beyond the point at which either side can possibly gain enough to justify its major losses. Instances of this type are all too common. For example, strikes and lockouts often persist for months, thus assuring enormous economic costs to both sides. Similarly, tragic wars often drag on and on, far past the point at which either opponent can hope to gain enough to justify its terrible losses. In short, many conflicts seem to be **entrapping**; once they begin, participants seem unwilling—or unable—to escape from them. But why is this the case? What is it about such situations that makes it so difficult for both sides to withdraw? According to Brockner and his colleagues, the answer is relatively simple.[46] Many conflicts are entrapping because once they start, both sides quickly have too much invested to quit.

Specifically, soon after such conflicts are initiated, each side experiences major costs or losses. These in turn generate powerful pressures to somehow justify their presence. Withdrawal from the conflict, of course, would make this impossible. Further, it would serve as an admission that entering it in the first place was an error. Thus, each

side feels compelled to "stick to its guns" and see the conflict through. Only in this way, they feel, can they obtain the tangible rewards needed to offset their heavy losses. As time passes and additional resources are committed, such pressures continue to mount. Thus, in the end, such conflicts take on a life of their own and totally entrap the parties to them (see Figure 12-11).

Given the "vicious circle" nature of such entrapping conflicts and their frequent occurrence, it seems reasonable to ask whether any steps can be taken to bring them to a close. Fortunately, research findings cast some light on this issue.[47] First, it appears that such conflicts are less likely to develop (and most likely to terminate) under conditions in which the decision to continue must be taken actively rather than passively. That is, entrapping conflicts may be avoided if at each step the participants must make an active decision to continue (e.g., they must actively vote against ending the strike, or actively reject an offer from their opponent). In contrast, if such decisions are taken passively (i.e., the situation continues as long as nothing concrete is done to stop it), conflicts may both persist and intensify. Second, entrapment may be avoided or ended by reminding participants of the major costs involved. Apparently, these are of-

from a very wide range of conditions. Thwarting (frustration) is included among these, but many others too play a role. Indeed, one of the major themes of recent research on aggression has been the identification of a growing list of factors that seem to play a role in its occurrence.[48] Included among these are many *social conditions* (e.g., direct provocation from others, exposure to media violence), *environmental factors* (e.g., heat, crowding, noise), and *personal factors* (e.g., gender, various personality traits). A detailed discussion of these conditions would require many pages, and take us far from the major thrust of this book. In order to give you a general idea of the very broad range of conditions found to play a role in human aggression, though, we have prepared the summary shown in Table 12-2. After examining this information, we think you'll be convinced that aggression does indeed stem from many different sources.

A second difference between conflict and aggression lies in the motives under-

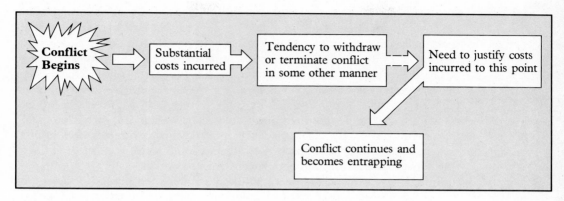

FIGURE 12-11   Entrapping Conflicts: Why Escape Is So Difficult to Attain

In some conflicts, participants incur substantial costs very quickly. Because they then feel a strong pressure to justify these costs, they are reluctant to withdraw or end the conflict in some other fashion. The result: the situation becomes *entrapping,* and escape is very difficult.

ten lost in the heat of battle. Bringing them sharply into focus may help terminate the process of continued investment and escalation. Finally, entrapment can be avoided by encouraging potential participants to adopt a cautious approach to such situations—one in which they are reluctant to incur initial costs.

Unfortunately entrapping conflicts are quite common. Thus, we predict that you will encounter them often in organizational settings. When you do, try to be an observer rather than an active participant. Allowing yourself to be lured into such conflicts can be very costly, for remember: once you are involved, there may be no easy escape!   □

lying each. In conflict, the parties involved are primarily concerned with attaining various goals—anything from increased profit through power or enhancement of their status. Attempts to reach these goals, of course, can sometimes lead to intense anger and even direct assaults against opponents. But the primary motive remains that of reaching some objective. Aggression, in contrast, generally stems from a different motive: the desire to inflict harm or injury on the victim. While this in itself may sometimes be a sub-goal on the route to other objectives (e.g., an individual may have to eliminate a rival in order to attain a promotion), harm or injury to the victim usually remains the major guiding impulse. Thus, while they are often similar in form, conflict and aggression usually differ with respect to their underlying motives.

Finally, aggression and conflict differ sharply in terms of the strategies that may prove effective in reducing or lessening their occurrence. As we have already seen, conflict may best be resolved through bargaining, the introduction of super-ordinate goals, and similar tactics. In contrast, sharply different procedures seem necessary for the control of aggression. Over the years, many such tactics have been suggested, but two have received by far the greatest attention: **punishment** and **catharsis.** Both of these procedures seem effective in controlling aggression under some conditions. But recent findings suggest that both may fail in this respect under other circumstances.[49] For example, punishment can often deter current violence. But because it is unpleasant, it often instills a desire for revenge among the persons who receive it. In this manner it may actually sow the seeds of future aggression, even while holding present violence in check. Similarly, certain types of catharsis (actions permitting the safe release of aggressive urges) can sometimes result in lessened tendencies toward aggression. But such effects seem to be quite short-lived in nature, and may totally dissipate within a matter of minutes. In sum, neither punishment nor catharsis seems to be as effective in deterring human aggression as was once widely believed.

Fortunately, as increasing doubt has been cast upon the efficacy of these techniques, other procedures for reducing aggression have been uncovered. One that has received considerable support from research findings in recent years is based on a simple fact: human beings, like other organisms, are incapable of engaging in two incompatible behaviors at the same time or of experiencing two incompatible emotional states concurrently. In accordance with this principle, it has been suggested that exposing angry persons to conditions capable of inducing emotional states or reactions incompatible with aggression will often tend to reduce such behavior. And in fact, many recent studies suggest that this is actually the case.[50] For example, it has been found that exposure to mild forms of erotica or to various types of humor can be quite effective in reducing later aggression. (You may already have witnessed the use of humor in this context. It is sometimes a major factor preventing tense and angry meetings from totally falling apart.) Because this general approach—often known as the **incompatible response strategy**—can be used in a wide range of settings, it seems very promising. Indeed, tactics for its direct application to group behavior are now being developed. And at present, it seems to offer an effective aid to persons whose inability to hold their own tempers in check often gets them into serious difficulty.

Aggression versus assertiveness.   Before concluding, we should note that aggression can also be distinguished from *assertiveness*. This latter form of behavior involves such actions as standing up for one's rights, and refusing to be "pushed around" by others. In contrast to aggression, assertiveness is often adaptive for individuals and can also play a constructive role in organizations. For example, it can prevent overly dominant supervisors from taking unfair advantage of their subordinates—and so totally wrecking company morale. Similarly, by enabling subordinates to speak their minds, even to high-level managers, it can provide these leaders with a greater range of input, and so, perhaps, contribute to the quality of their decisions. In sum, while there is little place within an organization for overt aggression, a degree of assertiveness among employees—provided it is not carried too far—can be a healthy characteristic.

SUMMARY

Group behavior may be viewed as varying along a dimension stretching from positive reactions toward others through negative actions toward others. At the positive extreme is **helping** or **prosocial behavior.** Such actions are enhanced by exposure to helping models (other persons who engage in prosocial actions) and by pleasant moods. Surprisingly, they are inhibited by the presence of other potential helpers, largely because of the impact of *diffusion of responsibility* and the *fear of social blunders.*

In many situations, individuals are faced with the choice of cooperating with others or competing against them. Many factors serve to tip the balance toward one or the other of these forms of behavior. **Cooperation** is enhanced by cooperative treatment from others and by the attribution of positive motives to these persons. It can also be facilitated by some types of *communication.* However, it is actually inhibited by threats and by direct visual contact, at least in some situations. Individuals differ greatly with respect to their personal preferences for cooperation or competition, and such differences affect their behavior in many settings.

Conflict occurs in situations in which one or more persons perceive that one or more others have frustrated or are about to frustrate their major concerns. When confronted with conflict, individuals show many different reactions, but most of these fall into five major categories: *competition, accommodation, compromise, collaboration,* or *avoidance.* One effective strategy for resolving interpersonal conflict is *bargaining.* A second is the induction of *superordinate goals.*

Aggression—behavior designed to harm or injure another person—is the most negative form of social behavior. At one time, it was assumed that aggression stems mainly from frustration. Now, however, it is known that it is stimulated by a wide range of social, environmental, and personal factors. *Punishment* and *catharsis* are both effective in deterring aggression under some conditions. However, they fail to exert such effects under other circumstances. A promising technique for the control of aggression developed in recent years is the *incompatible response strategy.* In this procedure individuals are exposed to stimuli known to induce emotions or responses incompatible with anger or overt aggression.

KEY TERMS

ACCOMMODATION A mode of behavior in conflict situations. Individuals adopting accommodation simply give their opponents what they desire.

AGGRESSION Any form of behavior directed toward the goal of harming or injuring a victim who is motivated to avoid such treatment.

AVOIDANCE A mode of behavior in conflict situations. Individuals adopting avoidance simply seek to withdraw from the situation.

BARGAINING A process in which two or more sides to a conflict exchange offers, concessions, and counter-offers in an attempt to resolve their disagreement.

CATHARSIS   A technique for the reduction of aggression. Catharsis is based on the performance of "safe" (i.e., non-injurious) substitute behaviors.

COLLABORATION   A mode of behavior in conflict situations. Individuals using collaboration attempt to arrange for both sides to attain full satisfaction of their goals.

COMPETITION   A basic form of social behavior in which individuals attempt to maximize their own outcomes, often at the expense of others. Competition often arises in situations in which two or more persons seek the same goal, and it cannot be shared among them.

CONFLICT   A process arising in situations in which one or more persons perceive that one or more others have thwarted or are about to thwart their major concerns.

COMPROMISE   A process by which each side in a conflict attempts to satisfy some of its needs and goals while permitting the opposing side to do the same.

COOPERATION   A basic form of social behavior in which two or more persons coordinate their behavior in order to attain a common goal.

DIFFUSION OF RESPONSIBILITY   Refers to the tendency of individuals to assume that others will take responsibility for needed actions. This type of diffusion seems to play an important role in the failure of many onlookers to aid the victims of crimes or accidents.

ENTRAPPING CONFLICTS   Conflicts in which both sides quickly incur substantial costs. Because of the need to justify such costs, neither is willing to withdraw. Thus, the conflict may persist long past the point at which there is any potential for gain.

FEAR OF SOCIAL BLUNDERS   Concern over appearing foolish in the eyes of others. This concern appears to play a key role in the failure of bystanders to aid the victims of accidents or crimes.

HELPING (PROSOCIAL BEHAVIOR)   Refers to actions by one individual that benefit one or more others. Often when individuals engage in such behavior, they anticipate receiving some benefit in return.

INCOMPATIBLE RESPONSE STRATEGY   A technique for reducing aggression based on the fact that human beings are incapable of engaging in two incompatible reactions or experiencing two incompatible emotions at the same time.

PUNISHMENT   A technique for reducing aggression based on the establishment of a direct contingency between aggressive actions and the delivery of aversive consequences.

RECIPROCITY   A basic principle governing many forms of social behavior. Reciprocity suggests that we act toward others as they have behaved toward us.

SOCIAL LOAFING   Refers to the tendency of individuals to exert less effort on a task when working together with others than when working alone.

SOCIAL RESPONSIBILITY   Refers to a social norm suggesting that we should assist other persons in need of our aid.

SUPERORDINATE GOALS   A technique for reducing conflict in which opposing sides are made aware of the fact that they actually share some common goals.

NOTES

1. Fry, L.W., Keimm, G.D., & Meiners, R.E. Corporate contributions: Altruistic or for profit? *Academy of Management Journal*, 1982, *25*, 94–106.

2. Baumann, D.J., Cialdini, R.B., & Kenrick, D.T. Altruism as hedonism: Helping and self-gratification as equivalent responses. *Journal of Personality and Social Psychology,* 1981, *40,* 1039–1046.

3. Batson, C.D., Duncan, B.D., Ackerman, P., Buckley, T., & Birch, K. Is empathic emotion a source of altruistic motivation? *Journal of Personality and Social Psychology,* 1981, *40,* 290–302.

4. Ouchi, W.G. *Theory Z: How American business can meet the Japanese challenge.* Reading, Mass.: Addison-Wesley, 1981.

5. Bandura, A. *Social learning theory.* Englewood Cliffs, N.J.: Prentice-Hall, 1977.

6. Bryan, J.H., & Test, M.A. Models and helping: Naturalistic studies in aiding behavior. *Journal of Personality and Social Psychology,* 1967, *6,* 400–407.

7. Bickman, L., & Rosenbaum, D.P. Crime reporting as a function of bystander encouragement, surveillance, and credibility. *Journal of Personality and Social Psychology,* 1977, *35,* 577–586.

8. Maruyama, G. Fraser, S.C., & Miller, N. Personal responsibility and altruism in children. *Journal of Personality and Social Psychology,* 1982, *42,* 658–664.

9. Cialdini, R.B., Kenrick, D.T., & Baumann, D.J. Effects of mood on prosocial behavior in children and adults. In Eisenberg-Berg, N. (Ed.), *The development of prosocial behavior.* New York: Academic Press, 1982.

10. Levin, P.F., & Isen, A.M. Further studies on the effect of feeling good on helping. *Sociometry,* 1975, *38,* 141–147.

11. Bell, P.A., Fisher, J.D., & Loomis, R.J. *Environmental psychology.* Philadelphia: Saunders, 1978.

12. Shotland, R.L., & Huston, T.L. Emergencies: What are they and do they influence bystanders to intervene? *Journal of Personality and Social Psychology,* 1979, *37,* 1822–1834.

13. Darley, J.M., & Latané, B. Bystander intervention in emergencies: Diffusion of responsibility. *Journal of Personality and Social Psychology,* 1968, *8,* 377–383.

14. Latané, B., & Rodin, J. A lady in distress: Inhibiting effects of friends and strangers on bystander intervention. *Journal of Experimental Social Psychology,* 1969, *5,* 189–202.

15. Moriarty, T. Crime, commitment, and the responsive bystander: Two field experiments. *Journal of Personality and Social Psychology,* 1975, *31,* 370–376.

16. Darley, J.M., & Latané, B. Bystander intervention in emergencies: Diffusion of responsibility. *Journal of Personality and Social Psychology,* 1968, *8,* 377–383.

17. Latané, B. Psychology of social impact. *American Psychologist,* 1981, *36,* 343–356.

18. Latané, B., Williams, K., & Harkins, S. Many hands make light the work: The causes and consequences of social loafing. *Journal of Personality and Social Psychology,* 1979, *37,* 822–832.

19. Williams, K., Harkins, S., & Latané, B. Identifiability as a deterrent to social loafing: Two cheering experiments. *Journal of Personality and Social Psychology,* 1981, *40,* 303–311.

20. Van Zels, R.H. Sociometrically selected work teams increase production. *Personnel Psychology,* 1952, *5,* 175–185.

21. Bjerstedt, A. Preparation, process, and product in small group interaction. *Human Relations,* 1961, *14,* 183–189.

22. Bixenstein, V.E., Potash, H.M., & Wilson, K.V. Effects of level of cooperative choice by the other player on choices in a prisoner's dilemma game. *Journal of Abnormal and Social Psychology,* 1963, *66,* 308–313.

23. Shure, G.H., Meeker, R.J., & Hansford, E.A. The effectiveness of pacifist strategies in bargaining games. *Journal of Conflict Resolution,* 1965, *9,* 106–117.

24. Brickman, P., Becker, L.J., & Castle, S. Making trust easier and harder through two forms of sequential interaction. *Journal of Personality and Social Psychology,* 1979, *37,* 515–521.

25. Wichman, H. Effects of isolation and communication on cooperation in a two-person game. *Journal of Personality and Social Psychology,* 1970, *16,* 114–120.

26. Deutsch, M., & Krauss, R.M. The effect of threat upon interpersonal bargaining. *Journal of Abnormal and Social Psychology,* 1960, *61,* 181–189.

27. Carnevale, P.J.D., Pruitt, D.G., & Seilheimer, S.D. Looking and competing: Accountability and visual access in integrative bargaining. *Journal of Personality and Social Psychology,* 1981, *40,* 111–120.

28. Kuhlman, D.M., & Marshello, A.F.J. Individual differences in game motivation as moderators of preprogrammed strategy effects in prisoner's dilemma. *Journal of Personality and Social Psychology,* 1975, *32,* 922–931.

29. Kuhlman, D.M., & Wimberley, D.L. Expectations of choice behavior held by cooperators, competitors, and individualists across four classes of experimental game. *Journal of Personality and Social Psychology,* 1976, *34,* 69–81.

30. Kelley, H.H., & Stahelski, A.J. Errors in perception of intentions in a mixed-motive game. *Journal of Experimental Social Psychology,* 1970, *6,* 379–400.

31. Messé, L.A., & Sivacek, J.M. Predictions of others' responses in a mixed-motive game: Self-justification or false consensus? *Journal of Personality and Social Psychology,* 1979, *37,* 602–607.

32. Johnson, D.W., Maruyama, G., Johnson, R., Nelson, D., & Skon, L. Effects of cooperative, competitive, and individualistic goal structures on achievement: A meta-analysis. *Psychological Bulletin,* 1981, *89,* 47–62.

33. Rosenbaum, M.E., Moore, D.L., Cotton, J.L., Cook, M.S., Hieser, R.A., Shovar, M.N., & Gray, M.J. Group productivity and process: Pure and mixed reward structures and task interdependence. *Journal of Personality and Social Psychology,* 1980, *39,* 626–642.

34. Thomas, K. Conflict and conflict management. In M. Dunnette (Ed.), *Handbook of Industrial and Organizational Psychology.* Chicago: Rand McNally, 1976.

35. Thomas, K.W. Toward multi-dimensional values in teaching: The example of conflict behaviors. *Academy of Management Review,* 1977, *2,* 484–490.

36. Thomas, K. Conflict and conflict management. In M. Dunnette (Ed.), *Handbook of Industrial and Organizational Psychology.* Chicago: Rand McNally, 1976.

37. Ibid.

38. Ruble, T.L., & Thomas, K.W. Support for a two-dimensional model of conflict behavior. *Organizational Behavior and Human Performance,* 1976, *16,* 143–155.

39. Hiltrop, J.M., & Rubin, J.Z. Effects of intervention mode and conflict of interest on dispute resolution. *Journal of Personality and Social Psychology*, 1982, *42*, 665–672.

40. Komorita, S.S., & Kravitz, D.A. The effects of alternatives in bargaining. *Journal of Experimental Social Psychology*, 1979, *15*, 147–157.

41. Breaugh, J.A., & Klimoski, R.J. Social forces in negotiation simulations. *Personality and Social Psychology Bulletin*, 1981, *7*, 290–295.

42. Pruitt, D.G. *Negotiation behavior*. New York: Academic Press, 1981.

43. Pruitt, D.G., & Lewis, S.A. Development of integrative solutions in bilateral negotiation. *Journal of Personality and Social Psychology*, 1975, *31*, 621–633.

44. Granberg, D., Jefferson, N.L., Brent, E.E., Jr., & King, M. Membership group, reference group, and the attribution of attitudes to groups. *Journal of Personality and Social Psychology*, 1981, *40*, 833–842.

45. Sherif, M., Harvey, O.J., White, B.J., Hood, W.R., & Sherif, C.W. *Intergroup conflict and cooperation: The robbers' cave experiment*. Norman: University of Oklahoma Press, 1961.

46. Brockner, J., Shaw, M.C., & Rubin, J.Z. Factors affecting withdrawal from an escalating conflict: Quitting before it's too late. *Journal of Experimental Social Psychology*, 1979, *15*, 492–503.

47. Brockner, J., Rubin, J.Z., & Lang, E. Face-saving and entrapment. *Journal of Experimental Social Psychology*, 1981, *16*, 68–79.

48. Geen, R.G., & Donnerstein, E. (Eds.), *Aggression: Theoretical and empirical reviews*. New York: Academic Press, 1983.

49. Baron, R.A. *Human aggression*. New York: Plenum, 1977.

50. Geen, R.G., & Donnerstein, E. (Eds.), *Aggression: Theoretical and empirical reviews*. New York: Academic Press, 1983.

13

Influence and Power:
Tactics for Getting Our Way

KEY CONCEPTS

Influence

Ingratiation

Conformity Pressure

Norms

Foot-in-the-Door Technique

Door-in-the-Face Technique

Guilt

Power

Reward Power

Coercive Power

Legitimate Power

Referent Power

Expert Power

Strategic-Contingencies Theory

Organizational Politics

□ □ □

It's lunchtime, and you and two of your best friends, Carol Murphy and John Aguerro, have just settled into a comfortable booth in your favorite local restaurant. The waitress takes your order and as soon as she departs, you start a spirited conversation.

"Boy, that Tom Franklin is really something," remarks Carol. "I heard that he's just done it again. The board okayed his latest plan this morning. That'll give him another big increase in his budget. And it won't hurt his chances for that vice-presidency either."

"Yeah, he's unbelievable," agrees John. "I don't know how he does it."

"Well," you reply, "if you study him closely, you can get some hints. I've watched him in a lot of situations, and it seems to me that he has a whole bag of tricks up his sleeve. He's a smooth talker—about as good as they come. And he sure knows how to put on the pressure."

"That's right," Carol agrees. "The other day I saw him trying to convince Frank Perotti to endorse his plan, and he made it sound as though Frank would look like a perfect fool if he didn't go along. By the time he got through with him, Frank couldn't wait to join the bandwagon."

Everyone laughs at this, for it sounds just like Tom and his usual style of operation. Then John adds: "And another thing. He sure knows how to use his power. He promises lots of goodies to people who support him—even things he can't really deliver. And he makes no bones about threatening people who hold out. He's subtle about it, but you still get the message."

"He also does his homework," you remark. "He's usually so well prepared at meetings that he comes across as a real expert. And we all know how much weight Gordon places on that."

John and Carol shake their heads in agreement, for they know that the company president really does value expertise greatly. The conversation is about to continue but just at this moment, your waitress arrives with the food. It's almost 2:00 PM, and you are all very hungry, so for the next few minutes the only sounds are those of three mouths chomping, punctuated by requests for the salt, pepper, or butter. . . .

At one time or another, most of us have had the following fantasy: somehow, we acquire a special power that permits us to control the behavior of other persons. Through this power, we can induce them to behave in any way we wish. This is a tantalizing daydream—and for good reason. Other people play a crucial role in our lives, both on the job and off it. Thus, the ability to shape their behavior to our wishes would provide us with a ready means of satisfying most of our needs, goals, and desires. Unfortunately, though, no magic formula for attaining such control exists. People have minds of their own, and are willing to do our bidding only on some occasions, and under some conditions. Thus, the fantasy of exerting total control over them must remain just that—an enticing but largely unattainable illusion.

While *total* control of others remains beyond our grasp, however, there are many tactics we can use to at least move in this direction. These are far from perfect in their impact, but if employed with skill and care, they can often yield impressive results. (Consider Tom, the character in the story!) Before reviewing such techniques, though, we must pause briefly to distinguish between two major concepts central to our discussion: **influence** and **power.**

In an important sense, these terms are closely related: both refer to the ability of one person to alter the behavior of one or more others in desired directions. But there are also important differences between them that should not be overlooked. First, influence and power differ with respect to the magnitude of their impact. Influence generally refers to the ability to change the behavior of others; power refers to the capacity to do so *regularly* and *strongly.*[1] Thus, in this respect, power is the more impressive phenomenon. Second, influence and power differ in terms of their scope or generality. Influence is generally exerted on a situation-by-situation basis, and in face-to-face interactions between individuals. Power is more general, and cuts across both situations and relationships.[2] Finally, power and influence differ in terms of the basis for their effects. Influence relies, primarily, on the specific tactics employed. If these are well-chosen and skillfully executed, it can succeed. If such tactics are poorly selected or utilized, it may fail. In contrast, power rests on somewhat broader foundations. For example, it can stem from the expertise, attractiveness, or legitimacy of the persons exercising it. Thus, it succeeds to the extent these bases are present; the specific manner in which it is employed is of less importance.

Because influence and power both play important roles in organizations, we will focus on each in this chapter. First, we will describe a number of techniques used by individuals to exert influence on others—to change their behavior in some manner. These include *persuasion, ingratiation, conformity, pressure, multiple requests,* and *guilt.* And as we will soon see, several of these can be highly effective. Second, we will turn to a discussion of *power.* Here we will describe some of the important bases on which it rests and the limits to which it can reach. Finally, we will offer a brief discussion of *organizational politics,* specific tactics often used by individuals to seize and hold power within an organization.

INFLUENCE: CHANGING THE BEHAVIOR OF OTHERS

How can we induce others to act in ways we desire? This is an age-old—and practical—question. Indeed, as noted recently by Sussmann and Vecchio, attempts by managers to "motivate" their subordinates (and so increase their productivity) can be viewed, basically, as attempts at social influence.[3] Further, this issue is one we all confront on a daily basis. Every day we seek to influence other persons—our friends, family, lovers, co-workers, subordinates. And we, in turn, are the recipients of similar attempts from these persons. As you already know, many tactics are employed for this purpose—everything from *persuasion,* which we considered in Chapter 7, to threats and even force (see Figure 13-1). But which of these techniques for exerting influence are most effective? How can they best be used? And why do they sometimes work and sometimes fail? Research on the nature of social influence has provided intriguing answers to these questions—answers that have important bearing on behavior in organizational settings. We will now summarize some of these findings for you.

Ingratiation: Liking as a Basis for Social Influence

One extremely common tactic for exerting influence rests on the following assumption: If other persons like us, they will be far more willing to comply with our wishes than if they don't like us. On the basis of this eminently reasonable suggestion, we often engage in a technique known as **ingratiation.** Basically, this involves attempts to influence others by first increasing their liking for us, and then, after this is accomplished, "hitting" them with various requests. Several procedures can be employed to enhance our appeal to other persons. For example, we can seek to convince them that we share their opinions or are like them in other respects. A large body of research findings suggests that perceived similarity

FIGURE 13-1   Tactics for Exerting Influence: The Range Is Great

Attempts to influence the behavior of others take many different forms! (Source: CROCK by Rechin and Parker © 1981 Field Enterprises, Inc. Courtesy of Field Newspaper Syndicate.)

is often an important basis for increased attraction.[4] Similarly, we can concentrate on demonstrating excellent task or job performance. In general, persons who perform at high levels are evaluated more favorably than those who perform less adequately. And such favorable evaluations seem to generalize, spreading from job or task performance to a wide range of personal characteristics.[5] By far the most common tactic of ingratiation, however, involves the communication of high personal regard to the target persons. This technique—which has been termed *other-enhancement*—frequently takes the form of flattery: exaggerated and undeserved praise of others, their work, or their traits. And often, it succeeds; praising the persons around us enhances their liking for us. In some cases, though, this tactic can backfire. If the recipients of flattery perceive that we are using it as a tool of social influence, they often react with anger rather than enhanced liking. For this reason, less direct techniques for communicating positive evaluations to others (e.g., hanging on their every word, encouraging them to tell us about themselves) are often more successful.[6] In any case, regardless of the precise tactics used, if ingratiation is carried out with skill and care, it can serve as an effective strategy for exerting influence over others.

Conformity Pressure: To Get Along, Often, You Must Go Along

Have you ever found yourself in a situation in which for some reason you stuck out like the proverbial sore thumb—where you were somehow different from the other persons present? If so, you are already familiar with pressures toward conformity. In such situations, we often feel tense and ill at ease. We don't like being different, and would prefer to be back in the comforting safety of the group. In order to reduce or avoid such feelings, therefore, most of us tend to act, speak, dress, and even think like others most of the time. The origins of such tendencies are not hard to discern. First as children and later as adults, we learn that being similar to others often results in praise, feelings of belonging, and other positive outcomes. In contrast, being different often leads to criticism, rejection, and other negative results. Given such experience, our strong tendencies toward conformity are hardly surprising.

As you probably know, however, such tendencies have often been the object of strong criticism in recent years. The 1960s and 1970s were decades during which individuals were urged to "do their own thing." Thus, conformity was strongly condemned as a totally negative force. Actually, though, it is quite useful in many situations. To see why this is so, simply consider the total chaos that would develop outside theaters or sports arenas if all the persons present did not form lines and wait their turn. Similarly, consider the impossibility of running a large office if all the employees used their own personal systems for filing and correspondence. In these and many other settings, a degree of uniformity in behavior is both efficient and rational. Thus, it seems reasonable to view conformity as negative or objectionable only when it proceeds to extremes or when it exists in situations where there is little justification for its presence (see Figure 13-2).

FIGURE 13-2   Conformity: Beneficial or Restrictive?

In some situations (left photo), conformity can play a useful role. In others (right photo), however, it seems excessive and unjustified. (Source: Photo [left] by Kirk Williamson; photo [right] © Frank Siteman MCMLXXXII.)

Regardless of the benefits they yield or the costs they incur, however, our pervasive tendencies toward "going along" provide the basis for an important form of social influence. Briefly, we can often induce others to act in ways we desire by suggesting that failure to do so will lead to their being viewed as "out of line." Since most persons wish to avoid such outcomes, they may then shift their behavior in the directions we recommend.

Conformity pressure is often used in this manner; indeed, you can probably spot it at work in any large organization. Usually, though, tendencies toward conformity operate in a self-enforcing manner. Individuals conform to accepted standards of behavior in their group or organizations (standards known as **norms**) without any outside urging to do so. In short, they go along voluntarily because they wish to avoid the real or imagined costs of doing otherwise. This important fact was first demonstrated several decades ago in a series of famous studies conducted by Solomon Asch.[7] In these experiments, subjects (college students) responded to a number of simple perceptual problems such as the one in Figure 13-3. That is, on each they indicated which of three comparison lines matched a standard line in length. Subjects made these judgments while in the presence of several other persons (usually six to eight) who also responded to the problems. Unknown to participants, however, *all these individuals were accomplices of the experimenter.* Thus, the stage was set for studying the impact of conformity pressure.

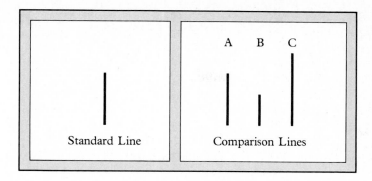

Standard Line

A B C

Comparison Lines

FIGURE 13-3 Asch's Line-Judging Task

An example of the type of problems used by Asch in his research. Subjects were to indicate which of the comparison lines (A, B, or C) matched the standard line in length. They gave their answers only after hearing the responses of several other persons—all accomplices of the experimenter.

On various prearranged occasions (twelve out of the eighteen problems), the accomplices offered answers that were clearly false. For example, referring to Figure 13-3, they unanimously stated that line B matched the standard, even though line A was clearly correct. On such trials, subjects faced a dilemma: should they go along with the group and report obviously false answers? Or should they "stick to their guns" and give what they felt were the correct responses? Surprisingly, most individuals yielded to the group pressure at least part of the time. Indeed, fully seventy-five percent of those tested in several separate studies went along with the accomplice's false answers at least once. These results have been confirmed in many later studies.[8] Together, the findings of these investigations point to the following unsettling conclusion: Many persons find it less disturbing to go along with conformity pressure than to speak up for what they know—or at least strongly believe—to be true. Thus, conformity pressure appears to be a powerful technique of social influence indeed.

Factors mediating the impact of conformity pressure: Group size, social support, and gender.   While the type of conformity first studied by Asch seems to be an all too common aspect of human behavior, even a moment's reflection suggests that it does not occur to the same degree in all settings or among all groups of persons. This observation, in turn, raises an interesting question: What factors determine the extent to which individuals yield to conformity pressure? Several decades of research on this issue have generated a long list of variables that play a role in this regard—factors that mediate the impact of conformity pressure upon individuals. Among the most important of these, however, are the following: *group size, social support,* and *gender.*

Common sense seems to suggest that the larger the group exerting conformity pressure upon us, the stronger our tendency to yield. Surprisingly, though, experimental findings have not confirmed this belief. Instead, it appears that up to some relatively small number (e.g., five), conformity rises with group size. Beyond this level, however, it may fail to show further increments.[9] The reason for this state of affairs seems to be as follows: as group size rises beyond five or six members, we no longer perceive all members as making independent judgments. Rather, they are seen as forming a unit, and we suspect collusion between them.[10] In other words, they are seen as working together to change our attitudes or our actions, and we often resist for this reason. Of course, if the persons involved are perceived as unrelated or as not communicating with one another, such effects will not occur. Then, our tendency to conform may in fact increase as group size rises.[11] In any case, what seems to be crucial is the number of independent sources of influence—not simply the actual number involved.

As you may recall, subjects in Asch's initial studies were exposed to conformity pressure from a *unanimous* group. That is, all the accomplices reported the same false judgment. Such conditions exist in many situations, for we often confront unified groups of opponents. (Circumstances of this type are far from rare in staff meetings within large organizations.) But in other cases, a crucial factor is different: We may have an *ally*—someone who shares our view of reality. Will this help us to resist conformity pressure? The findings of many studies indicate that it will. Specifically, when individuals learn that another member of a group shares their views or even simply disagrees with the majority, the tendency to yield decreases sharply.[11] Further, such effects appear to be at a maximum when the ally voices a dissenting opinion early—before the rest of the group has had a chance to "close ranks."[12] The practical implications of this latter finding are clear: if you ever find yourself in a situation in which pressures toward conformity are rising, speak out as quickly as possible. In such cases, delay can be very costly indeed.

A third factor often assumed to play a major role in yielding to social pressure is that of sex. Many early studies on this topic reported that women are much more susceptible to conformity pressure than men. And this finding, in turn, was interpreted as reflecting greater tendencies toward "submissiveness" or "dependency" among females. More recent evidence, however, has called these conclusions into question. For example, it appears that some early studies reporting greater conformity by females seem to have employed tasks or stimulus materials more familiar to males than females. Since it is well known that individuals are more willing to yield to conformity pressure when uncertain about their judgments or behavior than when they are confident about these, this factor may well have contributed to the greater conformity shown by females in some experiments. While this possibility has been questioned by some authorities, it is supported by the results of several studies.[13] For example, in one well-known experiment on this issue, Sistrunk and McDavid exposed male and female subjects to three types of items: ones more familiar to men than to women ("masculine"), ones more familiar to women than to men ("feminine"), and ones equally familiar to both sexes (neutral).[14] Subjects were then asked to make judgments about all three types in the presence of conformity pressure (the supposed responses of 200 other students). As you can see from Figure 13–4, results were quite revealing. On masculine items (ones more familiar to males) women showed greater conformity than men. On feminine items (ones more familiar to females) men showed greater conformity. And on neutral items, there were no differences between the sexes. These findings and those of similar studies suggest that there

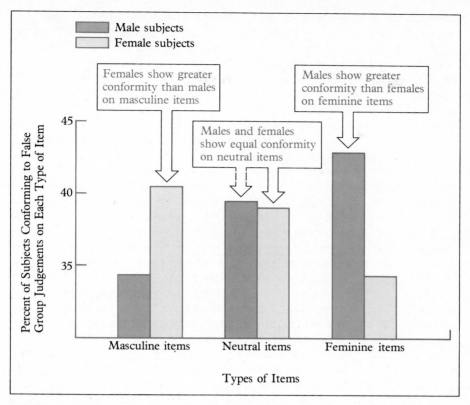

FIGURE 13-4   Sex Differences in Conformity: Apparent or Real?

In the study represented here, males conformed more than females on "feminine" items, females conformed more on "masculine" items, and the two sexes showed equal conformity on neutral items (ones equally familiar to both genders). (Source: Based on data from Sistrunk & McDavid, *Journal of Personality and Social Psychology*, 1971, *17*, 200-207.)

really are no overall differences between males and females in willingness to conform.[15] Rather, both sexes tend to yield to such pressures when they are uncertain about what constitutes correct or appropriate behavior. And both show less conformity when they are confident in these respects. Thus, it appears that this particular sex difference is much smaller in magnitude than was once believed and may actually be more imaginary than real.

Conformity pressure and organizational behavior.   We trust that our discussion so far has convinced you that pressures toward conformity are common and that their impact is affected by several different factors. As yet, though, we have not addressed a related question: Do such pressures operate in organizational settings? The answer, we believe, is yes—and with a vengeance. We base this general conclusion on two major grounds.

First, informal observation suggests that pressures toward conformity are present—and often pronounced—in many large organizations. As social settings, organizations often have clearly established norms governing a wide range of behaviors—everything from proper work procedures through informal rules about who can use certain equipment or facilities, and who is eligible for special "perks." Given the existence of such norms, it is only to be expected that individuals will often be exposed to subtle (or not-so-subtle) pressures to conform—to go along with the accepted status quo. As we're sure you already know, such pressures are quite common in large companies. Indeed, they often extend far beyond work-related activities, reaching even to such matters as how one should dress, where one should live, the kind of clubs one should join, and the types of hobbies one should adopt. While there is some indication that pressures of this type have decreased somewhat in recent years, they are still present and remain a potent force.

Second, a growing body of research evidence points to the important impact of conformity pressures upon many types of organizational behavior—especially work-related judgments and decisions.[16] As an example of this work, we will now describe a study conducted by Weiss and Shaw.[17]

These researchers hypothesized that subtle social pressure might strongly affect individuals' reactions to a specific job-related task. That is, they reasoned that subjects might report more favorable or less favorable reactions to a task depending on what they heard others say about it. In order to examine this possibility, Weiss and Shaw asked male students to view a training film supposedly designed to teach them how to perform an electrical assembly task. The film showed two persons working on this task, and in one version both commented favorably on it. In another version of the same basic film, these persons discussed only unrelated matters (e.g., spring break, the weather) and did not mention the task. Following exposure to one of these two films, subjects actually worked on the task themselves. Half performed an enriched version, designed to be both interesting and challenging. The remainder worked on an unenriched version that was somewhat less interesting. In a final phase of the study, all subjects rated the task on several dimensions. As you can see from Figure 13–5, results offered strong support for the hypothesis that social pressure would operate in this situation. That is, subjects exposed to positive statements about the task by others *did* report more favorable reactions to it than subjects not exposed to such comments. Further, this was true both for the enriched and unenriched versions.

These findings, those obtained in several related studies, and the informal evidence described above combine to support the following conclusion.[18,19] Pressures toward conformity are quite common in many organizational settings (see our discussion of *groupthink* in Chapter 11), and often exert powerful effects upon a wide range of work-related actions and judgments. Thus, this particular type of influence is a force well worth considering in our attempts to understand our own behavior, and that of the persons around us. (For a concrete example of pressures toward conformity within an organization, see the **CASE IN POINT** box on pages 430–431.)

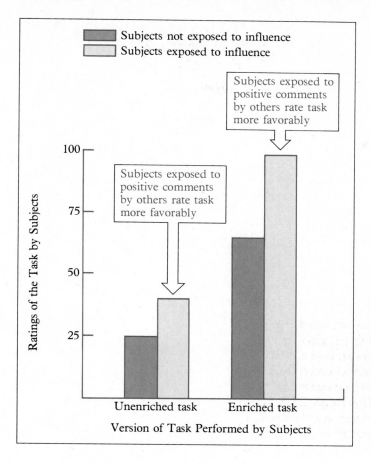

Subjects not exposed to influence
Subjects exposed to influence

Subjects exposed to positive comments by others rate task more favorably

Subjects exposed to positive comments by others rate task more favorably

FIGURE 13-5 Conformity Pressure: Its Impact on Work-Related Judgments

Subjects who heard two other persons make positive statements about a task later reported more favorable reactions to it than subjects never exposed to such influence. These findings suggest that many job-related decisions and judgments can be strongly affected by social influence. (Source: Based on data from Weiss & Shaw, *Organizational Behavior and Human Performance*, 1979, *24*, 126–140.)

Multiple Requests: The Old "One-Two Punch" Strikes Again

In many areas of life, persistence is an effective strategy. Contrary to the comments of perpetual cynics, hard work and repeated practice *do* often pay off in terms of goals reached and rewards attained. In this respect social influence is no exception to the general rule. Individuals seeking to exert influence over others often employ strategies based on multiple or repeated efforts. The basic idea behind such tactics is simple: one attempt at influence can serve as a kind of "setup" for another. That is, an initial request can help raise the chances that a second—and perhaps more important one—will succeed. Several different strategies based on this general approach exist. The ones you are most likely to encounter, though, are the **foot-in-the-door approach** and the **door-in-the-face tactic.**

"Gee, No One Told Me That!"

Today is your first day with the famous advertising firm of Fitch, Pitch, and Quod. You are very happy to have landed a job with the company, for it is one of the best and most respected in the business. For the next couple of weeks, you'll be working closely with Pam Clark, a junior copywriter like yourself, but one who has been with the firm for two years. Her task is that of showing you the ropes—making you part of the Fitch "family," so to speak. Pam is very pleasant, so you are sure things will work out well.

When you arrive, she shows you to your new office. The first thing you do is open a package you have been carrying and begin unrolling several large posters. They are among your favorites, and you want to put them up right away so you'll feel at home. When Pam sees what you are doing, she gives you a look of horror.

"For goodness sake, Marc, put those things away. They don't like posters around here. If you want to put up a picture or two that's okay. But they have to be conservative—old masters and things like that. And make sure they're in nice frames."

Hurriedly, you start to re-roll the posters. "Gee, thanks Pam. I had no idea. At my last job you could put up anything you wanted. I'll do what you say."

The rest of the morning passes pleasantly, and now it's time for lunch. Pam takes you to the company dining area, a plush and quiet room. When you enter, you spot a table near the window and start toward it. Pam grabs your arm and says, "No, Marc, not over there. That area's reserved for middle-level people. We have to stick to this section."

"But there's no sign or anything. How do you know?"

"Trust me. We have to stay over here where the junior people eat. At Fitch, Pitch, and Quod there are a lot of unwritten rules like this one. And you better learn them fast if you want to stay around."

After lunch there's a staff meeting during which the President, Kenneth W.

The foot-in-the-door: Small request first, large request second. There is an old saying that goes: "Give them an inch and they'll take a mile." What it refers to is this: individuals seeking to exert influence over others often begin with a small or trivial request. Then, once this has been granted, they escalate to a larger or more important one. Presumably, by following this strategy of escalation, they are more likely to get their way than would be true if they presented the large request cold. This tactic for gaining compliance with one's wishes is known as the *foot-in-the-door approach* and can be observed in many different settings. For example, door-to-door salespersons often start their pitches by asking poten-

Carlisle, describes recent developments and some new company policies. Near the end of the session, he asks for questions. When no one else raises their hand, you begin to raise yours. Again, Pam intervenes.

"No, Marc, not now."

"But he asked for questions."

"It doesn't matter. Junior staff *never* take the floor at these Monday afternoon meetings. Save it for Thursday. That meeting is less formal, and less top brass are present."

The rest of the day is filled with rules—most of them unwritten and also unspoken. There are guidelines for using the phone (never place calls yourself; always have your secretary do it for you); rules about proper dress (conservative, conservative, and more conservative); rules about handling correspondence; and even rules about socializing with other employees. As you travel home that evening, you try to sift through all these guidelines and requirements. You know that you'll soon master them all, but one fact is already clear: learning "the ropes" at Fitch, Pitch, and Quod is going to be even more demanding than you imagined. . . .   □

Questions:

1. Fitch, Pitch, and Quod has a large number of unwritten rules designed to govern employee behavior. Do you think the company is unique in this respect? Or do many other organizations have similar informal norms?
2. What would be the likely consequences if Marc failed to follow these unspoken rules?
3. Do you see any value in the existence of such norms or rules? Or are they merely an unnecessary irritation serving no useful function?

tial customers to accept a free gift, or even simply some literature about their products. Similarly, friends, co-workers, or subordinates wishing to extract a large favor from us (e.g., help with their work, substantial loans) may begin with a small request, and only then, after this is granted, present their larger one. The basic rationale behind such tactics is much the same: if an individual can somehow be induced to consent to a small request, the chances that he or she will also agree to a larger one are increased. But is this actually the case? Does the foot-in-the-door technique really work? That it does is suggested by the results of many separate experiments.

For example, in the first and most famous of these investigations, a study conducted by Freedman and Fraser, male experimenters telephoned several hundred homemakers.[20] The callers identified themselves as members of a consumer's group and in one condition—the *foot-in-the-door group*—they phoned twice. The first time they presented a small request: would the subject agree to answer a few simple questions about the kinds of soaps used at home? A few days later the same individual called again. This time, however, he made a truly gigantic request: would the subject permit him to send a five- or six-man crew to her home to conduct a thorough inventory of all the products on hand? Further, he explained that the men would require complete freedom to search the entire house—including all closets, cabinets, and drawers! In a second condition of the study—a *control group*—subjects were phoned only once, and presented with the large request cold. It was predicted that more persons in the foot-in-the-door group would agree to the complete household inventory, and results strongly confirmed this hypothesis. While only 22.2 percent of those in the control (one-request) group agreed, fully 52.8 percent of those in the foot-in-the-door condition consented! Thus, it appeared that the strategy of starting with a small request and then escalating to a large one was highly effective.

That the findings obtained by Freedman and Fraser cannot be attributed to some specific aspect of their study is suggested by the fact that similar results have been reported in many additional investigations. Further, the findings of these more recent studies indicate that the foot-in-the-door effect may be quite general in scope. It occurs when requests are made in person as well as on the phone.[21] And it has been observed in many geographic locations among a wide range of subjects, and with respect to many different requests.[22] As you might suspect, though, there do seem to be limits on its effectiveness. For example, it may fail when the target behaviors in question are very effortful or costly.[23] And it does not seem to operate with all types of persons.[24] In general, though, the foot-in-the-door strategy appears to be a simple and highly useful tactic for exerting influence on others.

The success of this strategy, in turn, raises an intriguing question: Why does it work? What accounts for its success? At present, it is difficult to offer a definite answer to these questions; the evidence needed for doing so is not yet available. One possibility that seems quite promising, though, is as follows. When individuals agree to a small request from another person, they experience subtle shifts in their *self-perceptions*. They begin to see themselves as the kind of person who does that sort of thing—the kind of person who complies with requests from others. As a result of these shifts in self-perceptions, they are more likely to agree to a second and even larger attempt at influence (see Figure 13-6).[25] Regardless of the precise mechanisms underlying its success, though, it is clear that the foot-in-the-door strategy can often be highly effective. Thus, it is one tactic for exerting influence you may wish to use on others—and to resist yourself—in the years ahead.

The door-in-the-face: Large request first, small request second.   While the technique of beginning with a small request and then moving to a larger one is

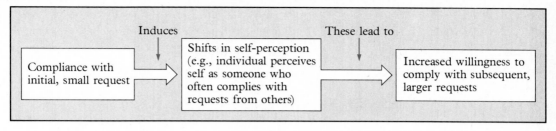

FIGURE 13-6   The Foot-in-the-Door: One Potential Underlying Mechanism

When individuals agree to a small request from another person, they may experience subtle shifts in their *self-perceptions*. For example, they may come to view themselves as the kind of person who does that type of thing—one who complies with requests from others. As a result of such shifts in self-perception, they may be more likely to agree to a second, larger request.

quite successful, an opposite strategy, too, may often succeed. That is, we can start by asking for a very large favor—one the target person is certain to refuse. And then we can shift to a smaller one—the favor we really wanted all along. For example, the following type of scene is quite common in many organizations. An individual in the sales department calls someone in the production unit and indicates that a specific order must be ready by the end of the week. The production manager utters an agonized groan and argues that it can't possibly be completed for at least a month. The caller then counters with a request that it be finished within ten days—what he wanted all along. The production manager, somewhat relieved, makes a tentative commitment to at least try to meet this deadline. (Please see Figure 13-7 for a more humorous example of this strategy.) The technique we have just described is often termed the *door-in-the-face* approach, and growing evidence suggests that it, too, can be quite effective as a means for getting our way. For example, in one study on this topic, Cialdini and his associates stopped college students on the street and presented them with a gigantic request: Would they agree to serve as a nonpaid counselor two hours a week for a two-year period?[26] As you can probably guess, none complied with this suggestion. When the experimenters reduced the magnitude of their request considerably, though, fully fifty percent agreed. (The smaller, "fall-back" proposal involved taking a group of juvenile delinquents on a single two-hour trip to the zoo.) In contrast, a much lower proportion of individuals approached agreed to this small request when it was presented cold—without the first, giant request (16.7 percent). Similar results have been obtained in additional studies conducted in other settings, and with other requests.[27] Thus, it appears that the door-in-the-face approach, too, may often be an effective means of exerting influence on others.

One basis for the success of this strategy may involve pressures toward *reciprocal concessions*. When an individual who starts out with a very large request backs down to a much smaller one, the persons receiving these requests may feel compelled to make a corresponding concession. After all, the requester has agreed to

FIGURE 13-7   The Door-in-the-Face Technique

One technique that is often effective in influencing others is the *door-in-the-face approach.* This involves beginning with a very large request and then, after this is rejected, backing down to a smaller one—the one actually desired all along. (Source: © King Features Syndicate, Inc., 1972. World Rights Reserved.)

meet them halfway, so the least they can do is reciprocate. For this reason, they may become more willing to comply with the second, scaled-down request.

The foot-in-the-door and the door-in-the-face: Can they both succeed?   At first glance, it might seem that the foot-in-the-door and the door-in-the-face techniques are contradictory in nature. After all, how can starting with a small request and shifting to a larger one *and* starting with a large one and then backing down both result in increased compliance? The answer lies in a simple fact: Because they are based on different underlying mechanisms, the two techniques can both be effective, but under somewhat different conditions. For example, in order to succeed, the door-in-the-face approach must involve two requests by the same person. If, instead, these requests are presented by different individuals, the effect fails to occur.[28] This is not surprising; if an individual has refused a large request from one person, there is no reason why he or she should experience pressure to make a concession to a different person. In contrast, the foot-in-the-door technique seems to work quite well even when different persons make the first and second request. Again, this is as we might expect. If an individual has experienced shifts in self-perception as a result of agreeing to an initial small request, these changes may well carry over to a new situation—one in which a larger request is presented by another person.

In sum, both the foot-in-the-door and the door-in-the-face techniques may represent effective means of exerting influence over others—means for getting them to behave as we wish. However, each may work best under somewhat different circumstances.

Guilt: Another Technique for Influencing Others

Have you ever harmed another person (e.g., hurt his or her feelings) without intending to do so? And have you ever engaged in some behavior you knew was wrong and which you later regretted? If so, you are already familiar with the impact of **guilt.** These feelings exert several different effects upon us. Most are familiar and far from surprising. For example, pangs of guilt are quite unpleasant and can threaten our peace of mind. One of these effects, however, is closely related to this discussion of influence. Briefly, feelings of guilt often lead us to engage in attempts to make amends for our "bad" behavior. And one important way of accomplishing this goal is that of doing things for other persons—consenting to their requests for favors, helping them with their work, and so on. In short, feelings of guilt can often increase our susceptibility to influence from others, especially those we have harmed or disappointed.

As you probably know from your own experience, many persons are aware of this link between guilt and influence, and attempt to turn it to their advantage. Thus, they seek to affect the behavior of others through tears, playing the martyr, and similar tactics. You may well meet such tactics in work settings in the years ahead. For example, when reprimanded by their supervisor, some employees burst into tears, or at least look very hurt. In this way, they seek to induce guilt and remorse in their critic and so cause him or her to "back off"—or perhaps do something nice for them to make up for this harsh treatment. Similarly, salespersons courting a major customer may hint at the possibility that if they don't close the deal, they will lose their bonus, or even their job. And this will wreak havoc on their career, or their lovely family. In such cases, the salespersons involved hope that the desire to avoid guilt over causing such negative outcomes will help push the customers into placing an order.

Direct evidence for the effectiveness of guilt as a technique for exerting influence has been obtained in a number of interesting studies.[29] In these experiments participants were first induced to experience guilt in several ways (e.g., they were made to knock over piles of carefully arranged index cards or to break a complex piece of equipment). Following such experience, their willingness to comply with requests from various persons (the ones they harmed, unrelated strangers) was measured. In almost all cases, persons induced to feel guilty showed greater acceptance of influence than those in control groups not made to experience guilt. Further, such effects appeared to be quite general in nature, spreading to persons not directly involved in the situation as well as to the "victims" of their misdeeds.[30] In sum, it appears that guilt is indeed a highly effective tactic for exerting influence over others. Before you decide to use it yourself, though, please consider the following point: guilt depends for its success on the induction of highly unpleasant feelings among others. Thus, the costs associated with its use are high. For this reason, we believe that it is one influence tactic you should be quite reluctant to use.

Tactics of Social Influence: A Concluding Note of Caution

Throughout this discussion we have emphasized the success and effectiveness of various strategies for exerting influence. In an important sense, this is fully appropriate; the tactics we have described *do* work in many cases. It is also important to note, however, that this is not always so. Human beings possess great resistance to influence from others. Thus, they can often withstand even highly skilled and carefully executed attempts to change their attitudes or behavior. Several factors contribute to this ability to stand firm in the face of pressure. First, there is what we might term sheer "behavioral inertia." Individuals often possess well-established patterns of behavior—patterns they have acquired and practiced for years. Changing these is far from an easy matter. Second, they often have strong and entrenched views on various issues. Again, producing shifts in these is a difficult chore. Third, and perhaps of greatest importance, most individuals know all about the tactics of influence we have described. They have had direct experience with them and know how they operate. And in terms of resisting influence, it appears, *forewarned* is indeed often *forearmed*.

This is not to say, of course, that attempts at influence are doomed to failure. On the contrary, they do often succeed. As is true of any tool, though, they are most appropriately used in certain situations. In particular, it appears that the strategies of influence we have described are most likely to succeed when the target persons are uncertain as to what constitutes appropriate behavior, when the changes we are attempting to induce are neither very costly nor effortful, and when the behaviors we seek to alter are not deeply entrenched. Under these circumstances—which do often exist—tactics of social influence can be highly successful. Where these conditions do not prevail, though, they may meet with much more limited success. Our closing words, then, are these. Before you decide to use specific influence tactics in your own life, examine the situation carefully. Then, proceed with caution. And above all, do not expect too much. (For information on the extent to which various tactics of social influence are actually used in organizational settings, please see the **"FOCUS"** box on pages 438–439.)

POWER: BEYOND INFLUENCE OR PRESSURE

Power. The very word itself is enough to make our pulses beat faster. Indeed, for many persons, it conjures up images of titanic struggles and heroic battles, all stemming from the pursuit of this elusive goal. But what, precisely, is power? And why do people seek it? As we have already noted, power can be viewed as lying along the same continuum of control over others as social influence, but much farther toward the high end or extreme. Thus, as noted recently by Grimes, power can be defined as the ability to control the actions of others to promote one's own goals even without their consent, against their will, and without their knowledge or understanding.[31] Of course, power does not always involve such coercion; often it is willingly granted to those who possess it, and simply involves the ability to mobilize resources, information, and energy to reach some goal.[32] Even in such cases, though, it remains a potent, seductive, and potentially dangerous force.

In this discussion, we will address several basic issues relating to power. First, we will examine the *bases* from which it stems—the foundations on which power rests. Here, both sources of individual and group (or subunit) power will be considered. Second, we will focus on the *limits* of this process—the extent to which it can affect human behavior, and some techniques for reducing this impact. Finally, we will examine the topic of *organizational politics*—strategies for seizing, holding, and exerting power within organizations.

Individual Power: Some Basic Foundations

The ability to change others' behavior regularly, and even against their will, is truly impressive. But how does it arise? In short, what foundations underlie this capacity? Scholars who have studied the nature of human power have called attention to many factors that seem to play a role in this regard.[33] Perhaps the most useful framework for understanding the bases of power, though, is one offered by French and Raven some years ago.[34] This theory focuses on five distinct sources, and we will now consider each of these in turn.

Reward power: Control of valued resources.   The first and in some ways most important source of power noted by French and Raven involves the ability to control valued resources. Generally, an individual able to determine who gains access to various **rewards,** and when, has considerable power over all persons seeking these rewards. The reason for this is simple: such persons can attain the positive outcomes they desire only to the extent that the controlling individual permits them to do so. Individuals possessing this type of power can, therefore, often get others to literally "jump through hoops." This is because they can arrange reinforcement contingencies so that persons seeking the rewards they control can gain them only by behaving in ways desired by the power-holder. (Recall our discussion of operant conditioning in Chapter 3.) The importance of gaining control over valued resources is well understood both in political and business circles. It is for this reason that individuals will often struggle long and hard to win election, gain committee chairs, or even a controlling interest in the company (see Figure 13-8). Once enthroned in these key positions, they can determine who gets what rewards at what times—and so exert tremendous power over others. In organizations, of course, those who control such resources as raises, promotions, desirable work assignments, recognition, or access to special "perks" possess reward power. And as you will undoubtedly discover in the years ahead, they frequently use it to advance their own ends.

Coercive power: Control over unpleasant outcomes.   The other side of the coin from reward power involves the ability to inflict punishment or aversive outcomes on others—a capacity known as **coercive power.** Basically, this is a form of power resting mainly on fear: If individuals do not behave as the controlling person wishes, they will be made to suffer unpleasant outcomes or events. Within organizations, such power often involves the ability to fire or demote indi-

FOCUS ON BEHAVIOR

Influence on the Job: Who Does It, How, and Why?

As we have seen, many techniques for exerting influence on others exist. Further, research evidence indicates that many of these work—they are quite effective in changing the behavior of target persons. But suppose you visited many different organizations; would you actually see the techniques we have described in operation? And if so, who would be doing the influencing, who would be the targets of such attempts, and why would they be performed? Revealing answers to these complex questions have recently been provided by Kipnis, Schmidt, and Wilkinson.[35]

These researchers began by asking 165 individuals employed in managerial roles in organizations to describe successful attempts at influence in which they had succeeded in getting a boss, subordinate, or co-worker to do something they wanted. Careful analysis of subjects' replies to these questions were then used to develop descriptions of a large number of influence tactics. These statements were then administered to a large sample consisting of 754 persons employed in organizations. Participants were asked to rate (on five-point scales) how frequently they had used each tactic to influence another person at work—either their boss, a subordinate, or a co-worker. Further, they were asked to indicate *why* they had engaged in these influence attempts.

The results of the investigations were very informative. First, it was found that most influence tactics described by subjects could be divided into eight basic categories. These are summarized in Table 13-1, and as you can readily see, many reflect the strategies we have already described. Thus, these findings suggest that basic forms of influence are quite common in organizations and that employees make frequent use of them.

Second, as might be expected, individuals reported using somewhat different tactics when seeking to influence their bosses, their subordinates, or their co-workers. When attempting to influence their bosses, they reported relying largely on tactics such as persuasion and logical argument. In contrast, when attempting to change the behavior of their subordinates, they often made use of orders or threats of sanctions. Still other tactics, such as ingratiation, offering a reciprocal exchange of benefits, or appeals to higher levels in the organization were used about equally, regardless of the status of the target person.

Finally, subjects reported using different tactics depending on the reasons behind their attempts at influence. The five major reasons for engaging in such attempts were as follows: attaining assistance with one's own job, getting others to do *their* jobs, improving another's performance, initiating change, and attaining personal benefits (e.g., promotions, raises). Each of these reasons was accompanied by the use of somewhat different tactics. Thus, when subjects sought personal assistance, they often relied on ingratiation. When they wished to improve others' performance, they made use of orders (assertiveness). And when they sought to gain acceptance for new ideas, they stressed persuasion and rational argument.

Taken as a whole, the findings reported by Kipnis and his colleagues offer the following picture of influence within organizations. First, contrary to popular belief, such attempts do *not* flow mainly from the top down to subordinates. Instead, they appear to originate at all levels and to be directed up, down, and laterally. Second, while influence attempts are quite common, the specific types used vary with the status of the target and the reasons for seeking influence. Thus, individuals appear to

TABLE 13-1   Influence in Organizational Settings: Its Basic Forms

A recent investigation conducted with several hundred employees at a large number of organizations indicates that influence attempts in work settings fall into eight major categories. These are summarized here. (Source: Based on information from Kipnis, Schmidt, & Wilkinson, *Journal of Applied Psychology,* 1980, *65,* 440-52.)

CATEGORY OF INFLUENCE	DESCRIPTION/EXAMPLES
Assertiveness	One person orders another to do something, or demands that it be done
Ingratiation	One person flatters another, acts humbly toward him/her, makes this person feel important
Rationality	Reasons for requests are carefully explained; detailed plans are prepared; logic used as basis for persuasion
Sanctions	Salary increase promised or denied; target threatened with loss of promotion for failure to comply
Exchange of Benefits	One person offers to do something for another if that person will return the favor; one individual reminds other of past help he/she has provided
Upward Appeal	A formal appeal for support is made to higher organizational levels; the support of higher-ups in the company is obtained
Blocking	One person ignores other or stops being friendly; work slowdown is threatened or instituted
Coalitions	Individual seeking to exert influence obtains support of co-workers or subordinates to back up requests

be quite flexible in this regard, striving to choose the tactics best suited to a given purpose. In conclusion, we wish to leave you with the following thought. Influence is both a basic and important fact of life in organizations. Thus, if you wish to survive and prosper in them, you should seek to understand its use, its benefits, and its potential costs.   □

"*Sans teeth, sans eyes, sans taste, sans everything. But a fifty-one-percent controlling interest!*"

FIGURE 13–8   Control over Valued Resources: A Key Form of Power in Organizations

Many persons are willing to go through quite a bit—or wait a long time—to gain reward power over others. (Source: Drawing by Ed Fisher; © 1980 The New Yorker Magazine, Inc.)

viduals, lower their pay, hold them up to public ridicule, or provide them with unfavorable references. And outside organizations, it can involve a much wider range of threats—anything from detailed tax audits to prison, torture, or even death. Not surprisingly, the open use of coercive power is generally frowned upon in organizational settings, and for good reason. First, exposing employees to strong punishment can often cause them to nurse a grudge against their manager or the company. Needless to say, this can be devastating to morale. Similarly, few persons enjoy inflicting suffering on others, and vivid exposure to such outcomes is intimately involved in the exercise of coercive power. For these and other reasons, such power is generally used as infrequently as possible in organizations. And when it *is* enforced, it is often concealed behind a "velvet glove." Even then, however, it is readily recognized by most persons and can exert powerful effects upon many aspects of their organizational behavior.

Legitimate power: Control based on consensus.   Have you ever seen a movie in which thousands kneel while their representatives beg some individual to accept the crown (see Figure 13–9)? If so, you are already familiar with a third major basis for power in human affairs. In some situations, individuals believe that particular persons have a legitimate claim to positions of authority over them, and willingly offer them power for this reason. As we have just suggested, one basis for such beliefs involves heredity, and claims of an especially "noble" birth. But other reasons for extending **legitimate power** to some persons exists as well. For example, in certain cultures, such power comes with age—it is widely agreed that older persons should be in charge. Similarly, in many organizations, employees accept the view that those above them in the corporate hierarchy have a legitimate basis for exercising authority. Regardless of its specific source, however, legitimate power is, perhaps, the type that ruffles fewest feathers. After all, most of the persons subject to it believe that it is somehow justified. As a result, they may follow directives from persons possessing such power quite readily, and with a minimum of resentment.

FIGURE 13-9 Legitimate Power: Authority by Consensus

As shown here, power sometimes stems from the belief, held by many persons, that certain individuals have a legitimate right to exercise authority over them. (Source: UPI Photo.)

Referent power: Control based on attraction. Some individuals are greatly admired by others. Certain characteristics they possess, such as a highly attractive appearance, great success in some endeavor, or considerable personal charm, lead many persons they meet—and even ones they never encounter—to identify with them. These positive reactions, in turn, can serve as a fourth major basis for power. When individuals admire someone and wish to be like that person in some respect, they are also often willing to change their behavior in accordance with the wishes of their hero or heroine. As a result, the persons fortunate enough to exert such attraction often gain the capacity to exert considerable power as well. Dramatic examples of such **referent power** in operation are provided by popular political leaders, sports figures, stars in the entertainment field, and the leaders of various social movements (e.g., civil rights). But this type of power can also be observed in organizations, where popular executives often inspire great admiration—and willingness to obey—among their staffs. In short, where power is concerned, being liked can often yield handsome dividends.

Expert power: Control based on knowledge. The final source of power considered by French and Raven is one we have all encountered: power based on expertise. When we visit a physician, we generally obey every request by this person without hesitation. Similarly, if we consult an attorney, plumber, or architect, we tend to follow *their* recommendations on matters relating to their fields. The reason for our willingness to accept influence from such persons is obvious: we believe that they possess expert knowledge in some area, and feel that it is in our best interests to accept their advice. In short, we willingly assign them power to affect our behavior—power based on their expertise. Such **expert power** is readily visible in many organizations. Individuals possessing expert knowledge in some area (e.g., the chief chemist, head engineer, top accountant) can exert strong effects upon the behavior of many other persons. Indeed, they can often wield power even over persons nominally higher than themselves in the status hierarchy. Such effects are generally limited in scope, however. In contrast to several other types of power we have considered, expert power is often quite specific, extending only to behaviors or policies closely related to the expert's knowledge. Of course, some "spill-over" occurs, so that persons possessing expertise in one area can sometimes exert influence outside their specialties. (Advertisers try to capitalize on such effects by hiring famous athletes or movie stars to recommend products.) In most cases, though, expert power is restricted in its domain.

The various bases of power: Interdependent, not independent. Before concluding this discussion of various bases of power, we should note that the five types described above are by no means independent. On the contrary, they can—and do—exist in various combinations. Moreover, the presence and use of one type of power can strongly affect the others. For example, use of coercive power can often reduce referent power; people usually dislike those who punish them. Similarly, because human beings are often attracted to high-status persons, the presence of legitimate power can often increase referent power. And referent power, in turn, can enhance both expert and legitimate power because individuals often seem to assume that attractive persons possess many other positive traits as well.[36] In short, different types of power are far from independent.

An interesting demonstration of this important fact has recently been provided by Greene and Podsakoff.[37] These researchers asked employees working in a paper plant to rate the reward, punishment, expert, referent, and legitimate power of their managers on two separate occasions. The first set of ratings was obtained while an incentive pay plan was in effect. (The plan was based on evaluations by the managers, and through it employees could obtain as much as a twenty-percent bonus each month.) The second set of ratings was gathered after this pay plan was terminated. Greene and Podsakoff predicted that removing the incentive plan would reduce the managers' reward power and that this would strongly affect ratings of their punishment, reference, and legitimate power. Only expert power was expected to remain unchanged. As you can see from Figure 13–10, results offered strong support for these predictions. Ratings of the managers' punishment power increased following termination of the incentive pay plan, while ratings of their reward, referent, and legitimate power all decreased. Similar changes were *not* observed in a second plant where the pay plan was retained. These findings and those of other studies suggest that changes in one base of power can strongly affect others.[38] Thus, while power can stem from many different sources, in actual practice, these tend to become intricately linked.

Group or Subunit Power: A Structural Approach

So far in our discussion of the bases of power we have concentrated on power as it is held by individuals. Within organizations, though, power can also be wielded by subunits (e.g., various departments). In short, one subunit can possess the ability to determine or change the activities of several others. For example, in many organizations, the finance or accounting departments are very powerful: all other units must work through them in one way or another. But what factors contribute to such power? How, in short, does a given subunit obtain power over others within the organization? Intriguing answers to these questions are provided by Hickson and his colleagues in the **strategic-contingencies theory** of intraorganizational power.[39]

Briefly, this theory suggests that subunits gain power when the activities of other subunits are dependent upon them. That is, they become powerful to the degree that other subunits are dependent upon inputs from them for performing their work. The theory further indicates that such dependencies develop when three conditions prevail: (1) the powerful subunit copes effectively with environmental uncertainty (e.g., with changes in market conditions); (2) this subunit is high in *workflow centrality*—its activities strongly affect the final outputs of the organization (high *immediacy*), and it is linked to the workflows of many other subunits (high *pervasiveness*); and (3) no other unit within the organization or outside it can perform this subunit's activities (*substitutability* is low). Under such

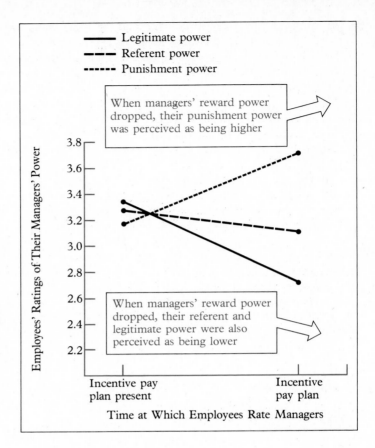

FIGURE 13-10   Different Bases
of Power: Evidence for their
Interdependence

When managers in a large paper
plant experienced a reduction in
reward power (an incentive pay
plan was canceled), their
subordinates perceived them as
changing in other forms of power
as well. Specifically, they were seen
as higher in punishment (coercive)
power, but lower in referent and
legitimate power. These findings
suggest that various bases of power
are interdependent. (Source: based
on data from Greene & Podsakoff,
Academy of Management Journal,
1981, *24,* 527–542.)

conditions, the theory suggests, a given subunit will gain power within the organization (see Figure 13–11).

Support for these proposals has been obtained in several studies. For example,
Hinings, Hickson, Pennings, and Schneck found that within several different
companies (breweries in Canada and the U.S., division of a container manufacturer), the higher the ability of a given subunit to cope with uncertainty, the
greater its workflow centrality; and the lower its substitutability, the higher was
its perceived power within the organization.[40] Moreover, only when all three of
these conditions were favorable was a given subunit perceived as dominant in
power.

In short, the strategic-contingencies theory calls attention to a crucial fact
about organizational power: Often it can stem from *structural* variables as well as
behavioral ones. And in many cases, it can reside in subunits rather than individuals. (Please see Chapter 15 for further discussion of organizational structure and
its impact on organizational effectiveness.)

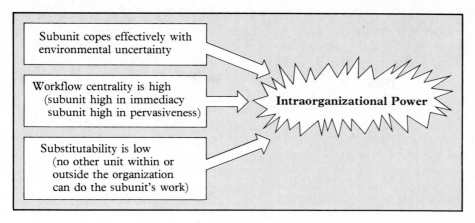

FIGURE 13-11   The Strategic-Contingencies Theory: Structural Determinants of Organizational Power

According to the *strategic-contingencies theory,* subunits within a given organization acquire power when other subunits are dependent upon inputs from them. Such conditions are most likely to develop when a given subunit (1) copes effectively with environmental uncertainty, (2) is high in workflow centrality, and (3) when no other unit can perform its work (substitutability is low).

Power: Testing Its Limits

Suppose that one day your boss called you into his office and made the following statement: "Listen, we've got a load of chemicals I want to get rid of. Make arrangements to dump them in the river. They're pretty dangerous, so be sure it's done at night when no one will notice." What would you do in this situation? Would you obey your boss's orders? If you did, this would be understandable, if not totally defensible. After all, he has a great deal of power over you. He controls your salary, your promotions, and even your very job. Thus, if you knuckled under and followed his directions, there would be strong reasons for doing so.

Now, imagine the same scene with one major difference: the person asking you to dump the dangerous chemicals is not your boss. Rather, it is the head of the Research Department—an individual with lots of status but no direct control over you. Would you obey in this case? Your immediate reaction is probably "No way!" While this person is an expert, she has no control over your rewards, so why should you comply with her wishes? This is a comforting answer but one, we're afraid, that can be questioned. Growing research evidence suggests that while power does have its limits, they are far harder to establish than one might suspect. Thus, even authority figures possessing relatively little power seem capable of inducing many persons to perform their bidding—and in ways we never predict. A dramatic illustration of this fact is provided by a famous and controversial series of studies conducted by Stanley Milgram.[41,42]

In these studies Milgram wanted to determine whether individuals would follow an experimenter's commands that they inflict considerable pain and suffering on another person—a totally innocent victim. In order to test this hypothesis, he informed subjects that they were taking part in a study of the effects of punishment on learning. Their task was then described as that of delivering electric shocks to another person (actually an accomplice of the researcher) each time he made an error in a simple learning task. These shocks were to be delivered by means of thirty numbered switches on the equipment shown in Figure 13-12. Further, subjects were told to move to the next higher switch each time the learner made an error. Since the first switch supposedly delivered a shock of fifteen volts, it was clear that if the learner made many errors, he would soon be receiving powerful jolts. Indeed, according to the labels on the equipment the final shock would consist of 450 volts! In reality, of course, the accomplice never received any shocks during the experiment. The only real shock ever used was a mild pulse given to the subjects from button 3 to convince them that the equipment was real.

During the session, the learner (i.e., the accomplice) made many errors. Thus, subjects soon found themselves facing a dilemma. Should they continue "punishing" this person with what seemed to be painful shocks, or refuse to participate? The experimenter pressured them to choose the former path, for whenever they hesitated, he made such remarks as "Please go on" or "It is absolutely essential that you continue."

FIGURE 13-12   Studying the Limits of Power

The photo on the left shows the apparatus used by Milgram in his famous experiments on obedience. The photo on the right shows the experimenter (wearing a lab coat) and a subject (standing at the back) attaching electrodes to the learner's (accomplice's) wrists. Please note: this person never received any real shocks during the study. (Source: From the film *Obedience,* distributed by New York University Film Library. Copyright © 1965 by Stanley Milgram. Reprinted by permission of the copyright holder.)

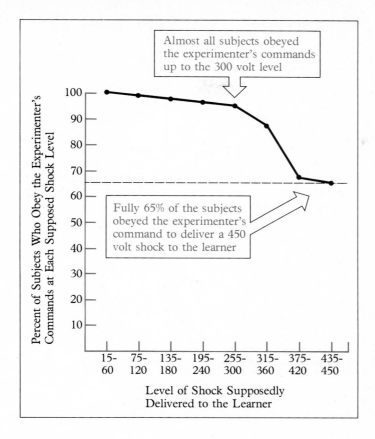

FIGURE 13-13 Power: An Unsettling Demonstration of Its Potential Impact

When ordered to deliver shocks of increasing intensity to another person (actually an accomplice of the experimenter), many individuals complied. In fact, fully 65 percent proceeded through the entire series, to the 450-volt level. (Source: Based on data from Milgram, *Journal of Abnormal and Social Psychology*, 1963, 371–378.)

Since subjects were all volunteers and were paid for their participation in advance, you might predict that they would be highly resistant to these demands. Yet, in reality, fully sixty-five percent showed total obedience. That is, they proceeded through the entire shock series to the final 450 volt level (see Figure 13–13). In contrast, subjects in a control group who were not exposed to such commands generally used only very mild shocks during the session. That these results were not due to special conditions prevailing in Milgram's laboratory is indicated by the fact that similar findings were soon reported in other studies, including ones conducted in several different countries (e.g., Canada, W. Germany, Britain, Jordan).[43]

The surprising nature of Milgram's findings raises an important question: why, precisely, do subjects obey in such situations? The answer seems to lie in the fact that the experimenter, though powerless to reward or punish them directly, appears to possess other sources of power. Dressed in a white lab coat, associated with a prestigious institution (Milgram worked on the campus of Yale University), and addressed by the title "Dr.," he seems to hold considerable expertise and legitimacy. And these sources of power seem sufficient to permit him to

FROM THE MANAGER'S PERSPECTIVE

Organizational Politics: Some General Strategies for Seizing, Holding, and Using Power

Modern organizations are highly political in nature. Indeed, in the 1980s they can be viewed as consisting largely of individuals or groups engaged in perpetual "jockeying" for influence and power. The rules of this game, which is generally known as **organizational politics,** are complex and ever changing. But the stakes are so high that sooner or later, nearly everyone chooses to play. As you might guess, the motives behind such political maneuvering vary greatly. Some individuals participate largely for personal gain; others take part for the good of their organization or department. Regardless of the motivation tapped, however, a wide range of tactics are employed. These include virtually every strategy of influence we have already considered and many others that are even more Machiavellian in nature (e.g., the spread of false rumors, the planting of misleading information, backstabbing, "dirty tricks").[45] Given the importance of the rewards involved (and the intensity with which such politics often proceed), we wish we could arm you with a firm set of guidelines for "winning"—for getting your share of power, holding on to it, and using it to your best advantage. Unfortunately, this goal is easier to state than attain. The situations involved are complex, and

little firm evidence about the relative effectiveness of various strategies currently exists. What we *can* do, though, is provide you with a summary of some general techniques that are consistent with what we know about power and influence, and so seem quite promising. Please note that in our list, we have tried to avoid those tactics that seem most questionable from an ethical point of view (e.g., the Machiavellian strategies mentioned above).[46] While several of these may be highly successful, they involve infringements on the rights of others or violations of basic principles of justice, fairness, and equity. Thus, we cannot in good faith recommend them to you. One final point: please regard the techniques we *do* list below cautiously. They are only suggestions, and we can offer no guarantee that they will always (or even usually) work. Since you are likely to encounter most in the years ahead, though, it is probably useful to become familiar with them for this reason.

First impressions count. A large body of research supports the belief that first impressions *are* important. Thus, you should always try to look good on any project right from the start. And of course, always try to be at your best when meeting important people for the first time.

---

strongly affect subjects' behavior. That the high level of obedience observed by Milgram and other researchers did in fact stem from these factors is indicated by the following evidence: when such research is moved away from high-prestige settings, and the experimenter's apparent legitimacy is reduced in other ways, compliance with his commands is greatly decreased. In short, removing these apparent sources of power goes a long way toward eliminating the experimenter's impact.

Taken as a whole, the research conducted by Milgram and other scientists points to important conclusions—ones we wish to call to your attention. First, this work suggests that reward and coercive power are not essential for producing major changes in the behavior of others; expertise and legitimacy may often be suf-

Cultivate a halo. As we noted in Chapters 6 and 8, "halo effects" are both real and powerful. Thus, if you can equip yourself with a positive image, it will strongly affect others' evaluations of your work. And this can be a big boost to your career.

Count on reciprocity. As a general rule, it is helpful to do favors for others. Once you do, you can remind them of this aid in subtle ways and then call in these IOU's at times when they will do you most good.

Learn to be persuasive. Forceful arguments eloquently stated are often quite effective in swaying others. And as we noted earlier (p. 000), they are especially useful when dealing with one's superiors. Thus, you should take pains to develop your persuasive skills to the highest degree possible.

Know the norms. It is important to know and understand both the formal and informal norms governing behavior in your organization. Once you are familiar with them, you can often use them to exert conformity pressure on others. That is, you can alter their behavior in ways useful to your ends by noting that these changes are consistent with—or required by—existing norms. And be careful to avoid situations in which your interests and these norms are at odds. When they are, you are almost certain to lose.

Develop an image of power. People often respond to the illusion of power just as strongly as they do to actual power itself. Thus, you should concentrate on appearing to have more power than you really possess. But be careful not to go too far; if you claim too much, your image may become transparent and do you little good.

Cultivate a reputation for expertise. Reward power, coercive power, and legitimate power must usually be granted from above. Thus, it is hard to attain these by yourself. But expertise can be cultivated without outside help. Thus, you should make every effort to add to your reputation in this regard. The outcome may be a substantial boost to your power.

Being liked is a plus. Referent power, too, can be nurtured. Through careful use of ingratiation and related techniques, you can often substantially raise your level of attractiveness to key persons in your organization. And being liked by such persons can add appreciably to your forward momentum. □

Good Luck!

---

ficient. (Recall our example on p. 445. On the basis of Milgram's findings, we might predict that you would follow the orders of the Head of Research, even though she has no direct power over you.) Second, it appears that often, even true expertise and legitimacy are unnecessary. If powerless persons can convey the illusion of possessing such characteristics, this in itself may be sufficient. This fact is well known to many "con artists," and also to the "operators" common in many organizations. Finally, on a more positive note, this research indicates that the impact of such pseudo-authorities *can* be countered. All that is needed is some means of punching holes in their aura of legitimacy. (In this regard, the presence of only one or two defiant persons who refuse to obey can be highly effective.[44]) Of course, we should hasten to add that such tactics do not apply when authority figures actually possess legitimacy and expertise, or when they control important resources. In such cases, the bases for their power are real, and our best word of advice must be: Deal with such persons cautiously—the career you save may be your own! (Please see the **"PERSPECTIVE"** box on pages 448–449 for a discussion of practical techniques for enhancing your own organizational power.)

SUMMARY

Individuals often wish to change the behavior of others in ways that are beneficial to their interests. Many techniques for exerting such **influence** exist. Flattery and *ingratiation* are effective in this regard. *Conformity pressure*—suggestions that others must behave in certain ways to avoid being out of line with existing norms—can also strongly affect behavior. Strategies based on *multiple requests,* too, are quite successful. Two of these are the foot-in-the-door approach and the door-in-the-face strategy. A final technique for changing others' behavior involves the induction of *guilt.* When people experience such feelings, they seek to make amends for their past wrongs by doing something for the victim. This, in turn, may increase their susceptibility to social influence. Influence is common in organizational settings, but the specific tactics used vary with the status of the target persons and the specific reasons for seeking to affect their behavior.

When one individual can affect the behavior of others regularly, strongly, and even against their will, he or she is said to possess **power** over them. Such power stems from several different bases, including control over rewards or punishments, expertise, legitimacy, and personal attractiveness. These sources combine and interact, so that possession or use of one type of power often affects the possession or use of others. Subunits or departments within an organization can also possess power. Power of this type often stems from aspects of organizational structure (e.g., workflow centrality). Research findings suggest that often even relatively powerless sources of authority can be highly successful in changing the behavior of many persons. Modern organizations are highly political in nature. Thus, growing attention has recently been directed to *organizational politics*—tactics for seizing, holding, and using power in organizational settings.

KEY TERMS

COERCIVE POWER   Power stemming from control over punishment and other aversive consequences. The use of coercive power is generally discouraged in organizations.

CONFORMITY PRESSURE   A tactic of social influence based on the suggestion that if individuals do not behave in certain ways, they will be in violation of existing social norms.

DOOR-IN-THE-FACE TECHNIQUE   A strategy for exerting influence based on multiple requests. First, target persons are presented with a large request and then, when they refuse this, a smaller request is made.

EXPERT POWER   Power based on the possession of expertise.

FOOT-IN-THE-DOOR TECHNIQUE   A strategy for exerting influence based on multiple requests. First, target persons are presented with a small request. Once they agree to this, they are exposed to a second, larger request.

GUILT   Negative feelings stemming from the belief that one has behaved in a disapproved fashion. Feelings of guilt can often enhance susceptibility to social influence.

INFLUENCE   The ability to change the behavior of one or more persons in some manner. Many tactics for exerting such effects exist.

INGRATIATION   A tactic for exerting influence in which individuals attempt to enhance their attractiveness to target persons. This is often accomplished through flattery or by emphasizing one's apparent similarity to target persons.

LEGITIMATE POWER   Power based upon a general belief that certain persons have a legitimate claim to positions of authority.

NORMS   Rules (either formal or informal) indicating what forms of behavior are appropriate in specific settings.

ORGANIZATIONAL POLITICS   Refers to the study of tactics for gaining, holding, and using power within organizations.

POWER   The ability to affect the behavior of one or more others regularly and strongly, even against their will.

REFERENT POWER   Power based on the personal attractiveness of persons who possess it.

REWARD POWER   Power stemming from control over valued resources.

STRATEGIC-CONTINGENCIES THEORY   A theory seeking to account for the power of various subunits or departments in an organization. According to this view, subunits acquire power to the extent that other subunits depend on input from them to complete their own work.

NOTES

1. Bonoma, T.V., & Zaltman, G. *Psychology for management.* Boston: Kent Publishing, 1981.

2. Grimes, A.J. Authority, power, influence and social control: A theoretical synthesis. *Academy of Management Review,* 1978, *3,* 724–735.

3. Sussmann, M., & Vecchio, R.P. A social influence interpretation of worker motivation. *Academy of Management Review,* 1982, *7,* 177–186.

4. Byrne, D. *The attraction paradigm.* New York: Academic Press, 1971.

5. Wall, J.A., & Adams, J.S. Some variables affecting a constituent's evaluations of and behavior toward a boundary role occupant. *Organizational Behavior and Human Performance,* 1974, *11,* 290–308.

6. Wortman, C.B., & Linsenmeier, J.A.W. Interpersonal attraction and techniques of ingratiation in organizational settings. In B.M. Swat & G.R. Salancik, *New directions in organizational behavior.* Chicago: St. Clair Press, 1977.

7. Asch, S.E. Effects of group pressure upon the modification and distortion of judgment. In H. Guetzkow (Ed.), *Groups, leadership, and men.* Pittsburgh: Carnegie, 1951.

8. Wheeler, L., Deci, E., Reis, H., & Zuckerman, M. *Interpersonal influence* (2nd ed.). Boston: Allyn and Bacon, 1978.

9. Gerard, H.B., Wilhelmy, R.A., & Connolley, E.S. Conformity and group size. *Journal of Personality and Social Psychology,* 1968, *8,* 79–82.

10. Wilder, D.A. Perception of groups, size of opposition, and social influence. *Journal of Experimental Social Psychology,* 1977, *13,* 253–268.

11. Reingen, P.H. Test of a list procedure for inducing compliance with a request to donate money. *Journal of Applied Psychology,* 1982, *67,* 110–118.

12. Morris, W.N., Miller, R.S., & Spangenberg, S. The effects of dissenter position and task difficulty on conformity and response conflict. *Journal of Personality,* 1977, *45,* 251–266.

13. Eagly, A.H., & Carli, L. Sex of researchers and sex-typed communications as determinants of sex differences in influenceability: A meta-analysis of social influence studies. *Psychological Bulletin,* 1981, *90,* 1–20.

14. Sistrunk, F., & McDavid, J.W. Sex variable in conforming behavior. *Journal of Personality and Social Psychology,* 1971, *17,* 200–207.

15. Goldberg, C. Conformity to majority type as a function of task and acceptance of sex-related stereotypes. *Journal of Psychology,* 1975, *89,* 25–37.

16. Pincus, S., & Water, L.K. Informational social influence and product quality judgments. *Journal of Applied Psychology,* 1977, *62,* 615–619.

17. Weiss, H.M., & Shaw, J.B. Social influences on judgments about tasks. *Organizational Behavior and Human Performance,* 1979, *24,* 126–140.

18. Hackman, J.R. Group influence on individuals. In M.D. Dunnette (Ed.), *Handbook of industrial and organizational psychology.* Chicago: Rand McNally, 1976.

19. Weiss, H.M. Subordinate imitation of supervisor behavior: The role of modeling in organizational socialization. *Organizational Behavior and Human Performance,* 1977, *19,* 89–105.

20. Freedman, J.L., & Fraser, S.C. Compliance without pressure: The foot-in-the-door technique. *Journal of Personality and Social Psychology,* 1966, *4,* 195–202.

21. Baron, R.A. The "foot-in-the-door" phenomenon: Mediating effects of size of first request and sex of requester. *Bulletin of the Psychonomic Society,* 1973, *2,* 113–114.

22. Pliner, P., Hart, H., Kohl, J., & Saari, D. Compliance without pressure: Some further data on the foot-in-the-door technique. *Journal of Experimental Social Psychology,* 1974, *10,* 17–22.

23. Foss, R.D., & Dempsey, C.B. Blood donation and the foot-in-the-door technique: A limiting case. *Journal of Personality and Social Psychology,* 1979, *37,* 580–590.

24. Wagener, J.J., & Laird, J.B. The experimenter's foot-in-the-door: Self perception, body weight, and volunteering. *Personality and Social Psychology Bulletin,* 1980, *6,* 441–446.

25. Snyder, M., & Cunningham, M.R. To comply or not comply: Testing the self-perception explanation of the "foot-in-the door" phenomenon. *Journal of Personality and Social Psychology,* 1975, *31,* 64–67.

26. Cialdini, R.B., Vincent, J.E., Lewis, S.K., Catalan, J., Wheeler, D., & Darby, B.L. Reciprocal concessions procedure for inducing compliance: The door-in-the-face technique. *Journal of Personality and Social Psychology,* 1975, *31,* 206–215.

27. Cialdini, R.B., & Ascani, K. Test of a concession procedure for inducing verbal, behavioral and further compliance with a request to give blood. *Journal of Applied Psychology*, 1976, *61*, 295–300.

28. Cann, A., Sherman, S.J., & Elkes, R. Effects of initial request, sizing, and timing of a second request on compliance: The foot-in-the-door and the door-in-the-face. *Journal of Personality and Social Psychology*, 1975, *32*, 774–782.

29. Wallington, S.A. Consequences of transgression: Self-punishment and depression. *Journal of Personality and Social Psychology*, 1973, *29*, 1–7.

30. Freedman, J.L., Wallington, S.A., & Bless, E. Compliance without pressure: The effect of guilt. *Journal of Personality and Social Psychology*, 1967, *7*, 117–124.

31. Grimes, A.J. Authority, power, influence and social control: A theoretical synthesis. *Academy of Management Review*, 1978, *3*, 724–735.

32. Tushman, M.T. A political approach for organizations: A review and rationale. *Academy of Management Review*, 1977, *2*, 206–216.

33. Tedeschi, J.T., & Bonoma, T.V. Power and influence. An introduction. In J.T. Tedeschi (Ed.), *The social influence process*. Chicago: Aldine, 1972.

34. French, J.R.P., & Raven, B. The bases of social power. In D. Cartwright (Ed.), *Studies in social power*. Ann Arbor: University of Michigan Press, 1959.

35. Kipnis, D., Schmidt, M., & Wilkinson, I. Intraorganizational influence tactics: Explorations in getting one's way. *Journal of Applied Psychology*, 1980, *65*, 440–452.

36. Goldman, W., & Lewis, P. Beautiful is good: Evidence that the physically attractive are more socially skillful. *Journal of Experimental Social Psychology*, 1977, *13*, 125–130.

37. Greene, C.N., & Podsakoff, P.M. Effects of withdrawal of a performance-contingent reward on supervisory influence and power. *Academy of Management Journal*, 1981, *24*, 527–542.

38. McFillen, J.M. Supervisory power as an influence in supervisor-subordinate relations. *Academy of Management Journal*, 1978, *21*, 419–433.

39. Hickson, D.J., Hinings, C.R., Lee, C.A., Schneck, R.E., & Pennings, J.M. A strategic contingencies theory of intraorganizational power. *Administrative Science Quarterly*, 1971, *16*, 216–229.

40. Hinings, C.R., Hickson, D.J., Pennings, J.M., & Schneck, R.E. Structural conditions of intraorganizational power. *Administrative Science Quarterly*, 1974, *19*, 22–44.

41. Milgram, S. Behavioral study of obedience. *Journal of Abnormal and Social Psychology*, 1963, *67*, 371–378.

42. Milgram, S. *Obedience to authority*. New York: Harper, 1974.

43. Shanab, M.E., & Yahya, K.A. A behavioral study of obedience in children. *Journal of Personality and Social Psychology*, 1977, *35*, 530–536.

44. Milgram, S. Liberating effects of group pressure. *Journal of Personality and Social Psychology*, 1965, *1*, 127–134.

45. Mayes, B.T., & Allen, R.W. Toward a definition of organizational politics. *Academy of Management Review*, 1977, *2*, 672–678.

46. Cavanagh, G.F., Moberg, D.J., & Velasquez, M. The ethics of organizational politics. *Academy of Management Review*, 1981, *6*, 363–374.

14

Leadership:
Its Nature, Emergence, and Effectiveness

KEY CONCEPTS

Leadership

Trait Theory

Leader Behavior

Leader Emergence

Great Man/Great Woman Theory

Authoritarian Leadership

Democratic Leadership

Initiating Structure

Showing Consideration

Implicit Theories of Leadership

Contingency Model of Leader
  Effectiveness

Normative Theory

Path-Goal Theory

Esteem for Least Preferred
  Co-Worker

VDL Approach

Substitutes for Leadership

□ □ □

It's the third day of your company's national sales meeting, and everyone around you is beginning to look a bit numb. The meetings are hard work, and some of the sessions seem to go on forever. Yet, no one really minds, because this is the one chance each year for people from all states and regions to get together. You are taking full advantage of this opportunity; in fact, tonight you are dining with three old friends who work in states far from your own. You haven't seen each other for almost a year, so the conversation is lively and varied. Mostly, though, it focuses on people you all know, and what has been happening to them recently. At one point, Bill Hammond makes a remark about Pat Pitrowski—a rising star in the company.

"Well, it looks as though Pat's done it again. She's only been head of the Southwest Division for four months, but I see that already their sales are up twenty-five percent."

"Right," agrees Linda Schacht, another member of your group. "She's really done wonders. And just talk to the people working with her—they love her to pieces. I've never seen morale this high before. And you all know what a problem it's been out there in the past."

Everyone agrees, and then Bob O'Meara remarks: "She sure does seem to be a natural leader. It doesn't matter where they put her. After she's there a few months, everything seems to go right—productivity, morale, motivation. Gosh, I wonder how she does it."

"I think I know," answers Bill. "In fact, I can give you the solution in one word: flexibility. Pat doesn't have a set style. She adapts it to whatever group she's in. When she was out in St. Louis two years ago, she really took charge. Made all the decisions herself, reorganized jobs, set firm deadlines—why she was a regular autocrat! But now in Dallas, she's totally different. She calls lots of meetings and makes all decisions in close consultation with her staff. Also, she spends a lot of her time working on personal relations. And she's doing a super job. In just a few months she's managed to end some feuds that have lasted there for years. Geez . . . she's almost a part-time therapist!"

At this everyone laughs. Then Linda adds: "You know, Bill, I think you're right. Flexibility really is *her magic formula. Somehow, she seems to sense just what style will work in a given setting. And oh boy, does she ever make it pay off!"*

456

Think back over all the groups and organizations to which you have belonged—everything from informal neighborhood gangs through large companies for which you have worked. Is there anything they all had in common? We believe that there is: in all probability, each had someone "in charge." That is, in every group or organization you can think of, there was one person who was more influential than the others—someone who could change, shape, and direct the actions of other members. Such individuals are usually described as being *leaders.* Thus, when we use the term **leadership,** we are referring to the exercise of a special type of influence—influence exerted by one member of an organization over many others.

In organizational settings, leaders are generally appointed to their positions of authority. That is, they are named as Office Manager, Vice-President, or Director of Marketing by the powers that be (see Figure 14-1). In other contexts, though, they may emerge in a relatively informal manner or are selected by group members. But regardless of how they gain their positions, leaders clearly play a key role in the functioning of the groups that they head. Thus, if they are suddenly or unexpectedly removed, through accident, illness, or acceptance of another job, their organizations may suffer greatly. Indeed in extreme cases, they may become totally paralyzed and incapable of carrying out their major functions, at least until a new leader is obtained.

Because leaders play such a crucial role in the functioning of organizations, leadership has long been a topic of central interest in organizational behavior. As we will soon see, this process has turned out to be quite complex—more complex than you might at first imagine. For this reason, many questions about it have not

FIGURE 14-1   Leaders: Appointed or Chosen

Many leaders gain their positions of authority through appointment (left photo). However, others gain this status through a less formal process (right photo). (Source: Photo [left] © T.C. Fitzgerald/The Picture Cube; photo [right] © David Strickler/The Picture Cube.)

as yet been fully answered. Yet, considerable progress *has* been achieved, and we now know much more about leaders and leadership than was true in the past.[1,2] In this chapter, we will summarize much of this information for you. Briefly, our discussion will proceed as follows. First, we will examine the view that leaders are "born, not made"—an approach often known as the **trait theory** of leadership. This idea is intriguing but as we will soon see, it is not supported by existing evidence. Second, we will focus on **leader behavior.** Here, we will see that several distinct styles of leadership exist, and that these have complex effects on both productivity and morale. Third, we will consider **leader emergence**—the process through which specific persons come to be perceived as leaders in their group. As you might guess, this process is strongly affected by characteristics individuals actually possess. In addition, though, it is influenced by *implicit theories of leadership*—ideas most of us hold about what behaviors constitute leadership. Finally, we will examine several modern *theories of leader effectiveness*—models that help us understand why leaders are relatively effective or ineffective in facilitating the major goals of their groups. As you will soon see, these theories go a long way toward explaining the success of the character in the story on page 456.

THE TRAIT APPROACH: IN SEARCH OF "BORN LEADERS"

Are some people born to lead? Common sense seems to suggest that this is so (see Figure 14–2). Such great leaders as Joan of Arc, George Washington, Jomo Kenyatta, and Mao Tse Tung do seem to differ from "ordinary" human beings in several ways. Further, they also appear to share certain traits—ones necessary for their important roles in history (e.g., possession of an iron will, boundless energy). And to a lesser degree, even leaders lacking such worldwide fame seem

FIGURE 14–2   Leaders: Born or Made?

Are some persons "born to lead?" Common sense suggests this is so. However, systematic research has failed to confirm this general belief. (Source: Reprinted by permission of King Features Syndicate, Inc.; © 1978. World rights reserved.)

different from their followers. Thus, top executives, high-level government officials, and sports heroes often possess an "aura" that sets them apart from other persons. On the basis of such observations, early researchers concluded that leadership is largely a matter of personality. Identify the key traits it involves, they reasoned, and the mystery of this process will be largely resolved. Carried to its logical extreme, this general approach leads to the **great man/great woman theory.** Briefly, this view suggests that (1) leaders differ from followers with respect to a small number of key traits, and (2) these traits remain unchanged across time. Thus, according to this view, persons possessing certain traits have the potential to become great leaders at any point in time, and in virtually any society.

The trait approach outlined above is certainly intriguing. Further, if it is accurate, it offers the potential for important practical payoffs. Specifically, if leadership is largely a function of specific traits, there is no reason why we cannot identify these characteristics and measure them in some way. Then, armed with such information, we can select for leadership only persons well-suited by their personality or temperament for such roles. As you can readily see, the practical benefits to society, organizations, and individuals from such near-perfect selection of leaders might well be immense. We wish we could now report that progress toward this enticing goal has been both steady and rapid. But—alas!—this grandiose vision has never been realized. Try as they might, researchers could not identify a set of traits that serve to distinguish leaders from nonleaders. A few positive findings were obtained; for example, leaders tend to be slightly taller, slightly more intelligent, higher in dominance, and higher in self-confidence than their followers.[3,4] But even here, the differences noted were quite small and not totally consistent. Further, there are serious difficulties of interpretation with respect to several of the most interesting of these results. For example, it may well be the case that dominance and self-confidence aid individuals in their rise to positions of power and authority. But it is also possible that once they are leaders, such persons undergo experiences that enhance these traits. (After all, leaders are often treated with respect, awe, and deference by others, and this may contribute to both their confidence and dominance.) In any case, after more than fifty years of research on the trait approach, investigators were not much closer to the goal of identifying the central traits of leaders than they were at the start. Thus, most reluctantly surrendered the goal of developing a quick and easy test for assessing leadership potential.

The Trait Approach: Why It Failed

We realize that at first glance, you probably find these negative results somewhat puzzling. Most of us have the subjective impression that given a few moments, we could generate a list of traits that accurately distinguish leaders from nonleaders. Why, then, did systematic research fail to verify this belief? The answer lies in a simple but crucial fact: in determining who becomes a leader, and how effective such persons will be in this role, situational factors and pressures are key. That is, different situations seem to require different characteristics, styles, and skills for effective leadership. For example, in some contexts, forceful, directive actions by the leader "work"—they enhance both productivity and morale. In others, such behavior is resented, and a more flexible, unstructured approach may be best. Similarly, in some settings an autocratic style of decision making, in which the leader gathers information and then acts entirely alone, may be effective. In others, a participative approach involving careful consultation with subordinates may be necessary to insure acceptance of each decision. In short, there is no single "best" style of leadership; rather, depending on specific situational forces, various approaches will be more or less successful. Our central question, then, should be: "What leadership style or leader behavior is best in a given context?" *not* "What kinds of persons make the best leaders?" This is a crucial point, and one that plays a major role in modern theories of leadership. Thus, we hope you will keep it firmly in mind as you read the pages that follow.

LEADER BEHAVIOR: SOME KEY DIMENSIONS

As we have just seen, leaders do not seem to differ from other persons with respect to a small number of concrete traits. Thus, we cannot differentiate leaders from followers or effective leaders from ineffective ones on these bases. This does not imply, however, that such persons fail to differ in *any* respect. In fact, informal observation points to another area in which such differences might well emerge: *behavior*. Specifically, it seems possible that effective leaders may engage in actions that inspire confidence in others, and encourage these persons to accept their influence. In contrast, ineffective leaders (and followers) may either fail to show such actions or demonstrate them to a sharply lower degree.

Research concerned with such possibilities has yielded more encouraging results than that focused on trait theory. While it has not provided us with a small list of actions that always distinguish leaders from followers, it *has* served to identify major styles or dimensions of leader behavior. Further, it has demonstrated that these dimensions play a key role in determining both the morale and productivity of subordinates. Several will now be considered.

Democratic versus Authoritarian Leaders: Contrasting Styles, Contrasting Effects

Think back to your days in elementary school. Did you ever have a teacher who wanted to control virtually everything—someone who made all the decisions, insisted on completing tasks in highly specific ways, and who generally ruled the room with an iron fist? In contrast, did you ever have a teacher who allowed the class much more freedom—someone who permitted students to vote on class activities, who allowed individuals to do things in their own way, and who generally created a warm, friendly atmosphere? If so, you have already had direct experience with two sharply contrasting styles of leadership: **authoritarian** and **democratic.**

These different approaches to leadership were first studied in detail many years ago in a classic investigation conducted by Lewin, Lippitt, and White.[5] In this study, ten-year-old boys met after school in groups of five to participate in enjoyable hobby activities. The adult leaders of these groups were specially trained to behave in either an authoritarian or democratic fashion. (In a third condition, the leaders adopted a *laissez-faire* approach, essentially surrendering all control over the groups.) The study continued for eighteen weeks, and during this period all groups were exposed to each type of leader. Careful observation of the boys' behavior revealed that as expected, the contrasting styles of behavior shown by the leaders did exert powerful effects upon group functioning. In general, morale was higher under democratic than under authoritarian leadership (e.g., the boys reported preferring the democratic style of leadership and were friendlier to the leader and one another under these conditions). However, all findings did *not* favor the democratic approach. Indeed, while productivity was relatively high in both the authoritarian and democratic groups (higher than that in the *laissez-faire* condition), it was actually somewhat better in the former. These findings suggest that contrary to what we might prefer to believe, a democratic approach to leadership is not always superior to a more autocratic one. And additional research conducted since the early Lewin, Lippitt, and White investigation has confirmed this fact. Specifically, it appears that under conditions of stress, or when great speed and efficiency are required, authoritarian leadership can yield positive outcomes. It can increase productivity. And, somewhat more surprising, it can also enhance morale.[6] The reason for these effects is clear: under such conditions, group members quickly realize that there is simply not enough time for democratic procedures. Thus, they may actually prefer leaders who "take charge" and help get things done.

Interestingly, most individuals seem to be aware of the potential benefits of authoritarian leadership. Thus, when confronted with stressful circumstances, even persons with a strong preference for democratic practices may shift in the direction of authoritarian tactics. Shifts of this type have actually been observed in an ingenious study conducted by Fodor.[7] In this experiment, employed foremen and supervisors served as the leaders of three-person groups, directing their activities in a simple construction task. The leaders could communicate with their groups verbally (over an intercom) and could give each of their three subordinates raises or cuts in pay at the conclusion of each construction trial. In one condition of the study, the leader was exposed to stress induced through disparaging comments and an uncooperative attitude on the part of one of his subordinates. (This individual objected to the task and criticized the leader in a harsh manner.) In a second (control) condition, no stress of this type was present. It was predicted that when confronted with stressful conditions, leaders would shift toward an authoritarian style, and as you can see from Figure 14–3, this was actually the case. Leaders exposed to disparaging statements from one of their subordinates became more directive, used more threats, and gave fewer raises to their groups than leaders not exposed to such treatment. In short, they behaved in a manner suggesting that they recognized the benefits of an authoritarian style under stressful conditions.

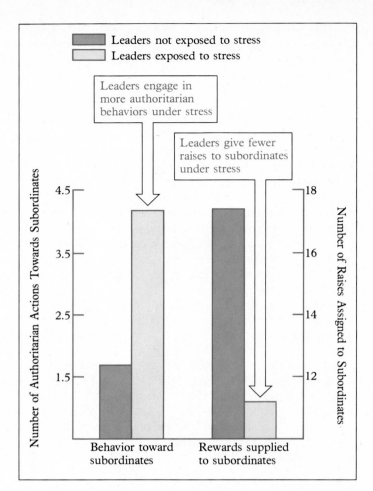

FIGURE 14-3   Stress and Authoritarian Leadership

When exposed to stressful conditions, leaders directing the actions of small groups shifted toward a more authoritarian leadership style. That is, they became more directive, and gave fewer raises to their subordinates than leaders not exposed to stress. (Source: Based on data from Fodor, *Journal of Applied Psychology*, 1976, *61*, 313–318.)

Before concluding this discussion of democratic and authoritarian leadership styles, we should mention one more effect they produce—important changes in leaders' perceptions of their subordinates.[8] When leaders adopt an authoritarian approach, they usually employ controlling tactics of influence with their subordinates (e.g., they give them direct orders, criticize poor work, etc.). The use of these tactics, in turn, leads them to conclude that the behavior of these persons is *externally* motivated—it stems from the leaders' commands or directives. And as such, it is often devalued; after all, if others' performance stems mainly from our orders, it deserves little credit (please refer to Chapter 6). In contrast, when leaders adopt a democratic approach, they often use less controlling tactics of influence (e.g., they *request* that their subordinates behave in certain ways, praise their successful work, hold discussions with them about how to proceed). The use of these tactics then leads them to believe that the behavior of these persons is *in-*

ternally motivated—it derives from their own desire to do a good job. And as such, it is often evaluated favorably. (Please see Figure 14-4 for a summary of these suggestions.)

Evidence for the occurrence of precisely such effects has been obtained in a recent study by Kipnis and his colleagues.[9] These researchers found that leaders instructed to behave in a democratic fashion perceived their subordinates' behavior as internally motivated, while those instructed to behave in an authoritarian fashion perceived it to be the result of their (the leaders') commands. Further, and also as predicted, leaders reported more favorable evaluations of their subordinates' performance when they behaved democratically than when they adopted an authoritarian leadership style.

Taking all the evidence we have reviewed into account, it appears that the authoritarian-democratic dimension is an important one for understanding leadership behavior. Where a leader stands on this dimension can affect (1) her subordinate's morale and productivity, (2) the leader's behavior toward these persons, (3) her perceptions of their motives, and (4) evaluations of their performance. Given the scope of these effects, it is clear that this aspect of leader behavior should not be overlooked.

Leaders Who Focus on Tasks and Leaders Who Focus on Persons: Initiating Structure and Showing Consideration

Have you ever seen a movie version of Dickens's *A Christmas Carol?* If so, you are already familiar with the extremes along another key dimension (or really two dimensions) of leader behavior. Prior to his miraculous experience, Scrooge was essentially interested only in one thing: carrying out his business in the most ef-

FIGURE 14-4   Leadership Style: Its Impact on Perceptions of Subordinates

When leaders adopt a democratic approach, they generally use noncontrolling influence tactics. As a result, they may perceive their subordinates' behavior as internally motivated, and evaluate it positively (upper panel). When leaders adopt an authoritarian approach, in contrast, they often use controlling influence tactics. As a result, they may perceive their subordinates' behavior as *externally* motivated, and so evaluate it negatively (lower panel).

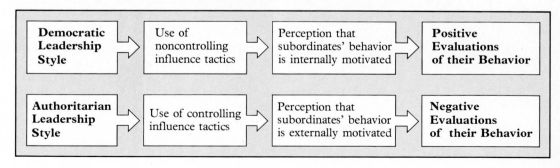

ficient manner possible. He had little if any concern for good, friendly relations with his subordinates or for their welfare. (Remember poor Bob Cratchit.) After his conversion by the spirits, though, all this changed. Scrooge's major concern became that of furthering the well-being of his poor, long-suffering clerk; completion of tasks relating to his work seemed to be of less importance (see Figure 14–5). In short, he shifted from a leader primarily concerned with getting the job done, to one primarily concerned with interpersonal relations.

A large body of research evidence suggests that these dimensions are key ones in leader behavior. Indeed, they may be *the* central dimensions to consider in many situations. Much of the evidence relating to these contrasting styles or concerns has been gathered in two continuing projects carried out at Ohio State Uni-

FIGURE 14–5   Before and After: Two Sharply Contrasting Styles of Leadership

Prior to his night among the spirits, Ebenezer Scrooge was clearly a task-oriented leader (left print). After his memorable Christmas Eve, however, he became much more interested in establishing warm, friendly relations with his subordinate (right print). (Source: Culver Pictures, Inc. by permission.)

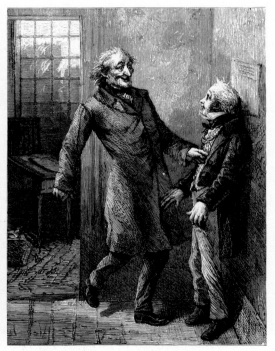

"It's enough for a man to understand his own business. . . . Mine occupies me constantly. Good afternoon, Gentlemen!"

"I'll raise your salary, Bob!"

versity and the University of Michigan. These important studies, begun in the late 1940s, have employed different methods and have focused on somewhat different goals.[10,11] Yet both have yielded highly similar results. Briefly, each suggests that leader behavior varies along the two dimensions mentioned above. One of these—often termed **initiating structure** or *production-orientation*—refers to concern with getting the job done. Leaders high on this dimension engage in such behaviors as organizing work, assigning people to specific tasks, and setting firm deadlines. Leaders low on this dimension are less likely to demonstrate such actions.

The second dimension—usually termed **showing consideration** or *employee-orientation*—refers to the leader's concern with establishing good, friendly relations with his or her subordinates. Leaders high on this dimension engage in such actions as helping subordinates with personal problems, attempting to gain their trust, and treating them as equals. Those low on this dimension, of course, are less likely to demonstrate such behaviors.

At first you might assume that these two dimensions are negatively related, so that leaders high in one are low on the other. Yet this is not the case. Actually, these dimensions appear to be largely independent. Thus, a particular leader can be high on both, low on both, high on one and low on the other, and so on.[12] And not surprisingly, the specific pattern a leader shows in this regard can often have important effects on both the morale and productivity of his subordinates. Years of research on this issue suggest that such effects are quite complex.[13] Thus, we cannot readily describe them in simple or definite terms. However, we *can* provide you with a brief overview of their basic nature.

We might expect that showing consideration will primarily affect subordinate morale, while initiating structure will exert its major impact upon productivity, and some research findings support this view.[14] It is also clear, however, that these effects are by no means exclusive in nature. That is, high consideration, by creating a positive group atmosphere, can sometimes enhance productivity. Similarly, a high level of initiating structure can occasionally improve morale—especially when time pressures are great.[15] Further, these two modes of leader behavior appear to interact, so that the overall effects on morale and productivity depend strongly on the specific pattern present. A brief summary of such effects, based on research findings, is presented in Table 14–1. But please note that the information in this table is by no means final or definitive. Rather, it is included simply to give you a basic idea of how the impact of initiating structure and showing consideration may combine under some conditions.

One final point: It appears that in many cases, a high level of showing consideration can make up for the "ruffled feathers" often produced by initiating structure. In general, then, it is useful for leaders to show at least moderate consideration toward their subordinates; if they do, they can often "get away" with even relatively high levels of structure. Of course, this is only a general suggestion; given the multitude of factors playing a role in leader effectiveness—not to mention group morale and productivity—many exceptions to it will probably exist. Our best overall advice then, is simply this: As a leader, be aware of where you

The Strange Mystery of the Leader Who Wasn't

"Well," says Sarah Carter with a sigh, "we might as well admit it—we goofed."

Looking pained and upset, Joe Halzi agrees: "Yeah, I guess so. He really isn't working out, is he?"

"No, you can sure say *that*," Sarah replies. "In fact, you might say that he's a total bomb . . . and we both know it. But I still can't figure out *why*. I never saw anyone who seemed more like a natural leader than Dan. What gives?"

"I don't know," remarks Joe, shaking his head. "He sure seems like he's well equipped. I mean, that deep voice, that self-assured air . . . what more could anyone ask?"

"And his appearance—he sure *looks* like a leader. If you met him at a party, you'd swear he's a general or something."

"Right. But he's a flop anyway. You know what the people in the plant up there call him? Dunkirk Dan. Get it? Dunkirk—a total disaster. And do they ever hate him! He's only been there a few months, but production's down, turnover is up, and they've missed three major deadlines. Another quarter like that, and heads will roll down here, too."

"But why?" Sarah interrupts. "I keep wondering how he can be so bad. What've you heard?"

"Only rumors, but here are a few things people have mentioned. First, he locks himself up in the office most of the day. No one can get to see him, and when they do, he's just not interested. Acts as though other people and their problems bore him to tears. Also, no one up there thinks he knows a thing about the business. And you know how deadly *that* can be. And maybe worst of all, he makes every single decision himself. They're not used to that in St. Paul. Old Dick used to give everyone a chance to have their say."

"Stop, I can't take any more!" Sarah snaps. "We made a mistake—a bad one—and now we'll have to undo it. I guess we really can't pick 'em like we thought." Then, after a pause, she continues: "Say, what was the name of the consulting firm—you know, the experts on—what was it—Organizational Behavior? Maybe we should give them a call. We can sure use some help. And one thing's certain. We can't stand another disaster like Dan."   □

Questions:

1. Before his appointment as plant manager, Dan seemed to possess all the traits we usually associated with leadership. Why didn't he succeed in this role?

2. Do you think Dan might prove to be an effective leader in some other situation or setting? If so, why?

3. If you were called in as a consultant by the company involved, what procedures would you use to help choose Dan's replacement? Why?

TABLE 14-1   Contrasting Leader Behaviors: Some Important Effects

As suggested here, the effects of initiating structure and showing consideration on both morale and productivity appear to be complex.

LEADER'S POSITION ON DIMENSIONS OF INITIATING STRUCTURE AND SHOWING CONSIDERATION	MORALE	PRODUCTIVITY
Low on both dimensions	Usually low	Usually low
Low on consideration, high on initiating structure	Usually low, but can be high in presence of stress or time pressure	Often high (if positive group atmosphere not necessary for productivity)
High on consideration, low on initiating structure	Often high	Often low
High on both dimensions	Often high	Expected to be high, but recent studies fail to offer strong support for this conclusion

stand on each of these dimensions; then try to adjust your behavior so as to maximize the chances of reaching your major goals. In short, as we will note again and again through this chapter, the key word for you to remember is *flexibility*. (See the **"CASE IN POINT"** box on the opposite page for an example of the difficulties involved in choosing an effective leader.)

LEADER EMERGENCE: WHO IS PERCEIVED AS A LEADER AND WHY?

In most organizations, individuals are appointed to positions of power and authority. As we noted earlier, they are named Vice-President, Manager, Director for Marketing, and so on. It seems reasonable to assume that such persons, by virtue of their assigned positions, will then be perceived as leaders; and often this is the case. But as you probably know, this is not always true. Sometimes even persons occupying positions associated with high prestige or status are *not* perceived as leaders by their subordinates. In fact, their failure to attain the appropriate "image" may be the subject of many jokes and cutting remarks. The existence of such instances raises an intriguing question. Just what factors cause specific individuals to be perceived or not perceived as leaders? (See Figure 14-6.) And what factors cause such persons to be identified as effective or ineffective in these roles? It is with these and related questions that we will be concerned in the present section.

FIGURE 14-6   Who Is Perceived as a Leader?

Contrary to the conclusion suggested by this cartoon, many factors play a role in determining which specific persons are perceived as being leaders or as possessing "leadership material." (Source: Reprinted by permission of King Features Syndicate, Inc.; © 1976.)

Competence: One Important Basis for Being Viewed as a Leader

As we noted in Chapter 13, competence is often a basis for influence in organizations. People are usually more willing to change their attitudes or behavior for others they view as being expert in some manner than for persons they perceive as lacking in competence. Further, *expertise* is often an important basis for power over others. Together, these facts suggest that individuals perceived to be competent in some respect are often more likely to be viewed as leaders than individuals perceived to be incompetent.[16] That this is true is suggested by the findings of several recent experiments.[17]

For example, in one of the clearest of these investigations, Price and Garland had participants work on a simple construction task under the guidance of an appointed leader.[18] Before beginning, individuals received information suggesting either that the leader was highly competent in such tasks or relatively incompetent. Results indicated that this information strongly affected subjects' willingness to follow the leader's suggestions, and also their ratings of his effectiveness in this role. Subjects were much more willing to be influenced by the leader, and expressed stronger endorsement for his leadership, when he was described as competent than when he was described as incompetent.

When combined with similar findings in other studies, these results offer a clear message for managers and other persons occupying positions of leadership in organizations. If you wish to succeed in influencing your subordinates and to be perceived by them as an effective leader, cultivate an aura of competence. To the extent you do, your impact on your subordinates may well be enhanced.

Does Sheer Output Count? The Effects of Rate of Verbal Participation on Emergent Leadership

In many Hollywood epics leaders are portrayed as being the strong and silent type. They are people of few words, but the forcefulness of their personalities leaves little room for doubt about who is in charge. Is this image accurate? Are persons who remain silent or choose their words with great care more likely to be perceived as leaders, or as possessing leadership material, than their more verbal peers? Actually, research evidence fails to confirm this view. In fact, it points strongly to the opposite conclusion—in many cases, the higher an individual's verbal output, the more likely he or she is viewed as a leader.[19,20] Thus, it appears that in terms of seeking leadership status—as in several other spheres of life—"fast talkers" often have an edge. Of course, we should hasten to add that there are probably definite limits on this relationship. Spouting total nonsense is unlikely to enhance one's image, no matter how high the volume. But provided that one's statements are of at least modest quality, high quantity of output appears to be a useful strategy. In sum, while silence may well be golden in some contexts, cultivating the image of leadership does not appear to be one of them.

Consistency: The Rewards of "Sticking to One's Guns"

When Jimmy Carter was defeated in the 1980 presidential election in the U.S., he was only the third president in ninety-six years to be turned out of office. Many factors probably contributed to his political downfall, but one the press mentioned over and over again was high lack of consistency. At several points during his administration, Carter seemed to shift his positions on economic, social, and military matters, and it was suggested that this accounted for his sharp drop in popularity. As one author put it:

> The American people find it easy to forgive a leader's great mistakes, but not long meanderings. (Hughes, 1978, p. 58)[21]

Events and observations like these suggest that one factor that often plays a key role in perceptions of leadership and leader effectiveness is *consistency*. Apparently, most people expect leaders to be consistent—to choose a position or a course of action and then to stick to it—at least until it is obvious that they have made a serious mistake. This seemingly powerful preference for consistency was recently confirmed in an ingenious study conducted by Staw and Ross.[22]

These investigators presented three groups of subjects (psychology students, business school students, and practicing managers) with a case history describing the actions of a fictitious government administrator. The case outlined this person's decision to pursue one of several policies in an attempt to reverse a decline in housing facilities in two large cities. To vary the character's apparent consistency, information in the case was altered so that half of the participants learned that after making his decision, the administrator stuck to it on two later

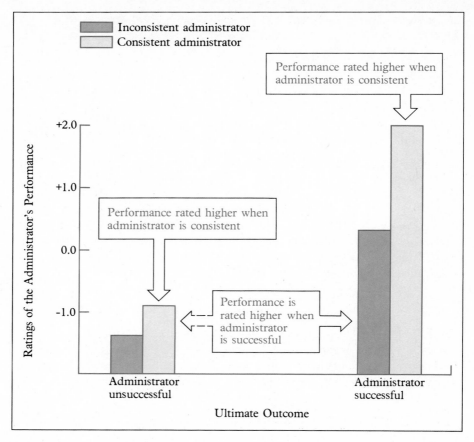

FIGURE 14-7   Perceiving the Effectiveness of a Leader: The Role of Consistency and Success

Ratings of an imaginary administrator's performance were strongly affected both by his apparent degree of consistency and by the success of his policies. Specifically, he was rated more favorably when he was consistent or successful than when he was inconsistent or unsuccessful. (Source: Based on data from Staw & Ross, *Journal of Applied Psychology,* 1980, *65,* 249–260.)

occasions, despite negative initial results. In contrast, the remainder learned that he was *not* consistent; each time he received information suggesting that his policies were not succeeding, he shifted to another strategy. A second variable included in the study concerned the administrator's ultimate success. Half of the subjects in each of the conditions just described learned that ultimately he succeeded in improving housing facilities; the remainder learned that despite his efforts he failed.

After reading one of these contrasting versions of the case (consistent leader who succeeded, consistent leader who failed, inconsistent leader who succeeded, inconsistent leader who failed), subjects rated the administrator's performance. That is, they rated the overall quality of his work and indicated whether he should or should not receive a raise and a promotion. As you can see from Figure 14–7, results indicated that these ratings were strongly influenced by both variables in the study. Specifically, the administrator was rated more favorably when he was consistent than when he was inconsistent, and more favorably when he ultimately succeeded than when he ultimately failed. Further, and perhaps of greater importance, these two variables interacted. Thus, the administrator received the highest ratings of all when he was both consistent and ultimately succeeded. This condition, of course, resembles what we often describe as "heroic leadership"—instances in which a leader sticks to his or her guns despite public pressure to change and is ultimately shown to be correct.

One further finding is of interest. While similar results were obtained with all three groups of participants, the effect of consistency appeared stronger among the business school students and practicing managers than among psychology undergraduates. This pattern suggests that belief in the virtues of consistency may be quite strong in actual organizations—a possibility you may wish to keep firmly in mind in the years ahead. In any case, the overall findings reported by Staw and Ross suggest that anyone wishing to be perceived as an effective leader would be well advised to be consistent. While this characteristic may indeed sometimes be the "hobgoblin of little minds," it still appears to be one we often seek in the persons who control our fate. (Are our perceptions of leader behavior accurate? For a discussion of this issue, see the **"FOCUS"** box on pages 472–473.)

LEADERSHIP: THREE MODERN VIEWS

At one time leadership was viewed as being very much a "one-way street." That is, leaders command, followers obey, and this is the essence of the process. Consistent with this view, attention was focused almost exclusively on the leader. First, his or her traits, and later, his or her behavior or style, were seen as being crucial. In recent years this picture has altered substantially. Investigators concerned with leadership have become increasingly aware of the fact that in reality, leadership is a complex social process. To understand it fully, therefore, we need much more than knowledge of leader traits or behavior. We also require information about the nature of the situation in which leadership occurs, follower characteristics, subordinate perceptions of the leader, and the tasks being performed. As this newer and more sophisticated conception of leadership has emerged, several elegant theories concerning its nature have developed. In this final section, we will briefly examine three of these frameworks, including Fiedler's **contingency theory**,[23] Vroom and Yetton's **normative theory**, [24] and House's **path-goal approach**.[25] In general, all may be viewed as focusing primarily on the factors and conditions that affect leader effectiveness. But all are far-ranging in scope and touch on several other issues as well.

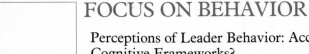

FOCUS ON BEHAVIOR

Perceptions of Leader Behavior: Accurate? Or Captive of Implicit Cognitive Frameworks?

What are leaders like? How do they behave? Most of us have ready answers to such questions. That is, even without thinking of a specific person, we can list behaviors we believe to be characteristic of most leaders. This simple fact suggests that most of us possess *stereotypes* or **implicit theories of leadership.** That is, we have implicit notions about how leaders behave and which of their behaviors covary (go together).

At first glance, this might appear to be an interesting but unimportant fact. Actually though, it has major implications for the study of leader behavior. The reason is as follows: when we are asked to rate the actions of a specific leader, our reactions may be strongly affected by these implicit cognitive frameworks. Indeed, it is possible that our ratings stem even more directly from our stereotypes and expectations than from the leader behaviors we actually observe in a given situation. Some indication that this can be the case is provided by the findings of recent studies.[26,27] In these investigations, subjects were asked to rate imaginary supervisors on scales traditionally used to describe the behavior of actual leaders. Results indicated that the dimensions underlying subjects' ratings were virtually identical to those shown when individuals describe *real* rather than imaginary supervisors. One interpretation of these findings suggests that ratings of actual leaders may in fact be heavily influenced by implicit theories about how leaders usually behave. And to the extent this is true, such ratings can be quite inaccurate. At the very least, they will be far less informative than has previously been assumed (see Figure 14–8).

But is this actually the case? Do such factors strongly affect ratings of leader behavior? At present the issue is far from resolved, but we can report that the findings of several recent studies are somewhat encouraging. That is, while effects of the type we have just described do seem to occur, their scope and magnitude may be smaller than some researchers have feared. For example, even after a two-day delay, subjects' ratings of a leader's behavior are strongly influenced by the actions they have seen this person perform. Thus, such ratings do not seem to stem entirely from implicit theories about leader behavior.[28] Similarly, individuals differing in degree of cognitive complexity do not differ in terms of their implicit theories of leadership or leader behavior ratings.[29]

Of course, these results do not suggest that cog-

The Contingency Model: Matching Leaders and Tasks

Leadership, as we have just noted, does *not* occur in a vacuum. Rather, leaders attempt to exert their influence on group members within the context of specific situations. Given that these may vary greatly along a tremendous number of dimensions, it seems reasonable to expect that no single style or approach to leadership will always be best. Rather, the most effective strategy will vary from one situation to another.

This basic fact is given full attention in a theory of leader effectiveness developed by Fred Fiedler.[31,32] Fiedler describes his model as a *contingency* approach. Its basic assumption is that the contribution of a leader to successful performance by his or her group is determined both by the leader's characteristics and by various features of the situation. Thus, to fully understand leader effectiveness, the theory contends, both must be taken into account.

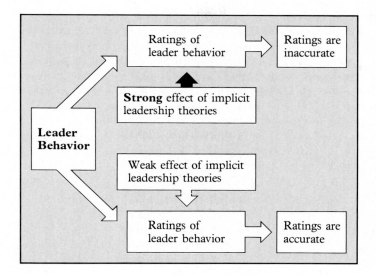

FIGURE 14–8   Ratings of Leader Behavior: Accurate or Inaccurate?

If ratings of leader behavior are strongly affected by implicit theories of leadership (upper path), they may be quite inaccurate. If, instead, such ratings stem mainly from actual leader behavior (lower path), they may be highly accurate. Fortunately, the results of recent studies lend support to the latter conclusion.

nitive frameworks are unimportant. On the contrary, other evidence indicates that they *do* influence our impressions and ratings of leaders—and of other persons in general.[30] But it also appears that ratings of leader behavior are *not* totally determined by such frameworks. In short, what we report in many cases *is* really based upon what we see.   □

With respect to characteristics possessed by leaders—and carried with them from situation to situation—Fiedler has focused most attention on what he terms **esteem for least preferred co-worker (LPC).** This refers to leaders' tendency to evaluate the person with whom they find it most difficult to work in a favorable or unfavorable manner. Leaders who perceive this person in very negative and rejecting terms (*low LPC leaders* in Fiedler's terms), seem primarily motivated to attain successful task performance. In contrast, leaders who perceive their least preferred co-worker in a positive light (*high LPC leaders*) seem concerned mainly with establishing good, friendly relations with other group members. But which of these two types of leaders is more effective? Since it is a contingency model, Fiedler's theory suggests that neither will be superior in every case. Instead, the success of both depends strongly on situational factors. Specifically, Fiedler suggests that whether low LPC or high LPC leaders prove more effective is strongly determined by the degree to which the situation provides the leader with *control* or *influence* over group members. (At one time, Fiedler referred to this dimension as *favorability of the situation,* but he has recently changed this terminology.) Situational control, in turn, is determined largely by three factors—the nature of the leader's *relations with group members* (the extent to which he enjoys their support and loyalty), the *structure of the task* faced by the group (ranging from unstructured to structured), and the *leader's position power* (his ability to enforce compliance from subordinates). Combining these three factors, the leader's situational control can range from very high (positive relations with group members, a highly structured task, and high position power) to very low (negative relations with members, an unstructured task, and low position power).

With this information in place, we can now turn to specific predictions concerning the relative performance of low LPC and high LPC leaders in different settings. Briefly, Fiedler suggests that low LPC leaders will be superior when situational control is either low or high. However, high LPC leaders will "shine" when situational control is moderate (see Figure 14-9). The reasoning behind these intriguing predictions can be summarized as follows. Under conditions of *low* situational control, the group needs considerable direction and structure to accomplish its tasks. Since low LPC leaders, with their focus on task accomplishment, are more likely to provide such direction than high LPC leaders, they will usually be superior in such cases. Similarly, low LPC leaders will also have an edge in situations that afford the leader a *high* degree of situational control. Under these conditions, low LPC leaders realize that their goal of task accomplishment will very likely be met. As a result, they may relax and adopt a "hands-off" nondirective style—one that aids task performance in this type of context. In contrast, high LPC leaders may actually become *more* directive and managing in such cases, and so tend to interfere with effective group function. (The reason for this is clear. Since they already enjoy good relations with their followers, they shift their attention to task performance—and begin to behave in ways their subordinates perceive as needless meddling.)

Turning to situations affording the leader *moderate* control, a sharply different set of circumstances prevails. Here conditions are mixed, and considerable attention to interpersonal relations is often required for successful task performance. Under these circumstances, high LPC leaders, with their greater interest in maintaining friendly relations, may have an important advantage—especially since in such situations, low LPC leaders become concerned about task performance and tend to behave in highly directive, managing ways.

To summarize: Fiedler's theory predicts that low LPC leaders, with their focus on task performance, will prove more effective under conditions of either low or high situational control. In contrast, high LPC leaders, with their focus on personal relations, will have a significant edge under conditions where situational control is moderate. (Please refer to Figure 14-9.)

The contingency model: Current evidence. Because it is quite sophisticated and makes intriguing (if complex) predictions about the impact of both

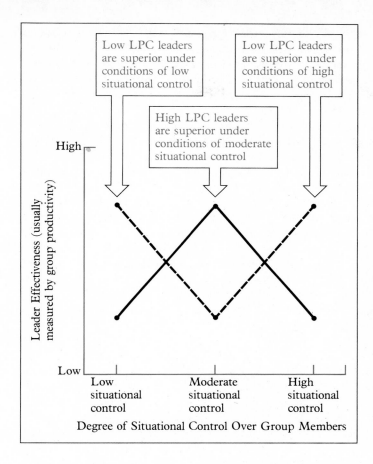

Low LPC leaders are superior under conditions of low situational control

Low LPC leaders are superior under conditions of high situational control

High LPC leaders are superior under conditions of moderate situational control

High

Leader Effectiveness (usually measured by group productivity)

Low

Low situational control

Moderate situational control

High situational control

Degree of Situational Control Over Group Members

FIGURE 14-9   The Contingency Model: Some Basic Predictions

According to the contingency model developed by Fiedler, task-oriented, low LPC leaders are more effective than relations-oriented, high LPC leaders under conditions of both low and high situational control. Under conditions of moderate control, however, this relationship is reversed, and high LPC leaders tend to be more effective than low LPC ones.

personal and situational factors on leader effectiveness, the contingency model has been the subject of intensive study. While all investigations performed to examine its accuracy have not yielded positive results, considerable evidence seems to confirm its basic validity. Indeed, one recent review based on 178 separate tests of the model concludes that support for the contingency approach is quite strong.[33] (Please note: This does *not* mean that all 178 tests were positive—many were not. But taken as a whole, this large body of evidence tended to favor the model.) In addition, several predictions from Fiedler's theory that seem at first glance to contradict common sense have also been confirmed. For example, consider the impact of increasing *experience* on leader effectiveness. Initially, we might predict that as leaders gain in this respect, their effectiveness in handling their groups or organizations will improve. Yet surprisingly, research findings do not support this view. In general, highly experienced leaders do *not* seem to be much more effective than inexperienced ones.[34] The contingency model helps explain this puzzling fact—and actually predicts its existence. The theory suggests that increased leadership experience will in fact increase a leader's situational control. But whether this will then enhance or detract from leader effectiveness depends on two factors—the degree of situational control present initially (before the increased experience), and whether the leader's orientation is high LPC or low LPC. If, prior to experience, the level of situational control is low, increased experience as a leader would be expected to *enhance* the effectiveness of high LPC leaders. This is so because it shifts the situation to one of moderate control—and high LPC leaders "shine" in such circumstances (refer to Figure 14-9). In contrast, however, it will actually *reduce* the effectiveness of a low LPC leader. But now, imagine that situational control is moderate to start with. In this case increased experience will raise situational control to high levels, and according to contingency theory, this will improve the performance of low LPC leaders but reduce that of high LPC leaders (see Figure 14-10 for a summary of some of these suggestions). Interestingly, these predictions, complex and counter-intuitive as they seem, have actually been confirmed in recent studies.[35]

Leader Match: A promising application of the contingency model.
Stated in simple terms, the contingency model suggests that leader effectiveness is largely a function of the match between two key factors—leaders' LPC orientation and the degree of situational control. If this basic assertion is correct (and we have already examined evidence suggesting that it is), then an intriguing possibility

FIGURE 14-10 Leader Experience: Some Complex Predictions Concerning Its Effects

The contingency model suggests that increased experience will result in greater situational control for leaders. Whether this then enhances or reduces their effectiveness depends on two major factors: (1) leaders' LPC orientation, and (2) the level of control present initially. For example, as shown here, if situational control is low to begin with, increased experience will enhance the effectiveness of high LPC leaders, but reduce that of low LPC leaders. (Note that if situational control were moderate or high initially, different predictions would be made.)

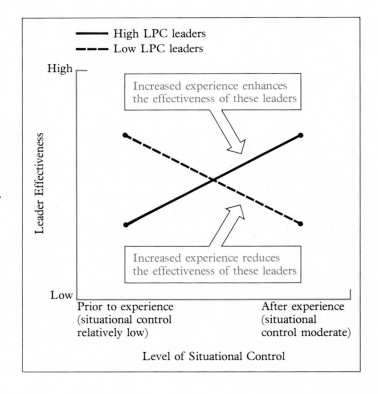

with practical implications follows. Perhaps we can enhance a leader's effectiveness by improving the closeness or appropriateness of this match. But how precisely can this be accomplished? One possibility would involve alterations in leader characteristics—attempts to somehow change a leader's LPC orientation or style to match the current situation. Obviously this presents a formidable task: modifying stable traits or characteristics is often difficult, if not impossible.

A second approach—and one that seems to offer greater potential for practical application—would involve altering situations. That is, these would be changed so as to provide a more congenial environment for specific leaders. This idea forms the basis for a program of leader training developed recently by Fiedler and his colleagues: *Leader Match.*[36] This approach focuses on training leaders in techniques they can use to modify specific situations, in order to obtain a closer match between their own personalities and degree of situational control. The program itself can be viewed as consisting of three major parts. In the first, leaders complete the LPC scale and learn how to identify their own motivational structure. In the next phase, they receive instruction in measuring situational control. And in the final phase they learn how to modify various aspects of the environment to yield a closer match between their own personality and degree of situational control. The effectiveness of Leader Match training has been assessed in a number of studies, and results to date have been quite encouraging. Leaders exposed to such training are generally rated as higher in effectiveness than those not provided with such experience.[37] Thus, at present Leader Match seems to offer a promising technique for enhancing leader effectiveness. Whether this potential will be fully realized in the years ahead remains to be seen. But in closing we should note that Leader Match—in contrast to several other techniques of leader training—rests on a firm and well-established theoretical framework. For this reason alone, we believe, it is worthy of further, careful study.

The contingency model: A concluding comment.   Before concluding, we should note that certain features of the contingency model remain controversial. For example, as Fiedler himself has noted, a degree of ambiguity persists concerning the location of specific situations along the dimension of control by the leader. Similarly, some critics have questioned the adequacy of the questionnaire used to assess leader esteem for least preferred co-worker (LPC). Specifically, they have noted that the reliability of this measure is not as high as would be ideal.[38] Despite these criticisms, there can be little doubt that the contingency model has already had a major impact upon our knowledge of leadership and leader effectiveness. Thus, with continued refinements it may well offer additional contributions of a practical as well as a theoretical nature in the years ahead.

Vroom and Yetton's Normative Theory: In Making Decisions, How Much Group Participation Is Enough?

One of the major tasks leaders perform is making decisions. Indeed, one defining characteristic of leadership positions is that they are ones where "the buck finally stops," and concrete actions must be taken. As you probably recall, we have already examined decision making in some detail (see Chapter 11). Thus, our purpose here is certainly not to return to full consideration of this basic process. Rather, we wish to address a question pertaining specifically to decisions as leaders make them. The issue is this: In making their decisions, how much participation should leaders allow subordinates? Obviously this can vary tremendously. On the one extreme, leaders can gather appropriate information and simply make their decisions alone, without any input from subordinates. On the other, they can consult these persons closely and reach a decision with them through consensus. Which of these approaches is better? Research designed to answer this question failed to provide a clear-cut answer.[39] In some studies, participative decisions seemed better, while in others such an advantage failed to appear. The reason for these inconclusive findings now seems clear. Just as there is no single best style of leadership, so too there is no single "best" strategy for making decisions. Rather, situational factors play a key role in determining which approach will yield the best results (i.e., the highest quality decisions and the greatest degree of acceptance by subordinates). But what situational factors are crucial in this regard, and how can we use information about them to select the most appropriate—and effective—decision strategies? Intriguing answers to these questions are suggested by a model of leader decision making developed by Vroom and Yetton.[40,41]

These investigators begin by identifying five contrasting methods of reaching such decisions. As you can see from the descriptions in Table 14-2, they run the entire gamut from decisions made solely by the leader through ones that are fully participative in nature. Vroom and Yetton then note that there is something of a

TABLE 14-2   Making Decisions: Alternative Approaches

Leaders can adopt any one of several different approaches to making decisions. As suggested here, these vary greatly with respect to the degree of participation by subordinates. (Source: Based on information from Vroom, *Handbook of Industrial and Organizational Psychology.* Chicago: Rand McNally, 1976.)

LEADERSHIP METHOD	DESCRIPTION
AI	Leader solves problem or makes decision alone, using information available to him or her at the time.
AII	Leader obtains necessary information from subordinates, then reaches decision alone.
CI	Leader shares problem with subordinates individually. Then the leader makes a decision alone.
CII	Leader shares problem with subordinates as a group, obtaining ideas and suggestions from them. Then, he/she makes the decision alone.
GII	Leader shares problem with subordinates as a group. Then, a solution is reached through discussion to consensus.

trade-off between these various strategies. In general, decisions reached through participative means stand a better chance of gaining subordinate acceptance and support. But at the same time decisions reached solely by the leader may be made more quickly and efficiently. The trick for a good leader, then, is to choose the specific decision-making strategy that will maximize these potential benefits. But how is this to be done? Vroom and Yetton offer specific suggestions.

Basically, they suggest that leaders should attempt to zero in on the best approach (or at least begin to identify ones that are feasible) by answering several basic questions about the situation—questions relating to key attributes of the problem they face. As you can see from Table 14-3, these questions relate to such issues as the importance of making a high-quality decision and the likelihood that this decision, once made, will be accepted by subordinates. Vroom and Yetton contend that as a leader answers each of these questions, various potential approaches to reaching the decision will be eliminated. They will be seen to be unfeasible, given present conditions. For example, imagine that in answer to Question A in Table 14-3, a leader replies "Yes—quality *is* important." This answer eliminates method AI (see Table 14-2), since that approach runs the risk of yielding a low-quality decision. Similarly, imagine that in answer to Question D, the leader replies "Yes—acceptance by subordinates *is* critical to effective implementation." In this case options AI and AII are both eliminated. After all, each involves an approach in which the leader makes the decision alone, and under these conditions acceptance by subordinates may be difficult to obtain. In a similar manner, answers to the remaining questions in Table 14-3 help the leader eliminate other unfeasible options and identify those that are most appropriate in the present setting.

In using the Vroom and Yetton model, a *decision tree* like the one shown in Figure 14-11 is often very helpful. Depending on the answers to each of the key

TABLE 14-3   Key Questions in the Vroom and Yetton Model

According to Vroom and Yetton, attention to these basic questions about a situation or problem can help leaders identify the most useful decision-making strategy to follow. (Source: Paraphrased from Vroom, 1976.)

Question A:	Is a high quality decision required?
Question B:	Do I have enough information to make such a decision?
Question C:	Is the problem structured?
Question D:	Is it crucial for implementation that subordinates accept the decision?
Question E:	If I made the decision by myself, is it likely to be accepted by my subordinates?
Question F:	Do subordinates share the organizational goals that will be obtained through solution of this problem?
Question G:	Is conflict among subordinates likely to result in the context of preferred decisions?

Key Questions to be Asked/Answered About Situation or Problem

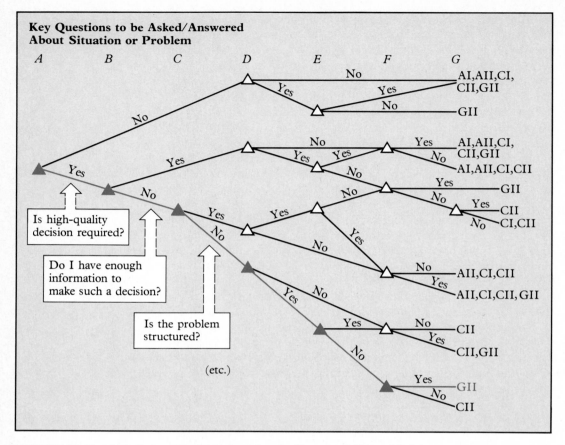

FIGURE 14-11   A Technique Useful in Applying the Vroom and Yetton Model

By answering seven key questions and tracing a path through this type of *decision tree*, leaders can identify feasible approaches to decision making in almost any situation. Note: a path leading to the conclusion that only GII (full participation by subordinates) is appropriate is shown in *colored ink*. Feasible decision-making approaches are shown at the end of each potential path. (Source: Victor H. Vroom, "Leadership" in Marvin D. Dunnette (Ed.), *Handbook of Industrial and Organizational Psychology*. Chicago: Rand McNally, 1976. By permission of the author and editor.)

questions mentioned in Table 14–3, a leader can quickly trace a path through this type of diagram and arrive at those decision-making approaches that are most feasible. As a concrete example of such procedures, consider a case in which a leader's answers to the seven key questions are as follows:

• Question A: *Yes*—a high quality decision is needed.
• Question B: *No*—the leader does not have sufficient information to make a high quality decision alone.

- Question C: *No*—the problem is not structured.
- Question D: *Yes*—acceptance by subordinates is crucial to implementation.
- Question E: *No*—if the leader makes the decision alone, it is not certain that it will be accepted by subordinates.
- Question F: *No*—subordinates do not share organizational goals.
- Question G: *Yes*—conflict among subordinates is likely.

As you can readily see, this series of answers leads to the conclusion that only one decision-making approach is feasible in this situation: full participation by group members (GII). The path leading to this conclusion is shown in color in Figure 14-11. Of course, different answers to any of the seven key questions would have guided the leader into different branches of the decision tree and so to a different conclusion. Regardless of the specific outcome, though, this technique for applying the Vroom and Yetton model seems to be a helpful one.

But now we must address another question: What happens when, after the seven key questions and tracing an appropriate path, we discover that several feasible options exist? How do we go about choosing among them? Vroom and Yetton indicate that several potential strategies exist. For example, we might adopt an approach that emphasizes efficiency. Here the decision approach that requires the smallest number of work hours would be selected. Alternatively, we could follow a strategy that focuses upon the development of decision-making skills among subordinates. Here we might choose an approach that offers such persons maximum participation in the decision process. In sum, there is no single best technique for choosing among feasible approaches. Rather, leaders should complete this final step in accordance with broad organizational goals.

In conclusion, we should note that while relatively little research has yet been conducted to test the accuracy of the Vroom and Yetton model, some encouraging results have been obtained. For example, when managers are asked to describe recent problems and how they solved them, their answers suggest that they follow rules similar to the ones outlined by Vroom and Yetton.[42] Further—and perhaps even more important—they report a high degree of flexibility in their decision styles or approaches. Thus, they report using participative decision making in some situations and nonparticipate strategies in others. Thus, as suggested by the theory, actual managers report "going with the situation." To the extent they do, Vroom and Yetton would suggest, their chances of selecting the best strategy— and so being an effective leader—will be enhanced.

Path-Goal Theory: When Leaders Serve as Guides

Individuals rarely work for nothing. Rather, as we have repeatedly noted, they seek—and expect to attain—specific goals through their on-the-job behavior. This basic fact about human motivation serves as the basis for a third major approach to leadership—the **path-goal theory.**[43] This theory suggests that leader behavior will be accepted by and satisfying to subordinates to the extent they perceive it as instrumental to their goal attainment. That is, leaders will be able to influence their subordinates and will be viewed in a positive light by them to the degree that their actions are seen to provide something not provided by the situation, and so as aiding them in their efforts to reach various goals (see Figure 14–12).

But how can leaders best perform these functions? The answer, as in other modern views of leadership is: *it depends*. According to path-goal theory, leaders can adopt four basic styles of behavior:

1. *Instrumental*—here they focus on planning, organizing, and coordinating the activities of subordinates.
2. *Supportive*—in this style they concentrate on supporting their subordinates and showing concern for them.
3. *Participative*—here leaders share information with their subordinates and consult with them.
4. *Achievement-oriented*—leaders adopting this style focus on setting challenging goals and seeking increments in performance.

FIGURE 14–12   Path-Goal Theory: A Simplified Overview

Path-goal theory suggests that leader behavior will be viewed as acceptable and satisfying by group members only to the extent that it is seen as aiding them in goal attainment.

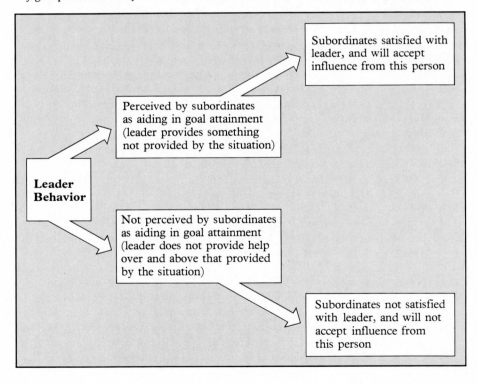

Note that while these styles of leader behavior differ in scope, they are by no means mutually exclusive. Thus, a given leader can demonstrate a combination of all at any given time.

But which pattern is best? This depends largely on the impact of several mediating factors. First, the leadership style of choice seems to be strongly affected by several characteristics of subordinates. For example, if followers are high in ability, an instrumental structured style may be unnecessary; a less structured, supportive approach may be preferable. On the other hand, if subordinates are low in ability, just the opposite may be true. Such persons may need a directive leader to help them attain their goals. Similarly, the needs of subordinates must be considered. Persons high in need for affiliation often prefer a leader who is supportive and participative; subordinates low in such needs will prefer a different pattern. In short, the style selected should be compatible with the abilities, needs, and personalities of followers.

Second, the most effective leadership style also depends on characteristics of the work situation. For example, path-goal theory predicts that when tasks are unstructured, instrumental behavior by the leader may be best—it will help clarify paths to goal attainment for subordinates. When tasks are highly structured and routine, however, subordinates may resent such leadership.

Direct support for several predictions derived from path-goal theory has been obtained in recent studies.[44] For example, in one carefully conducted investigation carried out by Schriesheim and DeNisi, employees of a bank and a manufacturing company were asked to rate their superiors' behavior and also to report on their job satisfaction.[45] They also completed a questionnaire designed to determine the extent to which their jobs were varied or routine, provided much feedback or little feedback, and offered much or little opportunity to interact with others. On the basis of path-goal theory, Schriesheim and DeNisi predicted that when individuals perceived their jobs as varied, low in feedback, and offering little contact with others, satisfaction would *increase* as the level of instrumental behavior shown by their supervisors rose. That is, persons performing such unstructured jobs would find planning, direction, and coordination from the leader useful in reaching their goals and would respond to it favorably. In contrast, when individuals perceived their jobs as routine, high in feedback, and high in opportunity to interact with others, the opposite pattern would hold. Here, reported job satisfaction would *decrease* as the level of instrumental behavior shown by supervisors rose, because employees would perceive instrumental, directive behaviors by the leaders as unnecessary and as *not* aiding them in their attempts to reach important goals. Results offered clear support for these hypotheses. Thus, as predicted by path-goal theory, employees did not prefer a specific style of leader. Rather, they reacted most positively to leaders whose style or approach seemed most likely to help them toward their goals.

To conclude: Path-goal theory suggests that the success of leaders in influencing their subordinates, and the satisfaction of these persons with them, depends on certain key perceptions by subordinates. And foremost among these is

FROM THE MANAGER'S PERSPECTIVE

Enhancing Leader Effectiveness: Some Steps in the Right Directions

If a common underlying theme lies in the present chapter, it is probably this: Leadership is a tremendously complex process—far more complex than was once assumed. Faced with such complexity, you may have concluded by now that there is little we can do to enhance the success of specific leaders—the task is beyond our capacity. If you have reached such conclusions, you are wrong. While we can't offer you a magic formula for improving leader performance, the theories we have examined and recent attempts to apply them to leader training point to concrete steps that can greatly improve others' effectiveness (and your own) in leadership roles. Several of these are described below. Needless to add, they are only general guidelines for enhancing leader effectiveness; each must be carefully adapted for use in specific situations. But we firmly believe that, together, they may often prove quite useful.

1. Above all, be flexible.   If modern theories of leadership tell us anything, it is that *flexibility* is a

virtue—at least with respect to leadership style. Since no single approach or set of behaviors is always best, the guiding principle for leaders should be: always adopt the approach most suited to a given situation. Doing so may prove highly useful, for in the world of organizations, the best leaders are often the most adaptable ones.

2. In setting policy, be consistent.   While flexibility is good as a general rule, there is one area in which it should *not* be applied—the setting and pursuit of policy. Once you have adopted a specific position, it is usually best to stick to your guns. Most persons expect leaders to be consistent in this manner, and departures from this pattern may prove costly. Thus, while you should remain flexible in terms of your style or approach, once committed to a specific course of action, remain firm. If you flinch, the leadership image you damage will probably be your own.

3. Strive for a good match between leaders and tasks.   While flexibility is a valuable goal, there

---

the belief that their leader is in fact helping them to attain valued goals. (How can leader effectiveness be enhanced? The **"PERSPECTIVE"** box above offers some suggestions.)

A GLANCE AT SOME NEW PERSPECTIVES: THE VDL APPROACH AND SUBSTITUTES FOR LEADERSHIP

Leadership is clearly one of the most central topics in the field of organizational behavior. Reflecting this importance, dozens of articles and several books dealing with this issue are published each year. Given the volume of such work, we cannot possibly summarize all of it here. In this final section, though, we would like to provide you with a sample of some of the new and sophisticated perspectives on leadership that have been offered in recent years. Among the most interesting of these are the **VDL approach,** and **substitutes for leadership.**

are obvious limits on its attainment. Often individuals have strongly preferred modes of behavior—patterns they cannot readily alter or abandon. For this reason, it is useful to seek appropriate matches between leaders and tasks or situations. Of course, this goal is often easier to state than attain—situations change quickly, and leaders cannot be shifted on demand. But in some cases, latitude for choice among several potential leaders exists. And in such instances, careful attention to leader characteristics, situational demands, and the match between them may prove well worthwhile.

4. *Choose the most appropriate strategy for making decisions.* As we noted earlier, one of the key tasks leaders perform is making decisions. And several contrasting strategies for performing this vital function exist. Fortunately, it is not necessary to choose among them by guessing. Through application of the simple questions and rules developed by Vroom and Yetton, the best approach can readily be selected. Given the logical nature of this technique, we recommend its use. While it can't help guarantee the best decisions in every situation, it at least helps set the stage for their emergence. And good decisions are certainly a basic aspect of effective leadership.

5. *Always remember—subordinates expect you to help.* Path-goal theory suggests that in the eyes of subordinates, the major function of leaders is straightforward—helping them toward goal attainment. Thus, it is crucial for leaders to do everything in their power to convince subordinates that they are in fact accomplishing this task. In actual practice this often translates into such actions as standing up for one's subordinates, removing obstacles from their paths, and helping them to get the job done. Leaders who engage in such behavior can usually count on strong reciprocal support from their subordinates. Leaders who do not may find that they are perceived—and treated—as being superfluous. □

The VDL Approach: Focus on Leader-Subordinate Dyads

Do leaders treat all of their subordinates the same? Most theories of leadership we have considered assume that they do and that for this reason, it is appropriate to study leader behavior in general. Yet a moment's reflection suggests that, in fact, leaders often behave quite differently toward different subordinates. Further, these differences may strongly shape the nature of their relations with these persons and so, ultimately, key job-related behaviors. These basic insights lie at the core of a new approach to leadership developed by Dansereau, Graen, and their colleagues—the *VDL approach.*[46]

This perspective suggests that because leaders often treat various subordinates differently, they develop different kinds of dyadic relationships with them. And these contrasting relationships, in turn, exert powerful effects on the behavior and perceptions of both leaders and subordinates. According to the VDL approach, then, our focus in the study of leadership should be on *vertical dyads*—specific leader-subordinate pairs.

In research on such dyads, Dansereau, Graen, and others have found that in at least some organizations leaders tend to treat their subordinates in one of two contrasting ways. First, in dealing with most of these persons they adopt an approach based largely on formal authority. That is, they seek to influence the behavior of these subordinates through roles and powers granted to them by the "employment contract." This process is termed *supervision*. Second, in dealing with a much smaller group, leaders adopt an approach in which they seek to influence subordinates' behavior *without* recourse to formal authority. Here, they rely on such techniques as offering certain employees greater job latitude, influence in decisions, support, and communication when they behave in certain ways. Dansereau and Graen term this process *leadership*, which they distinguish from supervision. Basically, then, research on the VDL approach suggests that leaders often develop two groups of subordinates: ones to whom they extend little latitude in negotiating job responsibilities and whom they perceive largely as "hired hands" or an "out-group," and others to whom they extend greater latitude and whom they view as belonging to a trusted "cadre" or "in-group."

Additional findings obtained in research on the VDL approach suggest that these contrasting methods of dealing with subordinates strongly affect both their behavior and perceptions. Thus, subordinates in a leader's "in-group" tend to report fewer difficulties in dealing with the leader and perceive her as more responsive to their job needs than those in the out-group. Further, they spend more time and energy in communicating and administering activities than those in the out-group.[47]

In sum, it appears that leaders do *not* treat all subordinates the same and that differences in their approach to specific persons may strongly affect the nature of the dyadic relationships that develop. And recent findings suggest that such differences, in turn, can exert strong effects upon employee attitudes and satisfaction.[48] By calling attention to these facts, the VDL approach provides new and significant insights into the leadership process—ones that may well prove valuable in future research.

Substitutes for Leadership: Why Sometimes Leaders Are Superfluous

Theories of leadership differ greatly in their details and in their assertions. Yet, all begin with one central idea: leaders are important. Basically, they assume that leaders perform crucial functions for their organizations and so affect them profoundly. At first glance, this assumption seems eminently reasonable; indeed, it is tempting to conclude that leaders are important almost by definition—to a large extent, this is what makes them leaders! But is this really so? According to a framework proposed by Kerr and Jermier, there is actually room for considerable doubt on this score.[49] These researchers agree that the functions usually ascribed to leaders—providing task structure and showing support for their subordinates—*are* important. But they also suggest that in some cases, these can be accomplished apart from the leader. For example, in some cases the ability, knowledge, and experience of subordinates may make guidance from the leader unnecessary. Similarly, a high level of cohesiveness within a work group or a high degree of intrinsic interest in the tasks being performed may make support and consideration from the leader superfluous. According to Kerr and Jermier, conditions such as these, which they term *substitutes for leadership,* tend to neutralize the functions of a leader—to make the leader, in short, unnecessary. A list of such factors is shown in Table 14-4 and as you can readily see, a wide range of circumstances seem capable of playing such a role.

Some evidence for the existence of substitutes for leadership has been obtained in recent field studies.[50] For example, in one investigation involving university and city police, Kerr and Jermier found that leader behaviors actually exerted *weaker* effects on several aspects of work-related activities (e.g., willingness to strive for organizational goals) than did substitutes for leadership (e.g., feedback from the tasks being performed). When one recalls that leadership roles are given high importance within police departments, these findings seem doubly impressive.

TABLE 14-4   Substitutes for Leadership: A Partial List

As shown here, a number of different conditions can serve as substitutes for key aspects of leadership. (Source: Based on information in Kerr & Jermier, *Organizational Behavior and Human Performance,* 1978, *22,* 375-403.)

FACTOR	ASPECT OF LEADERSHIP FOR WHICH IT CAN SUBSTITUTE	
	TASK-ORIENTED FUNCTION (INITIATING STRUCTURE)	RELATIONSHIP-ORIENTED FUNCTION (SHOWING CONSIDERATION)
1. Ability, experience, or knowledge of subordinates		✔
2. Indifference toward organizational rewards on part of subordinates	✔	✔
3. Tasks are routine and unambiguous		✔
4. Tasks provide direct feedback		✔
5. Tasks intrinsically satisfying	✔	
6. High degree of formalization (goals, plans, responsibility all clearly stated)		✔
7. Inflexibility in rules and procedures		✔
8. Organizational rewards not under leader's control	✔	✔
9. High degree of cohesiveness in work group	✔	✔
10. Distance between superior and subordinates	✔	✔

On the basis of such results, Kerr and Jermier conclude that the importance of leaders to their groups actually varies. If other sources of structure and support are absent, their role may in fact be crucial. But if these are present, in the form of factors such as the ones shown in Table 14-4, leaders may have little downward influence; indeed, they may be seen as largely superfluous by their subordinates.

Before concluding, we should note that these suggestions are somewhat controversial in nature. Many experts argue that leaders are still important, even in cases in which substitutes for some of their key functions exist. For example, in such cases they may affect their subordinates by serving either as models or as spokespersons for them. Such arguments aside, though, it is clear that Kerr and Jermier have called attention to a crucial fact. While leaders *are* often important to their organizations, we should take care to avoid assuming that this is always the case.

SUMMARY

Leadership can be viewed as a special type of influence—the influence exerted by one member of a group or organization over many others. It was once assumed that leaders differ from followers in terms of a small number of key traits. However, few differences of this type were uncovered in several decades of empirical research.

Leaders differ greatly in their approach or style of leadership. *Authoritarian leaders* wish to be totally in control of the groups they direct, while *democratic leaders* afford subordinates a degree of choice in such matters as choosing group activities. Some leaders seem primarily concerned with task accomplishment. Leaders high on this dimension (*initiating structure*) engage in such actions as organizing tasks and setting deadlines. Other leaders seem primarily concerned with personal relations. Leaders high on this dimension (*showing consideration*) often help subordinates with personal problems and attempt to gain their trust.

Several factors influence how individuals are perceived as leaders, and how effective or ineffective they are perceived in this role. Persons who are *competent, consistent* in their policies, and who engage in *high rates of verbal participation* are usually rated higher as leaders than persons who are incompetent, inconsistent, and who demonstrate low rates of verbal participation. Perceptions of leaders and leader behavior are also affected by implicit cognitive frameworks (e.g., *implicit theories of leadership*).

Modern theories of leadership emphasize the importance of situational factors and conditions. The **contingency model** developed by Fiedler suggests that the effectiveness of leaders who are primarily task-oriented and those who are primarily relations-oriented differs in situations affording the leader varying degrees of control over subordinates. The **normative theory** proposed by Vroom and Yetton suggests techniques through which leaders can select the most effective strategies for making decisions. Finally, the **path-goal theory** developed by

House and others suggests that the success of leaders in influencing subordinates, and the satisfaction of these persons with them, is strongly affected by subordinates' perception that leaders are aiding them toward goal attainment.

Two new perspectives on leadership are the *VDL approach* and *substitutes for leadership*. The VDL approach calls attention to the fact that leaders treat different subordinates differently and suggests that interest should be directed to specific leader-subordinate dyads. Substitutes for leadership notes that many of the key functions leaders perform can sometimes be fulfilled either by other members of the group or by impersonal factors (e.g., feedback from the tasks being performed, high cohesiveness among work group members). Thus, it suggests that in some cases, leaders may be perceived as largely superfluous by their subordinates.

KEY TERMS

AUTHORITARIAN LEADERSHIP   A style of leadership in which the leader attempts to control virtually every aspect of group functioning. Authoritarian leadership often results in reduced morale but can promote high productivity under some conditions.

CONTINGENCY MODEL OF LEADER EFFECTIVENESS   A theory suggesting that leader effectiveness is jointly determined by certain aspects of a leader's personality and the degree of situational control he or she can exercise over subordinates.

DEMOCRATIC LEADERSHIP   A style of leadership in which the leader allows subordinates considerable input into the nature and sequence of group activities. Democratic leadership often results in high productivity and high morale.

ESTEEM FOR LEAST PREFERRED CO-WORKER   Refers to the tendency of leaders to describe the person with whom they have most difficulty working in positive or negative terms. High LPC leaders appear to be primarily concerned with establishing good relations with their subordinates. Low LPC leaders appear to focus mainly on successful task completion.

GREAT MAN/GREAT WOMAN THEORY   A theory of leadership suggesting that (1) great leaders differ from other human beings with respect to a small number of key traits, and (2) these traits remain stable across time.

IMPLICIT THEORIES OF LEADERSHIP   Refers to cognitive frameworks concerning the characteristics and behavior of leaders. Implicit theories of leadership are held by most persons and may strongly affect their ratings of leader behavior.

INITIATING STRUCTURE   Refers to a style of leadership focused mainly on successful task accomplishment. Leaders high on this dimension engage in such actions as organizing work, setting deadlines, and assigning individuals to specific tasks.

LEADER BEHAVIOR   Refers to behaviors shown by leaders. More specifically, this term is used to refer to distinct and recognizable styles of leadership adopted by different persons when serving in this capacity.

LEADER EMERGENCE   The process through which specific individuals come to be perceived or recognized as leaders. Both characteristics of these persons and implicit stereotypes about leadership play a role.

LEADERSHIP Refers to a special type of influence—influence exerted by one member of an organization over several others. The greater the extent to which specific persons can influence the attitudes or behavior of others, the more they are perceived as being leaders.

NORMATIVE THEORY A theory of leadership concerned primarily with selecting the most appropriate strategy for making decisions in a given situation. The theory suggests that no single strategy is best. Rather, different approaches involving more or less participation by subordinates will succeed to varying degrees under different conditions.

PATH-GOAL THEORY A theory of leadership suggesting that leader behavior will be acceptable and satisfying to subordinates only to the extent that they perceive it as aiding them toward goal attainment.

SHOWING CONSIDERATION Refers to a style of leadership focused mainly on the establishment of warm, friendly relations with subordinates. Leaders high on this dimension engage in such actions as showing support for their subordinates, helping them deal with personal problems, and treating them as equals.

SUBSTITUTES FOR LEADERSHIP An approach suggesting that sometimes key functions performed by leaders can be accomplished by other group members, or even by impersonal conditions relating to tasks and group structure.

TRAIT THEORY The view that leaders differ from other persons with respect to specific traits. According to this theory, if the key traits involved in leadership could be identified, the nature of this process would be clarified.

VDL APPROACH A perspective calling attention to the fact that leaders treat different subordinates differently. The VDL approach suggests that these differences in turn affect leader-subordinate relations, and also the behavior of both parties.

NOTES

1. Hunt, J.G., & Larson, L.L. (Eds.). *Crosscurrents in leadership.* Carbondale: Southern Illinois University Press, 1979.

2. Hollander, E.P. *Leadership dynamics: A practical guide to effective relationships.* New York: The Free Press, 1978.

3. Gibb, C.A. Leadership. In G. Lindzey & E. Aronson (Eds.), *Handbook of social psychology.* Reading, Mass.: Addison-Wesley, 1969, 205–282.

4. Bass, B.M. *Stogdill's handbook of leadership: A survey of theory and research.* Riverside, N.J.: The Free Press, 1981.

5. Lewin, K., Lippitt, R., & White, R.K. Patterns of aggressive behavior in experimentally created "social climates." *Journal of Social Psychology,* 1939, *10,* 271–299.

6. Rosenbaum, L.L., & Rosenbaum, W.B. Morale and productivity consequences of group leadership style, stress, and type of task. *Journal of Applied Psychology,* 1971, *55,* 343–348.

7. Fodor, E.M. Group stress, authoritarian style of control, and use of power. *Journal of Applied Psychology,* 1976, *61,* 313–318.

8. Kipnis, D. *The powerholders.* Chicago: University of Chicago Press, 1976.

9. Kipnis, D., Schmidt, S., Price, K., & Stitt, C. Why do I like thee: Is it your performance of my orders? *Journal of Applied Psychology,* 1981, *66,* 324–328.

10. Halpin, A.W., & Winer, B.J. A factorial study of the leader behavior descriptions. In R.M. Stogdill & A.E. Coons (Eds.), *Leader behavior: Its description and measurement.* Columbus: Ohio State University, Bureau of Business Research. Research Monograph No. 88, 1957, 39–51.

11. Katz, D., Maccoby, N., & Morse, N.C. *Productivity, supervision, and morale in an office situation.* Ann Arbor: University of Michigan, Institute for Social Research, 1951.

12. Weissenberg, P., & Kavanagh, M.H. The independence of initiating structure and consideration: A review of the evidence. *Personnel Psychology,* 1972, *25,* 119–130.

13. Fleishman, E.A. Twenty years of consideration and structure. In E.A. Fleishman & J.G. Hunt (Eds.), *Current developments in the study of leadership.* Carbondale: Southern Illinois University Press, 1973.

14. Vroom, V.H. Leadership. In M.D. Dunnette (Ed.), *Handbook of industrial and organizational psychology.* Chicago: Rand McNally, 1976.

15. Fleishman, E.A. Twenty years of consideration and structure. In E.A. Fleishman & J.G. Hunt (Eds.), *Current developments in the study of leadership.* Carbondale: Southern Illinois University Press, 1973.

16. Patchen, M. The locus and basis of influence on organizational decisions. *Organizational Behavior and Human Performance,* 1974, *11,* 195–221.

17. Michener, H.A., & Burt, M.R. Components of "authority" as determinants of compliance. *Journal of Personality and Social Psychology,* 1975, *31,* 606–614.

18. Price, K.H., & Garland, H. Compliance with a leader's suggestions as a function of perceived leader/member competence and potential reciprocity. *Journal of Applied Psychology,* 1981, *66,* 329–336.

19. Hollander, E.I., & Julian, J.W. A further look at leader legitimacy, influence, and innovation. In L. Berkowitz (Ed.), *Group processes.* New York: Academic Press, 1978.

20. Sorrentino, R.M., & Boutillier, R.G. The effect of quantity and quality of verbal interaction on ratings of leadership ability. *Journal of Experimental Social Psychology,* 1975, *11,* 403–411.

21. Hughes, E.J. The presidency versus Jimmy Carter. *Fortune,* December 4, 1978, p. 58.

22. Staw, B.M., & Ross, J. Commitment in an experimenting society: A study of the attribution of leadership from administrative scenarios. *Journal of Applied Psychology,* 1980, *65,* 249–260.

23. Fiedler, F.E. Contingency model and the leadership process. In L. Berkowitz (Ed.), *Advances in experimental social psychology* (Vol. 11). New York: Academic Press, 1978.

24. Vroom, V.H., & Yetton, P.W. *Leadership and decision making.* Pittsburgh: University of Pittsburgh Press, 1973.

25. House, R.J. A path-goal theory of leader effectiveness. *Administrative Science Quarterly,* 1971, *16,* 321–338.

26. Eden, D., & Leviatan, V. Implicit leadership theory as a determinant of the factor structure underlying supervisory behavior scales. *Journal of Applied Psychology,* 1975, *60,* 736–740.

27. Rush, M.C., Thomas, J.C., & Lord, R.G. Implicit leadership theory: A potential threat to the internal validity of leader behavior questionnaires. *Organizational Behavior and Human Performance,* 1977, *20,* 93–110.

28. Rush, M.C., Phillips, J.S., & Lord, R.G. Effects of a temporal delay in rating on leader behavior descriptions: A laboratory investigation. *Journal of Applied Psychology,* 1981, *66,* 442–450.

29. Weiss, H.M., & Adler, S. Cognitive complexity and the structure of implicit leadership theories. *Journal of Applied Psychology,* 1981, *66,* 69–78.

30. Sims, H. Limitations and extensions to questionnaires in leadership research. In J.G. Hunt & L.L. Larson (Eds.), *Crosscurrents in leadership.* Carbondale: Southern Illinois University Press, 1979.

31. Fiedler, F.E. Contingency model and the leadership process. In L. Berkowitz (Ed.), *Advances in experimental social psychology* (Vol. 11). New York: Academic Press, 1978.

32. Fiedler, F.E., & Chemers, M.M. *Leadership and effective management.* Glenview, Ill.: Scott, Foresman, 1974.

33. Strube, M.J., & Garcia, J.E. A meta-analytic investigation of Fiedler's contingency model of leadership effectiveness. *Psychological Bulletin,* 1981, *90,* 307–321.

34. Fiedler, F.E. Leadership experience and leader performance—Another hypothesis shot to hell. *Organizational Behavior and Human Performance,* 1970, *5,* 1–14.

35. Fiedler, F.E., Bons, P.M., & Hastings, L. The utilization of leadership resources. In W.T. Singleton & P. Spurgeon (Eds.), *Measurement of human resources.* London: Taylor & Francis, 1975. Pp. 233–244.

36. Fiedler, F.E. Contingency model and the leadership process. In L. Berkowitz (Ed.), *Advances in experimental social psychology* (Vol. 11). New York: Academic Press, 1978.

37. Fiedler, F.E., Mahar, L., & Schmidt, S. Four validation studies of contingency model training (Tech. Rep. 75-70). Seattle: University of Washington, Organizational Research.

38. Ashour, A.S. The contingency model of leadership effectiveness: An evaluation. *Organizational Behavior and Human Performance,* 1973, *9,* 339–355.

39. Wood, M.T. Power relationships and group decisionmaking in organizations. *Psychological Bulletin,* 1973, *79,* 280–293.

40. Vroom, V.H., & Yetton, P.W. *Leadership and decision making.* Pittsburgh: University of Pittsburgh Press, 1973.

41. Vroom, V.H. Leadership. In M.D. Dunnette (Ed.), *Handbook of industrial and organizational psychology.* Chicago: Rand McNally, 1976.

42. Vroom, V.H., & Yetton, P.W. *Leadership and decision making.* Pittsburgh: University of Pittsburgh Press, 1973.

43. House, R.J., & Dessler, G. The path-goal theory of leadership: Some post hoc and a prioro tests. In J.G. Hunt & L.L. Larson (Eds.), *Contingency approaches to leadership.* Carbondale: Southern Illinois University Press, 1974.

44. Schriesheim, C.A., & Kerr, S. Theories and measures of leadership: A critical appraisal of current and future directions. In J.G. Hunt & L.L. Larson (Eds.), *Leadership: The cutting edge.* Carbondale: Southern Illinois University Press, 1977.

45. Schriesheim, C.A., & DeNisi, A.S. Task dimensions as moderators of the effects of instrumental leadership: A two-sample replicated test of Path-Goal leadership theory. *Journal of Applied Psychology,* 1981, *66,* 589-597.

46. Dansereau, F., Jr., Graen, G., & Haga, W.J. A vertical dyad linkage approach to leadership within formal organizations: A longitudinal investigation of the role making process. *Organizational Behavior and Human Performance,* 1975, *13,* 46-78.

47. Ibid.

48. Vecchio, R.P. A further test of leadership effect due to between-groups variation and within-group variation. *Journal of Applied Psychology,* 1982, *67,* 200-208.

49. Kerr, S., & Jermier, J.M. Substitutes for leadership: Their meaning and measurement. *Organizational Behavior and Human Performance,* 1978, *22,* 375-403.

50. Ibid.

Part Four

Enhancing Organizational Effectiveness

15

Organizational Design:
Planning for Effectiveness

KEY CONCEPTS

Organizational Structure
Job Specialization
Departmentalization
Scalar Chain of Command
Centralization
Formalization
Complexity
Systems Approach
Organizational Design
Bureaucratic Model
Behavioral Theories of
    Organizational Design

Role Theory
Linking-Pin Model
Contingency Approach
Environment
Technology
Sociometric Approach
Theory Z
Project Design
Matrix Designs
Free-Form Designs

□   □   □

It's Thanksgiving, and as you do almost every year, you have returned to your home town for a visit. Although you're something of a gourmet and enjoy a wide range of exotic cuisines, there's still nothing quite like Mom's turkey and home-made dressing—to say nothing of her famous pies! And you do enjoy seeing your family and old friends. As luck would have it, Joe Poulman, one of your best pals, is also home this year. You haven't seen him for many months, so it's a pleasure to get together and talk over old times. Right now, the two of you are sitting in his parents' home, sipping steaming cups of coffee.

"Well," Joe begins, "How do you like working in Silicon Valley? I heard from Hazel that you took a job out there last spring."

"I like it a lot," you answer with enthusiasm. "I'm in the research department of my company, and the atmosphere there is great. There's a top man—Dr. Stiles—but you'd never know it. He doesn't throw his weight around at all. Everyone acts pretty much like equals. And is that ever a change for me! At Chemco, where I worked before, I couldn't make a move without getting permission from at least five different people."

Joe laughs, and then asks, "But what exactly do you do? I mean, what's your specific job?"

"That's kind of hard to answer. No one really has a formal, set job. We all work on whatever has top priority at the moment. And we team up with different people at different times, depending on who's available, and what's needed."

Joe looks a bit disturbed at these comments. "Gee, I don't know . . . I guess that would be okay, but I like a little more structure myself."

"Well, Joe, that doesn't make much sense for us. We're a small company in a brand new field—one that's changing every day. So, we have to be flexible to stay on top of things. Change or fade away—that's almost the motto out there."

"I can buy that," Joe replies. "But it sure wouldn't work for us. You know the government—rules, rules, rules! Everyone knows exactly what their job involves and

what falls within their jurisdiction. And there's sure never any doubt about who's in charge. I mean, it's a real pecking order. But I don't see how we could do it any differently. Our work is pretty routine, so having things structured seems to help."

"Yeah, sure," you agree. "I guess we just work for very different outfits. There's no reason why what's right for one has to be right for the other."

The two people mentioned in this story both seem happy in their jobs. Yet it is clear that they work in sharply different settings. One is employed by a small, "high-tech" company—a business operating on the cutting edge of scientific and technological knowledge. In it, there are few set jobs, few rules, and little overt concern with status. The atmosphere is informal, communication is open, and decision making appears to be shared (see Figure 15-1). In contrast, the other person works in a large government agency. And this organization is, in several respects, the polar opposite of the first. The nature of all jobs is clearly specified, and there are numerous rules telling employees exactly how to proceed. A rigid line of command exists, decision making is centralized, and communication is more formal, often consisting of memos or other written documents.

Obviously these two organizations are very different places in which to work. But do these differences count? Are they reflected in the behavior, satisfaction, motivation, and performance of employees? In short, is one better—in terms of reaching its goals—than the other? These are important questions, and together, they serve as the basis for major areas of study in the field of organizational behavior—**organizational structure** and **design.**[1,2]

Work on these topics has generally been concerned with two basic issues. First, what are the dimensions along which organizations can vary, at least with respect to the ways in which they are "put together" and operate? Second, and perhaps

"I think it's time we established new guidelines for corporate behavior."

FIGURE 15-1 Organizational Structure: One Extreme

The organization shown here has clearly adopted an informal structure and climate—perhaps, as the speaker suggests, a bit *too* informal. (Source: Drawing by Stevenson; © 1981 The New Yorker Magazine, Inc.)

even more important, what are the effects of variations along these dimensions on organizational effectiveness? As you can readily see, the answers to these questions have practical implications. Thus, it is far from surprising that they have been the subject of intensive study for several decades. In the present chapter, we will attempt to summarize the knowledge gathered in such work. As will soon become apparent, much has been learned and we *do* know a considerable amount about the nature and impact of organizational structure.[3] But please be forewarned: taken as a whole, our knowledge in this area points to the conclusion that—alas!—there are no simple answers. That is, no single organizational design appears to work best in all cases. Rather, as suggested by the story on page 498, the most effective design appears to vary with a large number of situational factors (e.g., the *environment* confronted by an organization, the type of *technology* at its disposal). This is an important point—one to which we will return several times in the pages that follow.

But in a sense, we are getting ahead of our story. For the moment, let us simply provide you with a brief outline of the topics we will cover in this chapter. First, we will offer a description of several *basic dimensions* of organizational structure. Familiarity with these is essential for comprehending the materials that follow, so please read this section carefully. Second, we will examine several early perspectives on organizational design, including the *classical approach* and the *behavioral perspective*. At one time these enjoyed considerable support. Recently, however, they have been largely replaced by the **contingency approach**—a modern perspective that takes full account of the fact (noted above) that there is no single best organizational design. And finally, we will describe several recent innovations, including *project, matrix,* and *free-form* designs.

ORGANIZATIONAL STRUCTURE: SOME BASIC DIMENSIONS

Organizations are highly complex entities. Further, they differ tremendously in nature. General Motors is an organization, as is the Amalgamated Brotherhood of Pickle Packers. And so, too, are the San Francisco 49ers, the Rolling Stones, and even Hell's Angels (see Figure 15-2). Faced with such diversity, we might be tempted to conclude that organizations differ in an almost infinite number of ways. And then, we might despair of ever being able to describe them in systematic terms. In fact, this is not the case. While organizations *do* differ along many dimensions, some of these appear to be key. That is, differences along certain dimensions appear to be the ones that matter—the ones most likely to be recognized by members, and to have important implications for member behavior and organizational effectiveness.[4,5] Familiarity with these underlying dimensions, therefore, permits us to draw a rough roadmap or chart of virtually any organization. At the least, it permits us to compare one organization with another on certain central characteristics. A number of these key dimensions are described below. Please consider them carefully, for we will have reason to refer to each repeatedly in later sections.

FIGURE 15-2   Organizations: Diversity without Limit

As these photos suggest, organizations are tremendously diverse both in their major functions and in their internal structure. (Source: Photo [left] by Lew Hedberg/Global Focus; photo [right] by Bohdan Hrynewych/The Picture Group.)

Job Specialization: Few Tasks or Many?

One important dimension along which organizations vary concerns the manner in which tasks or work are divided among employees. At the high end of this dimension of **job specialization** are organizations in which each person performs a highly specialized job—one operation on the assembly line, one type of chemical analysis in the laboratory, defense of the company in a single type of legal proceeding. At the low end are organizations in which each employee performs a wide variety of tasks—all steps in the manufacture of some product, sales as well as general office work, and representation of the company in every conceivable type of legal action. As you might suspect, a high degree of job specialization often accompanies bigness; after all, it is impossible to have high levels of specialization in an organization consisting of five persons. But degree of specialization is also affected by many other factors, so this relationship is far from a perfect one.

Departmentalization: Parts within the Whole

In a very small organization, one person may perform each major function or task. As organizations grow, however, several persons may come to perform the same or similar jobs. When this occurs, it often makes good sense, from the standpoint of efficiency, to group these persons into subunits known as *departments*. These can be based on *function*—in which case there might be separate units concerned with personnel, marketing, and operations. Or they can be used on specific *products* or product lines—in which case there might be units devoted to the manufacture of consumer products (e.g., cosmetics and other grooming aids, sports equipment) and ones concerned with commercial items (e.g., the semi-artificial "food" now served by most airlines; those unremovable plastic bubbles used in packaging many products). While virtually all organizations show some degree of **departmentalization,** they vary greatly on this dimension, both in terms of the number of subunits they possess and the degree of integration between them. Thus, departmentalization is a second aspect of internal structure worthy of careful attention.

The Scalar Chain of Command: Who Reports to Whom?

In some organizations employees are on a first-name basis with their bosses. In others they treat these persons more formally; indeed, they may sometimes bow or salute when they meet them. Regardless of such differences, though, the line between superiors and subordinates is usually easy to discern. And while such a chain of command is present in virtually every organization, it can vary greatly in length. In some cases only one or a few levels separate top persons from those on the lowest rung of the organizational ladder. In others, literally dozens of levels intervene. Clearly, organizations differing in this respect are sharply contrasting places in which to work. Thus, understanding the *chain of command*—who reports to whom—is crucial to comprehending just how a given organization operates.

The Span of Control: Flat Structures and Tall Structures

As we have just seen, organizations differ sharply with respect to the length of their chains of command. But this is not the only way in which they vary in terms of superior-subordinate relationships. Another key dimension involves the *span of control*—the number of persons reporting directly to each superior. In some cases, this number is small, and the span of control is narrow. Here, a *tall* organizational structure, involving many levels of supervision may result. In other cases, in contrast, a larger number of subordinates report to each superior. Here, the span of control is wide, and a *flat* organizational structure may exist (see Figure 15–3).

Interestingly, differences along this crucial dimension may reflect the contrasting views of human behavior we described in Chapter 1—Theory X and Theory Y. As you may recall, Theory X (the traditional management view) assumes that people are basically lazy and wish to avoid work and responsibility. To the extent this view is accepted by top management, a narrow span of control (and an accompanying tall structure) may be encouraged. After all, it affords the close supervision of employees Theory X demands. In contrast, Theory Y suggests that how people behave at work depends very much on how they are treated. If they are given responsibility, it is argued, they may in fact be highly motivated and act as self-starters. To the degree *this* view is accepted by management, a wide span

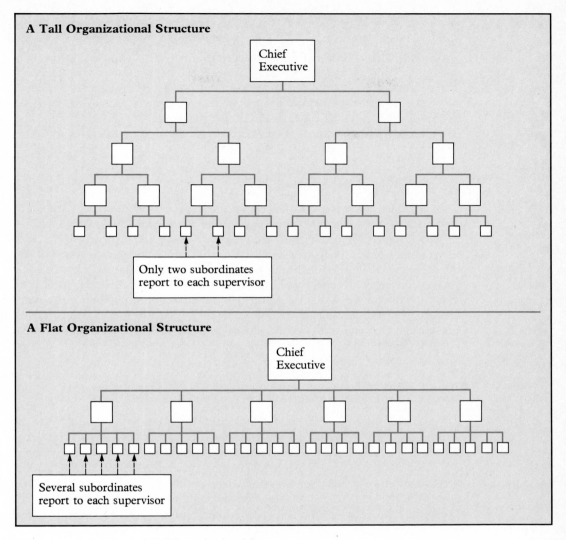

A Tall Organizational Structure

Chief Executive

Only two subordinates report to each supervisor

A Flat Organizational Structure

Chief Executive

Several subordinates report to each supervisor

FIGURE 15-3   Flat and Tall Organizational Structures

A *tall* organizational structure is shown above. Here, the span of control is narrow—only a small number of subordinates report to each supervisor. A *flat* organizational structure is shown below. Here, the span of control is wide—several subordinates report to each supervisor.

of control, involving lower levels of direct supervision, may be preferred. Regardless of whether span of control actually reflects these contrasting views of human behavior, however, it is clear that it represents a key aspect of organizational structure—one we should not overlook.

Centralization: Who Makes Decisions?

A fourth dimension along which organizations often differ involves their degree of **centralization.** In some, decisions are made only at the highest levels by a small number of key persons. In others decision making is shared quite widely, so that even individuals far down in the corporate structure can offer their input. Given the impact of participation in decisions on employee morale, satisfaction, and motivation, there can be little doubt that the degree of centralization or de-centralization present in an organization constitutes a key element of its basic structure.

Formalization: Rules or Flexibility?

The characters in the story at the start of this chapter worked for very different organizations. And one of the key dimensions along which these organizations differed involved **formalization**—the degree to which employees' behavior and responsibilities are clearly specified (often in written rules and procedures). As you probably recall, the small high-tech company had few formal rules. In contrast, the government agency was literally flooded with them. Indeed, it probably issued to all new employees fat handbooks containing information on precisely what their jobs involved and how they should be performed. Differences along this dimension often exert powerful effects on employees' attitudes and behavior. Thus, degree of formalization represents another key dimension of organizational structure we must consider.

Line versus Staff: Orders or Advice?

As organizations grow in size and complexity, they often require the services of persons possessing specialized knowledge or skill (e.g., lawyers, financial experts, personnel specialists). Such persons are often hired for *staff positions.* Individuals occupying such positions can advise but cannot order various courses of action. In a sense they serve as permanent, in-house consultants. In contrast, other employees occupy *line positions* and do have the authority to issue commands to others. The distinction between line and staff is important and must be taken into account in descriptions of organizational structure.

Complexity: An Index of Internal Differentiation

Considered together, several of the dimensions we have already examined contribute to a final aspect of organizational structure we wish to describe: degree of **complexity.** Basically, this term refers to the level of internal differentiation present in a given organization. Two basic types of differentiation exist. First, organizations may be described as *vertically complex* to the extent that they possess many levels of management (i.e., a long chain of command). Second, they may be viewed as *horizontally complex* to the degree that they contain many different departments or specialized subunits. As organizations grow in size and scope, complexity, too, usually increases. As it does, the task of coordinating or integrating the various departments and subunits becomes more effortful and costly. As we will note at later points, the success with which this crucial task is carried out can often play a key role in determining organizational effectiveness.

Organizations: Dynamic, *Not* Static

Organizational structure: the very term itself seems to imply something stable and unchanging—an entity or framework that will be very much tomorrow what it is today. To a degree these implications are accurate. Organizational structure *is* often constant. And this is only reasonable: if it changed repeatedly and precipitously, the result would probably be chaos—and reduced organizational effectiveness. Yet at the same time, organizational structure is far from totally static. When environmental conditions shift, structure too may be altered. Departments may be formed or dissolved; chains of command may be lengthened or shortened; formalization may be increased or reduced. In short, virtually every aspect of organizational structure may be modified when shifting external conditions dictate that this is required. Indeed, it is probably safe to assume that organizations failing to show such flexibility will often fade away: there is little room for immobility in the fast-paced modern world (see Figure 15–4).

FIGURE 15–4   The Costs of Inertia

When organizations fail to adapt to changing conditions in the external environment, their survival may soon be threatened. (Source: UPI photo.)

The fact that organizational structure is far from changeless stems, in turn, from another and even more basic principle: organizations themselves are *dynamic* rather than static. They are in constant interaction with the external environment and are, as a result, subject to pressures for change from this source. Similarly, they usually generate a complex internal environment or climate of their own—one that serves as an additional source of pressures toward change. Perhaps the dynamic quality of organizations is most effectively captured by the modern **systems approach**—a perspective that views organizations as open systems involving *inputs* from the environment, *transformation* of these inputs, and resulting *outputs*.[6] Input can be supplied by human beings or machines and can involve raw materials, information, or other resources. Transformation processes are ones used by the organization to act upon input and to change it in some manner. Finally, outputs are the products or services provided by the organization. For example, consider the case of a gourmet cooking school. Inputs here may include the expertise of the staff, raw materials from suppliers, ovens and other equipment, and the students who enroll. Transformation processes involve the instructional techniques and other procedures used to change the novice cooks into gourmet chefs. And the outputs, of course, are services provided by the school and its well-trained graduates.

As you can readily see, the systems approach or model emphasizes the fact that organizations are dynamic in nature; indeed, within this perspective change (or transformation) is—quite literally—their middle name. Thus, contrary to popular belief, they are neither fixed nor static. On the contrary, they are actually among the most fluid and dynamic—as well as the most fascinating—of human social constructions. (For a discussion of the impact of organizational structure on organizational effectiveness, see the **"FOCUS"** box on pp. 508–509.)

ORGANIZATIONAL DESIGN: EARLY PERSPECTIVES

Noting that organizations differ with respect to internal structure is one thing; determining which of these possible arrangements is most effective is quite another. And it is on this latter task that the field of **organizational design** focuses. Briefly, it seeks to establish basic principles that will help identify the most effective internal structure for any given organization—the one that will be most helpful to it from the point of view of reaching its major goals. In their attempts to accomplish this crucial task, scientists and practitioners have adopted several different perspectives. Among the earliest of these were *scientific management* and the **bureaucratic model.** Together, these are often described as the "classic approach" to organizational design, and both will now be briefly described.

Scientific Management: Some Key Implications

As we hope you will recall, the basic principles of *scientific management* (as outlined by its leading proponent, Frederick W. Taylor) were summarized in Chapter 1. At that time, we noted that this approach focused mainly on two issues: effective job design and enhanced work motivation.[7] Supporters of scientific management believed that through careful and systematic attention to these matters, tremendous advances in efficiency and productivity could be attained. Here, we simply wish to add that several features of scientific management hold important implications for organizational design. First, Taylor strongly recommended the scientific selection and training of workers for specific jobs. Thus, he called for a high degree of *job specialization*. Second, he emphasized the importance of cooperation between management and workers, as well as a fair division of both work and responsibility between them. These recommendations can be interpreted as implying a relatively short chain of command, and perhaps some minimal degree of decentralization as well. In sum, several of Taylor's basic principles for effective management relate quite closely to key dimensions of organizational structure.

The Bureaucratic Model: In Search of the Ideal Structure

In the 1980s, the term *bureaucracy* has a distinctly negative flavor. For many persons, it conjures up images of huge organizations filled with a maze of departments, and thousands of bland employees. Further, the inhabitants of such bureaucracies (those infamous bureaucrats!) are usually perceived as dull, colorless beings—creatures far more concerned with sticking to the letter of needless rules and following pointless procedures than with attaining any real or useful goals (see Figure 15-5).

Given this popular view of bureaucracy, you may find it surprising to learn that at one time it was strongly recommended as the ideal form of organizational

"I'm sorry, dear, but you knew I was a bureaucrat when you married me."

FIGURE 15-5 Bureaucrats: One Common View

As shown here, the public image of bureaucrats is far from flattering. (Source: Drawing by Weber; © 1980 The New Yorker Magazine, Inc.)

FOCUS ON BEHAVIOR

Organizational Structure and Performance: How Close a Link?

As we have just seen, organizations differ greatly along a large number of structural dimensions. Identifying these is clearly worthwhile, for it arms us with key insights into the basic ways in which organizations can be put together. But this is not the major reason for studying such variables. Far more important, we believe, is their possible impact upon organizational effectiveness. In short, we also wish to know whether these aspects of organizational structure influence the ability of organizations to reach their major goals.

Surprisingly, it has proven far easier to pose this question than to answer it. While many skilled investigators have sought to determine whether various structural factors such as those discussed earlier influence organizational performance, no definitive or clear-cut picture has as yet emerged. For almost every factor investigated, some studies report significant relationships between structure and organizational performance, while others fail to observe such effects. Even worse, in many cases different studies report directly opposite results.[8,9] For example, consider the variable of *degree of centralization*. In a recent study, Glisson and Martin found that this factor was positively linked to the productivity and efficiency of thirty social/health service organizations.[10] Their study was carefully conducted, and this pattern of findings seemed quite clear. Yet several other investigations—equally well conducted—have reported contradictory findings; they actually observed a *negative* link between degree of centralization and organizational performance.[11,12] Unfortunately, as we have already noted, inconsistencies of this type appear to be the rule rather than the exception in research on organizational structure and performance.

At first glance, this state of affairs seems quite discouraging. Indeed, after completing a thorough review of the literature in this area, Dalton and his colleagues remarked: "The literature on structure-performance relationships is among the most vexing and ambiguous in the field of management and organizational behavior."[13] But what precisely do these puzzling findings mean? Do they really indicate that there are no important links between structure and organizational performance? Or is there some other interpretation? We strongly favor the latter alternative. In fact, we contend that the present pattern of inconsistent findings stems mainly from three sources, all of which can be adequately handled in further research.

First, careful examination of the present literature on structure and performance suggests that investigators in this area have used many different measures of performance or effectiveness. These have ranged from "hard" indices such as profits, sales, or production, through "soft" measures such as supervisor appraisals or self-perceptions. Given this diversity of dependent measures, it is far from surprising that results, too, have been inconsistent. Second, the impact of structural variables is probably mediated by many other factors not directly related to organizational structure. For example, the impact of structure is probably affected by both the *internal* and *external environment* an organization confronts. The presence of such mediating factors makes it difficult to obtain a clear picture of the impact of various aspects of structure on performance.

Third, and perhaps most important, we believe that the influence of structural variables is indirect. In all probability these factors exert their initial impact upon group processes (e.g., patterns of communication, decision making, style of leadership). Then, these effects influence employee motivation, morale, satisfaction, and—ultimately—performance (see Figure 15-6). Some indirect support for this possibility has been obtained in research studies. For example, in one recent investigation, Oldham and Hackman found that structural variables such as formalization and centralization influence key

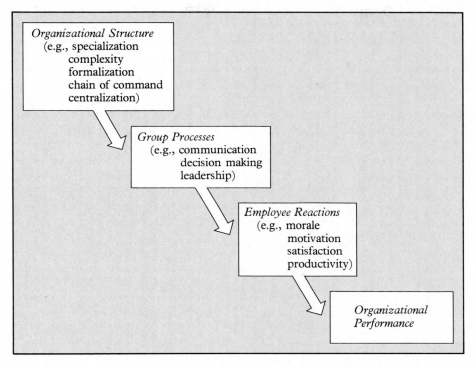

FIGURE 15-6 The Impact of Organizational Structure on Performance: One Possible Mechanism

Various aspects of organizational structure may influence group processes such as patterns of communication, decision making, and leadership. These effects, in turn, may affect the motivation, morale, and performance of employees.

aspects of various jobs (e.g., the degree of autonomy and feedback they provide). And these factors, in turn, affect crucial employee reactions such as motivation and satisfaction.[14] In short, it appears that organizational structure affects productivity indirectly rather than directly. To the extent this is true, the inconsistent findings of past research become less puzzling: there are simply too many intervening steps in the process for simple patterns or answers to emerge.

In sum, it is our view that structural variables *do* play an important role in determining organizational effectiveness. In order to gain a clear picture of these relationships, though, it will be necessary to conduct research specifically designed to separate their effect from those of many other factors. ☐

structure. Perhaps the most vocal proponent of this view was Max Weber, the noted sociologist.[15] (You may already be familiar with Weber's famous thesis that modern capitalism was stimulated by what he termed the *Protestant ethic*—the view that accruing wealth in this world is perfectly acceptable and may even be a sign of spiritual election in the next.) According to Weber, bureaucracy represents the most efficient organizational design—one that should be adopted as widely as possible. But what, precisely, did he mean by this term? On this score, Weber was quite precise. He felt that in its ideal form, bureaucracy was characterized by five major factors. First, it would involve a high degree of *specialization* and division of labor. Each bureaucrat, in short, would perform a limited job. Second, all positions in the bureaucracy would be arranged in a *hierarchy*. Thus, there would be a clear and orderly chain of command. Third, all tasks would be carried out in accordance with a consistent system of *abstract rules*. In this way the impact of individual differences among employees on the central business of the organization would be minimized. Fourth, contact between managers and their subordinates would be *impersonal*. This would prevent friendships or grudges from impinging on decision making and other key processes. Finally, employment would be based on *qualifications*, and promotions on *merit*. As a result, only the best persons would be hired for various jobs, and only those who performed well or who gained seniority would rise to the top.

As you can see, the underlying theme in Weber's conception of bureaucracy can be stated in one word: *rationality*. He felt very strongly that an organization that adopted this rational, rules-oriented approach would by its very nature be highly efficient. After all, the "noise" frequently generated by personal feelings, individual differences, and similar factors would be largely eliminated! We should also note that Weber believed that bureaucracy, as a strategy of organizational design, was totally consistent with a basic underlying trend in Western civilization—a shift toward rationality in *all* spheres of life (politics, religion, economics, etc.).

As we're sure you realize, bureaucracy is very much with us, even today. While few modern organizations are "pure" bureaucracies showing all the characteristics outlined by Weber, many demonstrate several of these in their internal structure. The key question, therefore, is this: does bureaucracy live up to Weber's high expectations? Is it as effective as he maintained? The answer, unfortunately, is: *only sometimes*. There are certainly some organizations structured along bureaucratic lines that seem to be quite effective and efficient. At the same time, though, there are others with a similar internal structure that do not demonstrate these characteristics. On the contrary, they are models of inefficiency and waste, and account for the negative reputation usually associated with the term bureaucracy. (If you have had any dealings with a large government agency in recent years, you are already familiar with these problems.) Many factors contribute to the failure of bureaucracy in such cases, but the underlying reason can be simply stated: several of the basic features described by Weber have hidden costs he did not anticipate.[16]

For example, consider the hierarchical nature of bureaucracy. One outcome of this arrangement may be the thwarting of upward communication (see Chapter 10). That is, individuals at lower levels of the organization are prevented from transmitting information and suggestions to those at higher levels. As a result they come to feel that no one cares about their views. At the same time, top management may be effectively isolated from what is happening within their own organization. Reliance on abstract rules can lead to other difficulties. Often, these regulations take on a life of their own, with the result that rules become ends and actually block attainment of organizational goals. Third, bureaucracy often stifles personal growth. Since individual differences are viewed as a nuisance (remember, the rules are designed to minimize their impact), creativity and innovation are discouraged, while conformity, groupthink, and a dull sameness are fostered. In short, bureaucracies are truly places where "to get along, one must go along" (see our discussion of conformity in Chapter 13). As a result of these weaknesses, bureaucracy often becomes a captive of the characteristics claimed to be its strength. Thus, contrary to statements by Weber, it is certainly *not* a perfect or ideal form of organizational structure. Several of its features may well prove useful under certain conditions; but under others they may actually get in the way of organizational effectiveness and success.

BEHAVIORAL THEORIES OF ORGANIZATIONAL STRUCTURE: FOCUS ON INDIVIDUALS AND GROUPS

Organizational charts consist of boxes representing various departments or positions within an organization and the relationships among them. In an ultimate sense, though, organizations consist of individuals. Awareness of this basic fact has led a number of theorists to argue that in order to gain full comprehension of organizational structure and to develop effective designs, we must direct at least part of our attention to the actions and reactions of employees. In short, they have adopted a *behavioral* approach to the topic of organizational design. A number of different theories of this type have been proposed.[17,18] However, most of these focus either on individuals or on the groups to which they belong. Thus, we will briefly describe one example of each type—**role theory** and the **linking-pin** model.

Role Theory: The Impact of Expectations

Specific positions within an organization usually carry with them expectations about how the persons occupying them should behave. That is, they involve firm expectations about the duties of such individuals, their degree of authority, and their place within the chain of command. Such expectations constitute *roles* and often exert powerful effects upon individual behavior. On the one hand, such expectations are usually widely shared: many persons within an organization hold similar views of the duties and functions accompanying various positions. As a result, pressures toward conforming with these expectations may be great. Second, the requirements of various roles are often general and far-reaching in nature.

Thus, they may dictate a wide range of personal matters as well as specific job-related duties. For example, consider the case of a man who is promoted to the position of Assistant Director for Marketing. His new position carries with it new responsibilities and an increased degree of authority. In addition, though, his new role also dictates changes in other aspects of his behavior. He may now be expected to dress in a more conservative and "business-like" fashion. Others now assume that he will stop eating lunches at his desk, and come, instead, to the Executive Dining Room. And he soon realizes that he is now expected to treat employees in a more formal and aloof manner. In short, his new position—and the new role it involves—may require many shifts in his behavior and general lifestyle.

Roles are also important for another reason. As we saw in Chapter 9, the demands they place on individuals sometimes conflict. For example, a manager may find that his role requires disciplining subordinates—a task he finds very distasteful. Here, conflict between an individual's preferences and his role exists. Similarly, a person occupying a given position in an organization may find that different groups of individuals hold contrasting expectations about his or her responsibilities. Consider the case of the head of some department. Top management may perceive her as *their* person on the scene—someone who will focus on carrying out policies and directives from above. In contrast, the members of her department may view her as *their* representative—the individual whose job it is to go to bat for them within the company. Here *intrarole* conflict exists—conflict between the expectations held by important groups in the individual's life.

Impressed with these and other effects, role theorists suggest that understanding such patterns of interlocking expectations can often shed important light on organizational function and organizational structure.[19] Thus, they focus on uncovering the precise expectations associated with various jobs or positions. Information on this basic issue, they contend, can often tell us much about the behavioral forces at work within an organization—including many links and relationships not shown on the organizational chart. And such knowledge, in turn, may yield important practical benefits.

The Linking-Pin Model: Work Groups and Organizational Design

In many organizational charts, attention is focused on relationships between specific individuals. For example, the chart may indicate—and very precisely—who reports to whom. Such person-to-person relationships are important and play a key role in organizational structure. But several theorists (especially Rensis Likert) believe that relationships involving groups may be even more crucial.[20] Briefly, Likert and others feel that each member of an organization may actually be viewed as belonging to at least two groups: one that he or she leads or represents, and one to which he or she belongs or reports. For example, consider the manager of a single sales division within a large company. This person may feel that she belongs to—and leads—the employees working in her division. In addition, however, she also reports, along with four other division managers, to a regional manager. As a result, she may also perceive that she is a member of *this* group too. Continuing the process, the regional manager may feel that he is part of the group consisting of himself and several division managers. And since he reports, with two other regional managers, to a national director of sales, he also recognizes his membership in this second group (see Figure 15–7).

As diagrammed in Figure 15–7, the linking-pin model may not strike you as very different from the traditional model presented earlier. Indeed, if you are a true devil's advocate, you might suggest that it simply draws triangles instead of squares! Actually, though, the difference is very real. But since it is largely one of perspective or perception, it is difficult to represent on paper. Verbally, it can be stated as follows: according to the linking-pin model, the members of a given organization often perceive that they belong to various groups. And these, in turn, can be quite independent of the formal organizational chart. Further, membership in these groups can exert powerful effects upon both their attitudes and their behavior. Indeed, since commitment and loyalty to such groups can often be quite strong, motivation, morale, and productivity can all be affected. In short, the linking-pin model places great emphasis on the role of groups and group processes in shaping the structure and actual functioning of many organizations.

But what precisely is the relationship between this model and organizational design? Does it offer any specific recommendations for structuring organizations

FIGURE 15-7   The Linking-Pin Model: Groups and Organizational Structure

According to the *linking-pin model,* employees often perceive that they are members of two groups, one they lead or represent and one to which they belong or report.

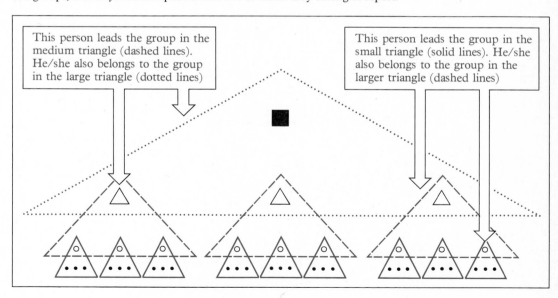

in ways that will enhance their goal attainment? In point of fact, it does. According to Likert, the linking-pin model implies that managers should devote careful attention to establishing *effective work groups*. More precisely, they should be concerned with encouraging work groups with challenging performance goals— groups to which employees can become committed. Once such groups exist, Likert contends, they will make an important contribution to overall organizational effectiveness. But how can such groups be encouraged? Here too Likert makes specific recommendations. Basically, he suggests that the formation of such groups can be facilitated through a series of steps termed *System 4*.[21] These include such strategies as encouraging open communication, decentralizing decisions, and setting goals in a participative manner. Likert strongly urges the adoption of this approach, for he believes that it will usually generate the most effective organizational design. Unfortunately, we must note that little direct evidence for the success of System 4, or for its relationship to the linking-pin model, currently exists. By calling our attention to the key role of groups and group processes in effective organizational design, however, these frameworks have yielded important insights. Thus, in this respect at least, they have offered a considerable contribution to the field.

THE CONTINGENCY APPROACH: MATCHING DESIGNS TO SITUATIONS

The approaches to effective organizational design we have considered so far differ greatly. Yet, they all have one thing in common: each assumes that there is one best organizational design. Identify this, it is reasoned, and the problem will largely be solved: all organizations can then simply adopt this ideal strategy, and so maximize their performance. The appeal of this assumption is obvious. Human beings have a strong preference for simple answers, and strive to attain them whenever possible. But is such a solution feasible with respect to organization design? Is there really a single type that is best for all organizations in all settings and at all times? Unfortunately, the answer provided by decades of systematic research is "no." Organizations face such a wide range of internal and external conditions that there cannot be a single structure or design that will prove successful for all. As this basic fact has become increasingly apparent, a new perspective on organizational design known as the **contingency approach** has taken form.[22,23] Supporters of this approach reason that there is, in fact, no best single structure. Rather, the one that will prove most effective varies with a number of situational factors. In short, the contingency model suggests that we must match organizational design to prevailing situational conditions. But what conditions, specifically, are of central importance in this respect? While many play a role, two seem especially crucial: the **environment** faced by an organization and the **technology** it uses.

The Role of the Environment: Change versus Stability

Organizations do not operate in a social, political, or economic vacuum. Rather, they are surrounded by a complex *environment* involving many factors. Often, these remain relatively stable: public attitudes and tastes go unchanged, political policies are held constant, and economic conditions remain steady. In other cases, however, they demonstrate rapid change. It seems reasonable to predict that different organizational structures may vary in their effectiveness under these contrasting conditions. While some operate efficiently under stable circumstances, others may prove more effective in dealing with rapid change. In short, one key aspect of the external environment, from the point of view of effective organizational design, may be its degree of stability. That this is in fact the case is suggested by the findings of several different studies.

In one of the first and most famous of these investigations, Burns and Stalker examined the organizational structure of twenty different companies.[24] Included in their sample, and of special interest, were a rayon manufacturer, an engineering company, and a newly formed electronics-development firm. The external environment confronted by these organizations differed sharply. While environmental stability was high for the rayon manufacturer, it was lower for the engineering firm, and lowest of all for the electronics company. Burns and Stalker predicted that these differences in environmental stability would be reflected in the structure of the organizations, and results offered support for this prediction. The rayon company showed a relatively formal structure involving highly specialized tasks, limited flow of information, high centralization, and a clear chain of command. In contrast, the structure of the engineering company was more flexible. Tasks were not as clearly defined, and less emphasis was placed on the chain of command. Finally, the electronics-development firm showed the least formal structure of all. Tasks were not rigidly specified, decision making was participative, and information flowed freely both up and down the organization. In short, the internal structure of these companies *did* differ sharply according to the type of environment they faced. Further study of additional organizations confirmed these findings and led Burns and Stalker to a more general conclusion: many organizations adopt either an *organic* or a *mechanistic* style of management (see Table 15-1). And which of these approaches is more effective depends upon the nature of the external environment. When conditions are relatively stable, a mechanistic approach may prove effective, but when conditions show rapid change, the organic approach may be more efficient. In short, neither is necessarily "better"—their relative success is contingent upon situational factors.

Further support for the importance of environmental stability in determining the effectiveness of organizational designs is provided by another well-known study conducted by Lawrence and Lorsch.[25] These investigators compared highly effective and less effective organizations in three different industries: plastics, food, and container manufacture. On the basis of interviews with executives in these companies, they rated the level of *environmental uncertainty* facing each organization. Lawrence and Lorsch expected there would be a clear relationship be-

TABLE 15-1   Organic and Mechanistic Management Systems: Contrasting Approaches
to Internal Structure

Many organizations seem to adopt either an organic or a mechanistic management system.
Several major characteristics of these contrasting approaches are shown here.

ASPECT OF ORGANIZATIONAL DESIGN	ORGANIC STRUCTURE	MECHANISTIC STRUCTURE
Specialization	Low	High
Communication	By advice, counsel	Orders, direction
Locus of authority	At the level where skill or competence exist in the organization	Concentrated in a select group at the top of the organizational hierarchy
Mode of resolving conflicts	Discussion and other forms of interaction	Decision by superior
Flow of information	Relatively free, both up and down the hierarchy	Relatively restricted and mainly downward
Formalization	Low	High

tween this factor and certain aspects of organizational design. Specifically, they
predicted that each department or subsystem within these companies would show
a structure reflecting the degree of uncertainty it faced: the greater the degree of
uncertainty, the more rigid and formalized the structure. Three types of departments or subsystems were examined for each company: *production, sales,* and *research*. As you can probably guess, the degree of environmental uncertainty was
lowest for production units, intermediate for sales, and greatest for research departments. In accordance with their predictions, Lawrence and Lorsch found that
the internal structure of these subsystems did vary with environmental uncertainty. Production units had the most formal structure, research departments had
the least, and sales units were in between. Thus, once again level of environmental
stability was found to be an important determinant of organizational design.

The studies conducted by Burns and Stalker and Lawrence and Lorsch are
viewed as "classics" in the field of organizational design. Indeed, they were responsible, in part, for the development and growth of the contingency perspective. But these investigations, impressive as they are, certainly did not answer
all the complex questions about the impact of the environment on organizational
structure we wish to answer—far from it. Thus, in recent years, many additional
studies have been conducted to further clarify the impact of this important variable. To provide you with the flavor of this newer and even more sophisticated
research, we will briefly describe one additional study—a project conducted by
Lindsay and Rue.[26]

These investigators were interested in examining the impact of the external environment on *long-range planning* within organizations. On the basis of the contingency model, they reasoned that such planning would become increasingly im-

portant—and more complete—as environmental complexity and instability rose. This would be the case because only through adequate planning can organizations adapt their internal structure and operations to meet changing environmental conditions. In addition, Lindsay and Rue predicted that the more complex and unstable environmental conditions, the more organic (as opposed to mechanistic) the long-range planning process would be. (This prediction, of course, was based on findings reported by Burns and Stalker and others, as described earlier.) In order to test these hypotheses, Lindsay and Rue gathered information on the long-range planning activities of 198 different organizations. On the basis of this information, the companies were divided into three categories: those with no long-range plan, those with a moderately complete plan, and those with a highly complete plan. Other information was then used to classify the environments faced by these organizations as stable or unstable, and complex or simple. Results generally offered support for the major predictions. The more complex and unstable the environment, the more complete the long-range plans adopted by the organizations under study (see Figure 15–8). Further, in the case of large companies (those with sales of $108 million or more per year), the greater the degree of environmental complexity and instability, the more organic the process through which long-range plans were formulated. For example, the higher the complexity/instability, the greater the degree of participation afforded to lower levels within the organization. (Interestingly, similar findings were not obtained for small companies, a result suggesting that the management of such organizations may react to adverse environmental conditions differently from the management of larger companies.)

Together, the findings reported by Burns and Stalker, Lawrence and Lorsch, Lindsay and Rue, plus many other researchers point to the conclusion that the environment in which an organization operates plays a key role in shaping its structure and determining its effectiveness.[27] Not all results have been consistent in this respect, but generally, existing evidence suggests that it is impossible to select the most effective design for a specific organization without careful attention to several key aspects of the external environment.[28]

The Role of Technology: Do Tools and Methods Shape Structure?

Organizations differ tremendously in their *technology*, the means they employ to produce their outputs. These can vary from simple tools and hand-performed operations at one extreme, to complex processes employing sophisticated, computer-controlled equipment at the other (see Figure 15–9). Clearly, the tools and methods selected by a given organization are closely related to the functions it serves and the goals it seeks to attain. Thus, in an important sense, technology is shaped or chosen by the organization. But what about the reverse of this relationship? Are organizations themselves also shaped or affected by technology? In short, does the selection of some specific set of methods and processes make it more likely that an organization using them will also adopt a particular type of internal structure? Research findings suggest that in some cases, at least, this may be

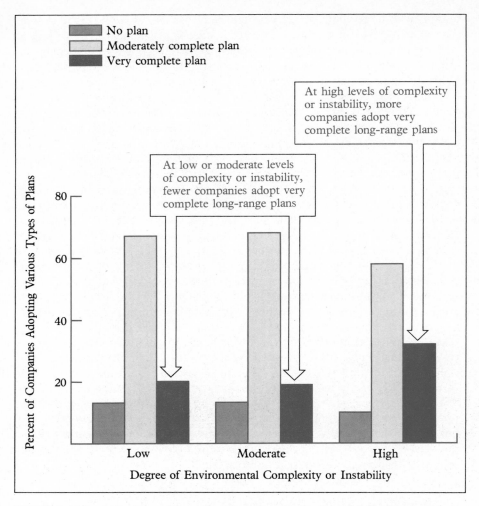

FIGURE 15-8   Long-Range Plans: One Technique for Dealing with Environmental Instability

One way organizations can deal with environmental complexity and instability is through the development of adequate long-range plans. That they do respond in this fashion is shown by the results of a recent study by Lindsay and Rue. As shown here, the greater the complexity or instability confronted by 198 companies, the more complete the long-range plans they adopted. (Source: Based on data from Lindsay & Rue, *Academy of Management Journal*, 1980, *23*, 385–404.)

so. Again, we will begin with some classic work and then turn our attention to more recent evidence.

Perhaps the best-known study on the impact of technology on organizational structure is one conducted by Woodward.[29] She and her colleagues collected data on the organizational design, success, and technology of one hundred companies

FIGURE 15-9 Technology: A Key Determinant of Organizational Structure and Performance

As shown in these photos, the technology used by organizations varies greatly. (Source: Top left photo by Dave Plank/Global Focus; top right photo by Larry Lawfer; bottom photo by Ed Hof/The Picture Cube.)

operating in England. Initially, Woodward expected that organizations classified as highly effective would share many similar characteristics, while those classified as being low in effectiveness would share other characteristics. Surprisingly, though, results did not confirm this reasonable expectation. Instead, various aspects of organizational structure appeared to be randomly distributed among successful and unsuccessful companies. At this point, Woodward and her colleagues turned to the possibility that technology might act as a mediating factor, some-how determining the impact of various aspects of structure upon organizational effectiveness. And here they hit the proverbial jackpot. When the organizations were divided into three categories on the basis of the technology they used (unit and small batch manufacturing; large batch and mass production; long-run process production), important findings emerged. First, it was clear that the companies using these different technologies *did* differ with respect to internal structure. For example, chains of command were longest in organizations using process production and shortest in those employing unit or small batch methods. Similarly, organizational complexity was greatest in companies using process production and lowest in ones relying on unit or small batch procedures. Span of control for first-line managers, too, varied with technology. Here, though, it was the mass production companies that had the largest spans; those employing unit and small batch or process production had somewhat smaller spans.

Perhaps even more important than these findings was the fact that the characteristics distinguishing highly successful from unsuccessful companies also varied with technology. Briefly, at the low and high ends of the technology dimension (unit and small batch production; process production), an *organic* management approach seemed best: companies showing this strategy were more successful than those demonstrating a *mechanistic* approach (see our discussion of these strategies on pp. 515–516). In contrast, in the middle of the technology dimension (mass production), the opposite was true. Here, companies adopting a mechanistic approach were more successful (see Figure 15–10). In short, Woodward's study indicated that there are important links between technology and organizational structure on the one hand, and between technology and performance on the other.

Additional support for the impact of technology on both organizational structure and effectiveness has been obtained in several studies conducted since Woodward's ground-breaking research.[30] We should also note that within the context of this work, a heated debate has arisen over the question of whether the *size* of an organization or its *technology* exerts a stronger impact upon structure and performance. Woodward's findings, of course, emphasize the role of technology. But other researchers have disagreed with this conclusion and stress the potentially powerful influence of size.[31] In fact, support for the impact of both variables has been obtained. But recent findings seem (to us) to give the edge to technology. For example, in one large-scale study, Marsh and Mannari obtained measures of the size and technology of fifty Japanese companies.[32] (Size was assessed in a straightforward manner; it simply involved the total number of employees. Technology was measured both through Woodward's categories, and also in terms of *automaticity*—the extent to which machines replace human labor.) When these two factors were related to several dimensions of organizational structure, results generally favored technology. Specifically, technology exerted a stronger effect than size on five aspects of organizational structure (e.g., span of control of the chief executive, level of education of employees, labor costs). In contrast, size outweighed technology only with respect to two factors: formalization and complexity.

We should hasten to add that while several studies have reported findings confirming the powerful influence of technology, others have failed to observe this pattern.[33] Thus, the overall picture is far from entirely consistent. Perhaps these negative results stem either from the difficulties involved in assessing technology or from the fact that many organizations employ several different technologies si-

FIGURE 15-10   Technology: A Mediator of the Impact of Internal Structure on Organizational Effectiveness

In a classic study on the effects of technology on organizational effectiveness, Woodward found that at high and low levels of technology, an *organic* management approach was best. However, at moderate levels of technology, a *mechanistic* approach was more effective.

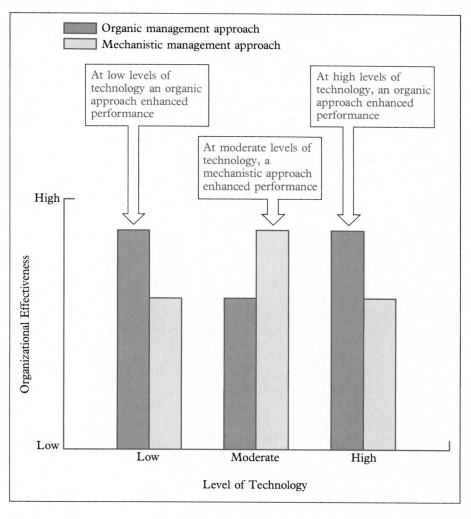

multaneously. Whatever the reason, however, there seem to be sufficient grounds for assuming that technology does play an important role in organizational structure and effectiveness. Thus, while organizations often shape and select technology, we should not overlook the fact that they themselves are often changed and molded by this factor.

The Contingency Model: A Concluding Comment— And a Glance toward the Future

In recent years, the contingency approach has gained widespread acceptance. In fact, it is probably reasonable to state that it is now the most popular framework for comprehending the impact of structure upon organizational performance.[34] This general acceptance, however, by no means implies that the theory is fully developed or that it has been exhaustively verified. On the contrary, much remains to be done. As we have already noted, many difficulties exist with respect to the measurement of technology and various aspects of the environment. Further, there is not even full agreement on just how these basic variables should be defined. These issues must be resolved if further progress is to occur. In addition, critics have called attention to several weaknesses in the contingency model itself—ones that must be rectified. For example, in a recent paper, Claudia Schoonhoven has noted that the basic assumptions and predictions of contingency theories are often lacking in clarity.[35] This makes it difficult to test them adequately. Similarly, contingency theory often fails to describe the precise nature of the interactions between technology, environmental uncertainty, and the performance it predicts. Again, such ambiguity renders firm empirical tests of the theory difficult. Fortunately, none of these problems strikes us as being "fatal" in nature. Thus, in our view they can—and will be—handled in future research. To the extent they are, contingency theory will be strengthened and will rest on even firmer scientific foundations than is true at present.

But now, permit us to speculate for a moment. Assume that the problems mentioned above, plus several others, are all resolved. If this comes to pass, will contingency theory prove to be the "last word" where organizational design and performance are concerned? Or is there room for additional advances as well? Predictions along such lines are always tricky, to say the least. But it is our impression that one further theoretical step may well occur. This would involve the construction of conceptual bridges between the *macro* variables examined in contingency theory (e.g., design factors, the environment, technology) and *micro* factors relating to groups and group processes. In short, such a theory would suggest how macro variables impinge on group processes such as patterns of communication, decision making, and patterns of influence within the organization. And this information, in turn, would help clarify effects on organizational performance. Actually, some steps along these lines have already been taken, and a new perspective known as the **sociometric approach** has begun to take shape.[36] Briefly, this framework seeks to explain how structural variables affect organizational effectiveness by understanding their impact on individuals and groups. To date, little work has been conducted on this new model, and it is too early to know whether—or to what extent—it will prove useful. If this framework does manage to construct theoretical bridges between contingency theory on the one hand and group structure and process on the other, however, it may constitute a major contribution. After all, in one real sense, such a theory will draw on, and integrate, the very best of two "worlds." (See the **"PERSPECTIVE"** box on pp. 524–525 for a discussion of a newly developed outlook on organizational structure and organizational effectiveness.)

SOME RECENT INNOVATIONS: PROJECT, MATRIX, AND FREE-FORM DESIGNS

Change is a byword of life in the late twentieth century. Economic, political, and social conditions seem to be in constant, rapid flux. Technology, too, has taken giant leaps forward and promises to progress at least as far in the next two decades as it did in the 1960s and 1970s. One implication of this dynamic state of affairs for organizations is clear: those that don't measure up and fail to adapt or change rapidly stand little chance of surviving; the competition is simply too intense. As this fact has become increasingly apparent, many managers and organizational theorists have expressed dissatisfaction with traditional forms of organizational design. They feel that while these certainly have their place, greater flexibility too is needed. With these needs in mind, they have developed several new approaches to organizational design—ones quite different from the standard "divide into departments on the basis of function or product" formula. Several of these are described below. But please note: they are not in any sense suggested as total substitutes for more traditional designs. On the contrary, these persist and will continue to do so in the future as well. The newer techniques we will describe here are simply designed to handle special types of situation in a more efficient manner. Thus, it is probably more appropriate to view them as *supplements* to, rather than as replacements for, older and more traditional forms of design.

Project Designs: Mobilizing Available Resources

Suppose that at some future time, you are the president of a medium-size toy company. One afternoon your top aide rushes into your office with bad news: Gametronics, your chief competitor, has just hit the market with an unexpected bombshell. Their new toy is a remote-controlled flying saucer that actually takes off, hovers, and lands on command. Further, it comes complete with little green women and men who also move about on electronic cue. You are shattered. This toy is sure to be a giant success and may crush your own hopes for the coming Christmas season. What should you do? One possibility is to work within the regular structure of your company. That is, you can call a meeting of the heads of research, marketing, and sales, and instruct them to have their individual departments start work on the problem. Perhaps a better plan, though, would be to es-

FROM THE MANAGER'S PERSPECTIVE

Theory Z: A Potential Answer to the Japanese Challenge?

Sony; Minolta; Panasonic; Honda; Toyota. In recent years these names have acquired the ability to send shivers up and down the spines of top managers at many American, Canadian, and European companies. The reason for such reactions is simple: these and other Japanese corporations have developed into *very* serious competitors. Indeed, in the eyes of some, they have become nothing short of invincible! This success, in turn, stems from a central and all-important fact: productivity in these companies is extremely high; indeed, it is currently the envy of most of the industrialized world (see Figure 15-11). Evidence for the high productivity in Japanese industry abounds. For example, companies such as Datsun, Toyota, and Honda are capable of building high-quality automobiles, shipping them thousands of miles to the U.S., and *still* selling them for thousands of dollars less than their home-grown competition. The same pattern also exists with respect to a number of other products. Little wonder, then, that American business is very uneasy about this challenge from the East.

But what factors are responsible for this phenomenal Japanese success? How, in short, do these companies attain their superb levels of productivity? Many answers have been offered, ranging from attention to the newness of Japanese industrial plants to almost mystical statements about the unique characteristics of Japanese workers. Perhaps the most comprehensive attempt to unravel this mystery to date, however, has been undertaken by William Ouchi.[37] In his widely read book *Theory Z*, Ouchi suggests that the major reason for this great success can be traced to a special set of conditions prevailing in many Japanese companies—conditions which, in his view, induce extraordinarily high levels of commitment among Japanese workers. Briefly, the key conditions mentioned by Ouchi are as follows:

1. Lifetime employment. Employees in many (but by no means all) Japanese companies are virtually assured a position for life. Feeling that their future is intimately linked with that of their company, they become deeply committed to it.

2. Slow evaluation and promotion. Evaluation and promotion are both relatively slow in most Japanese companies. Thus, an individual's performance can be appraised by many persons over a period of several years. This leads employees to realize that the company has a "memory" and will ultimately reward faithful service. And it also instills great confidence that their performance will be fairly and accurately evaluated. Together, these factors foster a high degree of commitment to the organization.

3. Non-specialized career paths. Many employees in Japanese companies—especially those at high

FIGURE 15-11 Japan, Inc.: A Major Challenge to American Business

As this cartoon suggests, the label "Made in Japan" was once held in low regard. Now, however, it is often perceived as a guarantee of high quality. (Source: Reprinted by permission of King Features Syndicate, Inc.)

levels—perform several different jobs during their careers. This leads to lessened commitment or identification with their own occupation or field, and to greater involvement with the company.

4. Consensual decision making. Decisions in most Japanese companies are made collectively, through a process in which all persons affected have a chance to provide input. This, too, strengthens feelings of involvement within the organization.

5. Collective responsibility. Responsibility for success is shared, while blame for failure, too, is spread among all members of a work unit or department. Since each person's fate is intimately linked with that of many others, feelings of general commitment and involvement are enhanced.

6. Wholistic concern for employees. Finally, Japanese companies are not simply interested in their employees during working hours and in work contexts. Rather, they show concern for their welfare off the job. Such concern fosters a high degree of intimacy between employees and enhances involvement with the organization.

Now consider how these conditions differ in traditional American companies (and in many Canadian and European ones, too). In such organizations (which Ouchi labels *Type A* to distinguish them from the Japanese or *Type J* pattern), there is no guarantee of long-term employment. Evaluation and promotion tend to occur rapidly. Decision making and responsibility are largely individual matters. Career paths are highly specialized, and there is *segmented concern*—the organization is interested in employees only within the scope of company business. Ouchi believes that together these conditions foster a much lower level of commitment or involvement on the part of American workers. And this, in turn, contributes to the relatively low level of productivity they have shown in recent years.

As Ouchi also points out, development of these sharply contrasting organizational types in Japan and the U.S. is no accident. Rather, they reflect basic differences in cultural and social climates. As a small nation with limited resources, Japan developed cultural values emphasizing cooperation and coordination. In contrast, the U.S., with its vast size and huge resources, tended to foster beliefs in "rugged individualism" and related values. Given these contrasting cultural features, Ouchi feels that

U.S. companies cannot simply adopt the Japanese model—the U.S., after all, is *not* Japan. What American managers *can* do, though, is to adopt those features of the Japanese approach that are compatible with American culture. Specifically, he suggests that American companies can benefit from moving to an intermediate approachmone he labels *Type Z.* Here, many features of the Japanese model prevail: Type Z organizations are characterized by long-term employment, slow promotion and evaluation, consensual decision making, and wholistic concern for employees. But consistent with American values, they retain moderately specialized career paths and individual responsibility.

According to Ouchi, a number of American corporations have already made the shift to a Type Z structure. And these, he notes, are among the most successful and admired companies in the U.S. (e.g., Kodak, IBM, Levi Strauss). Additional evidence that adoption of the "hybrid" approach recommended by Ouchi can yield substantial benefits is provided by the findings of several recent studies. Generally, these investigations suggest that the application of key Japanese strategies to American or European-based companies can result in major improvements in productivity. For example, one Japanese-favored tactic that has proven helpful in this respect is *JIT* (Just in Time). Briefly, this principle focuses on providing all materials needed in the manufacture of a product just when they are required—in some cases, down to the specific day or even hour! To the extent this goal is attained, inventories (and associated paper work) can be held to a minimum, and major economies gained.[38]

To conclude: **Theory Z** is clearly thought-provoking and insightful. But does it offer a solution to American managers for stemming the tide of Japanese industrial might? Only time—and further research—will tell. In any case, Theory Z does point to key differences between American and Japanese companies—ones that may well contribute to their contrasting levels of productivity. Thus, it is certainly worthy of careful study. Regardless of the ultimate fate of Theory Z, though, one basic fact is clear. Given recent shifts in patterns of world trade and the continuing decline of productivity in their businesses, many American (as well as Canadian and European) managers would agree on the following point: *it is definitely time for a change!* □

tablish a special crash project, headed by one of your brightest and most able employees. As project manager, she would have full authority to assemble a team of people from the regular departments to work under her direction. These would all be top individuals—with the skills needed to put the project over. And they would report solely to her, at least for the project's duration.

If you actually adopted this plan, you would be employing a **project design.** Designs of this type cut directly across the traditional structure of organizations. Specifically, employees are "pulled" from their home departments as needed and report directly to the project manager. The key advantage of such an approach, of course, is that it permits the rapid assembly of the appropriate employees into a working unit, one in which their skills and talents can be put to best use. As our example suggests, project designs are most useful in situations in which some specific goal must be met, a special unique effort is required, and the outcome is critical to the organization. In recent years, many companies have actually made use of such designs. For example, when faced with the challenge of the energy crisis, General Motors responded with a special project aimed at producing workable plans for down-sizing all of its cars. That the project was eminently successful is suggested by the fact that as a result of this approach, GM beat its competitors into the marketplace with fuel-efficient cars, and substantially increased its market share.[39] In short, project designs appear to represent a valuable managerial tool that should not be overlooked when a sudden crisis occurs.

Matrix Designs: A Hybrid Approach

Closely related to project designs is another approach useful in handling special problems—**matrix designs.** Actually, designs of this type can be viewed as the result of superimposing a project design on a functional organizational structure. Here, employees work in functional departments and report to the heads of these units. In addition, however, they may be assigned duties within a specific project and report to the manager of that activity as well. For example, consider the case of a marketing expert. He may normally work within the marketing department of his company. On some occasions, however, he is asked to serve as an instructor in a series of seminars conducted by his organization. At these times, he reports to the person in charge of running these sessions. Thus, in a sense, he serves "two masters." For this reason, it is important that the managers involved agree on the amount of time each employee will devote to his or her regular duties and to special project assignments. If such agreement is not reached, the possibility of serious conflict arises.

Like the project format, matrix designs offer the key advantage of utilizing employees' skills and abilities to maximum advantage. Further, they also make it possible for an organization to respond rapidly to special needs on the part of its customers or clients, or to sudden changes in the marketplace. A simple matrix design is illustrated in Figure 15–12; please examine it carefully so that you grasp the nature of this useful innovation in organizational structure.

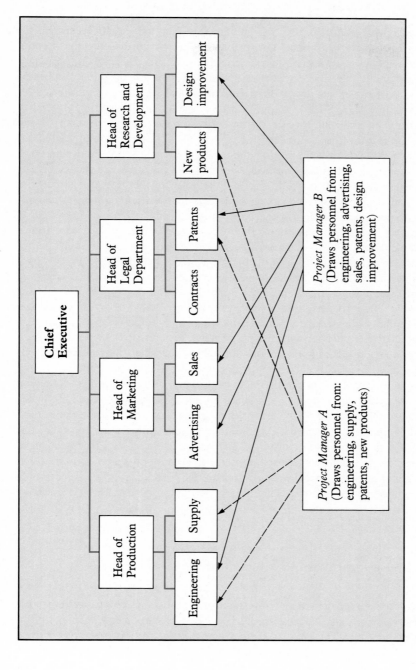

FIGURE 15–12   A Simple Matrix Design: Projects Combined with Regular Functional Departments

In *matrix designs* such as the one shown here, employees with special skills are assigned to specific projects and work under the direction of a project manager. In addition, they have regular jobs in functional departments and report to supervisors in these units as well. Note that in the example shown here, the two Project Managers draw personnel from somewhat different departments. This reflects the fact that their projects are concerned with different problems.

**CASE IN
POINT**

"Hardly Anything Is None of Our Business"

How do you organize a company that (1) develops new breakfast cereals, (2) assesses the health effects of road salt, (3) finds out why teabag strings become tangled in shipment, (4) designs instruments for scientific research on the moon, (5) analyzes the new business opportunities provided by the growing number of retirees, and (6) constructs lead balloons? This is precisely the question faced by Arthur D. Little, Inc. (ADL), a large, Boston-based consulting firm founded in 1886. During its almost 100-year history, the company has dealt with all the problems listed above, plus hundreds of others just as diverse and unrelated. In short, its major task is that of advising almost anybody on just about anything.

But to return to our initial question: how should a business like this be organized? The answer—at least at ADL—has been a cross between the project, matrix, and free-form designs described above. When a potential client comes to the company with a problem, it is first screened by a special management committee. If the committee concludes that the problem is an appropriate one, a case leader trained in some area relating to the task is selected. This person then invites other consultants within the firm to join his or her team. Together, these experts pool their varied knowledge and attempt to solve the problem at hand. For example, one recent case involved the planning of a new industrial city on the Red Sea for Saudi Arabia. Here, the case leader was a political scientist with special expertise in city planning. He assembled a team consisting of civil and chemical engineers, a pharmacologist, a telecommunication specialist, economists, mathematicians, a marketing expert, and a public relations specialist. Together, these persons developed a workable and comprehensive plan for building the new metropolis.

The style of management within ADL can best be described as free-wheeling. Thus, a case leader can ask anyone to serve on his or her project—even the president of the firm himself. And while working on the case, these persons are under their leader's direction, even if they nominally outrank him or her in other contexts. To add flexibility, any consultant can refuse to serve on a particular case, and this right is frequently exercised, sometimes because of a lack of interest and occasionally because of opposition to the project's stated goals. The basic idea is to have on hand a pool of highly talented experts who can be assembled and reas-

Free-Form Designs: When Flexibility Is the Guiding Rule

By far the most daring departure from traditional models of structure is provided by the **free-form** designs. Organizations adopting this approach seek flexibility above everything else. In doing so, they often avoid the restrictions imposed by a set internal structure. Rather, this is allowed to change in accordance with current needs. And instead of the traditional product or functional departments, self-contained *profit-centers* are created. These assemble the team of employees they need

FIGURE 15–13   Flexibility in Organizational Design: Some Surprising Results

Because they permit great flexibility in the utilization of employees' talents and skills, project, matrix, and free-form designs often yield impressive results. These "silk purses," actually made from pigs' ears by a team of scientists at Arthur D. Little, Inc., provide an amusing illustration of this key fact. (Source: Smithsonian photo by Dane A. Penland.)

sembled into different working teams, depending on the unique problems posed by clients. As one employee, Martin Erns, has put it: "The whole object of a consulting firm like this is to hold together an amount of ability that normally would be fissionable" (p. 119).[40]

That this unique organizational style—often described as a kind of Oriental bazaar—works is suggested by the success of the firm, both from the point of view of profitability and the wide range of problems it has solved. Perhaps the extreme example of just what such flexibility can accomplish is this. In 1921, an industrialist suggested to the firm's founder, Arthur Little, that even science couldn't make a silk purse out of a sow's ear. To prove him wrong, Little immediately assembled a team of chemists and other experts. These scientists reduced pigs' ears to their basic tissue, and from this produced thread. The result: the purses shown in Figure 15–13!

The methods used by ADL are clearly not for everyone or every organization; it is a special type of business, serving a highly specialized function. But its success underscores an important fact: where organizational design is concerned, there is often considerable room for innovation—perhaps much more than at first meets the eye!   □

to complete various tasks and are highly results-oriented: their success is measured in terms of the degree of profit they generate. Needless to say, free-form designs are suitable only under special circumstances. In particular, they seem most applicable to organizations working on the frontiers of technology, or in new consumer markets. One example of an actual company that has adopted a design approaching the free-form model is described in the **"CASE IN POINT"** insert above.

In sum, in designing their organizations, managers are by no means restricted to the traditional, bureaucratic model. Rather, they can draw on several intriguing innovations developed in recent years. When these are used in appropriate circumstances and with adequate planning and care, each can contribute substantially to the ability of organizations to reach their major goals.

SUMMARY

The internal **structure** of organizations differs greatly among several dimensions. Among the most important of these are *job specialization, departmentalization, scalar chain of command, span of control, centralization, formalization,* and *complexity.* While organizational structure is often quite stable, it frequently changes in response to shifting external conditions. Thus, organizations should be viewed as dynamic rather than static in nature.

Together, *scientific management* and the *bureaucratic model* constitute what is often termed the "classic" approach to organizational design. Scientific management recommends that organizations adopt a high degree of job specialization, a relatively short chain of command, and some degree of decentralization. The bureaucratic model also stresses specialization. In addition, however, it emphasizes reliance on abstract rules for carrying out the organization's functions, an impersonal style of relations between managers and their subordinates, and promotion on the basis of merit. *Behavioral theories* emphasize the importance of understanding the actions and reactions of employees. Within this context, *role theory* concentrates on the impact of sets of interlocking expectancies among employees. Another behavioral theory, the *linking-pin model,* devotes most of its attention to the impact of group membership. Specifically, it suggests that organizational effectiveness can be enhanced by establishing effective work groups to which employees become committed.

In contrast to the classic and behavioral approaches, modern **contingency theory** suggests that there is no single best organizational design. Rather, it contends that each organization's design should be matched to the specific situational factors it faces. Among the most important of these factors are the degree of *environmental stability* and the level of *technology* employed by an organization. A new approach—the *sociometric model*—has begun to take form in recent years. It seeks to build conceptual bridges between the macro variables examined in contingency theory, and micro factors relating to groups and group processes.

Recent innovations in organizational design include the *project, matrix,* and *free-form* designs. A basic element in all of these is the assembly of temporary teams of employees possessing the skills and knowledge needed to deal with specific problems.

KEY TERMS

BEHAVIORAL THEORIES OF ORGANIZATIONAL DESIGN   Theories of organizational design emphasizing the behavior of employees. Some of these theories focus on the importance of roles, while others concentrate on group processes and membership.

BUREAUCRATIC MODEL A model of organizational design emphasizing a high degree of specialization, impersonal relations between managers and subordinates, reliance on abstract rules, and a hierarchical arrangement.

CENTRALIZATION Refers to the degree to which decisions are made by a small number of key persons.

COMPLEXITY Refers to the level of internal differentiation present in a given organization. Vertical complexity involves the number of levels of management within an organization, while horizontal complexity refers to the number of different departments or sub-units.

CONTINGENCY APPROACH A modern approach to organizational design, emphasizing the fact that there is no single best structure for all organizations. Rather, internal structure must be matched to the specific situational conditions faced by a given organization.

DEPARTMENTALIZATION Refers to the number of departments or subunits within an organization.

ENVIRONMENT In the context of organizational design, refers to both the internal and external conditions faced by an organization. These often involve a complex array of social, political, and economic factors.

FORMALIZATION Refers to the extent to which the behavior and responsibilities of individuals holding specific jobs are described in written rules.

FREE-FORM DESIGNS Innovative organizational designs in which there is no set structure. In such designs, self-contained profit-centers replace traditional departments.

JOB SPECIALIZATION Refers to the extent to which employees in a given organization perform specialized jobs of limited scope.

LINKING-PIN MODEL A behavioral theory of organizational design, emphasizing the importance of group membership on organizational effectiveness.

MATRIX DESIGNS A form of organizational design in which employees serve in special projects but also retain responsibilities in more traditional departments.

ORGANIZATIONAL DESIGN The field concerned with identifying basic principles that will permit selection of the most effective internal structure by a given organization.

ORGANIZATIONAL STRUCTURE Refers to the way in which a given organization is "put together." Key dimensions of organizational structure include departmentation, chain of command, span of control, formalization, and decentralization.

PROJECT DESIGN A form of organizational design in which employees possessing special skills or expertise are assembled into teams that work on specific problems.

ROLE THEORY A behavioral theory of organizational design emphasizing the importance of interlocking sets of roles.

SCALAR CHAIN OF COMMAND Refers to the number of levels in the "organizational ladder." Chains of command vary greatly from one organization to another.

SOCIOMETRIC APPROACH A new theory of organizational design seeking to construct conceptual bridges between macro variables on the one hand and micro processes on the other. In short, it attempts to explain how structural variables affect organizational effectiveness by understanding their impact upon individual employees.

SYSTEMS APPROACH An approach that views organizations as open systems. According to this model, organizations receive inputs, operate upon these through transformation processes, and generate specific outputs.

TECHNOLOGY Refers to the means used by an organization to transform inputs into outputs. Technology can range from simple tools and hand-performed operations at one extreme, to complex computer-controlled equipment and processes at the other.

THEORY Z A framework that seeks to explain the high productivity of many Japanese companies. In essence, Theory Z attributes such productivity in these companies to certain conditions (e.g., lifetime employment) that induce high levels of commitment among their employees.

NOTES

1. Mintzberg, H. *The structuring of organizations.* Englewood Cliffs, N.J.: Prentice-Hall, 1979.

2. Robey, D. *Designing organizations: A macro perspective.* Homewood, Ill.: Richard D. Irwin, in press.

3. Mackenzie, K.D. *Organizational structures.* Arlington Heights, Ill.: AHM Publishing, 1978.

4. Ouchi, W.G., & Harris, R.T. Structure, technology, and environment. In G. Strauss, R.E. Miles, C.C. Snow, & A.S. Tannenbaum (Eds.), *Organizational behavior: Research and issues.* Madison, Wis.: Industrial Relations Research Association, 1974.

5. Miller, E.J., & Rice, A.K. *Systems of organizations.* London: Tavistock, 1967.

6. Miner, J.B. *Management theory.* New York: Macmillan, 1971.

7. Taylor, F.W. *Principles of scientific management.* New York: Harper and Brothers, 1911.

8. Child, J. Managerial and organizational factors associated with company performance—Part I. *Journal of Management Studies,* 1974, *11,* 175–189.

9. Vinson, E., & Holloway, M. The effects of formalization on perceptions of discrimination, satisfaction, effort, and performance. *Journal of Vocational Behavior,* 1977, *10,* 302–315.

10. Glisson, C.A., & Martin, P.Y. Productivity and efficiency in human service organizations as related to structure, size, and age. *Academy of Management Journal,* 1980, *23,* 21–37.

11. Pennings, J.M. Dimensions of organizational influence and their effectiveness correlates. *Administrative Science Quarterly,* 1976, *21,* 688–699.

12. McMahon, J.T., & Ivancevich, J.M. A study of control in a manufacturing organization: Managers and nonmanagers. *Administrative Science Quarterly,* 1976, *21,* 66–83.

13. Dalton, D.R., Todor, W.D., Spendolini, M.J., Fielding, G.J., & Porter, L.W. Organization structure and performance: A critical review. *Academy of Management Review,* 1980, *5,* 49–64.

14. Oldham, G.R., & Hackman, J.R. Relationships between organizational structure and employee reactions: Comparing alternative frameworks. *Administrative Science Quarterly,* 1981, *26,* 66–82.

15. Weber, M. *Essays in sociology.* New York: Oxford, 1946.

16. Levy. R. Tales from the Bureaucratic woods. *Dun's Review,* March 1978, pp. 94–96.

17. Bennis. W.G. *Changing organizations.* New York: McGraw-Hill, 1966.

18. Simon, H.A. *The new science of management decision.* New York: Harper & Row, 1960.

19. Kahn, R.L., Wolfe, D.M., Quinn, R.P., Snowe, J.D., & Rosenthal, R.A. *Organizational stress: Studies in role conflict and ambiguity.* New York: Wiley, 1964.

20. Likert, R. *The human organization.* New York: McGraw-Hill, 1967.

21. Likert, R. *New patterns of management.* New York: McGraw-Hill, 1961.

22. Galbraith, J. *Organization design.* Reading, Mass.: Addison-Wesley, 1977.

23. Meyer, M.W., et al. *Environments and organizations.* San Francisco: Jossey-Bass, 1978.

24. Burns, T., & Stalker, G.M. *The management of innovation.* London: Tavistock, 1961.

25. Lawrence, P.R., & Lorsch, J.W. Organization and environment: Managing differentiation and integration. Boston: Division of Research, Harvard Business School, 1967.

26. Lindsay, W.M., & Rue, L.W. Impact of the organization environment on the long-range planning process: A contingency view. *Academy of Management Journal,* 1980, *23,* 385–404.

27. Burack, E.H., & Negandhi, A.R. *Organizational design: Theoretical perspectives and empirical findings.* Kent, Ohio: Kent State University Press, 1977.

28. Coulter, P.B. Organizational effectiveness in the public sector: The example of municipal fire protection. *Administrative Science Quarterly,* 1979, *24,* 65–81.

29. Woodward, J. *Industrial organization: Theory and practice.* London: Oxford University Press, 1965.

30. Perrow, C. A framework for the comparative analysis of organizations. *American Sociological Review,* 1967, *32,* 194–208.

31. Child, J. Predicting and understanding organizational structure. In D.S. Pugh & C.R. Hinings (Eds.), *Organizational structure: Extentions and replications.* Farnborough, Hants, England: Saxon House, 1976.

32. Marsh, R.M., & Mannari, H. Technology and size as determinants of the organizational structure of Japanese factories. *Administrative Science Quarterly,* 1981, *26,* 33–56.

33. Mahoney, T., & Frost, P. The role of technology in models of organizational effectiveness. *Organizational Behavior and Human Performance,* 1974, *11,* 122–138.

34. Meyer, M.W., et al. *Environments and organizations.* San Francisco: Jossey-Bass, 1978.

35. Schoonhoven, C.B. Problems with contingency theory: Testing assumptions hidden within the language of contingency "theory." *Administrative Science Quarterly,* 1981, *26,* 349–377.

36. Tichy, N. Networks in organizations. In P.G. Nystrom & W. Starbuck (Eds.), *Handbook of organizational design.* London: Oxford, 1980.

37. Ouchi, W.G. *Theory Z: How American business can meet the Japanese challenge.* Reading, Mass.: Addison-Wesley, 1981.

38. Schonberger, R.J. The transfer of Japanese manufacturing management approaches to U.S. industry. *Academy of Management Review,* 1982, *7,* 479–487.

39. Burck, C.G. How GM turned itself around. *Fortune,* January 16, 1978, pp. 92–96.

40. Wolkomir, R. And now, from the people who brought you the lead balloon . . . *Smithsonian,* 1981, *12,* 113–120.

16

Organizational Development: Intervening for Effectiveness

KEY CONCEPTS

Organizational Development (OD)
Outcome Variables
Process Variables
Sensitivity Training
Team Building
Management by Objectives (MBO)

Grid Training (Managerial Grid)
Quality of Work Life (QWL)
Quality Circles
Alpha Change
Beta Change
Gamma Change

□ □ □

November winds are howling and gray clouds are scuttling across a darkening sky as the top brass of Panacea Drugs, Inc., files into the board room for a special meeting. The room is plush, warm, and cozy, yet somehow the outside chill seems to have crept inside. Faces are gray and a deep air of gloom hangs over the group. This is far from surprising. The company has just posted the worst quarter in its history—an actual loss of considerable size. This is quite a comedown for a firm that only a few years ago was the darling of Wall Street—a favorite on every analyst's list of glamour issues. Sales are down, and market share has shrunk considerably. Even worse, morale and motivation have slipped badly. The optimistic climate of the recent past has all but disappeared. Instead of planning eagerly for growth and searching for challenging new opportunities, key executives have begun to adopt a defensive posture, seeking merely to hold onto what they already have. Faced with these uncertainties about the future, some of the best people in the company have begun to leave; in fact, several have taken jobs with key competitors in recent months. Perhaps worst of all, a company-devised plan for coping with these problems and "getting back on track" has failed miserably. In fact, that's the purpose of today's meeting—to see if something better can be devised.

At this moment, D. J. Fleming, CEO at Panacea and a strong supporter of the aforementioned plan (known as "Project Upbeat") calls the meeting to order. "I guess you all know why we're here today," he begins. "The numbers speak for themselves." (He now points to several charts showing alarming trends in sales, productivity, and costs.) "Project Upbeat is a failure and we might as well admit it. After six months we're worse off than when we began. And I can't understand it. I really thought that new incentive plan, coupled with all those pep talks and rallies, would do the trick. But there's no point in looking back. We've tried one approach and it failed. What's next?"

At first, there is only silence. But then Carole Chalmers, a young V.P. known for her outspoken style, clears her throat and remarks, "Well, D. J., we all know that you and everyone else involved in Project Upbeat did your best. But as you say, it hasn't worked. So now, I think, it's time to get some outside help. There are a lot of outfits that specialize in helping organizations like Panacea solve their internal problems. And I think we should hire one right away."

At this remark, D. J. scowls. It's well known that he doesn't like consulting firms. "But what do these people do?" he asks with irritation. "I mean, what can they dream up that's so different from what we've tried already?"

Carole has a ready answer (she's rarely at a loss for words). "I've looked into that, D. J., and the answer seems to be: a lot of things. The firm called in by U.S. Motors last year used something called MBO. It centered around establishing specific goals and a concrete plan for reaching them. Standard Electric hired a different company, and they used another approach—team-building. That concentrated on increasing cooperation within departments. And at Chem-Food the consultants seemed to rely mainly on questionnaires and feedback from them. Anyway, what's most important is this: whatever they do, it seems to work. I've checked with people at a lot of different companies and almost all were positive. They felt that these consultant-run programs were a big plus. In fact, some were downright enthusiastic."

D. J. shakes his head in disbelief. "Well, you know my feelings about this kind of stuff. I'd much rather see us solve our own problems. But let's put it to a vote. All those in favor of calling in a consulting firm signify in the usual manner." At this point, D. J. really begins to scowl, for he's quickly deafened by a chorus of loud and emphatic "Ayes!"

Organizational effectiveness has been a major continuing theme of this book. At many points, we have focused on the following question: What factors and conditions help to enhance the success of organizations in reaching their major goals? Our emphasis on this question appears to be quite justified, for as we noted in Chapter 1, concern with such effectiveness is central to modern O.B. Indeed, one of its major goals is that of applying knowledge about human behavior to the attainment of positive organizational outcomes such as enhanced productivity and improved morale. As the pages since Chapter 1 have indicated, many different variables play a role in this respect. Thus, key aspects of organizational effectiveness are strongly influenced by factors as diverse in nature as job-related stress, the quality and style of leadership, the nature and adequacy of performance appraisals, and many aspects of organizational structure (see Figure 16-1).

But much more has been accomplished than the simple identification of such factors. Their impact on organizational effectiveness, too, has been clarified. Thus, while we are far from knowing everything about this central topic (many questions remain unanswered), we *have* learned much. And our possession of this growing body of knowledge points to an intriguing possibility—putting this information to practical use. Can it form the basis for comprehensive strategies designed to aid organizations in their continuing quest for excellence? The answer appears to be a resounding "yes." During the past two decades, interest in accomplishing this task has literally exploded. The result has been the emergence of a huge and growing literature on the process of **organizational development** (or **OD** for short).[1,2] Because OD has been the subject of considerable attention, and because it offers the promise of valuable practical benefits, it deserves our careful attention. In order to acquaint you with this important topic, we will proceed as follows. First, we will offer a *definition* of OD and describe some of its major goals. Second, we will examine a number of different *OD strategies*—contrasting

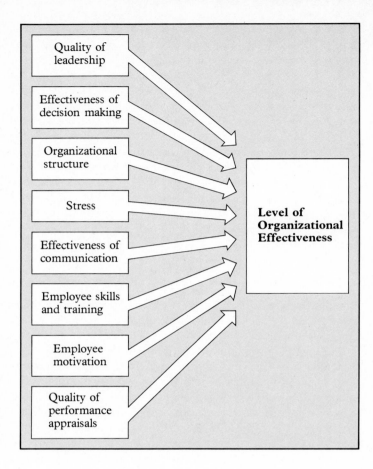

FIGURE 16-1   Organizational Effectiveness: Multiply Determined

As shown here, organizational effectiveness is influenced by a very large number of different factors.

methods for enhancing organizational effectiveness. Finally, we will address the key question of whether these tactics really work—whether they actually enhance productivity, satisfaction, morale, efficiency, and other related outcomes.

ORGANIZATIONAL DEVELOPMENT: ITS NATURE, ORIGINS, AND GOALS

We should begin by noting that the term OD is often used in two related but distinct ways. First, as previously mentioned, it refers to a *process*— one involving planned change within an organization. Second, it refers to the *study* of this process. Both uses are common, but since we view OD as falling within the broad scope of the field of organizational behavior, we will generally employ this term to refer to the basic process it encompasses.

Organizational Development: What It Is and What It Isn't

The study of organizational development is relatively new; indeed, authors writing about this topic often note that it is still in its infancy.[3] For this reason, OD has as yet no universally accepted definition. However, careful examination of a large number of books and papers on this subject indicates that researchers and practitioners alike view it as involving three major features:[4,5]

1. attempts to induce *planned change* within an organization
2. a focus on *enhancing organizational* effectiveness
3. a firm basis for these changes in *behavioral science knowledge.*

Taking these points into account, we can define OD as *a process aimed at enhancing organizational effectiveness through planned change suggested by behavioral science knowledge* (i.e., knowledge about human behavior). In short, OD involves systematic efforts to enhance an organization's attainment of its major goals.

Now that we have indicated what OD is, we should insert a word about what it is *not*. OD procedures are helpful in many different contexts, but they definitely do *not* constitute a no-fail formula for attaining perfection. Rather, it is much more reasonable to view them as helpful tactics for moving in the right direction—useful steps for enhancing certain aspects of organizational effectiveness under some conditions. We realize that by now you are quite sophisticated about the complex nature of organizational behavior and would probably recognize this fact even without our calling it to your attention. But we also know that in the years ahead, you may well encounter strong (perhaps exaggerated) claims for the efficacy of one or more OD strategies. When you do, we urge you to adopt at least a degree of caution. OD procedures *can* be helpful—as will become apparent in later sections of this chapter. But they are not yet ready to usher in a new era of near-perfection within organizations, and this fact, too, should be kept clearly in mind.

Organizational Development: Why It's Often Needed

At the beginning of this chapter, we described an organization on the brink of disaster. Profits, sales, morale, and motivation were down to discouraging levels. Clearly, something would have to change or the company might well "go under"—slip into financial ruin. It goes without saying that OD can be extremely helpful in such situations. Indeed, in cases like this one, its role can be viewed as nothing short of "organization-saving." In point of fact, it is often under just these circumstances that experts in OD are consulted. Their task is then straightforward, if complex—find out just what has gone wrong and help get the organization back on track.

But saving "endangered companies" is not the only function of OD. It is often applied to healthy organizations as well. Such use stems from the view that there's always room for improvement—a belief that we, too, share. In short, it is a rare organization indeed that cannot achieve even higher levels of productivity or morale, and OD can often be extremely helpful in producing such gains.

Finally, we should note that OD is often necessitated by a central fact of life in the modern world—rapid and far-reaching *change*. As we noted in earlier chapters, both the external and internal environment confronted by an organization can change quickly and extensively. When this occurs, the organization must either anticipate change and prepare for it in advance, or adapt to it once it has taken place. Unfortunately, though, human nature is such that people often seem to resist change. They cling to old patterns and tactics that are no longer effective. To the extent that such rigidity blocks necessary adjustments, OD, with its emphasis on planned intervention, may prove exceedingly helpful. Indeed, by assisting an organization in its efforts to adapt, OD can markedly improve its chances for success—and continued survival.

Organizational Development: A Note on Its Major Goals

As we have repeatedly noted, OD is aimed primarily at enhancing organizational effectiveness. This goal is self-explanatory. We all have at least a rough idea of what such effectiveness involves. But for purposes of this discussion, more precision is required. Thus, we will spend a moment in specifying those aspects of organizational function that usually serve as the major focus of OD programs. These fall into two major groups.

The first—often known as **outcome variables**—involve the concrete outputs produced by an organization. Included here are profits, productivity, group and individual performance, employee satisfaction, absenteeism, and turnover (see Figure 16-2). OD often seeks to induce major gains in all these areas. The second focus of OD programs—often termed **process variables**—involves the nature of

"This is just charming. Charming. Charming."

FIGURE 16-2   Maximizing Outcome Variables: One Basic Organizational Goal

As this cartoon suggests, organizations usually seek to maximize *outcome variables* such as profit. (Source: Drawing by Vietor; © 1979 The New Yorker Magazine, Inc.)

human relationships and interactions within an organization. Included here are such processes as motivation, decision making, influence, communication, and conflict resolution. When both groups of factors are taken into account, an important fact emerges. OD is not aimed simply at making organizations more productive and efficient; it also strives to make work places satisfying and pleasant.

ORGANIZATIONAL DEVELOPMENT: SOME SPECIFIC APPROACHES

In our discussions of several other topics (e.g., leadership, organizational structure, decision making), we noted that no single approach or strategy is always best. Rather, the most effective type of leadership, organizational structure, or mode of decision making varies greatly from situation to situation. Given the complexity of the processes it involves and the diversity of the goals it seeks, we might suspect that the same is true for OD. That is, it seems reasonable to predict that no single approach to this process will be most successful under all circumstances. In fact, careful examination of existing evidence suggests that this is actually the case. Many distinct approaches to OD have been devised, but none stands head and shoulders above the others with respect to overall effectiveness. Instead, different strategies seem most applicable—and successful—under different environmental conditions. In this section, we will describe several of these contrasting approaches. All are designed to enhance organizational effectiveness, and all employ systematic procedures for inducing planned organizational change. Apart from these underlying themes, however, they differ in almost every imaginable way.

Sensitivity Training: Effectiveness through Insight

Interpersonal friction is an all too common part of life, both in organizations and outside them. Individuals argue, criticize one another's work, place roadblocks in each other's way, and generally make life far more difficult and stressful than necessary. Negative social relations of this type can interfere with organizational effectiveness. Indeed, when carried to extremes, feuds, ill will, and smoldering resentment among employees can bring an organization virtually to its knees.

As you probably realize, such friction stems from many different sources. Often, individuals seek contrasting goals, and so come into direct conflict with one another. Similarly, employees may possess such different personalities or attitudes that a degree of mutual irritation is almost guaranteed. Perhaps the single most common cause of interpersonal friction within organizations, however, involves the absence of accurate perceptions. Frequently, individuals lack insight into their own feelings and into those of the persons around them, and—most importantly— do not comprehend their own impact on fellow employees. As a result they anger, irritate, or annoy these persons unintentionally, and often unnecessarily. Perhaps a simple example will help illustrate this crucial point.

Consider the case of a manager whose efforts to increase productivity among her subordinates are constantly thwarted by these persons. The more she exhorts them to greater effort, the less they actually accomplish. The manager is upset by this outcome and concludes that her subordinates are basically lazy and incompetent. Actually, though, their poor performance stems from totally different causes. Because she is young and inexperienced, the manager lacks self-confidence. As a result, she unconsciously adopts a superior, condescending tone whenever she addresses her subordinates. They, of course, don't realize that her annoying style stems from self-doubt. Thus, they come to view her as an "arrogant young twerp," who cares nothing about them or their welfare. In fact, she *does* care and wants desperately to be liked, but since there is no way for her subordinates to know this, they come to resent her instead. In sum, a chain of interlocking misperceptions and misunderstandings leads to negative outcomes for everyone involved—and for their organization as well (see Figure 16–3).

Unfortunately, situations of this type are very common. It is probably safe to suggest that they account for a substantial proportion of the social friction within organizations. But can they be avoided? Do any techniques exist for enhancing individuals' insight into their own feelings and behavior, as well as that of others?

FIGURE 16–3   Inaccurate Perception: A Major Cause of Personal Friction in Organizations

In the situation shown here, friction has arisen between a manager and her subordinates because of an unfortunate chain of misperceptions on both sides.

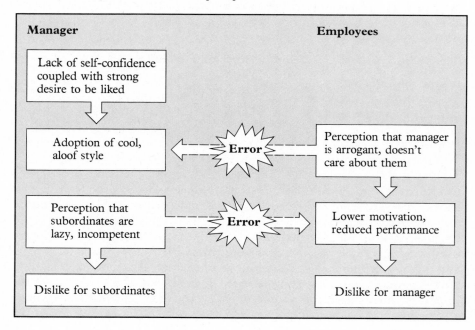

The answer appears to be yes. In recent decades several procedures for accomplishing these goals have been devised and used in organizational settings. That is, they have been employed as strategies of organizational development.[6,7] We will now describe the most popular of these techniques—one known as **sensitivity training.**

Sensitivity training: What it is and how it works. Advocates of sensitivity training generally accept three basic assumptions: (1) under ordinary conditions, individuals are far from open and honest with one another; (2) this lack of openness often blocks the development of important insights about oneself and others; and (3) such insights can be encouraged if individuals are placed in a setting where honest, direct communication is the rule rather than the exception. In accordance with these assertions, sensitivity training itself usually involves the participation of small numbers of persons (about ten to fifteen) in extended group discussions. These discussions take place in a setting geographically removed from the pressures and distractions of the home organization and often last for several days. An expert trainer is present at all times, but he or she does *not* actually direct the group. Rather, participants are actively encouraged to discuss anything they wish. It is emphasized, however, that the major purpose is to attain greater understanding of oneself and others. In some cases, all the participants are members of the same work unit and are acquainted before the start of training *(family groups);* in others, they belong to the same organization but do not work together *(cousin groups);* and in still others, participants are totally unacquainted before starting the group sessions—they may even work for different companies *(strangers groups).* Regardless of the composition of the group, two features remain constant. First, great stress is placed on *openness;* participants are encouraged to express their feelings directly and openly. Second, *immediate feedback* is provided. Whenever an individual expresses some feeling or reaction, other group members are encouraged to respond with their own comments and interpretations. It is reasoned that under these conditions, individuals will learn much about themselves and others. And in this way, perhaps, they will become more skilled or adept at handling interpersonal relations.

The role of the trainer: A guide, not a leader. Earlier, we noted that the expert trainer present during all sessions does not seek to direct the group's activities. In a general sense, this is true. The trainer acts neither as a leader nor as a therapist. Yet, she or he *is* an expert and performs crucial tasks—ones that may determine the success of the entire undertaking. (Please note: it is essential that trainers be experienced professionals. Individuals without formal training in this role can often do more harm than good.) First and most important, the trainer seeks to establish and maintain the atmosphere of openness. This in no way involves pressuring participants to reveal things they wish to hold private. It simply centers around encouraging them to be honest and direct in describing feelings and reactions they do wish to discuss.[8] Second, the trainer offers support to participants who, by revealing much about themselves, are in a vulnerable position.

And finally, the trainer protects group members from unfair criticism or treatment at the hands of other members. In sum, the trainer's role is to help the group stay on target and avoid blind alleys that will contribute little to the enhancement of personal and social insight.

Sensitivity training: Its potential value. After employees participate in sensitivity training, they return to their organizations. What happens then? Presumably, quite a bit. If the training has been successful, they now have clearer understanding of their own feelings, and have learned how to "read" those of others more effectively. Further, and perhaps most important, they now have a firmer grasp of their own impact upon others—how their behavior is interpreted by and affects the persons around them. Together, these new insights and skills may contribute to improved social relations. For example, consider the young manager in the example on page 542. Following sensitivity training, she may realize that her subordinates resent her largely because of the condescending style she adopts when interacting with them. Further, she may also have learned that other young managers, too, face self-doubt and that it is not necessary for her to hide these feelings behind a mask of cold arrogance. If she is successful in translating these insights into changes in her behavior, positive outcomes may well follow. She may be perceived more favorably by her subordinates, and this, in turn, may contribute to their productivity. To conclude, the major goal sought by sensitivity training is to help individuals toward better relations with others. And this, in turn, can yield important benefits for an entire organization.

Team Building: Focus on Task Performance

As noted earlier, interpersonal friction is one important factor often standing in the way of organizational effectiveness. Thus, attempts to overcome or reduce such a problem through sensitivity training and related techniques can be extremely helpful. Unfortunately, though, such friction is far from the only roadblock organizations face on the path to maximum efficiency. Many others exist as well. Among the most important of these are problems relating directly to *task performance*. Such difficulties stem from many sources and, unfortunately, few can be eliminated even by high levels of employee sensitivity or awareness. Because of this fact, other OD techniques that focus directly on task performance are required. A number of approaches seem promising in this regard, but the one that has received the most attention—and support—in recent years is **team building**.[9,10]

In several respects, team building resembles sensitivity training. Like such training, it involves employee participation in special learning or training experiences, conducted away from the pressures of daily organizational life (see Figure 16-4). Similarly, it involves an open and frank exchange of views and reactions during prolonged group discussions. The key difference between team building and sensitivity training lies in the focus of these sessions. In sensitivity training, interest is focused primarily on individuals and on the task of enhancing their per-

FIGURE 16-4   Team Building: One Important OD Approach

In *team building*, employees belonging to some work unit meet and discuss problems relating to their work (i.e., task performance). These discussions are held away from the regular organizational setting and are as frank and open as possible. (Source: Photo by Sandra Johnson, © 1981.)

sonal and social insight. (We should add, the ultimate goal remains that of enhancing organizational effectiveness.) In team building, interest is directed specifically to problems relating to task performance. Thus, in a typical team building exercise, members of some work unit or group engage in a discussion of factors affecting their productivity. Such sessions generally begin with attempts to identify current problems—those factors interfering with the group's productivity. As you can guess, a wide range of issues may be discussed. Thus, faulty equipment, ineffective policies, inefficient procedures, and a lack of clarity in roles and responsibilities may all be examined. Personal relations, too, may be considered, if they are perceived as task-related in nature. Once agreement on the key problems has been reached, the discussion shifts to specific tactics for overcoming these difficulties, and later sessions may focus on the question of assessment—have these tactics actually worked, or are other, additional steps necessary?

The use of team building has increased rapidly in recent years. In fact, it now seems considerably more popular than sensitivity training.[11] This shift may reflect the fact that team building offers a more direct route to enhanced productivity than other OD procedures. (After all, it concentrates directly on task performance.) Regardless of the basis for its growing use, however, you should be familiar with its basic procedures; the chances are quite good that you will encounter it yourself in the years ahead. (Why are organizations often so resistant to change? For a discussion of this important issue, see the **"PERSPECTIVE"** box on pp. 546–547.)

FROM THE MANAGER'S PERSPECTIVE

Organizational Development, Organizational Politics, and Resistance to Change

In a key sense, the central core of organizational development is *change*. OD procedures are designed to produce alterations in the way an organization functions—and so in its overall effectiveness—through shifts in the attitudes and behavior of its employees, changes in its structure, or both. Unfortunately, it is often easier to visualize such change than to produce it. As we noted in Chapter 13, human beings often resist change—and with a vengeance! Thus, they frequently cling to existing attitudes and behaviors even in the face of powerful pressures for shifts in these areas. Not surprisingly, organizational development is no exception to this general rule. In many cases, the employees of a given organization may engage in passive resistance against the change suggested by an OD program. Even worse, some may actively seek to sabotage these alterations, thus condemning the entire program to certain failure. There are many reasons for such resistance. First, people fear uncertainty; the OD expert promises benefits, but will these actually occur? Many persons are reluctant to take the risks involved in finding out. Second, individuals fear that the coming changes will inconvenience them. Even if an organization is functioning inefficiently, many persons within it have attained comfortable niches. Why should they jeopardize their orderly, pleasant lives for the possibility of future gains? Additional factors acting against change include fear of social disruption (e.g., loss of valued friends during reorganization), economic losses, reductions in status, and the derailment of one's career. In short, powerful forces are often marshaled against OD and the change it seeks to induce.

Given the existence of such barriers, managers and OD experts wishing to implement change face a basic problem. How can they overcome this entrenched resistance? Fortunately, a number of tactics for overcoming resistance exist. First, managers and OD experts can draw on several of the techniques of social influence described in Chapter 13. When these are used with care, they can help to overcome even powerful resistance to change.[12] For example, eloquent persuasion, supported by convincing facts about the benefits to be gained, can often be effective. Similarly, shifts in existing organizational norms that favor *change* rather than the *status quo* can put considerable conformity pressure on employees to cooperate. And exposure to high-status, highly competent models who demonstrate acceptance of the recommended changes can often persuade many who are wavering to "jump on the bandwagon" and accept the OD program. In sum, many techniques of social influence can be enlisted in the service of planned organizational change (see Figure 16–5).

But there is also another general strategy that managers (and OD experts) can follow to gain acceptance for OD programs. They can turn to *organizational politics* as a means for attaining change. As we noted in Chapter 13, organizations are highly political in nature. Indeed, they can be viewed as being composed of individuals and coalitions engaged in a continual struggle over resources, information, and power.[13] Given this state of affairs, it is clear that the success of any program of planned change will depend, to an important degree, on its interface with organizational politics. Specifically, OD programs that are rejected by powerful opponents stand little chance of success. In contrast, those supported by powerful allies within the organization may quickly gain general acceptance. But how, precisely, can managers and OD consultants turn organizational politics to their advantage? Two basic strategies have recently been described.

In the first, which has been labeled *political moderation*—managers or OD experts concentrate on creating a political climate favorable to change. Thus, they seek to win over powerful employees or groups within the organization by convincing them that they will suffer no loss of power as a result of OD. Similarly, they may act as a mediator between opposing factions, pointing out the benefits of the proposed changes to all such groups. In short, em-

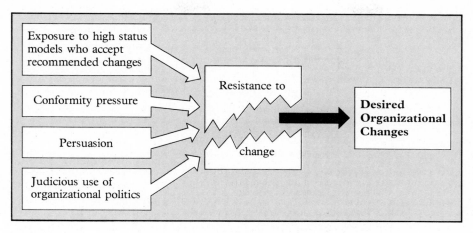

FIGURE 16-5   Overcoming Resistance to Change: A Basic Task in OD

Because they fear inconvenience, uncertainty, and other negative outcomes (real or imagined), employees are often wary of change. Fortunately, several techniques for overcoming such resistance exist.

phasis remains on the benefits of the OD program, but active steps are taken to assure that it does not fall victim to political sabotage.

The second approach—described as *political activism*—is much more extreme. Managers (or OD experts) adopting this approach do not merely attempt to create a favorable political climate. They actually engage in coercive political maneuvers designed to crush opposition to the OD program.[14] For example, they may limit and channel communication, use hidden agendas, and generally seek to manipulate others into positions where they have no choice but to go along. In a sense, this approach adopts the stand that "the ends justify the means"— almost any tactics are acceptable as long as they aid in adoption of the "good" OD program. Needless to say, most OD practitioners (and many managers as well) object to this Machiavellian approach—and with good reason. It violates basic values implicit in OD (e.g., the view that the client's welfare

should always be of foremost importance). And it may soon lead to a serious backlash, in which faith in the ultimate goals and intentions of OD is totally destroyed. At the same time, though, we can imagine situations in which managers, faced with a choice between radical change in their organization or its imminent demise, might well be tempted to consider this "no holds barred" approach as a last resort.

To conclude, regardless of the specific tactics adopted, it is clear that no OD program can succeed unless resistance to the change it recommends is overcome. Thus, managers (and OD experts themselves) interested in enhancing the effectiveness of their organizations through planned change must devote careful thought to this issue. Unless they do, even excellent OD programs may come to ruin; indeed, it is almost certain that they will be dashed to bits on the shoals of human inertia.   □

Survey Feedback: Information as a Basis for Change

There can be little doubt that the group discussions employed in sensitivity training and team building are often highly informative. Participants frequently learn
much about themselves and their organizations. But in a sense, these procedures
are somewhat inefficient. Only a small number of individuals can take part in each
session, and the discussions themselves sometimes occupy many hours or even
days. Given the costs associated with conducting such OD programs, managers
sometimes raise the following question: Is there some alternative procedure, less
costly in terms of employee time and effort, for obtaining information about the
strengths and weaknesses of my organization? Fortunately, there is. Much valuable information about an organization's functioning can often be attained both
quickly and efficiently through the OD technique of *survey feedback.*

This procedure—which now enjoys widespread use—consists of three major
phases. First, a carefully designed questionnaire is administered to selected
groups of employees (or perhaps to all employees). This self-report questionnaire
can be tailored to a specific organization and designed to answer highly specific
questions, or it can consist of a standard instrument useful in many settings.[15] In
either case the items contained focus on such key organizational issues as quality
and style of leadership, various facets of organizational climate (e.g., internal
coordination, decision making), and several aspects of employee satisfaction.

In a second phase of the process, the information gathered by this questionnaire is reported (fed back) to employees. Usually, this takes place in group discussion or problem-solving sessions. During such meetings, the OD expert conducting the survey feedback program attempts to summarize and interpret the
major findings in a clear manner, and also to elicit employee reactions to them. A
high level of expertise is needed in conducting these sessions for two major reasons. First, it is crucial that the survey results be presented and interpreted accurately. Given the complexities of survey-generated data, this is often a difficult
task. Second, the findings often contain information that certain individuals or
groups find upsetting (e.g., results indicate that they are not perceived as doing an
adequate job; some work unit is rated very low in terms of efficiency or productivity). In such cases, the consultant must use all of his or her professional skill to
ensure that results are presented in a non-threatening and constructive manner
(see Figure 16-6). In a final phase, specific plans for dealing with and overcoming
problems uncovered by the survey are devised and fully discussed.

As you can readily appreciate, survey feedback offers several important advantages. It can yield a large amount of informative data quickly and efficiently; it is
flexible and can be applied to many different organizations and to many different
questions; and the information it provides often serves as the basis for concrete
plans to enhance organizational effectiveness. It is important to note, however,
that survey feedback is useful only to the extent that four conditions are met: (1)
the questionnaires it employs must be valid and reliable; (2) employees must be
willing to report their views and reactions honestly; (3) the consultant conducting
the program must be skilled at interpreting—and describing—survey data; and (4)
top management must be willing to use the information it gathers. Fortunately,

FIGURE 16-6 Summarizing Key Findings for Employees: The "Feedback" Component of Survey Feedback

Reporting key findings to employees is a crucial part of *survey feedback*. This information must be presented clearly and accurately. (Source: Photo by Ken Robert Buck/The Picture Cube.)

survey feedback derives from a long and sound tradition of attitude measurement and survey research.[16] Thus, you can be quite confident that when it is used, these conditions are generally given careful thought. And when they are, survey feedback can be a valuable, informative, and efficient technique for fostering organizational effectiveness.

Management by Objectives: The Benefits of Having Clear-Cut Goals

There is an old saying that goes something like this: "It is usually easier to get somewhere if you know where you are going." In slightly different words, this statement implies that it is generally easier to reach specific goals if they are clearly defined or identified. As you can readily see, this suggestion makes a good deal of sense. After all, if we are uncertain about our final objectives, it may be difficult to develop pathways to them—or even to know when they have been reached! You may be surprised to learn, therefore, that this basic notion is often neglected in large organizations. Goals are stated in such general terms as high profits, high efficiency, or a good public image, and little attention is directed to the task of specifying just what these mean. As a result, employees—from top management on down—are uncertain as to just what they are trying to accomplish, and the entire organization can be seen as being very much adrift. (Please refer to our discussion of the benefits of setting specific goals in Chapter 5.)

The potential costs of such uncertainty were forcefully called to the attention of modern managers several decades ago by Peter Drucker.[17,18] Drucker, who was then a vice-president at General Electric, suggested that contrary to what common sense suggests, an organization's goals are *not* always obvious. Rather, they must be carefully and clearly defined. Drucker (along with a close associate, Harold Smiddy) noted that specifying objectives is a key part of managing—perhaps the most important part of all. Thus, he urged careful attention to this issue. As Drucker himself put it:

> . . . The important factor is that every member of management should have *specific* goals which he agrees to attain by *specific* dates, and which will obligate him to examine and explain the reasons for variance or deviation. . . . (1957, p. 78 [italics added])

Drucker's suggestions—which were subsequently refined and developed by many other scholars and practitioners—lie at the heart of an important approach to management, **Management by Objectives** (or **MBO** for short).[19,20] In Chapter 8 we considered MBO in the context of performance appraisal; here we will focus instead on its implications for organizational development.

MBO: A capsule view.   Before turning to MBO as a technique of organizational development, it is probably useful to say a few words about its general nature. (Again, please refer to our earlier discussion in Chapter 8.) At present, most MBO experts agree that four central themes are involved. First, superiors and subordinates should agree on specific goals and objectives. That is, these individuals meet, discuss alternative goals, and choose the ones they view as most important to the organization. Second, these goals should be *measurable, time bounded,* and linked to a plan for their attainment. Third, progress toward these objectives should be measured and monitored in a systematic manner and on a regular basis. Finally, each employee's responsibilities should be clearly defined in terms of specific results he or she is expected to achieve. In sum, MBO focuses on the development of specific, measurable objectives, plans for attaining them, and assessment of progress toward them.[21] Clearly, MBO is entirely consistent with the general notion that we should always try to know just where we are going.

MBO and organizational development.   Now that we have briefly described the major tenets of MBO, we can turn to its use as a technique of organizational development. When employed in this context, MBO involves four distinct steps. First, the persons who will be involved in the MBO program must be oriented to its basic principles and procedures. This is essential, for MBO may be a totally new concept or approach to many employees, including high-level managers. Second, subordinates and their supervisors meet and agree upon clear-cut, measurable objectives. At this time, specific steps for reaching these goals should also be determined. Third, after some predetermined interval, progress toward the chosen objectives is reviewed and feedback is provided. (Interestingly, recent findings suggest that feedback generated by employees, as well as that provided by their supervisors, can be very helpful in this context.)[22] Finally, an overall review is used both to assess current progress and to initiate the next cycle of objective-setting and planning (see Figure 16–7).

At this point, we should note that MBO is a very popular technique. Indeed, several authors suggest that a majority of the companies in the U.S. now use it.[23]

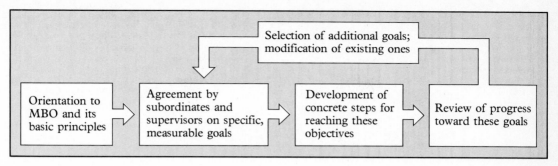

FIGURE 16-7   Management by Objectives: An Overview

When used as an OD procedure, Management by Objectives (MBO) involves four distinct steps. First, individuals who will take part in it undergo orientation to its basic principles and procedures. Next, subordinates and supervisors meet to select specific, measurable goals. Third, concrete steps for reaching these objectives are developed. Finally, progress toward these goals is reviewed, and this information is used to select additional goals or to modify existing ones.

One reason for this popularity may lie in the fact that in a key sense, MBO is "self-correcting" in nature. Since it states quantifiable, objective goals and insists on periodic assessment of progress toward them, it is a continuing process open to adjustment and feedback. Needless to say, this is a highly attractive feature. Second, through its emphasis on agreement between supervisors and subordinates, MBO may contribute to close cooperation between employees. This too probably facilitates its widespread acceptance. That the current popularity of MBO is at least partially justified is suggested by a recent review focused on the results of more than 185 studies concerned with the effectiveness of MBO.[24] While findings were not uniformly positive, a large majority pointed to the conclusion that MBO is, in fact, often quite successful.

Of course, all is not a bed of roses where MBO is concerned. Like other complex procedures, it confronts several problems. Perhaps the most important of these centers around the fact that the goals sought by organizations are often inconsistent or conflicting in nature. For example, a company may wish to maximize productivity and maintain good labor-management relations, often a difficult task. Similarly, an organization may wish to meet its social obligations by controlling pollution or by following equal opportunity employment practices, but may discover that these goals conflict with that of maximum profits. In such cases, MBO, with its emphasis on the selection of concrete objectives, may dictate that a choice be made. That is, one of the conflicting goals must be selected over the other. Then efforts must be concentrated on attaining the chosen objective at the expense of progress toward the other.[25] While such choices must certainly be made, MBO may tend to make them final or irrevocable, and this is a situation no manager wishes to confront. Another potential drawback to MBO lies in the fact that its implementation often requires a long period of time—as many as two to five years.[26] Many organizations find this requirement burdensome and may be tempted to terminate MBO programs long before they realize their full potential.

Despite these potential drawbacks, it is our impression that MBO is a valuable OD procedure. Indeed, as we noted earlier, growing empirical evidence supports this conclusion. Thus, having specific goals—and a concrete plan for their attainment—can often be useful in terms of enhancing organizational effectiveness.

Grid Training: Managerial Style and Organizational Effectiveness

In Chapter 14 we noted that the behavior of leaders seems to vary along two key dimensions. The first, known as *initiating structure,* refers to concern with production—completing the job at hand. The second, known as *showing consideration,* refers to concern with people—with maintaining warm, friendly relations with subordinates. When we described these two dimensions, we noted that some experts on leadership believe that persons high on both dimensions tend to be the most effective leaders. That is, such persons are most successful in enhancing the morale and productivity of their groups. In a very basic sense, managers are leaders. Thus, it seems only logical to expect that their relative position along these two dimensions will influence their success in this role, and so also the effectiveness of their organizations. This basic assumption underlies another major technique for organizational development, the **Managerial Grid** (or **grid training**).

According to Blake and Mouton, the originators of this approach, two key dimensions underlie managerial behavior—*concern for people* and *concern for production.*[27] As you can see, these are closely related to the dimensions of showing consideration and initiating structure. In order to measure a manager's position on each dimension, Blake and Mouton have developed a special questionnaire. On the basis of replies to this instrument, managers are assigned two numbers, one representing their relative position or concern with production, the other representing their position on concern for people. For example, a manager who shows little concern with both would receive a score of 1,1. (Blake and Mouton describe this style as one of *impoverished management.*) A manager who shows great concern with production, but little concern with people would receive a score of 9,1. (Blake and Mouton term this *task management;* see Figure 16–8). The opposite pattern is one in which a manager is greatly concerned with people but shows little concern with production (1,9). This is described as the *country club style* of management. Finally, a manager who shows moderate concern with both people and production would receive a score of 5,5. (Blake and Mouton term this *middle-of-the-road management.*) Of course, other scores too are possible (e.g., 3,8; 5,2; 2,2). In fact, since concern with both people and production are assessed on nine-point scales, a total of eighty-one different combinations exist. Blake and Mouton often employ a grid such as the one shown in Figure 16–9 to represent an individual's precise position in this array.

But which of these many patterns is best? Again, Blake and Mouton agree with experts on leadership; they hold that managers who are high on both dimensions

"I daresay you're right about the view, Hollingsworth. I've never looked out the window."

FIGURE 16–8 Task Management: An Extreme Case

The person speaking in this cartoon almost certainly shows the 9,1 pattern of management (task management). While he is greatly concerned with production, he has little interest in people or other matters. (Source: Drawing by Stan Hunt; © 1980 The New Yorker Magazine, Inc.)

(those attaining a score of 9,9) are best. (This pattern is described as *team management*.) Such persons are assumed to be most successful in enhancing the effectiveness of their organizations because their concern for subordinates leads to a high level of commitment among these individuals while their high concern for production enables them to remain efficient doers. If the 9,9 pattern is in fact best, then a straightforward implication for organizational development is suggested: In order to maximize organizational effectiveness, we should assist managers to adopt this approach. It is on this basic task that Blake and Mouton's *grid program* (or *grid training*) focuses. In essence, the program consists of six distinct steps or phases.

Phase 1—Seminar Training: The purpose of this phase is to introduce participants to the concepts and procedures of grid training. During these seminars, top managers discuss their current position on the grid and engage in evaluating their own behavior and problem-solving abilities.

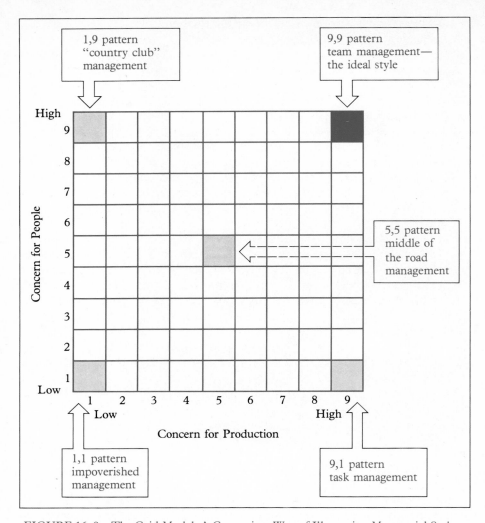

FIGURE 16-9   The Grid Model: A Convenient Way of Illustrating Managerial Style

By means of a grid such as this one, a manager's position on two key dimensions—*concern for people* and *concern for production*—can be represented. (Source: Based on a figure developed by Blake, R. & Mouton, J.S., *The Managerial Grid.* Houston, Texas: Gulf Publishing Company, 1964.)

Phase 2—Team Development: During this phase, teams of five to nine members formulate specific plans for moving toward the preferred 9,9 position. Specific objectives are set, and the information gained in Phase 1 is applied to the actual organization.

Phase 3—Intergroup Development: The first two phases of grid training focus primarily on individuals and single work groups. During the third phase emphasis is shifted to relations between various work units within the organization. Sources of conflict are analyzed, and ways of fostering cooperation are considered.

Phase 4—Organizational Goal Setting: At this time, top managers discuss and agree upon an ideal model for their organization—one encompassing description of its major goals, structure, reward system, and decision-making procedures. The model developed is then reviewed by lower-level managers, and commitment to its attainment is fostered among both groups.

Phase 5—Goal Attainment: During this crucial phase, participants attempt to accomplish the goals developed during the fourth stage. In short, they seek to translate their thoughts about an ideal model for their organization into reality.

Phase 6—Evaluation: During the final phase of grid training, the program's overall success is evaluated. The current state of the organization is compared with its state prior to the grid intervention, and areas requiring further work are pinpointed.

Blake and Mouton suggest that these procedures aid many participants in shifting toward the preferred 9,9 pattern of management. As a result, they become better managers—ones more capable of leading their organizations to a high level of effectiveness. Supporters of the grid approach believe that it is highly effective and empirical findings offer some confirmation of this view.[28] (We will return to this evidence later.) In any case, there can be little doubt that grid training has been extremely popular. Through the mid-1970s, more than 200 thousand people had participated in it, and this figure is certainly higher by now. Thus, it seems safe to conclude that many organizations find the possibility of enhancing their own effectiveness through improvements in managerial skill an enticing one.

Quality of Work Life: Effectiveness through Humanization of Work and Work Settings

During the 1960s and 1970s, major changes swept through most Western societies. These alterations were varied in nature, but most centered around a common theme—the quest for greater freedom and personal choice. Consistent with this basic notion, persons in many different nations called existing social, political, and even sexual norms into question. Indeed, it is probably safe to say that virtually no area of life remained untouched by this process of re-examination. Given the powerful pressures toward change during this period, it would be surprising to find that the world of work remained totally unaffected. In fact, it did not. At the same time they were questioning long-held assumptions and values in other spheres of life, many people also scrutinized attitudes and beliefs relating to work. For example, they questioned the view that one's job must always take precedence over one's personal life, or that advancement in one's career is always the most important goal to pursue. Not surprisingly, experts in organizational behavior shared concern with these and other complex issues, and the work they soon conducted led to the emergence of a new area of investigation—one often termed the **quality of work life.**[29,30]

Scholars and practitioners concerned with this important topic focus their attention on factors serving to enhance the experience of human beings at work. In their investigations, they often start with the basic assumption that positive business outcomes (e.g., high profits, productivity, efficiency) are *not* necessarily incompatible with positive human outcomes (e.g., fulfillment of basic needs, the enjoyment of work). In fact, such investigators strongly believe that both of these goals can be enhanced simultaneously. Consistent with this view, a major theme of research on the quality of work life (or *QWL*) has been the development of specific techniques for enhancing its overall level. That is, much attention has been directed to the task of devising procedures that will *humanize* the world of work— make it more pleasant, satisfying, and enjoyable for employees—while simultaneously contributing to high levels of productivity and efficiency.

We will now examine several approaches that have been employed for accomplishing these tasks. Before turning to such techniques, however, we will pause briefly to examine a basic question. Why should managers be interested in QWL?

The quality of work life: Why is it important?   Actually there are two related answers to this question. First, it is clear that improvements in the quality of work life are positive in and of themselves. Work is a crucial part of most people's lives, and there is no reason why it should not be as pleasant, fulfilling, and enjoyable as possible. Indeed, assuring that this is in fact the case is consistent with important societal values. Second, it is also apparent that improvements in QWL can lead to enhanced motivation, commitment, and satisfaction among employees.[31] These changes may contribute to heightened organizational effectiveness. In short, conditions that improve the quality of work life can be viewed as yet another general strategy of organizational development (see Figure 16–10). Viewed in this light, there are certainly powerful reasons for concern with QWL on the part of managers and employees alike.

FIGURE 16–10   Improved QWL: Benefits for Organizational Effectiveness

Improvements in the quality of work life (QWL) can enhance employee motivation, commitment, and satisfaction. Such changes, in turn, can contribute to higher levels of organizational effectiveness.

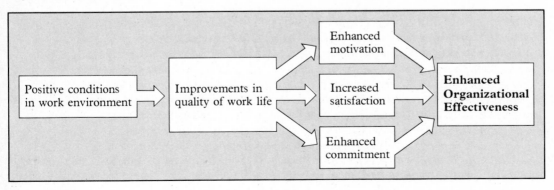

Quality of work life: How can it be enhanced? But returning to our original question, how can QWL be enhanced? What steps can we take to improve the quality of work life in many different settings? Actually, some of the answers now emerging from current research will come as no surprise. Many of the procedures that seem effective in this respect are ones we have already examined in other contexts (e.g., in our earlier discussions of motivation and job satisfaction).

Perhaps the single approach to enhanced QWL that has received most attention involves a cluster of changes recently termed *work restructuring.*[32] Briefly, such procedures center around changes in the nature or content of jobs. These changes are designed to provide employees with more interesting and varied work, more autonomy, and greater satisfaction. Since we have already considered several aspects of this process in Chapter 5 (e.g., *job enlargement, job enrichment*), we will not describe them again here. We simply wish to note that these techniques often seem effective in enhancing the quality of work life for employees.

A second tactic that seems effective in this regard concerns changes or reformulations in the role of supervisors. In this approach, attempts are made to narrow the status gap between employees and the persons to whom they report. Thus, for example, supervisors are trained to treat their subordinates in a more open and democratic fashion. As we have noted earlier (Chapter 14), most persons react positively to such treatment by managers or leaders, so it is hardly surprising that shifts in this direction tend to exert a positive influence upon QWL.

A third approach to enhancing the quality of work life is also one we have previously considered—the design and implementation of appropriate pay systems. Crucial here is the employees' perception that such systems are fair or equitable and responsive to a high level of effort on their part. As we have noted repeatedly, human beings strongly prefer clear contingencies between their behavior and their outcomes. Thus, careful attention to this fact can often yield important dividends with respect to overall QWL.

All steps we have outlined so far should be familiar to you. Further, they can all be viewed as relatively conservative in scope. Before concluding, we should note that more radical approaches to enhancing QWL have also been proposed. For example, some investigators have recommended the adoption of *industrial democracy*—procedures in which employees participate in key decisions, receive management-level information, and share in the economic benefits gained by their organization.[33] Similarly, other authors have called attention to the potential benefits that may accrue when employees actually own and manage their companies.[34] Needless to add, these tactics for improving the quality of work life are fairly extreme and cannot be adopted in many contexts. Some evidence suggests that when they *are* appropriate, however, they can yield many positive outcomes.

To conclude, the level of QWL present in any organization depends on a number of different factors.[35] As a result, the task of raising such conditions to new highs is often complex. Yet, as we have seen, many promising techniques for accomplishing this goal have already been uncovered. Whether, in the face of difficult economic conditions and other uncertainties of the 1980s, they will be put to actual use remains to be seen. To the extent they are, there are grounds for some guarded optimism. Perhaps under the guidance of enlightened managers, organizations will become increasingly attractive—and human—places in which to work. Perhaps. In this respect, as in many others, only time (and the course of future events) will tell.

Quality Circles: Building Effectiveness from the Ground Up

As we have noted in earlier sections of this book, motivation among employees to reach important organizational goals is often enhanced when these persons become involved with their work. One way to increase such involvement is to provide employees with a direct say in decisions concerning their jobs. Together, these basic ideas form the foundation for another technique aimed at enhancing organizational effectiveness, **quality circles.**[36] In essence, such circles are voluntary groups of employees who work on similar tasks or share some area of responsibility, and who agree to meet on a regular basis to discuss—and perhaps solve—key problems relating to their work. Typically, they consist of members of a specific work group and their supervisor, but this structure is far from rigid, and other persons may participate as well.

During quality circle sessions, team members first seek to identify key problems that interfere with the quality or efficiency of their work. Then they select one of these for careful analysis and attempt to arrive at specific recommendations for its solution. These recommendations are then transmitted to management, which considers them carefully. If they are deemed acceptable, steps are taken for their immediate implementation. If they are rejected, the reasons they are judged unfeasible or impractical are provided to team members. A final step involves evaluating the success of solutions that *are* adopted. Since the major goal of quality circles is to improve the quality of whatever product the work group produces, attention is focused on such indices as improvements in the number of defects per hour worked, shortages or delays stemming from workers' errors, and the number of defects per unit of work completed.

As you can readily see, quality circles have a great deal of intrinsic appeal. They seem to tap organizational resources that often go unused (the expertise and practical experience of workers); they can be applied in a wide range of settings; and they yield specific recommendations for dealing with specific problems. Perhaps most important, they focus on getting employees involved with their work—an effort that can yield many positive outcomes. But are they actually effective? Do quality circles really enhance organizational effectiveness? At the moment, it is difficult to draw firm conclusions, for little systematic research on these questions has been completed. But we should note that initial results seem quite promising.[37] Quality circles *do* seem successful in getting employees to take more pride in their work, and so tend to enhance both quality and overall efficiency. Thus, there seems every reason to expect that quality circles, with their intriguing "bottom to top" approach, will soon provide us with yet another effective technique for enhancing organizational effectiveness.

ORGANIZATIONAL DEVELOPMENT: DOES IT REALLY WORK?

Sensitivity training, team building, MBO, the managerial grid, quality circles. By now, we have examined many different OD procedures. In presenting these contrasting strategies, we have followed a largely descriptive approach. That is, we have simply summarized the major steps in each and indicated how they are applied in varied organizational settings. So far, however, we have made little mention of a basic and crucial question: Do these tactics really work? In short, are OD procedures actually successful in terms of enhancing organizational effectiveness? This is a practical issue, for as we have already seen, several OD procedures are quite costly, in terms of both time and effort. Obviously, then, their use is justified only to the extent that they yield concrete, measurable benefits.

Given the central importance of this issue, you will not be surprised to learn that experts on OD have devoted considerable attention to it. Indeed, they have conducted literally hundreds of studies to assess the impact of several of the OD strategies we have discussed.[38] But what precisely do these studies suggest? Does OD really work? Or is it actually a colossal waste of time? A recent review of existing evidence on these questions, carried out by Porras and Berg, is quite revealing.[39] Further—we are happy to note—it is also quite encouraging in its conclusions.

The Impact of Organizational Development: Some Basic Findings

In their review, Porras and Berg examined 160 different studies concerned with planned change in organizations. From these they selected thirty-five that made the clearest use of specific OD tactics. The methods and procedures used in these investigations varied greatly. All, however, reported evidence concerning the impact of OD procedures on two central aspects of organizational life—concrete outputs (*outcome variables* such as profits, efficiency, productivity, absenteeism) and human processes/relationships (*process variables* such as openness, motivation, influence, decision making). Each of the studies selected was then examined to determine whether the OD procedures it employed yielded "substantial change" in either or both of these two major categories. (*Substantial change* was defined as statistically significant shifts in the measures reported, or at least a thirty-percent change in these variables). The findings thus obtained by Porras and Berg were quite informative, and in a few cases quite surprising.

First and of greatest importance, there was fairly strong evidence for the effectiveness of all the major OD techniques considered *(sensitivity training, team building,* the *managerial grid, survey feedback)*. Indeed, as you can see from Figure 16–11, all these procedures yielded positive effects in a substantial proportion of the studies that employed them. Thus, it appears that OD *does* in fact work. When applied to actual organizations, it tends to induce the increments in organizational effectiveness that its supporters predicted.

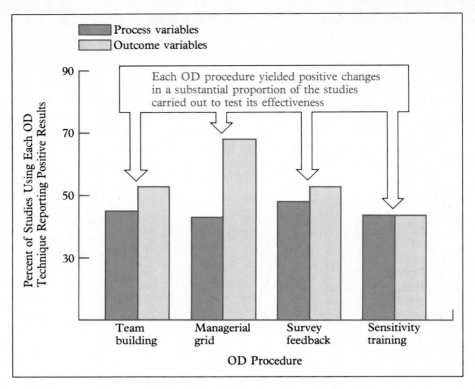

FIGURE 16-11   OD: Evidence That Often It Really Works

As shown here, existing evidence points to the conclusion that several OD procedures really work. That is, they seem capable of inducing positive change in the organizations to which they are applied. Further, they seem capable of inducing such shifts in both process and outcome variables. (Source: Based on data from Porras & Berg, 1978.)

Second, and also apparent from Figure 16-11, OD procedures seem equally effective in influencing outcome and process variables. This finding was somewhat unexpected, for it has often been assumed that OD exerts a greater impact upon process than outcome factors. Actually, though, a tendency in the opposite direction was noted. Thus, OD is not simply a technique for improving the "human side" of organizational life; it also seems capable of enhancing concrete, profit-related outcomes as well.

Two additional findings are also worthy of brief mention. First, the impact of OD seems to vary with its duration. Maximum benefits seem to occur when individuals are exposed to such procedures for moderate periods of time (about eleven to twenty days). With either shorter or longer periods of exposure, positive changes seem less likely to occur. Second, where OD is concerned, the standard phrase "more is better" seems to apply. Studies employing four or more separate

OD steps reported positive findings more frequently than ones employing a smaller number of intervention tactics.

In sum, the research examined by Porras and Berg seems to provide some support for the effectiveness of several popular OD procedures. Of course, we should hasten to note that the studies these authors reviewed vary tremendously in scope and in degree of scientific rigor. Indeed, some fail to meet the basic requirements for effective research outlined in Chapter 2. And we should also add that in many cases, research on the impact of OD has involved the simultaneous use of several different procedures. Under these conditions, of course, it is impossible to determine which of these techniques (or which combination of them) produced the positive results obtained. For these and other reasons, a healthy degree of caution seems indicated in assessing research findings in this area. Yet, taken as a whole, the weight of available evidence does seem to point to at least mildly optimistic conclusions. OD is probably *not* the no-fail panacea some of its more ardent supporters suggest, but when used with caution, skill, and care, it does seem capable of enhancing key aspects of organizational effectiveness.

Organizational Development: One Possible Basis for Its Effectiveness

The fact that several contrasting tactics of OD seem to work is certainly comforting. After all, this finding suggests that many different procedures can be useful in enhancing organizational effectiveness. But this fact in itself is somewhat puzzling. How can procedures as different in scope as sensitivity training, MBO, and survey feedback all yield positive outcomes? What is the underlying theme tying them together? Several different answers can be suggested to this seeming puzzle, but here we would like you to consider just one.

In essence, our arguments rest on two basic facts. First, all of the OD tactics we have considered possess fairly firm foundations in behavioral science knowledge. That is, they are derived, at least in part, from basic information about human behavior in group and organizational settings. Second, in many real organizations, a large number of executives and managers are unfamiliar with such knowledge; they have never been exposed to the topics and findings presented in this text. Given these two facts, it would probably be surprising if OD procedures did *not* often yield positive findings, and for a very basic reason—when such techniques are applied to an organization, they serve to raise the level of understanding about human behavior among high-level managers. To the extent this occurs, many major benefits may follow. At the very least, such persons will begin to think about employees (and human relationships generally) in a somewhat more sophisticated way. At best, they may gain considerable insight into key processes such as decision making, motivation, persuasion, power, and leadership. For this reason, we believe, many different OD procedures can yield similar positive effects. The specific steps and procedures certainly vary, but one of the key outcomes that all produce is much the same. Needless to add, we offer this suggestion primarily as food for thought; we have no hard-and-fast evidence for its

FOCUS ON BEHAVIOR

Measuring Organizational Change: More Complex Than It Seems

Change is a central concept in organizational development. OD programs are designed to induce planned shifts within organizations—changes that enhance their functioning and effectiveness. And in evaluating the success of any OD procedure, the direction and amount of change it produces are central criteria. But how precisely do we go about measuring change in such contexts? How do we ascertain whether an OD program has actually yielded the effects we desire? At first glance, you might conclude that this is a trivial task. We simply measure some aspect of an organization before the OD program, and then again after it has been completed. Any change observed is then evidence for the success of this intervention, right? Wrong! In point of fact, assessing organizational change in this manner is far more complex than at first meets the eye. Perhaps a specific example will help clarify why this is so.

Imagine that an OD consultant conducts a program designed to enhance the leadership abilities of managers in a large organization. Being a careful practitioner, she measures employees' perceptions of their managers as leaders prior to the start of the program, and then again after it is completed. Results are clear—these ratings improve substantially. Can the consultant then conclude that the OD program has induced real changes in managers' leadership behavior? Unfortunately, she cannot. The change she observes may stem from this happy cause (in which case, it would be termed **Alpha change**). But it may also stem from two other sources as well. The first of these, known as **Beta change,** involves shifts in the way employees respond to the leadership questionnaire. At first, they may have perceived the high end of this scale as appropriate only for great leaders—famous heros and heroines. After the OD program, though, they come to realize that leaders should be assessed within their present context. As a result, they now assign somewhat higher ratings to their managers. Note that this is *not* a result of changes in the behavior of these persons; rather, it stems from shifts in the way employees interpret and use the leadership scale.

But this is not the only possible complication. Changes in employees' responses to the scale may also stem from another source—a basic shift in their concept or idea of leadership. This is known as **Gamma change.** Imagine that initially, employees perceived leadership as involving the ability to bend other persons to one's will, largely through the exercise of a forceful personality. Now, however, they view it as consisting mainly of the ability to get the job done, whatever this entails. As a result of this change in concept or definition, they assign higher ratings to their managers. Again, however, this is *not* a result of alterations in the behavior of these persons (see Figure 16–12).

Fortunately, several techniques for distinguishing between these alternate sources of change exist.[40] One involves close examination of the manner in which responses to a questionnaire cluster together (the underlying *factor structure*).[41] If shifts in employees' responses stem from change induced by the intervention, similar patterns of clusters should exist on both the pre and post measures. If change stems from a redefinition of the concept being measured (Gamma change), these patterns should be very different. And if change stems from alterations in the use of the rating scale (Beta change), the patterns should be moderately dissimilar. Another technique relies on close examination of the specific patterning of responses—a procedure known as *profile analysis*.[42] Regardless of the specific technique used, however, attempts should always be made to separate Alpha, Beta, and Gamma change. Only when this is done is it possible to distinguish real, OD-induced shifts from other, spurious ones.   □

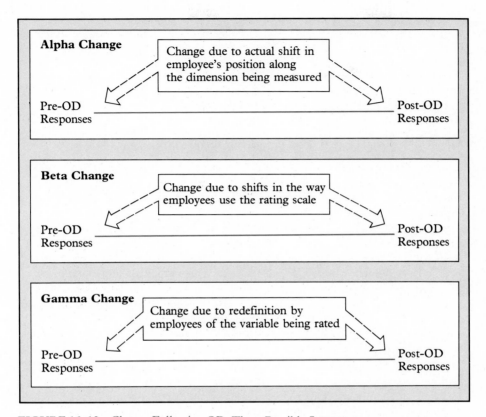

FIGURE 16-12   Change Following OD: Three Possible Sources

When scores on self-report measures (e.g., questionnaires) change following an OD intervention, these shifts may stem from at least three different sources. First, they may reflect actual change in employees' position along the dimension being assessed *(Alpha change)*. Second, they may reflect changes in the way employees use the rating scales *(Beta change)*. Third, they may stem from a redefinition of the variable being rated *(Gamma change)*.

accuracy. But you may well find it worth considering when, in the years ahead, you encounter one or more programs of planned intervention in your own organization. (Please see the **"FOCUS"** box on pp. 562–563 for a discussion of a basic issue relating to OD: how can change within an organization be measured?)

SUMMARY

Techniques of **organizational development** seek to enhance the effectiveness of organizations through planned, systematic change. *Sensitivity training,* one long-established OD procedure, seems to accomplish this general goal by reducing interpersonal friction. This is accomplished through group discussions designed to enhance individuals' awareness with respect to their own feelings, those of others, and their impact on fellow employees. *Team building,* a related OD strategy, focuses on the identification of specific problems relating to task performance, as well as concrete plans for their elimination. In *survey feedback,* a third OD procedure, employees complete a questionnaire designed to assess their views on the quality and style of leadership, decision making, and other aspects of organizational climate. The information thus obtained is then used to develop plans for overcoming any problems uncovered.

A fourth OD procedure, *management by objectives* (MBO), focuses primarily on the development of specific goals and concrete plans for their attainment. It also involves periodic assessment of progress toward these objectives. MBO is very popular and has been used by hundreds of organizations. *Grid training,* another popular OD approach, focuses on enhancing managers' leadership skills. Specifically, it seeks to encourage managers to show high concern both with persons and with production. In recent years, many OD experts have turned their attention to the *quality of work life (QWL).* Thus, they have studied factors affecting the experience of human beings at work. Many procedures for enhancing QWL have been devised, including work restructuring, redefinitions of subordinate-superior relationships, and the design of appropriate pay systems. *Quality circles* consist of groups of employees who meet on a regular basis and attempt to formulate solutions to key problems relating to their work. Such groups seem effective in raising employees' involvement with their work, and so their overall performance.

Existing evidence suggests that in general OD works. Several different OD procedures seem at least moderately successful in enhancing organizational effectiveness. One reason for this success may lie in the fact that OD programs are based on solid behavioral science knowledge. Thus, they may serve to enhance the sophistication of many managers with respect to human behavior.

KEY TERMS

ALPHA CHANGE　Refers to change in self-report data (e.g., responses to a questionnaire) stemming from actual shifts in the variable being measured.

BETA CHANGE   Refers to change in self-report data (e.g., responses to a questionnaire) stemming from shifts in the manner in which respondents use the rating scales provided.

GAMMA CHANGE   Refers to change in self-report data (e.g., responses to a questionnaire) stemming from a redefinition of the variable being rated by respondents.

GRID TRAINING (MANAGERIAL GRID)   An OD procedure focused primarily on enhancing the leadership skills of managers. According to this approach, managers who show high concern with both persons and production will often be most successful in enhancing the effectiveness of their organizations.

MANAGEMENT BY OBJECTIVES (MBO)   An OD procedure that focuses primarily on the establishment of specific, measurable objectives and concrete plans for their attainment.

ORGANIZATIONAL DEVELOPMENT (OD)   A process aimed at enhancing organizational effectiveness through planned change. The changes sought and the techniques for achieving them are suggested by basic behavioral science knowledge.

OUTCOME VARIABLES   Variables relating to the concrete output of an organization. These include performance, productivity, profits, absenteeism, and turnover.

PROCESS VARIABLES   Variables relating to the behavior and attitudes of employees. These include motivation, decision making, influence, conflict, and communication.

QUALITY CIRCLES   Groups of employees who meet on a regular basis and attempt to develop solutions to specific problems relating to their work. Participation in such a group seems to increase employees' involvement in their work, and so enhances overall efficiency.

QUALITY OF WORK LIFE (QWL)   Refers to conditions affecting the experience of human beings at work. QWL is affected by many different factors.

SENSITIVITY TRAINING   An OD procedure concerned primarily with enhancing employees' awareness of their own feelings, those of others, and the impact they have upon other persons.

TEAM BUILDING   An OD procedure in which employees discuss problems relating to task performance. Once specific problems are identified, concrete plans for their elimination are devised and implemented.

NOTES

1. Huse, E. F. *Organization development and change.* New York: West, 1980.

2. Margulies, N., & Raia, A. P. *Conceptual foundations of organizational development.* New York: McGraw-Hill, 1978.

3. Friedlander, F. The facilitation of change in organizations. *Professional Psychology*, 1980, *11*, 520–530.

4. Porras, J. I., & Berg, P. O. The impact of organizational development. *Academy of Management Review*, 1978, *3*, 249–266.

5. Blackburn, R. S. Dimensions of structure: A review and reappraisal. *Academy of Management Review*, 1982, *7*, 59–66.

6. Argyris, C. T-groups for organizational effectiveness. *Harvard Business Review*, 1964, 68–70.

7. Dunnette, M., & Campbell, J. Effectiveness of T-group experiences in managerial training and development. *Psychological Bulletin,* 1968, *70,* 73–104.

8. Aronson, E. Communication in sensitivity-training groups. In *The social animal* (3rd ed.). San Francisco: Freeman, 1981.

9. Crockett, W. Team building: One approach to organizational development. *Journal of Applied Behavioral Science,* 1970, *6,* 291–306.

10. Dyer, W. G. *Team building: Issues and alternatives.* Reading, Mass.: Addison-Wesley, 1977.

11. Porras, J. I., & Berg, P. O. The impact of organization development. *Academy of Management Review,* 1978, *3,* 249–266.

12. Baron, R. A., & Byrne, D. *Exploring social psychology* (2nd ed.). Boston: Allyn and Bacon, 1982.

13. Cavanagh, G. F., Moberg, D. J., & Velasquez, M. The ethics of organizational politics. *Academy of Management Review,* 1981, *6,* 363–374.

14. Cobb, A. T., & Margulies, N. Organization development: A political perspective. *Academy of Management Review,* 1981, *6,* 49–59.

15. Taylor, J. C., & Bowers, D. G. *Survey of organizations: A machine-scored standardized questionnaire instrument.* Ann Arbor: Institute for Social Research, University of Michigan, 1972.

16. Oskamp, S. *Attitudes and opinions.* Englewood Cliffs, N.J.: Prentice-Hall, 1977.

17. Drucker, P. F. *The practice of management.* New York: Harper & Row, 1954.

18. Drucker, P. F. *Management: Tasks, responsibilities, practices.* New York: Harper & Row, 1974.

19. Odiorne, G. S. *M.B.O. II.* Belmont, Calif.: Fearon, 1979.

20. Greenwood, R. G. Management by objectives: As developed by Peter Drucker, assisted by Harold Smiddy. *Academy of Management Review,* 1981, *6,* 225–230.

21. Kondrasuk, J. N. Studies in MBO effectiveness. *Academy of Management Review,* 1981, *6,* 419–430.

22. Ivancevich, J.M., & McMahon, J.T. The effects of goal setting, external feedback, and self-generated feedback on outcome variables: A field experiment. *Academy of Management Journal,* 1982, *25,* 359–372..

23. Jun, J. S. A symposium: Management by objectives in the public sector. *Public Administration Review,* 1976, *36,* 1–5.

24. Kondrasuk, J. N. Studies in MBO effectiveness. *Academy of Management Review,* 1981, *6,* 419–430.

25. Barton, R. F. An MCDM approach for resolving goal conflict in MBO. *Academy of Management Review,* 1981, *6,* 231–241.

26. Kondrasuk, J. N. Studies in MBO effectiveness. *Academy of Management Review,* 1981, *6,* 419–430.

27. Blake, R., & Mouton, J. *Building a dynamic corporation through grid organizational development.* Reading, Mass.: Addison-Wesley, 1969.

28. Blake, R. R., & Mouton, J. S. *The new managerial grid.* Houston: Gulf, 1978.

29. Herrick, N. Q., & Maccoby, M. Humanizing work: Priority goal in the 1970s. In L. E. Davis & A. B. Cherns (Eds.), *The quality of working life* (Vol. 1). New York: Free Press, 1975.

30. Walton, R. Quality of work life activities: A research agenda. *Professional Psychology,* 1980, *11,* 284–493.

31. Drexler, J. A., & Lawler, E. E., III. A union-management cooperative projective to improve the quality of work life. *Journal of Applied Behavioral Sciences,* 1977, *3,* 373–386.

32. Hackman, J. R., & Oldham, G. R. *Work redesign.* Reading, Mass.: Addison-Wesley, 1980.

33. Bernstein, P. *Workplace democratization: Its internal dynamics.* Kent, Ohio: Kent State University Press, 1976.

34. Zwerdling, D. *Democracy at work.* Washington, D.C.: Association for Self-management, 1978.

35. Walton, R. E. Quality of working life: What is it? *Sloan Management Review,* Fall 1973, pp. 11–21.

36. Scott, B. A. *Quality circles: An employee participation program that works.* President's Papers, Fall 1980 OD Network Conference, San Francisco, California, October, 1980.

37. Konarik, R. B., & Reed, W. Work environment improvement teams: A military approach to quality circles. *OE Communique,* 1981, *5,* 94–101.

38. White, S. E., & Mitchell, T. R. Organization development: A review of research content and research design. *Academy of Management Review,* 1976, *1,* 57–73.

39. Porras, J. I., & Berg, P. O. The impact of organization development. *Academy of Management Review,* 1978, *3,* 249–266.

40. Howard, G. S., Schmeck, R. R., & Bray, J. H. Internal invalidity in studies employing self-report instruments: A suggested remedy. *Journal of Education Measurement,* in press.

41. Golembiewski, R. T., & Billingsley, K. R. Measuring change in OD panel designs: A response to critics. *Academy of Management Review,* 1980, *5,* 97–103.

42. Terborg, J. R., Howard, G. S., & Maxwell, S. E. Evaluating planned organizational change: A method for assessing alpha, beta, and gamma change. *Academy of Management Review,* 1980, *5,* 109–121.

Name Index

Subject Index

John R. P. French jr.

John R. P. French, Jr.
Dr. French's work has shed considerable light on the key topic of power, including its basic nature and how it is used within organizations. (Please refer to Chapter 12.)

Donald T. Campbell

Donald T. Campbell
Dr. Campbell has helped to develop several effective and sophisticated methods for the study of behavior in organizational settings. A number of the techniques he has devised are widely used by organizational researchers. (Please refer to Chapter 2.)

B. F. Skinner

B. F. Skinner
Dr. Skinner's research on operant conditioning has greatly altered our view of the causes of human behavior and has exerted a profound impact upon many different fields. Within O.B., it has found major application in the process of O.B. Mod. (Please refer to Chapter 3.)

Greg R. Oldham

Greg R. Oldham
Dr. Oldham (along with his colleague Dr. Hackman) has made important contributions to the areas of job enrichment and task design. (Please refer to Chapter 5.)

Bertram H. Raven

Bertram H. Raven
Along with his colleague Dr. French, Dr. Raven has contributed greatly to our understanding of the nature and exercise of organizational power. (Please refer to Chapter 12.)

Frederick Herzberg

Frederick Herzberg
Dr. Herzberg is best known for his important research on factors affecting job satisfaction and work motivation. His *motivator-hygiene theory* has contributed to the areas of job design and enrichment. (Please refer to Chapters 5 and 7.)